SUNDAYS AT EIGHT

C-SPAN is directing any royalties from the sale of this
book to the nonprofit C-SPAN Education Foundation,
which creates civics and history teaching materials for
middle and high school teachers.

Sundays at Eight

25 YEARS OF STORIES FROM C-SPAN'S *Q & A* AND *BOOKNOTES*

Brian Lamb

C-SPAN

PUBLICAFFAIRS
New York

Library of Congress Cataloging-in-Publication Data

Lamb, Brian, 1941-

Sundays at eight : 25 years of stories from C-Span's Q&A and Booknotes / Brian Lamb. — First edition.

   p. cm.

Includes index.

ISBN 978-1-61039-348-5 (hardcover) — ISBN 978-1-61039-349-2 (electronic)

1. C-SPAN (Television network)—Anecdotes.   2. Booknotes (Television program)

3. Authors, American—20th century—Interviews.   4. Books and reading.

5. Authorship.   6. Lamb, Brian, 1941- —Interviews.   I. Title.

PN1992.92.C2L36   2014

384.5506'5—dc23

2014006359

First Edition

10 9 8 7 6 5 4 3 2 1

For Victoria

Contents

MEDIA AND SOCIETY

MONEY AND POLITICS

POST-9/11 AMERICA

A Note to Readers on Style

THE ESSAYS IN THIS book have all been crafted from televised C-SPAN interviews. They were selected from more than 1,360 interviews conducted over the twenty-five year history of our two Sunday night interview series, *Booknotes* (1989–2004), followed by *Q & A* (2004–present).

As in the style of previous C-SPAN books, the transcripts of the interviews have been excerpted and the interview questions were omitted to achieve an essay style. Essays were minimally edited in order to preserve the individual voices of our interviewees. We took care to remain faithful to each person's original meaning. Brackets and ellipses were used to indicate where words were, respectively, added or deleted within paragraphs. An extra space between paragraphs of an essay signals that we have pieced together non-sequential portions of the interview for clarity of thought.

All of the essays in *Sundays at Eight* are presented in traditional C-SPAN style—without commentary, allowing readers to form their own opinions about the people and issues we have selected for inclusion.

While the interviews presented here have been shortened and edited into essay format, in keeping with C-SPAN's public affairs mission and commitment to providing the entirety of what we produce, complete transcripts and videos of the original hour-long interviews are available online at www.c-span.org/SundaysatEight.

Introduction

WHAT MAKES FOR A good interview? It's a question I've pondered throughout my journalism career and earlier—ever since I was a teenager hanging out in my Lafayette, Indiana, bedroom listening to talk programs on Chicago radio stations. Many of the lessons learned over the years are demonstrated in this, our latest interview book, *Sundays at Eight*, which gathers forty-one selections from the last twenty-five years, from *Booknotes* and *Q & A*, our two sequential C-SPAN Sunday night series, airing at 8pm ET/PT.

The most essential ingredient of a good interview is, not surprisingly, a guest with an interesting story to tell, who can tell it well. Over twenty-five years, the various producers of our Sunday night interview programs have booked more than 1,360 interviews. Our producers are always on the lookout for people whose expertise complements our network's public affairs programming: nonfiction authors, documentary producers, historians, public figures, or journalists. And, whether the stories they tell are contemporary or historical, they should be able to compel viewers with their humanity or insight into events. Once a guest is booked, however, it's really up to the interviewer to get these stories told in an interesting and engaging way. For me, that translates into good preparation that's followed by asking concise and open questions, and listening carefully to rarely interrupted answers. The hour-long interviews that result then air exactly as recorded. In today's media world, our long-form, unedited production style is a polar opposite of Twitter's 140-character universe.

This "focus on the guest" philosophy is why you'll find this collection of interviews different from the standard TV interviewer's book of verbatim transcripts. To emphasize our guests' stories, *Sundays at Eight* has transformed forty-one interviews into essay-style chapters with all of my interview questions omitted. We've used a light touch with our editing, hoping to capture each featured guest's unique perspective in their own voice. (For a guide to the editing cues we've incorporated into the text, be sure to read our "Notes on Style" in the front section of this book.)

Sundays at Eight is our eighth published collection of interviews. Peter Osnos, PublicAffairs' founder and emeritus publisher, suggested this latest collection when he learned that the spring of 2014 marks the twenty-fifth anniversary of C-SPAN's Sunday interview series. This book features never-before published interviews from both series assembled into broad themes reflecting the times in which we live: Money and Politics, American History, Media and Society, and Post-9/11 America.

The book's initial section is titled simply, "Stories," and has become a favorite of our book team. Be sure to read the tale of Ishmael Beah, a conscripted boy soldier in Sierre Leone's civil wars, ultimately rescued by international relief groups and adopted by a caring American woman. There's Alfredo Quiñones-Hinojosa, known more familiarly as "Dr. Q." His is a quintessential American tale. Today, he's a world-famous brain surgeon at Baltimore's Johns Hopkins Hospital, but in an amazing "up from the bootstraps" story, he came to this country as a young immigrant from Mexico with little education, crossing the California border illegally. April Witt is a former *Washington Post* reporter who recounts a tale of the American Dream gone bad: West Virginian Jack Whittaker, a big-time lottery winner who learned through family tragedy that money is no key to happiness. And then there is the riveting story of Shin Dong-hyuk, born inside a North Korean labor camp. Journalist Blaine Harden, whose work has taken him all over the world, is a great storyteller who has you on the edge of your seat as he tells of Shin's perilous escape. Shin, who had no knowledge of the world outside the camp as he left its confines, remains the only person known to escape its horrors.

"American History" is a collection of nationally recognized historians who help provide context to the public affairs content served up daily on the C-SPAN networks. Don Ritchie and Richard Baker are two fine public servants who have devoted their professional lives to curating the history of the United States Senate. Their chapters provide insiders' expertise on the history of the Senate, capturing its essence. David McCullough, a great friend of this network and the dean of popular historians for his many book and television projects, recounts some of the stories told in his recent book, *A Greater Journey.* In his chapter, historian Richard Norton Smith, a longtime friend and a consultant for C-SPAN's history series, shares some of his encyclopedic and entertaining knowledge of presidential history. Isabel Wilkerson's chapter is based on her Pulitzer Prize–winning book, *The Warmth of Other Suns,* which tells the story of the twentieth century phenomenon of the great northern migration of American blacks through the lives of four such migrants.

It's often said that "money makes the world go 'round," but perhaps nowhere is that more evidenced than in Washington's political culture. Our "Money and Politics" section aims to capture this. Bob Ney is a one-time powerful House committee chairman whose chapter documents his downfall, vividly describing his time spent in a federal prison for corruption connected to the Jack Abramoff lobbying scandal. Peter Wallison's chapter on the housing giants Fannie Mae and Freddie Mac might make your blood boil. His is one of several chapters related directly to the 2008 financial crisis. My goal with the interviews we did in its aftermath was to help teach the public something about the system and its dysfunction. What has developed in the banking system and financial markets over the last couple of decades is so complicated, with short-selling of stocks and instruments like subprime mortgages, credit default swaps, and derivatives, that the journalism of financial reporters like Michael Lewis and Gretchen Morgenson, featured in this section, provides an important service to the public in understanding what went wrong and why.

Just as Vietnam shaped the sixties and seventies, September 11th and its aftermath has shaped this generation. In the section entitled "Post 9-11 America," we hear how Special Master Kenneth Feinberg approached the impossible task of assigning monetary value to 9-11's lost or injured lives. Richard Miniter reports on the background of Khalid Shaikh Mohammed, the convicted 9-11 mastermind now incarcerated in Guantanamo. He explains that KSM had personal knowledge of the society he attacked—he went to college in North Carolina. Michael Weisskopf, a Washington-based journalist well known to C-SPAN, went to Iraq to cover the military effort for *TIME,* and ended up joining the ranks of the wounded himself after losing his hand to a grenade. David Wood won a Pulitzer for his moving ten-part series on the enormous challenges for patients and their families and for the health care system following the traumatic injuries sustained by our fighting forces in the two post-9-11 wars.

Finally, a section called "Media and Society" acquaints you with some of journalism's old guard and its vanguard, to longtime colleagues in the Washington political journalism community, and to people whose technology innovations changed the way we communicate. Robert Kahn has had an enormous impact on the world as the lesser known co-creator of the Internet, along with the more frequently cited Vint Cerf. Mr. Kahn details the background of the Internet's creation, and the public-private partnership that allowed it to take root. Ken Auletta reports on one of the transformational companies made possible by the Internet—Google. Onetime CBS newsman Roger Mudd's reflections on what he calls the "glory days of television news," provide a meaningful contrast to internet video journalist Michelle Fields, whose professional aims included "going viral" with one of the opinion videos she produced for the online publication "Daily Caller."

"Media" has one entry that's particularly poignant, a chapter with Christopher Hitchens, journalist, intellectual, and social critic. He gave us his final television interview in 2011, just before succumbing to esophageal cancer. Christopher was truly his own, unique character. Intentionally provocative, he forced people to think about what they truly believed. We were not personal friends, but he was a great friend of C-SPAN's, giving freely of his time and intellect—twenty-five interviews over the years, beginning in 1988 when he was a self-described ex-pat British socialist writing commentary for *The Nation*. An atheist, Christopher's coming-to-terms with his impending death makes this chapter a compelling read.

These twenty-five years of Sunday interviews begin in April 1989 with the initial installment of *Booknotes*. Intended as an antidote to the three-minute author interviews generally offered up on network television, *Booknotes*' mission was to pay respect to the years of research, scholarship, and writing that generally goes into the production of a nonfiction book with a full hour of television. We broke most of commercial television's conventions—there was no editing of the finished product; it aired as it was produced, on a simple set, with only a black curtain for a background; we took no production breaks for summers or holiday seasons, producing fifty-two programs a year, and had rules such as "no return bookings for our guests." For the next fifteen years, we booked 801 authors, each focusing on one nonfiction book for an hour. Eventually, the demand of continuous reading for the series took its toll. What had been a joy was becoming a challenge, with stacks of unread books waiting at every turn. Calculating the 2.5 years of my life spent reading books for the series made it clear that it was time to transform it into something more manageable. It was then, in 2005, that *Booknotes* gave up its 8pm Sunday time slot to a successor program called simply, *Q & A*. Still an hour; still unedited; and frequently featuring nonfiction authors, *Q & A* permitted us to explore other media such as documentary films and online journalism; to visit historic sites; and sometimes to book people who simply had a good story to tell. By March 2014, *Q & A* will have logged 560 programs and counting; hopefully, each week we continue to introduce our viewers to interesting people with something useful to say.

Reflecting back on a quarter-century of interviews, we can only be appreciative of the more than 1,360 guests who have given us the benefit of their expertise, the generations of producers and technical staff who have assisted in creating this intellectual feast, and the numerous editors at C-SPAN and PublicAffairs who have helped create collections of books based on these series.

So, what makes for a good interview? Sitting down with genuine experts, people who help us to fill in some of the gaps in our understanding of our society, is an incredible opportunity. But another essential ingredient is the interviewer's curiosity, that itch to understand how things work and why things happen. And that, my friends, is exactly what we have tried to bring to the interview table over this past quarter-century. Thank you for giving us this opportunity with your continuing interest in C-SPAN's efforts.

Brian Lamb
Washington, DC
November 2013

Stories

Escape From North Korea

BLAINE HARDEN

Shin Dong-hyuk was born in a North Korean prison camp and knew of no other life outside the camp. Tortured and forced to witness the executions of his brother and mother, Shin made a remarkable and perilous escape at age twenty-three—the only person ever known to have escaped to the West. Journalist Blaine Harden, who spent twenty-eight years covering foreign policy for the Washington Post, *tells Shin's story and details the horror of North Korea's prison camps during his April 29, 2012 interview with* Q & A *and recounted in his book,* Escape From Camp 14: One Man's Remarkable Odyssey from North Korea to Freedom in the West.

NOBODY HAS SEEN A camp other than North Korean guards and officials, and people who go to them almost never come out. There are now five or six of these camps and they contain between 150,000 and 200,000 prisoners. With the exception of one camp, they are no-exit places where one goes if you are believed or imagined by the North Korean government of having done something wrong, of having been a wrongdoer or a wrong-thinker. You go there without trial. Usually, you're taken away at night and you stay there for the rest of your life. Very often, you go with your kids and with your parents…. Half of the people now in the camps are believed to be just the relatives of wrongdoers or wrong-thinkers.

Collective guilt is very much a part of this system. The reason the camps exist and have existed for more than forty years is because they're an instrument of terror of the Kim family dynasty. What they do is they put away those who might cause trouble and they terrorize the twenty-three to twenty-four million people in the country to not even think about causing trouble. To that end, they've been pretty darn successful. North Korea has been the longest-lasting totalitarian state in world history.

[SHIN DONG-HYUK] IS A survivor of Camp 14. He was born in the camp and he escaped in 2005. As far as we know he is the only individual born in those camps to get out and tell what it's like to grow up in the camp. His crime was to be born and his parents were there for reasons that are almost as flimsy. His father was in the camp because his father's brothers after the Korean War had fled to South Korea. After the authorities heard about that, his father and his father's many brothers and parents were all rounded up and taken to Camp 14. That's where Shin was born. He doesn't know why his mother was there. She never told him and he never asked. They didn't have the kind of relationship where they would talk.

His parents conceived him because they were chosen by the guards for something called a "reward marriage," and Shin was bred like a farm animal in the camp and raised by his mother. Physically, his mother gave birth to him, but he was raised with the values and the rules of the guards and was not close to his mother at all. He had to memorize ten rules of the camp, most of which end by saying, "If you don't do this you will be shot immediately." The first rule of the camp, the most important rule, is, if you try to escape, you will be shot immediately, and a corollary to that rule is, if you hear about an escape and don't report it, you will be shot immediately. These were basically his ten commandments, his ethical guideposts as a little guy growing up in that camp.

[PRISONERS] WERE SHOT OFTEN. One of the only forms of entertainment in the camp, where people actually get together to watch something, was an execution. So the rules were taken very seriously, particularly by the kids who saw the results of disobedience very clearly.

[THE FIRST EXECUTION THAT Shin saw] was the one that begins the book when he was four years old. I've said, "What's your first memory?"

He said, "I remember going with a crowd of people with my mom and being very excited," because it was the first time he'd ever been around a crowd of people. The rule of the camp is that you don't spend time with a lot of people. So that's what I think triggers his memory, that he'd never been in a crowd of people. He'd never heard this sort of hubbub of people whispering and being close together in a big crowd of many thousands of prisoners.

[Putting rocks in prisoners' mouths when they're shot] is a very common practice. I've talked to three others who saw this happen. They do it so that people don't denounce the guards or particularly the leadership of the country. They can't say anything. Sometimes they put a hood on them, sometimes they don't.

The real heart of this book and the psychological trauma of the rest of his life comes out of the escape plan of his mother and brother. What happened is when Shin was thirteen, he was living in a boarding school. All kids leave their parents and go to live with other kids in a boarding school in the camp, and this was only a couple of blocks, actually, from where his mom was staying. Shin had been in the boarding school for a while, and on a Friday night, his teacher, a guard, a guy who wore a gun, told him, "You go home and stay with your mom tonight. You can do that."

Shin didn't particularly want to because he didn't particularly like his mom, but he did it because he was told to. So he went home, and when he went home that night his brother was also at the house. This was very unusual because his brother also lived away from home; [he] lived in a concrete factory, which was about a mile and a half inside—the camp was big. His brother was eight years older. Shin hardly knew his brother; he knew who he was but he had no relationship with him. They had supper—the only meal he had ever eaten in his life, which was salt, corn, and cabbage. That's all. That was breakfast, lunch, and dinner. They put salt and corn in cabbage soup. It's a kind of gruel and that's the primary thing other than small animals that they could catch in the camps like mice and rats, but this meal was that classic meal.

He had the meal and he went to sleep. The house that he lived in had a central kitchen and one bedroom. The central kitchen was for three other units besides the room where his mother slept. So he went into this bedroom, fell asleep, and then he was awakened by the conversation of his mother and brother at about midnight. He heard them talking, and he crawled out and looked. He also saw his mother cooking rice for his brother. Rice is something that hardly exists at all in the camp, but it's grown there so sometimes farm workers can steal it. His mom worked in the farm at the camp so she must have stolen some over time. She had never made rice for him. He was thirteen years old and he was really jealous about that. That piqued his interest and then he heard them talking. Shin understood that his brother was in some kind of trouble in the camp.

He had apparently violated the rule and had left the concrete factory without permission and had gone to see his mother. Guards would soon come for him, take him away, and punish him. Probably not execute him but beat him up, which is the common way of punishing people.

Shin listened even more and then he heard his brother mention the word "escape" and Shin's heart started to pound. He became very, very, very upset and very afraid because of these rules: "If you don't report an escape then you'll be executed." Then he heard his mother countenancing that conversation about escape. Shin listened for a while, and it was clear that they were talking about trying to escape the camp. The rice she was cooking was food for flight for him to take and to eat after he got out of the camp.

Shin got up, told his mom he had to go to the bathroom, went out and found a guard and reported them. First, he went to a classmate and said, "What should I do?" and that classmate said, "We should report them."

So they went together, and when he reported this escape he was thinking, "How can I turn this to my advantage?" So he asked the guard if he could have more food as a result of his snitching and if he could also be made class leader, a position that would allow him to do less work, take fewer beatings, and maybe have more food as well.

The guard said sure, no problem, and called his superiors. He told Shin to go to bed. Shin went to bed in the school where he lived. The next morning he was awakened and told that there were guards waiting for him. They put a blindfold on him outside the school, put him in a Jeep, and drove him off to this underground prison inside the camp, which, before that, he did not know existed.

He was taken inside and then he was interrogated. He went in thinking they would see him as a good snitch, so when they started asking him questions about his involvement in the escape, he was frightened and confused, and he did not answer in any coherent way for his first two rounds of interrogation....

HE DIDN'T HAVE GOOD answers; he was very afraid and very confused. At one point in that underground prison, he was taken into a room that looked like a machine shop; he was stripped and with his clothes off, hung upside down from his ankles and his wrists in a kind of U, with his back hanging down. A cart was brought in with a coal fire, bellows were put on the flames, and the flames came up; the cart was rolled underneath his body and he was burned as they asked him questions. He passed out. [His injuries are] still visible. He has terrible burn marks on his lower back and buttocks, [representative] of a most severe burn that you would get from being held over a fire....

IN THE THIRD INTERROGATION, he was too weak to get up because he had been burned so badly. He was lying on the floor in his cell [and] he told them, "I did a good job. I turned in my mother. You can check this out with my classmate that I told." They did check it out and Shin was allowed to recover in that underground prison. Then he was taken out after seven months. He was taken back to the same officers who had originally interrogated him. He came out and saw that his father was in the camp. His father had also been tortured and looked horrible when he saw him. His father's leg was all akimbo. It had been broken in the torture, and his father could hardly move, hardly walk. Then they were both taken together in that Jeep with blindfolds on, to the execution grounds.

...Shin had his blindfold taken off and he thought, "Oh, they're going to kill me now." He was terrified that he was about to be shot. But they took his father, helped his father up to the front of the row, and they helped Shin up to the front of the row, and then they dragged out his mom and his brother. What's really interesting about this is that when his mom came out she was put on a makeshift gallows right in front of them. She was not blindfolded, a hood was not put over her face, and she tried to catch Shin's eye.

He hated her for the horrors he had just gone through in this underground prison and for her reckless talk of escape. He refused to catch her eye. She was hanged in front of him. Then his brother was shot in the head three times by the guards. Then Shin went back into the camp population at fourteen years of age.

His father lost his good job as a lathe operator. He began work as a common laborer, limping around the camp. Shin had a very strange relationship with him after this execution. His father tried to say, "I'm sorry that we were so selfish as to have children in this camp. I'm sorry you had to live through this. I hope somehow you can get out of here." Shin just said, "No, I don't care what you say." And he rarely saw him.

Shin escaped a decade later when he was twenty-three, in 2005. The escape is really a very important part of the book. One thing I want to say about the experience of the execution is that Shin was raised in such a way that he didn't really love his mother. He did not have feelings of affection or trust towards his father or his brother.

I asked him about those things: "How could you hate your mother? How could you not look her in the eye when she died?" And he said, "These people were competitors with me for food. They did nothing for me that was useful," as he saw it.

He had never heard of God. This is a concept that he heard about when he got to South Korea. Learning how to trust other people and learning to feel guilty for what he did with his mother is something that he has had to do since he has gotten to South Korea and the United States.

He's seen other families. He's seen other mothers and sons together. He has begun to feel terribly guilty about the kind of boy he was and what he did. But back then he wasn't guilty.

[IT'S NEVER HAPPENED BEFORE that somebody born in the camp escaped the camp.]...This camp existed, according to some South Korean authorities, since 1958. Nobody is known to have escaped it until Shin in 2005. So, it's really damn hard to get out of there.

He did it because he met someone who inspired him to think of the outside world. This was sort of Shin's birth as a human being. He was in the camp working in the sewing machine factory when he was assigned to work with an older guy who I think was in his early forties. His name was Park. Park had lived in Pyongyang. He had traveled and been educated in the former Soviet Union. He was a worldly and nice guy. Shin's job was to snitch on him because Shin had proved himself as a snitch over the years. He had done it with his parents and with many other people.

Shin started talking to Park about the world and Park said, "I grew up in Pyongyang," and Shin was interested in hearing these stories. Then Park started talking about something that Shin was really interested in, which was food. Park liked to eat and he talked about the joys and wonders of grilled meat in China. You could get grilled chicken, grilled beef, grilled pork, and you could eat until you were full, and you didn't even have to be rich or important. "That's the way people live outside this fence." That was a revelation that Shin could not get out of his imagination. He dreamed about it; he fantasized about eating well. Park told him many other things that were news to him: that the world is round, that China existed, that South Korea existed, that the United States existed, that the leaders in North Korea were a bunch of thieves and thugs. But none of that was very interesting to Shin, because he had no context for understanding that. His context was that he'd been hungry his whole life and he learned that if he could just get out of this cage, he could eat.

Camp 14 is about 300 miles [from the Chinese border], and it's about 50 miles just north of Pyongyang in the mountains of central North Korea. It was surrounded by a barbed wire fence of between 8 and 10 barbed wire lines, electrified. This was not a kind of fence where a cow touches it and jumps; this is the kind of fence that [if] you touch, it will grab you and it will kill you.

Shin heard about grilled meat in China; he got very excited and he said to Park, "Let's try to escape." Park was OK with that idea. He said they would try. He had met Park just two months before he decided to escape, so this is all very sudden.... They were really lucky in their escape planning, because they were assigned on the first of the year to go up to a side of the camp to gather firewood that was close to the fence. It wasn't near the guard towers, where guards looked down on the prisoners with weapons, where they would have shot people running for the fence.

They waited until late afternoon on January 2, 2005, until dusk, the glomming light, and they ran towards the fence. In fact, when Shin decided to go, he said, "Let's go" to Park, and Park said, "I'm not so sure."

Shin actually grabbed his hand and pulled him towards the fence, and then Park started to run. As they ran, Shin slipped and fell on an icy part of the snow, because it was cold, the middle of the winter. Park got to the fence first, shoved his torso between the first and second strands of wire, and was electrocuted and fell dead on the fence. [His body] pulled that bottom strand down. Without a moment's hesitation, Shin crawled over his body and had gotten most of the way across that fence when his legs slipped off on both sides.

He got these terrible burns from the voltage. I talked to an expert on electrocution at the University of Washington who knows the people who deal with all the power lines around the hydro dams in the Pacific Northwest. This scenario, which struck me as pretty weird and pretty odd and not very believable, he said, is completely believable; that this would happen and this would be the only way: Shin needed that insulator of a human body grounding the voltage so that he could get through that fence without taking a lethal charge. So, yes, he was lucky to get through the fence. But it's not like winning the lottery. It's something that is conceivable to do, according to experts, and he got through the fence.

The plan was for Shin to be the "Mr. Inside." In fact, he was the one who helped them get to the fence in a way where they wouldn't get shot as they approached it. But once they got through the fence, Mr. Park, who had been outside the fence and who grew up out there in the world, was supposed to be "Mr. Outside." He was supposed to take them to China, he had an uncle there, and then arrange for their shipment to South Korea. But Park was dead.

It took Shin a month to get across North Korea, a month of walking and riding in trucks. He hopped a train. One of the things that's really interesting about his journey across North Korea, [which is] a totalitarian police state, is this is a kid who didn't know which way was north and it really is an incredibly lucky trip that he made. But Shin had a couple of things to his advantage. He was very smart. He had this cunning sense of self-survival. That's why he had managed to survive in the camp. He also was smart enough to keep his mouth shut. He didn't tell anybody that he was from a camp. A few hours after he got through that fence, he came to an old barn that nobody was around and found some military clothes that he put on. This was in North Korea just outside the camp.

North Korea is the most militarized society on earth with a million-man army. It's actually 1.2 or 1.3 million people, so there are military uniforms in virtually every barn that you would find. So he found a military uniform, a change of clothes so he was no longer dressed like a camp inmate in distinctive clothes. He then walked into a town and he looked very much like a lot of young North Koreans. He was skinny, he was filthy, he was wearing an old military uniform, and he didn't have much to do. There were a lot of unemployed people who drifted around North Korea in the wake of the great famine there in the 1990s when almost a million people died.

North Korea at the lowest level is a very disorganized place where the food distribution system is very informal. It depends on smugglers from China, it depends on farmers selling food from cooperative farms when they're not supposed to. The North Korean government has no choice but to put up with this sort of messy informal market system because it's the only way that people can eat.

There are estimates that 80 to 90 percent of the calories in the stomach of any North Korean come from this system now. Shin fell into this system. He didn't know it existed, but he was lucky. Within a few days he had broken into a house, stolen some more clothes, warmer clothes, and stolen a big bag of rice. It was a 10-pound bag of rice, which he put in a backpack that he also stole. He walked past a market and a market lady said, "What have you got in the bag, boy?" He said, "I've got some rice." And she said, "Well, I'll give you money for it." So he was given some won, and this was his first transaction with money. Park had told him only a few weeks before that money existed. He sold the rice, got the money, bought some crackers and nuts and a few other snacks, and went walking out of the town and saw some other traders who were basically moving north towards China to do more trading. He fell in with them and that was his route out to China.

SHIN IS TWENTY-NINE NOW. What I hope is that he will use the money from this book to get a bit more education and to learn English and to pursue his dream as a human rights advocate on North Korea and other issues. He has not done exactly as everyone hoped, in terms of education, language, training, psychotherapy; he's his own individual person, but he is now doing Webcasting in South Korea and he's very excited about it.

He's in a much better place now than he was when I first met him in 2008. He's thrilled that this book is selling in the United States and that people are learning about the camps. That was the goal; that was the reason he went through the misery of talking to me.

HE LIED TO ME about his role in betraying his mother. When he got to South Korea, he did not say that he betrayed his mother. He simply said that they were executed and he saw it. The reason he didn't [tell the truth] was because when he got to South Korea, he thought if he told that story, the South Korean government might arrest him and certainly other people would think of him as not human. So he decided that he would expurgate his story a little bit. Finally, about a year into our interviews, he decided that he would tell me the truth. He said the reason he did it is because he was surrounded by people who were telling him the truth and who cared about him, and he felt an obligation to tell the truth.

He has become less wary, less suspicious, and a little bit more at peace with himself because he has told the truth about the betrayal of his mother. Yesterday, we were talking about a human rights convention and he talked about selling out his mother and why he did it and what he hopes will come of the truth that he told. He wants people to know that this is the kind of human being that they're trying to raise in these camps. There is the human rights abuse of starving people, shooting people, but there is also that of raising children to be little monsters.

He got mad at me sometimes because he didn't want to talk about all this stuff. Journalists just want to keep drilling. I say in the book that it was like being a dentist and not using anesthetics. It was painful and miserable for him, and sometimes he would just say no and leave.

THE REASON PEOPLE WILL be interested in this book is because it's a great story. It's an adventure story, and it's also a psychological story, because it's about how a person goes from having no human emotions to figuring out that they have got a good idea, and then developing it.

The normal trajectory of escape stories or of concentration camp stories is you have someone who comes from a sophisticated, civilized family, they're taken to the camp, all their other relatives are killed, they have to behave in an inhuman way to survive. Then they come out and they tell their story about a descent into hell, and then survival. Shin's story is completely different because he was born in hell and thought it was home and thought the values that he learned there were what it was to be a human being.

He has now discovered that the world and what it means to be a human being are completely different.

Profiling Extremists

JON RONSON

Welsh journalist and documentary filmmaker Jon Ronson appeared on Booknotes *in March, 2002 to tell the story of the year he spent with extremists, chronicled in his book,* Them: Adventures with Extremists *(Simon and Schuster, 2002). His premise for the book was that if he could study "them"—the extremists, he could discern common characteristics among the disparate organizations, whether the Ku Klux Klan, Islamic fundamentalists, or neo-Nazis. In our interview, he recalls his experience of sneaking into Northern California's Bohemian Grove, where global leaders gather and participate in torchlight ceremonies. He also explains the Ruby Ridge, Idaho story, where a deadly confrontation occurred between federal agencies and Randy Weaver.*

I SPENT A YEAR with an Islamic fundamentalist leader in London called Omar Bakri Muhammed, and it was just going to be for a newspaper article, actually. He was so unlike one's mental picture of a Muslim extremist. He was buffoonish and silly and burlesque. I thought, "That's so interesting. He's not the one-dimensional demon we're led to believe." I wondered if other extremists would be like that, so then I spent a lot of time with a Klan leader who was giving his Klan an image makeover. He figured that the Klan had a bad image, so he wanted to ban the "N" word and ban the robes and the hoods and the cross burnings, and replace those things with personality seminars, teaching their Klansmen to work out whether they're melancholics or sanguines, and so on. So again, he was very unlike my mental picture of a Ku Klux Klan leader. He was nebbishy. He reminded me of Woody Allen, and I thought there was an irony there. So then I figured, maybe there's a whole book in these unexpected portraits of extremist leaders. I thought it would be funny and there would be an interesting narrative. Maybe it would be an interesting way of trying to see our world through their eyes because all the extremists in the book are people who are living among us. They're trying to overthrow our way of life from within. Maybe the "them" could be us, as well as them.

I went all around the world. About 50 percent of the book is set in the States. There are a couple of British chapters.... There was Thom Robb, the Klan leader in [Harrison, Arkansas, in the foothills of the Arkansas Ozarks], who was giving his Klan a positive spin. Then there was the Weaver family. I spent a lot of time with Randy Weaver and one of his daughters, Rachel, and I re-tell the Ruby Ridge story in what I believe is a more accurate way. It benefited everybody to spin the story as white supremacists getting what they deserved, [as if] the government made a mistake, but they were white supremacists so it was basically OK. I've re-told that story in a more humanist way.

Bohemian Grove, as all the conspiracy theorists said, is this shadowy cabal, but once a year they go to a clearing in a forest [halfway between Occidental and Monteria, which is just above Napa Valley] in northern California. They undertake an owl-burning ceremony, where men like Henry Kissinger attend this robed torchlight procession, which culminates in a human effigy being thrown into the fiery belly of a giant owl. I figured, "That can't be true. I'm going to have to somehow infiltrate Bohemian Grove and find out if this is true."

It was an ill-thought-out plan. I was going to shimmy up a mountain and find the camp amongst the redwoods. Then I was told if I did that, I'd get myself killed, and not, I should add, by the Bohemians but by the terrain. Someone told me that the way to infiltrate Bohemian Grove is to pretend to be a Grover, to go to Eddie Bauer and get some chinos and some cashmere sweaters and just walk up the drive, giving the security guard an "I rule the world" kind of wave, which is what I did. Sure enough, I infiltrated the camp and witnessed this owl-burning ceremony.

DAVID ICKE WAS A BBC sports personality and a household name in Britain. He announced in 1991 that he was the son of God on the Terry Wogan chat show on the BBC. In Britain, this was a big splash. It's like Geraldo suddenly announcing he's the Son of God. It would become a big deal.

David Icke said, "Not only am I the son of God, but the world is about to be destroyed by cataclysmic earthquakes and tidal waves and floods." What I thought was interesting back in the nineties is that we were amazed and laughing, but a little bit of us thought, "Maybe he is the son of God. Maybe he's right...." The audience was laughing nervously, and the nation looked to Terry Wogan, the presenter, for guidance because part of us thought, "Maybe this guy is a soothsayer." Terry Wogan said, "They're laughing at you. They're not laughing with you," and there was a huge sigh of relief from the nation. It was OK to laugh at this guy.

He vanished and then returned a couple of years later with his new theory, which is that the Bilderberg Group exists, and they're also genetically descended from twelve-foot lizards. So is George Bush. So is Henry Kissinger. So are Kris Kristofferson and Boxcar Willie. I didn't quite understand where they fit into it. David Icke does people's genealogies to work out whether or not they're genetically descended from these malevolent lizards. What confuses me is how he actually even decided to do Boxcar Willie's genealogy. I asked him once if he'd done Dennis Healy's genealogy, who is the founding member of the Bilderberg Group, and he said no. I said, "So you haven't done his genealogy, but you've done Kris Kristofferson's genealogy?"

A lot of people agreed with the lizard theory. Some David Icke supporters said, "I don't necessarily agree with the lizards, but I respect his right to believe in lizards." Then you had a large anti-racist coalition form all over the world—in America, in Canada, in England--who were convinced that when David Icke said giant lizards ruled the world, he was using code, and what he actually meant was that Jews ruled the world. David Icke said, "No, I really do mean lizards." They said, "Oh, no, no, no. When you say you really mean lizards, what you actually mean is Jews." This was a very funny, burlesque way of examining the burgeoning cold war of paranoia. The crazier the extremists get, perhaps the crazier the response is towards them.

I was outed as a Jew at a jihad training camp in south London. It wasn't the best place in the world to be outed as a Jew. I was outed by Omar Bakri, bin Laden's man in Great Britain, as he used to call himself until September the 11th. Then, on September 12th, he phoned me up and said, "Why is everybody calling me bin Laden's man in Great Britain?" I spent a year with Omar, and it culminated in him inviting me to his jihad training camp. This was in about 1997, and it turned out to be in a place called Crawley, which is a very incongruous location for a jihad training camp. It's near Gatwick Airport. We were driven there and it turned out to be a scout hut in a forestry center, with maybe forty or fifty young jihad trainees beating punching bags. No guns, but still not the most comfortable place to be. Omar suddenly hushed the crowd and said, "Look at me with an infidel. Look at me with Jon, who is a Jew," and the whole room went, "Oh!" I'd never told him. I'd hidden that from him. He said he knew all along. He could see it in my eyes. I don't know when he discovered I was a Jew, but it wasn't the best place to reveal it.

I started looking more into these secret cabals like the Bilderberg Group. "Secret cabal" is a very pejorative term for what they actually are, which is a private, secret think tank. Men like Kissinger and Rockefeller do get together once a year at these hotels and talk without the media glare. They say, "Oh, the politicians who come to Bilderberg would just grandstand if the media was there," and the conspiracy theorists say, "The reason why they're there is because they're ruling the world from there."

The Bilderberg name is from the first hotel where they met, in 1954, the Bilderberg Hotel in the Netherlands. [The Bilderberg meeting I tried to get into was at the Caesar Park Hotel and Golf Resort in central Portugal.] About 120 people go [to the Bilderberg Group meeting] once a year at the end of May or beginning of June. David Rockefeller is one of the founding members. He certainly goes every year. [Henry Kissinger goes every year.] Bill Clinton's been. What tends to happen is that they go before they become president or prime minister. Of course, the conspiracy theorists will say, "That's because they go there, and that's where it's decided that they will become president or prime minister." It's three days with golf on the Saturday morning.

THE BILDERBERGERS STARTED CHASING me through Portugal, so I telephoned the British embassy to tell them that this was happening. I got really frightened. I was suddenly being followed by men in dark glasses who obviously presumed I was a crazy extremist, rather than a chronicler of crazy extremists. I telephoned the British embassy and said, "I'm being followed right now by a dark green Lancia belonging to the Bilderberg Group." The woman said, "Oh! Go on…Did you say the Bilderberg Group?" I said, "Yes," and she said, "Do they know you're in Portugal?" I said, "No." She said, "Look, you've got to understand. We're just a little embassy. The Bilderberg Group is much bigger than we are…What are you doing here?" I said, "I'm essentially a humorous journalist who's out of my depth. Maybe you could phone the Bilderberg Group and explain that to them," which is what she did! She called me back to say, "I've spoken to the Bilderberg Group and they say that nobody's following you and how can they call off someone who doesn't exist?" So I said, "He's behind the tree," and he was. This man in dark glasses was poking up, staring at me from behind a tree. When I tried to explain to him that I was a journalist, he swatted me away. He didn't want to know who I was. That was kind of frightening.

I FILMED MY BILDERBERG car chase. I thought I was going to die that day, so I was phoning up everybody to tell them I loved them. I phoned up my wife and said, "I may never see you again."

I've never been chased by shadowy henchmen. I had nothing to compare it to. You see, when I was shouted at by Aryan Nations, I could say, "OK, I've been to places like this before. I've been to the Klan. It's going to be OK." But I couldn't say, "Oh, this is like the time I was chased by the shadowy henchmen of the secret cabal back in '86." I was completely out of [my] depth. I had nothing to root it in. My wife laughed at me that time. She said, "Oh, you're loving it," and I said, "I'm not loving it." It was only when I got home and showed her what I'd filmed, which was deserted lanes at twilight with cars with blacked-out windows following me everywhere I went, that she thought, "OK, now I can see why you were scared."

THERE'S NOT REALLY ANY connection between Bilderberg and the Bohemian Grove. There is in the minds of the conspiracy theorists; it's all part of the new world order. In reality, Bohemian Grove is quite right-wing and Bilderberg is center-left. Bohemian Grove is Republican. That's why you get Dick Cheney and the Bush family going, and so on. Bilderberg is much more internationalist, globalist.

[People go to the Bohemian Grove] once a year for three weeks. Quite a lot of the really big names—the Dick Cheneys and the George Bushes—go for the second week. Apparently, the second week is the most popular week. The second week begins with the "Cremation of Care," the owl ceremony. They say that the human effigy they're throwing into the fiery belly of the owl symbolizes all their troubles in the marketplace. I've got to say, I don't blame the conspiracy theorists for thinking that when you put Henry Kissinger together with a berobed procession, culminating in this mock human sacrifice, it's no wonder you've got yourself a conspiracy theory.

The Bohemian Club in San Francisco [owns the Bohemian Grove], which was set up when the railroads came into town…. About a thousand people [go each year, all at the same time]. That's why I managed to walk up the drive so easily in July 2000. I snuck in with Alex Jones, a far-right-wing conspiracy theorist who believed that the "Cremation of Care" proved that the secret rulers of the world practice human sacrifice. Alex Jones was in Austin, Texas. I'd actually met him at the remnants of David Koresh's place in Waco, with Randy Weaver. Alex Jones was rebuilding David Koresh's Branch Davidian church with money donated from his radio listeners. He did a good job. He rebuilt that church, and it's good that [he did]. The Branch Davidians and the Weaver family [from Ruby Ridge] were victims of a government that on both occasions became slightly out of control and messed up and did wrong. I could be wrong, but I believe that neither the Weavers nor the Branch Davidians really were doing anything wrong. They were innocent parties.

Alex Jones [was at the time] twenty-six years old and looked ten years older. He's a hero to the militias. He's a burgeoning new hero. On one hand, he's kind of like Texe Marrs, the popular underground radio talk show host, but he's also much more than somebody like Texe Marrs. He's an activist. Infowars.com is his web site. He broadcasts in about forty cities across America on the Genesis Communications Network. I've listened. He's fantastic. If he wasn't so crazy, he'd be the new Bill Hicks….

What happened with me and Alex is that we both witnessed this owl burning ceremony, and I realized that it was silly grown-up frat nonsense. The only thing that shocked me was that the president of the United States wants to spend his summer vacations witnessing this torchlight procession, which I thought was kind of odd. Alex, of course, had his own spin on it, that it was human sacrifice! Maybe that's a real person! So I went off with my spin, which was a moderate spin: that it's not that crazy, it's understandable. Alex went back to his people with his own incredibly crazy spin.

I HAD A LITTLE camera; Alex was shooting too because he wanted to secretly film the owl ceremony. He was filming a little documentary about himself trying to break in. He brought along his girlfriend, Violet, and his producer, Mike....

We got the whole thing. We got in. We witnessed it. We just walked up the drive, waved, and were dressed preppy. That was very important. What I found very funny was that Alex is a far-right-wing Texan, plain-talking kind of guy, but he had to pretend to be preppy. He had to pretend to be a Yalie, so he took off his Wild West clothes and put on his chinos and his Polo shirt. He was so nervous about coming across as too right-wing and not preppy enough that he rehearsed preppy conversations while wandering up and down in his motel room. His version of preppy was camp, slightly effeminate, talking about the dot-com business. I don't know why they didn't check us. It's a mystery to me, because we just walked in.

[The attendees were all white men. Alex's girlfriend] had to stay behind in the motel. Out of all the people I researched, Danny Glover is the only black man I know of who's been. It's WASP-y. It's right-wing, white, male, pretty elderly. The average age is sixty-five, seventy.

IN TERMS OF BOHEMIAN Grove, I concluded that their worst crime was being dumb. These are the men that rule the world, yet they're doing these silly ceremonies. It's a beautiful place, Bohemian Grove. It's a clearing in these giant redwood forests, an absolutely wonderful place. I would picture myself sipping cocktails with world leaders and discussing the natural beauty. I could completely see why people want to be there. Then you see the photos of the parties they had the night before on the notice board, and you've got all these men, these CEOs, not only dressed up in drag, which is kind of OK, but dressed up with burlesqued, over-sized, fake breasts and ridiculous makeup. [It was] misogynist, I thought. What clearly struck me about the place is not that they really are Satanists or doing all this stuff that the conspiracy theorists say they're doing, but that the leaders of our world seem to be emotionally trapped in their college years.

RANDY WEAVER WAS A conspiracy theorist who figured that the federal government was out of control and determined to destroy the lives of simple people who wanted to live free, so he moved his young family up to a cabin in Idaho. He lost his job in Iowa City and moved to Idaho and had some pretty crazy beliefs, although, of course, Ruby Ridge is the place where all those conspiracy theories came true. Randy's big mistake was to go and visit Aryan Nations, which was the local neo-Nazi hangout…just near Coeur d'Alene in Idaho, although it's now been bulldozed to the ground. They lost a lawsuit against the Southern Poverty Law Center and it's been bulldozed now, and I'm glad, because it was a really horrible place.

I drove up past all the "No Jews" signs and jumped out of the car and said, "Hi. I'm a friend of Randy Weaver's." It didn't wash with them at all. They really didn't like me, but I survived….Now, Randy always has said that he was not a white supremacist, but that he was a white separatist. That may seem like a pedantic point to people like us, but it's not a pedantic point to him. He doesn't feel supreme. He wanted to be separate.

I wouldn't have gone to Aryan Nations, and I think separatism is a crazy belief system. Nonetheless, I felt utterly supportive of the Weaver family. Randy and [his daughter] Rachel Weaver were really, really good people who deserved to be left alone on top of that mountain in Idaho and had no intention of doing anything wrong.

The deaths were in [August] 1992. What had happened was the feds had seen Randy at Aryan Nations and thought, "Here's a guy we can work with." This is what I presume happened. "He's a slightly crazy person who is friends with far crazier people. Let's get him to be an undercover guy. Let's get him to be an informant." They offered Randy this deal, and Randy said no. Then they sent somebody in and asked Randy to saw off a shotgun, and Randy agreed to saw off the shotgun, and that was an illegal act. So they said, "OK, now we're going to send you to jail unless you join our team," and Randy still said no. He buried his head in the sand. He stayed at home with his family.

I don't think he was utterly innocent. He was stupid and pig-headed, but it escalated and escalated. In the end, some U.S. marshals got too close to the cabin, and the dogs started barking and chasing the marshals down the hill, and Randy Weaver's little boy chased the dog down the hill with a gun. They'd gone crazy in that cabin, really. They fed each other's paranoia. Sam, the little boy, chased the dog to the bottom of the hill, and then all the U.S. marshals jumped out of the bushes in full camouflage and shot the dog. Sam said, "You shot the dog, you son of a bitch. You killed my dog," and opened fire. He didn't hit anybody. The marshals shot back and hit his arm. This boy is [so young], his voice hadn't broken. He shouted, "Dad, I'm coming home, Dad," and ran home to his father. The U.S. marshals shot him in the back and killed him.

One of the U.S. marshals was killed in the gun battle. There has always been a debate as to whether he was killed by this family friend, Kevin Harris, or whether it was friendly fire. Four or five [U.S. marshals were involved] at the time, but after this marshal was killed, 400 turned up within 24 hours in these hostage rescue vehicles, which look like tanks, and with face paint. It was insane. It was a war. America declared war on this family whose son had just been killed. The next day, they put the boy in the shed, and Randy went to look at his son's body one more time. As he opened the door, a federal sniper shot Randy in the shoulder. Randy ran back to the cabin, and his wife, Vicki, was standing in the cabin, unarmed, nursing a baby. The same sniper shot her through the head and killed her. They pulled her in, locked the door, and put her under the kitchen table with the kids. Rachel was nine years old. That's when the siege began. They were shining the lights through the windows and using megaphones, saying, "Vicki! Vicki! Tell Randy to pick up the phone." Randy would shout back, "You son of a bitch, you know she's dead. You shot her." The FBI says they didn't know that Vicki Weaver was dead.

I spoke to the chief U.S. marshal, and he's very contrite. He thinks what happened up there was terrible. I would like to have spoken to the FBI in charge of operations up there, but they wouldn't talk, and they've never really spoken about it.

After a week, Randy Weaver [was in contact with] Colonel Bo Gritz. "Rambo" was based on Bo Gritz, I've been told. He was a highly decorated Green Beret in Vietnam, but he turned. He'd become a hero to the militants. Now, what you've got is 400 troops surrounding this mountain. The mountain is an emergency disaster area with troops, state police, FBI, helicopters; everybody's there. You've got 2,000 people down by the roadblock. It's at that roadblock that the militia movement really began in the United States. This became the touchstone.

[Convicted Oklahoma City bomber] Timothy McVeigh visited Randy Weaver's cabin a couple of years later. It showed that the government had become just what the conspiracy theorists have always said the government was—out of control and determined to destroy the lives of simple people who wanted to live free. The government had fit into that stereotype. They became the monsters that the extremists always said that they were.

I LOVED MY TIME with the Klan. I was Jewish and in the middle of the Ozark mountains. I figured I was the only Jew within hundreds of miles, but I started not feeling so alone because there was a Klan girl wearing a Calvin Klein T-shirt. I looked at the raffle stall, and the first prize in the raffle was a Walter Matthau video. The leader, Thom Robb, would make all these nebbish jokes. I say in the book that it was surprising to find myself toning down my Jewish character traits so as not to alienate a grand wizard who reminded me of Woody Allen. I found that very funny, the amount of Jewishness that the Klan didn't even realize was right in their presence!

Thom Robb eliminated the title Grand Wizard. He was a grand wizard, but he called himself "national director." He banned the "N" word and he banned hatred from the Klan, but he also banned all the language. They did this rally in Michigan, and I went along to witness it. It was funny, though: I remember being in Michigan, and they were doing interviews, and I was with them. The people who were interviewing them didn't realize I wasn't a Klansman, and I was desperate to tell them, "I'm not a Klansman, I'm a nice guy." They must have thought to themselves, "Who's that slightly sweet-looking English Klansman with the other guys?" They did this rally...in a parking lot with 300 yards between the stage and the audience, with patrolmen fencing off the entire place. They were really marginalized. There were thirty people in the crowd, fully 80 percent of them protesters, so they were having a really bad day, the Klan.

Thom was trying to be so upbeat and talking to all the policemen, saying, "Hi, everybody! We're the happy Klan," because that's what he wants to be. He wants to be the happy Klan. What he doesn't realize is America doesn't want a happy Klan. He thinks if they're upbeat and charming and don't hate people, then they'll get on Jerry Springer. Of course, Jerry Springer wants the kind of Klansman who looks like he's in the World Wrestling Federation. An upbeat, non-hatey-type Klan is confusing to people, and rightly so. That's not what the Klan's about.

So you've got the media, who want Thom Robb to be a racist. You've got Thom Robb's own members, who think that hate is a pivotal Klan activity. They want to hate people. They think, "What's wrong with hating people? It's OK. We're the Klan. We're supposed to hate people." All that responsibility just got to Thom Robb that day in the parking lot. He ended up calling the protesters "faggot slime," and it echoed across the parking lot: "Faggot slime. Faggot slime." He just crumpled. One way of reading this is that the mask slipped, and I think that's true. The mask did slip a little bit, but what also happened was that Thom had slid into being the caricature that everybody else wanted him to be. His image makeover was heartfelt, but Thom became what the media and what his own members wanted him to be. It was a defeat. It was a sad moment, in a funny and ironic kind of way.

I'D ALWAYS KNOWN ABOUT the Klan and always been very frightened of them. To me, the iconography of robes and hoods and burning crosses was something I had nightmares about as a child. I was comforted by the fact that the Klan wouldn't come all the way to Cardiff to lynch a Jew....Even though they've given up the robes and the hoods, Thom allows his members to wear them one day a year for the annual convention. One of the Klansmen asked me if I wanted to try on his hood and his robes, and I said, "Sure," so I tried them on. It was so interesting because, as a child, I really did have nightmares of robed, hooded guys. I was having nightmares as I was leading up to spending time with the Klan. I'm a Jewish person. I was thinking, "What if the Klan kills me?" On the conscious level, I was OK. I was brave. But on the subconscious level, I was churned up. But that moment I tried on the hood and the robe was such a demystifying moment. It was just cotton with the eyes cut out by the wives. It was kind of silly, and the silliness of it was charmingly demystifying to me.

Winning the Lottery

APRIL WITT

April Witt appeared on Q & A *on March 6, 2005, to tell the compelling story of Jack Whittaker, a self-made businessman in West Virginia, who won $314 million dollars in the state lottery in 2002. He took an immediate payout of over $100 million and became a celebrity in an economically challenged state. April Witt, then a* Washington Post *staff writer, went to West Virginia to write a story about the impact of winning this money on the Whittaker family. Jack Whittaker's story, as told by April Witt, vividly demonstrates that winning the lottery can ruin your life.*

THE STORY WAS ABOUT a man named Jack Whittaker, who lives in West Virginia. In 2002, he won the single largest, undivided lotto jackpot in history.

He had a lot of good impulses initially, and said he was going to do good works with this. He was going to tithe 10 percent to churches. He was going to start a charitable foundation. But like most people, he also had some bad impulses. This large amount of cash allowed him to act on both his good and bad impulses in spectacular fashion, and putting this lotto jackpot down in a poor state like West Virginia was like dropping a boulder in a pond. It had tremendous consequences for Jack, his family, and all sorts of people who barely knew him.

[I had the idea for this story when] an editor came to me with four little news clippings of various briefs that had run on the national page and one of them was a one-paragraph account of a young man being found dead in Jack Whittaker's house in Scott Depot, West Virginia.

When I read these four little clips and I started looking into the Jack Whittaker story, I thought, "that's the story I want to tell." I thought it had a lot of fascinating aspects and a sort of universal aspect to it, in terms of how people act on their good and bad impulses.

I went to West Virginia for the first time in November, and stayed there for eleven days at the Super 8 in Hurricane, West Virginia. Neither Jack Whittaker nor his family [spoke with me]. When I went to West Virginia, I went on spec. I did not call in advance. I thought I would show up, explain what I was trying to do, and get his cooperation.

I immediately realized I was not going to get his cooperation, and it did not matter, because once I started talking to everyone I could find, I realized that some of the most interesting aspects of the story are the impacts that Jack's win had on all these people that were just tangential to his life. They talked to me in great detail, and, for most of them, I was the first reporter who had ever interviewed them about Jack's win and what it meant to them.

JACK WHITTAKER WON $314 million. It was on Christmas Day, 2002. He decided to take a one-time payout of about $113 million after taxes. The woman who sold him the ticket, Brenda Higginbotham, was one of the first beneficiaries of Jack's largesse. He, within days after winning, said that he was going to buy her a new house and a new car and give her $44,000 in cash, which he did.

I talked to Brenda very soon after landing in West Virginia. And as soon as I talked to her, I felt like I would begin and end the story with her, because she had learned a lesson. She had been given this sudden wealth through Jack, and it hadn't turned out to be quite the pure blessing that she thought it was going to be. By the end of the story, she's learned the obvious lesson: money doesn't bring happiness. She is a very sweet, warm, genuine person who's had a hard life. She grew up on welfare; big family, no money.

At the time that she met Jack, she had no home. She was just staying temporarily in a borrowed place. She did not have a car. She walked to work, made minimum wage; yet she was a genuinely happy person. That's her gift in life, because she just wanted to reach out to others and make other people happy.

Initially after Jack won, his good impulses were on display, saying he was going to give money away to churches, give money to individuals, and that caused Jack and his family trouble, because if you're in a poor state people flocked to you.

He became a celebrity in West Virginia and people had a very high opinion of him. They thought he was sort of a super-Christian. He's going to do only good works in West Virginia with this money. It turned out that he started acting on some of his bad impulses quickly, too. He started going to a local strip club, and taking large amounts of cash into this local strip club. At one point, he was robbed in the strip club, [which] created a furor. There was local news coverage and it had a terrible impact for Jack and his family, because people thought he was a hypocrite.

It also had this strange, unintended consequence for Brenda, because once people in West Virginia turned on Jack, they started looking at him differently. A news story broke that Brenda's boyfriend had a conviction for sexual contact with a minor, and once that got into the newspapers, her neighbors all shunned her in her beautiful new neighborhood. She had the first house she had ever bought, but with lotto money. Jack bought it for her. She ended up selling the home, because she felt so humiliated by the neighbors knowing that her boyfriend had been in this trouble with the law. And her beautiful lotto-bought home became a prison to her. She felt, for the first time in her life, like she was poor white trash and people were looking down on her.

She gave up the house that Jack bought her and moved out into the country. She does not even have a phone anymore, because she just does not want people bothering her. Once there was the news story about her boyfriend, the people who she thought were her friends started fleeing when they saw her. They would rush into their houses, slam the door, and pull their children away. For the first time, [she saw] herself through others' eyes in a way that was very upsetting to her. And she thought, "maybe they've always thought I was poor white trash. Maybe they always thought I didn't belong in this neighborhood…." She had a heart-breaking experience.

THE FIRST THING JACK did was tithe to three churches and set up a foundation. He started giving money away quietly to people like Brenda. He didn't really publicize it much. He mentioned on the radio he was going to help her out, but he didn't boast. On a more quiet track, he also started celebrating in some sort of nefarious ways with the money. Within two or three days after winning, he went into the Pink Pony, a strip club in Cross Lanes, West Virginia, and put $50,000 down on the bar.

People were not used to seeing that kind of money down on the counter. The managers were worried that that cash would attract trouble, and eventually, it did. Jack and an occasional entourage would go back over the months to the Pink Pony, and they would also go to places like Tri-State Racetrack and Gambling. Wherever he went, he attracted attention. He attracted the attention of young women, and he started to get into trouble.

In March of 2003, according to some women who have since sued him, he sexually harassed some attendants at the racetrack. He just got too big for his britches, [as] they would say in West Virginia, and was sort of rough with these female attendants.

[THE "CHURCH OF THE Powerball"] is the Tabernacle of Praise. It is one of the churches that Jack initially said he was going to help out by building a big new building, starting programs there, giving a substantial amount of money to the pastor. He had never been a big member of that church, but his wife, Jewell, who is very religious, had gone and prayed at that church regularly before they won; he wanted to single them out for help.

When I went, they were still in the original sanctuary. It was a tiny little brick building, next to the highway, with a metal awning. It was very inauspicious, but [housed] a very warm and loving congregation. When I last visited, the new church hadn't opened yet. There were still only twenty or thirty souls. I went to two different services with them, and they had not really attracted a lot of people. They were controversial in town because a lot of the fundamentalist Christians felt like they should not have accepted gambling proceeds, and those people would never go worship at that church because it had been built with gambling proceeds.

By all accounts [Jewell and Jack] had a very strong marriage. They were childhood sweethearts who came from poor families in the hills. He was always a character, dressed in black like Johnny Cash, [in a] big black cowboy hat. Jewell was very quiet with very strong religious beliefs. She went to church, prayed, dealt with their family, had a small number of friends, and was not an outgoing person. She has since said that winning the Powerball ruined their lives, and that if she had it to do over again, she would have ripped up the ticket instead of collecting the winnings.

[Jack was] very successful for West Virginia. He had no education, but he had, through smarts and hard work, built a water and sewer pipe-laying business. He was worth on paper more than a million dollars, and he worked long hours to earn that money. He had built a nice life with a nice little brick house and a daughter and a granddaughter and a wife who adored him.

As Jack was seen around with other women, [and as] public signs of trouble started to arise, Jack and Jewell split. They tried to reconcile, but it has not worked out.

[BRANDI BRAGG, JACK'S GRANDDAUGHTER, is] the most heartbreaking strain of this story. Brandi had lost her father to suicide when she was very young. Her mother had had lymphoma. She had not had an easy life. She was a beautiful young woman. When Jack won, she seemed shy. She seemed overwhelmed and started to get into trouble. She started using drugs, [and became] addicted to crack, eventually injecting drugs.

This became a tragedy, not just for Brandi, but for a whole posse of young men in West Virginia who were drawn to Brandi's money. They started running together. It was a combustible mix. Who knows who corrupted whom? But with Brandi, the boys, the drugs, and the money, lots of trouble ensued. At one point, Jack's car was broken into, his Lincoln Navigator, and $100,000 in cash was taken from the Lincoln. Three boys who had been friends of Brandi's were eventually charged with multiple felonies and were facing spending a good chunk of their lives behind bars.

Jessie Joe Tribble was one of the young men who ran with Brandi; they were boyfriend and girlfriend. He was completely captivated by all the glamour that the money represented in that kind of setting. His family didn't have money. His dad was a small businessman just scraping by, making baseball bats for a living.

Jimmy Tribble, [Jessie Joe's father,] tried from the start to get his son away from Brandi, because he saw these young men were being arrested around her. He saw that his son was using drugs, and felt like he would never get his son off drugs as long as [Jessie] had a ready supply of cash. Brandi had thousands of dollars every day, and she was generous with [the boys around her].

Mr. Tribble felt he had succeeded. He tried tough love. He tried turning his son into the police. He struggled in all the ways you think a parent would struggle to get his son away from a bad situation. He thought he had succeeded when Brandi dumped Jessie Joe.

Jessie Joe came home. He finished high school in summer school. He was working in his dad's shop. Then, one day, Jessie Joe did not show up. Unbeknownst to his dad, he had recently gone back to Brandi and was found dead in Jack Whittaker's house of an apparent drug overdose.

That brief was how I started in on the story. There was just a brief in the *Washington Post*, saying that a boy was found dead in the home of a lottery winner in West Virginia. I thought, "how could that happen?" I went to West Virginia and started unraveling how that happened. While I was reporting the story, something else tragic happened. I quickly realized that Brandi [and her drug problem] were a nexus in the Whittaker family life.

I tried to interview her. She slammed the door in my face. I found her at a townhouse that her grandfather had [bought] for her after Jessie Joe had died in one of the family homes. They had moved her into this townhouse. It was like a crack den. There was graffiti on the walls. It was completely a mess; drawers were all askew, furniture was askew. I thought I was looking into an inner-city crack den, but it was the Powerball granddaughter's home.

She would not talk to me, which didn't particularly surprise me. But then, within a matter of weeks, she was dead of an apparent overdose. She was found abandoned in the back of a house that I had visited. A young man named Brandon Crosier lived there with his family, on Scary Creek, which was appropriately named. There were rusted-out automobiles in the yard. Brandi, according to Brandon's father, had had an overdose in their home. Brandon panicked and dumped her body. She was found rolled up in a tarp, after her body had gone missing for days.

There was a lot of public criticism of Jack Whittaker after she died. Everybody was saying it was an apparent overdose, and the young man who had been with her had told his father she had overdosed.

Jack Whittaker hired an expert to reexamine the autopsy and toxicology reports. He questioned whether it was an overdose, or whether there was some foul play. One of the interesting aspects of this for me is that I had never heard him take responsibility for his role in it.

Jessie Joe Tribble's father lays awake at night thinking, "What could I have done differently? How could I have acted more effectively to get my son away from the bad influence of the money and the drugs?" Brandon Crosier's father, [whose] one daughter died of cancer just while these deaths were unfolding, blamed himself; he was tending to the child who was dying of cancer and the other child, Brandon, was going down the tubes using drugs with Brandi. These were all people who were blaming themselves, questioning what they could have done differently.

Jack Whittaker has basically blamed other people. He's blamed drug dealers for corrupting his grandchild. He's blamed newspaper reporters for writing about some of the less savory things he did with his money. I don't know what he does at 2:00 a.m. because he hasn't talked to me. But at least publicly, he has not taken responsibility for any of this.

[Since] he would not talk to me, and his wife would not talk to me, I cannot say definitively his life was absolutely like this before the money, and it absolutely changed afterward. But from my outside perch, interviewing people who were close to him, he functioned extremely well. He had made more than $1 million. He was up at dawn to go to work every day. He was not drinking and carousing. As one person who knew him well put it, he got up early, he worked hard all day. He went home at the end of work and spent the evening with his family.

Clearly, there was a dramatic change. Places like the Pink Pony, the dog track, a lot of bars that I went into doing interviews, did not see him before he won. After he won, he became a regular. The money allowed him to act on some bad impulses.

People have asked, "How could he have changed so suddenly?" Shakespeare showed us how it could happen. Othello didn't go around strangling women every day. But when he finally murdered Desdemona, it grew out of impulses and character flaws that he had had all along. The best that I can make of it is that Jack's tragedy unfolded in that way. He had predilections. He had character flaws like all of us, along with his good impulses. Both his good impulses and his bad impulses helped take him down.

[ANOTHER LITTLE SIDE STORY is that the Putnam County detectives both worked for Jack Whittaker in the off hours and then investigated some of these things that went on].... They were an example of the corrupting influence that this money had.

Jack had said he was going to do all these good things with his money, and [he] did do many good things; he helped people and started the foundation. People came out of the woodwork to ask for the money. He needed security for the first time in his life. His family hired off-duty Putnam County sheriff's deputies to provide security for him, for his family, the house.

These crimes began to happen around Jack. He was arrested for drunk driving twice, the [Lincoln] Navigator was broken into, the $100,000 was stolen, and Jessie Joe Tribble died in the house of an overdose. The same detectives who were earning money from him to provide private security were involved in investigating some of these crimes.

This raised questions about whether they had enough independent judgment to be both earning money from Jack on one hand and investigating crimes that involved him, as a victim or otherwise. Even the West Virginia state police were investigating why one of their troopers testified in one of Jack's drunk driving cases in a way that allowed Jack to get off.

BRANDI HAD TROUBLES LIKE any teenager has troubles adjusting in life. She had not had an easy life because of the suicide of her father and the cancer of her mother. But I did not find any evidence that she used crack cocaine before she was the Powerball winner's granddaughter.

I am very surprised by how many people have e-mailed, written, and called me to say that they cannot stop thinking about the story because it does touch on universal themes about human nature....A few people have been angry that I wrote about West Virginia in a way that they thought made West Virginia look bad. I had a couple of people say that that has reinforced stereotypes of West Virginia, which surprised me. I don't agree with them, because I loved the people I met in West Virginia. I came away with a pretty high opinion. Even young drug addicts would call me "ma'am" and open the door for me. That doesn't happen in Washington all that often in my experience.

I have heard over the years that winning the lottery is not necessarily all good. It's a mixed experience. But I think everybody has the fantasy that they would know how to do it right. If they won the lottery, they would remain stable and they wouldn't blow up their lives.

Jack's troubles didn't grow just out of his bad impulses; they grew out of his good impulses of wanting to help. By wanting to help...people came out of the woodwork. He had to change his life almost instantly. He said from the start, "I'm not going to change my life. I'm going to be the same guy." But then the world changed around him. He went every morning to the C&L Super Serve to buy biscuits from Brenda Higginbotham and gas up his car. He couldn't go there after a number of days, because people would show up in the pre-dawn darkness and wait for him to arrive and hit him up for money.

...BRENDA SAID THAT THERE were heartbreaking stories. People would be crying, and say that they had a child who was dying of cancer. They were out of work. They were desperate. If that was uncomfortable for people who had just had ancillary roles in Jack's life, imagine what that must have been like for Jack and his family, just overwhelming.

Jack still has money left based on a few things. One, he was a savvy businessman before, and he [did not lose] that entirely when this tsunami hit. One of his few interviews was with a wire service in West Virginia; it was the one-year anniversary of his win. He talked about how much he had spent at that point, and said he'd spent about $45 million. But a lot of it was to acquire property that he said he bought under market value.

[THIS STORY] WAS ONE of the most memorable to me, because I found what it showed about people, to be so fascinating. In terms of significance,

I did hard…investigative stories. I spent a year of my life investigating Prince George's [Maryland] police, who were coercing false murder confessions from innocent men. A story like that has a lot more impact in terms of helping correct massive injustice in the system. A story like this seems maybe softer, less significant. But it apparently has a lot of people thinking, because they keep writing to tell me that they are thinking.

Memoirs of a Boy Soldier

ISHMAEL BEAH

A Long Way Gone: Memoirs of a Boy Soldier *by Ishmael Beah (Far-rar, Straus and Giroux) is his memoir of life as a child soldier in Sierra Leone, West Africa. He joined us on Q & A on April 1, 2007 to discuss his life story. After his family was killed when he was twelve, he explains how he and other young boys were forced into an army. Ishmael Beah was a soldier through age seventeen, attacking villages, often under the influence of drugs. He explains how he was brought to the United States and adopted by a woman, creating a new life for himself.*

M Y COUNTRY IS SIERRA Leone. It's in West Africa, a very tiny na-tion in West Africa. The population before the war used to be about five or six million people, but it's very less now, because a lot of people were killed during the war.

MY BOOK TRACES ME from when I'm about seven or eight, but more heavily on when I'm twelve, thirteen, fourteen, fifteen, sixteen, and then seventeen. That's really most of the book.... [I never thought I would be alive to this day, much less write a book.] The war that I was able to survive was so vicious and so brutal, to the sense that my life became just surviving each passing minute, and actually being uncer-tain about what the next minute would bring. Surviving that war that I was pressed in as a child soldier had nothing to do with me being smart or knowing how to run fast, or anything. It was [through] pure luck and the grace of God. So, for me, being able to get out of it is lucky enough. I never imagined this would be possible, that I would have a life beyond another day.

I LOST MY MOTHER, father and two brothers, who had been killed by the RUF [Revolutionary United Front] in the war. I was pressed into this conflict...[and] we were fully embracing this war that we were in, as children fighting in this war. Our conversations were limited only to the violent things we wanted to do, because there was no sense of something existing beyond this reality that we were in. The way the life was, we would go out and fight and then use drugs and then watch American war films—*Rambo, First Blood, Commando*. Sometimes we would want to be like those things and re-enact some of those things we had seen in the film....

In the beginning of the war, when you were pressed into it, you were afraid of holding the gun. But then when we went to the first battle and we fought and I shot somebody, killed somebody, it does something to you. You start a descent into this hell and it's very difficult in the beginning. But after time went on, it became easy. It became normalized, this world. In the context of war, this is what happens. You normalize the situation so you can live through it, because if you don't, you die. In the context we were in, if you second-guessed anything that you were doing, the commanders would kill you. Children who cried for their mothers were shot immediately. After a while, this becomes our world and we embrace it, and these groups become our surrogate family after we had lost everything dear to us....

The war started in 1991, to get rid of a political party called the APC [All People's Congress] that had been ruling and embezzling funds for so long, and that had driven the country to be really poor, so there were no schools and things like that. But at some point during the war, the reason for that got lost. As with most wars, it starts for a good reason and that reason gets lost. So it became a war of survival for the limited basic necessities that were available, and you had disenfranchised army squads, like mine that I was in, that just looted and pillaged the countryside while their friends were embezzling funds in the capital. So, it became a war and you were in it if you were part of a military group, or if you were pressed into it, you became part of it and you went out to look for whatever....It became kill or be killed.

My first gun was given to me by a gentleman called Corporal Gaddafi. He was part of my squad, and a lieutenant; he was the second-in-command there. It was an AK-47. The first time he gave it to me, I was so scared and so shaken. I had never held a gun in my hand in my entire life. I was shaking. I was so scared I didn't want to look at it. But it didn't have the magazine in it, [but] the second time around it had the magazine. But as time went on, it came with the rhetoric of saying that "this gun is your protector, your provider, your safety—everything. It does everything for you in this conflict, so you'd better learn to love it. And if you don't hold it, we're going to shoot you at some point." So you held it and you became attached to it.

After I had lost my entire family, I ended up at a military base—a disenfranchised group of the Sierra Leone army. It was the Sierra Leone army that recruited me into the war. Basically, I was not given a choice, along with over thirty other orphans who were in the village at that time. You either become a part of it or you were kicked out of the village. The thing about being kicked out of the village is that the rebels were surrounding it and they would kill you, because they would consider you a sympathizer of the other side. Now, everyone who was fighting this war believed that they were fighting the right fight. The rebels would use the same rhetoric to the children they were recruiting. We later found out, after we were taken out of this war, that they would tell them, "The army is responsible for everything—the atrocities and killing your families. So you are actually doing a service to them." But you had no choice. You couldn't leave. The army would use the same rhetoric. So you have everyone blaming everyone, but everyone was doing the same thing.

I was thirteen [when I first killed a person]. We had been pressed into this conflict because we had come to believe that the rebels were going to attack this village to take it over, so the safety that we knew was going to end. And because of this, we were pressed into it. We trained for less than a week, how to shoot the AK-47 and some basic military things—you had to crawl and follow small commands, and then we went to the warfront to try to repel the rebels. I remember laying in ambush and the commander, Lieutenant Jabati, saying, "Wait. I will give you the command when we see people moving in the swamp." And then we saw people moving and, actually, some of them were kids, just like us, wearing similar half-and-half combat and civilian clothes, and some were adults. They started shooting, exchanging fire. I could not pull the trigger. I was numb. Where I was lying, I could not do it. But as I was lying there, all the friends that I had joined with were being blown up. Some of them were shot and their blood was spilling all over me. That whole chaos and that madness just pushed something within me, and I started shooting whoever was moving from one bush to the other. And that's when it started.

I was in the war for over two years.... The way it was is that each day, each second of when you're engaged in any form of combat or violence, it was either you kill somebody or you are killed. This is the basic thing that happens in war. When you are there, you have to live. And when you live, somebody else dies.

Cocaine was available a lot.... We didn't have a strong supply route. It wasn't like there was somebody bringing in stuff. [So] we attacked other bases, other armed groups, in order to get ammunition and drugs. When we attacked other places, we killed people. We took the ammunition that was in their base and we took over. If we needed food, if it wasn't there at that base, we would go to civilian villages and take the food from them. This war was that kind of madness. You didn't know what was coming. But what was coming to Sierra Leone, from what I know now, is that because of the diamond trade, they took it out and sold it, and exchanged it for guns and other drugs that came in through that.

Because we had been using all these drugs, at some point, they weren't as effective anymore, because we would develop a strong tolerance to them. So, "brown-brown"—I don't know who really came up with it— was a concoction of cocaine and gunpowder. You mix it up and you sniff it. In the beginning, it burns the insides of your nose and it hurts. But after a while you get used to it, and it doesn't hurt inside. What it does to you is that it has more potency and effect than regular cocaine. It gives you a tremendous rush of energy and it numbs you to everything. You're not afraid of anything. You have no feeling for anything. Say, for example, you're in a bush and a shrub goes through your skin and you're bleeding, you don't even feel anything. You don't care. I think that's one of the powerful things they use also to keep us in that state.

A day was [like this:] you get up in the morning, the commander says we're going to the next village. We're going to scope out some villages, or we're going to attack some place. So, you go attack people, shoot people, kill people, and then you recruit more children if you capture them. Then you also have people to carry the loads of your loot back to your base. And then when we returned, we did drugs and then we watched war films. And then we went back to fight. So, this was the life. That was it.

SIERRA LEONE BEFORE THE war…was a beautiful country, nice weather. Really amazing people—the kindest people I've met anywhere. But then this came about, which is why I always say, before the war in Sierra Leone, none of us knew that any of us would be capable of doing these things or would have neighbors who can do it. But then it happens there. So, for me, it really goes to show that losing one's humanity in extreme violence is not specific to any particular country, people, or nation. It could happen anywhere. If people are put in that circumstance, no one knows what you might do.

Sierra Leone is a former British colony, so we are surrounded by Guinea, which is a French-speaking country. And then on the other side is Liberia, which has a strong connection to the United States. The capital is called Freetown, because when the slaves were freed in the Americas and in Europe, they were taken back to Freetown. This is how Freetown came about, as a freedom town for them to be removed. Early on, during slavery, there were actually a huge number of slaves who were brought from Sierra Leone to the Carolinas, because in Sierra Leone there's a strong love for rice, and people have rice-planting skills. So, because of that, slaves were brought from there to the Carolinas. I think they still have an island in the Carolinas—I forgot which one, but it's in the Gullah islands—where there are people who speak dialects that are very similar to those in Sierra Leone. There have been some anthropologists doing documentaries about people tracing their lineage back to there.

Growing up as a kid, one of the things that I had in my childhood was a strong sense of oral tradition in my culture. I'm from the Mende tribe, which is one of the biggest tribes in Sierra Leone. One of the things that we did in my village was that we'd sit around the fire and the adults would tell stories, orally, and you were supposed to retain them and remember them exactly—even with the hand gestures. Then, maybe two or three days later at another gathering, they will point randomly at somebody and say, "You retell the story we just told." And you will retell it. So, because of this at a very young age, you learn a sense of narrative, a sense of how to remember things very deeply and internalize them. And also, there is such a strong connection to the land, to nature, and a very strong feel for things. So, when all these things stop, when they were shifting, I could feel it and it said so much. And because I have such a strong photographic memory—which is actually a curse and blessing in my opinion, for me, because I remember everything so vividly—especially because I have so many bad things that I saw, it becomes quite heavy.

At that time, when I was drugged, it seemed that all of this [remembering] had stopped, because there was no thinking process going on. We were not allowed to do that. But after I was removed from the war and I went to rehabilitation, the drugs wore off. Then all this memory started pumping in, and the [memories] were just there waiting. They were lying dormant in my head; it was just the drugs that were numbing them. And then I started to remember everything. When I would see certain people, they would look like certain people, and I would remember those instances. Certain snaps would bring up certain memories in my head. And I also have a very visual recollection. So sometimes, because of the shock of it at that age, I remember certain things not just visually, but also [in an] auditory [way]. I can hear certain things. I can hear the sparks of certain fires and things of that sort. And the smell—it's something that will stay with me for the rest of my life. It's not something that I could forget at all.

I was talking to my mom—my American mother who adopted me, Laura Simms—the other day about how before, my life was, "Could I survive each minute?" Now my life is basically, "What journalist don't I need to talk to so I can have my own time just to rest?" So, it's gone from one different world to a completely different thing that I never imagined. But I think one thing that this shows, in my opinion, is the fact that, when you are caught up in that life of violence, it actually limits you from knowing your humanity, from knowing what you are capable of doing. So, at some point, I never thought I was intelligent or I could write or I could do anything. If you met me at that time, you would never think you and I could have an intelligible conversation.

[If you had met me back in the jungles,] you probably would have never liked me. I guarantee that. First of all, I had a very strong, tense face. I didn't think about anything except the violence. That was my life. [I hated] anyone who the commander said was the rebel—they were responsible for the deaths of my family or all the things like that. [In] my initial group, there were over thirty boys that were recruited. Then, as time went on, we had more and more. So, sometimes we would have five, six people and sometimes we'd have ten, twelve. Depending on what given moment, there were all kinds of people. Some—most—of them died along the way. I got shot a couple of times. There are lots of bullet piercings on my body and in my foot. At some point I got shot, and some bullets went in and out, and others got stuck in me. They had to do a minor operation and take them out. But my foot is fine, so I can still walk around. I am one of the very fortunate ones to have survived.

I was back in Sierra Leone in 2006. There are a few who came to rehabilitation with me, so I was able to see about six or seven of them. I don't know where the rest of them are. Some of them died during the time when I was in the squad with them, maybe we lost about ten, fifteen to twenty of them. And more of them came on. There are a few that are still in a rehabilitation center. What happened in my case was [that] my mom, now, from the United States, during the second part of the war, came to the capital city. She was able to get me out. So I had an option. I left. Some people who didn't get that option to leave were drawn back into the war, because it's either that or they will kill you....

The first time I came to the United States was at the end of 1996, after I had finished rehabilitation, to speak at the United Nations about the issue of children being used in war in Sierra Leone. UNICEF invited me. My local angel that I was with put forward my application as somebody who could come and speak about this. I think they selected me—I don't know—because they probably thought I was eloquent enough to speak about it. I'm not sure. At a very young age, I had two strong interests. One was hip-hop, American hip-hop music that I got drawn to. And another one was Shakespeare. So, because of those two things, I was always going to the dictionary and looking for new words and practicing reciting soliloquies from Shakespeare, writing American hip-hop lyrics down and trying to recite them. Because of that at an early age, I had a very strong fascination for language. But during the war, that didn't play out. So, after the war when I was at the rehabilitation center, we had some preliminary schooling and they tried to rekindle that again. So, that interest showed again.

When I was eight, I saw my first music video. It was this group called Sugarhill Gang and their song called, "Rapper's Delight." For me, growing up in this culture where English was not my first language or second or third language—I learned it in school only—I had come to believe that people who were black did not speak English. So, to see somebody on television so versatile in the language and speaking it so fast was very fascinating to me. And also [I liked] the poetry of it. So, I got drawn to it because of that. I would write it, and if I didn't know a word, I would look in the dictionary. My father would always say, "Why don't you listen to the BBC? This is better English. That's bad English." But I liked both worlds....

Shakespeare was introduced to me in school. Because of our colonial heritage, Shakespeare was the literature that I learned in all of my school years. I grew to love it a lot, but one of my favorite quotes in Shakespeare is from *King Lear*, when he's in the storm with the fool and he realized what had happened with all his daughters, and he said, "When we were born, we cry that we've come to this great stage of fools." That makes a lot of sense to me, especially with the state of the world and where I am, and what I saw. Because, in a sense, human beings don't really learn. So I'm a big fan of Shakespeare.

I knew a little bit of Shakespeare before I fought. One of the things that I did in primary school was, I would memorize soliloquies from Shakespeare, or little monologues. Then I would go to the town square, where adults would gather in the evening. All kids would do this. We would recite, "Friends, Romans, countrymen, lend me your ears. I have not come to bury Caesar..."—things like this. People would clap. Parents were very proud of this, because this showed that their kid had a mastery of the English language to some extent. When I did this, then people in the community would start coming to me so I could read their letters. If their sons and daughters who lived in the town sent them letters, sometimes I would write them letters. So, at a young age, I got to know some of the secrets of the community. And so, it was quite good to know the English language.

My mother and father separated when I was six, when I was very young. My older brother and I went to live with our father in a town called Mogbwemo. My grandmother was ten miles away from Mogbwemo and my mother was another two miles away in another town. My dad worked as a lab technician for this American company that mined rutile and bauxite, and things of that sort. So, growing up to begin with, we were considered misfits, because most people didn't have their families divorced at that time. So, we were the kids who, when we did something, it would be because we didn't have a mother at home, and things like that. When my mother left, we had a few stepmothers who came and went, and they were very mean to us, so they always created a rift between our father and ourselves.

When the war broke out, we went to Mattru Jong, which is where I was born, just sixty miles away, to partake in a variety show with some friends. We would mimic these American hip-hop songs and do the dances. Then, the next day, Mogbwemo was attacked; we tried to return, but we couldn't. On our way back we saw so many dead bodies and people who had been touched by this. It was the first introduction to war. And after this, we continued running. Mattru Jong was also attacked and then we continued running. But we would come across people who knew our family, and they would say, "Oh, they are in this village." So, that kept us going. We finally arrived at the village where all of my family had made it, including my older brother. But we were too late. We got there maybe a few minutes late and there was an attack right when we were on the outskirts. We heard the gunshots and the fire being set to places and people screaming. Everyone in that village was killed. People were lined up and shot in the back of their heads. People were locked in houses and burned alive. So, all of my family was massacred. I saw the ashes and the burned bodies and things.

I was so angry. I think it was one of the first times that I started to become quite violent. I was so angry because on our way to this place, we had encountered a gentleman called Gasemu, who used to live in Mog-bwemo, as well. He slowed us down so we could help him carry some trunks of bananas. The pain of seeing what had just happened and knowing that one minute that you had a family, and knowing that you're the only one left, was so severe, that I wished I had been there to die with them. I blamed Gasemu for stopping that from happening. I actually struck him....I was absolutely angry. I felt as if my veins were being pulled out of my body. My head was warm and it felt like it was heavy. My neck was hurting. I was in physical pain by just being there. Even to this day, when I think about it, it just makes my entire body uncomfortable. It's a very unpleasant feeling, at twelve, knowing that your family is all gone, just like that. But I think one thing that war showed me, and when I was running from it at that moment, was how fragile life really is. It had become so apparent in that context; you really see it right in front of your eyes.

I STARTED WRITING THIS book when I was at Oberlin College. This was during my junior year at Oberlin College. When I first came to the United States, I quickly realized that a lot of people didn't know Sierra Leone was a country. That upset me a lot, so I started speaking about it. The war had been going on there for seven years....But every time I would speak at the U.N., Human Rights Watch, at the Security Council—wherever I was speaking—I felt that ten or twenty minutes was not enough time for me to really explain and give a context to what happened, so people can really see and feel the humanity of the people of the Sierra Leone that I know. Because oftentimes, when people hear about these countries, they hear about Sierra Leone through the amputation, through the war. But for me, when you say Sierra Leone, it's much more than that. There was a culture that existed—a beautiful one before the war disintegrated it. So I wanted to show that. And also, I felt like it was very important to put a human face to what seemed so distant to a lot of people, to expose this continual use of children in war and how it comes about. So that's one of the reasons why I started writing it. It was a very difficult process to remember but I felt that remembering and the difficulties of it was a very small price to pay to expose what continues to happen to a lot of children.

I WROTE THE BOOK all myself. I had help from people who looked at it and said, "Well, why don't you write more about this?"—things that I was reluctant to write about. And then I would go and try to write about it. I had a professor at Oberlin, Dan Chaon, who is also a writer, who helped me a lot, who basically became my mentor. He would read it and give me feedback. But I did the work myself. I didn't do any research. I just sat down and wrote everything out, because I knew everything was in me so much. It was very difficult to write, but I would balance it out by writing about times before the war when it got too difficult. For example, I would write about my mother's cooking and how the air smelled that day; or how going swimming and things like that balanced out things for me.

LAURA SIMMS, [MY AMERICAN mother,] is a storyteller, a very good storyteller. When I came to the United States, in '96, at the UNICEF conference, that's how I met her. There were a lot of people introducing themselves saying that "I am this, I am a UNICEF psychologist, I do this." She said, "I'm a storyteller." So, now, coming from a very oral tradition, storytelling culture, I was very curious how this woman in New York City was a storyteller. So I got to know her through that. But also because, when we came in '96, I came with another young man who is in the book, Bah. We had no winter jackets. We were so cold. And this woman saw us and felt so sorry for us, and ran home, grabbed her winter jackets, gloves, and hats and gave them to us. So, because of that, we started knowing her a little bit. When the conference ended, I went back to Sierra Leone, and she gave me her number, so we kept in touch. She sent me money to start school. The war hadn't reached the capital yet, so I started school there. When the war reached the capital, she got me out. She had sent me money right before the war hit the capital. I told her that I would go to Guinea, a neighboring country. I asked, if I made it out, if I can come to live with her, and she said yes.

So then I left and went to Guinea. And I called her from Guinea, from the capital, Conakry. Then she put some things in place, [and] took me to South Africa to live with a friend that she knew there. From there, I went to Ivory Coast, and then I got a visa in Ivory Coast, and I eventually ended up in New York City, in 1998. She worked really hard, because, at that time, no one wanted to give me a visa to come, because I couldn't prove that I intended to return back to Sierra Leone. The country had collapsed. You couldn't prove that.

I lived with her in the East Village for the years of my schooling, for the last two years of high school. And then when I went to college, I would come back. I lived there. I still have the keys. I go into the house all the time and steal food from the fridge, just as a regular young person would. I went to the United Nations international school that she was able to get me into. When I came, it was very difficult, because one of the things in the war, when you run away, you don't have school records. When I started school in the capital city, I only went for two semesters. I didn't have those school records either, because I had to flee, so I had to be tested a lot to determine what level I was. They decided eleventh grade was my level, so they put me there. And then I went on. I lived with her. It was very wonderful. And one of the things that's really great about it, is that she is a storyteller. She knew stories that were from Sierra Leone that were very specific to my tribe. So when she would tell them to me sometimes, I absolutely felt like that she was giving me back a piece of my childhood that I had lost so much. She gave me a chance to be a child. Before, when I came in the summer in '98, before school started, we went around the country. She was going to storytelling festivals. We went to California. I went bike riding and swimming. I had my first burrito....

When I was in high school, my college counselor spoke about Oberlin College a little bit. But then, since I was in the human rights stuff a lot, I went to a lot of conferences and there's a thing called State of the World Forum in San Francisco. I was there and there was a gentleman from Oberlin who spoke about human rights, the need for international norms in the world, and things like that. I talked to him and he said, "Oh, yes, I went to Oberlin. It's this little school in Ohio. I think you'd like it. You should look at it." I was very taken by this gentleman, so I decided to talk to my college counselor, and they sent me to look at Oberlin. I went in the spring—it's a beautiful campus. The size was very small, and I was drawn to it. And then I went back in the fall. And then winter came. It's very cold in Ohio but I loved the school. The academics were very good. The class sizes were really small. It was ten-, fifteen-person class sizes, and

I needed that, because I was coming from a place where I hadn't been to school for so long. So I needed to be somewhere where I could get that personal attention, and it's the best place.

When I started high school, I didn't tell most of my friends [about my past]. Some teachers knew and a few other people. But most people didn't know. I didn't think it was a good introduction. "Hi, my name is Ishmael. I used to be in a war." You know, that won't go [over] so well. But, later on, when people found out—because people got to meet me and know me as just the Ishmael who lives in the East Village. Then, when they learned about all this, really, I think they understood perhaps why I had certain tendencies, perhaps why I was so calm, why I never tried to engage in any form of ruffle with anyone. And so, people got to understand certain things about me. If anything, they said, "I always knew there was something you didn't tell me." Some would say that, but I don't think people's reaction changed. Before, when I used to go around and speak, I encountered a few people—from Sierra Leone, actually, and sometimes elsewhere—who were still unsettled about where children who were pressed into this role stand in terms of being victims or perpetrators. I've encountered people like that who absolutely do not like me, because they think, if anything, I should be looked at as a perpetrator, or all the kids who participated in the war should be looked at like they're not victims. There are people who are of that notion. I think it's because they don't understand what really happened. A lot of those people are people who did not live in these countries, who don't know what really happened there.

WHEN THE USE OF children had become really rampant in the war in Sierra Leone, in all sides of it, U.N. agencies, UNICEF and other places, started creating local angels, and they would go into the bushes and talk to the commanders. I guess they were really convincing, because the commanders would release a number of kids at a given time. I happened to be one of the first lucky kids who was released and brought to this center. Those [rehabilitation workers] are like my heroes, because they were willing to see us as children, regardless of what we had been part of….It was the genuine care and compassion behind it; we had hurt some of these people, because we were so violent, and when they returned they would say, "It's not your fault. Have you eaten?" Those were their concerns. These people were so kind, that when they looked at us, they still looked at us as children, and nothing more. As time went on, this really began to touch some of us, to rekindle that joy we had known as children, to know that we were capable of regaining ourselves again.

I HAVE A LOT of nightmares, even to this day. Before, I used to have a lot of them, and it used to disturb me so severely. But through lots of therapy and writing the book, as well, I've been able to cope with a lot of it. When I wake up from a frightening dream, when I'm sweating or when I dream that somebody's killing me, or that I'm running from something, I wake up and realize that, "OK, I'm not there. I'm here now." There is still a healing process going on. When I walk down the street, different sounds remind me of different things, trigger different things in my head. But my life before the war, during the war, and after the war is what makes me who I am. I live with all of that. I've just been able to transform those experiences more into instructional tools rather than things that will harm me.

Gaining Sight

ROBERT KURSON

Robert Kurson is a former lawyer turned magazine feature writer and bestselling author who appeared on Q & A on June 24, 2007 to tell the story of Mike May, captured in Kurson's book, Crashing Through: A True Story of Risk, Adventure, and the Man Who Dared to See *(Random House). Mike May was blinded at age three in a chemical accident and lived a very full life as a blind man. Kurson reports on May's difficult decision to undergo surgery to regain his sight as an adult. We hear about May's life after the operation, including a time when he began to lose his sight again, his family's reaction, and what it's like to learn to see.*

*C*RASHING *T*HROUGH IS THE true story of Mike May. He's a businessman and inventor from Davis, California, who was blinded in a chemical explosion at age three, and who lived the next forty-three years of his life totally blind, until a chance encounter with a world-renowned ophthalmologist gave him the chance to see. About three years ago, I was having a sleepless night, tossing and turning. I started to ponder these crazy thoughts that sometimes we have in the middle of the night, and the thought I had that night was, "What is the single greatest human experience possible? What is the one most beautiful and perfect thing that could happen to a human being?" I tossed around various possibilities. Was it a night of romance with Charlize Theron? Was it the world's greatest steak dinner cooked by the most magnificent chef? Or was it, as my dad had often suggested, a night of listening to Mozart under the stars at the outdoor Ravinia Music Festival near our home? Those all sounded wonderful. But then I decided—and it was very conclusive—that the single greatest human experience possible is to live a life completely blind, and then open one's eyes. That had to be better than anything.

So, the next morning I started to do research on the subject.... I knew nobody by name [at that point]. I'd never even met a blind person in my life. For all I knew, people got their vision after a lifetime of blindness every day. What I discovered in the library was that this was extraordinarily rare, that there were fewer than twenty cases known to all of history in which a person had lived his life, or nearly all his life, blind, and then opened his eyes and got vision. Even stranger than that, the vision they got was this weird hybrid in which certain parts of the visual system work perfectly, but other parts didn't work at all. Every one of these patients seemed able to see motion and color perfectly and instantly. Yet none of them seemed able, for example, to understand or identify human faces. None of them seemed able to see in-depth. They saw instead what looked like an abstract painting full of bright and colorful but meaningless shapes. None of them seemed able to readily identify common objects, no matter how hard they tried. Even more astonishing to me than all of that was that every single one of these patients suffered a profound and deep depression for their daring to see the world. That's when I came across the name of Mike May, a person who seemed different than all the rest of his predecessors. There was only one other person that I could tell that was living that had had that experience. The first of these cases went back to ancient Arabia in the year 1020. The only other living candidate that I found, I couldn't locate, and that person seemed to have [had] a terrible result, just like all the rest.

The single worst part [of getting your sight back] seems to be that new vision after a lifetime of blindness requires a massive amount of cognitive heavy lifting, an incredible amount of conscious work to decipher this new world of images and objects. None of it comes automatically, instantaneously, or unconsciously to that newly sighted person, as it does to us. We simply look around and see the world and understand it. Every image to them, every moment requires work, requires translation in the way that speaking a foreign language for the first days does to us. We have to order the words, think of the vocabulary, conjugate the verbs, and then put it into a sentence. This is what vision requires of the person with new vision, but it never ends. They never seem to get better at it, so it's this constant workload that never eases.

AT THE TIME [I found Mike May], he was about fifty or fifty-one years old, and the only mention these cases in the literature made of Mike May was that he had gained vision from a very rare and revolutionary stem cell transplant surgery. Nobody made any mention of his emotional state. I had to know what this person had gone through and what his life was like. So, basically, I just looked up his name and phone number, found him in Davis, California, and gave him a call, introduced myself and was ready to hear someone who sounded to be on the verge of suicide. All these cases are filled with reports of suicidal thoughts, of clawing at the eyes, of fury at the surgeon who cured them, of reverting to dark rooms and blindfolds. In the best documented case, the person simply was so disappointed in the visual world that he gave up and died. So I expected to hear someone in desperate straits. Instead, the person on the other end of the phone sounded extraordinarily busy to me. I introduced myself and told him that I had read about these cases and had to know about his life. He very politely but firmly told him, "No thanks. I'm too busy."

I don't give up that easily. I kept at it, kept bothering him, and finally he agreed to see me... and I went to his house in Davis, California, and rang his bell. When he opened the door, he put his hand out and shook my hand perfectly, then proceeded to show me around the house flaw-lessly. He went from room to room, introduced me to his two sons, to his wife. He poured me a cold glass of water from the refrigerator, and then asked me if I'd like to play flag football. I distinctly did not want to play flag football. I'd come all the way from Chicago to see him, but he had arranged a game with high school and college kids, and I watched him make beautiful running catches over his shoulder. I saw him run around trees and concrete picnic tables. I thought I'd arrived at the wrong house. I thought this must be a different Mike May. There's no way that this person could have been blind for a day in his life. He moved too perfectly and too beautifully. Finally, when the game was over, we sat down on the couch. I asked him, finally, to tell me the story.

HE BEGAN TO TELL me about the accident that had blinded him at age three. I watched, and he made perfect eye contact with me during the story. He was locked in perfectly. Yet, as he continued the story, I had some sense, some vague sense, that he wasn't seeing me at all. I recalled what I had read about his predecessors, that they didn't understand human faces. I interrupted him finally and said, "Mike, can you see my face?" He said, "Oh, yeah. I can see your face perfectly. It's perfectly in focus, perfectly sharp. It's just that your face makes no sense to me." Now, I'd been told this many times in my life before but never under these circumstances. This was the beginning of a fascinating discussion that I had with him. He was looking at me perfectly, just not seeing me. He told me right then and there, "I don't understand faces. They make no sense to me. They're meaningless to me."

It was the second or third visit that I had with him [when I told him I wanted to write a book]. I found this to be about the most astonishing story I'd ever heard, and the most unexpected. I told him, "I'd like to write this book. There's so much to say. It's so unexpected." Again, he politely refused me. He said, "I'm very busy. I'm running a company now that requires my full attention. I'm on the road all the time. And, I think I'd like to write my own book someday." That's when I had to explain to him, essentially, "I'm going to write a much better book than you're going to write." He agreed. I gave him [my previous book] *Shadow Divers*, and when he was done with it, he was on board and ready to go with me.

I took my interview opportunities when I could get them. I found myself in London with him, in Kalamazoo, Michigan, on boats, on trains—all kinds of things, because I had to go where he had to go.

He had this hybrid of vision [when I met him]. He could see some things perfectly. He could do beautiful things in motion. He could ride a bike by himself. Yet, he still needed his guide dog to help him walk down the street, which seemed very odd to me. Here was a guy who can make spectacular running catches over his shoulder. He continues to be, to this day, the world recordholder in downhill speed skiing, sixty-five miles an hour, by a totally blind person. Yet, he couldn't tell the difference between a curb and a shadow, or a set of stairs and a series of painted lines.

He would invite me out [for our interviews] when he had time. I would prepare questions, sometimes for weeks at a time, in advance of our meetings, and then I just went, went, went. He could sit with me six, eight hours at a time. He was phenomenally capable of enduring my endless questions. He was a wonderful interview subject, just like the two divers were in *Shadow Divers*. He often thought to tell me things I couldn't have thought to ask myself, and some of those things make for the best moments in the book. He has a wonderful memory and a wonderful sense of what's important. That's a gift to an author any time you find that.

[AT AGE THREE,] MIKE got into some chemicals in the garage, plunged [a jar] full of powder into some water. It created an explosive gas that was ignited by a nearby flame. It blew up completely…six months in the hospital, and complete obliteration of his eyes. [Five hundred stitches] all over his body—his arms, his chest, his face, his legs—everywhere. It was a miracle he didn't die. In fact, the doctors told his mother repeatedly he would die and to prepare to say goodbye to him. When he pulled through, his total blindness seemed like such an inconsequential price to have paid in order to have her child back, that his mother was thrilled with the result and resolved on the spot that her son should live as full and rich and complete a life as any sighted child.

The family moved to a mining town in New Mexico when Mike was three, so that his father, who was an engineer, could pursue a new job. Mike had this accident, and because his mother refused to send him away to a blind boarding school, which is what happened to all blind kids in the late 1950s, the family moved itself 1,000 miles to California, where Mike was allowed to attend school for normal-sighted people. It's there that his mother began insisting that he live like everyone else and to try everything. That really is the story of the rest of his life.

He attended all public schools and mixed with sighted students all the time. He then went on to college at the University of California at Davis, and then took a master's in international relations from Johns Hopkins. At that point, he went out into the world. Even with that degree, an incredibly prestigious degree, he found it difficult to find employment, because it seemed people didn't want to take a risk on a blind guy, even one as accomplished and capable as he was. He spent a year in Ghana building schools and exploring Africa, because he was interested in it. He came back and started to find his inventor's heart. He became part of a team that invented the world's first laser turntable, the precursor to the CD. That started him on this next stage of exploration and of speaking to his curiosity in his life. He is a very busy guy.

[AT] FORTY-SIX YEARS OLD, he bet everything in his life—his family's future and their fortune—on a new product he invented, which is a GPS system for the blind. It's something that's handheld that will guide the blind about the streets and about the world, in the same way that GPS guides our cars. In a lovely kind of way, it's a product that gives a certain kind of vision to the blind. And that's the moment when he has a chance encounter with an ophthalmologist who says, "I think we can make you see."

This world-renowned ophthalmologist dropped this thunderbolt on him, that there was this very rare and revolutionary stem cell transplant surgery that can give him vision. It was a totally accidental encounter; it should have never happened. Mike's wife scratched her contact lenses while they were strolling about San Francisco one day. She was able to get a last-second appointment with an optometrist and asked Mike to come with her. He had no interest in coming with her. He would have rather walked up and down the streets of San Francisco, but she prevailed and said, "I'll only be ten minutes. Come with me." He thought, "All right. I'll wait in the waiting room." He went in, and the optometrist who saw his wife took a look at him and said, "How long has it been since an ophthalmologist looked at you." He said, "Ten or twenty years. As a child I was assured nothing could be done." [The optometrist] said, "I have a partner, world-famous, who does some very new and revolutionary things. How about if he takes a look at you?" Mike thought, "Well, I don't see why, but I guess it can't hurt."

The guy came in, took a look at him, and asked him how he'd been blinded. That was very important to the ophthalmologist. When the guy heard that it had been a chemical explosion, he told him about this stem cell transplant surgery that could give him vision. He said, ten minutes after Mike walked into the building, "I think we can make you see."

Up to that point, probably fewer than 300 people worldwide [have had the operation]. There were probably fewer than ten doctors in the

United States who even knew about the surgery, let alone could perform it, but he was sitting in the office of one of them who could. On the drive home, he and his wife discussed it a little bit. Mike had never yearned for vision a day in his life. They talked kind of jovially about it. What would he like to see? He said, "If I was made to see, I think I'd like to see panoramas." He loved hearing people talk about panoramas when he went skiing, but he'd never been able to touch them, so he didn't know what they were talking about. He said, "I'd love to see beautiful women." She said, after awhile and nervously, sweetly, "What about me and the kids?" And he said, "Honestly, I feel like I see you and the kids so deeply and so fundamentally as it is, in the true sense of what seeing means, to know you and love you and connect with you, that I don't think vision or anything else would help me see you any better at all." It was for panoramas and beautiful women. That's what he thought of first. The doctor had also explained to him the myriad risks involved in going forward with this, and that started to build up in his mind, even on the way home.

The doctor's name was Dan Goodman, from San Francisco. He explained to Mike that this stem cell transplant surgery—that uses stem cells from donors, not the politically controversial embryonic stem cells—could give him vision. But there were several risks, he said. The first was that there was just a 50-50 chance it could work. But even if it did work, Dr. Goodman couldn't predict the extent of vision restoration possible. Mike might get a little speck of vision, or he might be able to drive. Anything in between, Dr. Goodman couldn't say. Even if Mike got good and useful vision, Dr. Goodman said, "You could lose that vision at any time, for any reason or no reason whatsoever. So, you may have it for a year or two years or five years, and then it could be rejected and you could go blind again." Maybe worse than all of those, Goodman said, was the risk of cancer. Mike would have to ingest toxic doses of anti-rejection medication, Cyclosporine, to make this transplant work....Goodman said it's no small risk. He had, himself, a patient die recently from just such a cancer. So quickly, within minutes, the question became more than just, did Mike want to see. It became whether Mike was willing to risk dying in order to see. Goodman left it open. He said, "Call me if you're interested." This whole meeting was about ten minutes long.

I expected, when I met Mike, that he would tell me, "I got home and called him and signed up for the surgery." It took Mike nearly a year to contemplate this and to come to the decision to go forward with vision. The crux of his reluctance was that his life was already so full and rich without vision, it didn't seem necessary to him. He had not yearned to see—ever. And he was busy. And there were these risks.

Then he started to think about who he was as a person. He believed, from the bottom of his heart, for forty-three years, that while life with vision was great, life without vision was great, too, and that he was as satisfied as a person could be, being who he was. What would it mean, if, on a chance encounter with an ophthalmologist, he leaped into this new world of vision? Would it have meant he was wrong about who he was? He even worried about the prospect of, after forty-three years of being admired and looked up to by the blind and sighted alike, of suddenly turning average overnight, suddenly becoming ordinary when a man pulled the bandages off his eyes. These were all concerns to him, all the reasons not to do it. For months, he couldn't think of a single reason to go forward.

I talked to Dr. Goodman at length. He's a brilliant guy and a very plain speaker and a very honest man. He didn't encourage Mike. He didn't coax him one way or the other. He left it completely up to Mike, no promises, just a willingness to go forward, if Mike was willing.

WHAT THEY NEEDED TO do was first transplant donor stem cells around the cornea. Those forge clear pathways over the cornea and allow the cornea to remain clear, so that it can focus light and see clearly. They cut a doughnut of stem cells from the donor's eye. They shave it down to about a third of a millimeter, and then layer it on top of the patient's cornea. That's one part of the process. Then the person has to wait three or four months while the new stem cells forge clear pathways over the cornea. After three or four months, the patient then gets a routine cornea transplant, and that's the part that will either give him vision or not.

[The final operation was in early 2000.] Mike expected after the second surgery that it would be about three or four weeks before they could determine whether the surgery worked or not. The next morning Dr. Goodman asked him to come in the office, just to check the health of the wound. Something very unexpected happened that morning, which was he took the bandages off. Mike was just chatting away and when he lifted Mike's eyelid, this whoosh of color and motion and objects rushed into his eye. But it wasn't just before his eye. It was on top of him. It was in his hair, on his skin. It was behind him. It was on the wall, it was in the next room, in the next universe. This was a completely wondrous, unbelievable experience that Mike had no expectation of whatsoever. Within seconds, he saw Dr. Goodman's hand and could recognize it as a hand. A second later, he saw the color blue, but not just saw the color blue. He was able to name it, and say, "That's blue." We still don't know exactly [why he could do that]. It may be because he had experience with color for the first years of his life. Maybe because color is so primitively hardwired into our systems that we never lose it. But he could name them, not just see them—spectacular. He then saw his wife for the first time. As she moved over to him, he saw her blonde hair and said, "That's blonde. And now I know why I love blondes." One of the most beautiful things that happened was, when [his sons] came home he said, "I can see you!" and they said, "OK," and ran right past him and went up the stairs. Mike loved that, because it proved to him that his kids didn't think of him as a blind person or a sighted person. He was just "Dad" to them.

This is an astonishing moment: He's had vision for probably less than twenty-four hours after a lifetime of total blindness and goes into the backyard with [his son] Wyndham, who is a wonderful athlete, and he starts kicking balls, hard, right at him. Mike starts to make these running, beautiful catches. This is in the first day of vision. Things that are moving and things that are in color, he can see as well, or even better, than the rest of us. It's working perfectly for him. Yet, minutes [later], he cannot tell his wife from his sons, facially. Nor can he tell his wife from a stranger, facially. So, something was going on here.

He came very, very close [to losing his vision again]. He went in for a routine examination about a year into vision. He had always had very good checkups. Dr. Goodman suddenly told him, "You're going blind again. There's a vigorous rejection going on here. It's about the worst I've ever seen. We can try desperate measures if you want, but I've never seen one turned around that's this advanced." Here was one of the dangers; the risks he had put into the "don't do it" column come true to life.

When he asked the doctor, "What are we going to do about it?" the doctor said, "It's probably not going to work, but if you want to fight it, you're going to need to take a series of incredibly painful injections directly into your eye, and take many more doses of that very dangerous Cyclosporine. It probably still won't work, but it's up to you. But if you're going to do it, we've got to start now." [Without any kind of anesthetic.] Nothing.

The crux of it is that Mike had to decide on the spot to take the first shot, right then and there. He could, ironically, see the needle coming right toward his eye, because color and motion worked perfectly for him. So, he saw the glinting silver of the needle coming right for his eye, and then actually poking and puncturing the eyeball itself. He said it was so indescribably painful, that if it hadn't happened to him, he could not have believed such a painful thing was possible for a human being. I don't know exactly why [the doctor didn't anesthetize him] but this had to be done immediately, and Mike had to come back for a series of three or four more of them, all against huge odds that it would ever do anything to restore his vision. But Mike May doesn't quit, especially this far into the game. So he went forward with this and battled back.

It was only a matter of a couple of weeks before Dr. Goodman looked and said, "I've never seen something like this turned around, like this has done. But you're safe now." It was an incredible triumph for Mike. He has been able to see ever since. Nonetheless, there's still that small chance that gets smaller every year that this could happen again. I might see him tonight as a sighted person, and then, next week, find out that he lost it. I don't think [it makes him nervous]. I think the only thing that really makes him nervous is the idea of not having tried. I think he could deal fine with this, if he went blind again. He'd recover his blindness skills, and he'd live life just as fully.

THERE'S SO MUCH MORE to the story; the personal interactions with his family. The description just of his vision is very strange, a vision which was so difficult. The story of how he decided to get better at vision, even though the vision scientists told him, "Your brain no longer works for vision. No matter how hard you try, no matter how much of your heart you put into this, you can't get better at it." His decision not to go down the drain like every one of his predecessors seemed to, but to find a new way to see. That idea of how he decided to see in a way no one's ever thought to see before was an epiphany, really. That alone is worth knowing about. More than that, this is a story of how a person lives his life and what it means to breathe in the world fully and to allow yourself to fall. That's really what this is all about. That's really the story that people will get fully from reading the book.

Not everyone's comfortable with the concept of blindness. I remember having conversations with friends in which we debated, would we prefer to die or go blind. This is what vision means to people. Some people are uncomfortable even talking about blindness. But this book isn't really about blindness or vision at all. It's really about how a person best lives his life. That's why I think people respond to it.

An American Family
in Hitler's Berlin

ERIK LARSON

William E. Dodd was the U.S. Ambassador to Nazi Germany in the years prior to World War II. In a July 17, 2011 Q & A *program, Erik Larson explains how he discovered the diaries and memoirs of Dodd and his daughter Martha detailing their lives in Berlin. Through these first person accounts, he learned of the Dodd family's complex social obligations in Nazi Germany, the transformation in Berlin as Naziism increased, and the rise of Hitler, Göring, and Goebbels, and Rudolph Diels, the first chief of the Gestapo. His book about the Dodd family,* In the Garden of Beasts: Love, Terror, and an American Family in Hitler's Berlin *was published by Crown Publishing in 2011.*

M OST OF THE ACTION in my book takes place in 1933 and '34, [in the] very early days after the time when Hitler was appointed chancellor and including the point where he becomes the absolute leader, the Fuehrer of Germany in the summer of 1934. William E. Dodd became America's first ambassador to Nazi Germany, and, prior to that, he was a professor of history at the University of Chicago, a mild-mannered guy. In the State Department, the senior men were not really very pleased that Roosevelt went directly and hired Dodd to this position.

Martha Dodd was his daughter and half the reason I did this book is Martha, because when she arrived in Berlin with the family, she was in love with what she referred to as the Nazi revolution. She was enthralled by the Nazis, which really struck me as a completely surprising thing; given what we all know in hindsight, how could you actually be enthralled with the Nazi revolution? But there she was, and that was not an unusual position for somebody to have. Mattie Dodd was William E. Dodd's wife. She takes a background position, really, because, sadly enough, there just is not a lot of material out there about her. She's a stabilizing force in the family, a very, very charming, soft-spoken Southern woman, who finds herself in the midst of this cauldron of the Nazi regime. It seems that she liked some of the higher-ups, but she was just really unhappy with all the trappings and the malevolence of the Nazi regime.

WHENEVER I FINISH A book, I do not have a backlog of ideas to immediately go to. It's like all the other ideas that I ever entertained have disappeared, and I start with a blank slate. It's really a process at that point of putting myself in the way of luck, trying to find this next book I do. But about five or six years ago, after completing my previous book, *Thunderstruck*, I was again in this dark country. I was trying to think of something to work on. To jumpstart my thinking, I went to a bookstore in Seattle and started browsing the history section, seeking what covers of books would appeal to me, what covers were an immediate turnoff to me, what bored me, just to get my mind thinking in different channels. I came across a book face up on the shelf that I always meant to read, 1,200 pages, tiny print, kind of intimidating, no photographs, and that was William Shirer's *The Rise and Fall of the Third Reich*. Deciding I had nothing better to do, I took the book home, started reading, and loved it. But what really lit my imagination was the fact that Shirer, the author, had actually been there in Berlin in these early days. He came in 1934, had met these characters we know today to be icons of evil— Hitler, Goebbels, Göring, all these people—in a social context as well as a formal context. What occurred to me then is, what would that have been like, to have met these people when you didn't know the ending, when you didn't know what was coming down the pike? How would you have appraised them? How would you have viewed them at that time? I started looking for characters through whose eyes I could tell that story, ideally Americans and outsiders—and that's when I stumbled upon William E. Dodd, the first ambassador to Nazi Germany and his daughter.

I started reading as many personal memoirs and diaries from that era as I could, and came across William E. Dodd's published diary and read that. I liked Dodd as an individual. I liked his story, the fact that out of the blue he became the ambassador to Nazi Germany, when really, there was no good reason for him to be an ambassador. He had no diplomatic training, nothing, so I really liked that. But I wasn't so enamored of him at that point that I wanted to hang an entire book on him. It was when I stumbled across his daughter's memoir, which was soon after that; that was when I realized, yes, these might be my characters. These might be the people I want to follow into Nazi Germany, because they both had such different orientations at first, but then they both undergo very compelling personal transformations. In fiction, you can't write a good novel without having a character be transformed in one way or another. In nonfiction, since you have to go with what you've got, it is relatively rare to find people, let alone two people in the same family, who undergo a very satisfying real-life transformation.

I DON'T KNOW HOW many affairs [Martha Dodd] ultimately had. She had quite a few affairs, and she tells us that in her memoir and in her papers at the Library of Congress. She makes a lot of reference to the people she knew and became involved with in affairs. She was one of these people who had immense personal charm vis-a-vis the opposite sex. [In her early papers,] even when she was in what would have been late high school and early college, she was courted by people who ordinarily would be courting older and maybe more sophisticated women; she just had that thing. She had an affair with [historian Carl Sandburg]. In fact, I was going through Martha's papers at the Library of Congress and found she has seventy linear feet of documents at the Library of Congress. I came across a clear plastic archival envelope with two locks of Carl Sandburg's hair tied each at one end with a thick, black coat thread. I just found that absolutely charming. I don't think Martha Dodd had an affair with [novelist Thornton Wilder]. Even at this point, he had pretty much declared his interest in another direction. What is remarkable, though, is

that she managed to have these friendships with such potent literary figures in that time, which also speaks to her compelling character. Her affair with Thomas Wolfe occurs pretty much after the action in the book.
He comes into the picture fairly late in the program, but they had quite a
hot and heavy affair.

[ONE OF MY FAVORITE characters in the book] is Rudolf Diels who was
the very first chief of the Gestapo. The Gestapo was formed in April of
1933.... Diels lasted in that job for one year and was replaced by Himmler, who brought in his protégé, Reinhard Heydrich, and then the
game changed completely. They were as thoroughly evil as any human
beings could be. Rudolf Diels embodies the complexity and nuance of
this period. The message of this book was how complex this era was,
how hard it was to divine what was coming down the pike and how easy
in other ways, because of what was happening in '33, '34. He embodies
this complexity, this sense of nuance, because he was not a member of
the Nazi party. He was viewed by Dodd and by other diplomats in Berlin as one of the best men of the Nazi regime. He was the man you went
to if you wanted to extract a foreign national from Dachau, which at
this time was not a camp for Jews; it was a camp for political opponents.
Diels was also a very romantic figure, [who was] very handsome, at least
from the cheekbones up. From the cheekbones down, he was pretty
heavily scarred. This was from a practice common among students of his
generation, called bareblade dueling, where they would fight with actual
swords, sharp swords, the point being to so mark your opponent that
you became the victor, and everybody would be sewed up and presumably sent off to class. It was purely meant to demonstrate one's courage
and one's manhood. Diels [was] horribly scarred from the cheekbones
down; very handsome, though, to women. Martha was really taken with
him, obviously, and they became involved in what appears also to have
been a physical affair. It was pretty obvious that by the fall of 1933, they
were involved.

BORIS [WINOGRADOV] IS ANOTHER one of the characters that I found
very compelling. Martha meets him, this happens a little after she be-

came involved with Rudolf Diels, and she was not opposed to seeing numerous men at the same time. She was really far ahead of her time, in that respect. Boris was tall, 6'4", very handsome, Russian, and very charming. She meets him at a party, and as far as anybody can tell, it seemed to be love at first sight for both of them. They become involved in a very important love affair for her [that] she would describe later as one of the three great loves of her life. However, she appears not to recognize something that everybody else in Berlin seems to know: it's very likely that Boris is an operative, or at least in some way allied with the Soviet intelligence apparatus, the NKVD, precursor to the KGB.

THE "PRETTY GOOD CLUB" is a term that one diplomat, Hugh Wilson, the man who eventually replaced Dodd in Berlin, came up with to describe the diplomatic corps of the Foreign Service, the nature of it, that it was very clubby. The typical ambassador was very wealthy. The typical Foreign Service senior guy had gone to all the right schools—Harvard, Princeton, and they all kind of came from the same world. They knew each other and many were independently wealthy. The clubby idea extends even to the fact that if you weren't of that character of person, you were an outsider. Dodd was very much an outsider. He did not go to those schools and he did not have independent wealth. This became a serious source of low-grade and then, later, ultimately, career ending conflict within the State Department between the Pretty Good Club and Dodd.

FRANKLIN ROOSEVELT'S [MODUS OPERANDI] in terms of appointments was often to make a direct appointment himself without much consulting the person who was in charge of whatever department he was appointing somebody to. In the case of the State Department, there was Secretary of State Cordell Hull, but it was Roosevelt who appointed Dodd to be ambassador to Germany without [Hull] having really much to say at all. Dodd had this direct connection to Roosevelt, and Dodd would write handwritten letters to Roosevelt, telling him the real situation in Germany. Yet below that [there were] three senior

guys, in particular, in the State Department who weren't paying attention and not accepting what Dodd was telling Roosevelt and them
quietly. It's almost as though they felt that Germany was more an irri-
tant than the important center it would become even in just a year's
time. That was very interesting from the lines of conflict and force
within the State Department vis-a-vis Dodd.

JOSEPH GOEBBELS WAS THE head of the Ministry of Public Enlightenment, the propaganda chief of the Reich. Interestingly, in '33 and '34,
Goebbels was a coveted party guest, because he was perceived to have a
great sense of humor. Heinrich Himmler was a former chicken farmer
who became a senior police official in Munich, and had ambitions to run
all the secret police operations throughout Germany. Himmler ultimately
replaced Diels as head of the Gestapo or as head of the entire apparatus
that included the Gestapo. [He was a] thoroughly mundane and evil human being. No one knew exactly how awful this guy was going to be, so
one has to be very careful. In my book Himmler plays a fairly mild, fairly
minimal role, only because he doesn't take prominence in Berlin until
after, let's say, March of 1934. But, Himmler, the Gestapo after that,
their role in the Holocaust, that's all known and obvious. At this time,
however, he was just considered to be a rather mundane individual, always with the same kind of bland appearance, [who] looked like a school-
teacher more than an evil police agent.

ERNST SEDGWICK HANFSTAENGL, NICKNAMED Putzi, was a very
compelling character and a total surprise to me. I had not known of his
existence until I started the work on this book. He is a giant. He was
well over six feet tall. He was also a very talented piano player; he had a
broad repertoire, but he played with a certain kind of vehemence that
may have probably meant that you wouldn't want to hear a concert by
Putzi. He played piano for Hitler and was reputed to play late at night to
help Hitler calm his nerves at the end of a long day. Hitler would listen
to him play and perhaps even weep at times at the passion that Putzi was
putting into the music. One interesting note about Putzi is that his
mother was American. He was a Harvard graduate himself, but not a

member of the "Pretty Good Club," in any sense of the term. He had some pretty wild ideas, and, at one point, according to Martha's memoir, Putzi calls her up and says, "I think that Hitler would be a much better human being, a much more moderate individual, if he simply had a good woman in his life." He tells her this in this phone call. He says, "Martha, you are that woman." Then he arranges this very strange encounter at the Kaiserhof, which is one of the places that Hitler liked to hang out. Putzi orchestrates this meeting. He has Martha and himself sitting at one table. Hitler comes in, takes a seat at another table. Putzi arranges a meeting between the two of them. Hitler kisses Martha's hand at least twice, apparently, during this encounter. She sees him up close for the first time [and] judges him to be a very ordinary seeming man with a certain boyish charm, but what she's most struck by is, as others have reported as well, his eyes. They have this almost hypnotic quality when they make contact. Nothing comes of the meeting. Obviously, she does not have an affair with Hitler. It's just that one moment, and then it's over.

MARTHA WAS TWENTY-FOUR IN 1933. Her father was sixty-three or sixty-four when they first arrived. He died in 1939, before America actually became involved in the war. He died of a neurological problem that, as best anybody can tell, was made much worse by his distress of his time in Berlin. Dodd fancied himself a Jeffersonian Democrat to the core. He believed in yeoman farming values, and he owned this farm in Round Hill, Virginia, that he just adored. He loved spending time on this farm. Every summer he would go and essentially pretend that he was a farmer. He ran it as a working farm, and after his death, at some point, the family sold the property, and it became, ironically, this quite nice golf course.

MARTHA DODD HAD A very brief marriage to a New York banker. She was married to this guy after breaking two previous engagements. She had other love affairs with other younger men. She kept this marriage a secret from her friends; the only people who knew about this marriage were the husband and the families involved. But there is evidence that there was a problem to begin with, and sure enough, soon that marriage began to fall apart. Divorce proceedings were instituted, so by the time she arrived in Berlin at twenty-four, she was in the midst of a divorce and was probably, because of that, feeling even more free when she got there. In Martha's case, in this first year, 1933 to '34, she undergoes this change from loving the Nazi revolution to feeling she should ally herself with Soviet intelligence and provide information to them against the Nazis. In 1933, [the United States] had not yet recognized the Soviet Union officially. Recognition followed soon after that; we weren't exactly opponents, but we weren't necessarily the best of friends. It was a fairly status quo kind of relationship. Martha continued her alliance with Soviet intelligence and she tended to be more talk than action. Commie hunters started heating up their activities in Congress, they called her to testify. She and her husband, a husband she married soon after her arrival back in America, who was not one of the characters she knew in Berlin, fled to Mexico. They ultimately wound up in Prague, leading a very capitalist lifestyle, with a brand-new Mercedes and a big house, but essentially self-exiled from America, and eventually realizing that, they became very disillusioned with Communism, but were stuck there in Prague.

BOTH MARTHA AND ALFRED Stern, her husband, were agents. They had an alliance with Soviet intelligence. They were managed, apparently, by case officers with the KGB. But what they actually did or what kind of intelligence they provided is not at all clear. Whether they provided anything material in the way of intelligence is doubtful. She wrote her memoir in 1939 and it's called *Through Embassy Eyes*. Interestingly, in that book she makes no reference to Boris Winogradov, because it was 1939 and she was afraid that if she talked about him, he would be harmed, which ultimately was the case, but not because of her. Only by triangulation, only by going through her papers, do you find the materials necessary to show that this was Boris Winogradov who occupied a good chunk of her romantic interest in that first year. So 1939 was when she did the memoir, and the book was banned instantly in Germany and it actually did reasonably well in America.

MARTHA MADE A TRIP to the Soviet Union from Germany at Boris' suggestion. Boris was still attached to Berlin, but during that trip that she takes to the Soviet Union, he was actually in the Soviet Union as well. Martha had told Boris that she did not want to see him while she was in the Soviet Union because she didn't want to be influenced in her appraisal of what the Soviet Union was all about. Later, she writes a letter to Boris that gets him very annoyed, when she gets angry at him for not having tried to connect with her in the Soviet Union. He says, "Well, you didn't want to meet with me." He also hints that there was another reason he didn't see her, and that's because of what he refers to as "business." It seems pretty clear now, based on intercepts and KGB documents that have been unearthed, not by me but by others, that the handlers at Moscow's center wanted Boris to stay away so that the intelligence agency itself could court Martha and try to get her allegiance. She didn't like what she saw in the Soviet Union. She found it a very drab, depressing place, but apparently was able to overcome that, at least in terms of her ideological allegiances. She was really kind of dismayed by what she saw and experienced in Moscow. The sense that she conveys in some of her writings and her papers is that it wasn't so much that she was in love with the Soviet Union or communism, it was that she was really deeply opposed to the Nazis and the Nazi regime by the time this first year comes to an end. That's what seems to have tipped her into the Soviet's camp. Why she stayed in the Soviet camp is very hard to say, but it's clear that she did continue her allegiance.

WHAT WAS THE GERMAN hatred for the Jews based on? I don't think anybody knows. I don't think anybody can ever really understand what drives somebody to hate a particular race. What I was startled by, though, and intrigued by, is a thesis put forward by Sir Ian Kershaw about anti-Semitism in Germany. It is his contention that for the average German, the question of anti-Semitism was very much an abstract thing. For the average German, hatred of Jews was not something that was really high on their platform because there were relatively few Jews in Germany. Any kind of anti-Semitic attitude was very much an abstract. That was not the case as [Sir Ian] Kershaw points out, among members of the Nazi party, among the storm troopers, the self-selecting group who loathed Jews, for whom anti-Semitism was one of the key reasons to be in this movement. Anti-Semitism seemed to be a device. But again, Kershaw's thesis is so interesting, because it suggests that if it were a device, it had limited impact in terms of the broad German population, but a lot of power in terms of those who were already thinking in those directions....

The Journey from
Migrant Farm Worker
to Brain Surgeon

DR. ALFREDO QUIÑONES-HINOJOSA

Dr. Alfredo Quiñones-Hinojosa's journey from a Mexican migrant worker to a neurosurgeon at Johns Hopkins Hospital is the basis of his memoir, Becoming Dr. Q: My Journey from Migrant Farm Worker to Brain Surgeon, *published by University of California Press in 2011. In his October 16, 2011 interview with* Q & A, *he recounts his journey to the United States, his medical education, and the racism he has faced as a Mexican in the United States. Today, as he notes, the same hands that once picked cantaloupe in California's Central Valley now perform complex brain surgeries.*

I CAME TO THE United States in 1987...with literally $63 or $64 in my pocket. I spent $60 on my first trek and landed in Los Angeles with about $3 left, and then found my way all the way up to northern California where I began to work with these very same hands that now get to touch the human brain at one of the most prestigious institutions in the world, which is Johns Hopkins.

I started medical school at Harvard when I was twenty-six years old. And sometimes people have asked me, "Did you know you were going to be a doctor?" And I say, "No." "Did you know you were going to be a

71

brain surgeon?" And I say "No." How did I end up in this journey that I have lived for the past two decades?

Sometimes things happen for a reason. I used to think that chance and good luck comes to anybody who wants it, but I began to realize that it's not just that. Luck comes to those who look for it. One day I was walking in the hallways of Harvard Medical School, and a very distinguished brain surgeon looked at me on a Friday night around 11pm and asked me, "Where are you going?" I said, "I'm going to the library to study." And he said, "Have you ever done brain surgery? Have you ever seen brain surgery?" I said, "No." ...And he said, "Let's go right now." So, the next thing I know, I walk into this operating room, and imagine the magic that I felt when I saw that beautiful brain on a patient that was awake; which is, incidentally, what I do now. One of my specialties is doing brain surgery and taking brain tumors from patients that are awake.

This was 1997. I saw the human brain pulsating with a beautiful rhythm and a patient that was awake dancing with the heart. And right there, immediately right then, I was captivated, and the idea was born as to whether or not one day I would be able to do the same thing. And here I am.

I've been [at Johns Hopkins for awhile now]. So you can imagine thousands of times that I have seen the human brain. It doesn't matter how many times I see that brain. I still go back to the same feeling every time I peel back the dura and open it; I see the human brain pulsating with such a beauty. It makes me wonder—every patient, whether you're brown, whether you're black, whether you're Hispanic, whether you're Muslim—all our brains, once you peel back that dura, we all look the same.

THIS COUNTRY WAS BUILT upon people who have come and immigrated to this country, some of them legally, some of them illegally. In my case, I came in with no documentation and no ability to get a job or an education. So when I first came into the United States in the late eighties, I crossed the border between Mexico and the United States and ended up coming into the San Joaquin Valley to work as a migrant farm worker.

It was no challenge to find a job. There were not a lot of people trying to get the jobs of pulling weeds with the very same hands that are now doing brain surgery. I was pulling the weeds. As you can imagine, pulling the weeds from the land that is doing all the products—cantaloupe, cauliflower, corn, all those kinds of things—my hands were bloody, continuously being hurt.

I came in and asked for a job, and I immediately got a job. And then, eventually, right around that time Ronald Reagan had the immigration reform that gave a working authorization specifically for people who had been in the United States a certain amount of years, and then there was a special legislation for people who came and worked as migrant farm workers. That legislation allowed you to have a work authorization. That was the first thing. And to pay taxes. And, with that working authorization, you couldn't go back to your country. But it allowed you to work legally, pay taxes, and eventually apply for a Green Card, which is what I did.

The country was welcoming people like me who worked in the fields. It was a different time, and I felt that I was given an opportunity to live the American Dream…[but] times have changed. Our borders have gotten more strict. What I did back then wouldn't happen today; nonetheless, the American Dream hasn't changed. Some peoples' perception of how to achieve the American Dream may have evolved over time. But the American Dream is still [based on] the same foundation of hard work. People are coming into the United States with an idea that they can work as hard as they possibly can and still be able to put food on the table and to be able to give their children an education. That was my dream back then. It was that simple. All I wanted to do was work hard enough so I would have food on the table for myself, my future children, my parents, and my siblings. And that's exactly the journey that I took all the way from back then until where I am today.

[There have been patients who have said, "Is it true that the doctor is a dirty Mexican? Isn't there another surgeon I can see?"] It happened very often when I first came to Johns Hopkins in 2005. We've been so blessed that I have risen in the academic rankings all the way to now being nominated for full professor at Johns Hopkins. But when I first came and people didn't know my background, they could see that my skin color was different; they could detect a certain amount of an accent in some ways. And some of them, they could have known a little bit of my history of being at Harvard and then in San Francisco, training, but they couldn't get over the fact that I was from a different country. I always told my team that a lot of my patients who came to see me were not only suffering from [a] biological disease which is brain cancer, but they were also suffering from a social disease which is discrimination....My brain works [fine] with an accent. It works as well as anybody else's, and we know that. So I told my team continuously, "Don't worry, they will come around." And every single one of those patients always came around. After surgery, once they decided to trust me with their lives, I would come in and talk to them. They would turn around and many times, they would tell me or my assistants how sorry they felt for some of their comments. I attributed that to the disease—once again, their biological disease. They're dealing with a brain cancer that makes you think in ways that you really can't explain.

But it did happen often. I didn't pay much attention to it, to be honest with you. I turned all that negative energy into positive energy. How did I do that? By doing research. By continuously making every single one of my patients part of history, which is something that to me has been so simple. You'd be surprised how many brain surgeons have either given up fighting against brain cancer, or they have decided that they just want to go in and do their surgery every day and not necessarily fight the disease in the laboratory, which is something that I have done.

[MY PATIENTS ARE AWAKE during surgery, but do not feel pain.] Some of my patients have actually written about this. I have a wonderful patient that I talk about in the book who is a sportswriter. He talked about how it's difficult, it's challenging to be there awake and knowing that someone else is up in your brain, keeping you awake as they're touching your brain. But the truth is that the pain sensors are not in the brain surface. You can elicit painful memories, but there's no pain, per se, in the actual brain. The pain is on the scalp, on the skin; the pain is on the bone, and the pain is on the part that covers the brain. It's called the dura matter. It's a small layer of tissue. You put a local [anesthetic] that is no different than the way we do dental work. As a matter of fact, many of my patients tell me when they undergo the surgery that it was actually more painful to have dental work than to have awake surgery. The difference is the psychological pressure. But I tell you, it's amazing. Just about three weeks ago, one of my patients, a young man, fifteen years old...underwent an awake-craniotomy with me. Talk about being a true hero.

This young man was stronger than any patient that I have ever seen. He remained calm. He answered all my questions because I kept him awake. I interacted with him, I'm asking him questions–he is working with me. We are working as a team in trying to eradicate the disease and he did a beautiful job.

The surgeries range between an hour to sometimes up to three hours depending on the complexity of the tumor, the size of the tumor, how close they are. So they can be awake and sometimes I put them to sleep a little bit with a bit of local anesthesia. Having a wonderful anesthesia team is crucial because they keep patients nice and relaxed.

Yesterday morning, I did a case that lasted about twelve hours and I was the captain of this team. I had two EMT surgeons, I had two plastic surgeons, and then I was leading a team of neurosurgeons, obviously. Surgeons alone, we had about eight involved in this team, and this was a patient that came from far away with a very complex tumor that we had to remove at the base of the skull. In addition to that, we had three anesthesiologists. In addition to that, we had about four nurses helping us circulate in the morning and four nurses in the afternoon. So all together, I probably had a team of about twenty people. Some of these are very, very complex cases that we do.

I've been at Johns Hopkins for six years. Before that, I was at the University of California in San Francisco for six years, and before that, I was at Harvard for medical school, [where] I did four years, and then I spent one year with the Howard Hughes [Medical Institute] doing research investigation. Before Harvard, I was at the University of California at Berkeley, and before that, from '88 to '91, I was in a small community college in Stockton, California, northern California. Right before that, I was working in the fields. I worked in the fields for about a year and a half. Then, simultaneously as I was studying English in community college, I was working on the railroad.

Around this time, when I was in community college learning English, I fell. I guess we have to set up the story because it's a metaphor in many ways as to what it's like to fight for your own life and what it's like sometimes to give up control. Right after I worked in the fields, I was working in a railroad company, and I was doing the most menial job that you can imagine. I started first cleaning tanks that carry fish oil. At the bottom there'd be this fish lard that would accumulate, and I had to clean that. Then, I advanced to cleaning tanks that carried liquefied petroleum gas. I am working with one of my coworkers, Pablo, and I am in charge of fixing the security bottles so this tank wouldn't explode or wouldn't release all the gases that they carry (LPG).

I'm on the top of this 35,000 gallon tanker and I have a hole about this big and a big bolt falls into the tank, and I tell my coworker I'm going to go down and get it. Talk about arrogance. And my coworker, says, "Are you crazy? No. No. No. We'll let it be, we'll get someone else to do it." And I said, "It will only take me a minute." This is when I thought that I was in the top physical shape of my life, and I went down. As you can imagine, I didn't make it back out. But I did try.

As I landed at the bottom of this liquefied petroleum tank, I realized that there's no oxygen and I am [in there] with my whole equipment, steel-toed boots, big overalls, a lot of tools. I start dropping everything and I start climbing this rope. I am about eighteen feet down, right at the bottom, and I start going up on this rope. As I start doing this, my whole life starts flashing, just like when people talk about a near death experience. I'm thinking to myself, "Oh my gosh, I came to this country to fight for not only my life, but also to provide for my siblings and my parents and this is where I'm going to end up. But I'm not going to go without a fight."

I started going up, climbing that rope, little by little, with absolutely no oxygen in my lungs. I made it all the way up to the top and I grabbed Pablo's hands. Pablo relays the story as to how when he saw in my face the agony but also the strength—I could have almost crushed his hand—he thought we were safe and he went asking for help. Right around that time, my father comes because he was working on the railroad in the same place that I was working. And he comes out and he lands right on top of Pablo at the moment that Pablo couldn't hold me anymore because I'd completely lost consciousness. Pablo relays the story that right before I did this, I smiled, and then I went down to the bottom of this tank [again]. I fell all the way down completely unconscious. And then began the whole incredible journey and the work of a team…. My own brother-in-law went in not once, but twice to save my life.

It's an incredible story as to how they were able to get me out when I could have not only died, but the way that they got me out with a rope, and no resources, because we had nothing in this place. But they got me out of there. The next time I wake up I'm in a small hospital in Stockton, California, and I am vomiting and I am completely strapped in one of those yellow stretchers. My neck is protected and now I know what traumatic brain injury and a spinal injury is, and the way you have to protect it. The doctor is trying to examine me. He's telling me to relax. And I said, "How do you want me to relax?" I was vomiting. I needed to move to the side. I mean, I was completely sick to my stomach. My father relays the story that hours went by. They did all kinds of tests, CT scan, brain MRI, because I'd been down there for minutes with no oxygen. They thought I had a stroke. I couldn't feel part of my hands. I was having a lot of side effects from the liquid petroleum tank, the gas; not the fluid, but the gas.

I woke up a few hours later and I see my father and my brother-in-law crying. A few hours went by and then I noticed that there were some young nurses taking care of me. My father knew that I was going to be OK when I asked my dad, "Dad, how does my hair look?" And so, as you can imagine, the whole idea of that moment when I grabbed my co-worker Pablo, I knew that I had given it all that I had. It was at this point, it was symbolic of me trusting that things were going to work out for me.

MY WIFE'S FIRST NAME is Anna and her last name is Peterson. She comes from a Swedish family and she's absolutely brilliant, smart, and witty. She's beautiful. When I was in community college, learning English, right about the time that I fell into the liquefied petroleum tank, I was reevaluating my life. I also had so much energy; I cannot even relate to you. I would go for days without sleeping. Working all the time, and then I still had to do track and field. One day I had an injury and the coach sends me in the morning to run the swimming pool. I had a groin injury. When I come out of the swimming pool, there's a young woman who says hi to me, and I thought she was saying hi to someone else. I looked side to side and it was to me. I bolted the other way. I was so shy. People wouldn't believe this. I've seen this woman before. It turns out that, two weeks prior, I was sitting having lunch in the middle of this community college watching a Koi pond, and these two beautiful women sat right next to me and talked to me. My English was so terrible that I bolted out. I ran out of the place because I was so shy. It was the same woman. We didn't start dating until I was at UC Berkeley, a year before I went to Harvard. She's seen the growth. She saw me when I had nothing, when I was working in the school, going to community college with my steel-toed boots, my jeans smelling like sulfur because [for] many of the days I was actually shoveling sulfur. So she's been my life partner, as you can imagine.

I DECIDED TO TELL my story right around 2008. ABC did a beautiful show at Hopkins. How little did I know I was in the first episode, the so-called A story, and the last episode—I opened and closed the show. I had multiple interviews and…a lot of writers came to me and said we'd love to write your story. But I wasn't ready. Mentally and physically, I wasn't mature yet…. I needed to climb the ladder of academic medicine. I needed to go from an assistant professor all the way up to full professor before I released my story, which is what has happened now…. But right around that time, I realized that there was an incredible story to be told; not just my story, but my interactions with so many people that have mentored me. I realized that this was the American Dream and we were losing focus of what the American Dream is all about. I think the American Dream comes back to the same principle of hard work.

I wanted to tell the story about this underdog, this kid who came to the United States with nothing, and now, based on hard work, mentorship, doors being opened, opportunities being given and me taking those opportunities, I was able to show the world that you can still fulfill the American Dream and that America is still the most beautiful country in the world. That's why I decided to tell that story around that time.

[THERE ARE 600,000 AMERICANS living with primary brain or nervous system tumors; there are 130 different types of brain cancer; there are 124,000 who have malignant brain cancers.] These are the ones that are not only the primary brain tumors. Because we are getting much better at treating other cancers in our body, renal cancer, lung cancer, breast cancer, some of these tumors, when they are growing or when they release their little cells, they end up making it up into the brain.... Not only tumors that are born in the brain, like Senator Ted Kennedy's. That was a tumor that was born in the brain. But then, we have many others that make it up north.

Many times, patients present with a convulsion. They suddenly have a seizure. They've never been sick in their lives, and then suddenly, one day they're doing something and they start having a convulsion or they start having really bad headaches. I'm not talking about a small little headache that you resolve with Tylenol or aspirin. I'm talking about headaches that keep getting worse and worse. I'm not talking about migraine headaches here. Many patients know that they have migraines. These are patients that keep getting worse and worse and the patients are taking a lot of medications, and then suddenly, boom, they have a seizure. A convulsion. They drop on the floor just like a fish out of water, that's the best way that I can describe it; they end up in the hospital with a scanner, boom, big lesion in their brain. That is how they end up presenting, many of my patients....

This is something that I've committed my life to. I tell you, I can give up what I do today and go into a different job and make a lot more money. I'm not poor either, but I can assure you that in academic medicine you don't make the same amount of money that you would make in other jobs. And the job offers, I have gotten many. But I decided to be part of history. I want to help people. That's it. I want to continue to live the American Dream. I am thankful for the things that this country has done for me.

...I CANNOT SPEAK FOR all the physicians, but, to me, one of the most devastating things that I have experienced is that I'm always the last one to give up hope, but we reach a point in which we do things to patients that, instead of helping them, they're working against them. Once we reach that end of life where we know that nothing is working and the disease continues to progress, the worst thing that I have experienced myself from the family members of a patient, is their inability to realize that no matter what we do things are not going to change. [Sometimes] they are willing to see their loved ones continue to suffer rather than deal with their own inabilities to cope with the fact that their loved ones are going to die. That breaks my heart. I struggle and I meet with them and I say, "Please, this is not going to change. We need to help this patient make that transition. Put them in hospice care."

ONE OF THE THINGS that I began to realize that has made my relationship with my patients very strong is this: Sometimes what we do as surgeons in our specialty is to come in like the Special Forces. We just go in and we think about taking the tumor out, and sometimes we tend to think that's it; that's all we can do. When, in reality, what I've been able to do in my group and my team is to take that tissue work in the laboratory and try to find a cure. And then I get the patients involved in not only their own care, but also [in] being part of history. I [get their] consent so they can donate that tissue... so they feel part of history, and my relationship with those patients continues to evolve beyond just taking care of their tumor. I think that is a role that we can fulfill very well as brain surgeons, especially the ones who specialize in brain tumors.

TEN YEARS FROM NOW, we are going to be seeing more personalized medicine. Right now, for instance, in my profession in surgery, for a brain tumor we take as much as we can. We give the patient chemotherapy and radiation. Ten years from now, what I envision, thanks to the work that a lot of people around the world including our laboratory [are doing], is we're going to be able to take this tumor and say this patient specifically responds to this treatment. We're going to turn around and give personalized medicine to that patient. That's what I think is going to revolutionize our system. We can't allow our country not to be able to do that. That is why I feel so strongly that we still need to support research. We still need to be able to support those creative minds that are going to be able to help us to live a long and healthy life.

[PEOPLE WON'T STOP QUESTIONING whether I got where I am because of affirmative action.] It's never going to end. I bet you that people are going to see this interview and they are going to wonder, "Why is it that I am not there? Why is it that my son is not there? Why is it that my loved one is not there? He took a spot from someone else." I get this over and over…. When the show on Hopkins came out, I can tell you, I got death threats. I got e-mails. I got people who hated me and people who loved me and people who missed the message. They think that I have taken someone else's spot in medical school, that someone else who was born and raised in the United States should be the brain surgeon here in front of you doing this interview. So that's never going to end. I welcome it. I think that's what makes this country the most beautiful country, that people can express their opinions. I don't agree with them but I respect their opinions, as long as it doesn't affect my life, or the life of my patients, or the life of my family. Words come and go but what stays are ideas and what you do for people.

[Race is an issue in my life]…every day. Every day that I get a request for an interview, a possibility of doing something, people will always say we want to have this guy because he's famous, because he's Mexican, and no one else is like him. And I say, look, this is my agenda: I want to talk about my story and what I do as a brain surgeon. So there are things that I can do, but race plays a role every single day in my life. To be honest with you, I don't shy away from it. I welcome it. I realize that when I was in medical school, what I thought was a weakness—that I came as a poor immigrant and now I am a brain surgeon—turned out to be the greatest strength of my life. The true definition of the American Dream.

Discovering America

SIMON WINCHESTER

Author Simon Winchester was a guest on Q & A *on November 27, 2011, on the occasion of the paperback publication of his book,* Atlantic: Great Sea Battles, Heroic Discoveries, Titanic Storms, and a Vast Ocean of a Million Stories *(Harper Perennial, 2003). The British-born writer had a career as a foreign correspondent before turning to books and moving to the U.S. In the interview, he recalls his first trip to the U.S. as a nineteen-year-old. He describes replicating the 1919 journey of a young Army officer, Dwight Eisenhower, who was ordered to travel by car from the east coast to the west. Eisenhower took fifty-eight days; Winchester achieved it in eighteen. Years later, he still revels in the hospitality of the people he met.*

I [FIRST CAME TO America in 1963]. I had a girlfriend in Montreal and I was then eighteen, coming on nineteen. I took a year off between school and university and came over here on the *Empress of Britain*, which went from Liverpool to Montreal, and then saw the girlfriend and that was all lovely, and then hitchhiked to Vancouver. I had been utterly obsessed with America for years, because in the 1950s my father had been offered a job here. On the very eve of our getting on the ship to go to New York, he had gotten cold feet and decided not to go and my mother and I were desperately, desperately disappointed.

I vowed that one day I would visit America, so I had this spare year and I, as I say, hitchhiked to Vancouver and then entered America under the Peace Arch in Blaine, Washington. The first sign I saw after "Welcome to the United States" said it was illegal to hitchhike or pick up hitchhikers, so I thought, "Well, that's great, isn't it?" and just sat under the sign for a few moments. A chap in a convertible Triumph TR3 screeched to a halt because I had a Union Jack on the back of my rucksack. He took me to Bellingham.

That entire trip was 36,000 miles because I spent the better part of nine months hitchhiking around America. I entered with two hundred U.S. dollar bills, and when I left from Houlton, Maine, to go into New Brunswick, I had 182 of them left, so it cost me 18 dollars.

People were so overwhelmingly kind...and I got to meet people like Kirk Douglas and Johnny Carson and President Kennedy, whose hand I shook in Sault Ste. Marie, Michigan, when he was opening a lock on the St. Lawrence Seaway. I thought, not only is it beautiful, but the people are amazingly hospitable and generous, completely unlike us in Europe.

I went to Topeka to see the Menninger Institute, which is a very famous institute for the mentally unwell. Then someone said, "Oh, the other famous person that lives here [in Topeka] is Harold Stassen. He's very nice; go and see him."

I walked up to his door. He must have been in his eighties; fit as a fiddle. He said, "Do you ride horses?" And I said, "Well, after a fashion," and he said, "Come riding with me." We talked about running [for president] against Roosevelt. He said it was like jumping the front of an express train. It was completely impossible to get any votes at all. He was a marvelous, marvelous man.

[COFFEE WITH JOHNNY CARSON] was tremendous. In those days, if I remember rightly, the *Tonight Show* was taped in Burbank and the tapes were flown back overnight to be broadcast from New York. It sounds arcane and a Rube Goldberg way of doing things, but I think that's how it was done. I had gotten very friendly with the fellow that was responsible for taking the tapes to the airplane every night. He let me in the green room and said, "You should meet Johnny Carson." And Johnny Carson took a brief shine to this young schoolboy and didn't have me on the show, but he said, "Come and have a cup of coffee."

I'M NOT ENTIRELY SURE [where I got this wanderlust] because...I was an only child and my parents really didn't travel a great deal. It all went back to this deep disappointment. I sat next to a boy in school called Rollo Reid whose father built cranes and lived in America and...remember I was disappointed that my father didn't take us to America. Rollo lived in Connecticut and he would come back from the holidays to school and would show me pictures—it sounds ridiculous at this stage—of the Merritt Parkway, and I thought the Merritt Parkway was the most beautiful highway I'd ever seen, this vision of these endless beautiful roads. Then, obviously, I knew about things like the Grand Canyon and so forth. I thought this is where I want to go. I had no wanderlust before I got to North America. Once I did...it just occurred to me that, as they say, every journey begins with the first step. You take that first step in North America and you're rewarded handsomely by everything you see and everybody you meet. So it was here that the wanderlust was born.

...THE SPECIFIC TRIP [I took for my next book], was to follow the route that the young Captain [Dwight] Eisenhower undertook the late summer of 1919. Basically, the American Army, following World War I, was doing some planning on what would happen if America were to be invaded by what they called an Asiatic enemy. How quickly could they get troops from the big bases in the east and the south to the west? Of course, they could use the railways, but railways only have a certain amount of capacity. What about the roads? And so they sent a military convoy about three miles long, which assembled on the ellipse of the White House. It went north up to Gettysburg and then turned left and followed what was the Lincoln Highway.

Young Eisenhower was given a temporary rank of lieutenant colonel. He went as an observer and kept a diary, which I printed out and took with me. We followed the trip, which went from Pennsylvania into Ohio and Illinois and Indiana; my wife and I went the whole way. What we wanted to do, following Eisenhower's trip, was to camp. We took a tent and sleeping bags. The first few days it was fairly grizzly, the weather, so we stayed in B&Bs, but thereafter we camped, and it was absolutely fascinating. Twenty-odd days later, we fetched up in Lincoln Park in San Francisco, where beside a bus stop is a concrete marker; equivalent, but not nearly as grand as the [initial] one by the White House, but saying this is the endpoint of the expedition. They took fifty-eight days; I think we took eighteen. Of course, we were in a Land Rover rather than in a tank, but, nonetheless, it was fascinating.

A total of about 250 [people were on the Eisenhower trip]; it was quite big. The convoy itself was three miles long and there were armored cars, there were tracked vehicles, there were ambulances and cooking commissary type vehicles. They got the catalog of disasters every day. Things were breaking down and axles were being bent and cars and tanks were falling off the road. There was one particular vehicle called a Militor, which seemed bent every day on hauling people out of ditches. Then it got into trouble somewhere in Utah. The roads were reasonable up to Council Bluffs, Iowa, and across the Missouri River. After that, there were essentially no roads until you got to Lake Tahoe and California. So those 1,500 miles, for these vehicles, was almost impossible. When Eisenhower wrote his report, he said, "If there's an Asiatic enemy and we're going to take fifty-eight days to go from our bases, we've lost, basically." So it lodged in his mind there and then that we've got to have a decent road system. The conventional belief is that when he saw the German autobahn system in the 1940s, that's when he said America's got to have this road system. But I think that's not quite true. The real germ of this idea was planted thirty years before, in 1919, when he did it for himself.

THE BEST THING [I saw on this trip] has to be scenery. The road goes past Dinosaur National Monument on the Colorado-Utah border, and I'd never been to it. I've been to many of the national parks, but this was a new one. To drive into the park, it's forty-five miles off the main road. Thank heavens we had a Land Rover, because this particular campsite, you can't go down to unless you've got four-wheel drive. It's a twelve-mile switchback, down to the Green River, not far from where John Wesley Powell—another of my great heroes; the one-armed explorer of the Grand Canyon—launched into the river to begin his expedition. There you are in this sensational campground with only three or four campsites, a ranger who comes once a week to make sure the firewood and loos [bathrooms] are clean, and these great towers of sandstone right in the middle of the wilderness, and all sorts of extraordinary wildlife. It was magical.

THE DEPRESSING THING THAT I found on one particular trip that I remember were these huge agricultural industry plants that you see along the Columbia River, particularly where most of America's french fries are made in Idaho; these gigantic factories, which are not good for anybody, and these huge butchery plants and these vast feedlots for cattle. That side of America—agribusiness.

When I came here first in the sixties, I stayed with some farmers, the Judges, north of Ames in Iowa. They taught me how to drive a combine harvester. That was another wonderful thing I did when I was nineteen. I had heard over the years that the Judges had moved or disappeared. On the Eisenhower trip, I looked them up and I found them. They're still there. They're not elderly, but they're no longer young and he doesn't farm corn and soybeans as he used to. He had a quarter-section, which was perfectly adequate to make a living for himself and his family and his children. But now he said the economics of farming have completely changed and you can't make money unless you own thousands of acres, and it's all for industry. There's nothing romantic about farming anymore and I found that rather depressing....

Deliberately on the way back, I went through Texas, Louisiana, and Mississippi. The distance they feel from Washington, D.C.—the gulf is amazing. And, indeed, not wishing to be part of the United States is a very strong feeling, particularly in places like west Texas. They feel they're not part of the United States. "We should be independent; run our own affairs, keep our own tax revenues, arrange for our own defenses. We don't feel at one with those people up in Washington D.C." There are slightly similar expressions in places like Mississippi, but for different reasons. These are largely racial, because the Civil War has not been forgotten. That's something that I found very strongly in the deep South on this particular trip: a fractious mood, much more fractious than I imagined.

America is not as united as it seems.

American History

The Great Migration

ISABEL WILKERSON

Between 1915 and 1970, an estimated six million African Americans migrated from the South to points north and west. The exodus consisted of three streams of people continuously on the move northward: to Midwest cities like Cleveland, Chicago, and Detroit; up the Eastern seaboard to Washington, D.C., Philadelphia, and New York City; and westward to Los Angeles, Oakland, and beyond. This "Great Migration" included writers Zora Neale Hurston, and James Baldwin, poet Langston Hughes, and musicians Miles Davis and John Coltrane. Isabel Wilkerson's father and mother were among those on the move, migrating from Virginia and Georgia to Washington, D.C. On September 26, 2010, Ms. Wilkerson appeared on Q & A to discuss her Pulitzer Prize–winning book, The Warmth of Other Suns *(Random House, 2010), and the individuals she profiled representing the three migratory streams.*

I CAN'T SAY WHAT the moment was when I started thinking about doing this book because I have been living it all my life. My parents migrated from the South to Washington, D.C. My mother was from Georgia and my father from southern Virginia. Washington is where they met, married, and then had me, so without the Great Migration, I would not be here. I grew up with people from North Carolina, South Carolina, and Georgia all around me in the neighborhood. I was surrounded by the language, the food, the music, the ambitions, too, of the people who had migrated from the South.... It's been with me all this time.

When it came to the actual writing of the book, it probably started after I had been a reporter and Chicago bureau chief for the *New York Times* and talked to people in other parts of the country. I went to Chicago, Cleveland, and Detroit. I began to hear that there were similar migration experiences that people had. No one talked about it as a migration experience. They would just talk about it, "I can't talk with you today or this weekend; we're going to have to go back to Mississippi where there's a family reunion," or, "there's a funeral I have to go to." I began to connect the dots and see that this was so much bigger than just my experience in Washington, or the experience of Chicago, or even to Los Angeles. It was a national outpouring of people.

The book is about the migration experiences of three people who become representative of the larger whole, which was essentially the defection of six million African Americans from the South to the North, to the Midwest and the West, from 1915, World War I, until 1970 when the South began truly to change....

THE TITLE OF MY book comes from [a phrase used by] the author Richard Wright, one of the greatest novelists of the twentieth century. He was a migrant from Mississippi to Chicago. He grew up in Natchez, Mississippi, the son of a sharecropper, and always wanted to write. He set out on a journey in 1927 to get to Chicago. Almost everything he wrote had to do with understanding this migration experience that he was a part of; understanding his connection between the South and the North. [He moved to Paris to die.] He ultimately was searching for "the warmth of other suns," and he kept moving and moving. He went to Chicago, and then he went to New York, until eventually, he left the country altogether in search of it.

I interviewed about 1,200 people, but I stopped counting after that. I was setting out looking for three people who would represent each of the three strains of the Great Migration; that took me to Los Angeles, Chicago, and New York. I went to senior centers, AARP meetings, quilting clubs, Baptist churches, and Catholic mass. I even had a booth at the Juneteenth parade in Los Angeles, to collect the names of people who might have migrated from the South to the North. I was going to all these places where I might find people who were now seniors, and might have been participants in this migration. They were not hard to find. It's just a matter of going in and talking to them and hearing their stories....

At that stage, it was essentially like an audition. It was like a casting call for these three people. I began in 1995 and it took me fifteen years. It took me about eighteen months of interviewing, going from city to city, going from place to place...in order to find these three. One of the most interesting sources of people was the state clubs that exist in all of these cities. When you go to Los Angeles, there's a Lake Charles, Louisiana club, there's a Monroe, Louisiana club. There are multiple Texas clubs, multiple New Orleans clubs. I had to find a way to get access to them, and then I would begin to interview them. That's where you were hitting the huge source of people who had all done exactly what you're looking for. The same goes for Chicago, where there's a Greenville, Mississippi club and there's a Greenwood, Mississippi club. There is the Newton, Mississippi club, Brookhaven, Mississippi club. All of these were options there. In New York, there are churches where almost everybody is from South Carolina. I decided on the three [people I would profile] finally in 1996.

I wanted to write this book because I wanted to explore the reasons why these people left; what was the legacy of what they did. I really wanted to understand who they were and why they did what they did, and capture them before it was too late. I was really feeling a great sense of urgency because it began in 1915 and it ended in 1970. At least three generations were participants in this. They were getting up in years and time was running out. [There was a] real press of time to get to them while there was still time to tell the story.

[I PICKED THREE PEOPLE to tell this story: Ida Mae Brandon Gladney, George Swanson Starling, and Robert Joseph Pershing Foster.] In the writing of this book, it was essential that the three characters be easily distinguishable. You could turn to the page, be in their chapter, and know whom you are reading about. It was also important that they be from different backgrounds. I didn't want them to all be sharecroppers, or middle class, or working class. I wanted them to be distinctive. They all become one, because they all complement one another. It took me some time to actually look at the circumstances of all three. Where did they begin? Where did they land? What kinds of things did they do? What were their personalities? It was almost as if you have to have a board on which you have all of their characteristics. These will be the three that together will make the whole for the narrative. I had one character who left in the thirties, one in the forties, and one in the fifties. One went to New York, one went to Chicago, and one went to L.A.

IDA MAE BRANDON GLADNEY was from Chickasaw County, Mississippi. She was the wife of a sharecropper where they were working the land of a planter in that county, and once the Depression hit, they were still there. She was terrible at picking cotton and that was one of the things that was quite interesting to me; I never thought about a person being good or bad at it. It turned out that she was really bad at it, and was glad to tell you that. She had a wonderful way of incorporating both the South and the North into her psyche. She never changed her accent from the moment she arrived in Chicago.... She spent three times more years in Chicago than she did in Mississippi, yet when I met her, I could barely understand her the first time. By the time I spent a little bit of time with her, I could almost imitate her.

She left Mississippi when she was in her mid-twenties. The family left because a cousin of her husband was beaten nearly to death over a theft that he did not commit.... One particular night before her husband had returned from his errands, there was pounding at the door of her cabin. She had two young ones and a sister-in-law living with her. There was a posse of men at her door, and they were looking for a cousin of her husband's, named Joe Lee. She said Joe Lee wasn't there. She didn't know that he actually had come into the house and then gone through the back way to get away from the posse. She didn't know anything about what he had done. Later on, when the husband got back home, she told him and he went to try to find out what had occurred. It was too late. Joe Lee had already been captured, and was beaten with chains so badly that his clothes had adhered to his skin. He was thrown in jail instead of taken to a doctor. It was her husband and the other male sharecroppers who went to retrieve him. After seeing what had happened to his cousin, he then went home to his wife and he said, "This is the last crop we're making." Quietly, between the two of them, they began to try to divest of what little they had, the wash pots, kerosene lamps, and bed pallets. They went to her mother's house to position themselves to leave. As soon as the cotton was all picked, they got on the night train out of Okolona to up North, first landing in Chicago and briefly in Milwaukee, and then ultimately settling in Chicago in 1937.

At that time, there would have been about a million people who would have left [the South] by then, because there were about a half million in the first World War I migration. Then there were another half million, 480,000, who left during the Depression years, which is actually the smallest number for each decade. It really took off during World War II, which was the largest migration. Each decade, people who studied [this migration] were assuming that it would be over. They thought the economics of the North were the main impetus, but a precipitating factor had been World War I...because of the war in Europe, immigration had essentially come to a halt. All of the workers that were feeding the steel mills, foundries, and all of the factories of the North then had no labor. These Northern industries then began looking to the South for the cheap labor. That meant they had to go to African Americans and began trying to recruit them to go north.

Ida Mae Brandon Gladney very rarely ventured out beyond where she was [in Mississippi], because life was very controlled. They had so little free time, because they were working in the fields, and her life was fairly isolated. Every aspect of life was controlled then. For example, access to a physician was impossible; physicians did not come out to the country where she was.... Overall, in the South, Jim Crow had rules and laws that seem so arcane now. In some places it was illegal for a black person and a white person to play checkers together. She did not herself work in such a place, because she worked in the field, but blacks and whites couldn't walk up the same staircase in certain places where they might have worked together. In certain courthouses there was a black Bible and white Bible to swear to tell the truth on.

THERE WAS A GREAT angst, because if nothing was done to keep these people from leaving, if the conditions did not change to make it more possible for them to stay, they were going to lose their great source of labor, that cheap labor, which was the underpinning of the Southern economy. They depended upon that. It's an expensive proposition and great peril, to plant an entire field of cotton and not know what would happen to it....

There are so many factors that they were dependent upon, and the margin for error was so great, and they needed the hands available to pick the cotton once it was there. They could not afford to be losing this labor.

Ida Mae and I went back down to Mississippi to the cotton fields in the late nineties. I made arrangements for us to go back.... We first flew into Memphis, and then we drove down the legendary Highway 61, and then to the Natchez Trace Parkway. As we were driving and drew closer to the county where she lived, we came upon some cotton fields. It was fall of the year, which is the high picking season in Mississippi where she lived. We saw this cotton field that was wide open. There were no cars. This is still isolated land, and she wanted to get out and pick. She said, "Let's stop and pick some." I said, "Are you sure that we can do this? This land belongs to somebody. And we're in Mississippi, besides." She said, "Oh, they're not going to care what little bit we want to pick." She jumped out of the car and went out into the rows of cotton and started picking. I went with her, still wary. She seemed to be giddy; she hated picking cotton when she had to, but now that she didn't have to, it's almost as though you couldn't stop her.

In Chicago, Ida Mae and her husband had a really hard time making the adjustment. They had arrived from the South with the least education and the least skills. The men could find work, because strong backs were valued. They could find work in the slaughterhouses and the foundries and the steel mills. She had a much harder time. There also were many immigrant groups that they were competing against: there were Poles and Hungarians and Irish and Swedes, all kinds of Germans, who also were newly arrived. They often were further along in the queue, particularly for the women when it came to domestic work. Clearly, working in an office in a typing pool was not going to be something she would even be able to do. It took a very long time for her to be able to find work, and for her husband as well.... At first, he was hauling ice up four and five flights of those cold-water flats on the South Side of Chicago. He was willing to do it, because he had to haul that much in cotton, so it was something that he did. But it wasn't enough really to take care of the family. They moved a lot, from place to place to place as they tried to find the right location for them that they could afford. They had a difficult time making the adjustment. In the end, she was the kind of person to accept her lot, no matter what it would have been. But for all of the people in the book, there are many mistakes that they might have made in their lives, but moving from the South was not one of them. They did not regret it at all.

[Ida Mae] was the matriarch of her family. She was one of the wisest and most beautiful people I have ever met in my life, and doing this book changed me in so many ways. She had a kind of Zen perspective to accept what was, and recognizing what she could not change, and moving on and not living in the past. She was beloved by everyone who knew her…. When we returned south, one of the things we did was we looked up one of the men she was courted by…. Her decision of which of those two men [to go with] was ultimately the deciding point of her life. Had she not gone with one man, she would not have gone to Chicago. She did not know it at the time, but that's what had been her lot and that's what she chose. But the other man decided to stay. When we went back to Mississippi, we looked him up, and found him. He recognized her instantly and it had been sixty years. It's as if all those decades and the miles hadn't meant anything. He just said, "How are you, Ida Mae?" He reached for her arm. It was just a beautiful moment….

I CHOSE HER AS one of three out of 1,200. One of the places that I went was the retiree boards of the unions and of various trades. I went to the people who had been retired from the Chicago Transit Authority (CTA) and to postal workers. When I went to the retirees' meeting for the CTA, I passed around the flyer that I had and made my little statement. There were many people who signed up because most of them were from the South or had relatives from the South. A woman said, "I didn't actually make the decision to come from the South to Chicago. But my mother did." It was Ida Mae's daughter who signed her up…and when I met with her, she was wonderful. She was fine.

GEORGE SWANSON STARLING WENT from Florida to New York. He was a college student at the time the migration situation became relevant for him. He had to drop out of school, because at that time African Americans could not go to the segregated state schools. There was one school he could go to, but it was far from home. His father decided he wasn't going to keep sending him and that he had had enough schooling. Therefore, he had to go back to the primary work in central Florida, which was picking citrus. When he got out into the groves, he began to realize that people were being greatly taken advantage of; the working conditions were poor and the pay was worse.... He began to try to organize the pickers...to make a little bit more money. He would be asking for a nickel more a box as opposed to the ten or fifteen cents. This was a time when each of those boxes was commanding three or four dollars on the open market once they ultimately sold. He would speak on behalf of all the pickers. He had a very hard time keeping them organized. All of them wanted to say, "Well, while we're here, why don't we just go ahead and pick," and he'd have to keep them at bay to say, "Well it worked last week, so let's try it again this week."

He was born in 1918. The impetus for him to leave was the grove owners began plotting against him, since they did not like unions anyway, which is what this was becoming. Even his relatives told him that this was dangerous. He had to flee for his life. He caught the train and was very careful about not making himself too visible in those hours and days before he left. They did not apparently try to stop him. He actually discreetly asked a friend of his if he would take him to the train station. They drove carefully so as not to attract attention. In other words, he did not want to let anyone know that he was preparing to leave. He [ultimately] went to Harlem....

When he got to Harlem, he took a job as a railroad porter, where he ended up going right back to the South that he had sworn he would never go back to. He had no trouble finding work, because being male gave him something of an advantage in that era. It was during World War II when he left, as opposed to Ida Mae, who left during the Depression. Life was so much easier.... There are lots and lots of stories of him going back and forth, observing the migration, and then running into the experience of going back south. He was going from a place that was free, and then having to adjust oneself whenever he went back to the South. One of the adjustments was that if the conductors were Southern, they would often mistreat the porters. He got on the bad side of one of the conductors. There was a perilous moment for him in which the conductor did not like what he thought was an imperious dignity that George Starling had. He thought that he was not proper for an African American male, that he should be a little bit more humble. But George Starling had more education than a lot of the people he would be around, so he couldn't help that he had read a lot....He didn't like playing the game of being sort of the shuffling sidekick, and that didn't go over well with some of the Southern conductors....

[IN MY BOOK, I use language like "colored people," and at some points, "negroes," "blacks," and then "African Americans."] My approach was that I wanted the reader to be in the moment whenever something was happening. That meant, if I was talking about what it meant to be picking cotton or getting on a Jim Crow train, I wanted you to be able to imagine yourself there. The language all around them would have been that. All the signs said "colored" or "white," so it would be more consistent while we were in that era to be talking that way.

There are no pictures in my book. Both my editor and I simultaneously agreed there should be no pictures. We wanted people to lose themselves in the narrative, to imagine themselves in the hearts and minds of these people, to think about what they would have done if they were in that situation, black or white, whatever the situation might have been.

Jim Crow was a caste system by which African Americans were controlled. Their every move was controlled. But it also was something that hurt white people as well, because the word "caste" can have multiple meanings. It means a fixed thing;...if you have a cast on your arm, it means you cannot move. It meant that whites and blacks could not move freely within their own society. It's perceived as being something that hurt black people, but I believe that it actually hurt both.... Jim Crow began in Massachusetts. It was the first place to have segregated rail cars. Jim Crow was something that was actually applied more in the North. It would have been in the 1970s, very late, that the Jim Crow laws went away....

THE THIRD PERSON IS Robert Joseph Pershing Foster. The Pershing comes from John J. Pershing..."Black Jack" Pershing. It was the end of World War I when he was born, and Pershing was the hero of the day. His mother wanted her son to have this important name that would be in commemoration of the big hero of the day.... One of the things I write about is that the whole naming of a child was a very special thing for these parents in the South, because there was very little else that they could give their children. They didn't often have resources...they often had these imperious sounding names—Queen, Admiral, Major. Or if they were feeling very militant, they would name them someone like Ulysses from Ulysses S. Grant, because that was a way of affixing greatness to their children.

Dr. Foster left Monroe, Louisiana, and went to Los Angeles.... He had been in the Army in the Korean War, and performed surgery in Austria. But when he got back and was discharged, he found that he could not work in a hospital in his own hometown because of Jim Crow laws. [Hospitals did not allow] black people to be doctors, to perform any kind of medical work in a hospital. He had a brother who was a physician, too, and his brother found a way around it.... He created a portable hospital office in a car that he would carry around with him. He had essentially a bed that someone could lay on, and he had all the supplies in the trunk of his car. He would go out in the country and serve the people who were the sharecroppers.

But Pershing did not want that for himself. He wanted to be able to have everything he had been exposed to in the Army and wanted to live out a life as he imagined it. He set out on this journey, not anticipating that he would run into the trouble. In fact, at a certain point, that passage is just so heartbreaking.... He had to question whether he had made the right decision. But he had gone too far...

He found that no one would allow him to stay in a hotel for the night. He had the money to do it and had the standing to do it. He was an American citizen. He was well beyond what would be viewed as the reach or the boundaries of Jim Crow. By this time, he was in the state of Arizona in 1953, and no one would take him in. He stopped over and over and over again. And ultimately, the last place he went, he ran into some people who were from Illinois originally, and they thought about it. Actually, the wife had seen him first, and it gave him hope that he might be able to stay for the night there, that he might have finally met someone who would let him stay. But ultimately, she went back to talk with her husband. They talked for a long time. Then they came out and they said, "We're from Illinois, and we don't share the views of the people around here. But we would be ostracized if we take you in. We just can't do it."

I was surprised that the West was as hardened as it was. The people met great resistance wherever they went, because they were wanted by the industries, but not necessarily by the people that they would encounter, who would see them as economic competition. Wherever these people went…they were workers, who were used to much lower pay. That meant that there was a potential for them to drive down the wages of those people who were around them. Many of them were used as strikebreakers and there was a lot of resistance to their arrival. They had to put up with a lot, as many immigrants do when they arrive in this country. I was not surprised that there would be resistance. I was surprised that he ran into as much as he did, just trying to find a room.

[WRITING THIS BOOK HAS] changed my life, because it helped to answer so many questions for me about how the country came to be, about how African Americans made it to the North and West. The majority of people that you might meet who are African American in the North and the West are descended from this Great Migration. That's an enormous thing that I don't think people even thought about. It also reminded me of how much we have in common with one another. When I was growing up here in Washington, my mother went to the trouble of making sure that I went to the best schools she could find, which was a school west of the park. We lived east of the park. She arranged for a cab to take me there. I was five years old, and she would tell the cabdriver, "Now, don't pick anyone else up. I see your cab number. I'm going to pay you. Bring her right back home." And the cab was always there waiting for me. The cab would always look like it was empty, because it had a five-year-old in it. She always wanted to make sure they didn't pick up anyone else. When I got to the school, I would run into all kinds of people who were from all over the country; from Nepal since they were often diplomats' children, from San Salvador or from Chile, or from Finland. Even those who were American-born were descended from people from Ireland, Scotland, or wherever they might have been, Germany or Russia.… On certain days, particularly like St. Patrick's Day, there were all [these] stories that people were telling about life in the old country, or what their grandparents had done, or the food. I felt that I didn't have any stories to tell. It turned out that, actually, I did, and that there were many, many great stories that came out of this Great Migration.

The Nazi Raid on America

MICHAEL DOBBS

One of the more intriguing episodes in World War II took place on American soil. Known as "Operation Pastorius," it began when four Germans landed at Amagansett Beach on Long Island, New York on the night of June 12-13, 1942, with the goal of sabotaging the American war effort. Discovered by Coast Guardsman John Cullen, the Long Island crew attempted to bribe him and fled to New York City. Two of the men, George Dasch and Ernest Burger, turned themselves into the FBI and a manhunt ensued for the others. Foreign correspondent and non-fiction writer Michael Dobbs appeared on Booknotes *on March 28, 2004 to discuss his book,* Saboteurs: The Nazi Raid on America *(Random House, 2004).*

WHEN I FIRST DISCOVERED this story, I thought it was such an incredible yarn. The very idea of eight Nazi saboteurs coming to America, six months after America entered the war, by U-boat. Then they were tried by military tribunal. There's a historic Supreme Court session and finally, they were executed. That seemed so improbable to me when I first heard of it that I wanted to write a story about it. But then I was attracted by the huge amount of archival material available. There are whole shelves of boxes of FBI material going into great detail about every move they made. After I began the research, 9/11 happened, and I saw parallels between the way the U.S. responded to this case and the way the government responded to 9/11.

THE DATE OF THE first landing of Nazi saboteurs in this country was June 13, 1942, about six months after Pearl Harbor. Two U-boats came across the Atlantic. The first group landed in Amagansett, Long Island, on June 13; the second group landed six days later, June 19, at Ponte Vedra, Florida. There were four in each group. From Hitler's point of view, it was quite an intelligent response to America coming into the war. Hitler didn't fear an immediate U.S. invasion: the U.S. armed forces were at that time pretty ill-prepared, and certainly no match for the German army. But what he correctly feared was the long-term implications of America coming into the war, this huge industrial power with the ability to churn out huge numbers of tanks and airplanes. Hitler needed to somehow sabotage America's ability to make war. The target he chose was aluminum production. Aluminum was used to make airplanes, so the primary target or primary goal was to sabotage aluminum factories around America and disrupt the production of aluminum. The secondary goal was to disrupt transportation around the country. The U-boat war was going on in the Atlantic, up and down the American coast, and German U-boats were having a field day because America was really unprepared for this U-boat war.

This is one of the parallels with the situation here before 9/11. There's a false sense of security, that even though America had entered the war, nothing much had changed. Cities along the coast, for example, were very resistant to imposing blackout regulations. The city of Miami refused to impose a blackout because they thought it would be bad for tourism. German U-boats were able to patrol up and down the coast, which was lit up by the lights from cities, a perfect backdrop for providing silhouettes of targets. So [during] the first few months of 1942, they sank dozens of ships all up and down the American coastline.

This remained the largest German effort to insert saboteurs into America. What makes it a rich story for a writer is all the detail provided by the FBI. I began [to write the book] at the National Archives in College Park, Maryland, an essential first stop, particularly [in] researching this book because it's the location of the FBI files. But having gone through the entire FBI file, I followed [in] the footsteps of the saboteurs themselves. I went to Amagansett and was able to recreate for myself the events on the night of their landing. I went to New York where they traveled to after landing at Amagansett. The FBI was actually following a couple of the saboteurs around Chicago, so I was able to use that to follow precisely where they had been in Chicago over the course of a week. Here in this country, I went to Hyde Park, New York, President Roosevelt's retreat, where he took the decision to establish military tribunals. Then abroad, I went to Hitler's bunker, which is now in Poland, what used to be East Prussia. It was actually the place where Hitler took the decision to mount this sabotage campaign against the United States. In Germany, I visited the little town called Brandenburg, which is about half-an-hour's train ride from Berlin, where they were trained in sabotage techniques prior to getting on the U-boat to come to America.

The night they landed in Amagansett, the submarine got stranded on a sandbar a couple of hundred yards from the beach. Actually, they landed right next to a Coast Guard station, of all places, in Amagansett. It was a foggy night, so the Coast Guard, couldn't see the U-boat, but they could hear it. It was stranded there for about four hours, and I found the U-boat logs, which describe the panic inside the boat as they tried to get away. They were sure they certainly were going to be discovered. But the Coast Guard never thought to send a boat to investigate these noises of diesel engines trying to escape.

[The submarines were] each about the length of two subway cars, and very thin and very crowded with food provisions, torpedoes, all kinds of equipment, and incredibly cramped inside. There were about forty or fifty crew plus the four saboteurs. In order to move from one end of the U-boat to the other, people would have to get out of one side. There was also a kind of delicate system of balancing the thing, so too many people couldn't be at the front or the back. They would travel very slowly. The normal speed was about the speed of a bicycle. So imagine somebody taking a bicycle across the Atlantic. For the most part, they traveled above water; so they were really a submersible. They needed to travel on top of the water to charge their diesel engines, or to charge their electric motors and to charge their batteries. They needed to do that most of the time, and then they could submerge and be powered with electric power. But most of the time, in order to make any speed at all, they had to travel on top of the water. So they'd only go underneath the water when they were in danger or when they were about to mount an attack. It would be twelve, fourteen knots above water, about two-and-a-half knots below water, and a quarter of the time they were below water.

The eight men that came ashore were all German-Americans, and they all came out of a movement called the German American Bund, which was the American equivalent of the Nazi Party. They all had similar backgrounds and had been born in Germany just before the First World War. Then, after the war, their families fled Germany because the economic conditions were terrible, and came to America looking for new opportunities. Of course, it was the Depression in America, so it wasn't a great time to find jobs in America, and many of them had failed in America in different ways.

When Hitler came to power in Germany, they were attracted by Hitler and thought they wanted to support Germany in the war that was just beginning. They had become disillusioned with America and returned to Germany; but they knew of America and spoke varying degrees of English, so they were selected for this sabotage mission. The leader of the expedition was George John Dasch [who was on the first boat]. He had been a waiter in the United States [and had failed] in practically everything he did. He had been a traveling salesman and failed at that. He'd dabbled with communism, then became interested in Nazism. But he did have an intimate knowledge of American ways. He had a slang knowledge of English and American popular culture, such as baseball, which was one of the reasons that made him attractive to the people who organized this expedition.

...It took about three weeks to transverse the Atlantic. They left from the port of Lorient, which is on the Atlantic seaboard of France, and from where they launched many of their missions across the Atlantic. Hitler had approved the sabotage plan personally against the United States with the leaders of German military intelligence, in his bunker in East Prussia.... At the beginning of the war, Roosevelt insisted that some kind of rudimentary coastal defense be instituted. So they had the Coast Guard along the entire seaboard, patrolling the coastline. They were unarmed and patrolled alone, so they were not really prepared for anybody coming ashore. But each had a route that they had to follow, two miles out and two miles back. [John Cullen, who was in the Coast Guard] that night at Amagansett, was on patrol when the saboteurs landed. Amazingly, he actually ran into Dasch on this foggy, incredibly dark night.

The saboteurs were dressed in kind of rudimentary Nazi German army uniforms because they thought that if they were intercepted on landing, the uniforms would give them some kind of protection, that they would be arrested not as saboteurs, but as soldiers. And they brought with them each four boxes of sabotage gear, pretty sophisticated sabotage equipment: bomb-making equipment, fuses, detonators, liable to do quite a bit of damage. The sub had been submerged [in Amagansett] and it came to the surface. It sort of edged its way into the shore and as soon as they felt that there was sand beneath them, they knew they were pretty close to the shore. They had deliberately chosen a moonless night because they wanted it to be as dark as possible. But what they didn't know is they bumped into a false sandbar, which is actually notorious in Amagansett. There have been many shipwrecks on this sandbar.

THE SABOTEURS HAD TO come to the surface in order to communicate. That was one reason why they came to the surface frequently. The U.S. and Britain were able to track these communications and more or less get a pretty good idea of where the U-boats were through these communications. At one point, they were able to decipher the communications... with the help of a machine called Enigma. The Allies found a way of deciphering this at the precise moment when these people landed. At that particular time, the Allies didn't have the ability to decipher the communications, but they could locate the boats by triangulating where the radio signals were coming from.

PERHAPS, IN THEORY, PEOPLE talked about the possibility of saboteurs landing. But until this happened, it wasn't taken very seriously. Actually, one of the few people who took it seriously was FDR, because Roosevelt had been Assistant Navy Secretary during the First World War. He was an aficionado of spy stories and thought there was a real threat and tried to beef up the Coast Guard. For example, walkie-talkies had just been introduced, and he had seen his Secret Service people at Hyde Park and in Washington using walkie-talkies to communicate. He thought it would be a good idea if these two-way radios were also issued to the

Coast Guard. FDR made the suggestion a few months before the saboteurs landed, but nobody took him up on this. It was one of the suggestions from the commander-in-chief that people just ignored.

The saboteurs ran into Cullen [from the Coast Guard] on the beach.
Cullen went back to summon help, and by the time that he came back, they
had disappeared. They had moved inland...they just took the first train that
came along, which took them into Manhattan. [The second group that
went into Ponte Vedra Beach] had much less trouble than the Amagansett
group. Their landing went off pretty smoothly; they buried their sabotage
equipment and took a bus into Jacksonville. They checked into Jacksonville hotels, just as the Amagansett group arrived at Penn Station, and they
checked into the hotel just across the street from Penn Station.

THERE'S A QUESTION OF when Dasch decided to betray the rest of the
them and turn himself in to the FBI. He said that his name was Mr. Pastorius. The operation was called Operation Pastorius, after the first German settlers who came to America in the seventeenth century. He called
the FBI in New York and said his name was Mr. Pastorius. He'd just arrived by U-boat from Germany, and he had some very important information to impart to J. Edgar Hoover. He was dismissed as a crank. They
thought that he was a lunatic, made a note of the conversation, but they
didn't do anything about it. A few days later, Dasch took the train down
to Washington, checked into the Mayflower Hotel here in Washington,
and, the next morning, was brought to FBI headquarters, where he began
telling his story. Dasch says that he had become totally disillusioned with
Nazism soon after he'd returned to Germany, and that he'd secretly hated
Hitler, and that he wanted to use the money that they'd been given for the
operation to mount a propaganda campaign against Hitler using American radio facilities. That was his dream, to use this money to buy broadcasts on American radio, awaken the German people to the evil of Hitler.

This was about the same time as the landing of the group in Ponte
Vedra. Dasch said that he was asked why he waited so long to go to the
FBI. One of his reasons was that he wanted to give the Ponte Vedra group
the chance of also turning themselves in, that he wouldn't just betray
them without at least giving them the same chance that he had had of
going to the FBI. I spoke with Duane Traynor, who lives in Springfield,

Illinois. He's in his early nineties, but he still has an incredibly precise memory. He was head of the FBI's anti-sabotage unit, and the first FBI man in the United States to interview Dasch. Traynor was the first person to take him seriously, and said, "I'll send a car right over for you." At that time, the FBI treated him very respectfully, and they treated him as a free man. Instead of putting him in a jail cell at the end of each interrogation session, they permitted him to go back to the hotel. After the first night, Traynor went back with him to the hotel. Dasch told Traynor, "I've got something to show you." He brought out his suitcase and produced about 100,000 American dollars, which, Traynor told me, was more money than he'd ever seen in his life...it was one of the things that convinced him that Dasch was telling the truth.

THE FIVE-HUNDRED-PAGE TRANSCRIPT [OF Dasch's confession] had been published before.... Most had come out during the military tribunal hearings, because Dasch insisted that his entire confession be read into the record.

[THE TRANSCRIPT OF DASCH'S confession in 1942] reads: "The sense of American invulnerability was reflected in the low priority placed on homeland security. The defenses set up along the Eastern seaboard in the immediate aftermath of America's entry into the war were 'scanty and improvised,' in the words of the Army's official history. They were strengthened somewhat in April as a result of the growing U-boat menace and intelligence reports that Germans might be trying to land saboteurs along the coast. But there were many glaring holes, caused in large part by bureaucratic turf fights between the agencies responsible for homeland security." After 9/11, this sounds familiar.

Somebody [at the National Archives] did show me the stacks, which is where all these boxes of material are held. Quite a bit of attention had been paid to the transcript of the military tribunal proceedings. Those became public, actually, thirty, forty years ago. But the FBI files were only declassified about five years ago, so nobody had really systematically gone through them.

J. Edgar Hoover was an extraordinary person who built the FBI up into a remarkable organization, but he was also a vicious, bureaucratic infighter. He was determined that he and the FBI would take the credit for breaking the case. He hoarded information and refused to let any FBI agents inform other government agencies. There was infighting between the FBI and other government agencies, all of which you can follow in the files—particularly vicious with the Coast Guard and Naval intelligence. At one point, things got so bad that they were leaking rival stories to the press as the military tribunal was going on. Hoover was contemptuous of the way the Coast Guard had allowed the saboteurs to get away. He thought they were completely incompetent and didn't want to give any credit to the Coast Guard at all. Hoover had a PR guy called Lou Nichols who had made Hoover's reputation and [had many contacts in the media]. He strong-armed the Coast Guard into keeping quiet. In fact, he threatened the Coast Guard. He said that "if you bring out your side of the story…you wouldn't want all this unpleasant information about the Coast Guard to become public, the fact that you allowed the saboteurs to get away from the beach."

I WAS INTERESTED IN this case as a journalist since we journalists don't get to see what's actually happening in the bureaucracies. We don't read the memos; but sixty years later, you can read the memos. One of the things we find when we read these internal documents is that the infighting can become pretty vicious. Hoover made the announcement about a week after Dasch walked into the FBI headquarters in Washington. It took them a week to round up everybody else. At that point, Hoover made his own announcement that they had been caught, and that disturbed a lot of other people in the government. The military intelligence and the War Department were furious with Hoover, because they thought it would be much better if the whole thing was kept secret, and then perhaps other teams of German saboteurs would come, and they could roll them all up. But by going public, Hoover prevented that from happening. That was one of the controversies inside the government. By this time, they had arrested Dasch and stopped treating him as a free man. They eventually took them all [eight men] to jail cells in the New York FBI headquarters.

Once they decided to hold a military tribunal, the saboteurs were transferred to the Army and held in a military jail in Washington. The military tribunal took place in the Justice Department building in Washington. They landed on June 13th, were rounded up within two weeks of their landing, and the tribunals began in mid-July. That contrasts with what's happening now. In [the] two years after 9/11, and after the Bush administration announced that they were going to try [the] Al Qaeda people by military tribunals, no tribunals had yet been held. But in this case, the whole legal process was compressed into two months: the landing, the rounding up of the saboteurs, the military tribunals. There's a Supreme Court hearing, and six of them were executed, all within two months.

FRANCIS BIDDLE WAS THE Attorney General. He prosecuted the case himself, because he didn't trust any of his subordinates to prosecute it. The tribunals took about two weeks. They were all sentenced to death. But then the sentences on Burger and Dasch were commuted to life imprisonment. The six were put to death in the D.C. jail by the electric chair. There was the tribunal, and then there was a habeas corpus appeal to the Supreme Court, and the Court ruled against the saboteurs. The same thing is happening now. Some of the attorneys for some of the detainees in Guantanamo have appealed to the Supreme Court, based on the 1942 precedent.

Dasch [and Burger, another saboteur] were pardoned by Truman and they went back to Germany in 1948. Dasch spent much of his time trying to get back to the United States and died in 1972. Hoover vetoed all his attempts to get back to the United States. [There were two reasons why Dasch wasn't pardoned initially after turning the others in.] One was that Hoover wanted to take all the credit for rounding up the saboteurs. He didn't want it to be made public that the reason why the FBI was able to round up the saboteurs is one of them had gone and told the whole story to the FBI. But there was also a military reason, which is that they didn't want to let the Germans know why the operation had failed. They wanted to give the Germans the impression that American coasts were impregnable, and that the FBI was everywhere. That would be a deterrent to the Nazis to send further sabotage teams over to America. However, as a result of the publicity surrounding the case, the Germans had a pretty good idea of what had gone wrong.

The President's House

WILLIAM SEALE

White House Historical Association historian William Seale has been a regular contributor to C-SPAN's history programs over the last quarter century, including serving as one of four academic advisors to our 2012–13 series, First Ladies: Influence and Image. *He is the author of* The President's House: A History *(Johns Hopkins University Press, 2008, Second Edition) and joined us on* Q & A *in December, 2008 to talk about the White House and its many intriguing occupants.*

THE WHITE HOUSE IS an icon to the presidency and the president is the closest spot of human contact we have with our system, and I suppose that accounts for [the public's great interest.] It's where the president lives. There are no beds in the Capitol that we know of, and the man sleeps in the White House; that's his home, and I think there's that point of identity. Parenthetically, I don't think the White House would exist if Lincoln hadn't lived there because the whole nation, North and South, shared the melodrama of his family life as his family fell apart, just like other families in the nation fell apart and people had that in their mind's eye. [The White House was] the stage set for all of that....

[IF I HAD TO pick a president in history I would have liked to have known,] I'd probably pick James Monroe. It was a very interesting time in American history, the period of Monroe and the end of the War of 1812, when the United States felt at last they had defeated Britain and we were going into a boom situation. I think the years from 1817 on would have been very exciting at the White House. James Monroe looked a little bit like George Washington and he was like a younger son to the founding fathers. He was extremely popular. In his second election, one person voted against him just so that it wouldn't be unanimous and take the thunder away from George Washington…. He thought political parties were dead, that the nation was coming together as one, having finally defeated England, and was on its own and it was going to turn inward, which, in fact, it certainly did for the whole century. He did the White House up very grandly with old Napoleonic castoffs they bought in France, gold furniture—still in the Blue Room today—and dishes still used in the White House today that say, "President's House." They are always lovingly cared for. He made his grand progresses through the country, seeing the various areas, visiting people—no TV then—so they could see him. Interestingly enough, as grand as the White House may get, it's always a little down to earth. Monroe, of course, didn't have enough money to do these tours. They were very expensive. He had some French furniture that he and his wife had bought in France when he was an American minister there in the late 1790s, so he would sell that to the government, take the money and pay for his tours. Then when his salary of $25,000 a year, which was huge then, would come in, he'd pay it back. This pattern was repeated a number of times and never known until the next administration caught onto it, and it became a scandal. But his period was very vibrant. Of course, he soon learned with the panic of 1819 that there were political parties and there was financial disaster. But it was a brilliant eight years.

THE FIRST FIRST LADY to die in the White House was Mrs. Letitia Tyler in the 1840s. Mrs. Tyler was ill when she went there and died. Then the president, rather soon by most standards, married a much younger woman, a friend of his children. They only had a couple of months there. But that was very lively, in their time.

John Tyler became president on the death of William Henry Harrison, who was president only for thirty days. Harrison was the great hero of the old Northwest and he was swept into office. Actually, his election was far more of a people's election than Andrew Jackson's. Harrison was

"Old Tippecanoe and Tyler too," the song we all grew up with and the Log Cabin Campaign. The public swarmed around this man and brought him to Washington, and he lived for thirty days and then died. His wife never even made it over the mountains to live at the White House. Tyler took over and he proved much more of a project to deal with for the politicians. The politicians surrounding him thought they would, as they had expected with Jackson...tell him what to do, but Tyler didn't agree to any of that. And so there was a split and Tyler actually changed parties.

Tyler was president for almost four years, just thirty days under four years. [His wife died within about two years] and he remarried in New York. Julia was twenty-four years old. He had six [children at that point,], and then he had about eight with Julia. They were still having children by the time of the Civil War. He had quite a family. In fact, his son was the librarian at the College of William & Mary until the mid-twentieth century.

[WHEN HIS TERM ENDED, Millard Fillmore left the White House and moved into the Willard Hotel] to make way for the new president, Franklin Pierce. Then, Mrs. Fillmore died there at the Willard that first night. Fillmore is one of the most misunderstood of all of the presidents. He was a self-made man, as so many of them were, meaning he probably came from a stable family, let's say, but he had nothing to help him along financially, family-wise or otherwise. He was a surveyor, as many presidents had been, and he rose as a lawyer and politician. He and his wife, Abigail, were a very sophisticated couple. There are various things they did. One, they built the first White House library, which was relatively minor. But if you read the titles of those books, as one scholar is doing today, they were very sophisticated. They had all the latest books on landscape and poetry and history, and so forth. But affecting us even more is his enlargement of the Capitol. God knows what would have happened to that building if it hadn't been for Fillmore. But he had served there and he loved it. They were going to expand it, and he decreed, the same way Truman later did with the White House, [that] in no way could the original walls be violated. They were adding out to the side of the Capitol, and the original dome came to looking like a half an orange sitting up there. It was ridiculous. They needed a vertical piece for the Capitol to offset the long horizontal of the new wings. Of course, this led to the decision [to put an iron dome on top]. It was going to have a dome, because the state capitols have them, but you couldn't put a heavy masonry dome on those old brick walls. That's when they went to iron plates copied from Saint Isaac's Cathedral in Russia. It was light enough to ride those old walls, and that's really why we have the dome. It was Fillmore's idea.

Fillmore brought Andrew Jackson Downing, the great landscape architect, still great in America's annals of landscape, to Washington to improve the model. He changed the original plan a lot. That was an avant-garde thing to do in that day. Fillmore is remembered mostly because of a H.L. Mencken article about him putting the first bathtub in the White House. Fillmore's always been the butt of jokes, but he was a most interesting character and a sophisticated person. [He was an upstate New Yorker.] He became president on the death of Zachary Taylor. Taylor went to a Fourth of July oration by George Washington Parke Custis, who billed himself as the child of Mount Vernon. He was Ms. Washington's grandson and really trafficked on that fact, always. He built Arlington House that we know today in Arlington Cemetery. He delivered these orations and this particular one was four hours long. The sun was hot and the president was old and he went back to the White House famished and ate iced cherries. They led to something, and he developed pneumonia and died very quickly.

In the nineteenth century, death was very frequent with many a family. You could go out and get your feet wet—I guess that's why they didn't bathe so much—and have pneumonia and die in two days. It happened all the time. People were very careful about that. Harrison was the first [to die in office]; Zachary Taylor was the second to die in office. He was laid in state there, put in a receiving vault, and later buried in Louisville, Kentucky. In the old days they always were [embalmed right at the White House], just like people were embalmed at home. President Harrison, who died in the White House, was the first. The officials surrounding him went to Darius Clagett, an owner of a large store in town, and just said, "do it." There had been state funerals at the Capitol, so Darius [followed the model and] just went in, and draped the White House, everything. All the mirrors were covered in black crepe, the chandeliers, all the things like that. The president was in a winding sheet, and his body was put in the East Room, with his dress sword from the Mexican War on top of the coffin, and the funeral was held.

JANE APPLETON PIERCE WAS a very quiet, intellectual woman, very smart, probably a good advisor to Franklin, as all first ladies have been. She lost a son [Franklin Jr.,] who was ten, in 1836. Three years later, Frank Robert died from typhus. He was four and it broke her heart, of course. Then they had this little boy, Benny, who was eleven, and he was idolized by her. There's a very poignant daguerreotype image of the two of them together. On a train trip after Pierce's election, there was a train wreck, and the boy was thrown from the train and rolled down the hill in the snow. President Pierce jumped out of the train and ran down to him, and when he picked him up, his cap fell off and his head had been crushed, and he died. Mrs. Pierce took the unfortunate course of saying that it was God's punishment of her and her husband for [his] ambition of wanting to be president. She became a recluse. She would write letters to the boy [during] all the years at the White House. She just seemed doomed to problems. They were very close to Jefferson Davis and his very vivacious wife. The Davis' had a little boy, and Mrs. Davis, being very pushy and very bright, took it upon herself to bring Jane Pierce out, and so she did it through the little boy. Jane Pierce did become interested and started going places and did things, and then that little boy died and she went right back into where she was, from which she never recovered. But except for a rather unhappy home life, I doubt the tragedy had very much impact on Franklin's presidency. He was in a very tumultuous time. He took the states' rights side in the terrible Kansas battles and was a representative of the old Democratic Party. But he coped with it and had her along. She became extremely dependent for the rest of her life until she died.

[WARREN G. HARDING ALSO died while he was president.] He died in a hotel in San Francisco, and there are lots of mysteries surrounding it, as there are with every president's death. The funeral was the traditional White House funeral with a little less drapery. Mrs. Harding did not want all the mourning drapery. So there was a little bit of it in the East Room, but not a lot; then his body was taken to the Capitol, and then it was returned to Ohio.

[Some of Harding's conduct in the White House was wholly illegal.... Harding usually hosted several poker parties a week, and though it was during Prohibition, beside the poker table was a makeshift bar.] His explanation to friends was, this is my private area. I can do what I want. I won't do this in the state parts of the house. He is the only president who did that. Coolidge and Hoover were very particular in observing Prohibition, but Harding didn't think much of it.... Most of the Harding scandals unfolded after his death, but he knew about them. Jess Smith and Charles Kramer were the very first that were accused of corruption and graft in their federal positions, and these were close, close friends, and they were devastated and went home and were very depressed [and killed themselves]. A journalist, William Allen White, once asked him a question about his enemies, and he said, "My God, this is a hell of a job! I have no trouble with my enemies. I can take care of my enemies all right, but my damn friends, my God-damn friends, White, they're the ones that keep me walking the floor nights!"

PRESIDENT HARDING DIED SUDDENLY in California on a speaking tour, and Calvin Coolidge, former governor of Massachusetts, became president of the United States. He was a totally different kind of man. Harding was a glamour boy. He was the first president elected by women because he had an enormous appeal and a beautiful voice. There are recordings of his voice. Coolidge was a very different sort of man. He was very businesslike, very cryptic, and just as witty as he could be.... Calvin, Jr. died in the White House. He developed a blister on the tennis court and was dead in four days of blood poisoning, and naturally, it was a horrible thing for the family.

[CALVIN COOLIDGE LIVED OUTSIDE the White House at 15 Dupont Circle for six months while he was president.] He moved out because they needed more space...so they decided to tear the roof off and shape it in such a way that they could accommodate a third floor without seeing it from the street, and that's what happened in 1927. The Coolidges moved to the Patterson House, which still stands, and there they received [Charles] Lindbergh, [in 1927,] and then finally moved back into the [White] House. That third floor was pretty bad for the house... They didn't do an iron third floor. They did a masonry one and just squashed down on the White House, which was one of the reasons the house had to be reconstructed in '48 to '52, when, of course, Truman moved out for most of his administration. He lived in Blair House across the street while the house was being renovated. Theodore Roosevelt, in 1902, for his ninety-day wonder [construction project] on the White House did move out, finally. He said, "Oh, no, I can stay here. It'll be just great." Then plaster dust got to him, and after a month, he moved across the street to a row house on Lafayette Square.

The Clevelands weren't told to leave the White House. They just left. President Cleveland married his ward, a young woman of twenty-one. He was forty-seven, and he wanted her to have a normal family life. He made that very clear. He hated the press. The press was wild about her, and he tried to hide her from all that. So he built a house out by the present Washington Cathedral called Red Top, and they lived there just like a family, and she had some thirty pets there. They went to the White House for entertainment. They did the same thing [in his second term]. He was out for a term, and then he went back [in '93, after he] was reelected in '92, and they had another house in Washington. They didn't stay there quite as much. By then, they had children, and then another child was born in the White House, and so the Clevelands definitely lived between these other houses and the White House, but the White House was still their official residence....

Frances Folsom Cleveland was twenty-one years old when they married. There were Frankie Cleveland fan clubs all over the country. She went to Europe with her mother before the wedding, and when she came back, she had to be secreted through New York hotels. The streets were mobbed to see Frankie Cleveland. She was just so popular, and she was a very nice and interesting young woman. When Princess Eulalia of Spain came to visit in 1893, she wore the famous Spanish jewels, which were pearls the size of eggs that went from her neck to the floor, and diamonds. Mrs. Cleveland wore a white dress with one camellia pinned on the front of it, no jewelry at all, and won the day. She had a certain likableness about her, which was nice for him because he didn't. He was not much of a public figure. He'd take on after you if he got mad about something.

[WILLIAM MCKINLEY WAS ASSASSINATED in the first year of his second term.] The McKinley relationship was not totally unlike that of [Franklin] Pierce and Mrs. Pierce. They had lost two children, two little girls, long before the White House, and Ida McKinley was subject to depression. She also had epilepsy. She was a very smart, bright woman. She was the first first lady who ever worked in a salaried job long before they went to the White House. McKinley brought the country into the international world with the Spanish-American War, and then was killed at the Pan-American Exposition in Buffalo, New York. Theodore Roosevelt, the vice president, became president of the United States. So McKinley created Roosevelt. Mrs. McKinley lived a few years after McKinley, but not long. She was a very strong individual, but basically an invalid.

[CARY GRAYSON HAD AN impact on the Woodrow Wilson White House.] He was a doctor, and he was also one of the great horsemen of Virginia, of anywhere. After the inauguration, there was a luncheon at the White House and one of the relatives, a woman, an older woman, fell, and Dr. Grayson was attached to the White House as an assistant to Dr. [Presley Marion] Rixey, who was the White House doctor. There's always been a doctor assigned to the White House since the late nineteenth century. He was so gentle with her because she was in a fairly hysterical state, that he was detailed to the family. He became intimate to the Wilson family and became the White House doctor. He was raised to the rank of admiral and stayed there all during the Wilson administration. No one knew the Wilsons any better than Cary Grayson. He was there when Mrs. Wilson died in the White House in 1914. He was one of the ones who introduced the new wife, Edith, to President Wilson and was an old and dear friend of Edith's. He married "Altrude" [Alice Gertrude Gordon] and they had children, little boys; and when Woodrow Wilson had the stroke, one of the children—Gordon, who lived until recently—was very close to the president. Wilson would look forward to visits from him in his sickness. He pepped him up.... The little boy was attributed by the family and the doctor as being a great help.

HERBERT HOOVER WAS A brilliant man married to a brilliant woman.... He was secretary of Commerce and then became president. It must have been the busiest White House ever seen because the whole second floor was practically turned into a series of offices. He would be meeting with people in one, and she'd be meeting with people in another, and people who met with them said a five-minute meeting with the Hoovers was a long meeting. Then in the evening, they had the staff all come up and play Bridge. They just literally wore people out. They were the most energetic people. They built Camp Rapidan, the first presidential retreat in the Blue Ridge foothills of Virginia. They paid for it themselves and gave it to the government. You couldn't get there except by horseback, so it was definitely a retreat. Washington was very exclusive [in Hoover's day]. Mormons were not accepted socially and black people were not. The Hoovers did invite African Americans to the White House, [including the first African American Congressman since Reconstruction,] Oscar DePriest, from Chicago, and his wife. Mrs. Hoover had her to tea first to warm things up, and then they had them to dinners. [Guest lists for the teas were made up of what President Hoover described as "ladies previously tested as to their feelings," in other words, to find out whether they would allow themselves to be in the presence of African Americans.]...It's hard to imagine the White House and democracy [like that], but that's the way it was.

THIS BOOK WAS WRITTEN for history buffs because I've always been one, even though I'm a historian. I'd like to think that when my time is up, if these books still exist, there'll be 10,000 term paper topics in them for kids in school. So I tried to write it with that in mind. They could take, say, President Pierce's term and read that part of the book and get a picture of life in his White House. Most biographies of presidents, not even very long ago, really never had anything in them about the White House. It was very rare. It was about the presidency, but not about life in the house. So that is one of my personal motivations, that young people can get these stories out of the past—I hate to say it, but that's what they are—the First Families' reactions to living in that very strange situation that nobody can ever understand until they go there.

The United States Senate

DONALD RITCHIE

C-SPAN began providing gavel-to-gavel coverage of the House of Representatives in 1979 and the U.S. Senate in 1986. Over the years, Senate Historian Donald Ritchie has helped C-SPAN viewers better understand Congress. He joined the Senate Historical Office as Associate Senate Historian in 1976 and succeeded the chamber's first historian, Richard Baker, upon his retirement in 2009. He appeared on Q & A *on August 15, 2010 to discuss his book,* The U.S. Congress: A Very Short Introduction *(Oxford University Press, 2010). The book explains how Congress works and provides some history and background on the legislative branch of government. Mr. Ritchie also talked about Hollywood's portrayal of Congress in such movies as* Mr. Smith Goes to Washington *and* Advise and Consent.

I WAS ASKED TO write the book by Oxford University Press for a series called, *"A Very Short Introduction."* ...My job was to take this very complicated institution, which is really two separate institutions, and explain how it developed over time to an audience of people who are curious, including people outside the United States who live in parliamentary governments and wonder why we don't have a parliament in the United States.

We wonder why presidents of the United States don't come to the Senate chamber when they have big issues like treaties. The fact of the matter is it didn't work for George Washington. When Washington arrived in the chamber in August of 1789 with a series of questions, to ask the advice of the Senate as well as to get its consent, the senators didn't really want to debate this in front of Washington. He was quite an imposing figure. It was also summertime; the windows were open. It was hard to hear what was going on so they suggested referring the questions to a committee. Washington jumped up and said, "That defeats my whole purpose of being here," and stormed out of the Senate chamber. He came back a few days later to get their response. But after that, he decided he didn't want to go in person. And ever since then, there's been a big question: When the Constitution says that the Senate's role is to advise and consent, we know what the "consent" is: That's the vote, the two-thirds vote necessary for a treaty.... But what's the "advise?" What's the advisory role of the legislative branch? That's been a difficult issue ever since 1789.

[I JOINED THE SENATE Historian's Office in 1976.] Among the big changes I have seen in the Senate is security, which was very different in the 1970s. I could park on the plaza and walk into the building. The only metal detectors were those going into the chambers themselves. Any citizen could sort of wander at will. Over time, parts of the building have been closed off [and a badge is needed to go into those.] You need to show you are there on official business, or be escorted through those. But the major historical rooms are still open for the public tours, and the chambers themselves are open. Lots of other changes have happened over time. One of the biggest changes was television and C-SPAN televising the House in 1979 and the Senate in 1986. Whenever I do oral history interviews with long-time Senate staff members, I ask them what changed the most, and inevitably, they say television. Television is, both in terms of the campaigns that the members conducted and the type of people who get elected, the way in which people communicate with their constituents. Citizens are aware of what goes on in Congress because they get to watch the proceedings, and even how empty the chambers are. Even the press gallery is empty. They are watching on C-SPAN, too. They're not necessarily sitting in the press gallery. They don't need to be hovering near the chamber at any particular time to know what's going on. If something happens that catches their attention, they can quickly go into the Senate chamber.

Technology changed enormously. When I first came to work in the Senate, reporters in the press gallery were typing their stories on typewriters, ripping them out and yelling, "Western," and a little guy who worked for Western Union would come over and take their copy and run it back to the telegraph operator; they were actually telegraphing the news to their newspapers. The telegraph operation was not taken out until 1990. Now, everybody is using their laptops to send their stories as they are writing them in the committee rooms, which are all wireless. Even the telephone booths, where reporters used to run out and jump in a telephone booth and call their story in, are not needed anymore; everyone's on a cell phone. They actually have kept six of the booths, just so you can have some privacy while you're talking on a cell phone. But the need for the telephone booth has gone along with a lot of the other technological changes. Every staff member in the Senate is working on a computer using e-mail. There is all sorts of teleconferencing going on. None of that was happening in the 1970s when I first came.

I PROBABLY SAW THE movie *Mr. Smith Goes to Washington* [1939, starring Jimmy Stewart] on a late movie back in the 1960s for the first time, but I have now seen that movie many times and watched it under different circumstances. I've taught courses on the Senate, and I've also given lectures about the Senate using *Mr. Smith*. All sorts of visitors to the Capitol know *Mr. Smith Goes to Washington;* even non-American visitors have seen the movie. They think that's the way the U.S. Senate operates, and they think that's particularly the way filibusters operate; we always have to explain to them that it's a movie, and while some filibusters might resemble that, most don't.

But it's a wonderful film in the sense that they created a set in Hollywood that looks just like the Senate chamber at that time. They used Jim Preston, who was the superintendent of the Senate press gallery, as a technical advisor; he helped to really capture it. It's not totally accurate in the way the Senate does business...[but] surprisingly, there is a lot in the movie that's accurate. There is still the press gallery in that place, the members' gallery. We still have a diplomatic gallery. We have a lot of other set-aside galleries for the general public and other things. We still depend on Senate pages on the floor, although they're a little older now; they have to be high school juniors. The chamber looks the way it did in 1939; …what's different today, as Mr. Smith walked into the chamber, everybody wouldn't be sitting at their seat. The galleries wouldn't be packed, unless there was something really significant about to happen at that period. The chamber is usually fairly empty. Only the people who are engaged in the particular debate will be there at any particular time.

The very first time I ever went into the Senate chamber was in 1968; I was a graduate student, working at the Library of Congress…in those days, before the TV cameras were there, the chamber was much dimmer. Senator Everett Dirksen, (R-Illinois), the minority leader of the Senate, put his head down on his arms, and never raised his head the entire time that I was sitting in the chamber. I assume that he was probably taking a few winks. It was probably a lot more prevalent in those days when things were quieter and calmer in the afternoon. Members in those days did have to be on the floor more. I've talked to old-timers who say, the only way to know if your bill was actually up was to either be on the floor or be in the cloakroom. Even the people in the cloakroom didn't always know what was going on on the Senate floor. They would have to call somebody known as the chief telephone page, which was usually a senior page, who kept tabs on what was happening. Lobbyists, staff, and others hovered around. That meant you had to be there when other things were happening that you weren't particularly interested in. During those periods when you were waiting for the bills you were going to engage in, a number of people probably closed their eyes from time to time. These days, with the bright lights and the TV cameras, I have never seen anybody in modern times sleeping in the chamber.

Originally, the Russell Building was the Senate Office Building, and it was known by its acronym, the SOB. It was built in 1909, and it was the only office building till 1958, when the new SOB was built across the street. But in 1971, the Senate decided that it was time to name it for an individual. Richard Russell was chosen as the person to name the first building, and then Everett Dirksen the second, and Philip Hart the third building.… These buildings are along Constitution Avenue. Each one is a different style of architecture. The Russell Building is a classical style.

There's sort of a neoclassical style on the Dirksen Building, and a very modern style on the Hart Building, and they are all connected by tunnels and corridors. They provide offices for the senators and space for the committees to meet. Richard Russell was a Democratic senator from Georgia from 1933 until he died in 1971. He was known as a senator's senator. Even if you disagreed with him, people respected him. He had a great dignity and a bearing that the senators admired; he was the leader of the Southern Caucus. He often led the filibusters against civil rights legislation. I suggest that the Senate named the building in spite of his politics; they named it for him because of his character.

[People will say that Senator Russell was a white separatist who clearly thought the whites and the blacks ought to be separate.] Unfortunately, it was a reflection of representative democracy. Senator Russell believed that he was reflecting the views of his constituents. In those days, it was almost impossible for an African American to vote in the state of Georgia. Senator Russell's constituents were whites, and he felt that he was preserving a segregation system that his constituents wanted; he saw this in terms of states' rights. Senator Russell himself was a very complicated individual. He was a bachelor who fell in love with a Catholic woman. He felt he couldn't marry her, because his constituents wouldn't accept that. In a lot of ways, he was trapped by his need to represent what he thought was the viewpoint of his state.... Russell [was] feeling the weight of this representation [during the civil rights debates]; in a sense, it was a losing cause that even Senator Russell realized was doomed to fail.

The Philip A. Hart Building opened in 1982. Senator Hart was known as the "Conscience of the Senate." He was there seventeen years as a Democrat from Michigan and was elected in the big class of 1958. He was the kind of person in terms of representative democracy who actually stood against sometimes what his constituents were interested in. There's an issue as to whether or not you're there as a delegate for your constituents, or you're there as a trustee: Are you there just to reflect what they have in mind? Or are you there to reflect what you think is right and convince them that it's right? So here is Philip Hart, a senator from Michigan, who stood up against the auto industry and the gun lobby, a number of cases where a lesser politician would have simply gone with what the prevailing sentiments were, regardless of what he personally be-

lieved at the time. Everybody respected Philip Hart on both sides. Interestingly, Philip Hart is the only senator to object to naming the Russell
Building and the Dirksen Building after them. Hart thought they should
have waited longer to determine whether or not those individuals truly
merited that kind of historical recognition. But in December of 1976,
Senator Hart was dying. His term was coming to an end and his colleagues respected him so much that they named the building for him.
He's the only senator to know that one of the buildings was going to be
named for him.

Dirksen was meant as a committee building and it was built in the
1950s when television had come into its own. They wanted to set up the
committee rooms so that TV cameras could be brought in fairly easily.
The idea was that most of the committees…would be in the Dirksen
Building, and the chairmen of the committees would have the offices
adjacent to those committees, and that happened at first. However, the
chairmen, who were veteran senators, really liked the Russell Building
more. The Russell Building is just a classy building. It's got mahogany
doors, and marble fireplaces, and crystal chandeliers, and gorgeous views
of the Capitol. The Dirksen Building is much more functional. Over
time, a lot of the veteran senators moved back into the Russell Building,
so the idea of having the chairman right next to the committee went by
the wayside. But the largest number of committees is in the Dirksen
Building. That's the reason why fewer senators are there.

[SENATOR ROBERT A. TAFT was the ninth majority leader of the United
States Senate. On the Capitol campus is this huge monument to this
man, who was majority leader for only one term.] Senator Taft was a
dominant figure in the Senate for a long time; he was a senator from
1939 until he died in 1953. He had been in politics much of his life because his father [was William Howard Taft], the president of the United
States and chief justice of the United States. When I was doing my research on my doctoral dissertation, I was reading the papers of President
William Howard Taft. One day, I came across a letter from Robert Taft
to his father that was written on a piece of yellow legal paper that he had
ripped out and scratched out a message. Chief Justice Taft wrote back in
a nicely typed letter saying, "Son, someday historians will be reading our

mail. You must use better stationery than this." Here I was in the Library of Congress, reading their mail.

Robert Taft was Mr. Republican. He was the leader of the conservative forces in the Republican Party, a man of great integrity. Even people who disagreed with him admired him. John F. Kennedy, who certainly didn't vote the way Taft did, chose him for his book, *Profiles in Courage*. When Kennedy chaired the committee to pick the five most significant senators, he picked Robert Taft as one. Robert Taft also reflects that problem that a lot of senior senators who want to be president of the United States have. All the things that made them successful in the Senate make them less successful as presidential candidates. Senators have to vote on all sorts of controversial issues. You have to go on record; you can't dodge a controversial issue. The longer you serve in the Senate, the more difficult votes you cast; you reduce your political base rather than expand it. It's not surprising that the three presidents of the United States who have gone directly from the Senate to the White House have actually not been sort of the front row senators. They have been in many ways the back row senators, the newer senators, who had less of a track record: Warren G. Harding in 1920, John F. Kennedy in 1960, and Barack Obama in 2008. Whereas the famous senators over time—from Henry Clay to Robert Taft to Hubert Humphrey in many ways, made themselves too controversial as senators to be elected president of the United States. When Taft died, he had only been leader for six months when he became ill. He had tried for the presidency several times and he had a lot of supporters. He had really been running things in the Senate long before he became majority leader. He only formally took over when President Eisenhower took office, and he wanted to be there to guide Eisenhower's program through the Senate. But I think he had such a large body of support in the Senate and in the country, that they felt that some special memorial was needed. They constructed the Taft Carillon, which rings out every hour with a little bit of music in the background and the statue of Senator Taft in front of it.

A 1962 MOVIE, *Advise and Consent*, was written by Allen Drury from a 1959 novel. Every time I taught, I always showed this movie. This is a story based very loosely on real events and on real people. Allen Drury was a reporter from 1943 to 1945 in the Senate for United Press and later the *New York Times* and *Reader's Digest*. He kept a journal of his observations of the senators and events. One of the events that he observed was a clash between an old Southern senator, Kenneth McKellar, and the head of the TVA [Tennessee Valley Authority] David Lilienthal. The probability is that that was the clash that they were looking at, but he also grafted onto it the Army-McCarthy hearings. He grafted onto it the Alger Hiss case, a lot of other things that were happening. Drury always maintained that his characters in his plots were composites, even though they were clearly based on individuals. One of the great things about the movie is that much of it was filmed in the Russell Senate Office Building. Other than the major characters, like [the actor] Henry Fonda and the people who are the major senators in the movie, all the other personnel that you see [in *Advise and Consent*], the policemen, the elevator operators, the senators' staff, the committee staff, the reporters, the photographers, were all real people on Capitol Hill doing their regular jobs. They were recruited for the movie to do on screen what they did every day. The movie was filmed in 1961 and released in 1962. I came in 1976, and I actually knew many of the people that you see in the movie, and they were all real pleased with their roles there. But that movie was so disruptive, and so many people went down to watch it being filmed, particularly the United States senators, that the Senate Rules Committee said no more films inside the Russell Building.

THE VICE PRESIDENT IN *Advise and Consent* is very much based on Harry Truman. The president in the book is very much based on Franklin Roosevelt. The two majority and minority leaders in the book were based essentially on Alben Barkley, the Democratic leader, and Robert Taft, the Republican leader, who was the minority leader at the time. The reporters who were on the floor, they were doing what was then known as "dugout chatter." The reporters were able to come down on the floor and interview the majority and minority leader just before the Senate went into session. That is no longer done. Now they interview the leadership outside the chamber, not on the floor. But Drury, in 1954, was working at the *New York Times* and trying to write this novel, when a United States senator committed suicide in his office in the Russell Building. It was a very dramatic and shocking moment. Drury then grafted that story onto this novel about the 1940s that he'd been writing, and that gave him the dramatic centerpiece for his novel. That novel, when it was published in 1959, became a phenomenal best-seller. It [spent] 102 weeks on the *New York Times* best-seller list. It was a Book-of-the-Month Club selection, won the Pulitzer Prize, became a stage play, and then a motion picture. None of Drury's other books quite lived up to that story. I once corresponded with him about it. He always said that he wished that he had kept his journal longer than he did, because then he would have been able to cannibalize it for more stories. He clearly depended very much on that journal, which was published in a book called *A Senate Journal: 1943–1945*. It's a very good account of the Senate in the 1940s. As you read it, you can see lots of shadows of the characters that he would create in his novel.

THE PRACTICE OF "BLUE slips" for all judicial branch nominations began in 1913. At the National Archives [there are] judicial nomination file folders and the files are organized by the name of whoever was nominated to be a judge. When opening that file, stapled on one side will be a blue piece of paper with space for two signatures, and those are the two signatures from the senators from that state. Unless you see the two names of the senators from that state, you're pretty well sure that that person was not confirmed. If a senator from a state had a personal objection to someone from that state being nominated, the other senators would not vote that person in. That was senatorial courtesy, with the idea that if they had an objection, the other senators would similarly honor that. Now, that was the way it existed for a very long time. Then, in more recent years, in the last decade or so, as things got a little more politically divided, some chairmen of the Judiciary Committee began to move away from that automatic system, and only requested one signature from a senator from the state; they didn't want to have senators having an automatic veto over some of these nominees. You can still see the blue sheets in more modern files, but it's not as systematic as it once was. It was a way of showing that senators had a lot of influence over who got nominated. The president makes the nominations, but presidents consult with senators about the nominees from your state. I once did an oral history with George Smathers, who was a [Democratic] senator from Florida, and asked him, what was the best thing about being a United States senator? He said, "getting to name so many people judges and U.S. marshals." George Smathers recommended to the president, and the president then nominated the people that Senator Smathers had recommended.... He said that was a big difference between when he was in the House of Representatives. He never had that authority in the House. But when he became a senator, presidents began turning to him for that very reason.

FORTY-TWO PERCENT OF THE members of the Congress, House and Senate, between the years 1998 and 2004, now lobby for a living. A very large number of people who retire from Congress stay in Washington, D.C. In a sense, they use the talents that they developed while they were in office to promote issues to represent concerns, to give advice to people on how to get bills through Congress. There's a large lobbying contingent in Washington. Members used to have a great advantage because doors were always open to them. Their colleagues would always invite them in and they could go onto the floor of the House and Senate and use the dining rooms; this gave them an advantage over other lobbyists. Ethics rules have gotten much tighter, however. If a former member does lobby, a lot of the privileges of being a former member are very much restrained or taken away, and that includes going onto the floor, because no one is to lobby on the floor of the Congress.... Of course, lobbyists represent all sorts of interests, including interests like school teachers and environmental issues, and everything else.... But one of the things that lobbyists do is run fundraisers for members. It costs a lot of money to run for Congress.... Members of Congress are constantly seeking ways to raise funds. Lobbyists for issues that they support will run fundraisers for them. Then, there's always this question: Is there some quid pro quo? Again, ethics laws are much tighter now. But campaign finance has become a very difficult issue. The Congress has tried to pass a number of laws. The Supreme Court hasn't cleared those laws. Congress is still trying to address how to deal with campaign finance. But they want to avoid the perception that there's anything that is somehow giving unfair advantage.

ON AVERAGE, AMERICAN CITIZENS visit the U.S. Capitol twice in their lives. Once is as children with their families or with their classes, and again as parents bringing their own families. This is what the tour guides tell me when people talk about coming into the Capitol building.... There are all sorts of visitors who are coming. But then you also see the families coming in and taking their children around and pointing out what's happening in the Capitol building. Right now, with the Capitol Visitors Center, there's a lot more opportunity for them to learn more about what's going on in the Congress. I worked for many years in terms of the exhibits that are [on display there] to talk about what is the Senate, what is the House, what are the differences between them, how do they function? That's the same type of thing I tried to do in this book, to give an introduction to people about these very different bodies. Hopefully, they'll get curious enough and they'll have other questions to ask.

Americans in Paris

DAVID McCULLOUGH

In his book, The Greater Journey *(Simon & Schuster, 2011), historian David McCullough writes, "Not all pioneers went west." A number of nineteenth century Americans instead ventured east across the Atlantic Ocean to Paris, France. The names of those who made the treacherous voyage included the painters John Singer Sargent and Mary Cassatt, sculptor Augustus Saint-Gaudens, a young medical student Oliver Wendell Holmes, and politicians Elihu Washburne and Charles Sumner. Their experiences, he argues, changed them and changed America. A two-time winner of the Pulitzer Prize for his presidential biographies,* Truman *(1991) and* John Adams *(2001), McCullough joined us for a two-part Q & A in May 2011.*

PART ONE

The Greater Journey is about a journey but a different kind of journey, or a mission, or an adventure, or an odyssey. I kept working with these words and the word "journey" kept coming back. Then I was thinking about the voyage of these Americans who ventured off to France at a time when they were only able to go across the North Atlantic by sailing ship, and it was rough. It was anything but traveling on a cruise liner, and what a journey that was. They landed at Le Havre, almost all of them, and they then went by land to Paris, which was a two-day trip by a huge, cumbersome stagecoach affair. They would stop at Rouen halfway and they would see for the first time a European masterpiece and that masterpiece was the Rouen Cathedral.

Many of them wrote at length and very much from the heart about the impact of this one building, this one experience, and that they knew that something greater had begun by being in the Old World. The Old World to them was the New World. I thought that is it, the "greater journey." They know then that they are on a greater journey which will be their experience, their spiritual, mental, professional journey in the city of Paris where they are trying to rise to the occasion to excel in a particular field whether it was writing or music or painting or sculpture or medicine. Many of them in that day went as medical students because Paris was the medical capitol of the world. They are ambitious to excel and they are going against the trend because to go off to Europe then was not fashionable yet and it wasn't part of one's broadening education yet. Many of them had no money. Many of them had no friends in Europe, knew no one in Paris, and spoke not a word of the language and yet they were brave enough to go, to embark on the greater journey.

The Sorbonne on the Left Bank is where many of these young Americans went to study. They could go to the Sorbonne for free. They could go to the School of Medicine in Paris for free. The French government had a policy that all foreign students could attend their universities for nothing. They had to pay for their room and board, but once they got there, there was no charge for attending the university. It was the greatest university in the world. Imagine a country doing that. That Sorbonne experience changed several lives dramatically and consequently changed our story, our history. That is what interests me particularly. What did they bring home? What did they bring back? How were we affected? How did our outlook, our culture, our politics, and our country change as a consequence of the Paris experience of these Americans?

Mike Hill has worked with me for twenty-five years now as a research assistant. [He unlocked the mystery of the Elihu Washburne diary.] ...Elihu Washburne was a congressman from Illinois and was a very close friend of Abraham Lincoln's. When Lincoln became president, it was Washburne as much as anybody else who kept telling Lincoln, you have got to give this man, Ulysses S. Grant, a full chance to show what he can do. Washburne came from Galena, Illinois which is where Grant was then living before the Civil War started.... After the Civil War was over and Grant had distinguished himself conspicuously, Washburne was exhausted. When Grant became president, he first offered him the position of secretary of state. But Washburne was quite ill and he declined it three days later and said, "I can't do it." So he appointed Washburne our minister to France.

Washburne went over to France thinking, "This is going to be just what I need to recover my strength and have a little peace and quiet with my family." He arrived on the eve of the Franco-Prussian War. The Germans were marching on Paris and in very short order the Germans surrounded the city and Paris was cut off from the world. All the other ambassadors for all the other powers left the city, except Washburne. He said, "My duty is to stay here." He stayed through the entire siege, which lasted five months. He stayed through the horrific, God-awful, bloody Commune that followed, where the French were killing each other by the thousands in the city of Paris. He not only stayed and served admirably, helping Americans who were there, but also the Germans who had been living there as workers, who were innocent of doing anything wrong, to get them out of the city on the request of the German government, some 20,000 of them. He organized and arranged all that with special trains, a magnificent humanitarian successful mission. But, through all that, he also kept a diary every day. The diary wasn't just, did this, quick little notes, did that, lunch with so-and-so, met with so-and-so. No. They are long, superbly written entries of real substance. There is nothing like them in existence. They were unknown and Mike Hill found them in a place no one would think to look, in the Library of Congress....

In writing the book, I was able to draw on this experience and Washburne's attempt to save the life of the Archbishop of Paris, [Georges Darboy,] for example, who was in prison and going to be executed by the Communards, as they were known. Elihu Washburne was Protestant, but he greatly admired the archbishop and he knew that this was a terrible thing that was happening because they were killing priests, executing them. He was unsuccessful in saving that man's life; he was executed, but nobody tried harder to get him out. Washburne is a man that, again, was quietly heroic. His sense of duty was amazing and admirable in the extreme, but also he felt a strong sense of duty to keep that diary. He would come in after a terrible day of seeing the most heartbreaking, sometimes nauseating experiences and acts of human savagery and sit down at one o'clock in the morning and write long entries in superb English. His use and command of the language, is humbling. Here was a man who never really had an education as we would call it today. This is true of the letters and diaries I worked with through the whole book, people like Charles Sumner, people like Emma Willard, the great champion of higher education for women, or Elizabeth Blackwell, the first woman doctor in America. They were wonderful writers. They weren't writing to be published. They were writing letters. It was a time when people believed in writing letters and writing letters was a part of life, part of what you were expected to do.

Massachusetts Senator Charles Sumner's story is so arresting. Sumner is one of the most important figures of nineteenth century America. He was the most powerful voice for abolition in the United States Senate. He is the one that was nearly beaten to death on the floor of the Senate with a heavy walking stick by a Southern congressman, [Preston Brooks, of South Carolina,] who was offended by a speech that Sumner had given. Sumner had graduated from Harvard, went to Harvard Law School, practiced law for three years, and decided, "I don't know enough, my education is not sufficient. I want to know more. I want to learn more. I'm going to go to Paris." So, [in 1837,] he borrowed three thousand dollars from friends, closed up his law office, and went to the Sorbonne, attending lectures in everything—geology, classics. He didn't speak French so he had to learn French. He took a cram course that he had organized himself with tutors and, in about a month, was able to do it. The undaunted courage of these people is inspiring. He attended the lectures and he kept a journal. The journal is fabulous. It has been published in four volumes.

In the journal, he writes about what he is listening to or who he is meeting and what he is learning and so forth. But there is one entry where the speaker was tedious and he found himself looking around the lecture hall, his mind wandering. He noticed that the other students—

and there were several hundred, nearly a thousand people, in this lecture hall—treated the black students who were there just as though they were like everybody else; they dressed the same, acted the same. This is in 1838. He was young; he was still in his twenties. He wrote in the diary [on Saturday, January 20, 1838, something like this:] "Maybe how we treat black people at home is the result of what we've been taught and not part of the natural order of things." It was an epiphany for him. It was as if suddenly he saw the light, truly. Because we know that he had been to Washington on a trip before he went to Paris, and had seen slaves working in the field in Maryland and thought they looked like that was all they were good for. He had no sympathy for people in bondage, no sensible interest in African Americans at all. He came home with this new point of view, got into politics, was elected to the United States Senate in his early forties, and he became the powerhouse voice for abolition, changed by that experience in Paris. That is bringing home something that is not tangible. It is not a work of sculpture or a painting or a musical composition, but he brought home an idea and a new mission.

The beating left Sumner very damaged both psychologically and physically, and he went back to Paris several times to relieve himself of these anxieties that he felt and his inability to perform as a senator. It always helped him, so he came home and carried on. I think he is one of the most admirable figures in our story. His statue stands in the public garden in Boston. I doubt that one Bostonian in a thousand has any idea who he was. We all should know.

I LOVE ARCHITECTURE. I think in some ways architecture may be our most important art form because we live in it. It shapes us. Paris really is about architecture. There's no natural splendor there; no snow covered mountain range in the distance, no beautiful shoreline on the sea. The river's there, but rivers are in lots of cities. Paris is what people have built and what they've put their heart and soul into. It's not just what's in the museums, it's the museums themselves. There was no school of architecture in America [in the mid-nineteenth century], none. So these people who went over, these young men like Richard Morris Hunt, Louis Sullivan, Charles McKim, H. H. Richardson, who changed the look of our cities, changed the look of America. All went there to study architecture at the Beaux Arts, and came back different from what they had been. If you go to Boston's Copley Square, Trinity Church is on one side; H. H. Richardson trained at the Ecole des Beaux Arts. Look across the square, the Boston Public Library by Charles McKim, trained at the Ecole des Beaux Arts. It's very similar in many ways to the Bibliotheque Sainte-Genevieve, which is in Paris, and he said so. They were taking inspiration from Paris. Again and again, they all wrote that they wanted to bring something home to make things better here. They were doing something they felt was a service to their country, not just to their own ambitions.

PART TWO

This book is different, for me, in form, than anything I've ever done. Because if you are writing a biography or you are writing the history of an event or an accomplishment, there is a certain obvious track, a certain structure that is built into the subject and you are obligated to respect that and cover it, and write about it in all fairness to your reader. The cast of characters is already ordained. With this book, I could cast the book myself. I would pick the people that I wanted to write about. There are probably twelve major characters in this book, probably twenty people overall who appear are Americans. But that is a fraction of the number that went to Paris during this seventy-year period (1830-1900) that I am covering. So, in organizing the book, in organizing my approach to the subject, I was, in many ways, like a casting director. They would come in; show me what they could do; tell me their story and I would say, in effect, "Don't call me, I'll call you." So I'm picking the people that I want to keep company with for four years. I didn't pick anyone that I wasn't interested in or I thought would be uninteresting. There are none of them that I wouldn't give a great deal to meet, to talk to.

WE'RE SITTING HERE TODAY in a city [Washington, D.C.] designed by a Frenchman, L'Enfant, the French engineer and architect. The great symbolic work of sculpture at the gateway to the country in New York, the Statue of Liberty, was a gift from France by French sculptor Bartholdi. Countless rivers and some towns and universities and colleges all over the country have French names. We don't pronounce them the way they do, but the influence of France on this country is far greater than most Americans appreciate. We more than doubled the size of the country with the Louisiana Purchase, which, of course, was a decision made by Napoleon to sell.

FRANCE IN THE 1800's went from a king, a so-called citizen king, Louis-Philippe, who got power by a coup d'état. Then he was thrown out by an uprising, and escaped with his wife and their lives, and lived out the rest of his life in England. He's a very interesting man, in part because he spent a good time here in the United States when he was in exile from France because of the French Revolution. He had an aristocratic lineage, although he had fought in the Revolution as a soldier for the Revolution. He came to the United States. He sailed down the Ohio River and all the way down the Mississippi with his brother [when] he was still in his twenties. He was a guest of Washington at Mount Vernon. He worked for a while as a waiter in a restaurant that's still in business in Boston, the Union Oyster House. So when the Americans showed up over there [in Paris]— George Catlin was there with his Indians and his paintings in the 1840s— those Native Americans were astonished to hear the king say that he'd been out on the Great Plains. He had spent time there with their tribes and could speak some of their language. He really had seen more of what was then the Wild West than all but a very few Americans had. So from the point of view of the Americans who came to Paris, Louis-Philippe was a wonderful king. He was the kind of king who would take a walk in the Tuileries Gardens in the afternoon. It was sort of a quasi-republic with a monarchy. But it didn't last; it lasted about eighteen years.

Then came in another First Republic. Then, after that, came Napoleon III, as he called himself, who made himself the Emperor. That led to a complete rebuilding of Paris; the Paris that we see today is really the Paris that Napoleon III and his chief officer in charge of the reconstruction, George Haussmann, [built]. That's the Paris we know, with the grand boulevards, the opening up of avenues, the planting of all the trees, the expansion of the Bois de Bologne, and so forth. It was all done during that Napoleon III epic.

And then came another revolution, the great Franco-Prussian War. And after the Franco-Prussian War, another regime took charge after the defeat of the Communards, as they were called. This was, in effect, a French civil war where they slaughtered each other in the most atrocious fashion, irrespective, men, women, children; just a hideous bloodbath in Paris. The Americans, many of them, were witness to this, sometimes to their detriment and other times just as part of the adventure that they experienced in their life. One of the most admirable of all is a young woman named Mary Putnam who was the first American woman to get a degree in medicine from the Ecole de Medicine, who refused to leave during the siege of Paris and the Commune. It was a very dangerous time to be there, a very difficult time. People were starving to death. [She stayed] because she was determined she was going to get her degree and she came back to become one of the leading figures in American medicine.

AUGUSTUS SAINT-GAUDENS: HE, IN my opinion and in the opinion of numbers of others, is the greatest American sculptor, certainly of the nineteenth century, maybe ever. His most famous work is the "Shaw Memorial," in Boston, which is about Colonel Shaw and the 54th Massachusetts Regiment, the first all-black regiment in the Union Army. Alas, many, most of them, were killed including Colonel Shaw at Charleston. It is the first piece of American art to portray black Americans, African Americans as heroes. There is his famous Adam's Memorial, which is in Rock Creek Cemetery, which was for the wife of Henry Adams; it is a very mysterious sculptural work, which remains constantly of interest because of its mystery. Then there's the Sherman statue, which is in New York City. It's the equestrian statue of General Sherman with the goddess of victory leading him. It's at 59th street and 5th Avenue. It's a gilded, magnificent piece; I think it's the greatest equestrian statue in the country.

In many ways, Saint-Gaudens is the most interesting personal story. He was an immigrant shoemaker's son in New York who was put to work when he was thirteen years old cutting cameos, which was a craft form of real consequence then. Wearing cameos was popular with women and men. He learned the art of cameo cutting and also demonstrated that he had ability as an artist and sculptor beyond that. His shoemaker father helped to pay for him to go to take some art courses at Cooper Union in New York, which was one of the first art schools [in the country]…. He went off to Paris at age nineteen to become a sculptor. He was the first

American admitted to the Ecole des Beaux-Arts. To be admitted was a coup. It would be like getting into one of the greatest of our universities today. It is the school of art, architecture, and sculpture in Paris on the Left Bank. It is still there in the same place where he went. He was admitted as a student in sculpture and he studied in Paris up to the time of the outbreak of the Franco-Prussian War, when he then went to Italy to continue his studies there. He was three years in Paris as a student. He came back in the 1870s for another three years, by which point he was married. His wife was a painter. They had met when she was studying painting in Italy. The story of their marriage is extraordinary. I was able to tell that story because her letters, which number more than two hundred, have all survived and they are all in the library at Dartmouth College, which is very near Cornish, the home that they finally established on the Connecticut River in New Hampshire.

JOHN SINGER SARGENT WAS an American prodigy. He was a notably astonishingly gifted painter when he was not yet eighteen. He painted several of his major masterpieces when he was still in his twenties. His *Madame X*, as it's known. His *Daughters of Edward Boit*. His *El Jaleo*, which is about a Spanish dancer. All done in Paris. *Madame X* was Madame Gautreau. She was also an American. Most people living in Paris didn't realize that. This painting was, at the time, considered scandalous because of her pose and her low cut evening attire.

Mary Cassatt was a young woman from Pennsylvania who decided that she wasn't just going to be a woman who paints, but she was going to be a painter. She became the only American artist who was accepted by and taken in by the Impressionists as one of them in Paris. Her paintings are largely, almost entirely, about women, women seen in private life in the security of the home or the garden doing private things, knitting, reading, having tea. Their hold on the viewer has been consistent for well over a hundred years. Her importance as a master, as a genius of American art, only increases with time. She was a brave woman; she went to Europe, pursuing a career seriously as no American woman ever had. She was bound to excel and she certainly did, [despite] having, through much of her life, to look after her parents, with whom she lived in Paris most of her adult life.

GÉRICAULT'S *Raft of the Medusa* was a painting that simply froze, captivated, enthralled Americans first arriving at the Louvre, as it still does. One American who was swept away by it and wrote very passionately and eloquently about it was Harriet Beecher Stowe. Most people don't think of Harriet Beecher Stowe in Paris. But she was in Paris a great deal and loved it, and it had a very profound effect on her. She was there primarily to hide away from the publicity that surrounded her publication of *Uncle Tom's Cabin*. She'd been on a tour in England where the book was not only in print, but it had become a sensational best seller. It hadn't yet been published in French so when she got to Paris, she could go anywhere without causing any stir. She spent a lot of time at the Louvre. Spent a lot of time just walking the city. Wrote wonderfully about the experience. Started studying French. Came back again another time. It's fascinating how Paris affected her. She said it emphasized to her how much beauty had been denied her in her puritanical upbringing in New England. That beauty isn't just something you see that someone else has created. That beauty is in you and the love of beauty is part of being human. It's by being in a place where beauty is so respected and considered such an important part of life that you suddenly discover how much of that love and that respect is in you, a part of human nature.

I WORK ON A manual typewriter. I take it with me. If it can't go, I am not going to write. When I decided I was going to try and write a book in 1965, we were living in White Plains, New York. I was working in New York as an editor and writer at *American Heritage* magazine. I did my writing at the office on the job. I had a portable typewriter but I thought that if I am going to undertake a book, I had better get a real typewriter. I bought a secondhand Royal high-rise, black typewriter, the kind with the little glass covers on the letters, little dished letters. I probably paid fifty dollars for it, maybe less. I have written everything I have written on that typewriter and there is nothing wrong with it. It is a magnificent example of superb American manufacturing. It probably has 975,000 miles on it. I have to change the ribbons, obviously, and my children and my friends and others say to me, "Don't you realize how much faster you could go if you used a computer?" Well, of course I could go faster. I don't want to go faster. If anything, I want to go more slowly. I don't think all that fast and I love the idea of a key coming up and printing a letter. I can understand that. I would be horrified to think that as I was working if I pressed the wrong button it was going to zap out two weeks or two months of work. I am technologically challenged, I guess, is the explanation. Sometimes, I wonder, maybe it is the typewriter that is writing the books....

I am writing all the time. I am writing when I am flying in a plane. I don't mean literally writing; I am thinking about it. People often say to me, "How much of your time do you spend writing and how much of your time do you spend doing research?" It is a great question, but no one ever says, "How much of your time do you spend thinking?" That is probably the most important part of it—just thinking about it, thinking about what you have read, what you need to read, what you need to think more about. Putting things out literally on the table and looking at them. Putting a reproduction of a painting and really looking at that painting and thinking about that painting or the setting. Where things happened is very important to me. This whole book that I have just written is set in Paris. Another book I wrote was set in Brooklyn. Another was set in Panama. Much of several books have been set here in Washington. I believe that the setting has great effect on the way things happened, the way things went. The setting is part of history, just as the "who" is part of the why and so I really have to soak up the setting.

When my wife, Rosalee, and I went to Paris, I went there to walk the walk. I went there to see it in the winter when it is awful and damp and cold and grey, in the summer, the spring and the fall. If I read something that [said] it took Augustus Saint-Gaudens twenty minutes to walk from his apartment to his studio, I went over and made the walk from his apartment to the studio to see if that was right. I want to be out on the Pont Neuf the way Emma Willard and others were and feel what they felt.... I think listening, smelling, feeling what the chair feels like, rubbing your hand on the surface of the cathedral sculpture, on the exterior, all of that is part of getting closer to it. I'm always trying to get closer to those people, closer to that place, closer to that time and asking questions.

I spend a lot of time with students lecturing or visiting universities and colleges. They are so programmed for being able to answer questions that I wonder sometimes how much time they have spent asking questions. That is how you find things out. Ask a lot of people. People have a feeling that what I do and what others who do similar kinds of work, that it is a solitary endeavor. Not at all. I am with people all the time, talking to people, working with librarians, working with archivists, talking to experts. When I was writing about Augustus Saint-Gaudens, I spent the better part of one day just with a sculptor who does large pieces. Finding out how is it done. What is hard? What is easy? What is chancy? What's dangerous? The same thing with painters or politicians.... You have got to go and watch how it is done, listen to it, get a sense of the timing and also of the times when people are not doing anything much, the dead time, as it were, in their lives and how they handle that.

The Black History of the White House

CLARENCE LUSANE

In the early days of the nation, presidents were expected to bring their own staff to Washington. Many of them were enslaved. Jefferson, Madison, Monroe, Jackson, and Polk all brought their own slaves to the White House. And it was a slave who wrote the first White House memoir. Published in 1865, A Colored Man's Reminiscences of James Madison *was written by Paul Jennings, a personal servant to the fourth president. In a* Q & A *appearance on August 28, 2011, Clarence Lusane discussed Jennings and the contributions of other slaves to the early republic. His book is called* The Black History of the White House *(City Lights Books, 2011).*

[CITY LIGHTS PUBLISHING] WAS looking for someone to write about the importance of the Obama election. There are now probably hundreds of books out about Obama, and I didn't want to write what everyone else was writing—what this meant for today's politics and for the black community. In 2007, 2008, as the Obama candidacy was starting to rise, nationally and internationally, people would ask me, "What did I think? Could he win? What would it mean to have an African American as president?" But people also would ask, "What is the White House? Why is it called the White House? Will Obama change the name if he becomes president?" I didn't know the history of the White House, and what the history of African Americans was to that icon. I thought I would do a little research, write a short book, about 150 pages, and trace it through. I began to discover fascinating individuals whose mark on both the presidencies and the White House were virtually unknown except for a few scattered stories.

EVERYONE KNEW THAT GEORGE Washington and Thomas Jefferson had slaves, but most people probably didn't know that eight out of the first twelve presidents had slaves, or that there were slaves inside of the White House itself, and [in] the house where George Washington lived for his administrations when he was in Philadelphia. This history threw itself at me, and the book started to write itself. Instead of a straight-up political history of the White House, it has become a platform for presenting these fascinating individuals whose stories tell the history of the country.

I LITERALLY HAD NEVER heard of [Oney Maria Judge] at all. All of us who grew up in the United States learned the history of the first president. We may not know the history of all the presidents, but we certainly learned about George Washington and the stories about him cutting down cherry trees [and] about him never telling a lie; but what we had very little information about were the individuals who were actually enslaved to him. Oney was one of the nine slaves who traveled and lived with Washington during his presidency. She was not back in Mt. Vernon; she was actually with him initially for a short period in New York, and then in Philadelphia.

[She was a] young woman, in her early twenties. In 1796, Oney learned that Martha Washington was planning to give her away as a wedding gift. This was upsetting because the Washingtons had promised that when they died, they would free individuals who were enslaved to them. She had hoped that she would be out of this institution. But if she was going to be given away, that meant probably her whole life was going to be in slavery, and she made plans to escape. [She wrote in her memoir that] while the Washingtons were literally sitting at their dinner table waiting for her to serve them, she went out the back door. Eventually, they figured she wasn't coming and knew she had escaped. They put out advertisements for her and were very, very upset. We're talking about a young woman who basically had never traveled anywhere on her own, who escapes from the most powerful person in the country—the President, who has the entire government [and military] at his disposal.

Oney goes to New Hampshire, and she's discovered by a friend of the Washingtons, who informed them that he had seen Oney. George Washington was very image conscious, and he was living in the center of the abolitionist movement in Philadelphia. Of all of the thirteen states in the new country, [Pennsylvania] was the most active against slavery. George Washington was very sensitive to his image around slavery. He had also said that he opposed slavery, although he did not free any of his slaves, and did not initially want to be very public about going after her. He sent his nephew to meet with her.... The nephew said, "Oney, we would like you to come back. We can work it out. Things got out of control. You were scared. You know we didn't really like it, but all is basically forgiven. Come back and then eventually, you will be free." Oney's response was, "I am free now. I don't really see the rationale for giving up this freedom that I escaped to, to go back into slavery." The nephew goes back to George Washington and says, "Oney refused to come." Rather than say she escaped and "we don't like it, but we'll leave it alone," George decided they were going to kidnap her. The nephew goes back to New Hampshire and meets with the family that had initially exposed Oney to the Washingtons. The family is very anti-slavery, and once they found out what the nephew was up to, they delay the nephew, warn Oney, and she gets away.

ONEY GAVE INTERVIEWS. SHE lived to be in her eighties, learned to read, and became active in her community. She talks about being influenced by the Haitian Revolution, which happened in the early 1790s, but she was also influenced by the American Revolution. The individuals who were the closest to those debates that happened at the Constitutional Convention were enslaved, were serving tea and cleaning the rooms. They heard these debates and the arguments and some of these people were willing to risk their lives for freedom.

Hercules was Washington's cook, and Hercules also escaped. Now Hercules' story is interesting because he was considered one of the most famous cooks in the country at the time. He had been trained in Europe, and was well known across the country. [He was also known] as being extremely loyal to George Washington. Out of the nine individuals who were enslaved by Washington, Hercules was the only one that Washington would allow to go back and forth between Philadelphia and Mt. Vernon without being guarded. At the end of Washington's presidency, when he was preparing to move back to Mt. Vernon, Hercules escaped, and they never found him. They thought he was in Philadelphia, but he was gone. Now, it's my sense that Hercules was probably in touch with the brother of Sally Hemings…enslaved by Thomas Jefferson. Sally Hemings was the African American woman who was enslaved, but who was also a mistress of Thomas Jefferson. Her brother was also a cook. He had traveled with Jefferson when he lived in Paris and [attended] cooking schools in France. He was a very, very talented cook as well, like Hercules, and they were both in Philadelphia at the same time. [Sally Hemings' brother] bought his freedom at one point, with the stipulation that Jefferson said he had to train someone else to cook before he could actually leave; even though he had saved enough money to buy his freedom. So Hercules was in touch with him.

THE PHILADELPHIA CONNECTION IS important because in 1999 or so, the National Park Service decided to move the Liberty Bell from its old location to a brand new multi-million dollar pavilion. This was going to be an extremely fancy new pavilion, and they were building the pavilion over the land that held George Washington and his slaves when he was president. In fact, it was specifically over the part of the house where the slaves were kept. Once this was discovered by historians and other activists in Philadelphia, there were protests, and calls for honoring or remembering these individuals. You can't build this brand new artifice to the Liberty Bell, which is to celebrate American freedom, and not acknowledge or ignore what happened at this very site. So it took a ten-year or twelve-year battle. But finally, the National Park Service agreed; part of the new pavilion now, which opened in December 2010, is a commemorative section that notes the nine individuals who were held in slavery….

PAUL JENNINGS [IS] ANOTHER one of the individuals who pops out of the research. Paul Jennings was enslaved to James and Dolley Madison, and by the time he was ten years old, he was working at the White House.

Now, this turned out to be fortuitous because he happened to be there in 1814 when the White House was burnt down. He was there literally on that day when the British were burning and looting and headed towards the White House. The White House staff, both enslaved and [free], was trying to grab whatever they could before the British actually got to the front door. We know this story because in 1865 Paul Jennings wrote a memoir; one of the first, if not the first, memoir of someone who actually worked in the White House. He tells that story and the story of being at the bedside when James Madison died. He also tells the story how Dolley Madison reneged on the deal that he was supposed to be free after James Madison passed. For primarily economic reasons, Dolley didn't free him immediately; he had to earn enough to buy his freedom a few years later.

[Paul Jennings notes in his memoir] that Dolley Madison fell on very hard times. It's very different from today when someone leaves the presidency and they are guaranteed security for the rest of their life. But that really wasn't the case during that period; her friends and her family basically abandoned her. Although she did him wrong, he felt some compassion, and as he writes in his memoirs, he would often visit and bring her food, and probably give her some money when he had it. He stayed in Washington, D.C.; he ended up getting a government job, which he eventually retired from in the 1860s.

What he doesn't talk about in his memoir is his central role in a gigantic slave escape attempt in the spring of 1848. Washington, D.C. was bustling with parties that were celebrating the revolutions happening in Europe. This was a big contradiction: that while people were celebrating freedom in Europe, they were enslaving people in the United States. Jennings and two other freed African Americans had been part of this plan to bring a boat down to the wharf. People who were enslaved would come to the wharf on a Saturday night in ones and twos, and then sneak onto the boat. It wasn't unusual on Saturday nights to see African Americans walking around because that was generally the only night that people who were enslaved had some time off. The plan worked and close to eighty people got on the boat. By the time it was realized on Sunday that people had escaped, they had a [significant] head start. But they ran into problems. They hit bad weather [which] forced the boat to pull to the side;

then, back in Washington, someone who knew about the plan betrayed them. When the posse gathered, people initially thought they had escaped on foot and were heading north. This individual said, "No, they're in a boat headed south." The posse got into a faster boat. They caught up with the people who had escaped, captured everyone and brought them back to Washington D.C. Now, as it turned out, Paul [Jennings] was not on the boat, probably because he was free. But in any case, he wasn't on the boat, and he was never exposed. He left Dolley Madison's enslavement and became a slave to Daniel Webster, but [only] for a relatively short period. Webster essentially was working with him to get his freedom; later, Webster would be a key individual who challenged slavery.

DAVID WALKER WAS AN advocate in the 1830s, and a free black man who wrote a pamphlet called *David Walker's Appeal*, which called for slaves to rise up. He had no tolerance for the gradual evolution of the end of slavery. He condemned slavery in the harshest terms and issued a pamphlet which was distributed in the South. It actually became illegal to have a copy of the pamphlet. The seventy-six-page pamphlet advocated that blacks revolt against their white enslavers and called for nothing short of full liberation and equality for African Americans, enslaved and free. The pamphlet also argued against colonization.

ELIZABETH [KECKLEY BECAME THE] best friend of Mary Lincoln. Now, Elizabeth's own history is one of just amazing serendipitous encounters. She was a black woman, who grew up in Missouri, who was enslaved, and eventually was able to buy her freedom. She developed very good skills as a seamstress and dressmaker. Just to give a sense of her historic encounters, the individual to whom she was enslaved was one of the lawyers who argued the Dred Scott decision before the Supreme Court. The 1857 Dred Scott decision [was one of] the most important Supreme Court rulings prior to the Civil War regarding slavery. The Dred Scott decision [ruled] that slavery could exist anywhere in the country. This decision upset a delicate balance going back to the 1820s of bringing into the union one slave state with one free state to dampen the tensions within the country. The person who argued before the Supreme Court against Dred Scott owned Elizabeth Keckley.

Elizabeth Keckley was an independent businesswoman and she became the dressmaker for Mary Lincoln, [as well as] her confidante and friend. Elizabeth spent a great deal of time at the White House for her work, but also, [due to] her closeness to Mary, who was actually alienated from many of the people in Washington, D.C., Elizabeth also knew Abraham Lincoln, and she had a number of discussions and engagements with the Lincolns over the years. After Lincoln was killed, Mary left Washington, D.C. But she was in debt; in fact, she was in debt while Lincoln was president. [Mary Lincoln] and Elizabeth came up with a plan to secretly sell her dresses in New York City. But the plan didn't go that well; there was not a great market for her dresses.

IN THE ORIGINAL CONSTITUTION, The Fugitive Slave Clause stated that if a slave escaped from any state and went to another state, that state is obligated to arrest that person, or capture them and send them back to the other state. In 1793, the Fugitive Slave Act was signed by George Washington, probably while some of his slaves were standing around. There were very clear federal laws against people that had escaped from slavery; however, many of the northern states simply refused to enforce the laws. They would not allow law enforcement personnel to arrest people, [nor] would they arrest people who helped people escape from slavery. There was a contingent going on between the states long before the Civil War actually broke out. Part of the justification articulated by the states that seceded from the Union was that there were states in the North who were not enforcing the federal laws around escaped slaves....

[THE RULES OF SLAVERY] varied across the country, but people who were going to be enslaved for life had no citizen rights and virtually no human rights. Most of the slave owners, particularly in the South, but not exclusive to the Deep South, prohibited reading and writing. Other than work skills, there was very little opportunity for any kind of personal or professional development. Slaves became extremely skilled because they did the work around the plantations; but there were also a great deal of slaves in the cities of that period. All of the large structures that were built up and down the East Coast, from libraries, to universities, to city halls, to the mansions, were built by slave labor in many instances. People had carpentry skills, masonry skills, even some architectural and design skills. There was a whole other level of development that happened, but wasn't necessarily recognized or acknowledged, and certainly wasn't compensated. Peter was one of the carpenters who worked on the White House. What we know from the records is that there were five black carpenters who worked on the White House, and, for some period, also worked on building the Capitol.

I HAVE SLAVES IN my family background, but I don't know who they are. I have personally done a great deal of genealogical research. For many African Americans there are certain cut-offs. It wasn't until the 1870 census that people who were enslaved were listed as individuals. Prior to that, people were just listed, if they were listed at all, as John, who is twelve, or Bob, who is four. Unless you had very specific names and very specific locations, it's very, very difficult to do that tracing. I live in Washington, D.C. and have access to the National Archives. About twenty years ago, I found the diary of the family that owned my family in Alabama. This was a family that went back to about the 1500s, and there were some references to individuals who were enslaved. But it is very difficult to connect all those dots.

OVERALL, AFRICAN AMERICANS WERE probably about 30 or 40 percent of the country, depending on where you were [living]. If you were in some states (South Carolina, Mississippi, North Carolina, likely Alabama), slaves were the majority of the population. [A slave's economic worth] depended on how much had been invested in the individual or the age of an individual. There were different prices for men versus women, and children were a different price. It could vary from a couple of hundred to a couple of thousand, which was an exorbitant amount. But it depended if [the slave] was someone extremely skilled, or who was very young, or who had forty or fifty years ahead of them. They could potentially go for a higher price. Then there were issues of whether or not you took the whole family, or you took part of the family. All of this came into play over these negotiations around the buying and selling of individuals.

THERE WAS A FIERCE negotiation right after the Constitution was ratified over where to have the seat of government. The South wanted to
have the seat in the South, and the North resisted that. So a compromise
was worked out that for the ten-year period that it was estimated that it
would take to build this brand new city, the new government would not
be in one of the old cities. But at the end of that ten-year period, in
1800, it would come back to Washington, D.C. This land was deeded by
Maryland and Virginia at the time. It was trees and rocks, and this whole
area had to be cleaned, trees had to be cut down and dragged away. The
roads had to be paved, and buildings built, so that labor ended up being
slave labor. What we have not focused on in terms of our own historical
acknowledgement, though, is slave labor and the building of the White
House, and the Capitol. These institutions that were icons of liberty and
freedom also carry with them this history as well. That's part of what I
was trying to do with bringing that history out.

Now that I have given talks, particularly around Washington, D.C., I
am often approached by people who say, well, "my uncle used to be a
barber at the White House" or "my grandmother used to work upstairs at
the White House." These stories have not been told. As we think about
the history of the presidencies, we don't think of the particular relationship between the president's residence and how the White House is a
global icon. People all over the world know the White House, if they
know no other structure in the United States at all. People know the
White House, but we don't know the White House history.

I GAVE A TALK at the White House and was very surprised at how emotional it was. There were many young black people who work at the
White House, a lot of older black people, and whites who had no idea of
this history. I went through the presentation and talked about the different individuals, and people felt very, very emotionally attached. People
have come up to me and said, "I had no idea. I have had no idea whatsoever." I have spent many years writing about black politics and black history, and 80 percent of this book was new to me. I literally had not heard
of almost all of these individuals; in many ways, [it made me go] back
and look at some of the things I wrote before.

An Insider's History of the Senate

RICHARD BAKER

When the first Senate gathered at Federal Hall in New York in 1789, only eleven states were represented, as not all had ratified the Constitution. Each new senator was given a number upon their arrival—a tradition that continues to this day. To date, over 1,900 men and women have served in the U.S. Senate. Longtime Senate Historian Richard Baker, now retired, gave us insights into some of them when he appeared on Q & A *on July 7, 2013, to discuss* The American Senate: An Insider's History *(Oxford University Press, 2013). Baker co-authored the book with the late* TIME *magazine Chief Congressional Correspondent Neil MacNeil.*

THIS BOOK IS FILLED with Robert Byrd, [former Democratic senator from West Virginia]. It starts with Robert Byrd and it ends with Robert Byrd. I did not see any other way to do that because he really brings a focus to the Senate as an institution in the 1980s. He was interested in the majority leader's power to arrest senators when they were hiding and they did not want to make a quorum during a filibuster. He called me in one day in 1980 and he said, "I suppose you can give me a little piece on the history of arresting senators who are hiding from filibusters," and so I did. He liked it and he gave it as a floor speech. Then he had some other questions on other matters of Senate procedure. Before the 1980s were out, he had delivered a hundred speeches like that, and then they were published during the bicentennial of the Senate as a very large encyclopedic history of the Senate. So, he will be remembered for that, for sure, but I think also for being the conscience of the Senate. He evolved over the course of his remarkable Senate career.

[LOUISIANA DEMOCRAT] HUEY LONG had a huge impact on the Senate. He was in the Senate for just a very short period of time from the early 1930s until he was assassinated in 1935, but he decided that he was going to use the filibuster as a major legislative tool, and he did it almost like no one before him had done it. People really believed that he had a serious chance of becoming president of the United States, that he was lining himself up to run in 1936 in a populist campaign…. [He was assassinated] in the State Capitol in Baton Rouge by a disgruntled constituent. There were some financial dealings…. He had a lot of enemies and assassination was certainly very much on his mind as well as the minds of his staff who tried to protect him.

[His fellow senators didn't think much of him.] There were probably a few other Southern senators who engaged in some of the same kinds of oratory [as Long did], but the one senator who despised him beyond definition was Joseph T. Robinson, from the neighboring state of Arkansas. Joe Robinson was the majority leader, and his responsibility was to make the trains run on time. And Huey Long was the guy that was standing out there making sure the trains did not run on time until he finished his extended speeches, recipes for pot liquor and oysters—very amusing, but people said, "The Senate is going to blazes. The Senate is not getting anything done. What is going to happen to the Senate?" This is during the middle of the New Deal, trying to clean up after the Great Depression. "We cannot afford this kind of extended oratory. We've got to figure out a way to take this man off his feet," and somebody did.

[His son, Russell Long, who eventually succeeded him, was opposed to television coverage of the Senate.] He was a bit more moderate, although he had a significant drinking problem earlier in his Senate career. One of the best things that happened to him was to marry one of the staff members named Carolyn [Bason] Long, who, indeed, helped him get his act together, and he became an extremely powerful, knowledgeable tactician on the Senate floor. Any new senator who had any intelligence at all would try to cultivate him as a mentor just to get some of his distilled wisdom.

[There were a number of differences between the Senate in Huey Long's day in the 1930s and that of Russell Long's in the 1980s.] I would say number one is the method under which people arrived in the Senate, the whole campaign procedure. In my book, *The American Senate*, the first two chapters are about trying to answer that question. There were senators—George Aiken of Vermont comes to mind—who, as late as the 1960s, boasted that his campaign expenditures amounted to $147. Today, it is multiple millions of dollars. The senators of the 1930s were not exactly sartorially splendid; some were, but some of them were kind of frumpy and they didn't have to worry about spending a lot of time with their constituents. Generally, they would come to town, maybe go home four times a year; this was a long time before high-speed jet aircraft travel. They could just settle in and get to know one another and maybe get to know the families of their colleagues, whether they were Republican or Democrat, it didn't really matter. It was a much slower time, despite the national crises that they had to deal with.

[IN 1913,] JOSEPH ROBINSON was elected to serve as Arkansas's governor, but was immediately selected to fill a vacant seat in the U.S. Senate... the last senator chosen by the state legislature before the implementation of the Seventeenth Amendment establishing direct election of senators. In the Senate, Robinson took on leadership roles including majority leader. He was [known as] "the fightingest man in the United States Senate." He was a large man. He was given to rages; whether they were orchestrated or from the heart, hard to know, but his face would turn scarlet. He would get up there and he would beat his breast on the Senate floor. He would scream and yell and, as another senator said, you wouldn't want to incur the wrath of Joe T. Robinson because he indeed earned that moniker.

The Seventeenth Amendment to the Constitution was adopted, finally, in 1913. The first version of that amendment was offered in 1826. Institutional change comes slowly. The House, on a number of occasions throughout the nineteenth century, passed that amendment, sent it over to the Senate, and the Senate killed it. I think one of the main reasons was Southern senators who had a stranglehold on the procedures and floor proceedings were very much afraid that if you have direct popular election, you are going to have African Americans voting for senators. That was something, that until the Jim Crow laws began to really disenfranchise African Americans, that was a concern. By the turn of the twentieth century, they weren't quite as worried about it, and then, of course, there was the progressive reform movement.

The election of 1910 really brought a sea change into the Senate, with much more open, reform-minded members. Direct popular election of the senators was one of the constant points for reform, and finally, it got through. The main reason it got through is that there were a number of rather terrible corruption cases: senators who literally would go to their state legislatures and hand big packets of money off to the state legislators for their vote. Over and over again, the Senate was tied up in trying to determine whether a senator had secured his election by corrupt means. After it went into effect, one of the points that we make in this book is a perennial question: did it make any difference to have a direct popular election? We come down on the side of yes. It did make a difference. The senators began to act like House members, which, of course, is not something that any senators want to hear. That means that they were out scavenging for votes. They actually had to deal with the people.... After the direct election amendment went into effect, significantly, in the 1914 election, every incumbent who chose to seek reelection won.

[WHEN THE FIRST SENATE met,] there were initially twenty-two [senators] because not all of the thirteen states had ratified the Constitution when they first convened on April 6, 1789. Then, gradually, of course, through the nineteenth century, the numbers increased. By 1889, on their hundredth anniversary, they had seventy-six members, and that began to pose some major procedural problems. You got all these people out there seeking attention and whatnot. It was a lot easier when they were a smaller body. And then, finally, with the admission of Alaska and Hawaii in 1958 and 1959, they achieved their 100, but it is a far cry from the House of Representatives with 435 members. In the House, of course, they had to cap the number in 1911 because there was just no place for people to sit. They had to take the desks out of there and give everybody a bench to sit on in the House.

[THE U.S. SENATE CONTINUES as the most powerful upper house of any legislative body in the world. In France, Canada, and Great Britain,] the lower house passes the substance of legislation; it goes onto the upper house and the upper house reviews it. Maybe they do not like it, they send it back to the lower house, and the lower house says, "We respect your opinion, but we are going to pass it again," and then it becomes the law of the land. I think it is only the Italian Senate and the United States Senate, for sure, that have absolute veto over the work of the lower body. A fundamental issue at the Constitutional Convention in Philadelphia in 1787, and a major concern, was that you were going to have the House elected by the same people who are eligible to vote in state legislative elections and those people can be a little impetuous in their decisions. So, we need a "cooling body" to review and to stop and absolutely slow down and ask. As one senator said in the nineteenth century, the Senate is the place of sober second thought and that is what the framers of the Constitution had in mind.

EVERETT DIRKSEN WAS MOST remembered for making it possible to invoke cloture on civil rights legislation, shutting off debate with the proper amount of votes. At that point, they needed sixty-seven votes to end debate on this 1964 Civil Rights Act. Southern senators were determined not to pass that, and it was Everett Dirksen who managed to gather up enough of his Republican colleagues to give them seventy-one votes to pass it. That was huge because it was the first time ever that the Senate shut off debate on civil rights legislation. It was really the beginning of the end of Southern filibusters on civil rights. I saw him in action in the mid-1950s when I came to visit the Senate chamber one time. For many years in the 1970s and 1980s, I served on the board of directors of the Everett McKinley Dirksen Congressional Leadership Research Center in his hometown of Pekin, Illinois, a state-of-the-art research facility. In fact, Neil MacNeil did a biography of Everett Dirksen [*Dirksen: Portrait of a Public Man,*] that is still considered the best biography of Dirksen.

[DIRKSEN WAS A SHOW horse and a workhorse;] maybe a little more on the show horse-side. He was the Tournament of Roses Parade Grand

Marshal in 1968. He was cutting record albums, using his magnificent voice. I heard Ken Burns not too long ago at an event here in Washington respond to a question, "What is your favorite story about the Capitol?" He...did a film in the Capitol in the 1980s on Congress, and in that film there is a story about these ladies who came and stopped Everett Dirksen outside the door of his Republican leader's office. [Dirksen says,] "Oh! Ladies, you wish a word with me? What can I say to you?" And one of the ladies said, "Oh, nothing, Senator, we just wanted to hear you talk," because of his deep baritone voice. He was so theatrical. This is a man who grew up in the country, in the outdoor theater circuit. He was very proud of his voice and was indeed an actor on the Senate floor, but also there was a deeply serious vein. People criticized Dirksen for being "Oleaginous Ev." [They would say] he was too effusive, the grand old chameleon; that he changed position rather easily. I tend to think that although there may have been some of that, that this was a man who really knew how to make the Senate work the way that Lyndon Johnson did....

[RICHARD RUSSELL] DIED IN 1971. He had a huge impact on the Senate while he was a member. His lasting impact is hard to assess for sure, but there was a very large table that was in his office suite and the table is significant because around that table would sit members of the Southern caucuses. They ran the Senate throughout the 1930s, 1940s, and on into the 1950s, and he presided during the end of that period over the Southern caucuses. Certainly, the Civil Rights Act of 1964, he was having no part of that, and it took a lot to work around his opposition, but from Lyndon Johnson's point of view, he was a great mentor. Lyndon Johnson learned a lot about the Senate, when he came over from the House, from Richard Russell.

THE DIFFERENCE BETWEEN MIKE Mansfield and Lyndon Johnson as a majority leader is between one and a hundred. Mansfield was famous when he appeared on *Meet the Press* for going through many questions in the time available to him with his one-word answers; whereas Lyndon Johnson would take a question and he would embellish it, really go in, and maybe go off on a tangent here or there. So, [they had] profoundly different styles, but Mike Mansfield really was the product of Lyndon

Johnson. Senators, when they were electing a successor to Lyndon Johnson in 1960 and 1961, did not want another Lyndon Johnson. They
wanted somebody who would make the trains run on time and keep
quiet, so that's how Mansfield went about it: his philosophy was, "We
let 100 candles flicker." That was not really the way Lyndon Johnson
had approached his concept of leadership in the Senate, and before too
long, about a year or two into his leadership, Mansfield began to get a
lot of criticism from some of Johnson's friends in the Senate. Thomas
Dodd of Connecticut, the father of Chris Dodd, really blasted Mansfield one day, which caused Everett Dirksen—talk about bipartisan co-
mity—the Republican leader, to come to the defense of the Democratic
leader saying, "You should not talk about our leader this way. This is
sacrilegious to do that." It was Mike Mansfield who then had a speech
prepared that said, "This is the way I am as a leader. You basically can
take it or leave it." He was going to give that speech on November 22,
1963, and, of course, that was the date that John F. Kennedy was assassinated, so he never gave the speech.

When 1998 came along and it was time [to give] a speech, part of a
series of speeches by former leaders of the Senate that then Senate Majority Leader Trent Lott organized, my phone rang in the Senate Historical
Office. It was Mike Mansfield, the guy who was also responsible for the
creation of the Senate Historical Office in the mid-1970s, and he said,
"I've been asked to give a speech for this series. What should I talk about?"
Well, I knew about the famous 1963 speech on the nature of leadership
that he never gave; he did stick it in the record at that time, so I said,
"Senator, why don't you give that? Shape it a little bit." He said, "Well,
maybe I'll do that." And he did. And it was the first in a series of speeches
on leadership. They are all on the Senate web site, and, by golly, it was a
blockbuster. It was just magnificent.

I HAD NEVER KNOWN that [Republican Minority Leader] Senator Mitch
McConnell had polio as a young boy. It took a lot of courage and tenac-
ity on his part, and some help from a very determined mother to get over
that and to move on. At one point, he was interested in becoming a historian, and even today, [he is] very well read in American political history, but he had that tough decision: does he want to become an academic

or does he want to become a practicing politician? He had a goal of becoming the majority leader of the United States Senate. He had a very fortunate summer internship with Senator John Sherman Cooper of Kentucky, a liberal Republican; there were some then and he just soaked that up. All the more power to internship programs—that is such a crucial time in people's lives. Then, when he graduated, he went to work for another senator for Kentucky, Marlow Cook—a Republican senator, a very telegenic, interesting gentleman. He got involved in the Civil Rights Act, I believe in 1964, when he was with John Sherman Cooper.

[In my experience, senators that have ended up in leadership often came from the staff.] It was one of the major reasons why senators did not want to have professional staffs, and it really was not until after World War II that they decided they absolutely needed them; they could not operate without them. But you hire these staff and pretty soon you are going to have somebody smarter than you are and that person will be smart enough to know that he can probably beat you in a primary. In some cases that has happened and in other cases, they just succeeded their mentors.

[Is this the meanest time in the history of the United States Congress?] ...I had not realized the hatred, just for one example, of John Quincy Adams and Daniel Webster. John Quincy Adams called Daniel Webster "a man with a rotten heart" in his diary. It was Daniel Webster who blocked John Quincy Adams's one major aspiration in political life to be a United States senator. Daniel Webster did not want his other co-senator from Massachusetts to be John Quincy Adams, a former president who he could not manipulate. He wanted somebody less threatening and got somebody less threatening. For the rest of his life, John Quincy Adams resented Webster for that particular action. They hated each other, but they also loved each other. It was Daniel Webster who wrote the inscription that is on John Quincy Adam's coffin about his accomplishments. It was a love and hate relationship. It's just spectacular.

[Henry Clay himself could be savage, but so could many others. In 1832, Clay and Benton engaged in a shouting match so ugly that senators feared a fistfight on the Senate floor.] Thomas Hart Benton was a Democrat from Missouri. Henry Clay was a Whig, and so they were the opposing parties. Benton was a large, bullying type of man who was re-membered for moving down the Senate aisle in 1850 against a senator from Mississippi named Henry Foote. Foote was so intimidated by the presence of Thomas Hart Benton that he pulled a silver-plated pistol out of his inner coat pocket and pointed it at Benton.... It was Benton, at that point, who very theatrically opened his jacket and told other sena-tors that were trying to put this to an end, "Stand out of the way, stand out of the way. Let the assassin fire." Fortunately, the assassin did not become an assassin and cooler heads prevailed. But that was 1850, and members carried pistols.

These were pretty tough times. [Today's Congress] is certainly bad, no question, but it is not unusual. It's not the first ever. You start at the very beginning of Congress and certainly 1798, 1799, the Federalists ver-sus the Democratic Republicans, they hated each other. Thomas Jeffer-son said, "If we saw a member of the opposition party, we can cross the street to avoid having to tip our hat to that person and say hello to him." Duels stopped in the 1830s through the 1850s. There was a famous du-eling ground not far from Capitol Hill, out in Bladensburg, Maryland. There were many invitations—"Meet me out there"—from one senator to another.

[TELEVISION COVERAGE OF THE Senate] was inevitable, thanks to cer-tainly some members like Senators Robert Byrd and Howard Baker, who were receptive to the arguments. I do not see how it could be avoided. The House went on television in 1979. The Senate waited until 1986, [being] a more deliberative body. It took them a little bit longer but the pressure was so great. You know the old story of the House member and the senator walking through the airport in their home state. The people come up and they shake hands with the House member—"We saw you on television, on C-SPAN"— and the senator all of a sudden becoming the unknown member of the state's delegation. That, I think, did a lot to push the vote.

RICHARD NORTON SMITH

Presidential historian Richard Norton Smith has visited the gravesite of every American president, a journey that began at Calvin Coolidge's grave at Plymouth Notch, Vermont, in the summer of 1962, just a few months shy of his ninth birthday. He shared his fascination with the presidency during a Booknotes *interview on February 21, 1993; his scholarship and enthusiasm for presidential history helped spawn the C-SPAN television series* American Presidents: Life Portraits *in 1999 and its companion book,* Who's Buried in Grant's Tomb? *Smith is a significant and longtime contributor to the network's history programming, including our 2013 series on first ladies, and for that reason we chose to include him in this book, drawing from a March 21, 2000, event at Washington's National Press Club, during which he talked about the history that can be learned from burial grounds of our nation's presidents.*

THE TRUTH IS WE wrote this book, *Who's Buried in Grant's Tomb?*, to demonstrate that not all the stiffs are running for president—this year. The great thing about this hobby [of visiting presidential gravesites] is you can go out and meet the only politicians who can't talk back.

GEORGE WASHINGTON WAS A great actor. He had an extraordinary sense of theater. He even staged his own death. It was an amazing thing. He had understood for thirty years that his life was lived very much on the public stage. He was a real stoic, and he realized quite early on the morning of December 12–13, 1799, as he said, that his "condition was likely to be lethal." He actually died, in effect, of a fatally sore throat. Today, he could have been treated with antibiotics, or a tracheotomy might have been performed. The reason we know all this is because he had a secretary named Tobias Lear. Lear is a wonderful character. He once said, "No sound on earth compared with George Washington swearing a blue streak." Tobias Lear, thank God, preserved everything that happened in the last forty-eight hours of Washington's life. It is just an amazing pageant. About four o'clock on the last afternoon of his life, he gave instructions for Martha to go to his study and take two wills out. One was to be destroyed and one was to be preserved. He was surrounded by doctors who, of course, bled him. But don't blame the doctors. It was Washington who, in fact, at the very outset of his illness called for an overseer and had him bleed him. Over the next twenty-four hours or so, they would take about one third of his blood. I tell you, it's a great argument for Christian science when you look at eighteenth century medicine.

[There are two slave stones at Mount Vernon marking their burial place.] The Mount Vernon Ladies Association has really been very good at recognizing, some would say belatedly, the contributions made by the slave population at Mount Vernon. Washington actually employed more people at Mount Vernon than he did as president in the entire executive branch of government. Now, obviously, the vast majority of those people were employed against their will. This is an issue we dealt with in the *American Presidents* series, not only on the Washington broadcast, but on a great many broadcasts, and it's something Mount Vernon has to deal with. But those two stones and the language on those two stones illustrates the fact that history is not fixed. It's not a monument, it's not a totem. It's fluid, it does evolve. Every generation basically makes its own assessment, and fortunately, in the last twenty to thirty years, there's been a much greater appreciation and interest in the contributions of people who were for a long time marginalized.

[JOHN ADAMS AND HIS son John Quincy are buried at the United First Parish Church in Quincy, Massachusetts, in the middle of the town where they both lived. Both wives are also buried under the church in the little crypt area.] Probably the most famous, if inaccurate, final words in presidential history were uttered by John Adams on his deathbed. Remember both Adams and Jefferson died on the Fourth of July, the fiftieth anniversary of the Declaration of Independence. Adams's last words were, "Thomas Jefferson still survives." Well, he didn't. He died several hours earlier, but it's the thought that counts.

John Quincy Adams's coffin would not fit in the sarcophagus [at the church.] I love John Quincy Adams, and given his somewhat expansionist view of the presidency, I think that's very appropriate. They had to stop in the middle of the ceremony and bring stonemasons in and actually widen the sarcophagus to get the president in his place.

THOMAS JEFFERSON WROTE HIS own epitaph. Presidents, like historians, like to have the last word, and he wrote his own epitaph and didn't mention the fact that he was president. There's a wonderful story here because, as a very young boy his best friend was a man named Dabney Carr. They used to lie out on the slopes of what would become Monticello and they made a boyish pact that whoever died first would bury the other. Dabney Carr had a meteoric rise in Virginia politics, established himself as a rival to Patrick Henry, but died [in 1773,] before his thirtieth birthday, and Jefferson honored the pact. He had his remains moved to the oak tree on the side of the little mountain where they had laid as boys. That was the beginning of the Monticello graveyard, which, 200-plus years later remains, I guess, a source of some controversy. I think there is an ongoing controversy regarding the Sally Hemings's descendants, who I am willing to predict one day soon will be admitted to that graveyard.

JEFFERSON DAVIS, JAMES MONROE, and John Tyler are all buried in the Hollywood Cemetery in Richmond, Virginia. James Monroe died, as many of the early presidents did—impoverished. He had, in fact, to leave Virginia, sell his estate, and move to New York to live with his daughter. He died there on the Fourth of July, 1831, and was not reburied in Virginia until 1858.

[John Tyler] was the first vice president to become president because of the death of a president and frankly, no one really knew what to do. There was nothing in the Constitution that explicitly said [the vice president should become president upon the death of the president.] A lot of people thought that he was "acting president," but Tyler made it very clear that he was president and he was soon a man without a party. He, in that one moment, upon learning of the death of the president, William Henry Harrison, made his contribution to defining the presidential office. He was president from 1841 to 1845. He had two wives and fifteen children [and still has a grandson who is alive]. He's also the only traitor. He was a member of the Confederate Congress. He had tried, to his credit, to preserve the Union; there was something called the Washington Peace Convention that met at the Willard [in] 1860-61, and he was part of that but it went nowhere. Then he decided to throw his lot in with the Confederacy. He was elected, first to the House and then the Senate, [but] died before he could take his seat. So he is the only president to die a traitor.

[Jefferson Davis] had the biggest funeral in the history of the South. Two hundred and fifty thousand people turned out to remember the lost cause and the man who embodied it. In fact, he died in New Orleans and several years went by before Virginia appropriately claimed his remains. He is there in Hollywood Cemetery [in Richmond] and is part of that trifecta buried there.

[Martin Van Buren is among those presidents and vice presidents that are buried in the Hudson Valley. His gravesite is located in Kinderhook, New York.] There's almost nothing you can say about Martin Van Buren.... Martin Van Buren sort of reinvented himself several times as an ex-president. He'd been a pro-Southern president. Then he ran on the "Free Soil" ticket, unsuccessfully. He died in the middle of the Civil War, just before the 1862 elections, and Lincoln, being the brilliant politician he was, heaped praise on Van Buren. Not much of it was sincere, but it was politically well-timed. Van Buren's followers would say, "On to Kinderhook," and that was shortened to "OK."

William Henry Harrison. This guy, first of all, he is no master of the sound bite. William Henry Harrison was sixty-eight when he became president. He orated in the middle of a snowstorm for almost two hours, contracted pneumonia, and died. That's all he did as president after thirty days and look at what he gets: he gets this hundred-foot shaft overlooking the Ohio River. Now, there's a rule about Ohio presidents. There's an inverse relationship between what they accomplished in life and how they are memorialized in death. Wait and see. This is just the first. [The former president is buried there underneath the obelisk. Up beyond that is a family gravesite area where his son, John Scott, was originally buried. John Scott's son, Benjamin Harrison, who also became president, went to visit the gravesite a few days after his father had been buried there and found that he was missing. Benjamin Harrison was later visiting the Ohio Medical Institute and found his father on a hook there. It's a true story. He brought him back and put him back in the grave.] Someone had stolen the corpse. What had happened was, in those days medical schools looking for cadavers were not above hiring some lowlifes to go out [and steal corpses,] and, in this case, they robbed a rather distinguished corpse. It set off an enormous uproar and it finally led the Ohio legislature to pass legislation. It became known as the "Harrison Horror," not referring to either presidency.

ZACHARY TAYLOR IS BURIED in Louisville, Kentucky, in the Zachary Taylor National Cemetery. He died eating chilled cherries, strawberries, who knows what. On the Fourth of July, he sat out at the Washington Monument listening to these endless orations, probably got heat stroke and went back to the White House and drank chilled milk and iced cherries, or whatever, and he died. His wife had the coffin opened three times to gaze upon his lifeless features. One hundred and forty-one years later, an academic in Florida decides that he was poisoned. Her evidence did not hold up, but first of all, she persuaded descendants of the president to permit his remains to be exhumed. For several days and for the first time in 141 years, Zachary Taylor was back on the front pages. It was a perfect *USA Today* story. The only thing that was lacking was that there wasn't a poll and there wasn't a front page graphic of Taylor astride Old Whitey, his horse. But otherwise, it was made for *USA Today*. Then they find there was no arsenic, so they put him back and you haven't heard anything about him since. It's one of my favorite stories.

He's not one of my favorite presidents. He's the most famous man, famous for being obscure.

FRANKLIN PIERCE'S ONLY EXCUSE for his performance in office was that he was an alcoholic. That's the only thing he has going for him. This was a man who, perversely, brought on the Civil War. He wasn't even like Buchanan, doddering and incompetent and inept. This was a man who brought this on like a positive, the only thing he did. Then he went back to New Hampshire. It was kind of sad. His wife Jane was a New Hampshire Calvinist, hated politics. She was smart. When her husband was nominated—a dark horse in 1852—she fainted. The rest of the electorate should have had the same reaction, but they didn't. He was elected and then, tragically, just before the inauguration, as they looked on, their son was killed, an eleven-year-old boy, [the] last surviving son. It just shattered whatever chance there might have been for a successful Pierce presidency. Mrs. Pierce blamed her husband for the fact that they were going to Washington. It was not a happy term. After he went back to Concord, he basically did what came naturally; he surrendered to the bottle and drank himself into an early grave. [He is buried in the Old North Cemetery in Concord, New Hampshire.]

I WAS ABOUT THIRTEEN [when I visited Abraham Lincoln's gravesite in Springfield, Illinois]. I always loved Lincoln. Remember, Lincoln had the misfortune to die at the height of the Victorian Age when people liked nothing better than a good prolonged cry. His funeral lasted twenty days, which posed some very practical challenges. The train went through city after city after city, and eventually they began whitening the remains and, really, the worst was still to come. He was buried in May in Springfield in a temporary tomb. Plans were made to build this monument and on election night 1876, a group of conspirators made plans to steal Lincoln's body. They were going to hide it in an Indiana sand dune in order to spring their leader, who was in jail on counterfeiting charges. In fact, the gang had been infiltrated, but they almost made off with the "Great Emancipator," and in the wake of that, he was buried and reburied and buried and reburied. For several years, while people paid their respects to an empty sarcophagus, Lincoln was outside it, buried under a pile of rubbish. It was pretty awful. [Three of his four boys are buried there along with him and Mary Todd Lincoln.] The interesting thing is that Robert Todd Lincoln, the oldest son, who went on to be secretary of war in the government of the Garfield Administration, is buried in Arlington National Cemetery. He's buried there with his son Abraham Lincoln II, whom they called "Jack." He died at age sixteen from an infection after surgery to remove a carbuncle under his arm,] and with him died out the male heirs on the Lincoln side.

[ULYSSES GRANT'S TOMB AT Riverside Drive and 122nd Street in New York City] is the largest tomb in America—still, almost a hundred years after it was dedicated. Grant, of course, died in public. He died by inches. It's an extraordinary story. This man who had been swindled, and feared leaving his family penniless, spent the last months of his life writing his memoirs, a heroic struggle against time. He wrote what everyone regards as one of the great literary classics of American history, managed to complete it days before he died in July 1885. He died at Mount McGregor, near Saratoga, New York, in a cottage. You can still visit the cottage. The deathwatch was very public. People would come up by railroad, large groups of people, and stand outside the cottage, and just stare at the general as he sat clothed in blankets as the cancer ate away his jaw, while he was scribbling away on his memoirs. It's an amazing story.

[RUTHERFORD B. HAYES IS buried in Fremont, Ohio, on the grounds of Spiegel Grove, the thirty-three-room mansion where he lived.] The first presidential library in the country, which opened in 1916, is located there. Hayes is one of the underestimated figures in American history. I always say he's the gold in the Gilded Age. Lucy Hayes, she is so much more than the "Lemonade Lucy" of legend. She's patronized, but she was an extraordinary person. She persuaded her husband that women should vote fifty years before the rest of the country caught up. She took a great interest in politics and in social reform. As an ex-president, Hayes was very, very active in promoting education among Southern blacks. (They were not originally buried at Spiegel Grove.) Lucy died in 1889 and President Hayes went four years after that. Life was really never the same for him. He was struck with a heart attack in Cleveland and he said, "I would rather die at Spiegel Grove than to live anywhere else." They got him home just in time and he died. Remember, Hayes had been elected in a very controversial election in 1876 and the Democrats never let him forget it. Grover Cleveland, who was president then, went to Spiegel Grove in Fremont to attend the funeral and said, "He was my friend. He was coming to see me. But he is dead and I will go to see him." And, in doing that, he not only buried Hayes, he also buried that controversy over that disputed election of 1876. A real class act.

[JAMES GARFIELD'S SITE IS right outside of Cleveland, near Mentor, where he has a home and they've restored the home there. In the same cemetery are John D. Rockefeller and John Hay, who was secretary to Lincoln and secretary of state.] This is one of the great stories you can impress everyone with at your next cocktail party. Garfield, of course, was shot in July 1881 by a disappointed office seeker, who had another motive. He had written a book and he wanted to promote the sales of the book. Garfield lingered for three months almost. He was in the White House. It was summer and there was no air conditioning so they came up with the world's first indoor air conditioning system. They brought Navy engineers into the White House and they had six tons of ice. They blew air through the heat vent of the president's sickroom, and they managed to lower the temperature by twenty degrees. Well, he remained somewhat snappish, which was not surprising, given the fact that his diet consisted of oatmeal and limewater. In the course of his final weeks, he was informed that Sitting Bull, then in captivity, was starving himself in protest and Garfield said, "Let him starve." Then he thought and said, "I've a better idea. Send him my oatmeal."

CHESTER ARTHUR HAD GOOD taste. He refused to move into the White House after Garfield died because it was such a dump and he brought Louis Tiffany, his friend from New York, to come in and redecorate the White House. Only after Tiffany had done his magic did Arthur move into the White House. Talk about taste, [when he died,] he rode to his tomb on Cornelius Vanderbilt's private railroad car. [He is buried in Albany Rural Cemetery, in Albany, New York.]

IN LIFE, GROVER CLEVELAND was very conspicuous. He weighed 300 pounds. In death, it is impossible to find him. [His grave is] in Princeton, New Jersey. It was dark and they were about to close the place and I told my folks, "Park the car in the gate and I'll go and find him." I couldn't find him and I stumbled over Aaron Burr. Now I'm a Hamiltonian and I was really sorely tempted to do a jig on the old bastard's grave, but anyway, I couldn't find Grover Cleveland. Eventually, this light went on across the street and my mother said, "We're going to get arrested, we're going to get arrested." And, in fact, there was a rather curious caretaker who wanted to know what we were doing there, but once we told him— I'm twelve years old, what am I doing, grave robbing?—he was fine. So he had a flashlight and he took me over to Cleveland's grave. [Aaron Burr's father is buried there with him. He was the [second president of Princeton. John Witherspoon, who was a close friend of Madison's, and George Gallup Sr., are buried there,] and so is Baby Ruth, Grover Cleveland's daughter, who was born in the White House and who gave her name to the Baby Ruth candy bar.

[BENJAMIN HARRISON WAS THE only Hoosier president and he is buried in Crown Hill Cemetery in Indianapolis.] Now, if you can imagine being overshadowed by a man (William Henry Harrison) who was president for thirty days, that's Benjamin Harrison's fate. In fact, the person in the cemetery that people really go to see is John Dillinger. The poet James Whitcomb Riley and [Booth Tarkington, the novelist,] are both buried there, and a man named Larry Conrad, who was secretary of state of Indiana and wrote the Twenty-fifth Amendment dealing with presidential succession is also buried there. Crown Hill Cemetery is a very famous cemetery in the United States. They say it's the third largest in America. This is the only cemetery where three vice presidents are buried: Thomas Riley Marshall (Woodrow Wilson's VP), whose most famous words were, "What this country really needs is a good five-cent cigar," Thomas Andrew Hendricks (Grover Cleveland), and Charles Warren Fairbanks (Theodore Roosevelt).

ON THE NIGHT OF January 5, 1919, Theodore Roosevelt, who was in poor health and who had lost a son, Quentin, in World War I just a few months earlier, said apropos of nothing in particular to his wife Edith, "You will never know how much I love Sagamore Hill," and shortly afterwards he put a book down and went to bed; he told his valet, "James, will you please put out the light?" And they were his last words. Sometime in the middle of the night he died of an embolism. The news was relayed to Woodrow Wilson, who was in France at the time. Reporters saw Wilson, and the look on his face went from shock to something approaching triumph. Wilson's vice president, the aforementioned Hoosier (Thomas Riley Marshall) had a much more gracious response. He said, "Death had to take him sleeping, for if Roosevelt had been awake, there would have been a fight." He's buried today near Sagamore Hill, [about an hour outside New York] near a bird sanctuary, which, I thought, is very appropriate since he spent his lifetime, certainly in the White House, ruffling congressional feathers. Remember, of course, that he loved birds and swatted his share of them.

[William Howard Taft is buried at Arlington National Cemetery. This man, as you know, served nine years as the Chief Justice of the United States (1921-30). He is one of two presidents buried in Arlington National Cemetery. He was from Cincinnati, but he didn't go back there.] It's interesting, the Tafts had their roots in Cincinnati, the Taft dynasty continues in Ohio politics. He went to New Haven, [Connecticut,] for several years after he left the White House. Taft is often thought of as this jolly, fat, incompetent president, but there is so much more to Taft. He had this marvelous, wry sense of humor. Remember he lost reelection in 1912, coming in third in a three-way race and he said he took some consolation from knowing that no one in American history had ever been elected ex-president so resoundingly. He went back to New Haven, which was a second home. He had gone to Yale—the Tafts all go to Yale—and he was a law professor, which is what his temperament was suited for. Then, he did finally achieve what was the great goal of his life, when Warren Harding, another Ohioan, in 1921, made him chief justice of the United States. He lost a hundred pounds. He was so unhappy in the White House and his weight actually reached 360 pounds at one point. While he was chief justice, he lost a hundred pounds. People all over America wanted to know his diet secrets—today, he would write a book—and he said it was simple. He'd given up bread and potatoes.

[WOODROW WILSON] IS THE only president buried in the District of Columbia. Somehow very fittingly for the son of a Presbyterian minister and a man who brought a certain Messianic quality to the presidency, he is buried in the [National] Cathedral. He was originally buried in Bethlehem Chapel, which was the oldest part of the cathedral to be completed. I believe in the 1950s, as more of the cathedral was finished, his coffin was brought up and he lies there [in the main part of the cathedral]. His wife Edith is buried in the cathedral as well.

[WARREN HARDING'S GRAVE IS one of the biggest] and the most undeserved. Nothing so became Warren Harding in life as his leaving it. He died a rather messy death in August 1923. There were rumors, completely unfounded, that his wife poisoned him. In the years since, there is a scholarly consensus that she didn't, but should have. He was buried in Marion, Ohio. Years went by before a president really had the nerve to go and dedicate his memorial. Herbert Hoover did in 1930. Calvin Coolidge was in attendance as well. But that tells you how quickly the bottom fell out of Harding's reputation once Tea Pot Dome and the other scandals became public.

ONE OF THE MOST idyllic spots of the American Presidents series was Plymouth Notch, Vermont. This is the gravesite of Calvin Coolidge, and there with him is his wife, Grace Coolidge, and his young son, Calvin Jr., who died when he was sixteen in the White House of blood poisoning from a blister from a tennis match. And often they say that's the reason why he didn't want to run again in 1928. There's a village a very short distance from there, where the original house is where he was born, where he lived, and where he was sworn in as president. This was my first presidential gravesite that I visited. I was eight when I persuaded my parents to go up there. There were six houses there in 1872 when Coolidge was born there on the Fourth of July.

THE HOOVER LIBRARY [IN West Branch, Iowa,] is probably one of the most poignant of all the presidential gravesites. People think of Herbert Hoover as a man without drama.... [His grave is located at the end] of a gentle knoll, one quarter mile from the fourteen-by-twenty-foot whitewashed cottage in which Hoover's life began in 1874. Hoover, in his last years, gave instructions. First of all, he decided he would be buried in West Branch, where he spent the first eight years of his life. Then he gave instructions that nothing was to be built or planted that would ever intrude upon an unobstructed view. He wanted people to stand at those two simple marble slabs—remember, he was a Quaker, nothing more than names or dates—and gaze off at that little tiny cottage, which, in fact, is the size of a typical American living room today, and draw the conclusion in America that the origins of one's life were irrelevant to what one did with that life. It was a very emotional, patriotic message, if you will, that he wanted to deliver at the end, and it's very powerful.

[FRANKLIN DELANO ROOSEVELT IS buried on his estate in Hyde Park, New York. There are two dogs buried there: Fala and a German Shepherd named Chief that belonged to his daughter Anna.] It's interesting, it's very modest. One of the real paradoxes is we speak of the imperial presidency; Franklin Roosevelt invented the modern presidency, and yet if you look at the gravesites of these modern presidents, they're much simpler, much less elaborate than those associated with the nineteenth century presidents. They were much more remote because media weren't the same, but because they were remote, presidents were much more revered. [Hyde Park is an hour and a half from Manhattan.] About a mile or two from there is the house, Val-kill, where Eleanor Roosevelt kept her home after his death. She had, some would say, an irrational fear. George Washington insisted that he not be buried for three days. He had this fear of being buried alive. Mrs. Roosevelt, in her will, stipulated that her wrists were to be slashed because she, too, had this irrational fear of being buried alive.

[EVERY YEAR, ON THE birthday of each president, the president of the United States, in the name of the people of the United States, delivers flowers to their grave.] Those of you who know your history know that the Eisenhowers had a tragedy early in their marriage. Their first child [Doud Dwight] "Icky" died at the age of three, I believe, from scarlet fever and was buried in Denver. In his last years, President Eisenhower gave approval to the plans of this very modest chapel; it's called the "Place of Meditation," a non-denominational chapel. What no one knew was that it was intended as a tomb for him and Mrs. Eisenhower, and furthermore, no one knew that Icky was going to be buried there. One day, in 1967, amid great secrecy, Ike went out to Denver on his own, had Icky's remains disinterred and brought back to Abilene, and personally supervised their interment at the foot of the crypts reserved for him and Mamie. His health really gave way shortly after that.

I was out there during the centennial year, helping to organize it for the National Archives. If you have ever been out there, above the crypt, now there are quotes. One is from Ike's Guild Hall address in London at the end of World War II; the other is from a magnificent address called "The Chance for Peace," [that he delivered on April 16, 1953]. My one legacy from the Eisenhower centennial was that we added those quotes in 1990 and they have stayed. We're discovering things about Eisenhower that we never knew, and one of them was that he was capable of eloquence. Those words have a timeless quality to them and it just seemed to me that they were kind of a summing up, and what better place to put them than [in] his final resting place.

IT WAS BY NO means a sure thing that JFK was going to be buried in Arlington. In fact, on Saturday morning on November 23, it was assumed by the family that he was going to be buried in Massachusetts, quite possibly in Brookline, where his son Patrick had been laid to rest just a few months before. It was pouring rain and [Defense Secretary Robert] McNamara went over to Arlington Cemetery. It was really Robert McNamara who found this site, brought other people to see it. Before that Saturday was over—it's incredible to believe she had the time or the will to do it—Mrs. Kennedy went over to the site which is just below the Custis Lee Mansion. Only after the site was actually selected did McNamara run into a young man who had been there the day that JFK had paid a visit to the Custis Lee Mansion, and he (Kennedy) made the comment, "I could stay here forever." He was so taken with that majestic view of Washington, D.C.—and how appropriate.

Media and Society

MICHELLE FIELDS

In a December 25, 2011, interview for Q & A, *Michelle Fields discusses her work as a video journalist for the* Daily Caller, *where she covered politics. The Los Angeles native attended Pepperdine University, where she believes her activism brought her to the attention of the national political web community. Her video of a confrontation with actor Matt Damon over teacher compensation went viral, with more than two million views. She discusses the differences between traditional journalism and her video and social media approach to the craft, arguing that today's audiences want opinion journalism.*

I AM A VIDEO journalist. I would say that what we're doing is almost like citizen journalism…we're capturing raw and real moments, which is basically what people are doing with their iPhones and Blackberries. As a video journalist, you're now competing with people who have iPhones and Blackberries and are uploading on YouTube, and that's what going viral. So we're recreating that. We're asking questions that congressmen maybe don't have the answer to, they don't have talking points for, or when we're going to a protest, we're going on the ground….

[I went to an event on Capitol Hill organized by the Patriotic Millionaires, who advocate raising taxes on the wealthy, and asked people there if they would be willing to donate to the Treasury Department to help reduce the debt.] I didn't know what to expect. It was a question that a lot of people wanted answered when Warren Buffet first came out and said he wanted higher taxes. This was a question that a lot of people were asking: "Well, why doesn't he just donate?" I didn't see any reporters asking that question to him, so I saw this as an opportunity to ask a question that I felt a lot of people wanted answered. I thought that maybe one of them would end up donating because it's what they believe in, right? But no one ended up donating to the government.... I thought it was hypocritical. I think if you really believe in something, it doesn't matter if other people aren't doing it. You do it. So I just thought it was very hypocritical of them.... [None of these people gave me back talk off-camera,] but there were some people who were part of the Patriotic Millionaires who saw me interviewing. When I asked for an interview, they just turned their back on me and didn't even want to do an interview. We put the video up on the *Daily Caller* web site and it just took off from there. It went viral and went on a lot of political blogs and I think we got about 400,000 views on it. [I think it worked] because it's a combination of both news and entertainment. I feel like a lot of the [traditional] reporters that were there, they covered the event as well. They asked questions such as what are you doing here and a lot of general questions. But it doesn't have that element of entertainment, and that's what we're bringing. People want videos now; we are combining fun and news, and it went viral.

[DURING THE REPUBLICAN PRESIDENTIAL primary campaign, I attended a book party for MSNBC *Hardball* host Chris Matthews for his book *Jack Kennedy: Elusive Hero,* and interviewed Bob Woodward and Ben Bradlee, among others.] I figured that there would be a lot of interesting people there and it was a cocktail party. There would be lots of insiders there that may want to do an interview with me, and people like that. People want to see off-the-cuff stuff. They want to see people when they don't have their talking points, when they don't have their press person around, and that's the perfect opportunity. They maybe had a drink. They're in a comfortable environment. They're more willing to say the truth, what they really believe. I'm sure if I interviewed Ben Bradlee as a sit down interview in [a studio] environment, he probably wouldn't have said what he said. He was much more comfortable, much more relaxed, and that's what people want. I don't know if it's because we live in this world where reality television dominates entertainment, but people want to see real raw moments and that's what I gave them. My era knows [Woodward and Bradlee] because they've seen the films about the Watergate scandal.... I mean, they're the fathers of journalism, basically, over at the *Washington Post*. What I'm doing is much different than what they're doing, but I still consider it journalism.

I THINK [WOODWARD'S JOURNALISM is] a different world. Now, people want biased journalism, I feel. They want to hear journalism either tell them what they want to hear or tell them what their opinion is and what they think about it. We have such polarized news now. It's a much different world. I think it's different. I think it's impossible not to be biased. I don't think that there is a need to try not to be biased because it's impossible to be unbiased. Even if you were interviewing someone, you decide what you think is important, what you think people would like. You still have biases, and so I don't see the problem with biased reporting [or] reporting from a certain angle. People who read my stuff, or watch my videos, they feel as though their voice is not in the media and so I'm providing a voice for them and I think that's great...they e-mail me and tell me, "You're the only person in the media that I trust." I think that's important....

YOUNG PEOPLE, PROBABLY EIGHTEEN to thirty, are watching a lot of our videos. When videos go viral, they start on web sites like reddit.com that are filled with the thoughts of young people. Reddit.com is just a bunch of forums; it starts there, and it goes viral. What I do in the morning [to prepare for my day] is I do not really go to that many web sites. I go to my Twitter. I go to my Facebook and I look at what is posted. I look at what my friends liked and I click on it, and sometimes it links to the mainstream media, so I click on that, and I look at it, but I do not go out of my way to visit the *New York Times* or the *Washington Post*.

[I LOST MY FATHER, Greg Fields, in 2002.] He was a writer, a comedian. He wrote a lot of TV shows, *Full House, In Living Color, Back to School*. He was probably the most real person I have ever known. He grew up in Kentucky. He was a man of faith, of great values, and when he went to Los Angeles and became this big-time writer, he never changed. He never drove a luxury car. He was still the same guy from Kentucky. When he donated money, he did so anonymously. He taught us that money meant nothing. He told us that we should be who we are and stay true to ourselves. He led by example. He showed us that it is possible even in a world like Hollywood that you can remain yourself. I think that that has had a tremendous impact on me…. He was forty-six. He died of a heart attack. He was very, very conservative. My mother is more liberal. I would say she is a moderate who has liberal tendencies. I'm pro-liberty. I believe in economic freedom. I believe in social freedom. I respect people's individual decisions and I believe that people can make reasonable choices for themselves, and I am suspicious of this idea that government can make people better, can make the economy better by forcing people to do things they do not want to do. [The opposite of economic freedom would be] lots of regulation. I believe that individuals should have the ability to choose how they produce, how they sell their resources so long as they respect the rights of others.

I was very excited [when I first came to Washington] and now I feel as though it is just filled with power-hungry people. That's my impression. Everywhere you go, everyone just wants to know what you do. They are trying to figure out what your resumé is, and if they feel they can't get something from you, they move on. Everyone is going to cocktail parties, schmoozing with people that they may not like but they feel they can get something from. I think it's quite sad. [Before I came here] I heard people say that, but to me, Washington, D.C., just sounded so amazing. It was so different than Los Angeles and I figured it would be a wonderful opportunity. So many people are intellectual. In Los Angeles, all everyone talks about is how they want to be a model or an actress. And so I figured I'm going to go somewhere where people are educated. I can talk about so many issues with them and they will understand what I'm saying. I guess I am a bit disenchanted.

[Pepperdine University is in Malibu and it looks out over the Pacific Ocean.] The school is very conservative. I don't think I could have picked a better university. It's unlike any other. If you go to most college campuses, everyone is drinking. There are a lot of frats. Everyone is just partying. At Pepperdine, it's a whole other atmosphere. Everyone on the weekends is going to volunteer, and they're thinking of ways that they can join groups and maybe go to Africa or go to Central America for spring break to help out and build homes. So that certainly had an impact on me and I was able to really make a difference on campus. [It is a religious school]—Church of Christ. There is a lot of religion [in the school]. I don't consider myself a very religious person, so that was not that important to me. I believe in a higher power. I believe in doing good.... Their values aligned with mine, so it felt like a perfect fit.

[I COVERED THE OCCUPY Wall Street rally on November 17, 2011.] They were going to occupy and shut down Wall Street, and I felt like it was a perfect opportunity to go there and capture that moment, and I thought that it's something that people would enjoy watching. We were down on the ground, where we were obviously at risk, covering the protesters, and we ended up getting in the middle of it when the police decided that they wanted them off the streets and shoved them onto the sidewalks. We decided to put the video up because I think it shows a different side to Occupy Wall Street. Before I went to Occupy Wall Street, I thought that these people were violent. That's what I saw on the news, [that] these people were horrible. You read all these things that they're raping women and they're violent with the police officers, but when I went there, these people were so kind and they were not violent at all. The police officers were the aggressive ones. They were the ones instigating the violence. And although that doesn't follow the narrative that people who read our web site would like to hear, it was something that was happening—that these people are not as violent as people are making them out to be. They are actually quite kind and [when I got knocked down,] they helped me up.

With this new Internet world, one voice, my voice, anyone's voice can be just as loud as the *New York Times* or the *Washington Post*. You can put a video up on the Internet and it is distributed globally. [The police officers pushed me down during the rally.] My camera girl and I were in front of the protestors as they were marching down the street and we were getting footage of them marching. At that moment the police officers decided, "Oh, OK we do not want them on the street anymore. Let's just shove them back into the park." So, they came up with batons and I ended up just getting in the middle of it because I couldn't move. There was a car in front of me and there were cops and protesters around me. They wanted us to get on the sidewalks, but the sidewalks were completely filled with people, so there was nowhere for me to move. So, the police officer hit me in the back with the baton and I fell onto the car, fell to the ground, and I got back up. I am not sure if it was the same police officer, but I got hit down again.

[There was a picture taken of me on the ground.] It went up on the *Daily Mail* and my boyfriend called me and said, "Hey, are you OK?" I saw the photo on the *Daily Mail*. I tweeted the picture out and then people started retweeting it all over…. I feel as though Twitter and Facebook have enabled people who, maybe, are not in the media, who do not have a loud voice, to become one of the loudest voices in media. We see people like Matt Drudge who had no connection to the media. He was a political outsider and look how far he has come. He saw this potential, this new medium that is Internet journalism, and his voice is now just as loud as the media establishment.

I UNDERSTAND THAT THE [Occupy Wall Street protestors] are frustrated. I think that they should be targeting the government, not Wall Street, or targeting them equally, because it is both of their faults. I don't understand why they're on Wall Street, why not come here [to Washington]? It is crony capitalism that they are fighting, so why are they just singling out Wall Street? [People automatically take sides "for" and "against" when they don't know all the facts.] The protests are driven by unions and obviously, the Right doesn't like that. They believe George Soros, or someone like that, is helping to fund these protests, and the Left say the same thing about the Tea Party, that Koch is funding it. There are these narratives that people come up with. The video we posted where I am thrown down and Occupy Wall Street is helping me up shows them as very kind and I've gotten lots of hate mail from conservatives [who are] very upset with me for putting that video up. I think that is silly. If that's the truth, if that's really what happened, I don't see the problem with putting that online.

[I INTERVIEWED ACTOR MATT Damon at an event here in Washington and asked him on camera about tenure and job security for teachers.] It was a teachers' union rally. I had just graduated from college and Nick Gillespie from *Reason TV* contacted me and said that he would be interested in me hosting a few of their videos, to try it out. This was the first video that I did for *Reason TV*...and it ended up going viral. [Damon said, "A teacher wants to teach. I mean, why else would you take a shitty salary and work really long hours and do that job unless you really loved to do it?"]

He was arguing that teachers love to teach, that they want to do it, and there is no reason if they get tenure that they're automatically just going to become lazy, but that's not true. Teachers make great salaries. They get great compensation. They get great benefits. There is a reason why teachers want to teach. There are a lot of benefits and if you guarantee someone their job, with any profession, that may make them lazy. They don't have an incentive to work harder when they're guaranteed their job. [I developed my position on tenure when] I went to school and I saw teachers who had tenure who didn't care at all about their students, about their classes, about their lectures. You hear students say, "Oh, she has tenure, that's why she's like that," [and I believed that]. I went to Calabasas High School, in Calabasas, California. It's fifteen minutes from Malibu. It's right outside the Valley.... I didn't enjoy it. I wasn't really challenged. I didn't care about high school at all. There was no one challenging me. Teachers didn't really care about their classes. I think many of them gave the same lesson that they did ten years prior. It wasn't that great. Then, I went to Pepperdine, and it was a completely different situation. We were in classrooms with twelve people. We had professors who would invite us to their house for their lesson or we would go down to the beach and have a lesson. They really cared about me personally and professionally, probably because it's a private school. [Private versus public matters.] I speak to people who go to public schools and they're in classrooms with 300 students, so there is a difference in quality.

I think almost two million watched [the Damon video. People care,] I think, because there is a movie star in it, and he gets angry, and people like to see celebrities. They like unfiltered content. He was off-the-cuff. He wasn't expecting that question, and then he got very confrontational and aggressive. People like seeing that. I think he is like most Hollywood stars. They get sucked into that world, where everyone's liberal, and I think he argues from emotion, not from logic. [As for me,] I have values and it doesn't matter if I live in Hollywood or if I live in D.C. or if [I live] in a different part of the world, I stick to my beliefs. I'm not going to change because everyone else around me changes.

I THINK I STARTED using the Internet a lot when I was in about the sixth or seventh grades. I'm spoiled. I have so much information. Any answer I want, I don't have to go to an encyclopedia. All I do is go to *Wikipedia* and I instantly have it. It's allowed me to get information so much more easily and make friends and create a network of people from all over the world. I was interested in promoting the ideas of liberty, and when I was in college, the Internet provided me so much opportunity. I could talk to people from different countries, different universities who had questions and I could give them ideas that they could use on their campuses, so I think it's wonderful. I think there is a lack of privacy, but you get so much good in return.

[During] my freshman year of college, my brother introduced me to Robert Nozick and his book *Anarchy, State, and Utopia,* and he introduced me to Ayn Rand and Frédéric Bastiat. I instantly realized that that's what I was: I was a libertarian. It just so happens [that] at that same moment Ron Paul came on the scene, and so there was this explosion of young people like me who had just discovered libertarianism, and it was almost like we took over the Internet. The Ron Paul people were everywhere. Every forum you went on, every video you watched, there was some argument, someone saying you should vote for Ron Paul, and it was very exciting. There were the Ron Paul forums where you had thousands of people exchanging ideas and book recommendations. It was a very exciting moment.

[I think our country is in] a bad condition. I see that people are very unhappy. People are struggling. I think there was some poll that came out that D.C. is the only place where people feel that things are getting better. Inside the Beltway, it's so ridiculous. It's nothing like real America.

My brother found out about libertarianism on the Internet and I knew he was libertarian for quite a while. I remember thinking, "Oh, he likes this crazy guy, Ron Paul, and I don't know who he is…." Finally, I was asking him for reading recommendations and he gave some to me, and I said, "OK, I'll give it a shot." I was politically apathetic before then, and it was really life changing. I have always been fiscally conservative, but when I was around conservatives, I always felt uncomfortable when they would talk about gay rights or medical marijuana. I finally read something where there were people who were like me, who believed in both social and economic freedom.

I'D LIKE TO ONE day have a louder voice and represent a good portion of America who feels that their voice isn't [heard] within the media. I'd like to be a voice for them in the media as a journalist, maybe an anchor on a network. If you look at MSNBC, or you look at Fox News, there are lots of people who give their opinions. I think people want opinions. So I think people want biased journalism. They want someone to tell them what they think.

KEN AULETTA

From a garage in the Silicon Valley, Google has grown to a global behe-moth. Ken Auletta, media critic for the New Yorker *since 1992, and the author of more than ten books on media powerhouses, is the author of* Googled: The End of the World As We Know It, *published by Penguin Press in 2009. He interviewed Google's management team in their offices over several months for a book that explores the history of Google, analyzes the future of communications in the digital market-place, and explains how the search algorithms were created. Mr. Auletta appeared on* Q & A *on November 1, 2009.*

M Y BOOK, *Googled: The End of the World as We Know It,* [has that subtitle] because it is the end of the world as we know it. This is a book about how this company, Google, which is really a surrogate in many ways for the Internet, came along in 1998 and started a search engine, and ultimately said, "Hey, wait a second. The world of media is inefficient. Why can't we digitize books? Why can't we have Google News and collect and aggregate all the news from newspapers and magazines? Why can't we have YouTube do television for free on the Internet? Why can't we create Android for cell phones, a free cell phone operating system? Why can't we have cloud computing to take on Microsoft?" Suddenly, for traditional media, it was the end of their world as they knew it. They were suddenly confronted, not just by Google, but by the digital world—a world that was much more ef-ficient than theirs, and one that was really stealing their business.

Tom Curley, who ran the Associated Press, arguably the most powerful news organization in the world, said about Google, "They have the greatest business ever invented. They are taking everybody else's work, and they are figuring out how to do a deal with most other people in which, 'heads, they win, and tails, most everybody else loses.'" It's not everybody else; the customer wins. See, that's the great dilemma here; Google aggregating news harms the A.P. and newspapers, as does the Internet. If you can search from Pakistan about the developments today, you don't even know where it's coming from, but you're getting a lot of information. For the public, it's a wondrous thing. It's free, and it's at your fingertips. It's like having a library on whatever device you're using. So, Google is a miraculous service for consumers. The problem is that it hurts a lot of businesses, particularly media companies and they have been very slow to figure out a way to respond to it.

[I MADE THIRTEEN TRIPS to Silicon Valley, where Google is headquartered, and I stayed there for thirteen weeks.] I was visiting another planet. This is Silicon Valley. I'm from New York. I wrote a book on Microsoft, so I spent time out there. But I spend a lot of my time looking at traditional media on the East Coast and Hollywood. This was a way to visit a world of people, of engineers. When you spend time out there, you realize it's a world with a different set of values than you see in most traditional media or institutions. Engineers start from an assumption, and the two founders of Google, Sergey Brin and Larry Page, started from the assumption that most of the way things operate are inefficient. And they are right, they are inefficient. But you start from that assumption, and you empower an engineer with that assumption. An engineer asks a simple question: "Why?" Why can't we have free phone service? Why can't we digitize all the books in print, twenty million of them? Why can't we just do that? Why can't we put television for free on YouTube? Why can't we sell advertising much more cheaply, and tell the advertiser who is actually watching your ads? And why can't we just charge them when someone clicks on their ad, as opposed to whether it catches their eye or not, which is the way it's done in the traditional world.

Once you start asking those questions, you begin to invade other people's businesses, and it's not good for those businesses. But what I discovered is that, in the world of Google, the engineer is king...they get 20 percent of their time off from Google to work on anything they want. A lot of the innovations that come out of Google come from that 20 percent time, that freedom, that sense of liberation they convey to their engineers.... As I sat in the Google meetings, I understood maybe half their words. They could have been speaking Swahili. I had to have it interpreted. But Larry Paige (co-founder and CEO) and Sergey Brin (co-founder) and Eric Schmidt (executive chairman) are all engineers. They understand every word. What I came to understand sitting there, a little by osmosis over a period of time, is that, in fact, the engineer is the content creator at Google. They're the equivalent of the screenwriter or the director. They're creating content, different kinds of content, YouTube content and software that enables you to read or watch or do Google Maps. That's content.

[Google] started in a garage in 1998, and they got $25 million in funding in 1999 and said, "We're not going to figure out a way to make money. We're just going to create a great search engine and then, at some point, we'll figure it out." Well, by 2001, they still were not making money, but they had built a great search engine. But their venture capitalists were getting a little restive. Then they came up with an advertising system, which, when you do a Google search, on that right-hand side, there's a gray box, and those are ads. But what they did was very clever: they created a Vickrey auction system, [a type of sealed-bid auction, where bidders submit written bids without knowing the bid of the other people in the auction, where the highest bidder wins, but the price paid is the second-highest] and Google copied it. [This system says] if you want to bid on the word "sneakers," a sneaker manufacturer would bid on that. So, a sneaker manufacturer comes in and says, "Well, these are the key search words I'd like to bid on: 'sneakers, playground, basketball, sports'—and you come up with a series of key words. And I will bid fifty cents each time that comes." ...Let's say Nike bids fifty cents. And let's say New Balance bids twenty-five cents.... All of this is online. What the Vickrey auction system did, which is one of the reasons that advertisers loved it, is that it said Nike won with the highest bid, fifty cents. But they didn't pay fifty cents. They paid a penny more than the second-highest bidder did. So, they paid twenty-six cents. The second-highest bidder paid a penny more than the third bidder did. So the advertiser said, "This is great. And not only is it great financially for me, but I only pay if someone clicks on my ad. I could tell when they're clicking on my ad, and if they have a second click, they can actually purchase something." So, it's effective advertising. It's not a shotgun anymore, it's a rifle shot...Google learned from that. But they found out that almost half the people who do a Google search actually look at the ads, and they treat the ads as information. For Google and for the consumer, it's a win-win. And for the advertisers, it's a win-win. Twenty-two billion dollars a year of revenue comes in; $21 billion of it is from those search ads.

There are a lot of Google's twenty thousand employees at Mountain View [California] and in New York, and they are in offices in China, in Europe, in Asia, and South America. They have these data centers, which are secret locations, in most cases. They don't talk about them. They're very secretive about stuff like that. But they have at least two or three dozen of those. The numbers [of data centers] we don't know.

...[Google's] servers are basically laptop computers. They take the keyboards out and they stack them and they cool them. There's a space between each one, and they store and process and index the Internet. In an average Google search, when you type words in the Google search box, the average time it takes to get the results back from a Google search is four tenths of a second. One of the reasons it's so fast is that they know where you are physically. They send your search to the data center physically nearest to you. So, if you're on the East Coast, you're going to a data center on the East Coast...[I don't have any idea how many different locations they have, and they won't tell you]. Google loves talking about transparency, but if you ask them, "How many data centers do you have?" or "Where are they located?" [they respond,] "Sorry, we can't talk about that for security reasons." If you ask them how many employees they have who are from India, "Sorry, we can't talk about that for security reasons." They're very competitive. There's actually a reason for this which is kind of interesting. Larry Page, the co-founder, read a book as a teenager on Nikolai Tesla, who arguably is the person who really invented electricity. Tesla was a tragic figure, because he didn't get the credit; Thomas Edison did, Tesla died destitute and bitter. One of the reasons that Larry Page is convinced he died destitute and bitter is because he shared his secrets openly. Larry Page was determined that Google would not share its secrets openly. They are very paranoid about competitors getting knowledge. If you ask them what is the algorithm that determines what ranks highest in the search results, they won't tell you what's in that black box.

AN ENGINEER NEEDS TO quantify everything, which is one of the reasons why Google sometimes gets in trouble, certainly with government in Washington today. But they want to quantify everything, and they start from a logical premise. They ask you a simple question: "Why can't you do it this way?" If you have digital technology which lets you know who the people are…who are watching a regular television set, and you could actually tell whether someone is watching an ad, and for how long, or what they're reading, or what they're searching for, wouldn't that be incredibly valuable? "Why shouldn't we share that with advertisers?" And if they say, "Wouldn't it be wonderful to have all the twenty million books ever published digitized, so you can have access to it in school libraries, or me as an author at home?"…You can buy books, electronic books that way. For a consumer, it's wonderful. Why shouldn't you make that available to them? But they don't ask the questions that don't fit into their algorithmic, mathematical model, which: What do you do about copyright protection? What do you do about privacy with advertising? Those are questions that are soft questions that engineers tend not to dwell on.

An algorithm is a mathematical formula that says to someone who's doing a search…. I ask a question and it shoots back a list of things. We know at least two things that make up an algorithm. An algorithm is composed of the number of times that someone has visited a website. The most popular websites…would tend to rank higher in the search results and be on that first page of the search results. I know from reporting the book that they added a qualitative piece to the algorithm, though they won't tell you how much it is. That is to say, if an article is in the *New York Times*, it tends to get a boost in the rankings. That's also part of the algorithmic design. But it's basically a mathematical formula that's secret, that Google ranks where a search result should go.

[There are organizations that actually can be paid to try to get your name higher in the results when someone's searching for a particular subject.] It's one of the reasons why Google keeps the algorithm a secret. They don't want these people to know how to game the system. These are search engine optimizers...they are marketing consultants who basically tell a business, "We can figure out how to make you rank higher in the search results of Google." Some of that is witchcraft, and some of that is probably real. But Google is constantly changing and tinkering with its algorithms in order to fight off those people. One of the reasons they don't allow advertisers to pay to be ranked higher in search is because they want to keep it pure. That's to their credit. It's very noble and, in many ways, they do many noble things.

I DESCRIBE THIS SCENE in my book where Eric Schmidt, the CEO, walks into Larry's office in 2002 and Larry Page has a Lego set. He's creating this scanner, and Eric Schmidt says to him, "What are you doing, Larry?" Larry says, "I'm creating a scanner. We're going to scan all the world's books." He says, "Larry, how are you going to scan all those?" "Well, we'll go to colleges. I'll go to Michigan and I'll talk to the library." And he did. And they got Al Gore to talk to the Library of Congress, and they talked to other libraries and they got them on board. But they never thought to get the publishers and the authors on board, so they got a lawsuit instead. Again, it was a copyright issue. They settled with the publishers and with the Authors Guild. They agreed to pay $125 million over the years and, in return, they got the right to digitize all the books in print, and ultimately, to sell books, electronic books, online, and compete against Amazon.

The law says, fair use allows you to quote a minimal amount. They never define in the law what a minimal amount is. This was part of the battle. Google's definition of fair use was much broader. They assumed that they could take much more out of a book than the authors and the publishers did. For instance, if you're an author of a cookbook, if they could take your whole recipe for chicken or desserts, then, they've really destroyed the value of your book. A book like mine, I don't care if they take a paragraph out of it, but do they want to take more than a paragraph out of it? Do they want to take chapters out of it? That, I would object to.

[In one of my interviews with Sergey Brin, he suggested that I ought to put this book free out on the Internet.] He came in late [to the interview] on his rollerblades, and his hair was all spiked up. He had just come out of the shower. He plopped his bag down, and he said, "I don't understand." He said, "Why don't you just publish your book for free on the Internet? Many more people will see it than actually read the book. Wouldn't that be great?" I said to him, "Well, let me ask you a couple of questions, Sergey." I said, "If I put my book online, who's going to pay me to come out here thirteen times and live out here and pay for the hotel and the meals and the interview time and the airplane flights? Who's going to pay for that?" He said, "Oh." I said, "Well, let me ask you another question. Who's going to edit my book? Who's going to market my book? Who's going to do the index? Who's going to legally vet it for me? Who's going to pay for all that?" By that time, he wanted to change the subject. What insight I took away from that was twofold: One is, he's an engineer asking logical questions at thirty thousand feet. Everything looks the same. He has a very simplistic view of the publishing process and what it's like to actually write a book. I'm dependent on writing a book and that's my income. It's not like I'm doing this for fun; it's how I make a living. The other thing it teaches you is that he has a very expansive view of copyright laws, which is, just put it out there. If you're an author or you're a director or you're a screenwriter, if that's the way you make your living, you don't want to give it away. You want to be sure that you can earn some money.

The narrative conflict in this book is how slow traditional media, be it advertising or telephone or television or newspapers or magazines or Microsoft, was to wake up to the fact that Google was a bear coming at them. Google didn't start out to take over the world of media, but [they asked] the engineer's question which is "Why?" or "Why not?" As you start asking that as you're growing, you realize, "Oh, my God. We can grow from just being a search engine to YouTube, which is television, and we can grow to Android, which is a telephone operating/mobile operating system. And we can go to cloud computing, which really says, why do you need to pay software fees to Microsoft for packaged software? Store everything in our portable cloud." The world began to open up for them, and it opened up the reality of what Google was up to. The traditional media was very late to understand.

Cloud computing is not in a cloud. It's in a series of computers and servers that store information. When you do your e-mail, that e-mail is in a cloud. It's in a server. It's waiting there for you. You pull it down, and you open it up. But it stays there. It allows you, no matter where you are and whatever device you're working on, be it your BlackBerry or your iPhone or your laptop, or your workstation at home or in the office, that cloud follows you around, or you follow it around. That's what cloud computing is. What Google is saying is, instead of just doing e-mail in the cloud, and instead of paying $300 or so for Microsoft 7 Word, we'll charge you much less. It may even be free, and we'll figure out some other way to pay for it. All your apps will be there; your word processing programs, the other applications that you like to use. We'll just store them on our servers, which we call the cloud, and you can access them anywhere you want.

[Google has spent $3 billion on servers. They seem to have an infinite capacity for all this information.] What they've realized is, one of the incentives for these companies to do cloud computing is that they've spent all this money on infrastructure. Amazon spends all this money for books, but they have excess capacity. They say, "Well, why don't we just branch out and do cloud computing, and offer services to companies?" If a company is potentially very attractive, not just for individuals, it's much more lucrative for companies, when you think of it, as a customer. Of course, they'll say to the company, "Why do you need your own I.T. department? Why do you need to spend all this money on computers yourself? Farm it out; outsource it to us. We'll do it much more cheaply. And you can still have your experts to evaluate that this a good service, but you'll save a lot of money." You do, potentially. You also lose control.

ONE OF THE THINGS that is extraordinary about these two founders, and about this company, despite the fact that they were in their twenties when they started this company, is that they have such clarity of thought about some things. And one of those things was that they would not do a regular initial public offering…which happened in 2004 for them. They said, "We are going to control the majority of the voting stock, like the *New York Times* or the *Washington Post* does, or Warren Buffett does. And even though we don't own a majority of the stock, we're going to own the majority of the voting control, because we want to assure that we will make decisions for the long-range interests of Google."

One of the other things they said: "We're not going to give dividends, because we don't want to create a kind of a culture here among our investors that expects always to have rapid growth every quarter. We want them to look long term. If it means that we want to make an investment in servers for cloud computing, let's say, that will cut into our profitability this quarter or this year, we're going to do it, because we want to focus on long-term growth." That was an extraordinary amount of clarity for young men to have. They were just insistent on it and they wrote a letter to shareholders at the time they went public in 2004, telling them all this. "We want to be transparent," they said. "We want you to know our philosophy. If you don't want to invest in this philosophy, don't invest in Google."

[Today, Google] competes with Apple. They compete with Verizon. They compete with AT&T. They compete with Nokia. Google…is one of the most popular companies in the world. How can you beat free? Everything's free. It's wonderful. You love it. And it's efficient. So, Google has very good standing with the public. If you go out, on the other hand, and you talk to, as I did, the leading executives of phone companies, cable companies, movie companies, Microsoft, newspapers, magazines, books, Google is not in good order. They fear them. In fact, they dread them.

Eric Schmidt was one of Barack Obama's economic advisors. David Drummond, chief counsel, was an early and fervent supporter of Obama. Obama spoke of Google in 2007 and talked about an open net, and more broadband and more investment in infrastructure, and supporting the entrepreneurship of places like Silicon Valley, which is music to the ears of the Google people. But the reality is that engineers are brilliant at understanding science and mathematical formulas, but they often lack emotional intelligence, that's to say, a feel for what's going on. I saw this when I did a book on events leading to the Microsoft trial in '99 and 2000. I went out and interviewed Bill Gates in '98 for my book, and Gates was just enraged that the government would question his motives. He thought he was doing good. He thought he was creating an operating system that was almost universal. Wasn't that wonderful that everyone had the same system? You didn't have to build two sets of railroad tracks around the country. But the government sued him for antitrust violations. What Gates couldn't understand was fear, that people would fear a monopoly; people would fear a concentration of power. And Google has that same blind spot. They have trouble understanding that.

They've got powerful forces that are now appearing in Washington lobbying the government, as powerful forces did against Microsoft. But Microsoft now is on the other side, lobbying the government to rein in Google, saying that "over two-thirds of all the searches in the United States Google controls. That's too much. Google has too much sway over advertisers. Google has too much sway over digitizing all the twenty million books." So, you have a lot of people who have an interest in assuring competition, the same kind of people who had an interest in assuring competition in operating systems for Microsoft ten years ago.

[THERE WAS ABOUT $172 billion spent on advertising in this country in 2009.] Google has $21 billion of that, after only being in business eleven years. And, by the way, to put this in context, that's roughly the same amount of ad dollars that consumer magazines in the entire United States bring in.... And it's two-thirds of what all the newspapers in the United States bring in.

My own take, one of the things I take away from this two-and-a-half year visit to another planet, including visiting back with traditional media companies, is that I am harsher on the traditional media companies than I am on Google; though, I'm sure people at Google will think I'm too critical of them on some things. I am critical of Google on some things, but what really bugged me about the time I spent with traditional media is how late they were to understand the new digital world and how the Internet changed the game. They had to change and play a new game, and they weren't doing that.... I wrote a book called *Three Blind Mice* that was about how the three television networks, which were dominant, missed the threat from the new technology, which, in the eighties and early nineties, was cable. They missed that, and they were late. They could have invested in and owned cable. They didn't do it. They were afraid of the cost and had short-term thinking. The same thing happened here with traditional media. They didn't invest, didn't plunge into that digital world and the Internet world the way they should have. They waited too long. I came away with that sense when I hear people in traditional media today whine about, "Oh, woe is me. They're doing these terrible things." I have no sympathy for that at all.

The head of Nielsen Company said to me, "There are two types of people in this world. There are people who lean forward, and there are people who lean back." The people in traditional media were leaning back. In this new world, which is changing so fast, you've got to lean forward. The other thing I learned and I write about at some length in this book is there's a conceit that people in Silicon Valley have, that the Internet is the most transformative technology that the world has ever seen. That's crap. It's not the most transformative. Electricity was much more transformative. In fact, you wouldn't have an Internet without electricity. It powers everything, including the Internet, and our laptops and everything else. But what's different about this period of change than any other period of change is the speed of change. It is all happening in an eyeblink. And that creates an enormous amount of insecurity in the executive offices, and it should. People are terrified. And why shouldn't they be?

I believe [that Google believes their motto of "Don't be evil."] I believe that they are not like Microsoft was a decade ago. Microsoft was [full of] cold businessmen. They were out to harm Netscape, to harm Sun, to harm Apple, to harm their competitors and to build a giant, dominant company. Google people are cold, but they're cold engineers, not cold businessmen—and again, they are the cold engineer who asks the question: Why?

CHARLES KRAUTHAMMER

Nationally syndicated columnist and Fox News commentator Charles Krauthammer began his career as a medical doctor but pursued political journalism after coming to Washington, D.C., during the Carter Administration. In 1980, he was a Henry Jackson Democrat who worked for Walter Mondale; today, he refers to himself as a neoconservative who supported the Iraq and Afghanistan wars. He was awarded the Pulitzer Prize for Commentary in 1987. Charles Krauthammer suffered paralysis after a diving accident in 1972, and in this May 1, 2005, interview on Q & A, he recalls his rehabilitation and continuing medical school studies after his accident.

I HAVE HAD A very checkered, irregular career. I was once asked, by an intern at the *New Republic* magazine where I used to work, how to be a nationally syndicated columnist, and I said [jokingly], "Well, first you go to medical school." It was pretty unplanned; I had intended to be a psychiatrist and I practiced for three years. Then, I just had a tug, a feeling that there was a wider world out there I wanted to get involved in. I studied political theory as a graduate student and came to Washington and one accident led to another and I ended up doing what I'm doing.

The single most influential thinker when I grew up, which was late sixties, early seventies, the time of the student revolution, was a very short book by a political philosopher called Isaiah Berlin, *Four Essays on Liberty.* One of them was two concepts of liberty in which he made a distinction between what he called "positive liberty" and "negative liberty." It was a liberal credo. It was against the craziness, the left-wing radicalism of the age. It was a very clear essay in which he stood up for what he called "negative liberty," which is how we understand it in the West: being left alone. Whereas there were all these ideologies, Naziism, communism, socialism, fascism, which offered you a "positive liberty," which meant we were going to find your higher being, but by regimentation, which was odd and paradoxical. He pierced that in that essay. I've been sort of small "l" liberal ever since, cured of any radical impulses. That was the single most influential text, a single essay.

John Stuart Mill was my favorite political philosopher, and his famous essay *On Liberty*. As you can see, liberty is a theme here. Another favorite is a fiction writer, Jorge Luis Borges, who was an Argentinean short story writer, and wrote rather mystical and magical, very short, fictional stories with deep philosophical roots.

When I was an undergraduate at McGill, I read for my courses, but it wasn't until I went to Oxford afterward and studied political theory with a philosopher called John Plamenatz who made me read the great political writers, such as Hobbes and Locke, one a week, and write him an essay every week [that I read seriously]. I remember, I handed him my first essay one week, and he said, "Krauthammer, I don't know about your creativity, but you're certainly creative in your spelling." That put me in my place. Reading with him for a year was my first mind-expanding experience in political theory. That year-and-a-half is what has stayed with me all this time.

No American is serious when they go to Oxford. You go to Oxford to have a good time. It's always an interlude. You're between undergraduate and whatever school you're to go to after. Grades don't matter. It's a new country. The country is wonderful, it's all new and you tend to go and have a good time. A lot of Americans had gone to Balliol College, which specialized in political philosophy. It had a graduate dormitory, which, in 1970, when I was there, was the only one in town that was co-ed; that was its highest distinction. That's where I met my wife Robin, who was a student at St. Anne's. She was studying law and practiced law for a while. In July of 1978, I quit medicine and she quit law on the same day. She has been an artist, a painter and sculptor ever since. Our parents were somewhat disappointed with us given their investment in our professional education.

My family is a rather epic story. My father was originally from Ukraine, but he lived in France most of his life. A naturalized Frenchman, he was a lawyer. During World War II, he fought with the French army, but that only lasted six weeks. Afterwards, he went to Cuba and Brazil, back to France, then America, where I was born, and ultimately to Canada, where I grew up. By the end of his life, he spoke nine languages.... My mother is from Belgium; she left on May 10, 1940, which is the day the Germans invaded. She made her way through France, ended up in New York translating American Army manuals into French for the Free French. She met my father in Cuba, long story, and she now lives in New York and in Miami. My dad, at the time, was running a diamond factory, which was producing industrial diamonds for the U.S. military. My mom was visiting her parents, who didn't get into America since they didn't have a visa, but ended up in Cuba, as a lot of Jews did. She met him at the Hotel Internacional and the rest is journalistic history and a lot of other history.

It had a lot of influences on me; this was a very worldly upbringing. My parents had been everywhere. Their friends in New York and Canada had also been everywhere, not by choice, but scattered by the war, and I grew up with that confluence of influences. If you're Jewish, you're also post-Holocaust; you grow up with a sense of the tragic element in history. It tempers your optimism and your idealism. It gives you a vision of the world which is more restrained, conservative, and you don't expect that much out of human nature. You are prepared for the worst. The most interesting political aspect of that is you have enormous respect for the American political system, in which the founders had an equal skepticism about the goodness of human nature, and constructed a structure which would contain the impulses, good and bad, check and balance, to produce a stable and a just society. So, in a sense, all of that ends up giving you a deep appreciation and even love of America.

My parents were beyond politics. Life was involved in raising a family, trying to make a living, maintaining your friendships. Politics was not central to our lives. In a sense, I learned my politics when I left home. My father moved us to Canada when I was five. I grew up in Montreal. I went to McGill until I was twenty. I graduated in 1970. I went to Oxford and then I never returned to Canada. I was always an American citizen because I was born here. I went to medical school in Boston and then later I came down here [to Washington].

MY WHOLE MEDICAL EXPERIENCE was at Harvard; I was a student there and then I did a three-year residency in psychiatry at the Massachusetts General Hospital. In my last year, I was one of the chief residents, published a few papers on bipolar disease, and then came to Washington in 1978. I chose psychiatry when I went into medical school. I went into medical school coming out of a couple of years of political theory, and I thought psychiatry would be the perfect compromise between the broad thinking of political philosophy, a philosophy on the one hand, and the practical aspect of life in medicine. It wasn't exactly what I had hoped it would be so it's one of the reasons I left. There are no special insights that psychiatrists have into human nature. People assume if you have a psychiatric degree, you have a Delphic insight into what makes people tick. What psychiatry does is it gives the knowledge about mental illness. So when you deal with people who aren't well, you do have insight that laymen don't have. You also know how to treat it and about drugs and all that. I have tremendous respect for psychiatry. But in analyzing political or social life, it's of no advantage whatsoever, and I've tried not to pretend in my career as a journalist that it does. I didn't hide the fact that I was a doctor and psychiatrist, but I never highlighted it. In my last year of residency, when I had to look at the future, I said, "No, that's not what I want to do. I might have made a mistake here. I want to do something else."

IN 1972, I HAD a diving accident. I was a freshman in medical school and was hospitalized for a year and two months. But since it happened at Harvard Medical School, in one of the swimming pools at the complex, I ended up doing my year-plus stint as a patient in Harvard teaching hospitals so that I was able to do my second year of medical school in the hospital as a patient. Even though I was not able to attend any classes, I would study at night. They were very good at having the professors tutor me at night. Then I rejoined my class for the third year, and graduated a year later.

I hit the bottom of the pool with my head and it caused no injury except a breaking of the spinal cord. As a medical student, and that week studying neurology, it was rather ironic. I knew exactly what happened the second it happened. I knew exactly what the consequences were and what the future was. That was a help to me, because I never had any illusions. Many of the bedmates I had on the wards had a lot of illusions, and I didn't have them, which was useful. I knew I had two choices: give up or pretend it hadn't happened—or do everything you could to do that. What I resolved is that I would try never to let it change my life, or change the direction of my life. The irony is that I had intended to be a psychiatrist, which is about the only thing I could do. That is what I wanted to do, so I went ahead and did it.

First, I spent that initial year in physical therapy, exercising, regaining my strength. That was my whole day, eight hours a day, on the mat, training, weightlifting, and all of that. In the evening, I studied. My day now is all the routine stuff, except it takes a little bit longer, life is a little more expensive, but ultimately, it's not that different. [For example,] I drive with hand controls.

Everything is different about my life because of the accident. When I was in my teens, I spent 80 percent of my waking hours doing sports. That doesn't happen anymore. There are a lot of things that you lose, but, on the other hand, everybody has their cross. Mine is a particularly obvious one, difficult one. But I never asked the question, "Why me?" I mean, why not me? We all have our tragedies. I got mine early. In fact, as I age, and my friends are aging, some of them are in one way or other joining me and I've had thirty years of practice. So I have a head's up. Look, I'm not looking at the upside here. Parking is easier and that's about it. There are not a lot of upsides. But, you take the hand that you're dealt with and you do what you can with it.

I CAME TO WASHINGTON to work at the National Institute of Mental Health, as a director of psychiatric research, a continuation of my expertise. It was a nonpolitical appointment. But at the time, through a series of accidents, I ended up being asked to be a speechwriter for the vice president, Walter Mondale, and I did it. When we lost the election in 1980 and I was unemployed, the *New Republic* invited me to come to be a full-time editor, and that was the beginning of my journalistic career. At that point, I was a Henry Jackson Democrat. I was a Cold War liberal. I was a believer in the Great Society, but I was also a believer in a tough approach to the Soviet Union, which means I had pretty much of a home in the Democratic Party, [with leaders such as New York Senator] Pat Moynihan and Henry Jackson, the great senator from Washington State. Later on, that element of the Democratic Party shrunk to nothingness. As it did, I was without a home. I remain generally without a political home.

I think you could, fairly, call me a neoconservative now. There are several distinctions between conservatives and neoconservatives. One has to do with personal history: Neoconservatives generally are people who started out as liberals, and as the dean of neoconservativism, Irving Kristol, once said, "They were mugged by reality." They evolved, in time, into conservatism. So that's number one. If you ask a neoconservative, "How did you vote in 1964?" a seminal year, he'd say, "Lyndon Johnson." A conservative would say Goldwater. So that's one distinction. The second is that because of that, neoconservatives carry over some of the idealism, if you like, and objectives of liberalism. For instance, in foreign affairs, there is a critique by conservatives of neoconservatives, which is that they are too utopian, Wilsonian, if you like; we want to revolutionize the world. We want to democratize the world. What distinguishes us from liberals is that we don't rely on the institutions that liberals rely on: the U.N., treaties, and all that Wilsonian stuff. We believe in power, American power in particular. But what distinguishes us from other conservatives, the more traditional conservatives, [is that] they are more likely to be realists. They're not interested in the governance of other countries, if it's a democracy or not. They're just interested in how the government acts in relation to the United States. They're interested in [the] national interest. They're not interested in constructing democracies abroad. You might look at the traditional conservatives, the realists, as people who believe in the billiard ball theory of international relations: other countries interact with each other, they knock into each other, and that's what you care about. Neoconservatives care about what's inside the ball and how it governs itself because the idea is that if you can change the way a society governs itself—Afghanistan, Iraq, Lebanon, the Soviet Union—then the policies will change, and then you might have a safer world.

TIME MAGAZINE, TWO YEARS after I started at the *New Republic*, asked me to do an essay once a month…. The next year the *Washington Post* asked me to start a column. The year after that it was syndicated nationally. I write in one place, on one machine in one office. I don't know what it is, but if I'm anywhere else, I can think, but the writing is not going to happen. I write in my office which is in downtown Washington. It's my own office. I set it up about eighteen years ago…. I usually write all day. I mean, I don't have a specific [schedule]. I'm not one of those who wakes up at three in the morning, writes until seven, and then goes off and fishes…. I'm a fusser [about my language]. I know it's a problem…. I like dictating my first drafts, because I have a horror of a blank screen. The minute I start to type on a blank screen, I'm fussing and editing and I get nowhere. So what I do is, I think it out in advance, usually I put down an outline of a dozen or twenty words, so I know the structure. Once you've got the structure of anything, it's done. Then I speak it as if I were explaining it to you, or my friends, and then I have it all down on tape. It gets instantly transcribed, it ends up on my screen, and then I'm just editing. As you know, editing is easy, writing is hard. So then I'm editing myself and I spend hours and hours. You go over it and you make it right. I like to polish. And that's how I do it. But I don't sit there and compose. I just say it, and then I'll work it from there.

I WAS ASKED TO go on television for the first time in the eighties, a series called *Agronsky & Company*, which evolved into a show called *Inside Washington*, the same show which I have been on as a regular since the invasion of Kuwait in 1990…. Then I was asked whether I wanted to do Fox News regularly, and I have enjoyed it a lot. The most reaction to my work is probably a tie between Fox, because it's national, and the *Washington Post*, because it's read in Washington…. I think Fox is "fair and balanced." [The reason] it has raised the ire of so many people in the country is because it offered an alternative to the mainstream, which, for a generation, were just obviously and clearly liberal. I once said that the genius of Roger Ailes and Rupert Murdoch was that they discovered a niche in broadcast journalism of half the American people; meaning that you had half of the country rather evenly split between liberal and conservative. There's nothing wrong with having a liberal filter, but it's not good if that dominates the airwaves. By establishing a channel in which you [broadcast] a different filter, it had a huge response and it's a very, very necessary component [in terms of] the diversity of outlets people have available to them. If Fox wasn't successful, it would be ignored. But it commands an audience. People hunger for that kind of approach. That's the monopoly that the mainstream, the old style media had, the liberal media had, [and it] was broken. People hate losing monopolies, and this is the classic example of a monopoly shattered.

I WROTE ABOUT OUR Iraq policy in *TIME* a month before the invasion, saying that the real reason to do Iraq was not weapons of mass destruction, but to change the culture of the Middle East, which was a risky endeavor. There was no question about it. I never said it was a slam-dunk, to change that culture in order to change the conditions which had led to the terrorism, al Qaeda, 9/11. I was not very happy that we pinned it all, or at least a lot of it, on weapons of mass destruction (WMD). I understood why that was, because we needed U.N. support, and all of that hinged on a legality about the weapons of mass destruction. I've written about international law for years. I'm a great skeptic about international law. It is worthless in almost every important issue outside of the fisheries treaty with Canada. I was not impressed by the necessity of U.N. action or all of this explanation. I understood why the president had to do it, because a lot of Americans worship at the church of the U.N. and wanted U.N. action. Thus, we had to have the WMD issue. But I thought it was risky and a mistake. And, it turns out that it was a mistake.

Syria is the last remaining bad actor in the entire region, from the Iranian border to the Mediterranean. Turkey, Lebanon, Israel, a new Palestine, Iraq, Jordan, Kuwait, all democratizing to one degree or other, all rather tolerant, heading in the right way. Syria is the bad actor destabilizing everybody, destabilizing Lebanon, supporting the terrorists in Palestine and in Israel, working to help the insurgency in Iraq. If Syria's regime changes…I think it would completely change the complexion of that region and would secure it for the kind of democratization that we really want.

I believe in Israel's right to exist. I believe it has been unfairly attacked over the years, starting with the [belief that] Zionism is racism. It has been a target of the international left, which is a scandal. It's a shame to the international left. If Israel were ever destroyed, it would be on our conscience in the West for generations, like the Holocaust. The aid that we are spending on Israel is mostly military. Israel's economy is becoming stronger and stronger. Ultimately, perhaps within a few years, it will wean itself off the U.S. money.

I don't think the money is the real issue. [Our Israeli policy] causes a lot of Arabs to be angry with America and I understand that. But the answer is not to throw your friend into the sea. The Chinese are angry with America over our defense of Taiwan. The answer is not to throw Taiwan into the sea, but it is to try to find some accommodation. We have tried very hard to do that for the first time in many years; I'm an optimist on the fact that that might happen. I thought the Oslo agreements were a fraud and a deception from the first day they were signed, and, in fact, they turned out to be. But there is a new realism in understanding the issue and I think that, over time, if we can find some accommodation, which I think the Arabs may be getting ready to do, that will help to improve our relations with all of the Arabs.

For our generation, it's the war on terror that I'm most concerned about. No question that the problem today, the threat today, is that these guys will get their hands on a weapon of mass destruction and they will kill a million Americans in one day. That's an existential threat to the United States. That is, without a doubt, the issue of our time. I think we will prevail because of what we are now pursuing in the Middle East, the Arab spring that we're seeing. Our generation may be able to manage this issue and solve it. Then the rising issue will be China. China is the second issue, but it is not immediate, it's a long-range issue, it will be the issue in mid-century. Luckily, I'll be gone and others will have to deal with it. China today, to the world, is what Germany was a hundred years ago, a rising have-not power that's looking for its place in the sun. If we mismanage it the way that Europeans mismanaged it a century ago, we're going to have real problems.

GOING FORWARD, I WANT to write the book on foreign policy. I'd like to write not a memoir, but a pastiche of some of the incidents in my childhood, particularly of my parents' generation, which was a very picaresque and very interesting generation. And also, you want to live as long as you can because you want to see how things turn out. That's the real downside of dying. You just don't find out what's going to happen in the Middle East, what's going to happen with all the things you care about in the world. So I'm hoping to hang in there and learn what history is going to say to us.

ROBERT KAHN

In the 1970s, Robert Kahn led a team of scientists, academics, and government agencies that are credited with the development of the Internet. In an August 14, 2005, interview on Q & A, he recounts the dramatic story of the Internet's creation and the important role of federal funding to spur the initial innovation. In 1986, this engineer and Internet pioneer founded the nonprofit Corporation for National Research Initiatives, which he continues to lead, whose mission is to foster strategic development of network-based information technology.

I WAS CERTAINLY THERE at the beginning of the Internet, and the idea of federating different networks together was mine. I worked very closely with a colleague named Vint Cerf on the development of the protocols for the Internet. I've been involved in it for the last thirty years. But the reality is that the Internet itself is the result of many people's work over many years and we were just fortunate to have been there right from the very beginning.

There is a set of people, and they're all good friends of mine for the most part, that have worked in the field of computer networking for a long time. The first documents that were really produced on this field came back in the early 1960s. People like Len Kleinrock and Paul Baran were associated with that and they talked about the idea of packet-switching in slightly different terms, but the basic idea was there. Then you had people in Britain, Donald Davies in particular, who talked about it again from a British perspective. DARPA, the Defense Advanced Research Projects Agency, started a program to build the first computer network; it was called the ARPANET, which was started informally in the mid-sixties. It actually ended up with a request for quotation going out, and I was part of the team that won the contract to build it. I actually wrote the technical part of the proposal; it was a team that had a lot of experience in building networks like this. My background, of course, was from MIT. I had been on faculty there and it was more academic than engineering at the time. But we actually built the net. Everybody who was involved in that whole process saw this as the start of something big. The Internet itself, as people know it today, is really a federation of a lot of different networks and computers that are connected to those networks. There has been a separate effort to try and figure out how to do the federation and make the Internet work and a key part of that has been the TCP/IP protocol suite that Vint [Cerf] and I worked on…. Many people have a claim to pieces of this whole puzzle.

A PROTOCOL IN THE context of computer networking is a set of procedures that two machines might use in order to communicate with each other. We might have a protocol for you and me to communicate. Then you might say something back and then I might say something back, and we might view that as a simple form of a protocol. It's the way the machines handshake with each other in communicating and how they format their bits to communicate.

Packet-switching is a name that has been given to a particular form of moving data in a network that relates to sending chunks of data. In the telephone system, historically, what happens is, when you make a phone call, a circuit is established from you to the end user that you want to talk to, and all your data flows over that circuit. Packet-switching is more like sending postcards through a system or cars through a road system. The data is in discrete little addressed chunks. It's like a postcard, and it would be routed; maybe every packet, every postcard would be sent over a different route and reassembled at the destination into a continuous stream. It would simulate the equivalent of a circuit, but there would be no one circuit over which all of the data would go. If you had a fleet of a hundred cars going from point A to point B, they may take different routes, but you could put them together at the destination in the form that you wanted. That's what packet-switching was all about: the ability to switch little chunks of information that had addresses on them called packets.

I strongly doubt that [there would be an Internet without the United States government]. There would not have been as much emphasis on computer networking. Would it have shown up somewhere else, would the carriers have done it on their own? Possibly. But it would have been ten or twenty or thirty years later. Would we have been able to put together this international capability without substantial research funding from some dedicated source? I seriously doubt it. It was not in the plans of any of the carriers to create something like this. But given that it has now been created with a lot of support from the U.S. government over the years, particularly DARPA initially, and later, the National Science Foundation, it became the basis for which the carriers could then take over, and they are largely dominating what goes on now around the world.

I ended up running one of the offices called the Information Processing Techniques Office; it was, in fact, the office that originally caused the ARPANET to happen and where I did most of the work on the Internet. The ARPANET doesn't exist anymore. The first node in the ARPANET was installed at UCLA in September of 1969, and I was out there myself helping with the field testing unit. The ARPANET lasted for over twenty years. It was finally decommissioned in 1990, the last node of that net removed because the National Science Foundation (NSF) and others had played a key role in networking and [had] created some alternatives. The NSFNET was a major contribution of the National Science Foundation, [because it] had higher speeds and had broader connectivity to the university community. It had more temporals abroad and it became the backbone for quite a while. The NSFNET itself only lasted until the mid-1990s, at which point it was determined that there was enough commercial activity going on that you did not need a separate government supporting backbone in order for the Internet to operate.

In 1972, I was thirty-three. I actually thought I was going to DARPA to run a manufacturing program, applying artificial intelligence to advanced manufacturing…. I had started my career at Bell Laboratories. The program I thought I was going to run did not make it through as a congressionally supported program. The director of the office at the time, Larry Roberts, was the one who started the ARPANET program at DARPA and later hired me into the office, asked me to get back and involved in networking. He knew I had been principally involved in helping to create the ARPANET.

Very shortly thereafter, I ended up working on the development of two other networks, one of which was a satellite net on an Intelsat 4 that linked several countries in Europe with the United States in a packet-switching mode, a kind of Ethernet in the sky. The other activity was a ground-based radio system using packet-switching, which I called packet radio. It was a spread spectrum system that involved taking signals and spreading them over a very wide band in order to communicate. This is like the difference between FM and AM, FM being a wideband system and AM narrowband. This was an equivalent kind of system with a fairly new technology that has now been popularized as Code Division Multiple Access (CDMA)....CDMA uses essentially the whole band all the time, but they do it by coding their signals in a way that you need to know the code in order to decipher the signal that you're interested in listening to.

VINT CERF IS A very close colleague of mine. He's an engineer who is a computer science graduate from UCLA. I first met him in 1969 or 1970 when we were first starting the ARPANET where we got to know each other pretty well. When I first came up with the idea of linking together all these different networks that we were creating at DARPA, I knew that I couldn't do the implementation work myself because DARPA is a funding agency. I asked Vint if he would work with me on this, and together the two of us took some of these basic initial ideas and refined them to the point where they became really good enough to implement. Vint had been involved in some of the early work on host protocols for the ARPA-NET. These are computer-to-computer protocols, the means that computers use to talk to each other. So he knew quite a bit about the different operating systems, the software. I later recruited him to come on and work with us at DARPA in 1976.

DARPA, originally started as the Advanced Research Projects Agency (ARPA), is the agency of the Department of Defense that was created in the late 1950s by President Eisenhower in response to the Soviet launch of Sputnik. The question then was, "Why not us?" We had all the technology and we got into space very quickly thereafter. But it didn't seem to be anybody's responsibility. ARPA was created as the agency that would maintain this technological vigil for the nation, be responsive to the secretary of defense, a kind of quick reaction agency with the ability to find the best people in the country and work with them. The computer science and information-processing program got started a few years later. Subsequently, in the early 1970s, they put the "defense" in front of it.... I never knew the totality of what DARPA did. I know they had some number of programs that were classified, some number of programs that I'm sure I didn't have the appropriate ability to know anything about. But most of the work that we did was pretty much open, unclassified because it involved supporting a basic research community in the United States. Largely, more than half of the research was probably in the universities, but we funded some of the nonprofit organizations such as Lincoln Laboratories and RAND Corporation.

Vint and I made an intensive effort starting roughly in the spring of '73...to work out a lot of the details, to take a basic concept and make it more specific. We had meetings on the East Coast and on the West Coast, and we would often have our discussions walking through the streets of Rosslyn, Virginia, or working in the ARPA office late at night. When the actual paper that we wrote was published, we gave it at a conference in Sussex, England, in September of 1973. It was subsequently modified slightly for presentation in a publication and then published by the IEEE Transactions on Communications in May of 1974. IEEE is the Institute of Electrical and Electronics Engineers, a professional organization for electrical engineering. There really wasn't a computer science discipline at the time. We actually wrote the paper in that summer of 1973, and I recall Vint and I doing most of the writing in a little room in the Cabana Hyatt, which was a hotel on El Camino Real in Palo Alto.

We thought the connection of networks was a big deal from a research perspective and we saw it as a technical challenge. We thought it was neat to be able to work with potential organizations all over the country, to try out something nifty like that. In the context in which this was all being done, the personal computer revolution had not happened. There were very few organizations that even had large timesharing systems. The whole idea of these networks at the time was to link interactive timesharing systems together. There might have been fifty or a hundred organizations that might have been able to participate; this was not a commercial thing we thought we were doing. We had one basic carrier in the United States: AT&T. This was not high on their priority list because it was not a very promising commercial area back then. Much of business then was based on a more short-term prospectus, namely, what can be done in the next year or two or three looking at return on investment.

We did not think this was going to turn out to be a good thing outside of the research community, but we knew it could have a big impact on the way research was done and the things that it would enable. That is what we thought we were doing back then. Of course…on the ARPANET side, we were demonstrating how to build efficient networks to link computers. In the Internet side of the world, we were trying to figure out how to take multiple networks and cause them to work together because they were all different.

We understood that this could be important, but we certainly had no vision of where it has come. There were no personal computers so the idea that the population as a whole could be part of this really didn't cross our mind. We did not think it was going to go commercial because we did not think AT&T was going to be interested in the short term. They later became very interested in the long term. We knew this was being done with government support, so we thought that this would probably have to be limited to use for government purposes only. The government later changed its view of networking and there was a bill put forth by Congressman Rick Boucher of Virginia that passed in late '92; it enabled the NSF to take their network and open it up to commercial use.

The personal computer revolution started in the early 1980s; I got my IBM in 1981 or 1982…. I remember we got our first workstations in the DARPA office in the early 1980s. These were SUN Microsystems workstations, which was the outgrowth of another program that DARPA supported. The acronym SUN actually stands for Stanford University Network. So this was an outgrowth of some workstation development that had been done by folks at Stanford University using software that had been done by a fellow named Bill Joy at Berkeley. They later became the nuclei of this little workstation company called SUN Microsystems.

It was clear over time things were happening for which this was well positioned to be a big deal. When the personal computer revolution happened, it suddenly became clear, "Gee, an awful lot of people that I never thought would have a chance to get on a network like this now have the technological wherewithal to do that." The community, instead of being hundreds or thousands, could be tens of thousands, hundreds of thousands, or more. When the National Science Foundation opened it up more broadly to the research community and to the entire science and engineering community, it became clear that a lot more people could get on it. They could not only get on it because of policy, but because of the fact that equipment was now affordable. I remember the first time I saw on the nightly news on TV, somebody said, "We now have this new capability for you to communicate with us, you can send us e-mail." They gave an e-mail address that was literally out of the Internet regime. Suddenly I said, "Hey, the rest of the world is now going to be able to use this in some real sense." It was that time when the World Wide Web was just coming into people's perspective. That was roughly the same time that the NSFNET opened up to commercial use. An awful lot of commercial activity was now able to make use of those capabilities that were previously constricted to very localized and rather segregated private networks....

The way a typical organization would communicate with the Internet is they would procure some kind of a circuit from one of the carriers. The carriers would then have equipment and facilities of their own that would provide a network capability, and they could take traffic from that user and funnel it anywhere on their net. To the extent that you wanted to talk to users who are on other party's networks, they would have various arrangements with those other networks, peering arrangements either where they agree on how to swap money and traffic, or they would have other people who would just connect to their networks and be paying customers. The traffic, through the protocols that we started with and [that] have evolved steadily over the last thirty years, would somehow manage to route itself to the right places just like if you were in your car and you wanted to go somewhere, you would have intelligent cops at every intersection. You could say, "I'm going to this location." The cop would say, "OK, take a right turn there, take a left turn here," and eventually, you would get there if they were doing a good job of routing it.

[Is it possible to shut down the Internet?] Not practically. The Internet has its vulnerabilities and I'm sure there are ones that will continue to turn up; for every one that's found, people will try and figure out how to make it either less vulnerable or invulnerable. And others may show up. How do you shut down the world economy? Could it be shut down? I suppose that if somebody were just evil enough, you could find a way to make the entire population vulnerable. But the Internet is a big distributed system. It's everywhere. For somebody to actually bring the whole Internet down, they would have to have an orchestrated activity of such unprecedented proportions that it would be very unlikely. Those may be famous last words. There are vulnerability points. And if people go after those vulnerability points, they could cause serious trouble, like they could prevent an address from being resolved to the right place to go, and/or if you had bugs in operating systems. The more vulnerable issue, really, is in the actual user's computer itself, because they may not protect themselves properly with passwords. There may be bugs in those systems that can be exploited. It is just a continuing battle. We have it in every part of society…. Can you ever make [the vulnerability] absolutely zero? Probably not without becoming so repressive that nobody would want it. The same is going to be true of the Internet.

[TODAY, THERE ARE 4.2 million pornographic web sites, 12 percent of all sites.] I can believe those numbers. I'm disappointed, to say the least; certainly, this was not what we had anticipated, nor did we anticipate all the spam and the viruses and the like. But I believe that there are going to be technological solutions to some of the problems and the rest of it is going to have to be dealt with by either policy or other people deciding what they're willing to support. I think, technologically, one can build all kinds of filtering mechanisms; people have proposed that for keeping kids away from some of this material. I think standards could be developed to help with that…. But I think they are mainly policy issues for countries around the world, how they want to deal with that kind of thing. It's disappointing, but that's about as much as I can say, because historically, I think it's disappointing that we have as much crime as we do, or as much terrorism as we do. But ultimately, if that's in human nature, that's what's going to happen and we have to learn to deal with it and take the appropriate steps.

When I first started this work at DARPA, I was calling the program "interneting." It was an exploration of the text for internetworking and we might have even called it "internetworking" at one point. But the term Internet really got applied to the collection of networks mainly by the community. We have used the term "Internet" to refer to...some common information to be carried along. And we called the header that came to carry that the "Internet header." So the term had somehow shown up as a shorthand of interneting or internetworking, but I don't know that anybody ever took a discrete effort to name this collection the Internet, per se. It just sort of happened along the way back in the 1970s.

I don't know the exact numbers that the taxpayer, through the government, paid for the Internet, but I bet it's the biggest bargain that the American taxpayer and the economy has ever had. In fact, I remember in the late 1990s, when the Clinton administration was riding that big economic boom, they had come out with some numbers that said one-third of all the growth in the economy was due to Internet-related activities of one sort or another. When we built the ARPANET, the very first of the networks, the actual money that was spent on the network piece of it was less than $10 million.... But, if you compare that with what private industry is putting in even in one year today, private industry contributions dwarf everything that the federal government probably put in over its lifetime. That has to be one of the biggest or most successful investments that has ever been made by government....

The routing is actually done in a very distributed fashion. All the networks share information about who can get to whom. Every network, in principle, could do its job its own way.... The most prominent network in an organization is probably something called the Ethernet. This is literally a wire or a switch that allows everybody in that location to share information in a kind of a broadcast mode. Think of it as a means of you putting out a piece of information, and everybody's computer can ask, "Is that for me or not?" It can be encrypted or not, as the case may be. There is no routing that's done there. This is all done by essentially broadcasting it to everybody and people pull off that which is addressed to them. So you can do routing in various ways, but for the most part, the Internet relies on a system of routing that has an algorithm for sharing routing information.

There are a number of areas where the Internet really has great potential. For example, we have seen very little use of it for multi-party collaboration, where different groups in different parts of the country or of the world can get together to work on problems of considerable interest. We've also seen very little use of the net for the kinds of things that will be possible when you can discover things through its power. The potential is almost unlimited because you could get into full-time, twenty-four-hour a day kinds of life-blog situations, sensors that are always reporting.... But the biggest area by far that hasn't been explored is the use of the Internet, and computer technology more generally, to unleash new forms of creativity and expression.

There is really no way that any one organization can run the Internet, whether it's the U.N. or this government or anybody. The Internet is a big distributed system, all around the world. And there are parts of it that work well, parts of it that can use some more help, and things that have not been invented yet will need to be dealt with in the future. Many of the countries of the world, when those reports were first starting to be generated, really had the feeling that somebody needed to be in charge. In fact, that was the first question that people used to ask: "Who runs the Internet? Who's in charge?"

And I would say, "Who's in charge of the world economy? Who runs that? What about the weather? Who's in charge of that?" "Well, that's different." But the Internet has many of the same properties: It is ubiquitous; it's everywhere; and the pieces are separately run and controlled by different parties.... We need to worry about evolution of the Internet and make sure that it can make available all the new technology that comes out, get it integrated properly, coordinate all the developments around the world in some effective way, which we've been doing for a long time now.

The role of places like the U.N. will be to act in a way to get ideas out, get people to share notions, to help with the coordination of critical issues, but ultimately, governments in the world are going to have to weigh in on the issues that are important in their own country. We are going to need some mechanism by which we can then deal with the issues that are larger than those that can be dealt with by a single government. The U.N. might be able to help in that capacity. But there are other organizations that can help as well.

There is a system that is now around the world in a big way, and a lot of people contribute to that. I was instrumental and right there at the beginning. The idea of federating all these networks together and actually launching a program to do that did originate with me, but the work was done by a lot of different people. And the ideas that led to that were really contributed by multiple people. I mentioned Vint Cerf, who was one of my early colleagues, who helped a lot in getting us forward. We built a lot on the work in computer networking that had been thought about before by others. If the ARPANET had not been created, we would not have had a chance to link together multiple networks. It serves no useful purpose to try and credit something of this magnitude to any one person. When then Vice President Al Gore made his comments [about his creation of the Internet], it was unfortunate, because he actually played a pretty important role in helping to roll out the Internet. He was the first elected politician to really articulate the value of networking. Sometimes by saying the wrong thing, you can get yourself into hot water, as he did. But, from my point of view, the credit for this really needs to go to all the people who have contributed over the years. I was glad to have been a part of it right from day one. History will show what the roles of the different parties were.

Writing Bestsellers

MALCOLM GLADWELL

Malcolm Gladwell has had four books on the bestseller lists, often si-multaneously. The Tipping Point, *published in 2000, documents how ideas travel through a population.* Blink, *published in 2005, focuses on instant decision making and the criteria involved in those decisions.* Outliers *was published in 2008 and discusses why people live outside traditional parameters.* What the Dog Saw, *published in 2009, is a collection of essays from the* New Yorker, *where Mr. Gladwell has been a writer since 1996. He appeared on* Q & A *on May 14, 2006 and December 6, 2009, to discuss what's influenced his writing, including growing up in a biracial family in rural Canada. This chapter is drawn from both interviews. His books are published by Little Brown, Inc.*

FROM 2006 INTERVIEW

Why did I do what I do? Because I failed at everything else, is the short answer. But I'm just curious. I want to know about the world. I'm in a position where I get to wander around and take a look at all kinds of things I wouldn't ordinarily be able to take a look at. It's like being an eleven-year-old for your entire life, which is a fabulous thing to be. When I got to college, I realized that there was a virtually limitless amount of cool things to learn about the world.

I grew up in southwest Ontario about an hour west of Toronto, a little place called Elmira. My father taught at the University of Waterloo, which is the big Canadian science school. Waterloo is where the Black-Berry was invented and where it continues to be made. It was a little farming community of 5,000 people. We lived on the outskirts of town and it was a lovely, lovely place to grow up. My parents still live there. My mother is Jamaican and black and my father is English and white. They met in England where my mother went to college. I was born in England, and then we moved to Canada when I was six or seven. It had all those wonderful virtues we associate with small towns. When I compare my childhood to the childhood of my friends who grew up in New York, it's like they're living on a different planet. Canada was so much quieter; it's much safer; less hectic, less overwhelming. My universe of people was smaller. I'm very grateful for that kind of upbringing, because it gives me a base from which to explore the world. I didn't get jaded. I often talk to friends of mine who grew up in New York City, and by the time they were seventeen or eighteen, they felt that they had already seen the entire world. By the time I got to that age, I felt that I hadn't seen anything, which is a much better position to be in, because every day is full of excitement. I still wake up that way, thinking, "Oh, my goodness! There's so much more to know." That's the gift of starting small, because you always feel there's a great, wonderful thing around the corner. If you're going to Studio 54 when you're thirteen, life goes downhill after that. I think one should grow up in small towns and move to cities. I think that's the perfect way to live life.

Before I was born, my parents lived for a while in Boston in the fifties as a mixed-race couple. They lived in London, in Jamaica, and then we moved to Canada. There are Mennonites in southern Ontario. It was an extraordinarily tolerant place. Mennonites are a very special denomination; they have this combination of being conservative socially, but also extraordinarily open-minded. It was not until we moved to this tiny place in rural Ontario that my mother felt accepted and felt that the issue of race went away, which is an enormous paradox. You don't think of religious, small-town farming communities as being racially tolerant in the seventies, and yet, that's precisely what happened. She wanted to be treated for who she was, not the color of her skin. That happened in this kind of miraculous way in this little corner of Canada.

My mom was a writer. She wrote a very lovely and successful memoir called *Brown Face, Big Master* in the late sixties. Brown Face is her; Big Master is God. It was about growing up in Jamaica, and moving to England in the fifties as a black woman, and her spiritual and personal journey. It was a bestseller when it came out back in the sixties. It's recently been republished by an academic publisher in England and translated into many languages. The memoir is very much in vogue now, but this was very much ahead of its time. My mother was a housewife living in England and was in her thirties when she wrote this, and I always found the book to be very inspirational...it's so beautifully written. Clearly expressed and simple in a way that it's always served as a model for the way that I would like to write.

I've always felt, no matter what you write, that when you write, you cannot write in a calculating way. You cannot sit down to write a bestseller and you shouldn't think about that issue at all when you sit down to write. What you should do is write what you find interesting and follow your own curiosity. When I was writing *Tipping Point*, I can honestly say that I never for a moment tried to imagine how well that book would sell. I just wanted to write something cool. I was interested in this. I wanted to write something that my friends would read, that my mother would like.... You can tell when a book is written as a bestseller. It's not a good feeling; it seems calculated. The reason people like books and are drawn to books and read books is that they would like to participate in the world of the author. They do not want to be pandered to. They want to be led somewhere...I find writing such an immensely pleasurable act; I never get writer's block. I know some writers find it painful, which fills my heart with sadness, because how tragic to find the act, to find your life's work, painful. If I can find a couple of hours to write in a day, I'm just thrilled.

I STARTED OUT AS a business writer at the *Washington Post* and covered health care and the pharmaceutical industry. Then I was a medical writer, and covered HIV and the Federal Drug Administration and the National Institutes of Health. Tina Brown, editor of the *New Yorker*, hired me. I wrote a number of book reviews and smaller things for the *New Yorker*. Then I did a piece for the race issue about the differences in the way that Jamaicans were treated in New York versus Toronto.

In the seventies, there was a big wave of immigration out of Jamaica, of middle- and lower-class Jamaicans, simultaneously to Brooklyn, Flatbush, and Toronto. We are not talking small numbers; there were hundreds of thousands of people. Brooklyn, to this day, has been transformed by the West Indian presence and Toronto was transformed by the West Indian presence. Just arbitrarily, half of them go to Toronto and half of them go to New York. But the way in which they have been greeted has been profoundly different. In New York, to be a West Indian is an advantage. They are considered the "good" immigrants. They have privileged access to certain kinds of jobs; there are all [these] positive stereotypes attached to being a West Indian. In Toronto, on the other hand, they're considered the problem and there are all [these] negative stereotypes. They are considered to be the people who are running the drug trade and they are the bad blacks. It's the same people and that's what the article is trying to figure out: how did this happen? The answer was, in New York there is an existing body of black people who are lower on the totem pole of African Americans. The whole idea was that prejudice exists along a hierarchy, and as long as you're not at the bottom, you can be OK. There's an implicit hierarchy of ethnic groups in New York. There has been some really wonderful sociological work on this, and so long as there are black people at the bottom, black people who can distinguish themselves from those people at the bottom can thrive.... In Toronto, there was no one. Jamaicans came in and they found themselves at the bottom of the totem pole. That's what's been so painful for West Indians in Canada. The West Indians who immigrated to Canada were my cousins. My cousin is an executive at IBM with a wife with graduate degrees and kids who score at the ninety-ninth percentile of their class. My family in Jamaica is educated and sophisticated. They are the people who are principals of schools and think of themselves as every bit the equal, if not the superior, of their fellow Canadians when they moved to Canada. Yet, they're treated as if they are inferiors. It's baffling.

Someone looks at Jamaicans in Toronto and they think they are criminals. Me a criminal? Are you kidding me? That's a very different experience than African Americans have in this country who have this whole long, depressing history that they're dealing with. Jamaicans don't have a depressing history at all. They've come from the top of their world. So, they treat discrimination as a very psychologically different process when you're coming from a place where you were at the social top than if you're coming from a history where it's at the social bottom.

I mostly think of myself as a Canadian and that's odd, because I haven't lived there since 1984. My Canadian experience is so fundamental to who I am, and so formative, and I like Canada so much. We chose Canada, and the country that you choose is, in many ways, the country that always is closest to your heart. The Gladwells, back in 1969, decided that Canada was where our future lay. To totally go off on a tangent, this is why I find the whole debate going on right now about immigration in this country so frustrating, not because I don't think there are legitimate arguments to be made by people who are threatened by illegal immigrants. But we have forgotten something, which is, illegal immigrants chose the United States. They have affection for it. I know this, because I've been through this myself. I'm an immigrant twice over. If you choose a country, your love for it is overwhelming. When you're dealing with people with that level of affection for your country, for their country, you have to treat them with respect. They're here because they want to be.

TIPPING POINT, WRITTEN BACK in '98, '99, sold north of somewhere between 1.5 and two million copies. *Blink*, written in 2003, sold around 1.5 million copies. *Tipping Point*—I kept waiting for it to go away. It just wouldn't. It just kept chugging along. It kept on being discovered by some other group. The nonprofit world [discovered it first]...I went out and gave talks to community groups. That book deals with social change and they are in the social change business, and that book talks about making large differences with small inputs: they're trying to bring down the teen pregnancy rate in the town of X, and they have a budget of $20,000. It's an enormous problem.... They're thinking, "Can I do anything with $20,000 and with fifteen volunteers?" They found the book profoundly hopeful.

...Why were these books successful? I have always said that people are experience-rich and theory-poor, and that we have these lives that are dense with really interesting experiences. Things happen to us. Now more than ever, we're exposed, we travel. We have these jobs that are involving and fascinating. What we lack is some way of making sense of all that.

These books give people cognitive and intellectual tools to order their experiences…. In that sense, that is why, particularly now, they are so appealing. I don't know if they would have been as appealing thirty years ago, but [they are now,] at a time when people are overwhelmed with things that they don't know how to categorize and how to explain.

Advertising and marketers were the second group to discover the book. They were picking up on something quite different than what the nonprofit people were picking up on, the "word of mouth" idea…. Eventually, the people who were interested in it were businesses who saw it as a way of understanding internal change in their organization…. With the rise of the digital revolution, there was this feeling on the part of many organizations that they had to restructure. How do they get there? How do you renovate the culture of an organization? That's a perennial question, but it was very top-of-mind in the 2000–2001 era.

I DIDN'T NAME THE book *Blink* because of my hair, but the hair experience was so striking. I used to have very short hair, but then I had this huge Afro, and noticing how profoundly different the way the world treated me was just this eye-opener. Many, many different people have had this experience in one way or another. I had never had it before. I began to think, "This is something that is not central to who I am, yet it's having a profound difference in the way that I am received by the world." That difference is all in the moment. It's like, boom! Cops are suddenly thinking, "You're a lawbreaker." People began to think that when I grew my hair out, I was perceived as being far more dangerous, but also positive things as well; that I was far more interesting and hip. Funnier, kind of weirder. I remain pretty much a dweeb; I'm a guy who goes home and reads books. All of a sudden, I was plucked from that world and everyone thought I was Lenny Bruce, or something. That transformation was so remarkable that I thought, "These snap judgments we make about people, they're important."

It wasn't about race because I'm so fair-skinned and only black people ever really suspect that I am part black. That was not the key variable. We have a certain set of inferences that we draw about people, unconsciously and automatically, who have long hair. Long, crazy hair means something in our world. And…if you have long, crazy hair, you don't work at a law firm and you aren't a junior executive at GE. You can draw accurate conclusions about people from the length of their hair. We go much further than that, and we start drawing inferences—having long, crazy hair does not mean you are funny. It does not mean that you are charming. It doesn't mean that you're on the cutting edge. You could be quite out of it and have long, crazy hair…. This is what we do and this is part of what I wanted to explain [in *Blink*]: What are we doing when we make these snap judgments? Because we're running with them an awfully long way.

FROM 2009 INTERVIEW

I currently have four books on the bestseller list: *The Tipping Point* and *Blink*. *Outliers* [2008] is an investigation of success. It's an attempt to understand what the reasons are why certain individuals are outliers, why they lie outside normal experience. What sets them apart? It looks at culture, luck, generations, and all the things that feed into success.

The current book is *What the Dog Saw*, a collection of essays I'd published for the *New Yorker* over the past ten years. The title is from a profile of Cesar Millan, the dog whisperer on *National Geographic*. I was spending all this time with Cesar and my first thought was to write an essay about what does Cesar see when he sees a dog, because he has this extraordinary ability to calm dogs…. The interesting question is not what does Cesar see when he looks at a dog, it's what does the dog see when he looks at Cesar? So that was the title of the essay, and any time you can put "dog" in the title of a book, you are doing well….

ALL OF US WHO do this speech business know that it can be a very good living…. I don't get nervous before public speaking, even though I am kind of a nervous person. Years ago, I used to be a competitive runner and would get insanely nervous before big races, so much so that I wouldn't be able to sleep for weeks beforehand. Ever since then, everything else I've ever had to do, I think, "Is it as scary as running a race? No, it's not"…so, I never get nervous. I really like giving talks; the discipline of being forced to tell a story in front of a group of people and explain yourself through spoken word, as opposed to written, is very important for a writer. They are skills that beautifully translate to the task of writing on paper. Since I started to do my speaking, I think I have become a much better storyteller. The other thing crucial about it is that it forces you to get outside your world. That's hugely important if you are going to do as I do, nonfiction journalism. I am by nature somewhat reserved and reclusive. But I need, by virtue of my job, to meet people, hear about new ideas and stories, and get different perspectives.

I meet people I would never in a million years have met before. It constantly replenishes my store of information about the world.... More often, you start to chat with somebody who does something totally different from you, and they tell you something that is incredibly interesting. They do not realize it is interesting, because it is familiar to them.... This is one of my rules of conduct, since everyone is interesting. I really, honestly, seriously believe that when people are talking about the things that they know well and do well, they are almost always interesting. If they are not, it's generally your fault, because you are not asking the right questions, or you have not made them comfortable. Once I learned that lesson, my journalism became easier.

AFTER THE FINANCIAL CRISIS, I wrote a talk about the Battle of Chancellorsville during the Civil War involving Robert E. Lee and "Fighting Joe" Hooker. Lee beats Hooker, and he should not have beat him. Hooker had him outnumbered two-to-one. Hooker had him dead-to-rights, and Lee pulled it out. It was an incredibly interesting battle. There are reasons why Hooker blew it. But at the core of it was that he was arrogant. He was overconfident. He thought he had Lee so completely outgunned that he no longer had to take Lee seriously as an opponent. I thought that there was a truly extraordinary, fascinating lesson in that, because overconfidence turns out to be, psychologists tell us, the most common flaw of experts. If incompetence is the disease of the novice, overconfidence is the disease of the expert.

One of the ways to explain what happened on Wall Street [during the 2007-2008 financial crisis] is precisely this: these titans of the financial industry began to behave as Hooker did on the eve of the Battle of Chancellorsville. They believed themselves to be in such command of their world and environment and decisions, that they were no longer capable of failure. This notion that our experts and leaders need to be humble more than they need to be good is really important. It's not to say that they don't need to be good; of course they do. It is that, as we get better and better at what we do, we run an ever-increasing risk of overconfidence and arrogance. The task of the leader or the expert is to keep that psychological problem in check, and they need our help to do that.

...I HAD A CONVERSATION a couple of weeks ago where I was giving a talk and was seated next to a guy who ran a regional bank in Akron, Ohio. I was talking about his business, "How's your banking business?" He says, "Oh, we're fine. In fact, we're more than fine. We're about to buy a big bank in Chicago." I said, "Why are you fine and no one else is?" He was an older man. He was probably in his late sixties, and he said, "I've been through this three times before." I suspect that he was humbled twenty-five years ago, or in the early or late seventies, and never forgot that lesson. It is in times like [these] that we understand why experience and learning from experience is so important. That word is not a meaningless triviality. Experience matters, because there are certain things that you only learn when you have been humbled. You cannot explain to a twenty-eight-year-old that things are going to get bad. It is not going to sink in. But to this man to whom I was speaking, who saw it firsthand and dealt with it, and I am sure went through all manner of crises before, it is a lesson that he kept with him.

Colin Powell, before the Iraq War, was the in-house skeptic. Why? Because he had been through Vietnam in a very firsthand way, in a way that many of the other decision makers had not, and had never forgotten those lessons. This is another case of someone who appropriately was humbled and learned from experience. You have to have people like that around.

Writers have built-in support systems that do keep us humble. I have an editor at the *New Yorker* who is not dazzled by any of my book sales, and is, if anything, more willing today to tell me than he was ten years ago, that what I've written is nonsense. I have a mother who is resolutely unswayed by the opinion of the outside world. She said of *Outliers,* in a way that only a mother can, "I really like this book," meaning that she did not like the first two books so much. When you have people in your life who keep you in check, it's easier. And luckily, I do not have any real power. I am not running a major country or investment bank, so the damage I can do if I were to get overconfident is limited, thankfully.

The nature of influence that a writer has is very specific. We do not change the world. What we do is we start conversations. Maybe, if we're lucky, those conversations well down the road are developed and enhanced, and some idea gets in the hand of someone who can actually effect change. There is a piece in *What the Dog Saw* called "Million-Dollar Murray" about homelessness. It describes the work of a guy named Phil Mangano, who was an extraordinary public servant in the Bush administration. He ran the homelessness policy and was responsible for dramatically changing the way we treat the homeless in city after city after city. He was the Paul Revere of this new policy. He traveled incessantly for four years, making the argument that it is cheaper to solve homelessness than to treat homelessness, and that the homeless person who stays on the streets costs us all far more money than if we simply were to go and give that person an apartment, someone to watch over them, and, finally, a job. I wrote a piece about his ideas, his crusade, and also, the larger intellectual context in which he was operating. I did not create that movement, but I publicized what he was doing. Many people in that world tell me that it made their work easier to have a fully fleshed-out argument in a national magazine making the case for what they were doing. It helped to overcome some of the skepticism. That's the way in which writing of the sort that I do is valuable. When I shed light on something, it helps those people who are interested in creating change. It makes their life a little bit easier.

JUDITH RICH HARRIS IS a psychologist who I wrote about years ago when she wrote a book called *The Nurture Assumption*, which is an extremely interesting book. She makes a number of very sophisticated arguments in the book, one of which is what we mean by environmental influence—all of us are shaped in part by our genes, and in part by the world we grew up in. She wanted to argue—and I think she convincingly did so—about what we mean by that is really peers and not parents. In other words, parents provide less of an environmental influence on the lives of their children than do children's siblings, friends, cohorts....What appealed to me about that idea was that a lot of my writing is about trying to understand the nature of the environment, the influence of the environment. That's really what I come back to again and again and again. *Outliers* is trying to understand success in a context of the worlds people are born into—generation, culture. *Blink* is trying to understand what's going on around you, how does that affect the kind of snap decision you make? So, I keep coming back to this issue. What she did very brilliantly and very early on in my thinking was that she clarified what the environment means, and she said, even more powerfully, that we have only the dimmest understanding of what the environment means. We've been using all kinds of myths that are untested and untried, and we need to rethink that really important word. That was a crucial motivation for me to write some of the books I've written.

THE STORY I SPENT the most time on is "Late Bloomers," an essay in *What the Dog Saw.* It took three years to get into the magazine. It went through so many drafts. I read this book by an economist at [the University of] Chicago named David Galenson, in which he talked about how genius comes in two very different forms. He talked about the conceptual innovator, who is the person who has the big, bold idea, and the experimental innovator, who is the person who succeeds, creates through trial and error. The conceptual innovator is the prodigy, and the person who works through trial and error is the late bloomer. I loved this idea so much, because he was dignifying the late bloomer, but I had a devil of a time finding the right stories to illustrate that point. When I have an academic argument, I like to find narratives to complete it. It just was hard to find the right ones, but sometimes you have to be persistent.... I chose this novelist from Dallas named Ben Fountain, who wrote a collection of short stories called *Brief Encounters with Che Guevara,* which is magical. He was my late bloomer. He published that book in his late forties, after spending twenty years sitting at his kitchen table in Dallas, writing and being rejected. My prodigy was Jonathan Safran Foer, who is on the bestseller lists; he wrote a really interesting book about vegetarianism. They were such fascinating contrasts, and beautifully illustrated what David Galenson was talking about.... But sometimes, finding the right story is really difficult. If you rush into print with something that doesn't quite work, you throw away that idea. And that's something you should never do.

THE EASIEST STORY I wrote was a profile of Ron Popeil, the great kitchen gadget entrepreneur and king of late-night infomercials. It was far and away the most interesting, because he is so effortlessly interesting. Every now and again, this happens to a journalist about once every decade. You turn on the tape recorder. The person you are writing about starts talking. As they talk, you realize, "I have to do nothing else. I just have to go home and transcribe the tape, and it's done." It literally was that way with Ron. He just started talking, and then I talked to his cousin and the guy he worked with and one other guy. I just transcribed the tapes and literally just put blocks of text down, and it was done. It's amazing. Sometimes that happens. It's a miracle when that happens. You never forget it.

ROGER MUDD

Roger Mudd's memoir, The Place To Be: Washington, CBS, and the Glory Days of Television News, *was published by PublicAffairs Books in 2008. It recounts an era of transformational news events: assassinations, the Civil Rights Act, and the Vietnam War; years when Mr. Mudd served as the weekend anchor of the CBS Evening News and co-anchor of NBC Nightly News and moderator of NBC's* Meet the Press. *In a two-part March 2008 interview for* Q & A, *he explains how each network carved a role in the growing broadcast news business. A veteran of many presidential campaigns, he also discusses his pivotal 1979 interview with then presidential candidate Sen. Ted Kennedy, which is frequently cited as contributing to the senator's poor showing during the presidential primaries.*

PART ONE

[My publisher recommended I write about] life at the TV networks when being a television journalist was a profession of honor and when it was a substantive job. [He encouraged me to] write about that great bureau in the sixties and the seventies, the CBS News Washington bureau. I'd never thought about doing it quite that way, confining it to twenty years. There are a couple of chapters about where I came from and how I went from newspapers into radio and then to television, but it stops in 1980. [The twenty] years gave me a start and an end, and a chance to talk about all those marvelous people who made that bureau what it was. It's never been equaled, in my estimation.

[I WAS BITTER ABOUT what happened in 1980 and 1981,] when Walter Cronkite was the longtime anchor. He was the anchor of the news division and negotiated a new contract, which gave him two months off every summer.... Everybody assumed that when Walter retired, I would be his replacement.... Richard Salant, president of CBS News, said, "Well, Mudd, who had been doing the Saturday news, is going to be his regular replacement when he's gone on assignment. In the summertime, Mudd will come to New York and be the regular substitute, so we won't have this one and that one substituting. People get used to Mudd....'' But when the time came, Bill Leonard proposed a joint anchorship with Dan Rather. Dan was very much interested in succeeding Cronkite. Roone Arledge was then head of ABC and they were in a full-court press to hire Dan. The [CBS News] proposal was that we anchor together, and I declined because I thought a dual anchor with Dan would not work out for a lot of reasons. The only way they could keep Rather was to offer him a lot of money and the chance to be the anchor. Rather was offered the job, and I found out about it on the radio.... It was a public humiliation. They tried very hard to keep me, but I thought I really wouldn't feel comfortable staying....

I started as a weekend relief man at the White House.... I would go off on the weekends when [John F.] Kennedy was the president and went to Rhode Island and Newport and Boston.... Then I was assigned to the Hill and I loved it.

[In my book, I said, "Technology improved through the 1950s, of course, but not until 1963, when the *CBS Evening News* with Walter Cronkite expanded to thirty minutes, did the golden age of television news really begin."] ABC was a fairly weak sister during that period. They didn't have a big news department.... It wasn't until Roone Arledge came that they became a force.... NBC, on the other hand, was a distinguished news organization. They had so dominated television during that period with Chet Huntley and David Brinkley, and they were very used to being number one, because CBS was shifting from Doug Edwards to Walter

Cronkite. Huntley-Brinkley dominated the convention coverage. They dominated election night. As a consequence, I think they got a little lazy and the NBC bureau never developed the kind of strong bench or cadre of reporters that CBS did. Cronkite believed that reporters ought to report and gave us all the time that he could afford. And he loved hard news; he loved specific coverage.

[I wrote in my book, "Most of us thought of ourselves 'chosen.' It was as if we had been lifted up by a journalistic deity and dropped down in the middle of the Washington bureau to serve our country by doing God's work."] Those years were unlike any other twenty years, beginning with the Kennedy election and the assassination and Vietnam, and the race riots and the violence, and Lyndon Johnson's election, and Watergate. That era was so fraught with stories…. This marvelous bureau and these talented men and women all came together. One of our producers called it the perfect storm…. We all felt we were so good and knew what we were doing, and knew what our priorities were and knew that we wanted to be accurate and balanced. We were given this opportunity of a twenty-year period, a transition between the peace of the Eisenhower years and the violence of those twenty years…. The coming together of those two decades and those fifty men and women in that one bureau has not happened before or since. I felt that all of us, looking back, when I talk to all those people on the telephone and in recordings, all of them said, "Thank God I was there. Thank God I had the chance to be there during those twenty years."

Eric Sevareid had been a newspaperman and had been one of [Edward R.] Murrow's boys over in Europe during World War II, and came back after the war a hero. A striking-looking, tall man, six-foot four, who looked like a Viking…. He came to the bureau, and his assignment was to do a nightly, two-minute analysis…it was just a little oasis on television. [There was] nothing like it, to have a literate view of the world every night, Monday to Friday. It came at the end of the broadcast and people looked forward to it…. His words were strong, well written, well delivered, and thoughtful…. Today, there's so much competition…and attention being shorter and shorter, and the pie, which used to be cut up into 3 or 4 pieces, is now [in] slivers of 500, and everybody has to make the pie a little sweeter to hold the audience…. The quality of news broadcasting has declined, because of the pressure to hold the audience, because that TV remote can pop off to 500 different places.

THE SELLING OF THE PENTAGON was a really tough 1971 documentary about the $30 million-a-year budget that the Pentagon had for public relations, the selling of armed might as a solution to our problems. You had to have a public that enjoyed and understood the use of arms and tanks, and colonels who would travel around to advocate the use of force when necessary. Richard Salant, our news division president, proposed that we do a broadcast about the use of public funds for public relations campaigns.... It was a tough broadcast and it was not easy to do. It immediately resulted in an explosion of complaints from Capitol Hill, led by the Democrat chairman of the Armed Services Committee, and the chairman of the Interstate and Foreign Commerce Committee. Together, they attacked the broadcast for some of the editing that we did with an interview I had done with Dan Henkin, who was then the assistant secretary for public affairs [in the Department of Defense]. In the course of the editing, in order to make his answers clearer and more succinct, we had taken the answer from one question and combined it with the answer to another question. They attacked us on those grounds. They did not attack the accuracy of the broadcast. They did not attack the accuracy of our interviews or the conclusions that we reached. They attacked the editing; editing is a very difficult process for people to understand, and we were vulnerable.... [Congressional] hearings were held. The committee issued a contempt citation against Frank Stanton, the president of CBS, for his refusal to turn over outtakes from my interviews, my notes, and the citation came out on the House floor.

For the first time in the history of Congressional citations, Harley Staggers [Chairman of the House Committee on Interstate and Foreign Commerce] was shot down; they rejected the contempt citation, [but] it was a very close vote. Had the contempt citation been adopted, it would have been referred to the Justice Department, and then there was the possibility, remote as it might have been, that Frank Stanton would have been prosecuted and sent to jail. Unlikely, but the whole procedure was so shattering, so precedent setting, that CBS was really, really nervous. They debated it on the House floor. I was taken off the story, and I sat in the visitors' gallery while they debated. It was an almost out-of-body experience to hear my name bandied about on the House floor.... The pressure in the editing process is to make the interview interesting and to the point, and you don't want your interviewee to wander. It was standard procedure then, provided you did not distort a person's meaning, to combine two answers to one question, take two answers to a first question and to a follow-up question on the same subject. That was standard procedure. But when we were attacked so violently about that, CBS put out clarifying orders about combining answers to one question, and it was something that people are very careful about now...to be accused of taking me out of context, you can never win that argument. It's very difficult. You can't say I was misquoted, because you heard him say it. But if you can prove that the answers were moved around or were taken out of context, it's a battle you cannot win.

[There is also the story I recount] of Lillian Brown being with Richard Nixon right before he resigned.... Lillian was the premier makeup artist in Washington. She had started with the *Face the Nation* contract, and she had done [makeup for] John Kennedy when he was beginning to run for the presidency. She was also Eric Sevareid's regular makeup artist.... She got a call from the White House, "We want you over here for the Nixon [resignation] speech." She went over to the White House, and when she got there, the Secret Service agent, who knew her, said, "Lillian, President Nixon is not in very good shape." He was then meeting with the leaders of Congress, telling them that he was about to resign and the cameras were over there in the Oval Office setting up for his speech.... She waited in the anteroom near the Oval Office. He left the meeting with the congressional leaders. He came in and he sat down, and she began to apply the makeup, and he began to cry, weeping, and she couldn't keep the makeup on because of the tears; he was just sort of blubbering. Lillian began to panic; here it was, three or four minutes to air, and she couldn't keep the makeup on. It kept streaking. She finally remembered something that had happened the year before at the Christmas party when they were decorating the Christmas tree. Nixon's Irish setter kept bumping into the tree and knocking down the ornaments. So, Lillian said, "...I'll take the dog and lock it up in the bathroom." Before she could get the dog, she looked around, and there's the president himself with the dog. The two of them then go in toward the bathroom and they get the president of the United States and Lillian and the dog in the bathroom. Suddenly, the door behind them closes and locks. There's Lillian, trapped in the bathroom with the dog and the leader of the free world. She tells this story to Nixon just before he goes on the air, and he begins to laugh and finally gets control of himself, and she gets the makeup to stay on. And then he goes on [TV to announce his resignation]....

PART TWO

The idea for the CBS documentary about Edward Kennedy was [that he] was [as] close to being an unelected president as we could have had without ever being elected. CBS said the time had come to do an hour on him [since] his appearances on television had been limited to *Face the Nation* and clips from hearings, but never had he sat down and talked about it. We went to him and said we want to do an hour. We said, "We hope you'll cooperate, but we're going to do it anyway if you don't." But they cooperated happily.... We shot film of the summer and skiing and all that sort of stuff. We sat down and did the interview in two places. We said we wanted to do two interviews, one up at Cape Cod and one in his office. We did the first one up at the Cape and we talked about [the] Chappaquiddick incident, and we talked about his family and it did not go well. The Kennedys are not easy to interview. They don't like to talk about themselves a lot. They want control of the questions.... They don't like surprises, so it was like pulling teeth. The office said, "Because the first interview didn't go very well, we'd like to do a second." They had already agreed to do a second one, so the second one was in his office. We are talking about policy and his life in the Senate, and at one point he had said something about differing with Jimmy Carter's policies and there wasn't much difference between what he was saying and what the president was saying. I said, "So why do you want to be president?" meaning because the differences weren't so great, how would you be different than Carter?

[This piece became known as the "Teddy Documentary,"] and his responses enabled a lot of political writers who had not been critical of Kennedy before, but who really liked Kennedy...to write critical pieces of him, so he got beat up in the press. The Kennedy office explanation for his really hapless answer [on leadership] was that he had not really decided that he was going to run. It was not until well into November that he made his announcement, but everybody knew in Washington that he already made his decision to run…. [The Kennedy office] accused me of asking a lot of personal questions, which I had not asked, and they were trying to trash the interview as being unfair on my part.

The question, "Why do you want to be president?" was simply because he hadn't made up his mind. But, to me, what it meant was that he really hadn't thought about that. He felt that he was a natural and it was his turn, and he had ascended to the nomination without really having gone to the mountain and asked himself the questions that every candidate asks himself, "Who do you want to help, who do you want to hurt, what do you want to do with the country?" None of that came through in the answer…. [I also asked about his then-wife Joan Kennedy.] Here's a United States senator who's about to announce his candidacy for the presidency and given that circumstance, that question was appropriate. The voting public was entitled to know this is a man who campaigns as a great family man who has had difficulty with a marriage, and I thought it was appropriate to ask what the state of his marriage was…. Nobody knew exactly the state of their marriage. They knew that Joan was being treated for alcoholism [in Boston], but they didn't know whether the marriage was over, whether any legal proceedings had been instituted or not, so it was a legitimate question because I didn't know the answer to it.

My relationship [with the Kennedys] was really with Robert Kennedy and Ethel. We lived two or three miles apart out in suburban Virginia, and I had gotten to know them when I was working at the local TV station and Robert Kennedy was the chief counsel of the Senate's rackets committee, headed by John McClellan. We carried those hearings live and Mrs. Kennedy always came down and I got to know her. A few years later, we got an invitation to Hickory Hill, the Kennedy home in McLean, Virginia, where [there was] always lots going on, lots of interesting people, and it was a lot of fun…. I covered Robert's campaign in 1968, through the Ambassador Hotel and the assassination there, but it was inevitable that I would get to know Edward when he came to the Senate. I was covering him as the Capitol Hill correspondent; never was I as close to Edward as I was to Robert. But we were friends in a slightly confrontational way, so [if] they thought because of this past history with Robert Kennedy that it would be an easy hour on Teddy, they should have known better.

[Politicians routinely] dodge a question; it happens all the time, and when I watch interviews now with the candidates, at the end I say, "He didn't answer the question." It's standard procedure. I think the public picks up on that sometimes, but not enough.

In the early sixties, I got involved in the civil rights reporting from Capitol Hill...which revolved around the great filibuster of 1964. Fred Friendly, who was then the CBS News boss, said, "I want to cover that debate. I want to cover it morning, noon, and night, and I want Mudd to do the morning news, the noon news, the 3:30 news, the Cronkite news at 6:30, and the 11:00 news for the local affiliates, and I want him on every other hourly radio newscast." It sounded to me like a flagpole sitting stunt, but he said, "No, no, no. We're serious. This is serious." [Fred Friendly] thought, given the violence that had preceded it from 1962, 1963, and 1964, this was the government's final attempt to come to grips with racial violence and discrimination in the United States. The Kennedy Administration had introduced the bill, but really had not pushed it hard. After [Lyndon] Johnson became president, this was one of major pieces in his legacy, and using the martyred John Kennedy, the bill was introduced in his memory and it had a lot of momentum behind it. Either the bill would be withdrawn because they couldn't break the filibuster or it would pass in a modified way. It would be the twelfth time the Senate of the United States had tried to break a civil rights filibuster.

[The Senate was controlled by the Democrats] and Senator Mike Mansfield [D-Montana] was the majority leader and the leader of the opposition was Senator Richard Russell [D-Georgia]; they were very powerful senators...and the senator from Texas, John Tower, was the only Republican to join the filibuster. That was a very tough crowd and they knew what they were doing. Richard Russell knew the rules inside and out and he knew exactly what to do when he had to do it. The filibuster opened about Easter in 1964, and I was assigned to do it and that's all I did for a better part of three months on the Hill.

[In my book,] I noted the Southerners' belief that my big Eastern liberal employer [CBS News] was run by Jews who wanted nothing so much as to put the South in its place with a tough civil rights bill.... [I got that from] offhanded comments and from Senate staffers who would tease me. The Southern senators were anti-Jewish because they thought that CBS was a liberal network, owned and run by Jewish men and women who were liberal, and particularly motivated to see that this civil rights bill went through because they thought that the way that the South handled the black race was something that America needed to have corrected.

Housing and employment were the two big issues in this [civil rights bill]. Voting [rights] were set aside…. The bill of 1964 was significant in that the power of the South had finally been broken by invoking cloture, [a motion in parliamentary procedure aimed at bringing debate to an end], which ended the filibuster. Filibuster was never used successfully again for civil rights legislation, but it was the first time that there were equal accommodations; education and employment were all part of the Civil Rights Act of 1964…. It was a dramatic day because in Washington there's something special about the day [when] there's a roll call vote. Legislators have to stand up. You can't make any explanation of why. You just have to say yea or nay and it's as clear as the air. The Senate gallery was just absolutely packed, first time this was going to happen. After twelve attempts, they finally broke the filibuster…. Senator Everett Dirksen (R-Illinois) broke it. He was the hero and he got enough Republicans to come along with him.

THE TITLE OF MY book, *The Place to Be*, refers to the Washington bureau of CBS News, [as the place to be if you were a television journalist in the sixties and seventies]. What I want readers to learn from it is how good it used to be and what they are missing now. They are missing a daily, reliable, comprehensive account of what happened in the world during the past twenty-four hours; it's very hard to get that without spending three or four hours in front of the television. Television now is so sliced up into a hundred different pieces, the competition is so intense, and the standards have changed so much that it remains almost impossible to find one place or two or three places, even, that you can go to and count on it being straight, authentic, reliable news.

Misreported Stories

W. JOSEPH CAMPBELL

W. Joseph Campbell was a foreign correspondent for the Associated Press before entering journalism education at American University in Washington, D.C., in 1997. His fifth book, Getting It Wrong: Ten of the Greatest Misreported Stories in American Journalism, *published by University of California Press in 2010, lists ten media-driven myths. The 1898 Spanish-American War, the* War of the Worlds *radio program, and the reporting of Hurricane Katrina are some of the examples he presents. For each media myth he exposes, he describes the real story behind it. He was a guest on* Q & A *on August 1, 2010.*

M Y BOOK *Getting It Wrong* discusses and debunks ten media-driven myths. These are stories about or by the news media that are widely believed and often retold. These are prominent stories about journalism and journalists, but these stories, under scrutiny, dissolve as apocryphal or wildly exaggerated. I characterize them as akin to the junk food of journalism; they are appetizing, appealing, tantalizing, but not terribly nutritious or healthy in the long run.

I WAS TWENTY YEARS in the profession. I broke in at the *Cleveland Plain Dealer*, covering the police beats. I was in Cleveland until 1980 when I joined the Associated Press in Geneva, Switzerland, and also had some fill-in stints, substitute reporting stints in Warsaw, Poland, during the early eighties. [This was] when the solidarity movement was taking hold and posing a direct challenge to Soviet rule, and it was an electric time. I also reported from Abidjan and Cote d'Ivoire in West Africa for the Associated Press and was a national reporter for the *Hartford Current* in Connecticut before entering journalism education.

Here is a summary of the media myths debunked in this book:

Number One: "I'll furnish the war."
That was William Randolph Hearst's famous vow to furnish the war with Spain at the end of the nineteenth century. It's a widely known, widely believed, and widely retold anecdote. It's perhaps the best known anecdote in American journalism, and it's certainly one of the oldest. It's almost certainly untrue. Hearst himself denied having said that.

Number Two: "Fright beyond measure."
The *War of the Worlds* radio dramatization of October 1938 by Orson Welles was great radio entertainment and a very inspired show. Orson Welles was twenty-three years old when he supposedly set off nationwide panic and mass hysteria. But, on close inspection of the available evidence, there's very little to indicate that that was the case, and it was almost certainly apocryphal.

Number Three: Murrow vs. McCarthy, "Timing makes the myth."
Indeed, the famous Edward R. Murrow show, *See It Now,* in March 1954, supposedly stopped Senator Joe McCarthy in his tracks and his communists-in-government witch hunt. But, in reality, Edward R. Murrow was very late to taking on McCarthy. Other journalists had been addressing McCarthy and his bullying ways for months, if not years, before Murrow finally took them on. Murrow was very late, and he acknowledged it, too.

Number Four: The Bay of Pigs, the *New York Times* suppression myth.
The notion that the *New York Times*, under pressure from the Kennedy Administration, spiked or held back or suppressed its reporting about the pending invasion of the Bay of Pigs in April 1961 is [at] the heart of that myth. Upon close inspection, reading what the *New York Times* printed, for one thing, quite clearly shows that they reported an awful lot in a lot

of detail, and there was no evidence at all that Kennedy ever, in advance of publication, asked the *Times* to hold back or suppress any of its pre-invasion stories.

Number Five: Debunking the Cronkite moment.
The Cronkite moment is probably one of American journalism's best known anecdotes, certainly in the twentieth century. Walter Cronkite's famous program in February 1968 supposedly altered American war policy and swung public opinion against the war and forced or prompted Lyndon Johnson to reconsider running for reelection. All of that is untrue.

Number Six: The nuanced myth, bra burning at Atlantic City.
Bra burning at Atlantic City was…one of the first feminist protests of the late sixties. They protested the Miss America Pageant in 1968, which was held at Atlantic City. During the protest, they discarded into a large trash can, which they called the freedom trash can, instruments of what they called torture for women, and that included bras and girdles and high heeled shoes, as well as issues of *Cosmopolitan* and *Playboy* magazines. The notion is that the feminists set fire to their bras and waved them demonstratively over their heads in a fiery public spectacle. My research shows that that's almost certainly untrue, that if the bras and other items were set on fire, it was very briefly in the freedom trash can at this demonstration in '68.

Number Seven: It's all about the media, Watergate's heroic journalists.
The notion is that two intrepid and young investigative reporters for the *Washington Post*, Bob Woodward and Carl Bernstein, through their investigative reporting, brought down Richard Nixon's presidency. It's a very beguiling notion and appealing, delicious story, but it's untrue. Even the *Washington Post* principals, Woodward himself among them, have said over the years that the *Post* did not bring down Richard Nixon. What brought down Nixon was a combination of forces, including federal prosecutors, federal judges, the U.S. Supreme Court, and bipartisan Congressional panels. All of those were at work to bring down Nixon and expose the depth and dimensions and extent of the Watergate scandal. About twenty people went to jail for their criminality, and these

were either associated with Nixon or working for his reelection campaign in 1972.

Number Eight: The fantasy panic. The news media and the crack baby myth.

The "crack baby myth" is supposedly that women who took crack cocaine during pregnancy would give birth to offspring who would be forever dependent. Commentators both on the political left and political right forecast that there would be this bio-underclass of dependent young people who, as they grew up, would essentially be wards of the state, that there was this huge number of people who were forever damaged by the prenatal exposure to crack cocaine. It seems not to have been the case. It's not a good idea to take this stuff during pregnancy, or at any time, but nonetheless, it didn't seem to have that effect. There is no crack baby syndrome as there is a fetal alcohol syndrome.

Number Nine: "She was fighting to the death." Mythmaking in Iraq.

Jessica Lynch was the nineteen-year-old young woman who was caught in an ambush in the early days of the Iraq war. She was taken prisoner and then later rescued by a U.S. commando team early on April 19, 2003. Jessica Lynch's battlefield heroics were reported by the *Washington Post*. These were quite incorrect, quite in error, and the *Post* story about Jessica Lynch fighting to the death in Iraq was untrue and turned out to be almost certainly a case of mistaken identity. It wasn't Jessica Lynch in that unit who was fighting to the death, but another person, a Sergeant Donald Walters.

Number Ten: Hurricane Katrina and the myth of superlative reporting.

The landfall of Hurricane Katrina was in 2005. Supposedly, the news media were aggressive in their reporting and calling attention to the defects in the state, local, and federal response to the hurricane. But in addition, the news media coverage of the extent of the damage and lawlessness that was unleashed by Hurricane Katrina is quite wrong. It was hardly a moment of superlative reporting. The news media got that story quite wrong. Estimates of death tolls that exceeded ten thousand were wrong by an order of magnitude. The fact that widespread looting, pillaging, raping, and murdering were going on in New Orleans in the aftermath of the hurricane, all of that was untrue. It had the effect of really impugning a city and its people in an hour of their most urgent need.

[THE IDEOLOGICAL COMPOSITION REPORTED among national journalists surveyed by Pew in 2008 was 8 percent conservative, 32 percent liberal, and 53 percent moderate.] I would put myself in the moderate category.... The data are interesting because it does point to an imbalance that Pew and others have pointed to in American newsrooms. It does tend to be center-left rather than [in] any other direction. That does tend to lead to a certain element of group-think in American journalism newsrooms. It's a cause for some concern and probably more debate and discussion than it's been given.

A MESSAGE I TRY to get across in the book is that it's not a media-bashing book, but one that's aligned with a fundamental central objective of American journalism, mainstream journalism in this country, and that is trying to get it right. The book does try to set the record straight to the extent that we possibly can. So I think it's aligned with one of the fundamental objectives of American journalism rather than bashing the media. There's a lot of that going on, probably enough of it going on.

[THE CRONKITE MOMENT:] THE Tet Offensive, which was a surprise attack across South Vietnam by North Vietnamese and their Vietcong allies in the South, took the American military and the political establishment in this country by surprise. Walter Cronkite [of CBS] went to Vietnam as the Tet Offensive was winding down and did some on the ground reporting and came back and aired on the twenty-seventh of February 1968, a special report about Vietnam.

A few weeks after that, Lyndon Johnson told the country that he was not going to run again.

Supposedly, Lyndon Johnson was watching the Cronkite show, and when Cronkite intoned his "mired in stalemate" assessment, Johnson supposedly leaned over, snapped off the television set, and said something to the effect of, "If I've lost Cronkite, I've lost middle America," or

"If I've lost Cronkite, I've lost the war," or "If I've lost Cronkite, I've lost the country." There are a lot of versions as to what Johnson supposedly said, and that, in my view, right off the bat, is a tip-off. It's often a marker of a media-driven myth. If you can't get the story straight as to what the president supposedly said in reaction to this, then there's something probably wrong with it. But it doesn't take much research to find out that Lyndon Johnson was not at the White House that night in front of a television set. Lyndon Johnson was in Austin, Texas. He was attending the fifty-first birthday party of Governor John Connally. At the time when Cronkite was editorializing in his conclusion about the U.S. being mired in stalemate, and perhaps negotiations might be thought of as a way to get out of Vietnam, Lyndon Johnson was making remarks on the campus of the University of Texas at Austin about Connally turning fifty-one. He was saying something to the effect of, "Well, John, you've reached the magic number that all politicians shoot for, simple majority, you know, fifty-plus-one." It's not the greatest joke ever told, but Johnson's not sitting in front of the TV set bemoaning his fate and realizing his policy's in tatters; he's making light with an old political ally at a black tie dinner in Austin, Texas. Moreover, Johnson, in the aftermath of the Cronkite show, is out on the stump publicly saying we should recommit to end the war in Vietnam successfully: "Let's bring home a victory." He's saying this on more than one occasion in the aftermath of the Cronkite show. If this was such an epiphany for the president, he really didn't make it very clear that this had changed his mind in his public comments afterwards.

The power of this anecdote lies in the immediate, abrupt, and decisive effect that it supposedly had on Johnson and his thinking about Vietnam, [and] that Cronkite suddenly crystallized for him what was going on in Vietnam. That's just not the case because Johnson is clearly out there in the weeks afterwards saying, "Let's redouble our national efforts, let's recommit to a successful conclusion in the war in Vietnam." He's not saying, "Woe is us. The war is over; we're in bad shape. Cronkite told us, and now we have to leave."

It is one of the most memorable bits of Walter Cronkite's long career, this so-called Cronkite Moment. But it's an interesting thing about media-driven myths, in many cases the principals involved afterwards say that this really didn't have that kind of effect. For a long time, Walter

Cronkite made that same kind of comment. He said this on one occasion, "My comments about Vietnam represented a straw on the back of a crippled camel." He made that kind of remark in his memoirs, which came out in 1995, I believe. Cronkite, only later in his life, began to embrace the notion that it did have a powerful effect, but for the most part, his reaction was no, this is really not that dramatic; this really didn't have that powerful of an effect. But it's one of these neat, tidy, even delicious stories about the news media and their power. That's one of the reasons that it lives on. That it's so compelling and so interesting and demonstrates so vividly the power of the news media is certainly one of the reasons why it has endured for quite a long time and lives on to this day.

It's pretty clear that public sentiment about the war had begun to shift well before the Cronkite Moment, well before Walter Cronkite's editorial comment that he expressed on air. By October of '67, a plurality of Americans had said that sending U.S. troops to Vietnam was a mistake. The Gallup Organization had been asking this question since about 1965 and had been doing so on a regular basis, and by October '67, this plurality emerged and numbers like 47 percent thought it was a mistake. The numbers were pretty close throughout the fall and early winter of 1968, but sentiment had begun to shift well before Cronkite took to the air.

[*The War of the Worlds*:] On the eve of Halloween, October 30, 1938, twenty-three-year-old Orson Welles is a boy wonder who is the head of the Mercury Theatre on the air. He's directing and starring in this weekly hour-long radio program. They had been on the air since the summer of 1938. He and his troupe began the program that night with an adaptation from H.G. Wells's 1898 science fiction thriller, *The War of the Worlds*. H.G. Wells set the story in England [while] Orson Welles set it in the farmland of central New Jersey near a little hamlet called Grover's Mill. Welles made use of simulated newscasts, simulated radio bulletins to propel a sense of urgency, of danger and distress, and did so in a very imaginative way. Supposedly, Americans by the thousands, if not tens of thousands, thought the program was so realistic and so lifelike that they took to the streets and headed for the hills in utter panic, [while] mass hysteria gripped the country that night. Supposedly.

This was great radio entertainment. It's marvelous. It's amazing how seventy-plus years later *War of the Worlds*, the radio dramatization, holds up. I play this for one of my classes almost every year around Halloween time and often students are riveted.

Welles's characterization came many years afterwards in one of the biographies he did with one of his colleagues. But Orson Welles's immediate reaction to the radio show was one of astonishment. How can people really take this seriously? He was perplexed as to how people could have confused this. There were tips and cues embedded in the program that would give people the notion that [this] was [a] radio show, a radio show that was well done. Some of the best research that was done on this in the immediate aftermath indicates that maybe seven million people listened to this, and, of that number, 1.2 million were frightened or scared or upset by the show. That alone is a small minority, and what the person who did the research didn't really operationalize, didn't define, was what he meant by "frightened or scared." It's far from saying a mass panic seized the country that night, and that hysteria reigned across the United States, so most people who heard the show recognized it for what it was, good entertainment.

[At the time,] the FCC, the Federal Communications Commission, is an early entity, it's in its first days as a federal agency, and there was some movement to try to keep radio from doing this kind of thing again, but it proved to be unwieldy, improbable, and difficult to navigate that kind of terrain because those edge into censorship. Newspapers in the aftermath of the *War of the Worlds* seized upon this as a real opportunity to bash radio. Radio was an upstart medium and it had begun to encroach upon traditional print media in terms of its news delivery capability as well as an advertising medium. For newspapers, Orson Welles's broadcast represented a great opportunity to hector, to lecture radio on its responsibilities; that radio was a new medium but it still had a lot to learn and still had a lot to do to grow up. It had to learn how not to mix news with entertainment as newspapers had learned many, many years before, said some of these commentaries in the aftermath of this.

Orson Welles was a prodigy; he was really on a roll. As I say, twenty-three when he did the *War of the Worlds*, and then, three years later, in 1941, he comes out with *Citizen Kane*, which is his masterpiece, and he's only what, twenty-six? He did terrific work. I think *Citizen Kane* is perhaps the best American motion picture ever made. He played Charles Foster Kane, whose character was loosely based on the life and times of William Randolph Hearst. It's pretty clear that Welles meant this to be a jab at Hearst and his people close to him. Hearst tried through his subordinates to get the movie killed, to keep it from ever being shown.

William Randolph Hearst was a media mogul who owned a lot of newspapers, but also was into radio and television. He had an empire in the 1930s, the 1940s. He had begun with the newspaper in San Francisco; later, in the mid 1890s, he bought the *New York Journal* in New York City. That became his flagship newspaper and some of the more illustrious days of Hearst and his aggressive activist journalism were with the *New York Journal* in the run up to, and the aftermath of, the Spanish-American war.

["You furnish the pictures, and I'll furnish the war":] Frederic Remington was the artist whom William Randolph Hearst sent to Cuba to illustrate and draw sketches of the Cuban rebellion that had swept the island by 1897. Remington travels there in the company of Richard Harding Davis, who was becoming the best known, most eminent foreign war correspondent in the United States. This is a real coup for Hearst to send these two eminent individuals to Cuba, and supposedly, Remington found that everything was quiet in Cuba, that there was not going to be a war with the United States. He sent a cable asking Hearst if it would be OK if he returned. In reply, Hearst supposedly said, "Please remain. You furnish the pictures and I'll furnish the war."

Cuba was Spanish-run at the time and Spanish authorities controlled the incoming and outgoing telegraphic traffic. There is no way that they would have allowed a message like that, as inflammatory and meddling as William Randolph Hearst's "furnish the war" message supposedly was. There's no way that those messages would have flown freely from New York to Cuba. There was a war going on anyway, so for Hearst to vow to furnish a war makes no sense on its face. It's illogical. Why would he say that when war was the very reason he sent Remington and Richard Harding Davis to Cuba in the first place? The rebellion was going on, and by early 1897, when Remington was there, most Americans knew that there was a very vicious, ugly conflict going on. It was the forerunner; it gave rise to the Spanish-American War, fifteen months later. But for those and other reasons, it's almost certainly apocryphal.

The sole source for this anecdote was a journalist named James Creelman, who wrote about it in his book of memoirs called *On the Great Highway*, in 1901. Creelman had a reputation for exaggeration, for overstatement, for bluster, for putting himself in the stories, too. He loved to talk about himself as the journalist. He mentions this not in any great detail, but mentions it almost in passing, as an example of the forward-looking kind of journalism that William Randolph Hearst was practicing. He meant this anecdote "furnish the war" as a compliment to Hearst and the activist-oriented journalism that Hearst was practicing at the end of the nineteenth century. That it was anticipatory, forward-looking. It was only years later, particularly in the mid-1930s and early 1940s, did the interpretation get twisted or changed or altered to the malignant interpretation that we know it is today—as an example of Hearst at his worst, a warmonger.

[WATERGATE'S HEROIC REPORTING:] THE broader myth is the one of the heroic journalist; that Woodward and Bernstein brought down Richard Nixon's corrupt presidency. The subsidiary myth is that Woodward and Bernstein, being young guys—their book, *All the President's Men*, came out when they were thirty and thirty-one, respectively—they made journalism look glamorous, they made journalism look sexy. And the movie, *All the President's Men*, which came out in April 1976, solidified that notion, that journalism is a very sexy and entertaining and appealing profession, so thousands and thousands of young people decided to major in journalism programs in colleges and universities across the country. The best research on this topic clearly shows that this is not true, that the surge in enrollments in journalism and mass communication programs at U.S. universities and colleges had begun well before Watergate was underway, well before Woodward and Bernstein became household names.

Richard Nixon would have survived his presidency; he would have served out his second term had it not been for the existence of the Watergate tapes. That's my view. There's no way of knowing this. The Supreme

Court forced Richard Nixon to surrender the tapes that really, clearly showed his culpability, his guilty knowledge, his role in covering up or attempting to cover up the Watergate scandal. Had it not been for those tapes, Nixon would have survived as a wounded president but would not have resigned. It was only because of the existence of those tapes and the Supreme Court's forcing them out, under subpoena by federal special prosecutors, that Richard Nixon finally gave up the office.

In trying to take this apart, to unpack the Watergate story, the heroic journalist myth, it becomes pretty clear that journalists alone couldn't have brought down the presidency of Richard Nixon. It was too vast, too powerful, too much in control, and it had to be a combination of other forces and factors. There were the special prosecutor, federal investigators, grand juries, federal judges, bipartisan congressional panels, and ultimately, the Supreme Court. You needed that to get at the criminality of the Richard Nixon administration.

[MURROW VS. MCCARTHY:] I think that Edward R. Murrow probably would not today hold the prominent position in mainstream American journalism, had it been known that he was privately counseling a Democratic candidate or a Republican candidate for president on the finer points of using television. His résumé padding, a lot of that information is from biographers of Edward R. Murrow. This is not an unknown detail. Yet, the man's aura and his journalism tend to outweigh those deficiencies and those flaws.

By March 1954, most Americans were not waiting around for a white knight like Murrow to say, "Hey, this McCarthy guy, he really poses a toxic threat to the country." By then they knew. McCarthy's favorability ratings had been slowly declining since the end of 1953. Other journalists including a guy named Drew Pearson, who wrote the *Washington Merry-Go-Round* for many, many years…took on Joe McCarthy early, in 1950, right after McCarthy began his communists-in-government witch hunt, claiming that communists had infiltrated high levels of the State Department, of the Army, of the Democratic Party, and so forth. Pearson took him on and revealed McCarthy's claims as being largely hollow. Pearson paid a bit of a price for this because McCarthy—it's hard to even imagine this today—but sixty years ago, McCarthy attacked Drew Pearson in the cloakroom of the Sulgrave Club in Dupont Circle. There was a private dinner that they were both at where they were trading jibes and barbs all night long. At the end of the dinner, McCarthy, the senator, cornered Pearson, the columnist, and versions vary as to what exactly happened. Pearson said that McCarthy tried to knee him in the groin a couple of times. McCarthy admitted to slapping him real hard across the face. Another version was that McCarthy slugged Drew Pearson so hard that it lifted the columnist three feet into the air. Richard Nixon, then a senator, was also at the same party, intervened and broke up this confrontation. But it was emblematic of the difficulties and of the threats that McCarthy posed, and would follow through on them with journalists.

MURROW OFFERED ON HIS show, right at the outset, to give McCarthy ample time to respond to Murrow's allegations, and McCarthy took him up on it. About three or four weeks later, in April 1954, McCarthy goes on the air and does a very bad job, really a terrible job of trying to defend and explain himself.... His attacks on Murrow did Joe McCarthy no good, and by the time he was on the air in April '54, his favorability ratings were in decline and his career was in jeopardy. The Senate was about to begin investigative hearings about McCarthy, charges that had been raised by the Army that he had sought special treatment for one of his former aides on his sub-committee. Those charges were the centerpiece of a succession of hearings in the summer of 1954 and wound up leading to McCarthy being censured by the U.S. Senate in his political decline and eclipse. Three years later, he was dead at age forty-eight.

Murrow was very late to taking on McCarthy. The toxic threat that McCarthy posed to the United States was well demonstrated long before Edward R. Murrow's program. Interestingly, Murrow himself said that he really did not want credit for taking down McCarthy. Fred Friendly, who was mentioned earlier, Murrow's producer, also said as much. It wasn't the Murrow show that took down McCarthy, it was the Army-McCarthy hearings in the summer of 1954. The myth started pretty quickly. It was seeded very early on in a magazine called *Telecasting Broadcasting* which... extolled Murrow for his taking on McCarthy and being very courageous about it. At the time, television was making its clear entry into American households, into American living rooms. In 1954, it passed the threshold of 50 percent penetration, in other words, 50 percent of American house-holds now had television. So television needed a defining figure. It needed a white knight. It needed someone like Edward R. Murrow and it needed a defining moment. That defining moment became the confrontation that Murrow had in March of 1954 taking down Joe McCarthy. Also, it's very well timed. Murrow didn't plan it this way, but the Army's charges against McCarthy took hold and were announced a couple of days after his program. So this coincidental great timing helped place Murrow at the center of this unraveling of Joe McCarthy, but he really was a subor-dinate player.

JOURNALISM IS ABSOLUTELY BETTER off today. The more choices and the more variety, the more options that are out there the better, the better for American journalism, the better for American democracy, the better for the American public. Back in the day when there was the Fairness Doctrine and just three major networks, American journalism was not well served by that. The media-driven myths often invoke the "golden age fallacy," a look back to say, "There really was a time when American journalism was respected, that journalists did great work, that they told truth to power and their work had an effect." The Murrow-McCarthy confrontation, just as Watergate, just as the Cronkite Moment, all of those, fall victim to the golden age fallacy....

THE WAY TO COMBAT media-driven myths is to attack them directly and to point out how flawed they are. There's a school of thinking that says that when you do that, you repeat the essence of the myth, you actu-ally perpetuate the myth in trying to debunk it. That's a risk worth run-ning in order to try to combat these. I can't think of any other way to take them on and to debunk them. I think the weight of the evidence is the best friend that the debunker has.

WARREN BROWN

Warren Brown has written the "Real Wheels" column for the Washington Post *for over thirty years, traveling the world to test drive cars for his readers. A recipient of two kidney transplants, he undergoes dialysis wherever he travels. He appeared on Q & A on September 19, 2010, for a wide-ranging interview that covered his childhood in a still segregated New Orleans and his Catholic school education there, as well as the regulatory, safety, and production history of the automobile industry.*

[I GOT STARTED REVIEWING automobiles] when…a very wise colleague at the *Washington Post* told me that if I wanted to make it at the *Post*, I had to develop a franchise, find something that no one else was doing, and do it and live with it—try to love it if I could. So that's what I did. When I was on the national desk at the *Post*, I petitioned to join the business staff, much to the chagrin of my national desk editors, who thought that I was throwing away my career by doing that. But I also was lucky enough to have a friendship with Frank Swoboda, who thought I was crazy, but he gave me space to be crazy. And so that helped.

I've always been interested in automobiles. I grew up in New Orleans in the late 1940s and fifties and sixties, when I had to sit at the back of the bus—certainly in the fifties—and that always bothered me. It always bothered my father, boarding the bus and having to sit behind a sign saying "No Colored Beyond This Point." Freedom came to my parents and black neighbors who bought their own cars. That way, they could not only sit up front, but they could drive the things, and that, to me, was power; that, to me, was freedom.

Cars have always meant more to me than the sum of their parts. They were a way to escape or see other worlds. They were also a way for me to see my parents in charge of something rather than sitting behind a sign.

I'll tell you an interesting story about how our parents reared us. We went to Catholic schools in New Orleans—mostly Josephite and Blessed Sacrament schools in New Orleans. I came home from St. Augustine High School one day complaining to my father, who was a scientist and a researcher for the National Science Foundation, and also a teacher in New Orleans public schools, that one of my priests was a racist. This happened to be a priest who taught me geometry and chemistry. My father didn't say anything. He just told me to get my chemistry and my geometry books, and he said, "Well, show me where you are in these books." I showed him. In the chemistry book, he wanted me to work some formula. I couldn't do it. He didn't say anything. He said, "Show me where you are in geometry." I showed him and I wasn't up to snuff in geometry. He looked at me and he said, "The priest might be a racist, but you're stupid, and as long as you're stupid, it doesn't matter if he's a racist. So don't ever come home and tell me that he's a racist unless you know how to do the work."

That was a lesson that has just basically stuck with me. That sort of sums up the entire way my parents dealt with race in New Orleans. It was, "Yeah, it exists, but it's no excuse. We don't care if somebody calls you the N-word and any of this kind of crap if you don't know what you're doing, or if you're behaving improperly, or if you aren't trying your best." And so, that's how we were reared. Some people might call that bourgeois or close-eyed. I called it a blessing, because it's how we reared our children as well, not to base your life on what someone else thinks of you, but to base your life on what you think of yourself and what you want for yourself and what you are doing for other people as well.

After that, I never came home and told him that somebody was a racist; or, if I had a complaint, I made sure that I had researched the complaint thoroughly before bringing it to him. The best defense was to know what the hell you're talking about before you start talking about it in his house. And I studied, that's what I did. I stopped worrying about what I thought the priest thought of me or didn't think of me, and I started trying to figure out what he was actually trying to teach me in the academic subject matter at hand.

It's amazing how this church has changed. We used to live in the Lower Ninth Ward. There was a church there, St. Mary's Catholic Church. We could attend that church, but normally, by tradition, had to stand in the back of the church, behind the whites. The whites would have communion first. I always thought that was wrong. I was a cheeky little fellow, and so I would go up to communion with the whites. Sometimes, the priest wouldn't serve me communion until the whites were served. My late brother Daniel Thomas Brown, Jr. would clunk me in the back of the head at the mass, saying, "You trying to get us killed? You trying to get us in trouble?"

NORMALLY, TO AVOID THAT, we went to black Catholic churches, which were our true parish churches, now defunct in many cases. Holy Redeemer Catholic Church, just right outside of the French Quarter, we would go there. Those were black Catholic churches, mostly run by Josephite priests and Holy Ghost nuns, Blessed Sacrament nuns, Redemptorists, and people like that.

I don't mean this as a putdown. Understandably, a lot of blacks who were baptized Catholic and who grew up with me, left the Catholic Church, even people in my own family. I never did and married a woman who never did, because we never really identified the teachings of the Church with the way some people practice the teachings. We were able to separate that. I had good training. I remember once—I think it was on a Good Friday, as a matter of fact, at Holy Redeemer, I think the nun was a Sister Mary Vincent. We had gone to morning mass before going back to class. We were following her out of the church in our Holy Redeemer uniforms, and white kids in the park across the street, which was a whites-only park, started calling Sister Vincent a "nigger-lover." Seriously! We took offense to that and several of our number charged across the street and got into fisticuffs. It was a kind of knockdown thing.

We thought we were heroes. We got to the classroom and she told us how disappointed in us she was, that we had learned none of the teachings of the Church, nothing about forgiveness, nothing about turning the other cheek, that we behaved as hooligans first and Catholics second, and she would have none of that.

THE IMPACT OF RACE was that my siblings and I—I had six brothers and sisters; we're now a sibling group of four—could not have had better parents. I think about this every day. We were lucky in our choice of parents.

I had a father who had every reason to be an angry black man. He fought in World War II, was a U.S. Army medic; came home, tried to get into medical school—Tulane University, LSU, those schools down there then were not accepting blacks in their classrooms. He went to Xavier University—pre-med, what have you. Then Mother Katharine Drexel, later St. Katharine Drexel, took him under her wing. I recall him telling me what she told him, that if he couldn't become a doctor now, maybe he could train future doctors. He took that to heart. He taught science in Catholic schools in Louisiana and then he taught science for a long time in the black New Orleans public schools. The funny thing is that, even now, even when I'm overseas, I may wind up in somebody's pharmacy in Belgium or France and see a black person behind the counter, and I wonder if they came from the United States. On one or two occasions, in France, they had actually come from the United States, and I said, "Well, where'd you grow up?" He said, "In New Orleans." And I said, "Do you know a Daniel Thomas Brown, Sr.?" And he said, "Yes, he taught me in…senior high school down in New Orleans." It's just the greatest amount of pride that he chose not to hate. He chose to take Mother Katharine Drexel's guidance and he did train the black doctors and pharmacists of the future. That's a very special thing to me.

I BRING ALL OF my historical baggage to my coverage. People say, "Why are you so willing to give General Motors and Ford a break?" It's personal, but I have no problem admitting it. I'm willing to give GM and Ford a break because they were the companies that gave my people a break. It is justifiable to have an argument to say that we would not have a black middle class had we not had General Motors, Ford, and Chrysler. You go to Detroit today, to the old automotive neighborhoods. The difference in those neighborhoods [now,] and say, [the] 1950s, 1960s, is that the blacks who were working in the plants then, they did have a dream. They wanted their kids to run the plants. They wanted their kids to design the cars and to be lawyers and so forth and so on. And that's what their kids became. One of our chief foreign correspondents at the *Washington Post* is a guy who grew up in a UAW family. So, did I have affection for those companies? Yes. Now, does that affection translate to turning a blind eye to their failings? No. As a matter of fact, I think I was probably more harsh on them for their failings than people who fancy themselves as being so-called objective and not having any feelings for those companies, because, to me, they were throwing away our legacy— not only our legacy as black Americans, but our legacy as Americans, period.

The idea that you would throw away manufacturing superiority because you're just chasing bucks, and you don't really care what you're producing, the idea that you would throw away leadership and innovation, infuriated me. I was angry with those companies for a long time, but at the same time, I was also willing give them a break once I was convinced, as I became convinced, that you had people who actually cared about turning out top products.

I'VE HAD TWO KIDNEY transplants—one from my wife, and one from a very good friend, a wonderful colleague of mine, Martha McNeil Hamilton. Both transplants have now gone kaput, as sometimes happens with transplants. Martha's is still functioning in me, but not well enough to keep me off of dialysis, and that's going on about maybe nine to ten years. What it's taught me is that you've got to try to take advantage of life now. You'd better try to figure out what's important now. Would I have learned this lesson another way, without going through all of the pain and suffering of end-stage renal disease? Yes, probably. But I don't regret it, not one bit.

My first operation was in 1998, and that was my wife Mary Anne's transplant gift to me. And the second one was in 2001, which was from Martha Hamilton, who's one of the funniest, but at the same time, sternest, people you'll ever meet. She just came up to me—we worked together for a long time. We were friends—and she says, "Look, dummy, you need another kidney, right?" And I said, "Yes." And she says, "Well, I have two. You can have one." It went on like that. That's typically Martha. We did a book, *Black & White & Red All Over,* together, in 2001, [which came out in 2002] at the behest of the *Washington Post,* as a matter of fact.

The kidney stopped functioning as well as it should have, and that, of course, can create other problems. To avoid those other problems, we chose to go back on dialysis.... I don't know if I'm going to have another transplant. My youngest daughter, Kafi, who's a medical reporter for New York1, wants to give me her kidney. I'm now sixty-two years old. I'm doing quite well on dialysis this time around. I don't know if I want to put another life of someone I love [in danger]...when I'm actually doing OK.

I go three days a week for dialysis, but it's manageable. The only thing that going to dialysis has meant for me is that I had to do something that Martha, and my wife Mary Anne, and Louann Hamilton, who's a friend of mine out in California, have always criticized me for not doing, which is planning...and so the only thing this disease has done is make me grow up. I have an assistant, Ria Manglapus, who just basically shakes her head because I never really tell her anything. She just kind of figures it out. So now I've begun to tell people things. It makes life easier for me, for them, for everyone else.

[My wife Mary Anne is] a funny woman. She was very, very happy, as a matter of fact, insistent, to give me her kidney regardless of the pain, medical inconvenience, or anything it would cost her. It didn't cross her mind. She loves me, here's my kidney, take it. The impact was on my losing [her] kidney. I never saw anyone so devastated. She was absolutely devastated that her transplant only lasted for two years or so. She was depressed for a long time. The hardest time in my life was coming home and telling Mary Anne that I was losing her kidney because I knew how devastating that would be to her, and it was. That told me a lot about her....

Martha is one of God's children, really, truly. Martha and I were working together for at least a couple years after she gave me her kidney. It was like having a second wife in the office. I'd go out to lunch, "What are you going to eat? What are you going to drink?" And, "You can't have any of that because you have part of me in you." And, honestly, I took that seriously. When somebody gives you, physically, a part of themselves like that...the recipient has a moral obligation to do everything in his or her power to take care of that gift.

AND SO THAT WAS another part of helping me to grow up, understanding not only that Mary Anne, not only that Martha, gave me a physical part of themselves, they gave me something else of themselves, and I owe them. And it's not "owe" as in a dunning note. It's owe as in, I have to return that gift of love with how I behave and how I take care of myself.

So, to people who are receiving the gift of a transplant, the one thing I wish they would understand is that it is far different from receiving a car part. It's not like changing a filter. You are receiving a part of a life, be that life now snuffed out and you're getting a cadaver transplant, or ours, which is a living transplant. You're receiving a part of a life. As a recipient, you have to honor those people with how you live. That's very real to me.

The question that is frequently asked of me—I was kind of a poster child for kidney transplants—is, "Are you cured?" My answer is, no, you're not cured. If you read the Bible, you remember that, like Lazarus, you eventually die, and so will I. And so the question is, what happens after the transplant doesn't work out? Do you hang your head and feel bad about it? Or how do you think about it? And how I think about it, and what I want to write about, is that you have to look at every moment, particularly every gift of love, as an ultimate gift.

I've had two major gifts of love. It extended my life and it's extending my life now. The question is, what do you do with the extension? How do you use the extension to make a difference? If it's just an extension and you don't make a difference, then what value is the extension?

JOHN F. BURNS

As Chief Foreign Correspondent for the New York Times, *John F. Burns has had a front row seat to the world. Twice a winner of the Pulitzer Prize for International Reporting, his assignments have included South Africa during apartheid, the Soviet Union through the Cold War, and China under Mao Zedong, where he was arrested and deported as a spy, a charge he refutes. Now based in London, Mr. Burns continues to cover Iraq and Afghanistan and explains the security details involved with setting up the Baghdad bureau during the war. John Burns appeared on* Q & A *on December 5, 2010, while the series was on location in London. We begin by asking if he plans to write a book.*

I CAME BACK TO London a couple of years ago…after quite a few years at the Iraqi and Afghanistan wars, and I really didn't relish the idea of the solitude of writing a book. I would have told you when I was in Iraq and Afghanistan that I was relishing the assignment. I was. I loved every minute of it. I hated leaving. What I hadn't anticipated was the difficulty of readjustment. Partly, it's coming off of a very big story; partly, it's the loss of the camaraderie, exhilaration; but partly, I think, too, it has to do with the fact that you've been in a place which is beyond, in some respects, the consciousness or imaginings of people, notwithstanding television and everything else.

Probably, I'm talking now about the feelings as [having] receded, as I have come to be exhilarated by this assignment here, which has turned out to be somewhat against the odds, one of the more important assignments the *New York Times* has. We generate an enormous amount of news from London. It's probably normal when you come back from an extraordinary experience like [Iraq and Afghanistan] to want a period of reflection, and that's what I had when I came back from that. Hardly a day goes by without an agent or publisher coming to me and saying, "Write a book." So, I'm going to have to do it. One of our editors said to me once, "You will never really be taken seriously as a writer unless you do a book." I think I do have a story to tell, and I think I have to tell it. I think if I want to be able to continue to belong to a good golf club in my retirement, when it comes, I'm going to have to.

I already know the subtitle of the book, which would be something that the Iraqi information minister under Saddam, Muhammad Saeed al-Sahhaf, known in the United States as "Baghdad Bob," known here in England as "Comical Ali," to separate him from "Chemical Ali" [once said to me]. He was a rather comical fellow with Coke bottle specs. When American troops arrived at the heart of Baghdad on the seventh of April of 2003, we saw Baghdad Bob, Comical Ali, at a news conference on the mezzanine roof of the Palestine Hotel, which gave us a view to Saddam's palace....He was standing with his back to the palace, which was eight hundred or one thousand yards behind him across the river. He told us that the American army had been defeated at the gates of Baghdad and was in retreat and tens of thousands of American soldiers had been killed. At this very moment, over his shoulder, there were troops of the Third Infantry Division of the United States Army who were bootless, dangling their feet off a pier in what became known as the Green Zone, on the grounds of the Republican Palace, cooling their feet. I said to him, "Mr. Minister, I think if you look over your shoulder, you would see that the United States Army, far from being defeated at the gates of Baghdad, has actually captured the heart of Saddam Hussein's power." Unblinking, and certainly without any kind of glance over his shoulder, he looked at me and said, "I'm here to tell you, you are too far from reality."

My book would be about living, for a very long time, beyond the bounds of the common Western experience—China under Mao, the Soviet Union at the depths of the Cold War, North Korea, Afghanistan, Iraq, and the extraordinary people that you meet, the extraordinary evil that you encounter, but also the inspiriting goodness in the human soul, which is rather the larger theme for me. I'm not particularly religious. I hope I'm not particularly self-righteous, but that would be a very major theme for me...how in the midst of darkness there is always light.

[I was in China] in the first years working for a Canadian newspaper, the *Globe and Mail*, from 1971 to 1975, which was more or less the last five years of Mao Zedong's life. It was also the mid to late part of what was known as the Cultural Revolution, the Great Chaos, which Mao occasioned by trying to turn Chinese society upside down. Then I went back to China when they began to open to the world in the 1980s, an assignment which ended with my imprisonment for spying, of which I hasten to say, I was not guilty, and which the Chinese ultimately themselves...acknowledged two or three years later. [I was in the] the Soviet Union between those two [assignments]. I'm inclined to say [it was] during the time of Leonid Brezhnev, except that I felt that I had gotten season tickets to funerals in those days when we had three Soviet leaders in my time there. I was in South Africa [during] the depths of apartheid. I was extraordinarily lucky in my assignments; I didn't set out to be a foreign correspondent and I certainly didn't set out to have these assignments. I just felt like I had a kind of an angel on my shoulder that carried me to these places at times of particular interest, and there was somebody else who was prepared to pay me for it. You've often heard it said, [and] for me it's actually true, if I were a wealthy man, which I'm not, I would have done with my professional life exactly what I have done.

I have to say I'm apprehensive about Iraq.... I've always felt and I think the recent indications strongly support this, that as the American military presence diminishes...that we would see a resurgence of violence and possibly even a renaissance of civil war there because none of the fundamental problems have been solved. The problems that have occasioned all the troubles that have enveloped the United States and its allies in Iraq and the Iraqi people since 2003, all those problems remain. There has been no fundamental political reconciliation in Iraq, and I've felt from the time when I was there and since, that the keeper of the peace to the extent that it has been peace...has been the United States, which, for reasons that are not far to seek, is coming home. I think that's irreversible. But I don't think that what the United States will leave behind in

Iraq is likely to prove stable. We have to open our minds to the possibility that much of it will be washed away. There could be an onset of something like a civil war, perhaps not immediately. It might take a year or two or three. If I had to put my money on a likely outcome, it would be that peace in Iraq, and it might be a very harsh peace, is likely ultimately to be imposed once again by autocracy. We just have to hope that if that does happen, the new ruler, the new dictator, will be a lot more benign than was Saddam Hussein.

[MY FATHER, BORN IN South Africa, was in the Royal Air Force for forty years and once commanded sixty thousand men....] I'm sure my harshest critics would say that the impact of [my military family background] is an attempt to see both the best and the worst of the West, particularly the American military performance in these wars. Critics would say, "He would say that, wouldn't he, because his father was ultimately a quite senior officer in the British armed forces?" He became a one-star general at the height of the Cold War. It was that which gave me my first encounter with Americans, as it happens, playing golf with them. One of the air bases [my father] was responsible for in Germany had a golf course, and [we were] on the fourteenth fairway and passed this grassy dome surrounded by concentric rings of razor wire and defended by these curious looking characters in army camouflage, and he said, "You know who they are?" I didn't know who they were, and he said, "Those are Americans," something for which he probably could have been court marshaled. He said to me, "That's where we keep the nuclear weapons that we would carry to war in British aircraft if there was a war with the Soviet Union." ...So that was my first sighting of Americans. I was fourteen years old, and for reasons I've pondered ever since, because my father's been gone now for twenty years, he said to me, "Those are the people that keep the peace in the world."

I'M THINKING NOW FROM what I've learned about some of the internal conflicts in which he was engaged, the reason he said that was that, in the aftermath of the Second World War, and still vestigially, to some extent, there was a certain amount of unease in Britain and in the British military about what some people regarded as the usurpation of power in the world by the United States. Britain went from being the imperial power of the late nineteenth and early twentieth century…to being a power which, Prime Minister David Cameron put it to me, "we punch above our weight in the world because of our special relationship with the United States." So, the British–U.S. relationship changed substantially, and I think that the 1950s were a period of some unease. It's a little known fact that on D-Day, Britain and its Commonwealth partners, Australia and Canada principally, and New Zealand, landed as many troops on the beaches of Normandy as did the United States. That was probably the last moment, and the last moment in the Second World War, at which there was that kind of equivalence…. [My father] recognized he felt a slight discomfort with the unease that some British officers had about American power… I would confess out of all this that I came to America and I came to my encounters with the American military with a basically positive disposition. I still do believe that what my father said that day on that golf course in Germany is correct—that in a turbulent world, it is America more than any other power overwhelmingly that keeps the peace in the world.

MY WIFE WAS IN Afghanistan and Iraq as the manager of the *New York Times* bureau in Iraq when I was the bureau chief [and remained there after I left…]. She is in a position similar to me; she doesn't go to war. She doesn't embed, but she is living in and working in very dangerous places. Now that I have been back from those places for some time, I understand much better what it is like for those hundreds of thousands of American families, British families who have their loved ones at war. You keep your fingers crossed…. As my wife, she accompanied me for thirty years or so to far flung assignments and she always had the job, in effect, not just of raising our children, but also helping to run the operations of the *New York Times*. It wasn't called a job, but it was. That became formalized with these wars. She left for Pakistan, and later Afghanistan, within three weeks of 9/11, and she's never really come back. She comes back on leave. She, too, is now in her sixties. To say she loves it, how could anybody love war? But, she finds it exhilarating, like any woman of her age; she finds it very engaging to be needed, to be able to do something useful.

[THE *NEW YORK TIMES* had about a hundred people involved in the Baghdad bureau when I was bureau chief in 2007.] There's a kind of critical mass that you need if you're going to operate effectively at all. We have to provide our own security, and that accounts for fifty or sixty of those hundred people. In addition, this is another kind of bravery on the part of the *New York Times* and the people who make the decisions: foreign coverage by American newspapers and American television networks has shrunk considerably. It was already shrinking before the recession; it has shrunk further. The *New York Times* has had financial battles to fight, as have all newspapers in America, because of the recession, but also because of the rise of the Internet. I think we are going to prevail in this, but it would have been understandable if the people who make these decisions had decided that we could no longer afford to spend that kind of money in covering these wars. They didn't. They committed themselves to continuing to give full spectrum coverage to these wars. And we will. America is not out of Iraq.... There's going to be a huge American interest there for some time, and our editors have made it plain that we will continue to be there as long as there is an American interest there.

[WHEN I WAS IN China, back in the seventies and eighties, I did not think they would own a trillion dollars of the American debt.] I hadn't been back in China since the day that they put me into a paddy wagon from the Peking Central Prison, in 1986, and drove me to the airport literally in shackles, deporting me for the alleged spying incident. I have watched with wonderment what has happened in China. They've invited me back many times, it just hasn't worked out. I'm not avoiding going back to China; I have some apprehension because it's a bit glib. For the people of China, there's no doubt that this extraordinary accretion of wealth and power over the last thirty years [would happen].... It's not a surprise [because] the Chinese people, as you could see during the Cultural Revolution, have always had an extraordinary natural capability and resilience. These were people who, given their chance, were always going to rebuild China to something like the greatness that it had when it went into decline in the late 1830s [and into] the nineteenth century.

IF THERE'S A SORT of apprehension, it's because the China I first saw forty years ago was a China which, communism notwithstanding, had changed very, very little in the previous 150 years. I could get on a bicycle and cycle into traditional China in three minutes. That was an enchanting place, it was an enchanting kingdom; I loved it. I came to think during my second assignment in the 1980s, when the door was open to foreign investment, that the China that loved Mao Zedong was, for a foreigner living in China, a somewhat more agreeable place than a China that worships the dollar. Of course, there's no argument, the Chinese people are vastly better off than they were. Witness the fact that they can now afford to buy one trillion dollars of American debt. They're changing the entire configuration of the world we live in, and that's very good for the people of China. It's in many respects good for us, but in some respects, inhibiting. It's going to present us with all manner of problems, for our children's generation certainly. But I'm speaking only about the experience as a visitor. I think I will have a strong nostalgia for the China of my youth.

AS A GUERILLA LEADER, I would give Mao Zedong a grade of probably ten out of ten. Mao Zedong wrote his own epitaph really. On the first of October, 1949, this was the moment when the communists took control of all of Mainland China from Chiang Kai-shek's nationalists and he ascended the Gate of Heavenly Peace in Tiananmen Square and said something that will resonate forever in Chinese history. He said that after centuries of oppression and humiliation, the Chinese people have stood up. That had an enormously motivating power for the people of China and, of course, in their enthusiasm, they endowed, or allowed to be invested in Mao Zedong, absolute power. As always happens, that power was corrupted and corrupted terminally. By some estimates, ten million people died during the Cultural Revolution. More than that died during the Great Leap Forward that occurred some ten years earlier than that. An awful lot of people in China died as a result of the dictatorship imposed by Mao Zedong.... China is in a very conflicted state in its views of Mao Zedong. They have looked pretty honestly and openly at the disasters that were brought upon the country by Mao, but they've also recognized that 1949 marked a historic turning point of enormous importance. I find him fascinating enough a figure that at my home, to this day, in my living room, I have a rather wonderful porcelain bust of Mao Zedong acquired during the Cultural Revolution. Underneath it on the little wooden stand is his Little Red Book. Remember how the millions of Chinese walked through the streets waving this Little Red Book? The Little Red Book is actually quite a valuable little document partly because it's a kind of boiled down, synopsized version of Chinese philosophy through the ages. Confucius, Sun Tzu the military strategist, and some of the teachings in that Little Red Book I have found very useful in getting out of or avoiding getting into trouble of various kinds. One of them is his doctrine on guerilla warfare. I told my children about this when they were almost knee high to a grasshopper, having to do with disputes at school. Doctrine number one: don't engage the enemy unless victory is certain; number two: don't engage the enemy unless victory is essential to your cause. Now, if you apply those two provisos to many incidents in life where there's a potential for conflict, it turns out that you can avoid about 80 percent of them. First of all, because if you look realistically at it, in potential conflicts with people who employ you, potential conflicts with difficult officials in faraway countries, it's safe to assume that you're not going to win. If you're not going to win, don't engage. Now some people would say that this is a formula for ducking problems. I think it's a formula for at least a modest degree of success in life.

THERE ARE THREE OF us in our family. My son [who is twenty-eight years old now, but was born premature]. I'm another; my wife is a third. [We are] the beneficiaries of high technology American medicine. I don't want to be maudlin or melodramatic about it, but I think all three of us would not be walking around now if it wasn't for that.... [I spent a year at Sloan Kettering Hospital in New York for lymphoma treatment,] and it took them a year to turn me around and push me back out on the street. ...[Great Britain] has the system of socialized medical care, which is extremely expensive. The budget of the United Kingdom government is about £700 billion a year. That's in the region of a trillion American dollars. Of that £700 billion, something like £105 billion is spent on the National Health Service, and that figure has more or less tripled in the last ten or thirteen years. It's become a huge financial burden. Mr. Cameron, who as the present prime minister, is in the process of radically reducing government expenditures "ring fenced" [or, grandfathered,] as they say, the National Health Service budget. This means that while he's going to cut all other departments by an average of 20 percent, the health budget will not be cut. Why did he do that? He did that because, in 1948, a reformist labor government after the Second World War introduced the National Health Service in the face of fierce opposition from the Conservative Party and fierce opposition from the medical profession. It is now the jewel in the crown of this kingdom. No political party that came to be seen as likely to destroy or undermine the National Health Service could possibly survive. That reflects the lived experiences of the National Health Service. There are many things wrong with it including long waiting lists, including occasional denial of lifesaving drugs, and so forth, on the basis of cost. But there are many things right with it; principally, what they call medical care free at the point of delivery. When you go to a clinic or a hospital here, nobody asks about your ability to pay. You may get varying levels of treatment. The Royal Marsden is one of the best in cancer hospitals in the world, with excellent treatment. If you get cancer somewhere else in this kingdom, in more remote places, your chances of survival are going to be proportionally reduced. That's also true under the American system of medical care. So I've ended up conflicted.... But I said to [Joe] Lelyveld, [former executive editor of the *New York Times,*] I come to America, to this high technology system of medicine, which saved my life, and I see a New York City police officer weeping at patients' meetings because of the cost. And in my native country, which couldn't give me this kind of cancer care, nobody is going to ruin his family as he descends to the end of life through cancer or any other chronic disease.... And Joe said, "I don't think you need to puzzle too hard over that. I would see it as the United Kingdom has the kind of medical system I want from my country. The United States has the kind of medical system I'd want for my family." That's more or less how I keep saying about this, but coming back here after forty years away, I'd have to say that if I were to list the things about [England] that I find most admirable, the National Health Service would be right at the top and the BBC would be not far behind it.

[THE IRAQ AND AFGHANISTAN wars have been my most exhilarating assignment] because they pose the essential questions of life in its darkest form; because they bore so heavily on the interest of the United States and of my newspaper. In terms of sheer fun, exhilaration, I would say China during the Cultural Revolution. I used to say to colleagues of mine who were foreign correspondents for the *New York Times* and were moving from very desirable assignments to ones that they thought were less desirable, "There is no such thing as a bad foreign assignment for the *New York Times*...." To be a foreign correspondent of the *New York Times*...is to have a front row and very glorious seat. I've had an enormous amount of fun in my life. I've had an ongoing paid education. Had I won the lottery when I was twenty-five, I would have wished to do exactly what I've done. I can't think of anything else I would've been well suited for.

My father...persuaded me not to go into the Royal Air Force as a pilot, which had been my ambition.... Many, many years later, again on a golf course...he said, "When I persuaded you not to do that, I wasn't really thinking so much of your welfare." I said, "Well, what were you thinking of?" He said, "I was thinking of the welfare of the Royal Air Force. I had come to the conclusion by the time that you were thirteen or fourteen that you would have made the worst officer that the Royal Air Force ever had." He said, "I was saving myself from embarrassment." So, that was a turn well taken. I kind of fell backwards into this business and wouldn't change a day of it.

CHRISTOPHER HITCHENS

British-born writer and social commentator Christopher Hitchens made his first appearance on C-SPAN in 1983. His final appearance on television was an interview at his Washington, D.C., apartment on C-SPAN's Q & A *on January 23, 2011, when he reflected on his career and spoke about his battle with esophageal cancer, his various treatment regimens, and dying. He died from complications of the disease on December 15, 2011. A contributing editor to* Vanity Fair *and the* Atlantic Monthly, *Hitchens authored several books, including* God Is Not Great: How Religion Poisons Everything, *and his memoir,* Hitch-22.

I HAVE A TUMOR in my esophagus which has metastasized and it has spread to my lymph nodes and, I'm afraid they're not completely sure, to part of my lung. It's at stage four, and the thing to note about stage four, is that there is no stage five, so it concentrates the mind a bit. I have some wonderful oncologists working with me, and we're on the verge of a whole number of new treatments, some which may apply to me. The chemotherapy is holding it at bay. I have to practice staying alive and preparing to die at the same time, which, as my memoir says, is actually what one has to do all the time. You're never more than a breath away, but it's a bit more vivid to me now: doctors in the morning and lawyers in the afternoon.

I was wondering whether I wanted to [write about my illness in *Vanity Fair*] or not. I didn't want to make a parade of my condition, but I was very intelligently pressed to do it by my editor, Graydon Carter, of

Vanity Fair. I tried to do it in such a way as [that] it wasn't a parade of my feelings or some yellow-ribbon-type journalism. I've been told that some people have been comforted by it a bit, or identified with it to some degree. If you have a lemon, make lemonade, would be the other explanation. It's better than staring at the wall. It is a great subject. Everyone has to do this at one point or another: either survive or die off. It's one thing one is certainly born to do. As an extension of the memoir I published when I was hit with it, I thought I should keep up the narrative because this is very much a part of my life. Because of these experimental treatments, I've had my genome sequenced, for example. I'm very unique in this way, very lucky. I'm able to write about some really quite exciting new developments in the field of oncology which I hope will shortly become more available to more people. It's a rather tantalizing time to have cancer, for me, someone of my age, because there are treatments that I can see that are just out of my reach, probably, which is both encouraging and annoying. There are others that are probably just within it. My constitution is very good. All my other vital signs are excellent. Everything, from my liver to my blood pressure is excellent, superb, in fact; unjustly so, as a lot of my friends would say. If I can hang on, there are quite a few experiments I can, and intend, to try.

I had a very bad episode a couple of weeks ago. I crashed, as my doctor, who is normally a very aberrantly diffident guy, said. I had a meltdown in my bone marrow. That can happen with chemotherapy. I had a crisis with white blood cells at the same time as my gall bladder went rancid and I was in terrible pain. I thought I had a burst appendix. I was really flat out. I've now lost the gall bladder and I've gained some blood in transfusions, so I'm back, hanging on.

The worst part of the initial treatments was what's called "chemo brain" in the trade, where you feel fogged in the head. You barely even want to read, let alone write. That terrified me very much because I thought if I can't do that, my *raisons d'être* [would] have gone, in the literal sense. I wouldn't have a very persuasive reason to live and I didn't want to give in to despair. It turns out the chemo brain is transitory. I still suffer from terrible exhaustion. I've got it now physically, but I'm quite lucid, at least in my own opinion. I could write a column today if I was lucky, and if I had some strong coffee. I can certainly read and converse.

If anything was to spread in that direction, then I probably would feel that was the end.

The esophageal cancer is right in the core and too near the viscera to be really amenable to radiation, apparently, so I have to do chemo until a personalized genomic treatment—because this is a disease of our genes—can be found for me.

I HAD TO CANCEL a rather lavish book tour just as it was beginning back in the summer. I couldn't just do a fade and go into treatment. Because I was some kind of public figure, I had to make a statement about why I couldn't keep these appointments when people had gone to a lot of trouble; I had to say something. It became a news item overnight. I guess it must have been a slow week. I imagine it was partly because of my opinions about the supernatural and the religious life. I also got a lot of attention because people thought, "Well, surely now will be the time for him to make a reconsideration, withdraw from the principles of a lifetime, and make his peace with some church or other," and there was a lot of public talk about that. There was a national day of prayer for me, which I took kindly. I thought it was at least a gesture of solidarity. That was, by the way, prayer in my favor. There were other people who lobbied of the divine in the opposite direction. Presuming to instruct Him in either case seems to me a bit presumptuous, but people can't seem to help that. I've had an amazing number of letters from people. I still get them—handwritten ones to the house as well as e-mails to my office in New York saying really the nicest things. Most of them, not all. They're trying to assure me that, in their minds, my life hasn't been a waste of time, even if it ends prematurely. Believe me, that's been encouraging. I've learned something from it, which is, like most of the things one knows that are important, already known to me, but I really know it now. Never put off writing a letter to someone who's in distress. It's always very much appreciated. I'm not asking for more people to write to me, but if they have someone in mind, or someone known to them and they haven't quite got around to it yet, I'd urge them to do it. It's been a terrific help to me, I must say, and I'm not a particularly vulnerable person in that way. I'm not that easily stirred, but this has been very, very moving for me and very confirming.

Professional enemies are, I suppose, rivals or people that take the opposite view. All of them have been very nice. I've had newspaper columns written about me in the *New York Times* by David Brooks, a very generous column, and another one by Timothy Egan. There was an editorial in the *Times of London*. I began to feel a bit as if I was reading my obituaries, because I was still alive. Only the nice bits would be printed, as it were. I thought it was nice, but, of course, it gave me this slightly creepy feeling of it being premature as well.

I don't know how many personal enemies I have; people who just didn't like me, in other words. Ones on whose nerves I get. The number of people who've written to me saying they hope I suffer now, and then forever after I've died is, I'd say, hearteningly small.

I HAD A FREE gift from the National Portrait Gallery in London which publishes a magazine for subscribers about its upcoming exhibitions. There was an exhibition for the friends of Martin Amis, who was a friend of mine. [The exhibit included] some photographs, which included me. Because one of the people featured had died while the catalogue was going to press, they hastily put in the words "the late," but they put it next to my name. So, for the first time in my life, I saw the words "the late Christopher Hitchens" in print, and it does concentrate the mind. They wrote to me, groveling. I think they thought I was going to sue. They said, "They've all been withdrawn, we'll pull them, and only a few got out, so it's all right." I said, "No, no. I want you to send me as many as you've got because it makes a wonderful mini-introduction to my memoir," which I had nearly finished then. So, I wrote a...meditation on death, but at that stage, I had no idea how ill I was, none.

I WENT ON *The Daily Show with Jon Stewart* the day I was diagnosed. I'd been told in the morning. I'd woken up in New York feeling very ill and had to be taken to hospital. I thought I had a heart attack. They said, "It's not your heart, and you can discharge yourself if you want, though we recommend you stay in for observation. But, whatever you do, the next stop must be an oncologist. There's clearly a tumor, probably in your esophagus, but it's spread." I decided to discharge myself because I wanted to do the Stewart show, and also that evening, there was a big public event with Salman Rushdie at the New York 92nd Street Y. I managed to do both of these without showing any ill effects, but I'd just had the sentence read to me. I'd just buried the thought for what it took to do the show, then later, this onstage event with Salman, which also went very well. It was only at the dinner after that I began to feel I couldn't carry on anymore, but I should get through it. I don't think anyone noticed. But every opportunity between these events I was violently sick. I threw up very powerfully....

[My father died of esophageal cancer] at the age of seventy-nine.... I suppose because I used to smoke very heavily I was afraid of always getting it in the lung. I seem to lead a charmed life, but the thing about esophageal cancer is you can have it for quite a while. It's very hard to detect unless you have an upper GI almost every month and you're looking for it, so you're very likely to miss it. It doesn't usually present until it's metastasized. By the time I went to the doctor for a biopsy, it was very easy to do because you could feel it in the lymph node on my neck, which is not a good sign.

I began a Cysplatin treatment of chemotherapy, which made me then lose all my hair. It's growing back slightly with the new chemical I'm trying. It made me lose a lot of weight and made me very tired, but knocked it back perceptibly. It was measurably reduced. [The treatment was in Bethesda and started in July of last year.] It's still going on....

A wonderful American doctor, Francis Collins, who's the head of the National Institutes of Health...and I met because we're [on] opposite sides of the religion debate. We became friends that way. He's a very convinced Christian. We've become friendly debaters and he's taking a very kindly interest in my case and has helped me have my genome sequenced and is trying to look for a more perfect identifiable match for any mutation they can find that's peculiar to me that can be targeted by a special drug. [In three days] I'm going in.... I hope to try that, if I'm strong enough, and if my bone marrow has recovered enough. That involves six billion DNA matches of my tumor set against six billion DNA matches of my blood to look for something that was individually mutated that wasn't in my genes. It's absolutely extraordinary what can be done now. I had to go to St. Louis to do [the genome sequencing]. That seems to be where the project is for finding out how the genome can be applied to individuals' predicaments in medicine. It'll be commonplace soon. There's a terrible lack of funding. I might just say a word about this now so people can write their congressman. In the most recent budget, there was a terrible collapse in funding to the NIH. There's this stupid attempt to limit the extent to which actually existing embryonic cells can be used for this kind of thing, and I've become [even] more of an advocate for overcoming these pseudoscientific obstacles to medical research.

I've had various tests [at NIH,] but I just go to my regular oncologist. He's a very brilliant man called Dr. [Frederick] Smith, in Bethesda, who consults over the Internet with a panel of like-minded experts, and they work out of Sloan Kettering and elsewhere. They work out a protocol for me and adjust it every few weeks.

[I'm thinking of starting a] campaign to have a book of cancer etiquette published, which I might do. I was signing books in New York after a debate with Tariq Ramadan about Islam. There was a long line. A woman at the front came towards me. She didn't even have a book for me to sign, hadn't bought one. She said, "I'm sorry to hear you're ill." And I said, "It's very nice of you to say so." She said, "A cousin of mine had cancer." I said, "I'm really sorry to hear that," and she said, "Yes, in the liver." I said, "Oh that's dreadful; that's awful," and she said, "But he got better." I said, "Oh, good," and then she said, "But he got much worse again." I said, "Oh, I'm sorry," and she said, "Of course, he was a homosexual," and I thought, "I'm not going to say 'Of course,' because how was I supposed to know?" She said, "And all his friends and family abandoned him and he died alone and in great pain, agony, incontinence, piercing pain, humiliation, and indescribable horror." I said, "Oh well, I…." I was beginning to run out of things to say, but I expressed commiseration at that, and then she said, "I just wanted you to know I know exactly what you're going through," and then left, without buying a book. So, I thought, "Would she have treated me like that if I was well?" Of course not. But people think they have the right, if not a duty, to do it if you aren't. Patients also need to reciprocate by not inflicting [their illness] on people. I actually have a button I'm not wearing that says, "Don't ask and I won't tell."

Some people do make a huge parade of their condition. I've tried to write about it in other contexts. I wrote about the national day of prayer and why I wasn't joining it. I've written about imaginative new gene-based treatments. Things like that. I don't just want to write my own tumor diaries.

[IN THE PROLOGUE OF *Hitch 22*, I wrote "I personally want to do death in the active and not the passive, and to be there to look it in the eye and be doing something when it comes for me."] Death is part of life, so I'd like to be conscious for it, but this is what I thought then. Ideally I'd like to be making a speech perhaps, or making love, or sitting with friends, or, if I had more notice, conceivably to try a sort of synchronic terminus where people gather round and you try and make a fist of a decent farewell. I've had cause to reconsider that now because if this cancer doesn't go into remission, it's a very unpleasant way to die. One quite probable way of doing it is to choke in your own puke, for example. That's not a very good thing, and it can be preceded by all kinds of humiliations. It's not that you're going to die and you're resigned or reconciled to that as part of life, it's that the sentence includes that you be tortured for a bit before you die. I now feel a slight bravado about what I wrote then. I would still, if it were possible, like to be awake and looking at people, and, if I'm lucky, talking to them, but I'm not so sure I would insist on it. It might be as well to sort of slip away in a narcotic stupor. It might be, but still there's something about that. It may sound very old fashioned and you can say it strikes me as a bit ignoble. As I say, it's part of life. I want to get as much out of it as I can.

[During this period, I have talked about this kind of thing with Carol Blue, my wife,] a lot because she's been a great prop and stay for me. She does things I don't like to do, like going on the Internet, looking up every conceivable ramification of treatment and possibility, tirelessly looking for new doctors and new avenues and things like that. So we talk a lot about it, about losing, about what would happen when I've gone. Actually, we have barely talked about that. My determination is that I'm not going to die of it. Well, I'm not going to die of it now. I might die with it, perhaps some years from now, but that is a possibility and I'm certainly going to do everything I can to be an experimental subject for other treatments, even if they don't work for me. In the book, I quote the great American scholar Horace Mann, who said until you've done something for humanity you should be ashamed to die. So, it's quite a high standard to reach.... That would be doing something for humanity at a fairly small cost to myself; even if it involved protracting the treatment unnecessarily, I'd be willing to do it.

[A FEW WEEKS AGO, I debated former British Prime Minister Tony Blair in Toronto.] Because I had a lot of notice of the event, I timed my treatments so that it would come at the end of the treatment, when I'm usually much stronger. It was a huge event, and a lot of trouble and money went into fixing it up and getting Blair and getting security. I never like to cancel anyway, but I couldn't do that. I was feeling OK—very tired, but physically all right and mentally quite alert. It was the first time Blair had had a public debate since he stopped being prime minister, on any subject. [I then wrote about it in *Vanity Fair*.]

I debate with religious people all the time, like Tariq Ramadan, Rabbi Shmuley [Boteach], all kinds of people I have debated since I became sick. Blair is, of course, a new convert to Roman Catholicism so I wanted to question him a bit about that. One can only do one thing at a time in these debates, and the point I wanted him to concede was that the evils that people like myself speak about when we talk about religion, he and his co-thinkers will always acknowledge were done in the name of religion. I said, "You must drop that." There is scriptural warrant and authority very clearly in the holy books, which are supposed to be the word of God, for these evils. It's a cop-out to use a vulgarity to say it's in the name of religion; you have to face the responsibility. In fact, when we were asked by one questioner to say what had been the strongest point made by the other, he said that he agreed that I was right: that the problem is that there is scriptural authority for a great deal of atrocity and cruelty and stupidity in the holy books. That's my best memory of the evening.

I opened with a long quotation from Cardinal Newman, whose beatification he'd just recommended to the Pope and supported. It was a very wicked, in my view, quotation from Newman's *Apologia*. Then I wanted to know whether he thought the Pope was the "Vicar of Christ" on Earth, and whether the Catholic church was the one true church. It was quite strange. He didn't come up to the scratch to fight me on that. You could not have told in anything he said that he was a Roman Catholic at all. He could have been a very weak Christian socialist liberal. Basically, he says that Christianity is OK because it makes people do good works and give money to charity, which no one denies is true, but has nothing to do with the relevance or the truth of the matter. But he's a man with whom I sympathize in other ways. I've known him a little bit for quite a long time, so it was an unusual, interesting debate.

I WAS SMOKING UNTIL quite late on. I forget when it stopped. It's incredible now when I see that shot of Walter Cronkite announcing the president's death in Dallas in 1963, and the whole studio looks like Chernobyl with ashtrays stretching as far as the eye can see…. I used to write my columns in Timberlake's bar on Connecticut Avenue. My father was a pipe smoker and a reasonably consistent drinker, too, and I can't help but think that that's what contributed to [his death from esophageal cancer]. We didn't learn much from his death, my brother and I, because he was diagnosed and died almost right away. We didn't find out much about it. I know it was lower down than where mine is, and it was probably inoperable then, but it wasn't a teaching moment.

[My cancer] can't be cut out. It has spread, and it's too near my lungs and my heart to be properly radiated, so it has to be chemo and/or targeted gene therapy. Of course, I always knew that there was a risk in the bohemian lifestyle, and I decided to take it because, whether it's an illusion or not, I don't think it is, it helped my concentration, it stopped me being bored, and stopped other people being boring, to some extent. It would keep me awake; it would make me want the evening to go on longer, to prolong the conversation, to enhance the moment. If I was asked, would I do it again, the answer is probably yes. I'd have quit earlier, possibly, hoping to get away with the whole thing. It's easy for me to say, but not very nice for my children to hear. It sounds irresponsible if I say, "Yes, I'd do all that again to you," but the truth is, it would be hypocritical of me to say, "No, I'd never touch the stuff if I'd known," because I did know; everyone knows. I decided all of life is a wager, and I'm going to wager on this bit. I can't make it come out any other way. It's strange; I almost don't even regret it, though I should, because it's just impossible for me to picture life without wine and other things fueling the company and keeping me reading and traveling and energizing me. It worked for me. It really did.

I think acedia is actually one of the deadly sins. Boredom was the anteroom to despair; the feeling, that anomie, that nothing's interesting, nothing's worth it. I am too prone to it. I get easily tired of committee meetings, not that I have to do many of those, or waiting in line. I'm a very, very impatient person. I'm very happy by myself; I'm lucky in that way, if I've got enough to read and something to write about and a bit of alcohol for me to add an edge, not to dull it. It's been a formula.

THE MAIN THING [I'D like to tell people] is to emphasize the extraordinary innovations in medicine that are becoming available based on our new knowledge of our genetic makeup, insofar as these treatments are applicable to me, which some of them are. I'm hoping to write in some detail and alert people to possibilities that they may not yet know about that exist, even for quite hard, advanced cases.

I thought I'd write a book that was both about facing death and about the struggle for life, and how one motivation for the latter, in my case, apart from the obvious ones, is precisely to see if I can participate in pushing those boundaries back and enlarging the area of scientific knowledge.

A MEMOIR OF A person who has just passed sixty has to face [the topic of death]. I thought I owed that much to the readers. [The process] hasn't been all that surprising. It's a commonplace thing. I don't sit around asking myself, "Why me?"; and if I did, the cosmos wouldn't bother to favor me with a reply. It wouldn't even say, "Why not?" It's…almost laughably predictable. The only interesting thing about it is its possible amenability to treatments that were unknown until very recently; the outcome of brilliant work by devoted people, some of whom I'm very lucky to count as friends.

[MEDICAL PROFESSIONALS] HAVE GIVEN me more than a margin of hope it can be licked. They haven't pronounced on my chances unless I've asked them, which I decided not to do at first until it occurred to me that it would be very useful for accounting purposes to have a rough idea because one has to plan for one's loved ones and descendants. For actuarial reasons, I'd like to have a guess. They don't like being asked because they don't really know. The best answer I got was the following: If you took 1000 people who were myself—my age, my state of health, my gender—half of us would be dead within a year. Of the remaining half, others might hope to live more than a year, and of that number, quite a number would live for a considerable number of years. They can't do better than that. That was from a very senior person at the NIH who was expecting the question.

I'm a little bit [surprised that so many people want to talk about this story]. A lot of it I know has been to do with my stance on religion. A very large number of people have asked me, "Doesn't it change your attitude to the infinite, the eternal, the supernatural, and so forth?" I've said that I really don't see why it should. I've never thought it was a particularly searching question. I spent a lot of my life deciding that there isn't any redemption, there is no salvation, that there's no afterlife, that there's no supervising boss. If I was to tell you, "Now that I've got a malignancy in my esophagus, that changes everything," you would think, I hope, the main effect had been on my IQ. It's a complete logical non sequitur. It's nothing to do with it.

I've enjoyed taking part in that argument. There's a certain ghoulish element, even about the nice people who've been praying for me. They are not just praying for my recovery, they're praying for my reconciliation with religion. I proposed a trade-off the other day. I said, "I tell you what, what if we secularists stop going to hospitals and walking around the wards and asking if people are religious when they are in extremis and in their last days, and saying, 'Look, you've still got a little time, why don't you live the last few days of it as a free person? You'll feel much better. All that nonsense they taught you—you know you could still have every chance to give it up. Experience the life of a free-thinking autonomous person. Don't live in fear, don't believe in mythology.'" I don't think they'd welcome it. Of course, we don't do that, but it seems to be considered the right of almost everybody to do it the other way around. I don't resent it at all, because I like every opportunity for the argument, but a lot of it has been to do with that. I don't flatter myself as a public figure, I rate all that highly.

Since it's not really avoidable, the question is how to turn [hating people] to an advantage. One of the things I don't like about Christianity is the idea of compulsory love because I think it's bound to lead to hypocrisy: people pretending to love more than they do. Also, since it's coupled with the injunction to love a god you're also supposed to fear, there's every chance of that curdling. There's something very honest, by contrast, to finding someone completely unbearable, someone like Henry Kissinger, for example. It's bad, a bit like alcohol. It's a good servant, but it's a bad master. I have a completely cold hatred and contempt for Henry Kissinger, but it doesn't waste much of my time. It's just that it enables me to penetrate the sort of fog of sentiment and bogus reputation in which he's shrouded and protected. It doesn't eat away at me. It doesn't keep me awake at night, it doesn't poison me, it doesn't fill me with bile, but I can't pretend that it's just a matter of political disagreement. There is such a thing as evil in the world, and sometimes, it's personified....

What would change my mind about Mother Teresa? One couldn't exactly hate Mother Teresa because, in a way, she was a pathetic figure. I detested the influence that she had. I could tell you why in a sentence. The very reason is that she's so celebrated. We have this apparent concern for the poor of the world, or the poorest of the poor as she was always obliging us to say. As it happens, we know what the cure for poverty is, or what a certain cure for poverty is, and it goes under the name "the empowerment of women." It works everywhere: Bangladesh, Bolivia, name it. Give women some control over their reproductive cycle. Get them off the animal routine of breeding machine and the level of poverty will decline, sharply. It's never, never known to fail. It's a consistent finding. This is my central point about Mother Teresa: she spent her entire life opposing the only thing that works, opposing all forms of birth control, comparing them to abortion, which she called murder directly in her Nobel Prize speech. She said that was the main threat to peace in the world, which is a fanatical, stupid thing to say. That's basically it; that, plus the reputation for sanctity that she got for preaching this nonsense. One could add her friendship with the worst of the richest of the rich, people like Charles Keating of the savings and loan [scandal], who was a great friend of hers. She took sterling money from him, and refused when the court asked [her] to return it. She took money from the devaluated dictatorship in Haiti, which treated the poor like pigs and worse. She blessed them in return and gave them divine sanction. It goes on. Her whole effect was entirely retrograde, and no one ever wrote any but one story about her until I wrote my critique. In that book, it's very short. I make five or six other direct accusations against her, backed up by fact, and that book has been reviewed by every newspaper in the world, including all the religious press. No one's ever pointed out a mistake in it. Not one. If half of what I say is true about her, then none of what is commonly believed about her is true. I'm used to this now. People need, every now and then, a complete illusion, and this was one.

It would be extremely interesting [if Henry Kissinger decided to call me and bury the hatchet after all these years]. One of the reasons I detest him is I know that couldn't happen. He wouldn't even agree when I was writing my book about him to have questions submitted in writing, let alone to meet me. He's made it a condition when he appears on television programs that he not be asked about the book. I know this from several of the [television programs'] producers. He made it a condition of his appearance at the National Press Club, which I don't think should have agreed, that he not be asked about the book. Never mind his attitude to me—there's no reason to like me—but if I was him, I would have pretended, "Who's this guy Hitchens? I don't care," but I know I needled him. Think of the things he's been found out as having done—lying about Vietnam, lying about Chile, Bangladesh—the needless deaths of so many people for the vanity of himself and his criminal president. We have other people from that period in our history such as Robert McNamara, the Bundy brothers, William Colby, and others who, in their memoirs, tried to make some kind of restitution. They said, "Actually, this was pretty bad policy, and we suspected at the time that it was bad, maybe worse. We're sorry, and we have some evidence we feel we should share with you, some disclosures that you should have had at the time..." Kissinger has never said a word of self-criticism, not one. He gets very petulant and angry and spoiled and ugly when he's criticized. As Jeeves says, in another context, "The contingency, sir, is a remote one." If he was to try it, I'd be fascinated to meet him, of course.

YOU PROBABLY REMEMBER STEPHEN Solarz, the late congressman. He was a very interesting man. He had the same thing as me and died recently.

Before he died, he'd had cancer for years and he'd done a lot of traveling. He kept up his interest in human rights and international policy. Then he got word that the cancer was back and that was probably it, and he made fairly short work of dying. This was a few weeks ago. That's what I'd need to know. The great loss to me in the last few months is the inability to travel. I got to Toronto for Thanksgiving. That wasn't that hard. I've been to California. I've been by a private plane that was sent for me very kindly to do a speaking engagement in Montana. I've finally got to see the Little Bighorn, which I've always wanted to, and the wonderful national park. I've now only got three American states unvisited: the Dakotas and Nebraska. I've done all the others plus Puerto Rico.

It's sentimental, I know, but someone said to me randomly the other day, "Are you afraid of not seeing England again?" and I realized, yes, I was. I can't bear the idea of not going back at least once, but I couldn't do it now. I might have to be told I was on what they call a "chemo holiday."

CRYSTAL WRIGHT

Crystal Wright is sometimes described as a "triple minority" —conservative, African American, and female. She credits her family and her Virginia upbringing for the development of her political viewpoints. In this December 9, 2012, interview for Q & A, she describes her online political commentary via conservativeblackchick.com, which she edits and publishes. She is also a communications consultant in Washington, D.C.

[M Y BLOG IS CALLED ConservativeBlackChick.com because] it really illustrates what I am trying to convey. It also showed who I am. It's literal and it's fun. I was at a reunion for my alma mater, Georgetown University, talking to a good friend, and she said, "You should just do your own blog." Then I asked, "What should I call it?" and out popped the words, "conservative black chick." I started blogging in 2009 when President Obama got elected. I was very frustrated by his election early on because I felt as though he was trying to run a little more as a moderate Democrat.... In January 2009, when he started making his appointments and I began to see the same faces of the Clinton Administration that I had seen when I first came to Washington, I was becoming increasingly frustrated. Obamacare tipped me over the edge; with unemployment where it was in this country, I said, "Why isn't this president focusing on job creation? People don't want what was close to universal healthcare right now."

I don't know if it was a light bulb going off in my head [to become a conservative], but the way I was raised by my parents was to take responsibility for my actions and not depend on somebody to do something for me. We would all have dinner as a family together. My parents didn't ever talk to us about politics, but they talked to us a lot about values and keeping promises to people.... I really became a conservative when I moved to Washington in the mid-nineties [and] started working in television news and sitting in on hearings for ABC News. I remember walking up and down Constitution and Independence Avenue and seeing all these government buildings, and I thought, "What the heck do all these people do all day?" I just felt like the more I engaged with government, the more conservative I became. I felt like government wasn't doing a whole lot for Crystal Wright, so why was I paying all this money in taxes for it? Government should be there for the indigent and poor, and as a framework for how we conduct business, [and as a] structure for society, which, when you read the Constitution, that's what the founding fathers had in mind. I do not think government is there to prop [the majority] of us up, because then there would not be a safety net for the people who really need it; people who are disabled, who fall on hard times, and need a little help along the way. But government now has grown so much beyond what our founding fathers wanted it to be....

I grew up in Richmond, Virginia; when we all got home from school and my dad got home from work, [and my] mom was always cooking... we sat down and I remember watching Walter Cronkite and Ted Koppel when the Iran Hostage Crisis was going on. We just talked about current events, what we had done at school, our grades, what was going on in our lives.... It was such a meaningful thing to me; it left such a strong imprint on my life even to this day as an adult. As a country, somehow we have gotten away from that family time, and I do think that makes a difference in kids' lives.... Families that eat together tend to stay together, and their kids do well.

I don't know if I'm often picked [to appear at public events] as a balance, but I'm picked typically to go on panels and perhaps do news programs because people consider me an anomaly. Why, I don't really know, because there are a lot of black conservatives. I tend to become a punching bag when I go on some television [shows]. I'm the punching bag for the liberal host or the liberal guest; that is my perception of it. I don't like it. I know there are a lot of black Republicans out there. If people go back in history and do their homework, they will realize that the Republican Party was the home to black Americans up through probably the 1960s. It was really the Republican Party that did a lot to get blacks elected to office and make sure they would vote. They fought for civil rights, and it frustrates me. I don't like it; I get angry about it actually.

I am fearless to my own detriment. Just the fact that I speak out and write a lot of the things I write as a conservative black woman, is an example of my fearlessness. It goes back to the way I was raised.... As kids, my brothers and I were always told, "You can do it. There's no barrier to you doing it except yourself." [My parents] never let us quit. That's what they always told us. My mom said, "If you make a commitment, you are going to do it. I want you to follow through till the end." Dad was the same way. So when I hear these accusations that voter ID laws disproportionately affect minorities, it implies to me that somehow we have something missing in our brain, we're lesser than. To me, if white Americans can get IDs to vote and go through all the processes to follow the laws, what are you telling black people? That somehow they are not good enough, that they are lesser than? And that's what bothers me about a lot of the rhetoric coming from Democrats and the left; that there has to be a specialness when we deal with minorities because they're too feeble-minded; we really need to make concessions for them because they cannot follow the rules like everybody else. When you treat people like victims, then I do not think they want to aspire. I really resent it. It's bad to teach young people that kind of rhetoric. It's nothing to write home about or sing praises about when one in six Americans are on food stamps right now.

My father was one of the very first blacks to be admitted to the Medical College of Virginia in the dental school. He was the only black in his class, and he dealt with discrimination from his professors when he was in dental school. He would help other classmates study and produced the same work as his white counterparts, and he would get graded down and they would get A's. I hear stories from my parents talking about how they were called the N-word and all sorts of ugly things. My mom talks about sitting at lunch counters with my father during segregation. She talks to us often about when she was a little girl, she had to go to the segregated beach, but she could see where the line marked off, here's for blacks and here's for whites. She was on the black side and she could see the white kids and their families enjoying umbrellas and being able to rent all these great things for a day at the beach, and she didn't have access to those same things.... My mother tells me, "Before Rosa Parks did that, I had my own encounter on the bus." I said, "Mom, what are you talking about?" She said, "I'm serious." She was going to ballet class and got on the bus. She went to the back of the bus like she was supposed to in Richmond, Virginia. A white, older man got on and told her she needed to move. She looked at him, said, "Sir, I'm already in the back of the bus. Where do you want me to go?" So she sat there. The bus driver didn't make her move. I get a lot of my fearlessness from my mother, because my dad's a little more shy. But I get fortitude from him, and other strengths.... I can't help it, I guess; it's all in the genes, why I'm the way I am and why I speak out. Because I think we should all want to get more engaged in the political process, not less engaged.

MY MOTHER HAD TEARS in her eyes when Barack Obama became president in 2008. She voted for him and my dad said he voted for him. My father did not vote for him again. I haven't asked my mom.... I voted for him originally, but did not vote for him again.... It was historic for me, knowing how my [family lived] and to go into a voting booth in 2008 and see a black man running on the ticket that you had the option of voting for president. [It was] very moving, meaningful; it was great. I'm glad that we as a country got past that barrier.... I'm troubled, on the other hand, that the president isn't being held to the same standards as his predecessors because of his race. We have a coddling of his presidency by the mainstream media, because he's the first black president and they're fearful of offending. That really troubles me. I think it's great that we crossed the Rubicon as a country. People chose again, and they voted to give him another four years. I don't think that was the right choice, but we live in a democracy and that's the way it is.... There's a lot going on there for black Americans. I'm not so sure if all the black Americans who voted for him a second time around really looked at his record and what he has or has not done for them as a people or a race. It's complicated, certainly, but, for

me, the second time around, it wasn't that complicated. I wanted to believe that he wasn't going to govern in the way that he governed the first
term…. For me, it was a complicated vote. McCain and Palin weren't as
strong of a ticket as I would have liked to have seen.

[My parents do not] carry with them [the impact of their early up-
bringing] as a badge, or say, "Let me show you my civil rights work…."
My parents aren't going around saying, "Oh, woe is me, look at how
much we had to overcome, how much we had to fight to get to where we
are." No. Their parents instilled in them the same values my parents instilled in me. When we're going through bad times as children and we
needed some pep talks, that's when my parents said, "Hey, look, if we can
go through the crap we had to go through, you can suffer these minor
bumps in the road. Here's how you do it. You have fortitude, you keep
pressing forward." That's really the message I always got from my parents. But it's not to say that racism doesn't still exist, and in many ways
my parents are often telling me, "We feel like the country is more divided
now, maybe in a more subtle way than it was when they were sitting at
lunch counters."

MOST OF THE ATTACKS and vitriol that I get are coming from other
black people. People would think it would be counter that, right? That
people who didn't look like me are throwing all these aspersions at me.
It's situations when I'm in a predominantly black, liberal environment
[that] I get attacked viciously. It doesn't feel great, but I'm not going to sit
there and be somebody's punching bag and not set the record straight….

[I WROTE IN MY blog, "Old, white men just don't cut it anymore. They
are not reflective of the changing demographics of the country. America
is browning up, not whitening up, as evidenced by the U.S. Census findings that minorities will make up 54 percent of the population in 2050."]
…Mitt Romney lost because he ignored the minority votes. He gave lip
service to Hispanics and Latinos, threw up a couple of ads and thought,
"Hey, y'all! Come, come to the polls and vote for me." It doesn't work
like that. With blacks, there was virtually no outreach. While I don't
agree with the president's message, he filled the void with a message to all
groups, including women. Romney won five percentage points more

among white voters than McCain; that still wasn't enough to carry him to the White House. We know that the next election, those numbers are going to go down, down, down. If the Republican Party doesn't do something about fixing its image and bringing more people into this big tent that we claim we're all members of, we're not going to win elections; and…[the Republican Party will] probably be voted literally out of existence, if we don't get our act together…. If Mitt Romney actually had black people around him, and Latinos and Hispanics, he quite possibly could have won. I don't think they would have said, "It's phony," I think they would have said, "Wow. Look at this guy, he gets it. He gets it…."

Some people would have argued [that] it would look like he's pandering. I've heard that. But I think that's the biggest joke running. The big problem that I had with Mitt Romney is that, from inside the campaign, the people he was putting [forth] as spokespeople for the face of the campaign, [were] mostly white males and peppered with white females. But that's not saying, "Hey, I'm inclusive; I'm your guy." To his credit, Mitt Romney went to the NAACP and made his case to black Americans. I thought it was one of the best speeches he gave during the campaign, but he didn't follow it up with anything. If you look at that in hindsight, people would say, "That's pandering because he didn't follow it up."

I think the media swoons over President Obama an enormous amount…. Candy Crowley [CNN host who moderated the presidential debate], and the way she inserted herself to jump to the president's defense in that debate, was so inappropriate, it went beyond the pale. I really don't believe that if that was a Republican incumbent, Candy Crowley would have jumped in like that. [Another example of the media swooning over President Obama] was during the 2008 campaign, and the president's relationship with Jeremiah Wright…. Obama belonged to Reverend Wright's church, where Wright gave incendiary sermons. He baptized [President Obama's] children and presided over the marriage between President Obama and Michelle Obama. That really got very scant attention by the mainstream media. These were awful sermons [given by] Reverend Wright, saying America deserves what they got from 9/11. [In addition,] there is the president's failed record in his first term; the media did not hold the president accountable when the president said, "If I can't get the job done in four years, I should be a one-term president." Now,

President Obama said that. Why didn't we hear that on the campaign trail from the mainstream media? Why did no one at the White House press corps stand up to the president and say, "Mr. President, you yourself said if you couldn't get employment down, if you couldn't solve the country's economic problems, you should be a one-term proposition." Why isn't anybody calling him on his failed promises?

…Many things I have written have not even necessarily been in lock-step with the Republican Party. I don't do talking points. I do think that I'm one of the few black conservatives [who talks] about how the president's race [plays] into the liberal media not holding him accountable to his failed record….I also believe they have a love affair with President Obama, almost as though he is celebrity-like in their minds. This man can do no wrong and the liberal press is going to continue to prop him up and prop him up until the bitter end…. I almost wonder to myself, what would President Obama have to do that would be so egregious for the liberal media to turn on him? If you look back on the 2012 campaign, I find it strange that throughout the presidential campaign, all the questions were always directed to Mitt Romney. "What's your economic plan? What are you going to do to fix the country?" Well, Mitt Romney had an economic plan and he talked about it ad nauseam. He talked about reforming taxes and reigning in entitlement spending. But the media didn't do an equal job of grilling the president on his failed record. "Mr. President, what is your plan for a second term?" Was he ever asked that? No. He really wasn't. It's outrageous because those questions were asked of all his predecessors, Reagan, Bush. Every incumbent. Clinton, [who] actually had a record to run on, but they grilled him on his personal scandals, I will say.

FORTY PERCENT OF THE males in prison are black…. It's not the sentencing guidelines that are the reason why you have a disproportionate number of black males in prison. It's not…. Daniel Patrick Moynihan's [former senator, D-New York] report that he wrote for President [Lyndon B.] Johnson…is about how he saw a breakdown in the black family. Simultaneously, parallel to this breakdown, he was seeing a rise among blacks on welfare, and he said, "This is a disturbing trend to me. I'm seeing a lot of black families headed by single, black women. I'm very concerned about this." At the time…about 23 percent of all black babies born were born to unwed mothers. Today, it's 73 percent. The reason why we have more black males in prison is not because of sentencing guidelines for crack versus powder cocaine; it's because you have 73 percent of black babies born into homes without fathers, where you don't have a marriage to support and welcome this child and nurture this child. These are failed policies by Democrats, who think the solution is let's just throw money at it.… Our system rewards women for not having men in the home. No fathers. You get money. I'm not saying that white Americans aren't on welfare. This is the number people will tell you: there are more whites on welfare. True. But we blacks represent a smaller portion of the population and we have a disproportionate number of us on welfare. [This is] not a good thing and it's not empowering. If we look at what was happening in the 1960s, we haven't done much better. We have gotten worse. How is this empowering to black Americans? …Somewhere along the line as a country, we have said, "Marriage isn't sexy anymore. Family isn't sexy anymore." And the numbers are bearing this out.… Forty percent of babies are born out of wedlock…you're not doing kids a favor and you're not doing our country a favor. You change it by talking about traditional family values and not be accused of being non-politically correct. It sounds very basic; why aren't we talking to little kids about family? Maybe the family is changing a little bit.… But why can't we talk about family, and sex education? We need to bring that back into public schools. I remember learning about all of that, the biology of the body and all that, the birds and the bees, in middle school, in a very scientific way, and it was reinforced at home. But if we're going to talk about sex education, we also should be talking about abstinence and, "Hey guys, there's a great way not to get pregnant: not to have sex." There's nothing wrong with abstinence.

I've worked at CNN, ABC News, and left there and was one of the first folks to be hired by Fox News Channel when they started up their D.C. bureau back in the day. I covered the State Department when Madeleine Albright was secretary of state. I was the producer on site. So those were interesting days. Not always fun days, because we were the stepchild of all the cable networks, because we were a conservative venture trying to break into the scene.... I worked there a little over maybe a year and a half, and am now a public relations consultant. I also did some work for the Republican National Committee (RNC); I helped them with an out-reach web site to black Americans, but it has not yet launched. I was frustrated that the RNC didn't launch it before the election. They claim that they didn't have funding for it, which kind of boggles the mind when you think of the RNC and the money they raised in this election cycle. If they had launched it with activities behind it, [it could have] had a mean-ingful impact, but the decision was made not to.... We have got to grow the tent, but we can't give lip service to, "Oh, now we're the party of in-clusion, we really mean it, we really do." Because we lost. It was an epic fail, 2012.

WHEN I THINK BACK on my mother's generation, the majority of them had fewer choices as far as careers go, [but] if they wanted to be married, they were married [and] had families.... Our generation so much wanted us to take advantage of the opportunities before us, they forgot to go back to basics and say, "Marriage is OK." What bothers me with femi-nism is that you can do it all, you can have a baby without a man, you can bring home the bacon, you can cook it up in the pan. The fact is, you just can't. Women can't have it all. I don't think you can be a CEO of any company and have it all as a woman; you can't have a family and be a good mom at the same time. I think if you put women in a confessional situation, even if they don't necessarily believe in God, but whoever their Über-power is, and ask, "Do you really want to be alone?" I think most women [would say they] want to be with someone.... I think feminism is a bunch of garbage. I think it's written to brainwash women into be-lieving they can do it all on their own and the big, bad world is out there to hate them. Well, not all men hate women.

The Iron Curtain

ANNE APPLEBAUM

On March 5, 1946, former British Prime Minister Winston Churchill delivered his now famous forty-five minute address at Westminster College in Fulton, Missouri. The speech's official title was "The Sinews of Peace," but a line in the middle of the speech provided a metaphor for the Cold War that ensued after World War II and Churchill's warnings about the threat to Eastern Europe: "From Stettin in the Baltic to Trieste in the Adriatic, an iron curtain has descended across the Continent." Pulitzer Prize–winning journalist Anne Applebaum's book, Iron Curtain: The Crushing of Eastern Europe, 1944–1956 *(Doubleday, 2012) tells the story of those years in East Germany, Poland, and Hungary. Applebaum, whose husband Radoslaw Sikorski is the Polish Foreign Minister, was a guest on* Q & A *on December 16, 2012.*

CHURCHILL DEFINED THIS ERA probably without even meaning to do so. He coined the expression, the "Iron Curtain." It was such an emotive and evocative description of what had happened between 1944 and 1946. There is a long and complicated story to the phrase, "Iron Curtain." It is a theatrical term; there was an iron curtain that theaters used to use...to prevent fires in the theatres. It was a term in Victorian England, but it was Churchill who used it first in a private communication with his American counterparts, and then later in his speech.

My previous book was a history of the Gulag system. I became interested when writing about the Gulag of why people went along with it. Why do people go along with totalitarian regimes? What's the mentality? What are the institutional pressures? Why do camp guards do what they are told to do? Why does it happen? I decided to write about this period right after World War II because it is the time when the Soviet Union had reached a height; there was an apotheosis of Stalinism. Stalinism was created throughout the 1920s and 30s, and then it was reinforced by the experience of the war. By 1945, it was a fully developed system with a political theory, an economic theory, and a clear ideology. It was exactly at this moment when the Red Army marched into Central Europe and began imposing that system on the Central European states. [This book explores the questions:] What did the Soviets think their system was? What did they think was important to do first? How did they try and carry it out?

Stalinism was a developed system of complete control. The Stalinist State believed it could control everything. It could control not only politics and not only economics, but also social and civic life. It could control sports clubs and chess clubs. In the Stalinist system, there were no independent institutions of any kind, and no independent voices of any kind were allowed to speak. There was a cultural aspect to Stalinism, too. The arts were under Stalin's control. There was also a cult of Stalin himself, so Stalin's portrait hung everywhere. All of society was organized around his name and his image.

Stalin died in 1953, and after that, people began to want to reform his system. When Stalinism was brought into Eastern Europe, it was an attempt to put everything under state control. 1956 was really the revenge of civil society, when people began reorganizing themselves and social life independently and spontaneously.

I WANTED TO EXPLAIN how totalitarianism happens. We know the story of the Cold War and have seen the archives that described relationships between Roosevelt, Stalin, Churchill, and Truman. [What] I wanted to do was show from a different angle, from the ground up, what did it feel like to be one of the people who were subjected to this system, and how did people make choices in that system, and how did they react and how did they behave? I started very systematically. I went through archives in Warsaw, in Berlin, and Budapest. I looked at government archives and party archives. I looked at secret police archives, all of which are now open and some are easier to use than others. Some countries give you better or worse access.

I looked at specific institutions. I looked at the Hungarian film industry. How did the Hungarian film industry, which was one of the biggest and most powerful film industries in Europe before the war in the 1930s…become a Social-Realist film industry? I looked at German painters. Germany had a very vibrant abstract art movement in the 1920s and 30s, which was destroyed by Hitler. Many painters had left the country; they went abroad and came back to Berlin thinking they would finally be able to paint as they wanted. Many were Communists and were on the Left, and discovered to their horror that they weren't going to be allowed to [paint what they wanted]. So, how did they react? What did they do? Some of them taught themselves how to paint again. They tried to paint in Social-Realist or in a Stalinist way.

I looked at economic questions, in particular, small shops and retailing. This is, in some ways, the hardest part of the economy to control. I looked at the files of the Ministry of Economics in Germany and Poland. I looked at the secret police documents because I was looking for the origins of the secret police. How was it created? Who were the original secret police and where did they come from? How were they trained…? There is a wonderful collection in Warsaw. In about 1991 or '92, the Polish Military Archive sent a researcher and a couple of Xerox machines to Moscow. They Xeroxed all of the archives that had anything to do with the Red Army's liberation of Poland in 1944 and 1945 and its first encounters with the Polish resistance movement. It's all Xeroxed and can be read in Warsaw. I don't even know if those documents are accessible anymore in Moscow, but you don't have to go and see them there. There is a tremendous amount of material available.

MY HUSBAND IS THE Polish Foreign Minister. When I met him in 1989, we were journalists; he came to report on the collapse of Communism in Eastern Europe. We drove to Berlin on the November night when the Berlin Wall fell and spent the evening sitting on the wall chipping at it with a chisel. We were married about a year later.... People have forgotten how much fun it was; it was a very exhilarating time in history. But they have also forgotten how nervous people were. I remember sitting on the wall; it was about four o'clock in the morning and everyone was awake in Berlin and everything was open. There were hundreds of people sitting on top of the Berlin Wall. The East German guards were still there, because there was a wall and there was no-man's land and there was actually a second wall. They were standing in between the two walls and wearing riot gear. At four o'clock in the morning, everybody had drunk champagne and sung the national anthem. What do you do next? They started to, rather drunkenly, tease the guards. People started to jump off the wall from the West and to the East, and then the guards would rush over and throw people back over the wall. It wasn't an entirely satisfying moment and I discovered many years later that, as we were sitting there, the East German Politburo was trying to decide what to do about these people who were sitting on the wall, and should they start shooting? It could have all ended differently.

One of the things that has happened since 1989 is the region that we used to call Eastern Europe has become very differentiated. These countries no longer have much in common with one another except for the common memory of Communist Occupation. Poland is as different from Bulgaria and Albania as Greece is from Finland. Europe is really divided in different ways. There are a few elements of the Communist past in post-Communist countries. Sometimes there is a paranoid element in politics that comes from the legacy of people being spied on and people having lived in an oppressive system. They are more paranoid about secret deals being done behind their backs because secret deals were done behind their backs. In a way, that's understandable; there's an anxiety about being left behind or being left out by the West, and they're always keen to being inside the Western camp. The memory of the past continues to play out, but in truth, these countries are more different from one another than they are similar.

I CHOSE POLAND, HUNGARY, and East Germany in the book because they were different. They had different historical backgrounds; they had belonged to different empires in the nineteenth century. They had different political traditions and they had very different experiences during the war. Germany was, of course, Nazi Germany. Poland had one of the largest resistance movements in Europe, and the Hungarians were somewhere in between. They were reluctant collaborators with the Nazis at some points, but they also had some elements of resistance. I was interested in how they reacted to the Soviet invasion and then the subsequent process of Sovietization. All three of those countries are now democracies. East Germany is part of Germany. It is indistinguishable now in its legal system and its economic system from West Germany. East Germany is still much poorer than West Germany and in some ways, poorer than Poland, which has recovered more vigorously than the eastern part of Germany. Poland is a very vibrant democracy...and it now plays a very important and central role in Europe. It's a member of the European Union and NATO. It really is the largest of the former Eastern European countries, and it has perhaps a larger role in the region than anybody else.

Hungary is also still a democracy...but it has been badly governed in the last twenty years...and in many ways, there are many Hungarian institutions that haven't been reformed very much since 1989. There's an unattractive Far Right and unattractive Left in Hungary. It's a less happy and less stable state, but it is still a democracy and it is still a very open society.

When I read Communist Party archives, I discovered that, behind closed doors, the Communist officials are much more open than they are in public. They are always saying very surprising things to one another. They understand their societies fairly well. They are driven by and believe in their ideology. We often now tend to dismiss that; but no, they weren't mouthing them; they believed the proletarian revolution was coming, and that if we just do the right thing and press the right buttons, we'll be able to create it. They are constantly surprised by what goes wrong. It's supposed to be happening this way. The peasants or workers are supposed to be supporting us and they should vote for us in these elections. But they don't. Why? What's wrong? They argue about that. We need more ideology.... They discover the factories are not producing as much as they are supposed to be. Why not?...they have the statistics and evidence. They know it has gone wrong. They can't ever figure out how to fix it; this happens over and over and over again....

The leaders of these countries lived in very isolated communities. They lived in villas and were cut off from the rest of society. They had access to privileges that may not seem so extraordinary now to us. But, at that time, they had indoor plumbing and all kinds of food at a time when there were great shortages. The leaders were very isolated, very protected, often surrounded by servants, maids, and chauffeurs who were employees of the state, who were employees of the interior ministry. They were protected at all sides and at all times. They were often very nervous about making public appearances; they had a lot of bodyguards and were anxious. [Some asked, "How did that track with the idea that everybody should be equal?"] It's an interesting question—all the pigs are equal, and some are more equal than others. There was one of the things that developed during the course of the Revolution. They thought of themselves, "We are working hard." If they were asked to justify it, they would have said, "We are working hard on behalf of the state. We are the avant-garde of the proletariat. We will lead the proletariat into a full state of Communism. We aren't there yet, and until we've reached the full state of Communism, we have to have these temporary inequalities." That would have been the justification of it. What actually went through their heads, one doesn't really know.

I speak Polish and read Polish fluently and I speak Russian and read Russian fluently. With German, I have some extremely weak German, but with both German and Hungarian, I had translators, people who were more than translators; both of them were journalists who had worked in archives before and had done translation...I literally, physically, went around with them. We would go with my translator to the Bundesarchiv, the main German federal archive. [We would] sit in the back, open the documents, and she would start whispering in my ear. Everybody in the Bundesarchiv would turn around and go, "Sshh." We would have to be even quieter. I simply talked my way out of some of these things. We read books together. We spent a lot of time together, these finely tuned translators and I.... One of the reasons there are so few books like mine is because historians feel awkward about using translators. You never get regional portraits; there are many wonderful books about Poland in this period, Hungary in this period, Germany in this period, written both in those languages and in English.

The Russian Archives were opened in the 1990s when the Russians were in the wake of Glasnost and the end of the Soviet Union. There was a movement in Russia to end secrecy and to discuss the past openly. This was an authentic movement. It came from the ground up and people at the top supported and sympathized with it. The Archives, in some ways, were extraordinarily accessible, and archivists began working with western scholars.... I worked in Russia towards the end of the nineties, and had the impression that one of the reasons that they were open was the Russians were so preoccupied with other things and they did not care. People often said to me, "How is it that a young American woman could be wandering around these Archives? Is anybody stopping you?" The answer is, "No." The attitude was, "She wants to go look at some old documents? So what? We are busy with reforming our economy with massive change."

In 2000, Putin became president of Russia and had a much more instrumental idea of what history was, and he re-politicized history. He became much more conscious over what history was told and how it was being told: this always trickles down.... [But] I should add that they aren't totally closed and you can still work in them....

THERE WERE REALLY THREE or four institutions that the Soviets considered important. If you look at the world in 1945, Stalin did not have a ten-point plan such as, "We're going to do this, and then these will be Soviet satellites." He was an opportunist and a tactician and had a conviction that, sooner or later, these will become Communist countries, because Marxist-Leninist ideology says so. It says that there will be international revolutions and the Soviet Union will bring the international revolution to these countries. He had a conviction that it would happen, but not a lot of certainty about when and was still nervous about how the West might react. But [he wanted to] make sure that he had enough influence in three institutions in particular that he thought were important. Number one was the secret police. He created...secret police forces, speaking local languages; sometimes from people from the Soviet Union and sometimes from natives, and began training them in NKVD (KGB) methods right away.

In Poland, the Soviets began creating a Polish Secret Police force in 1939. They import those people back into the country in 1944 when they begin chasing the Germans out of Poland. [The Polish Secret Police] is an institution [that] used to target people. The Soviet Union...begins to look for potential opponents such as church leaders or resistance leaders. These are the first encounters between the Red Army and the Resistance Army, which is called the Home Army. These are very violent, with the Home Army expecting to collaborate with the Red Army in the fight against Fascism. Instead, the Red Army arrested [the Home Army], disarmed them, and sent them east to labor camps. This may sound paradoxical, but because the plan from the beginning was to eliminate or suppress those people that might be post-war leaders, that included the Home Army.

At the same time, the other institution [they were] obsessed with was the radio. They were interested in radio, as opposed to newspapers, because they thought of the radio as the most effective means of reaching the masses. There was not much television anywhere at the time in 1945; television eventually serves a similar function. But, in 1945, it's the radio. Everywhere they go, one of the first things they do is either take over or create new radio stations. In Central Berlin, they occupy the Nazi radio station immediately on the first day as soon as they get there. They protect it from harm. Some of the first East German Communists, who spent the war in Moscow, are flown in from Berlin and sent to work on the radio station. That's how important they considered it to be. In Poland, they create a radio station from scratch since all radio equipment had been destroyed during the war. They believe in the efficacy of their own propaganda. They believe that "once we begin to explain to people what we're doing and what we want, they will go along with us." Radio is going to be the means to do that. They care enormously about targeted organizations, and the secret police uses the radio.

The third element...is they begin to target what we would call organizations of civil society. Youth groups and other self-organized groups such as women's charitable organizations and church organizations are the groups they immediately want to put under state control. They do not want any independent institutions or associations of any kind to come into existence.

The YMCA had a building in Warsaw. It was one of the few buildings to survive the war, and very soon after the war, people began moving into it. The YMCA had some resources from outside. It was able to bring in clothing sent from the West and to feed people and to set up their soup kitchens. It also very quickly became, because of a shipment of jazz records that arrived at the YMCA, a center of social life in Warsaw. It was the place where you would go to parties in 1947 and 1948. Warsaw is a city where just everything is rubble and there's practically nothing standing, [while the] YMCA is an island of jazz music. The YMCA poses such a threat and such a problem at the very highest levels. The Communist leaders write to one another angry letters, "We must do something about the YMCA," "We must destroy the YMCA," and eventually, they shut it down. They closed it up, and at a very tragic moment, the Communist Youth Group is sent in to smash the jazz records because anything that is seen as an island of self-organized or spontaneous organization is a potential threat to the regime.

MANY THOUSANDS OF JEWS have moved back in to Eastern Germany, Poland, or Hungary [after the war], and many thousands have survived. Remember that many people were in hiding or disguise to survive the war. More survived in Hungary than is generally known, particularly in the city of Budapest, because the attack on the Hungarian Jews happened late in the war…when the Nazis took over Hungary in the end, that was when the Holocaust began in Hungary…. In Poland, they survived in all kinds of ways. Many of them survived by going to the Soviet Union, by coming abroad, and many people came home to find what's left…. As one very sad and moving archival document says, many come home just to see the cemeteries and leave because they don't want to live there anymore. But Jews do come back. Some try to make new lives there, and some join the Communist Parties. The Communist Party has an attraction for, not just Jews, but for anybody who's experienced the devastation of the war and the shattering of all ethics and all morality that war brought. Many people did see in Communism an alternative…. Liberal democracy has failed, the West did not come to our aid, capitalism was a disaster…maybe there's some sort of alternative here. There is a very brief period, where some people were listening to the radio station and they were attracted to it, and it was particularly attractive for Jews who really had nothing else and who had been excluded from all kinds of politics, not only during the war, but in some cases before. They come…and it's a strange and hard story to tell. Some join the Communist Party and come into conflict with the Communist Party because they are small traders or merchants, and subject to the nationalization and takeover of this period. There begins to be large groups to leave for Israel right in the late 1940s. Some leave with the aid of those countries. There are a couple of moments when both the Poles and Hungarians help train Jews who were going to go ahead and fight for independence in Palestine, to the irritation of the British.

…The Soviet Union and the Soviet system in Eastern Europe contained the seeds of its own destruction. Many of the problems we saw at the end began at the very beginning. [When] attempting to control all institutions and all parts of the economy, political life and social life, you create opposition and potential dissidence everywhere. If you tell all artists they have to paint the same way, and one artist says, "No, I don't want to paint that way. I want to paint another way," you have just made him into a political dissident; somebody who might have been otherwise apolitical. If you tell Boy Scout troops that they can no longer be Boy Scouts but they have to be Young Pioneers, which is what happened in a number of countries, and one group decides they don't like that, then they form a secret underground Boy Scout troop. This absolutely happened; underground Scouts were very important in Poland all through the Communist period, and you have just created another group of political opponents from other apolitical teenagers. The system created pockets of resistance and opposition all over.

The other element of the system that you can see from the beginning is the gap that begins to grow between the ideology and the reality. The Communist leaders continue to say, "This is what things are going to be like. This is what should be happening. We have read Marxist doctrine. This is how things will develop. This is how the economy will grow." It does not happen that way, or it happens but not really, or, there is some growth, but the West is growing much faster. The system is never able to fulfill its promises, which means that, by 1989, even the people leading it don't believe in it any more. The loss of faith in the system, which begins in the 1940s, and simply grows worse and worse over time, means there's no one left to defend it.

By 1989, not even the Soviet leadership at the very highest levels was able to defend the system. Gorbachev, in the late eighties, began the conversation about history. What's really wrong? How is our system set up? As soon as people did not have to collaborate anymore, and did not feel obligated to go along with the Party, to keep chanting "The Party is always right," then they stopped, and they stopped very fast.

THE QUESTION OF COLLABORATION [with authorities or secret police] is incredibly complicated. It is more complicated than we in the West like to think. People very often were not one thing or another.... There were some collaborators and there were some real heroes of resistance, but many people zigzag through their lives. They collaborated at times, or they marched in the May Day Parade, and then at other times, even told jokes behind the party's back or agreed to help somebody or hide somebody who's been imprisoned. People often tried to find a path which they felt was moral and which they felt was right. In a period when the state controls everything in everything, this is very difficult.

It often helps to think about if you have children: Would you be willing to say, "I won't march in the May Day Parade? I won't salute comrade Stalin? I won't do all these things," if you know that it means your child will be expelled from school and will not be able to study and will not have a future and won't be educated? These were really dramatic and radical choices people made. They had to give up things that would never occur to us that we would have to give up in order to make a political point.... It's more drastic to become a police informant, although, even then, there were degrees. There were people who thought, "Right. I'm going to inform just a little bit, and I won't really say anything important. I'll do it so that I can protect my wife who's ill and needs to get medicine from the hospital; and if I do this, then I'll get medicine for her and she won't die." Even then, sometimes the choices were much more grey and more complicated than we now imagine sitting here, now, in a free society.

...THE PEOPLE [IN THE United States who have power] dish out favors to people based upon whether or not you follow the party. The difference is there's no threat of violence behind it...if you don't vote for the

Republican Party or the Democratic Party, you don't go to jail and you're not going to be arrested and your child will not be expelled from school. There's a dramatic difference between the kinds of consequences and the radical nature of choices the people had to make. The second difference is, our system is more or less open. We know this stuff goes on and we can have an argument about it and discuss it. The Communist system was entirely closed. There was a high level of secrecy about all state affairs and all political affairs—you didn't necessarily know what was going on.

Money and Politics

2008: The Big Short

MICHAEL LEWIS

A onetime bond salesman turned financial journalist, Michael Lewis joined us on Q & A on April 4, 2010, to discuss his bestselling book, The Big Short: Inside the Doomsday Machine *(W.W. Norton, 2010). It tells the story of the financial crisis of 2008 and the people who created the complex financial instruments such as credit default swaps that led to it. The fallout from the subprime mortgage crisis was dramatic. The U.S. found itself in the worst recession since the Great Depression. Property values plummeted, unemployment rose to double digits, and the stock market lost half its value. While millions lost their jobs and personal wealth, Michael Lewis details the stories of the Wall Street few who got rich along the way.*

I WORKED AT SALOMON Brothers for almost three years. I got there in the summer of '85 and left in early '88. The oxygen for *Liar's Poker* was my own bewilderment that anybody was willing to pay me large sums of money to give investment advice. I had been an art history major at Princeton. I had, indeed, done an economics degree at the London School of Economics, but it really didn't have anything to do with giving investment advice. As interested as I was in finance at Salomon Brothers, I had a pretty strong sense that I wasn't particularly well-suited to be telling people what to do with their money. I didn't think I knew what was going to happen in the stock market and didn't feel like I was making a useful contribution to the global economy, but it was clear if I just sat in that seat, I'd get rich. That was a puzzle. Why on earth should I, or any-one, get paid all of this money just to sit in this seat? The trick was get-ting to the seat. So I left to write a nonfiction story about it [*Liar's Poker*] that also tried to explain what had happened on Wall Street to make these sorts of jobs possible, and to make them so lucrative.

I really did think when I wrote it, that this was it. This was the 1980s. I thought it was a strange little episode in American history. It was going to end. These seats would be less valuable, so I had to get the story down on paper just so future generations would believe it. Little did I know that twenty years later people would pity me for how little I made while I was there. The sums that were paid on Wall Street had gotten so big that my salary looked quaint.

MEREDITH WHITNEY WAS A catalyst for me to write *The Big Short*. She was, until very recently, what is called a sell-side analyst, which means she works for the Wall Street firms that offer stocks to the public. She worked for a firm called Oppenheimer, and she was a financial sector analyst. Meredith Whitney, whom I had never heard of, started saying things in late 2007, when I first started paying attention, about Wall Street that sounded different from anything I had ever heard. She was saying the Wall Street firms basically didn't understand the risks they were taking. They didn't understand their own balance sheets. She predicted Citi-group was going to have to cut or eliminate its dividend a week before they actually did. She seemed to know more about what was going on inside the places than the people who ran them. Her tone was almost as interesting as what she said. She was actually condescending to these Wall Street people. I called her up because she was making a different sound. I thought, "I haven't been writing about this world, but I'm curious who this woman is and why she thinks this." She made such sense that she persuaded me pretty early on that the Wall Street firms had become the dumb money at the poker table. She didn't put it that way, but I put it that way. When I left Salomon Brothers, the last thing you wanted to do if you were an investor was be on the other side of one of Salomon Broth-ers' trades. If there was a zero-sum bet to be made with Salomon Broth-ers, you did not make it because you were sure to lose money. What had happened was somehow the firms had turned stupid, or rather, as institutions, they had become the dumb money. I was curious how something this big had changed. Then the natural question, of course, was, "If they were the dumb money, who was the smart money?" That led me to my characters because they were the smart money.

I WAS LED TO Steve Eisman by Meredith Whitney because Meredith Whitney had trained with him. She was from the "school of Eisman," in a way. He was a New Yorker, born and bred. He had gone to the University of Pennsylvania and been a brilliant student. He went to the Harvard Law School and was a brilliant student. He instantly joined, like so many Harvard Law School grads, a corporate law firm and hated it immediately, so he called his mama, as one does when one's in trouble. His mother and father were both prominent brokers at Oppenheimer Securities. His mama got him a job as a "step-and-fetch-it." He was a junior analyst, but analyzing nothing at first. In the mid-nineties, when he joined the subprime mortgage market, it was in its earliest form. There was this new kind of company called a subprime mortgage originator, meaning the people who are looking for borrowers. Someone asked him if he wanted to be the analyst on it, so he became one of the first two or three analysts of subprime mortgage companies on Wall Street. Pretty quickly, he was the world's expert on the subject. When this happened, he was in his early thirties.

It didn't occur to me until one of his colleagues pointed it out that when *Curb Your Enthusiasm*, the Larry David show, came on to HBO, they stole [Larry David's character]—that was Steve. They said, he is Larry David. He runs around offending people. His own wife said to me, "My husband is rude. He has no manners. I know that. I've tried and I've tried and I've tried, and there's nothing I can do about it." He is tactless throughout the story, but there is a pattern to his tactlessness which endeared him to me. He was never rude or mean to little people. He wasn't mean to the secretary. He wasn't mean to his nanny. He was wonderful with them. He was protective and caring about the people beneath him. Who he was tactless to were people who were in power who he thought were abusing their positions. It made him angry. He would find himself in these situations where he was in meetings with Wall Street big shots and saying things that caused the meeting to come to an end or caused the Wall Street big shot to say, "I'm never going to set foot in the same room with this man again." It got to the point where the people who worked with him would stop their jobs for the day to follow Eisman wherever he was going because they wanted to see the show. They knew that if he was going to be meeting someone important on Wall Street, then something was going to happen that they were going to want to see. One of them said, "It's like watching a car crash when you're watching Eisman" in a social situation. You can't watch, but you can't not watch.

A MORTGAGE LOAN IS when you borrow money to buy a house. A prime mortgage loan is to a borrower who has a credit score of a certain number. Credit scores supposedly measure the likelihood you are going to re-pay your loan. There is a company called the Fair Isaac Corporation that generates something called a FICO score, a "Fair Isaac Corporation" score, that suggests what the likelihood is. On a scale of 800, above 660 is a prime mortgage, below 660 is a subprime mortgage....

The credit default swap is the mechanism that was created in 2005 to bet against the subprime mortgage market. The credit default swap is es-sentially an insurance policy on a security. If I buy a credit default swap on a subprime mortgage loan, I pay you, the seller, a premium as I would an insurance premium—a couple of percent a year. In exchange, you have to pay me the whole value of the subprime mortgage bond if the bond goes bad. I bought insurance on that bond. The general idea is that people who own subprime mortgage bonds might like to have the ability to buy insurance on them as a hedge. It is a silly idea because you can simply not buy the subprime mortgage bonds in the first place if you were worried about the risk, but that is why these instruments were sup-posedly created. They quickly became tools for speculation. Instead of buying a credit default swap on a subprime mortgage bond to hedge my risk of owning one, I buy a bet on a subprime mortgage bond. So what someone is buying is an insurance policy on the mortgage bond.

The whole financial system at this moment in financial history was organizing itself around a bet and the bet was on subprime mortgage bonds, which are essentially just pools of loans. There are a bunch of people who borrowed money to buy a house. Are they going to pay off their loans or are they not? The vast majority of the financial system was betting yes, they're basically going to repay their loans, and some people bet no.

[If you buy a house, you get a mortgage with a mortgage company. You owe them, for example, $100,000. Then you might find out your mortgage has been sold.] There could be lots of steps in the change, but the simple step is the bank sells it to a Wall Street firm that pools it together with lots of other loans in a trust, then issues bonds off the trust. The money coming in from you to pay off your loan is now going to some bondholder. It could be in Germany. It could be Japan. It could be anywhere. He is the ultimate lender. The ultimate lender now is very far removed from the ultimate borrower. It is very likely to be Goldman Sachs, but you don't see that. You are still writing checks to some servicer of your mortgage who is standing in between [you and the ultimate lender]. The Wall Street firm doesn't actually go and get your money from you.

The dollar volume [of subprime mortgages] is unbelievable. To put it in perspective, the subprime mortgage loan business did not exist until the mid-nineties. In the mid-nineties, it had a brief life and it was maybe $10, $20, $30 billion a year of subprime mortgage loans. There were several companies born all at once that existed to originate the loans, to go find people to lend to, and to package them into securities and bonds and sell them off. There were companies called Aims Financial, The Money Store, and Green Tree. These companies don't exist anymore, but it was small. It was tiny.

Why there was a need for subprime mortgages is a good question, and it has to do with what has happened in the American economy. There were lots of people living beyond their means and using their credit cards to do it. One of the big changes in American life in the last twenty to twenty-five years has been the extension of credit to people who previously had trouble getting it. Credit companies and auto loans got there first. There was an argument that the credit companies were charging some poor guy who cannot make ends meet 25 percent interest on his unpaid balances. That same guy owned a house and he had equity in the house. If we could get that same guy a home equity loan, we could justify lending him at a much lower rate than the credit card company because our loan is secured by the house as an asset. It would be good for everybody because he is going to pay off his 25 percent per annum credit card debt and instead owe a 10 percent home mortgage. Nobody should have been [getting scammed at this point]. In theory, it could have worked. The problem was the consumers were poorly protected. The minute that the Wall Street firms were in the business of harvesting middle class and lower middle class Americans for their home equity value, and making loans to them against it, there was a natural risk of abuse because generally in financial transactions, people are bewildered. The minute they get a little complicated, they get a lot complicated in people's minds.

...THE STORY I'VE TOLD is what happened in the private markets without a lot of government help. These loans were not being made because the government said, "You've got to make loans to poor people." That wasn't why they were getting made. They were being made because the lender was lending the money, packing them in the bonds, and selling them off, and didn't bear the risk of the loans not being repaid. It was a volume business. They got paid fees for doing the business. The trick was persuading people to take out the loans. Some people didn't take a lot of persuading, but there were lots of cases where the nature of the loan was disguised from the person who was borrowing the money. Teaser rates should be criminal. Essentially, you talk someone into taking a loan out that has an artificially low rate for the first couple of years so it looks very, very tempting, and then it skyrockets after two years. But the impression is left that you can flip this house within the two years. All of a sudden, if they make you that loan, what they have done is turned you into a property speculator because you are completely dependent on the price of the property going up to refinance the loan. If the value of your house goes down, you are stuck with this loan that is going to eat you alive.

This pernicious relationship between high finance and the American borrower is what Eisman becomes an expert in, and he starts to become very, very cynical about what Wall Street does in this situation. He asked, "How big were these subprime loans?" When we got to 2004 to 2007, there were about $1.6 trillion of subprime loans made, and another $1.2 trillion of what's called Alt-A loans. These are not subprime, but they are loans that for some reason lack the documentation, so the borrower is not required to file proof of income. In a lot of cases, those were sub-prime, too. This was about almost $3 trillion of loans that were dubious. Eisman was at first sitting there investing in the stock market with his little hedge fund, but then seeing again this explosion of lending in this beast he thought he had slain back in the nineties, the subprime mortgage lending business, he said, "This is all going to blow up again. This is all going to end badly because I know how this business is done," and it is a sinister business. He started to try to learn about the bond market, the market that's creating this credit. He and his colleagues were essentially starting from scratch. They did not know anything about the ratings agencies and they did not know what a credit default swap was, none of this. They learned that you could actually make bets against these loans, and he thought the loans were going to go bad. So he ended up making a massive bet against the loans. He bought credit default swaps on the subprime mortgage bonds.

MOODY'S (THE RATINGS COMPANY) biggest shareholder is Warren Buffett, and Standard and Poor's is owned by McGraw-Hill. They are both public corporations. They will tell you, "We're just like *Auto Trend* magazine for car buyers. We're just journalists. We give our views about the relative trustworthiness of these various securities and the relative likelihood they're going to repay." These ratings were taken far too seriously. They were meant as a suggestion of the way you should order them in your mind from riskiest to least risky, but their place in the world was, and is, much more serious than that. They are federally-sanctioned enterprises. Banks have to reserve capital against their assets, and how much they have to reserve against each asset depends on the rating of the asset. The rating is bestowed on that asset by Moody's and Standard and Poor's. Their ratings have a huge effect on the ability of the institutions to hold these securities.

A triple-A rating is what the U.S. government and the U.S. treasury have. S&P and Moody's slapped triple-A ratings on piles of subprime mortgage bonds, and then on derivatives culled from these piles. They were triple-A ratings priced at hundreds of billions of dollars on bonds that did not just decline in value, but went to zero, so the ratings in this world end up meaning nothing.

[STEVE EISMAN AND OTHERS were] betting that the subprime mortgage bonds would all collapse. [The party on the other side of his bet against subprime mortgage bonds was the financial products unit of triple-A rated insurance company AIG. Former Bush Treasury Secretary Henry Paulson and Federal Reserve Chairman Ben Bernanke] wanted to pay off the gambling debts of AIG because all of the Wall Street firms were on the other side of those bets. If AIG didn't pay off its bets, the firms would have experienced the loss. Think of it this way: Goldman Sachs had lost on its bet to [subprime mortgage investor] Michael Burry, but it wasn't that they thought they were just brokering the debt between Michael Burry and AIG. So they paid off Michael Burry and they were out of pocket. They wanted to get paid off by AIG, and if they weren't paid off, they would have had a $13 billion loss. I don't defend this. I'm just saying what they were thinking. Paulson and Bernanke and [then Obama Treasury Secretary] Tim Geithner were thinking, "If we don't make the Wall Street firms whole, the Wall Street firms are going to collapse. The market's not going to believe they're going to survive." [A couple of them did collapse.] Wall Street people were not hurt. The rest of the country got hurt by what the Wall Street firms had been doing the previous five years, generating this frenzy of finance where finance should not have happened. If you were a Lehman Brothers' bondholder, you got hurt. If you were a Lehman Brothers' employee, you got hurt. And that's about it.... But Dick Fuld, the CEO of Lehman Brothers, made many, many, many tens of millions of dollars that he got to keep after his firm collapsed.

HOWIE HUBLER IS THE *reductio ad absurdum* of this story. First, the financial system had organized itself around this bet. Second, no matter which side of the bet you were on, you still got rich personally. Your institution might have lost huge sums of money, but you, yourself, got rich. Howie Hubler was a trader at Morgan Stanley, the Wall Street investment bank. He was regarded as the hub of the smartest group of traders, and they traded subprime-backed mortgage bonds. They were not satisfied making just millions of dollars a year. They wanted to make tens of millions of dollars a year, so they started to agitate within the firm for a bigger piece of the action. They wanted to be given their own little hedge fund within Morgan Stanley, owned by Morgan Stanley, so they were given it. It became the Morgan Stanley proprietary trading group. Very soon, months after they were set up, they made an enormous bet. It was a complicated bet, but the gist of it was they bought, in a matter of a couple of months, $15 billion of triple-A rated CDOs backed by subprime mortgages. A CDO is a collateralized debt obligation. Now, what is that? The loans create the bonds. The bonds go into a trust. The trust is traunched up. It is sliced so that there are junior and senior claims on this trust. If you are entitled to get the first dollars that get repaid, you have less risk than the first person who gets the last dollars that get repaid, so you get a lower rate of interest and you have a higher rated bond—a triple-A rated bond. The person who experiences the first losses from the trust gets a triple-B-minus rated bond and a much higher rate of interest. Wall Street took the triple-B-minus rated bonds and piled them all into another trust. Slice that up and 80 percent of that is triple-A rated. So what Howie Hubler bought was essentially a pile of triple-B rated subprime mortgage bonds—$15 billion of them. He did this very quickly with Goldman Sachs and Deutsche Bank, which were the two big counterpoint parties.

THOSE BONDS WENT TO zero. There were some bets against it so he didn't lose all $15 billion, but he lost $9-and-a-half billion. It is, by far, the single largest trading loss from a single bet in the history of Wall Street. He was allowed to resign. He was allowed to keep all of his deferred compensation, and he is rich. The amazing thing to me, and this is another reason I got reengaged with the subject, is that nobody knows who he is. His name is not mentioned. He was just allowed to move on. Twenty years ago, when a trader lost a lot of money, he was shamed. Everybody knew his name. That this had happened and had been regarded as a private matter in a public corporation was an incredible thing to me, so I went and talked to all of the people involved and wrote the story.

GREG LIPPMAN IS THE one Wall Street trader who was actually on the right side of the bet very early on. He was the subprime bond trader at Deutsche Bank. He was betting against subprime. This is where it gets very strange. Here was this trader who was the senior trader inside a big

Wall Street firm. It's a German bank, but it's still a big Wall Street firm. His firm was creating these subprime mortgage bonds and creating the CDOs, and he was saying, "It's all going bad. I'm going to make a big bet." He spent eighteen months at war with his own firm because people were telling him he was crazy, he was stupid, and he was wasting money. He was telling them, "*You're* crazy, *you're* stupid, and *you're* wasting money." He was running around trying to talk people out of buying the stuff his firm was selling. He was an annoying character to a lot of people in his own firm, but he was the other principal short seller in this.

THE JARGON, OR MORE generally, the complexity of Wall Street is probably not self-consciously invented to hide what is going on, but that is the effect. People on Wall Street are happy it has that effect. It's a very interesting thing. The complexity is a form of obscurity no matter how putatively transparent it is. A lot of this stuff isn't even transparent. It is a lot of hidden deals, but you dissuade the public from taking too much of an interest. The only social purpose I had in writing this book…was if I could explain this to people, they are going to be outraged, and they really need to know. You need to know. There is a financial reform bill coming out and people need to know.

I WROTE A LITTLE magazine article for the now deceased *Portfolio* magazine a year-and-a-half ago when I met Steve Eisman, who was the center of that article. The phrase "The Big Short" popped into my head. I thought it would be a great title for the piece. I said to myself, "This isn't actually a piece; it is going to be a big book. It is an interesting story. There is much more than a magazine article here…." "Short" is to bet against something—to bet the price is falling. This was the single greatest opportunity to bet on prices falling in the history of mankind.

[THE CHARACTERS IN MY book had very mixed feelings about the subprime mortgage collapse.] One of them went to the SEC and tried to get them to take action. All of them were screaming to high heaven, "This is insane." They were torn up about it…I don't know [how much Eisman or Burry made]; $50 million, $100 million. They made for their investors $700 or $800 million. I was told by someone in Greg Lippman's firm that he was paid a bonus of about $50 million at the end of '07. So, he got rich. I think Steve Eisman was sincere when he said, "You feel like Noah. Yes, you built the ark and, yes, you are going to survive, but at that moment when the flood happens and you are on the ark, it is not a happy moment for Noah. It is a torn-up moment."

We are living through a really traumatic period and it is not over. We are at the beginning rather than the end. There are real structural problems. I'm not an economic forecaster but everything I read suggests we are going to be living with unusually high levels of unemployment and a lot of pain from over-indebtedness. A quarter of the country is on food stamps. It is not a Great Depression. We are not reprising exactly what happened in the thirties, but it is a version of that.

The Federal Takeover of
Fannie Mae and Freddie Mac

PETER WALLISON

On September 6, 2008, the George W. Bush Administration announced the federal takeover of two major government sponsored enterprises, Fannie Mae and Freddie Mac. Treasury Secretary Hank Paulson justified the decision to place them into conservatorship to avoid turmoil in the financial markets in the U.S. and overseas. The move also allowed for an infusion of billions of tax dollars and changes in leadership at the top of both organizations. In the wake of the government bailout, Peter Wallison, a financial policy studies fellow with the American Enterprise Institute in Washington, visited Q & A on September 14, 2008, to give his perspective on how the crisis unfolded.

I ALWAYS LOOKED AT Fannie Mae and Freddie Mac as key examples— maybe the poster children—of corporate welfare. They are the ones who were most helped by the federal government.... I wanted to be sure that when I started on this process, writing a book and doing other things, that I showed that this was not simply something that Republicans or conservatives were interested in, but people who were interested in a fair government, a fair economy, and government policies that really didn't favor corporations.

I'VE BEEN IN THE government a fair amount. I've never run for office, but I've helped people who are running for office. And then, in Republican administrations, I've had some roles. I'm a lawyer—graduate of Harvard Law School, and then I practiced law for many years. And during that time, I came in and out of government. I'm a New Yorker, actually, by birth, and so, I got to know Nelson Rockefeller. I became his counsel when he was vice president, and then, in the Reagan Administration, I was the general counsel of the Treasury Department. And finally, when Don Regan went over to become chief of staff in the Reagan White House, I went over about a year later—left my practice once more—and became a White House counsel for Ronald Reagan. So, I've had a fair amount of government experience and a lot of financial experience in the government. That's one of the things that gave me a real interest in Fannie Mae and Freddie Mac.

Fannie Mae was a fairly significant company in the early 1980s, when I was at Treasury, and even then, it occurred to me that this was an accident waiting to happen. They had a business model that seemed to me to be unworkable, and one that would eventually cause a lot of problems. I wasn't able to do anything at Treasury at the time; we were too busy with many of the problems, including the S&L collapse. But what I did remember when I left Treasury was that this is a subject that I'd like to return to at some time in the future. Fortunately, when I had an opportunity to go to AEI, I was able then to start looking more seriously at Fannie and start investigating a little bit more exactly how they were doing and whether my thoughts about what was going to happen to them were likely to come true.

...I THOUGHT, ACTUALLY, WHAT then Treasury Secretary Henry Paulson said was the truth at the time, and that is, he thought, that with the backing of the U.S. government made explicit through what Congress had authorized in July 2008, there wouldn't be any need to come in specifically and take over Fannie and Freddie. But what they found was that the markets didn't quite believe that Fannie and Freddie were going to pay all of their obligations, and what they found as the days went on was the spread of interest rates that Fannie and Freddie were paying over treasury rates was gradually growing. As it grew, it meant that mortgages in the United States would become more expensive because if Fannie has to pay more for its money, then the banks that they lend to will have to pay more for their money, and people will have to pay more money when they buy homes. What Paulson saw happening was that he had to reassure the markets that the government was actually behind these institutions, and the only way to do it was to actually take them over. He also knew from the investigations of Fannie and Freddie's financial condition that they were close to, if not, insolvent. I don't think Paulson misled anyone in the Senate. What he said was, "You give me this authority and I probably won't have to use it because the markets will believe that I could come in at any time and take over these companies, and therefore, they will know that their loans will be repaid." Well, they didn't quite believe it. We have read that the Bank of China was beginning to sell off part of its portfolio of Fannie and Freddie's. Fewer people were showing up at the auctions for Fannie and Freddie securities. They weren't bidding as aggressively, so Fannie and Freddie were beginning to have to pay more and more for the money they were borrowing, and the pattern was becoming very clear, so Treasury really had to act. Now, I happen to believe they did the wrong thing. He should not have appointed a conservator for Fannie and Freddie. He should have appointed a receiver for Fannie and Freddie. A receiver would be able to modify their business model substantially, and even in his statement Paulson said that they have flawed business models. That is true. That's why I thought from the beginning that they were going to cause trouble for everyone because they are partly profit-making companies and partly companies with a government mission with government backing. Those two things can't go together in the same institution. Paulson should have moved in and taken them over with a receiver so he could have changed that business model. He didn't do that.

ONE OF THE WAYS that Fannie and Freddie operate is to create pools of mortgages, and then they sell securities that are backed by those pools of mortgages. That's how you get a mortgage-backed security…. It's put into a pool with a lot of other mortgages; some of them are larger, some of them smaller, but thousands of them, all in the same pool. Then, securities are sold, backed by that pool, and the securities say that we will pay you your share of what we receive from the mortgages in the pool, and if the mortgages in the pool don't perform as we anticipate they will perform, we will pay you anyway. In other words, we guarantee a certain return out of this pool. That's what a Fannie or Freddie mortgage-backed security entails. Now, the reason you are able to get your $400,000 mortgage from some bank that is the lender [which] knows they can sell your mortgage to Fannie, which will buy the mortgage and put it into the pool, and then reimburse itself by selling mortgage-backed securities to investors.

A mortgage-backed security…would say [to its holder that] this security represents a one-millionth share of a certain pool of mortgages that we have created, and if we don't pay you the specified amount to come out of this pool, then you have us backing the pool. The security is absolutely solid, and that's one of the reasons why the government had to take over Fannie Mae and Freddie Mac, because so many individuals and mostly financial institutions around the world hold exactly those kinds of securities. [The Chinese own a] very large amount, probably running into maybe the hundreds of billions of dollars. Same with the Japanese. Very large. Most central banks own these kinds of securities, and not only the mortgage-backed securities, but they buy direct borrowings by Fannie Mae and Freddie Mac—that is, the two GSEs, Government-Sponsored Enterprises—use to buy and hold mortgages themselves. They don't securitize all their mortgages. They hold a certain number of those mortgages, amounting now to about $1.5 trillion, in their own portfolios. That is, in fact, the most profitable way that they operate. Mortgage-backed securities are not a very profitable business. It's a much less risky business and, as a result, it's not as profitable. When they really want to make profits, they buy and hold the mortgages themselves, because what is being paid on the mortgages is a lot more than they have to pay for the money they borrow in order to buy those mortgages.

A GSE is a government-sponsored enterprise. Fannie Mae was created in 1968 from an existing organization called Fannie Mae, which was started during the New Deal, and was an actual government agency. The trouble is that, by 1968, when we were in the middle of the Vietnam War, we were running deficits in the general government. The Johnson Administration realized that the way Fannie Mae was growing, it was causing these deficits, because it was putting out a lot more cash than it was taking in [in] any year, as it grew and bought more and more mortgages. They decided one of the ways to reduce this deficit was to get Fannie Mae off the government's books, which they did by selling shares to the public in Fannie Mae, and turning it into a quasi-public company—with private shareholders, but at the same time, with a kind of implicit government guarantee, because they were allowed to keep a number of ties to the U.S. government. Since that time, the capital markets have believed that the government would back Fannie Mae, and ultimately, Freddie Mac, which was created a few years later, in case they got into any difficulty. That's why they've never had any trouble raising funds, because there was always the thought in the markets that the government would back them if they got into any trouble. They denied this for many years. They said, "No, no, no. There's no doubt that we are independent of the government. The government has no responsibility for us." Their supporters in Congress said exactly the same thing. But now we realize that the markets were right all along: As soon as they got into trouble, the government stepped in and saved them.

IT'S VERY HARD TO say [whether the Johnson Administration decision was cynical] in Washington. This is called smoke and mirrors. The idea was to get Fannie, at that point, off the books of the government. If they had done it completely, if they had said, you won't have a congressional charter, what you will have is a charter from, say, the State of Delaware; you won't have any line of credit to the Treasury Department, as they initially had; we won't say it's possible for banks to invest in an unlimited manner in your securities; if we take away many of the benefits that Fannie and Freddie were given at the time they were privatized—then, it would have been a perfectly reasonable thing to do. That would have been a real privatization. Unfortunately, they only did a quasi-privatization, where they allowed the markets to believe that, over time, if it was necessary, the government would step in and back them.

[FORMER CHIEF EXECUTIVE OFFICER (CEO) of Fannie Mae, Franklin Raines's compensation from 1998 to 2003 was $90 million; the portion derived from components tied to attaining earnings per share goals, $52 million. Timothy Howard, chief financial officer, his compensation for the same time period, $30 million. Jaime Gorelick, the vice chairman of Fannie Mae, took away $26 million in those years, 1998 to 2003. Daniel Mudd, another CEO during that time, took out $26 million.] These are private companies, after all. If they have private shareholders, their obligation is to make sure that their shareholders earn profits. To the extent that they were successful doing that, they would claim, like any other CEO, or any other major officer of a private company, that they're entitled to the compensation that they were receiving. The problem with that argument is that they were helped substantially by the backing of the taxpayers of the United States. One would think that anyone who realized he or she was getting that kind of backing would be less demanding in the compensation that they wanted. Unfortunately, they didn't behave that way. They behaved as though they were entitled to all this compensation, when their jobs were made very easy by the fact that the government was seen by the markets as backing them up.

[As far back as 2002, President George W. Bush began arguing for greater regulatory control over the two companies, but was thwarted by Republicans who controlled Congress. Democrats eventually granted the authority, which provided the legal underpinning for the takeover.] I was for this. I was for a number of things President Bush was proposing, and still am. The point he was trying to make…was to separate the government from Fannie Mae and Freddie Mac to the extent possible. The way this thing was set up by Lyndon Johnson and his administration was to have a real quasi-government agency, in which the president appointed five members of the board, and the shareholders elected the remaining thirteen. That reflected a certain involvement of the government in their business. What the president was trying to do was to send a different signal, and that is: "No. We're not responsible for Fannie Mae and Freddie Mac." They were trying to get the markets to believe during this period that there really wasn't a connection between the United States government and Fannie Mae and Freddie Mac, and the markets simply would not believe it. The markets turned out to be right, because now we find, when Fannie and Freddie have gotten into financial trouble, that, in fact, the government did step in and back them. This has happened before. The markets are not crazy and they are not particularly prescient. They just look at what's happened in the past, and in the 1980s, the farm credit system had financial difficulties. That was also a government-sponsored enterprise and, of course, the government stepped in and bailed them out. So, the markets looked at that, and they looked at what Fannie and Freddie are in relation to the government, and they said, "Well, this is going to be the same thing. The U.S. government is never going to allow one of these organizations to fail." And the markets, of course, turned out to be right. We are not allowing them to fail.

Fannie Mae and Freddie Mac are *sui generis* in this respect. That is, it was always clear to me and to a lot of other conservatives that the government was going to bail them out if they got into difficulty, and that's why they would get into difficulty, because there wasn't any market discipline. We believe—and I think most economists believe—that the best way to control risk in private companies is to make sure the market is at risk; meaning, they will not get the funds that they need if they are taking risks and the market is wary.... But when they're backed by the government, that doesn't happen. That's how—at least in my mind—we get this kind of corporate welfare that we've had with Fannie Mae and Freddie Mac, in particular.

...At the time the Bear Stearns bailout occurred, the international financial markets were in a panic. There was, for the first time, certainly in my lifetime, and probably for the first time since the Great Depression, real concern worldwide in the stability of all of the major financial institutions in the world, in the global capital markets—the major banks in Europe, the major banks in the United States, the investment banks in the United States, and many other such institutions. The fear was, at the Treasury Department and at the Federal Reserve, that if Bear Stearns— which was not one of the larger investment banks in the United States— failed, the panic that was current in the market at the time would cause investors to run to all these other financial institutions and start withdrawing their funds—in other words, create runs throughout the world. They hoped to prevent that by showing that the government will step in and stop that from happening. This actually was the right thing to do under the circumstances.... If the government had not done that, the people of the United States and the people in the developed world, generally, would be far worse off now, because many of these financial institutions would have failed, and there wouldn't be the financing available that is necessary to keep our economies running.

[THERE ARE SEVENTY MEMBERS of the House Financial Services Committee; fifty of them got money for their campaigns in the 2008 election cycle from Fannie Mae and from Freddie Mac. There was the Fannie Mae Foundation, which was shut down in 2007, and Fannie Mae spent $75 million a year on advertising.] In fact, until they ran into their financial difficulties, there were many in the financial world, including mortgage lenders, who believed that Fannie and Freddie were trying to get into the business of originating mortgages, and so were trying to make themselves familiar to the American public, in general, as good guys. They were doing a lot of public service advertising, and trying to tell the American people that a Fannie Mae or a Freddie Mac mortgage would be something they should want. They never did get into the mortgage origination business. They stayed in the business of buying mortgages from other lenders, but only because they ran into financial difficulties in the early 2000s. That's why they were advertising.

All of these payments to Congress, that's only part of the story. This was truly a culture of corruption…a perfect example of what is wrong with this town. These organizations were made out of federal backing, taxpayers' backing. They were made into powerful organizations, and their executives and their shareholders took tremendous profits out of these companies— again, because of the backing of the [public]. They then took some of these profits, and they turned it over through campaign contributions to the people on the committees in Congress who were supposed to be supervising them…. [In 2004 alone, their lobbying expenditures were close to $16 or $17 million.] They practice a very tough business in politics, very tough on individuals who are critics, and a critic could get in a great deal of trouble. There were people whose careers had been ruined by criticizing Fannie Mae and Freddie Mac, and I happen to be very fortunate that I'm working at a place like the American Enterprise Institute, because they were not intimidated by Fannie Mae and Freddie Mac when I began to criticize those two companies…. They did that all through Washington, so that the media in Washington, and individuals in Washington, and people in Congress who wanted to stand up to them, were under threats all the time.

THE FACT THAT THEY brought in people from Washington for these companies' boards was a terrible mistake, but one that they could be expected to make, because they were purely political creatures. The reason they survived was because they had the support of the government. You would want people on your board who don't know anything about the financial markets, or anything about making mortgages, or anything about how to construct a financial system or a financial business. You don't need those skills on your board. What you need in Washington are people who are in the Washington cognoscenti, the people who go to the cocktail parties and know the congressmen and know the senators, and can make sure that you're getting heard when there is a challenge.

The Fannie Mae Foundation served their political purposes, like everything else at Fannie. The boards of directors served their political purposes and their foundation served their political purposes, because they gave money to community groups. Whenever there was a challenge to Fannie Mae or Freddie Mac of any kind, those community groups would write to the congressmen or call the congressmen or the senator and say, "Don't do anything to Fannie Mae. They're good people. They support us." So, even though the money was actually being used—probably, I assume—for good purposes within these districts, the reason Fannie Mae and Freddie Mac gave out this money was to gain the political support that it bought them in districts all over the country…. Presumably, when Dan Mudd came in at Fannie Mae after the accounting scandals, he said to himself, "We don't need this problem anymore. We'd better shut this stuff down." But, frankly, this is just another part of the scandalous process that was going on there. This is using essentially government money, taxpayer money, to lobby Congress indirectly through these groups. We see the same process continuing to work. Even though reform legislation was passed, it contains a nice slush fund that can be used by the officials of Fannie Mae and Freddie Mac to reward community groups.

Ordinary corporations, of course, give away lots of money to community organizations and charitable organizations and cultural organizations, and they do this in part to support their products. If General Motors gives a gift to a cultural organization, what they hope is that people will then think better of buying a General Motors car. Fannie Mae and Freddie Mac are different. Those gifts were given for the purpose of building political support for them, not their products. They weren't at that point selling any products directly to individuals. They were buying mortgages from banks. These gifts were given to organizations that would then, hopefully, come back and support them politically in Congress. They were using, in effect, the taxpayer money that was backing them to buy political support in districts around the country that then reflected back on the congressmen and senators here in the United States. That was the process that was going on.

THE CONGRESS IS PART of the problem here. They are implicated in creating Fannie and Freddie, keeping it alive, protecting those two companies against attack from any side within the political process and in the private sector, and they get benefits from Fannie and Freddie—they get campaign finances. Fannie and Freddie hire the [exiting] staffs of the congressmen, they hire the lobbyists who are the friends of congressmen and senators, they give out money to community groups who then, in turn, support those congressmen and senators who are their friends. It is a very unpleasant thing to watch, and ultimately, it is a way for Congress, without actually appropriating any money, to direct money to their friends....

THE TROUBLE IS THAT this [corruption] was known. This was known to everybody in Washington. This was known to the media. Where was the *Washington Post*? Where was the *Washington Times*? Where was the *New York Times*? These things were known. But Fannie and Freddie were huge advertisers in all of those media. Maybe that's the reason why all of this stuff was not exposed.... It is a very troubling thing to see that something as serious as this, which everyone in Washington knew about, everyone who was on the inside in Washington knew about and refused to do anything about. That's why you really do need a political revolution, if you will, someone coming in at the top who says, "I'm going to change the way this town does business."

The Hidden History of
the Financial Crisis

BETHANY MCLEAN

A one-time investment banker turned financial journalist, Bethany McLean wrote All the Devils Are Here: The Hidden History of the Financial Crisis, *published by Portfolio Hardcover in 2010. The veteran financial journalist, who currently writes for* Vanity Fair, *joined us on November 14, 2010, for another take on the origins of the 2008 financial crisis. She documents the twenty-year growth of the housing bubble and the lax oversight of quasi-federal agencies Freddie Mac and Fannie Mae. She notes that consumer activists in the 1990s were warning about predatory lending, but federal regulators did not respond. Ms. McLean voices concern over the "culture of greed" that continues to permeate Wall Street.*

[I N 2005, I WROTE a book called *Enron: The Smartest Guys in the Room*.... Back then,] I would almost say that I wasn't cynical enough, because if you had asked me back then if we were going to have another financial crisis, one much bigger that makes Enron look like a canary in a coal mine, or just a little hiccup before the big explosion, I would have said, "Oh, it can't possibly happen for a while. We've learned some lessons, surely," and I would have been completely wrong.

We started thinking about [*All The Devils are Here*] in the fall, as the financial crisis was hitting in full force in September 2008. My co-author,

Joe Nocera, who was my editor at *Fortune* and who edited *The Smartest Guys in the Room*, said, "We should do a book together about the financial crisis...." From the very beginning, we wanted to tell the history of the financial crisis. We wanted to go back twenty years in time and talk about all the various strands that had to come together in order to create this, and they are very different strands, and pull it together into a narrative....

Our book starts in the 1980s, with the invention of mortgage-backed securities, or the modern invention of mortgage-backed securities, through the characters who were there at that time. It traces the growth of both subprime lending and of Fannie Mae and Freddie Mac in Washington, D.C. It traces, on Wall Street, the growth of various means of measuring risk and other financial tools, like credit default swaps, and traces the changing morality on Wall Street. It tells you the history of Countrywide. It ends with the conservatorship of Fannie Mae and Freddie Mac in the fall of 2008. It is not a blow-by-blow of the meltdown, but rather a history of the events that led to the meltdown, told in a character-driven way.

[We start the book with this sentence: "Stan O'Neal wanted to see him,"] because it's a fascinating example of the power that one man has over a company. It's the untold story of how Merrill Lynch, once one of America's great companies, was brought to the brink of destruction, only [to be] saved by a last-minute merger. Through the actions of a few people and this chain of events that is almost remarkable in hindsight, where this incredible exposure to these disastrous subprime mortgages accumulated on its balance sheet without Stan O'Neal, then the CEO of Merrill Lynch, even knowing that that was happening. He is still trying to recover from what happened at Merrill Lynch. As much as I say I have become more cynical, I have also developed more sympathy for the mistakes that people make and the devastation that they suffer when they make those mistakes. It's easy to look at a man like Stan O'Neal or a man like Angelo Mozilo [former chief executive officer (CEO) of Countrywide] and say, "Send them to hell. Look at what they did to our economy. Look at the money they took out of their companies." But, on another level, these were very proud men who believed in the companies they created and will always be remembered as failures because of what happened. That, to them, is worse than any prison sentence could be.

Getting to know people through the course of reporting a book, I came to see what means the most to them and the extent to which people define themselves by their professional accomplishments and their pride in what they think they've built. It comes down to a question of what you call suffering. To Americans who have lost their homes and are struggling to meet their bills in the wake of the financial crisis, no, these people aren't suffering. They are not suffering in terms of material wealth. If you think about your sense of the world and your faith in yourself being destroyed when you're sixty, sixty-five, seventy years old, and having to look in the mirror with a very different reality than you would [have] thought you were facing, that can be devastating. I'm not saying it makes up for what people think they've done, and I'm not saying it's suitable punishment. I'm just saying there's a human level of pain there.

Merrill Lynch was a huge company. At its peak, it was one of the five big broker dealers on Wall Street, employing tens of thousands of people. It was the thundering herd. It was an immensely proud company with a really long history and legacy. All of that is gone. Stan O'Neal was a man, like some in American business, who really came from nothing and beat back incredible prejudice and rose to be a really prominent African American CEO. There's tragedy in his fall; however, you see that he brought it on himself.

John Breit is a risk manager who came to understand how bad Merrill's exposure to the subprime mess was. He had been sidelined under Stan O'Neal's Merrill Lynch, which is really how Merrill Lynch was able to accumulate all of this junk on its balance sheet without anybody knowing. It was the slow sidelining of risk management; a critical function on Wall Street, but one which we have all discovered exists in name only at many firms. Over Stan O'Neal's tenure at Merrill, it was slowly dismantled and pushed aside in a way that O'Neal didn't even understand. We told this story at the beginning of the book about this moment of realization that doom was upon them, and it's a very human story, which is part of the reason why we wanted to start with it.

ONE PERSON WHO I would have loved to have spoken to was Roland Arnall. He died in the spring of 2008, and he really was the pioneer, the founder, of subprime lending, despite the fact that Mozilo was often given that extreme negative. Arnall is just a fascinating character; he stayed a very, very private man, not a well-known name because he never took any of his companies public and never was the CEO of any of his companies. Other people were always the face persons. He became a huge political donor and was appointed the ambassador to the Netherlands by George Bush in 2006, when his company had just settled the largest predatory lending accusation by the state attorneys general ever. At the time, which is just astounding, no one paid attention to this: the largest subprime lender in the country just paid $325 million to settle accusations of predatory lending. Is something happening here we should all be aware of? And it rolled off. It rolled off all of us.

Subprime really started out as so-called hard moneylending, the practice of somebody buying a refrigerator and paying an exorbitant interest rate. The loans would be heavily collateralized. This grew into second lien mortgage lending, where people would take out these really high interest rate second liens on their homes in order to pay for their daily expenses. Hard moneylenders were a small, tough bunch who really excelled in knowing their consumer and getting enough collateral that they got their money back. With the slow liberalization of the laws surrounding mortgage lending, then the liberalization of the rules surrounding what S&Ls could do, and then the end of the S&Ls, there was a whole new breed of people in mortgage lending. It really took off in the 1990s, and the thing that fed it, in addition to this relaxation of the rules, was the advent of securitization. In the past, if you were a lender, you would have to find somebody to finance the loans. If you were a small, fly-by-night lender, how did you get the cash to go out and make mortgages? You knew to corral together investors and it was a slow, painstaking process. But, with the advent of securitization, you could bundle up these loans and sell them to Wall Street, which would sell them on to investors in the form of securities. These securities would get a really high rating from the credit rating agency by virtue of all these financial engineering techniques. The business just exploded…. You had had what we called "Subprime One" in the 1990s, which was the first wave of subprime lending and ended badly. It is just another shocking canary in the coal mine example, because people did not pay any attention to the fact that this ended really badly once before.

SECURITIZED PACKAGES OF MORTGAGES can be bought if you go through Fannie and Freddie. Right now, Fannie Mae and Freddie Mac, the two government sponsored entities which were taken over by the government, are basically the only game in town. Investors are unwilling to buy mortgages unless they have Fannie and Freddie's stamp on them, meaning that now they are explicitly backed by the full faith and credit of the United States government. In the so-called private market, these companies that would sell their loans directly to Wall Street and wouldn't have a government guarantee on them, have been pretty much shut down in the wake of the crisis.

FANNIE AND FREDDIE BECAME deeply embedded in our housing market. They are part of what is known as the secondary mortgage market, and it is this invisible part of the machinery of finance to most Americans, but a very critical one. Fannie and Freddie would buy mortgages that were made by mortgage makers and stamp them with their guarantee, meaning that nobody had to worry about the credit risk because Fannie and Freddie promised you would be paid back, and turn around and sell them to investors. Fannie Mae and Freddie Mac became enormously controversial companies, and politically and financially powerful. In the wake of this, when the government has to take them over and we are on the hook for untold billions of losses, you would think that they would be shut down. But without Fannie and Freddie today, we do not have a mortgage market, because there are no private lenders who are out there willing to make loans. Fannie and Freddie and the Federal Housing Administration account for the mortgage market today. So you are in this conundrum: How do you yank these enterprises out from under the market when they are the market?

FANNIE MAE AND FREDDIE Mac have always been such an odd mixture of partly public, partly private, partly government-owned companies. They were huge forces on Wall Street, but they were located in Washington, D.C., so they were always these strange breeds of companies. Now that they are owned by the government, they are even stranger. They are run by their regulator, that is run by the government, and it is really hard to determine for what purpose they are being run. Are they being run to minimize taxpayers' losses and make as much money as possible? Or are they being run to support the housing market, possibly at the cost to taxpayers? There's a shroud of secrecy over them now.

[The third chapter is "The Big Fat Gap." In it, I wrote: "In 1991, David Maxwell retired as the chief executive of Fannie Mae. He was sixty-one years old and had held the post one day short of ten years. He walked away with a lump sum of $27.5 million; most of it accrued retirement benefits, but still a shocking sum of money for Washington during that era."] You can argue that David Maxwell earned his money. He took what was a failing enterprise and turned it into a phenomenally profitable enterprise. He managed these twin goals of being profitable while also supporting the housing market. But, over time, and I blame the change in Wall Street culture for this, Fannie and Freddie got seduced by the same enemy that so many corporations fall prey to, which is relentless profit growth at all costs. If you're supposed to be a mission-oriented company that is supposed to have this other reason for its existence beyond producing profits, that becomes a pretty difficult conundrum over time.

The "Big Fat Gap" in the title refers to a way that Fannie and Freddie made inordinate profits, which was taking advantage of their ability to borrow money at a very low rate, because investors assumed they were backed by the U.S. government, and buying mortgage-backed securities with that, and earning the difference. It was Alan Greenspan who became a big foe of the government sponsored enterprise, who referred to that as "the big fat gap."

...FANNIE MAE WAS RUN like a government enterprise without a lot of focus on its bottom line at all. Like many of the S&Ls, it had bought mortgages at a time of rising interest rates. It was stuck with fixed-rate mortgages paying one thing, while its cost of funding was going through the roof. Money was just going out the door every single day. David Maxwell started to run it more like a business; he demanded accountability on the part of managers, changed some of Fannie's policies and procedures so that they would no longer commit to buy a loan at any interest rate from someone a year in advance, and then be stuck with that loan, even when it turned out to be unprofitable. You could argue that Maxwell set Fannie on the course of being a bottom-line oriented company, but like everything in life, there's a balancing act.

David Maxwell passed Fannie Mae onto Jim Johnson as CEO. Johnson was a Democratic operative, a tall, forty-seven-year-old Minnesotan and a graduate of Princeton; Johnson was a player. He spent his twenties working on the campaigns of Eugene McCarthy and George McGovern, and then served as Vice President Walter Mondale's executive assistant during the Carter Administration.... He did have these deep political connections, and David Maxwell was savvy enough to see how important those would be to Fannie Mae in the coming years, because Fannie was constantly fighting this battle with Wall Street and with others in the mortgage industry that wanted some of its very lucrative turf. But Johnson was also a businessman. He had worked at Shearson Lehman and had enough of a business background that he was not a pure political operative. He was very much regarded as a very, very tough operator by the people who worked under him and by people who dealt with him. He had a take-no-prisoners attitude, and some of that was bred into Fannie Mae's DNA. They always had this sense that people were trying to kill them off, and it was true. Fannie always had foes in the government who would have liked nothing better than to see the end of Fannie Mae.

[In 1990, Fannie Mae engaged Paul Volcker, the legendary former Federal Reserve chairman, to defend Fannie Mae's low capital levels.] It was a testament to the low risk that everybody believed mortgages had, and, in fairness, they probably did have. What people could not have foreseen at the time were the changes in the mortgage market that made mortgages carry a much higher level of risk and the changes in Fannie's business that led it to carry far more leverage than it did then.

People tried desperately, particularly the Bush Administration, to rein in Fannie and Freddie. Alan Greenspan would actually publicly say that the amount of mortgages they housed on their balance sheet needed to be capped. The very blunt answer is that Fannie and Freddie were simply too politically powerful for anybody to do anything. People were also scared. What happens if you take them out of the mortgage market? What happens if they are right and the housing market can't function without Fannie and Freddie? We'll get the blame. There was both a paralysis due to their political power and a paralysis due to fear.

Their foundation is a part of why Fannie's lobbying apparatus was regarded as the most politically powerful, potent force that people have seen. I have a quote from former Congressman Richard Baker saying, "General Patton couldn't have stood up to them." It was 24/7 and never anything left to chance. People talk about the sheer amount of money that Fannie and Freddie spent lobbying, but that pales in comparison to the other ways in which they bought influence, whether it was via the foundation or partnership offices that they opened all over the country or the revolving door, that people went back and forth between Fannie Mae and official Washington, D.C....

THERE ARE AN AWFUL lot [of people circulating between the government and the financial industry]. You can look at that through two prisms. You can look at it through one prism and say, "How great; people make their money in the financial world and they come to the political world to share their wisdom and their insights into the real world with the rest of us. How wonderful that these people, after making fortunes, are willing to give that up and devote time to public service...." Or, you could look at that through a far less benign lens and say that the ultimate form of corruption is not someone explicitly doing someone else a favor, but the form of corruption that happens when everybody already thinks the same way. If you have this revolving door, particularly between government and Wall Street, you are likely to get a lot of people who think the same way in positions of power. You do not need explicit corruption and don't need any favors, because you all already agree anyway.

THIS CRISIS WAS PREVENTABLE in the early years. By 2005, 2006, it would have been very difficult for one person stepping in to have taken an action to have prevented what was coming. The crisis isn't a story of big decisions made by big people. It's a story of corruption or venality or wrongdoing or invention simply gone wrong, pushed to a place they weren't meant to be taken, at all layers. There had to have been transformation of subprime lending. You had to have the mortgage become this product that it had never been in order to provide the raw material for the leverage that eventually took the system down. You had to have this unwillingness to rein in the amount of debt that was in the system for it to become a problem, and you had to have the invention of all these complicated financial tools on Wall Street. You had to have these disparate things come together to make a crisis of the size that we had. It was preventable in numerous ways, or, at least, negatable in numerous ways along the way, by regulation or oversight of derivatives, by tighter regulation of investment banks, by smarter regulation of banks and investment banks, by some sort of action in the mortgage industry. That was the shocking thing to me, the warnings from consumer activists starting in the 1990s about predatory lending, and yet federal regulators didn't do much of anything until 2006, when it was far too late. So, preventable, yes, but in the paths along the way; not in something someone could have stood up and shouted from the rooftops in 2006, "We're going to have a financial crisis unless we do X, Y and Z."

I WORKED FOR TWO years as an analyst in the investment banking department in Goldman Sachs's Mergers and Acquisitions department, and then I spent a year working for what's known as the Whitehall Funds, which, at the time, was a Goldman fund that invested in distressed real estate. I was very young when I worked there. I was a naïve kid from a mining town in Minnesota who found herself working on Wall Street. It was an eye-opening experience in terms of how hard people worked and how motivated people were by money. That stood out to me. I came away from Goldman Sachs and my time there as an admirer of the firm. I wouldn't say those were the easiest three years of my life; in fact, in some ways I would say they were the hardest, but I grew up a lot and learned an immense amount by working there, and so I have retained a level of loyalty to the place over the years.

My view began to change; I was always an admirer of Goldman's success, too, and of how, unlike other firms on Wall Street who merely talk about risk management, Goldman Sachs actually practiced risk management. But there was always this underlying complaint about Goldman Sachs that you would hear whispered. Nobody would ever say it on the record, but the Goldman culture had turned rapacious; that it was profits at any cost, that this whole notion that the first business principle that "our clients come first" was just completely meaningless; that they would run over a client in the search of enriching their own bottom line. I listened to the complaints and they were loud enough that it was hard to discount them, but it was also really hard to find any proof that this was happening, because nobody would go on the record to complain about Goldman. The really telling thing about the financial crisis was that it does show Goldman's culture had changed since the firm had become a public company. It's really hard to look at their actions during the financial crisis and say that this is a company who believes that our clients come first, unless you very narrowly define the word client.

IT IS INDISPUTABLE THAT a really sick, dare I say, byproduct of the financial crisis is that too-big-to-fail firms have become bigger, that we bailed out the biggest institutions, which became even bigger and more powerful, and now we have even less diversity among financial institutions. Why not just break them up? Make them into small firms, so we don't even need to go through all these legislative contortions. It will be very difficult if we are faced with the failure of one of these firms, to actually let it fail.

The underlying issues of the financial crisis have not been fixed at all and, indeed, there's no easy fix. One thing is similar to what we talked about when we talked about Enron five years ago, and it is this culture of short-term greed: if I can get mine and get out, then who cares what happens after I'm gone. That's an attitude that is pervasive across Wall Street. There isn't a sense of a larger right and wrong and I do not know how you fix that.

PEOPLE WANT TO PHRASE this as a crisis about homeownership; in other words, that this was a crisis caused by putting people in homes that they couldn't afford, and it really was not. If you look at most subprime loans, they were used so that people could do cash-out refinancing of their homes. In other words, they used their home like an ATM card, because people weren't making enough money to support the lifestyles that they and our economy had become used to. That's a huge underlying problem; that is not a quick fix about America's homeownership policy.

SOME OF THE BANKS who are engaged in the foreclosure mess today are not the same firms that were involved in pedaling subprime mortgages. It's easy to put everything under the rubric of the financial industry. In fact, it's quite a mass of disparate actors, so it would be nice to be able to hold Bank of America up and say, it owns Countrywide, therefore it's accountable for all of Countrywide's sins in the past. But if the executives and the people who ran Countrywide are no longer there, is Bank of America really accountable? Legally, they are....

FOR BETTER OR WORSE, the story of the financial crisis is a story trying to find the line among venality, greed, outright corruption, outright fraud, and most of it is somewhere in the murky middle. Just because you are disgusted by behavior, you cannot say it is criminal when it is not. I do not believe that firms are not being prosecuted because of some sort of political agenda not to prosecute. The Southern District of New York is a very independent and powerful prosecutor, and if they were finding myriad examples of prosecutable fraud, they would prosecute. The Countrywide case against Angelo Mozilo and former executives settled on the eve of trial because it was a civil case, and it settled because it was not ironclad. It is a very tough thing to come to terms with because, as a country, we like our villains. It makes us all feel better when we have suffered something as devastating as this to be able to hold up someone to blame. This murkiness makes the whole thing even harder to comprehend.

[THERE ARE STILL SUCH things as credit default swaps.] If you have a Wall Street firm that has made a loan to General Motors and has General Motors debt on its books, and they can buy an instrument that protects them should General Motors default, that is legitimate. But like everything on Wall Street, something that starts as a good idea gets taken to a speculative frenzy. Credit default swaps eventually became a means of betting on the demise of companies that had no connection to the underlying debt and of structuring these just insanely complex investments based on mortgages.

IN THE STOCK MARKET, I am a fan of short sellers. Short sellers are betting that the stock of a company is going to go down. Since they are making this bet they do detailed, extensive research in order to uncover financial frauds and to uncover weakness in a company's accounting. They do the sort of research that most people in the market do not do, because we live in an economy where everybody wants things to go up.

That leads to frauds going unnoticed, because most frauds, like Enron, take the complicity of the victim, and the victims are all too willing to be complicit, because all of our money is in it as well. Short sellers provide an incredibly important leavening for us against that. You really have to think twice about that when it comes to mortgage-backed securities. In an ideal world, the fact that there were people shorting the mortgage market would have sent a signal to everybody saying, "Wow. There are all these smart investors who think this thing is going to crash and burn." But the market was opaque enough that you could not see that the way you can see it in the stock market. The way these instruments work, you were not betting on real mortgages, but rather, you were betting on the casino version of a mortgage. It ended up multiplying the exposure to mortgages; to souring mortgages that were out there and multiplying the damage done by the financial crisis. It's hard for me to argue the social utility of short sellers in the mortgage industry.

I DON'T THINK YOU can still buy a subprime mortgage, which is a mortgage made to anybody with a low credit score. It used to be available to anybody who did not qualify for a Fannie Mae or Freddie Mac mortgage, anybody who didn't qualify for a conventional mortgage. You probably paid a higher interest rate and your mortgage might have some special fees that applied to it, and the higher interest rate was supposed to be because you were a worse credit risk. But you could still get credit by getting a subprime mortgage. Once again, in theory and in balance, that's a great idea. As a Fannie Mae executive said to me, "Do we want to live in a country where, because you have a blemish on your credit, you can never own a house?" Well no, probably not. But balance seems to be a thing that's all too often missing in this world. Things are created and they go to extremes without ever pausing at the proper middle.

MOODY'S, FITCH, AND S&P are the so-called credit rating agencies and were a hidden but very powerful part of the machinery of the financial markets. They rate debt and are supposed to be able to tell you when debt is going to be paid back on time and in full. A triple-A rating…means that you are pretty assured of getting your money back. Triple-As were supposed to be handed out very sparingly…. Credit rating agencies are funny because this ability to rate debt makes them incredibly powerful, because as a company you can't sell debt without their approval. People at credit ratings are academic, nerdy, and somewhat staid. They never made the salaries that people on Wall Street did. They were the little gremlins down in the basement making the gears work. With the advent of structured finance, which is making securities out of mortgages, they became even more powerful than they were, because the whole purpose of securitization was to take something that was risky, a subprime mortgage, and turn it into something that looked really safe. In order to do that, you needed the stamp of approval of the credit rating agencies. It was Moody's and S&P and Fitch who rated mammoth portions of these mortgage-backed securities with a triple-A rating. They handed them out like candy. So this once pristine, really highly cherished rating really became quite degraded over the years.

Many former people at Moody's point to CEO Brian Clarkson as the source of a cultural change at Moody's. Moody's used to pride itself on saying, "...We are all about serving investors; the people who buy this debt. If the issuers don't like us, despite the fact that you pay us, that's your problem." Under Brian Clarkson, the culture really began to change, to where Moody's really began to care about what the issuers thought and they began to care about what the issuers, their investment banking clients, in the case of mortgage-backed securities, thought more than they did the investors who were buying these things....

I do not think we are safer in any way. With all these complex financial products, I do not see why anybody in the world would want to own the stock of a financial company. There is just absolutely no way. If this crisis proved anything, it is that nobody on the outside can tell what's going on the inside of these companies, and that the balance sheets and financial statements of these companies may have absolutely nothing to do with reality. That's really scary for our system.... As a consumer, can you trust the financial products that people are selling you? Can you trust the people who are selling you these things to do the right thing? Well, clearly the answer is, "No...."

Part of it is the story of modernization and globalization and that the bigger a society we live in, the less people feel personally accountable.

The less people feel personally accountable, the more leeway there often is in their actions. It is why the corporate world has to be structured in a way that incentives are all. People will do what they are paid to do. I am not sure that that incentive structure has changed.

[THE PERSON TO RUN these financial organizations should be] both knowledgeable and an independent thinker, and the second is very, very hard to find. Most people like to think like other people, and there is a group-think mentality that takes over. Skeptics, like some of the ones profiled in our book, are often a little bit out there. Whistleblowers are often kind of weird figures. They are not the sort of people who blend into a mainstream discussion, because they're always saying, "Wait; what about this and what about that?" If I come away from this and the Enron story with one pleading, it's to listen to the skeptics and try to find people for those roles who have an ability to think independently.

Fannie Mae and the 2008 Crisis

GRETCHEN MORGENSON

Gretchen Morgenson, financial columnist for the New York Times, *tracks the history of the mortgage crisis and its role in the 2008 recession in her book,* Reckless Endangerment: How Outsized Ambition, Greed, and Corruption Created the Worst Financial Crisis of Our Time, *published by Times Books in 2011. She joined us on* Q & A *on July 1, 2012, to chart the role of Fannie Mae and Freddie Mac prior to the housing crisis, the lack of transparency, and the political connections of these agencies. She questions the role of government in financing housing, and notes that taxpayers have been charged with over $150 billion in losses.*

I N MY BOOK, *Reckless Endangerment*, I describe Fannie Mae Chief Executive Officer (CEO) President James Johnson as "a calculating political operative, who was the anonymous architect of the public-private homeownership drive that almost destroyed the economy in 2008." There is so much on his shoulders because a crisis this large doesn't happen overnight. To understand what happened to create this mortgage bubble, and then the ensuing crisis, we have to go back to early nineties when Fannie Mae and Freddie Mac were under pressure from Congress, because of the savings and loan crisis.

Congress was rightly concerned that there were losses sitting in these mortgage finance giants that were quasi-public, quasi-private. They were public in that the government had started them, but they had private shareholders, so they were operating for profit. Congress was concerned there might be losses like in the S&Ls in these giant companies, and wanted to make sure that they were overseen, that they were policed, and that they were not going to require taxpayer bailouts. In 1991, when James Johnson takes over as the head of Fannie Mae, he really takes this Congressional urge, or fear, and turns it on its head. Instead of having tougher regulators, higher capital cushions required at the companies, a Congress that was more vigilant and watchful for a taxpayer bailout, he turned all that on its head and created a piece of legislation called the ["Federal Housing Enterprises Financial Safety and Soundness Act"] that was virtually written by James Johnson of Fannie Mae.

James Johnson was a Democratic political operator who had run Walter Mondale's campaign for president, who bridged Wall Street and had worked at Lehman Brothers in a Washington lobbying effort, but did come out of Democratic Minnesota politics. He went to Princeton... [then] came to Washington, and understood that he had to protect the government subsidy to predict the implied government guarantee that stood behind Fannie Mae and its smaller brethren, Freddie Mac.

I've been writing about Fannie Mae as a political machine since the mid-1990s, so I'm not a friend of Fannie Mae. The enterprise essentially either owns or guarantees home mortgages. It was set up in the aftermath of the Great Depression to keep housing finance wheels moving. In a banking crisis, as [during the Great] Depression, home lending dries up; nobody's willing to make those kinds of loans. Fannie Mae was created to step in when the private markets for mortgages failed. Fannie Mae is a government-sponsored enterprise (GSE) with a sumptuous headquarters, and it allowed its CEO, Franklin Raines, to take $90 million out of it over a relatively short period of time. Fannie Mae, like any financial institution, borrows money from investors in the debt markets. They will go out to investors and say, "We want to raise $100 million or $10 million. What do you want for income that will make you buy that security?" Fannie Mae has a government-sponsored aura around it and can borrow money at a far lower rate than other banks that don't have the implied guarantee of the taxpayer. That difference between what an enterprise pays to borrow money from the public is very lucrative. It's a subsidy, and it is where the riches came from.

One of the things that Mr. Johnson devised was these grassroots efforts offices, or partnership offices, across the country. These were designed to create photo ops for politicians when they came home to their local constituents, and to participate in developments that look good for the constituents and that look good for the congressman. Fannie Mae was everywhere. It was really ingenious, just a brilliant strategic plan to really dominate the industry, to defang its regulator, to co-opt Congress, and to protect that very lucrative subsidy. On Freddie Mac's board, there are very high-level people in Washington and the elite power circles that are invited—both Republicans and Democrats. Both sides of the aisle are represented on the board, and this government-sponsored enterprise did not have to reveal what it paid its top executives.

PUBLIC COMPANIES DO HAVE to disclose in proxy statements the amounts that they pay their top five executives. Fannie Mae and Freddie Mac didn't have to do that, and when members of Congress had the temerity to ask for this information, they were shut down. This was the power of these companies. They would marshal their friends on the Hill and they would beat back any attempt to identify the riches that the top executives were making.

Johnson was crucial to the government's public-private partnership to push [home] ownership. [In 1995, during the Clinton Administration,] there was a goal to increase the rate of homeownership in the United States of America. The idea was that if more people could buy a home who have been shut out of the process—immigrants, first-time homebuyers, minorities—that that would be a greater good for the nation because homeownership is good, even though there really was no proof that homeownership was a boon to everyone.... There's something about homeownership that's very noble and uplifting, but there was an awful lot of money to be made in this partnership, and you didn't hear them talking about that, but that was also a huge motivator.

THEY WERE ABLE TO wrap themselves in the American flag of homeownership. Jim Johnson was able to argue that if you touch the system, if you fiddle with the system, are you going to be able to deliver a home loan at the cheap rate that Fannie Mae will? This was always the threat that was held over people who criticized the business model of Fannie Mae. It was always, "You're anti-homeownership, you're anti-the-American-way." But what he's not saying is that of that subsidy, he's only passing on to the borrower two-thirds of it; he's keeping one-third of it to himself, and that is an inefficient way to subsidize housing.

THERE'S A WONDERFUL ANECDOTE in the book where the CBO, the Congressional Budget Office, in the mid-nineties decides to do the unthinkable: to try to calculate what Fannie Mae and Freddie Mac had in terms of a government subsidy in this lower cost of capital. This had never been done. The company did not want it to be done because they didn't want anybody having any inkling of the billions of dollars of this subsidy that they were reaping every year. They also said that they passed along every nickel of it to the borrower, which CBO also wanted to test. So Marvin Phaup, who was a research analyst at CBO, took this on as a study, came up with the figure, a kind of calculation of how much the subsidy was. It was $6 billion in one year. This was in the nineties, when that was real money. He is going to deliver this research to Congress through June O'Neill, who's the head of the CBO at that time. There's a wonderful moment, where, after they've done all the work and all the analysis, Fannie Mae asks for a meeting with June O'Neill, so she invites them in…. The researchers are in the meeting with three henchmen from Fannie Mae, and they try to persuade June O'Neill not to publish this research. It was a big threat to them because nobody knew that $6 billion was the size of the subsidy. Mr. Phaup had also determined that two-thirds was all they passed along to borrowers, that they kept a third of that to themselves every year. That's a lot of money. This was a threat to them, and they wanted to make sure it wasn't public. They pushed and they pushed. June O'Neill told me she felt like she had been visited by the mafia. But she stood up and said, "I'm sorry, gentlemen." They couldn't poke any holes in the arithmetic. It was, again, all these bromides about homeownership. You're going to make it harder for people to own a home if you print this research. This is their typical default position. She said, "Gentlemen, I'm sorry we're going to publish this research. We're proud of it. We know we did a good job." And so they did. She went to deliver it to Congress and was savaged by all of the Fannie Mae and Freddie Mac protectors who were members of Congress at that time.

THIS IS THE CONVERSATION we need to have in this country that nobody is willing to have: what role should government play in housing finance? If you want to subsidize housing in this country, and the populace agrees that it's something we should subsidize, then put it on the balance sheet, and make it clear, and make it evident, and make everybody aware of how much it's costing. But we deliver the subsidy through a public company with private shareholders and executives who can extract a lot of that subsidy for themselves. That is not a very good way of subsidizing homeownership. We've seen the end of that movie in 2008.

At the moment, taxpayers have had to pay $151 billion to bail out Fannie and Freddie. It's possible that the loss will decline somewhat but never break even; it is always going to be some sort of a loss to the taxpayer. The shareholders' losses were caught at the end of the line when all the troubles were coming forward and all the losses were accumulating. A lot of the smaller banks who bought the debt issue and preferred stock of Fannie and Freddie were losers...but the debt holders came out fine because the government backstopped it. All those years that Jim Johnson and all of his colleagues said that no taxpayer dime would ever have to be extended to Fannie Mae, of course, was proven to be false in September 2008.

Fannie Mae [officials] had to come up with a masterful way to extract money for themselves while pretending to do something good for the country. Homeownership does sound like a good thing. If you can pass on savings to borrowers, that is a good thing; if you can allow people who are not typically homebuyers to enjoy homeownership, that's also a good thing. But, in this way, it was actually corrupt, because it was a company that was designed to make profits for the shareholders, and paid its executives immensely well, and used a lot of that subsidy again that the taxpayers stood behind. The reason that Fannie Mae was so wealthy was because it didn't have to pay as much to borrow money, and used that money to buy members of Congress, to put out these partnership offices, to put the public relations out there that Fannie Mae was a do-gooder. It helped them get the message out with advertising that actually inserted themselves in presidential elections. This was all about protecting the subsidy. They would do whatever they had to do. The partnerships would often hire family members of congressional members to make sure that you were helping your friends back in Washington. Another ingenious thing that [Johnson] came up with was to fund the Fannie Mae Foundation with Fannie Mae stock, which was at that point in time going to the moon because the company was so profitable. With the Foundation money, he would pay academics to write articles that were very pro-housing, pro-homeowners, pro-Fannie Mae and -Freddie Mac. He ended up co-opting almost the entire academic community, as well, by paying them well to write favorable research about the benefits of homeownership, and how Fannie Mae was delivering on its goals. The Foundation was immensely wealthy, and they could deploy that money to get the word out about the good deed-doers of Fannie Mae.

FANNIE MAE IS NOT allowed to lobby anymore. They're not allowed to contribute to political campaigns. They had to give up the Foundation and the partnership offices. So it was a changed world after Labor Day, 2008.

THERE ARE TWO KINDS of people in this story. One is the housing zealots, the people who really believe that homeownership is a worthy goal and we should push for it no matter what. I would put Barney [Frank, retired Democratic Congressman from Massachusetts,] in that category. It wasn't that he really personally benefited. And then there were the people who want the personal enrichment from the public-private partnership, people like Johnson and Franklin Raines. There are two kinds of people in this story; zealots and personal enrichment schemes.

FRANKLIN RAINES WAS THE CEO at the time of the accounting scandal, and the *pièce de résistance* is that the United States taxpayers continued to pay the legal bills of Franklin Raines and two of his cohorts in their defense against shareholder litigation in the accounting scandal. Jim Johnson is keeping a pretty low profile, but he's on the boards of Goldman Sachs and Target. He is the compensation committee chair of both Target and Goldman Sachs. But it was interesting [when] a very prominent shareholder of Goldman Sachs came out with the public letter urging investors to vote against Jim Johnson's reelection on the board of Goldman and Target because the investor said he had been involved in quite a few questionable scandals, or had been near to them—and then cited his years at Fannie Mae.

Angelo Mozilo [former CEO of Countrywide Financial] sold stock worth about $500 million in the last few years of the company's history before it was sold in a fire sale to Bank of America. This was when the boom was ending and he was selling stocks hand over fist. He was a founder of the company. He took a lot of money out of it, and had a huge salary. The SEC contended that because Angelo Mozilo was making these private statements that were different from his public statements, and that he was selling stock at the same time, that this was insider trading; that he had nonpublic information, and that he had increased the amount of shares he was selling because he knew that the end was near. The SEC settled with him for $22.5 million.... Countrywide was the largest single supplier to Fannie Mae of loans. Mr. Mozilo didn't have to worry about every loan he made because [many] of them went to Fannie Mae, and were at the taxpayers' bottom line.

TIM GEITHNER WAS THE PRESIDENT of the New York Fed during the years when regulations became extremely lax in this country for financial institutions, and particularly in New York. Citibank was the purview of the New York Fed, and obviously, they were not paying attention, because Citibank became one of the biggest nightmares of the bailout brigade. Tim Geithner was present at the creation of this belief that banks could set their own capital standards, that derivatives were a wonderful thing that spread risk, and that financial innovation was not to be stopped. It was this mindset that came down from [former Federal Reserve Chairman Alan] Greenspan, which really was anti-regulation, and was not interested in making sure that financial products that were sold to people were not going to blow up on them five minutes later. There was a tone that bankers would never do anything so silly and stupid as to take the risk that would blow themselves up. That was the Greenspan notion. He later apologized for it, saying he can't believe...they didn't understand that they were taking these risks. Geithner was a big part of that mindset, and a big part of that regime were bankers who were really allowed to set their own rules in capital standards.

I HAVE A GRUDGE about what's happened if it means weighing the taxpayer down with $151 billion in losses. I have a problem with allowing companies to take reckless risks and pay themselves immensely as they're doing it, and when the bill comes, when the risk shows up to be problematic and the loans that they made go bad, they don't have to pay the freight; the taxpayer pays the freight. I have a problem with that and I think a lot of people in this country have a problem with it. I don't have a problem if people are operating within [the] confines of prudent business practices, and if they are being paid very well to manage risks, and they do that well. I have a problem with taking reckless gambles, reaping enormous profits doing it, and then walking away with your money and leaving the taxpayer holding the bag.

BUSINESS REPORTING IS A lot cleaner and a lot easier than political reporting. There's a lot of public information. There are a lot of government documents that companies have to file that really can reveal immense amounts of information. I get people calling me over the transom who are whistleblowers, who are upset about what they see happening in an organization, or in some practice. I was a broker myself on Wall Street long ago, so I have a lot of contacts from my years on the Street. And, believe it or not, there are a lot of people who know that Wall Street can be honest. It is an honest place for many people, and they don't want the bad apples any more than I do. They will call me and tell me about practices that they find disturbing.

In many types of reporting, you're relying on people to deliver something that you can't get any other way, particularly in political reporting, Washington reporting. You're relying on someone dropping a classified document in your lap. You're thrilled to have it, but then your trick is to explain to the reader how you got it.... In business reporting, you don't need to do that; you can do your work. There's so much more information available. You can do what we call "write arounds," where you write around the person. They don't have to participate. It's much harder in political reporting. I am the skunk at the garden party, and I like it that way. But I stay to myself. I go home every night to my husband and my son, and that's the way I like it. I don't believe in socializing with the people that I'm covering. It's just that simple…. The downside is that I will not get the piece of information that someone wants me to have that makes them look good.

Interestingly, covering the financial crisis from Wall Street was easier than when it moved to Washington. Washington became a much more confined, closed shop, and [it was] harder to get information. I remember an example, when Treasury started one of their programs for loan modifications, and we were trying over and over to get information on how many borrowers had been helped by this program, and it was like pulling teeth. You might as well have been asking for the formula for Coca-Cola. Nothing. They would not tell us. It was ultimately because the program wasn't doing very well.

WE HAVE NOT RESOLVED Fannie Mae and Freddie Mac. We have not had that conversation about the role of housing finance in this country. We need to have that conversation. I was hoping that this [crisis] would create that conversation, so people could have a robust discussion and then decide. But we haven't done that. We haven't got near to that, and therefore, I think the chances of another crisis are pretty great.

Bailing Out Wall Street

NEIL BAROFSKY

Neil Barofsky was Special Inspector General (SIG) charged with oversight of the Troubled Asset Relief Program (TARP). He joined us on Q & A on September 23, 2012, and reported that a total of $23 trillion of public money was used to protect the financial institutions after the 2008 crisis. He recalls conversations with several leaders of the Treasury Department, one of whom warned him about his tone when discussing the TARP program. He describes his view of the role of an Inspector General, and notes the contrasting directions he received from members of Congress, his colleagues, and federal agencies. His book is Bailout: An Inside Account of How Washington Abandoned Main Street While Rescuing Wall Street *(Free Press, 2012).*

$2 3.7 TRILLION [IS THE total amount of government money spent to shore up our financial system after the 2008 crisis. The number] is so big that it almost defies understanding. One way to understand it is that when we had a financial crisis, the government was in a full-blown panic. There's really no other way to explain it. They were worried about the next Great Depression, and they threw the kitchen sink at the financial system. They made promises and guarantees across the board and almost anything that you could imagine to help support the largest financial institutions to keep them from failing.

That included the $700 billion, which is the point seven in that $23.7 trillion number. It also included a wide array of guarantees. If you add them all up, the number comes to $23.7 trillion. That includes more than $3 trillion to guarantee all the money market funds. All the money market funds weren't going to fail at once, but even if they did, we put up three-point-something trillion dollars. It was adding up those different programs which gave a sense of the total level of commitment.

We thought it was very important to get that number out there because this was at the very beginning of the regulatory reform debate. We thought it was important for Congress to know, the American people to know, and frankly, I wanted to know. I didn't know what that total number was when you added it all up, and no government agency had done so, so they could understand just how broken our financial system was and just how extraordinary the government response had to be....This number created this huge controversy. The number had gotten twisted out of context, so that [others] were saying that we're going to lose $23 trillion which...we never said. What was probably most surprising were the attacks that we got from the White House and the Treasury Department, who we naively thought would be really supportive of the idea of painting a picture of how extraordinary the bailouts were, but that was definitely not the case.

TARP STANDS FOR THE Troubled Asset Relief Program. In 2008, the banks were hemorrhaging huge, huge amounts of losses, mostly coming from bets on real estate. We had a huge bubble in this country in housing, and banks had a lot of exposure through very complex, financial instruments. The very simplest way of looking at it is that housing went down and it took the banks who had investments in housing down with them, and that created all sorts of runs in the banks and a general crisis. The original idea of TARP was that it was going to buy these real estate related assets: bonds that were made up of bunches of mortgages, and then these other bonds that were made up of a bunch of other bonds. They get to be really complicated, and the government was going to buy them from the banks to try to stop the bleeding and bring back some degree of financial stability. That's what a lot of members of Congress thought they were voting for when they voted for TARP.

An RMBS is what is called a residential mortgage-backed security. In simplest terms, the way to think about it is that, in the run up to the crisis and even before that, financial institutions would take a whole bunch of mortgages and bundle them together into a bond. People would buy different parts of the bond. When people would invest in the bond, they would be getting a claim to each of the monthly payments that everyone who has a mortgage behind that bond would make. So thousands and thousands of mortgages get put into one bond, and people invest in that by buying these bonds, which give them a right to those flows of income. Those are called mortgage-backed securities because it's the mortgage that backs the bond. The "R" is because these are home mortgages as opposed to other types of mortgages. We still have them. The private market for them where Wall Street was putting them together has almost disappeared. Right now, it's almost entirely government-funded through government entities.

PPIP is the Public-Private Investment Program that…was originally envisioned to be a trillion-dollar program to help ultimately buy those same toxic assets. After TARP was passed, the money wasn't used to buy the bonds. It was used to plug the holes in the banks directly by buying shares of their stock, increasing their capital and their ability to withstand future losses. The PPIP was an idea of marrying up Treasury money with private money, as well as Federal Reserve money, in a very complex program to try to recreate that idea of buying these RMBS, these mortgage bonds and other things that were created from them. Ultimately, the program was a failure and maybe $20 billion actually got spent.

A CDO is that bond of bonds; it's a collateralized debt obligation. When people talk about troubled and toxic assets, this is what they were talking about, because they would take a whole bunch of mortgage bonds and package them together, and then sell a right to buy pieces of that bond. If that sounds hopelessly complex, it is. They were created with some of the most poorly performing and riskiest mortgages that were riddled with fraud, because the banks that were putting them together didn't really care what the performance was; they were just selling them off to investors. These all got concentrated in these CDOs, and when these CDOs blew up, they took the financial system down with them.

AT THE TIME, HERB Allison was the Assistant Secretary of the Treasury for Financial Stability, which meant that his job was to oversee the implementation of TARP, the $700 billion funded bank bailout. Prior to that, Herb had a storied career on Wall Street. He had [held] just about every major job you can imagine at Merrill Lynch including being its president and CFO. He then went on to become the CEO of TIAA-CREF. He actually retired in 2008, when Hank Paulson, who was then Treasury Secretary, called him as the financial crisis was just beginning to take off and asked him to come to Washington to run Fannie Mae after it had been put into conservatorship and basically nationalized by the United States government. Then, in April 2009, he came in and eventually became the head of TARP. I was providing oversight of TARP, and many times I had been very critical of the things that he, the Treasury Department, or Secretary Geithner were doing. He was my main portal into Treasury.

We had had a number of conflicts. As you can imagine, our jobs were not necessarily going to create a long-lasting friendship. My job was to criticize him and make recommendations where I thought he and the program had gone off the rails, which, by 2010, was pretty often. We decided to have a meeting offline, if you will, to clear the air, have a couple of drinks, and try to diffuse what was a building tension between the two of us. Our weekly meetings had often devolved into shouting matches. At this meeting, though, I got a real taste of how Washington works. We had a little chitchat and [made] small talk about our families. I told him that my first daughter was about to be born. She was about three weeks away at that point. He talked to me about his commute to Washington, back and forth from Connecticut, where he lives, and about his grown children. He eventually turned the conversation and pointed out that I was young, that my job as Special Inspector General was, by its very nature, a temporary one, and started asking me about what my plans were and what I wanted to do next. As we started discussing it, he gave me a warning. He said that I was doing myself real harm for my "future prospects," in his words, and by that, he explained that I had a very harsh tone. I was very critical of Wall Street and very critical of the Obama Administration as I was carrying out my job as SIGTARP and providing oversight. He warned me that if I didn't change my tone, it was going to hurt my ability to get a job after SIGTARP when I left the government, presumably to go get a job on Wall Street. When I explained to him I wasn't really interested in that, he then said, "Well, even within the administration," but if I changed my tone and became a little bit more upbeat and positive, good things could happen to me. He mentioned even perhaps an Obama appointment as a federal judge, if only I would change my tone. At the time when I heard that conversation, I thought I was being threatened or bribed, to be honest with you. I thought I was hearing, basically, "If you don't shape up, mister, you're going to ruin your entire career, but if you change your tune, good things can happen to you." Later, I realized that he was just explaining to me how Washington worked and what it means to be a regulator in Washington. That means pull your punches, go with the flow, and great things could happen to you, including a rich career on Wall Street. But, speak your mind and be effective, and you could do yourself real harm....

I certainly didn't have any power over him. All I really had was the power of the logic of our arguments. What I learned over time, from advice from others as well as just sort of figuring it out, was that I wasn't going to be able to directly influence Treasury officials—Herb Allison or anyone else. I could do my recommendations, and if they were easy to implement, they would probably take them.... They did adopt a number of them, sometimes without putting up too much of a fight, but for the big issues, they tended to, at least initially, ignore us entirely. What I learned was that I had to use the press and Congress to try to get external pressure on Treasury to see what we were doing....

SIGTARP IS THE SPECIAL Inspector General for the Troubled Asset Relief Program. When Congress passed TARP in 2008, the act gave Treasury the ability to bail out the banks with $700 billion of taxpayer money. They also created this brand new entity called SIGTARP. Our role is to provide oversight. Part of that was done by creating a brand new law enforcement agency. We are like a mini-FBI for the TARP to police the program and catch criminals who are trying to steal from it. The second part [of the act] was an oversight mechanism whereby we would report to Congress every quarter, as well as create special reports on special audits we would do of specific TARP programs. Our authority came from Congress, from this legislation, and it provided that we had all the authority of any inspector general, which are similar types of oversight agencies attached to each department in many agencies within the federal government.

There are about sixty-four different Inspectors General (IG). When I first came down to Washington, I didn't really know what an IG did. In my experience as a prosecutor, we only occasionally would run into their law enforcement arms. They would be our agents. For a while, I was doing mortgage fraud cases. I had started up a mortgage fraud unit and I was dealing with the inspectors general from HUD who were very good law enforcement agents, but I didn't know the big picture of what an IG was doing. When I got the SIGTARP job, one of the first things I did was go around and meet the different IGs. Starting with those meetings, and over the next couple of years, I found that the inspectors general are supposed to be fierce watchdogs looking out for waste, fraud, and abuse. Those are the magic words that are written into their statute and what they're supposed to be doing. They had really become just like any other governmental agency. Their number one concern seemed to be how to preserve their budget. They were very worried about clashing with management. They were very worried about too much interaction with Congress. It was really very much a go-along-to-get-along type of attitude. What I kept hearing was [that] there were three types of different IGs: a lapdog who would presumably curl up in the lap of management, and that was discouraged; a watchdog, which is sort of in between; and a junkyard dog. Ultimately, I was told by Senator Max Baucus, who was the head of the Finance Committee which oversaw one of my confirmation hearings, that I needed to be like a junkyard dog, but the IGs were telling me that I shouldn't be too aggressive and should be more like that watchdog. Unfortunately, in practice, it seemed often that IGs were more concerned about keeping their job and not being offensive, rather than necessarily being that strong advocate to the taxpayer that they're supposed to be. There are some IGs who do their job well, and usually those are the ones that you hear about in the news. When Glenn Fine was the Inspector General at the Department of Justice, he helped use his office to lead the investigation into the politically motivated firings of U.S. attorneys. That's an example of an extremely aggressive, very effective IG. Often, you don't hear about them. I was once asked the question about why a particular agency didn't have an IG doing what we were doing, and it turned out that they did. It's just that you never heard of them because they are not out there, not aggressive. I was once told by an IG point-blank that he wished he could do what I was doing, but he was afraid because he had kids in college and he couldn't afford to lose his job. That's one of the problems. They live in fear of being fired if they are too aggressive in carrying out their duties.

We had an original outlay of $50 million from Congress to use until we ran out. We would have to go through the normal budgetary process through Treasury in the White House to get additional funds. I will say, in this age of a lot of agencies being denied funding, we never had a problem. We were always more than adequately funded. Senator Richard Shelby kept good on his promise, as did Congress, to make sure that not only did we always have the adequate resources to do our job, but also had support and backing, which was absolutely instrumental, especially from both parties. We had the Republicans, such as Senator Shelby, but probably even more importantly, the Democrats once the Obama Administration took over. They also strongly supported what we were doing and helped keep the pressure up on Treasury.

SENATOR JIM BUNNING (R-KENTUCKY) was very much opposed to TARP in the first place, the whole legislation, and he wasn't comfortable with creating yet another new federal agency with, as he said, a $50 million budget. That's an understandable concept. There are a lot of people out there who similarly feel that more government agencies are not the solution. Eventually, we brought Senator Bunning over to our side. He co-sponsored a bill that expanded our power and jurisdiction. One of the most remarkable things is, at a hearing right before he stepped down, he said I did a pretty good job, which, from Senator Bunning, was a pretty remarkable compliment; he was coming from an understandable place given what we've seen in government. As an agency, we more than pay for ourselves many times over; in just one case, we kept more than half a billion dollars from going into an ongoing fraud because of our investigative functions.

A program like this is designed at its outset to bail out banks and help Wall Street institutions, but people running that program within Treasury all came from the same mindset. This was the same when it was

Hank Paulson's Treasury Department, under President Bush, and continued under President Obama with Treasury Secretary Tim Geithner. There were people who all saw problems with a Wall Street perspective. Their biggest concern, over and over again, was protecting the banks, and, as they saw it, by protecting the banks, we protect a financial system. They didn't have people who are sensitive to the issues. If you're shoveling hundreds of billions of dollars out, you have real vulnerabilities to fraud. There are going to be those who are going to try to steal that money. They are not as attuned to conflicts of interest. They weren't really cognizant of the fact that you needed a degree of skepticism with the people and the institutions that they were interacting with. The role of all IGs should be, that voice of the taxpayer, to be that institutional concept of pushing back when money is being pushed out. There were not enough strings attached when there were potential vulnerabilities to fraud that, frankly, if you have a career at Goldman Sachs, you're not really going to be sensitive to when you're pushing this money out. One of the things I saw over and over again was that presumption of goodness that these banks and these executives would never ever, ever take advantage of the taxpayer by putting their profit interest over that of the public interest, and our voice was one of skepticism to help try to rein that back in.

For example, [Charles] Antonucci was essentially the CEO of the smallest bank in New York and tried to get TARP money by cooking his books and committing a type of accounting fraud by making it look like they had more bank capital, which is the cushion that a bank has against losses. It's what prevents a bank from failing if it has a certain number of losses or makes it able to withstand that impact through their own shareholders. Antonucci had engaged in some trickery to make it look like the bank was healthier than it was to try to get $11 million of taxpayer funds. We worked with the U.S. Attorney's Office in the Southern District of New York to investigate and prosecute him, and ultimately, he pleaded guilty to those charges.

HOME AFFORDABLE MODIFICATION PROGRAM (HAMP) was the program that the Obama Administration launched to try to meet the requirement that Congress put forward that TARP be used not just to help the banks by bailing them out, but also do something about the foreclosure crisis that was raging in 2008. Congress insisted when they gave the Treasury authority to go bail out the banks, then they also had to do something for homeowners. That program was launched with the intention to help up to four million people stay in their homes. Unfortunately, it's falling far, far short of that goal. It has helped around 800,000 now, about 20 percent of its goal. In the book, we talked a lot about the program design flaws, but also some of the intentions behind the program. My book also recounts conversations that I had with Secretary Geithner and others discussing the program as more about helping the banks survive the crisis than it was necessarily trying to get four million people to stay in their homes. A tremendous amount of politics [was played with HAMP]: in the way that they fought back against some of those recommendations that we had made to try to deal with the foreclosure crisis head-on, and later, how they defined success under the program. For example, they originally said up to four million people would get helped by the program. When it became pretty obvious that they were never going to come anywhere near that, they said, "Oh, no, no. That was never our intent. Our intent was just to make four million offers. Whether people accepted those offers and whether those modifications were actually successful and people actually stayed in their homes, that was never really part of what we wanted to do." That was one example of how politicized the program became.

I had anticipated a major change [in attitudes towards Wall Street and the big banks] because of the political differences [in the Bush Administration with Henry Paulson, to the Obama Administration with Timothy Geithner,] but, substantively, there was almost no difference. That level of deference to the banks, and putting the banks first, was really the same under Paulson's administration as it was under Geithner's administration.

On a personal level, the two were very different. Paulson was very welcoming. He swore me in on my first day. He had sent a message out to the Treasury Department that he wanted to make it work with SIG-TARP. On my first day, they were just about to put the money into the auto industry bailout and [he wanted to know] what thoughts we had, and agreed in concept with a lot of the ideas we had to protect taxpayer money. Geithner was much more dismissive. I didn't really meet with him all that often. We had maybe a couple of meetings. He was at times very combative, at times very aggressive, at times profane. Stylistically, there was a difference, but substantively, unfortunately, we really saw a lot of the same, which was pushing back on what we thought were pretty commonsense approaches to protect the taxpayers and bring more transparency.

ELIZABETH WARREN WAS THE head of another oversight institute that was created in that same TARP legislation called the Congressional Oversight Panel. Congress wanted to have its own eyes and ears and created this special entity to provide another level of oversight. This was a body of five panelists—three Democrats, two Republicans—and Elizabeth was named its chair. We had different roles in providing oversight. We were, on one hand, inside of the Treasury Department. We were a part of the Executive Branch, and our job was helping with program formation as well as our law enforcement goal. They had more of a Congressional type of role, which is why they had the ability to call hearings, take testimony, and try to bring transparency in that way. They took more of an academic approach in analyzing the programs from an after-the-fact perspective. They brought a very specialized skill. On the panel you had some members of Congress initially, but you also had a professor like Elizabeth Warren, and other experts. They were able to cull through their own budget, bringing a pretty impressive array of experts on different issues. Could Congress have done it themselves? Probably, but this level of specificity and depth, which they had in their reports, I don't think you would normally see that from a Congressional panel.

[THE GENERAL MOTORS (GM) bailout] is an example of the government and the Treasury Department talking a perfectly good story, and then trying to make it look a lot better than it was for PR and political purposes. As a result, you end up with a confused mess that ultimately seems a little bit misleading. What had happened was that GM had paid back part of its loan.... Ultimately, when they repaid that loan, which was made with big announcements from the White House and from the Treasury Department, they used other TARP money that they had received as part of the bailout from some of that stock that we have, and used it to pay off the loan. It was good news that they paid back the loan. That was a lot of TARP money sitting around that they didn't need in order to keep the company afloat, and they used it to pay back the loan. That was a good thing. They didn't really disclose where the money came from, and they made it sound like it came from just selling a bunch of cars. They had all this cash and they paid back their loan. Look, part of my job was to rain on the parade a little bit and clarify where this money was coming from and bring that level of transparency.

We saw that a lot in TARP and I think we see that a lot in government: taking something that is good news, [and making it sound better]. GM didn't need the money that we originally gave it and was able to pay down its loan and try to turn it into something else. As a bigger question, what would have happened had we not bailed out GM and Chrysler? The estimates of the job losses are all over the map. All I know is, from my own experience, I was in Hank Paulson's office on my first day, December 15, 2008, and he told me that if they didn't use TARP funds to bail out GM and Chrysler, that those institutions were going to go bankrupt and disappear. The impact on our economy at that time was too frightening to contemplate, so it was probably the right call.

It was comical as I went through my interview process. I went to different offices around the Treasury Department. I saw Eric Thorson, the IG of Treasury, who had these remarkable four offices combined into one with sweeping views of the White House. One looked like a museum. Actually, it was a roped-off part of the tour of the Treasury Department. After my meeting, I got sworn in by Secretary Paulson and had this really remarkable meeting. He said, "OK, we're going to take you to your office," and we just kept walking down the stairs and down the stairs and down the stairs, and eventually, I was hit by the smell of bacon and eggs because we're right next to the Treasury cafeteria. We walked into a very dismal, grungy basement office where we had this smell, I'll never forget, that hit us right as we opened the door and was there for months. We later found out it was actually an open sewage pipe right underneath the office. Instead of palatial views of the White House, all we had were some gated windows—I call them "Laverne and Shirley-like" windows—right by the top of the office, where you could see the ankles of people walking by. I'd come from a pretty dilapidated, seventies-style building in Manhattan when I was at the U.S. Attorney's office, so I was used to modest accommodations, but it was quite a contrast seeing the palatial offices that are reserved for what was known in Washington as presidentially-appointed, Senate-confirmed officials, and then see that they had dumped us into the basement.

IT WAS ACTUALLY A big point of contention [whether or not Timothy Geithner had any say over my position]. The way we use the statute, and the way Congress wrote the bill, made it very clear, in our view, that we were an independent agency within the Treasury Department, which meant that, essentially, the president of the United States had the ultimate authority over me. He could fire me at will, didn't need to have any reasons or cause. He could fire me with the stroke of his pen. Ultimately, we operated independent of any supervision from the Treasury secretary. They didn't like that. They went to the Department of Justice and actually sought to get a ruling that I was under Geithner's supervision, which would have given the secretary the potential ability and the authority to shut down audits he didn't like, shut down investigations he didn't like, and keep me from releasing certain reports. We ended up fighting tooth and nail using some of our friends in Congress to help push back on that, and they walked away from that fight. After they withdrew that request, they didn't have that authority.

Tim Geithner and I had a meeting I had asked for. Essentially, it was after the Treasury had refused for almost a full year to require TARP banks to report on how they were using their funds. We thought that was a real failure in transparency and there had been other transparency failures that had followed. I wanted this meeting to try to personally impress upon him, because I have been saying it to Herb Allison and his predecessor, and everyone else would listen, but I hadn't had a chance to voice to the secretary that they were really doing themselves harm, doing the country harm, and doing the president harm because there was this perception out there that those bailouts were just a giant transfer of wealth from the taxpayer to a handful of executives. The secrecy, by not being more transparent, was fueling a degree of cynicism that could have a lasting impact on the ability of our country to govern itself.

I wanted to make an impassioned plea that we needed to reverse these policies and be more transparent. As I lay that case out to him, and explained to him that he was not being sufficiently transparent, the meeting got very contentious. He, to put it mildly, disagreed with my contention. He used a lot of obscenities and expressed his view that he had been one of the most transparent secretaries of the Treasury in the history of the country, and that he had forced the banks to disclose things that no one else would. It followed this pattern for about forty minutes of really very explosive obscenity-laden tirades against me as I was trying to make that argument. Let me make this clear, I'm not complaining about that. It was the nature of a very contentious meeting. But still, inside, I'm just a line prosecutor from Manhattan, and now I've got one of the most powerful officials in the world dropping F-bombs on me. It was a very remarkable moment. After the meeting, my deputy who came with me from New York, Kevin Puvalowski, and I looked at each other. Here we are trying to advocate for what we think are some pretty commonsense changes, and we faced this deep level of animosity and condescension....

I go back to how Secretary Paulson approached the job. He understood that I was a prosecutor and someone who was outside of that Wall Street bubble. When Paulson, and then later, Geithner completely surrounded themselves with people from Goldman Sachs, Bear Stearns, Merrill Lynch, and other banks, an outside perspective, especially one that's very sensitive to the issues of fraud and abuse, such as one from my background, would be a valid voice to hear. Even if you disagree with that voice, even if you think that voice is wrong, it's still valid to get that input so you get something to pierce the echo chamber of pro-Wall Street-centric voices.

I don't want to speculate on Tim Geithner's motives, but what I can comment on is his own ideology. It really reflects that Wall Street ideology, this sense that what's best for the top banks is best for the country. The banks were telling him that more transparency would be dangerous. What I heard [from him] was that more transparency, like having banks account for how they spent the money, could...be dangerous. It could take down TARP. It could take down the banking system. He accepted those voices from Wall Street without questioning them, and I was trying to give him counter-arguments and lay out examples of how these things could get done, but he saw it as completely invalid. That's a real sense with the regulators in the Treasury: if you're not among those bankers, you really have no business having an opinion.

TIM MASSAD IS THE current successor to Herb Allison. He worked with Herb as the Chief Counsel for TARP. When Herb Allison stepped down in early October of 2010, he took over. When I came to Washington, I didn't give a fig leaf about protocol. I didn't really understand it and usually violated it. Under protocol, I was a presidentially-appointed, Senate-confirmed official. At that time, Mr. Massad was an acting official, which means he was not presidentially-confirmed, which meant, by any degree of protocol, I should have [testified first at a hearing presided over by Congressman Darryl Issa (R-California)]. The funny thing is, now I saw red. I was so upset at this "slight" that I had imagined that, afterwards, I went to my Legislative Director and I used my own salty language, and said, "You need to tell his staffer that...I outrank him and that this is Issa's first hearing, and he's got to understand the basic rules of protocol."

I went home that night and told my wife about it, and she burst out laughing. She said, "What's wrong with you? What happened to you?" As I started explaining, I realized, my God, she was right. Literally that night, I started working on my letter of resignation, because this was part of the influence of Washington and of power. I had so much become part of this system that I had abhorred when I came there, that I was now getting upset about something as trivial and stupid about who testifies first. At that point, I was thinking about stepping down. This was in January of 2011, and that solidified for me that I was becoming part of the very mechanisms of power that I'd so detested when I first got there.

WHEN I STARTED OFF, it was just me and [my deputy,] Kevin [Puvalowski]. We were two people. We had an agency. I realized that we needed to have a press person. I'd already realized that I had no idea how to deal with the media and I'd gotten good advice that I should hire a press person. When Kris Belisle came in to interview, it was like she was explaining a whole netherworld that I had no idea existed, which is the world of press flacks in Washington. The first thing she said to me was, "I'm not going to lie for you." I said, "I never asked you to lie for me."

I asked her what she was talking about and she really explained how the press works, and how she believed it was very important, as a new agency, to be completely upfront with the media, to never spin, and never do what a lot of the agencies do, which is to say things off the record or on background, which means telling the press something, but not putting your name behind it. One of the great tactics in this town is that you could say anything when your name is not attached to it; you can lie. You can make things up. You can exaggerate. She was basically saying that, if I were to hire her, we're not going to play any of those games. We're going to be straightforward. We're going to tell the truth. We're going to expose when we make a mistake, which we did, and we're going to admit it. Her strategy—and it was a strategy, it wasn't just being kindhearted—was that we were going to build up so much credibility with the media and with Congress, that when we were under attack (and she knew that we would eventually be attacked), we would have this level of credibility that we could use to fight back. I didn't really think of that back in December of 2008. I was ready to hire her on the spot. I had never met anyone like her. I never heard of these things, but it all that made perfect sense to me.

When I stepped down, around 120 or 130 people worked for me. There is still a SIGTARP. It will continue as long as Treasury has some outstanding assets that it has purchased under the program. A lot of the TARP money hasn't been paid back. There are still hundreds of banks that have not repaid their TARP funds. We still have that HAMP program limping along. It's now at a glacial pace. The largest banks have mostly paid back. Ally Financial, [formerly GMAC,] is a big bank that still owes a ton of TARP money.

I WANT EVERYONE WHO votes to read *Bailout.* I want people to understand and to care about the financial system and what's happened to our government. I want them to read this book, because there's so much anger out there. I'm furious and I'm still angry, and part of the reason why I wrote this book is to express that anger. But there's an anger out there now that people are understanding that Washington isn't being run for them, but it's being run for the interest of the small group of too-big-to-fail banks and their executives whose welfare has been put before the American people time and time again.

They understand this on the Left [with the Occupy group]; they understand it on the Right, in the Tea Party; and a lot of other folks in between understand this. But oftentimes, they're derided as crazy or as conspiracy theorists. I wrote this book so I could give them the evidence for their anger: the stories, the anecdotes, the individual things. I tried to bring the reader along with me as I went to Washington and to sit by me as you hear the things that these officials say and the policies that they implemented. Those are the people I want to [read this book,] so they can understand that their anger is justified, and frankly, for people who aren't angry, I want to make them a little bit angry.

IF YOU'RE AN EXECUTIVE at a too-big-to-fail bank, you're not going to be very happy that this book explains the power and the influence that you exercise over the government. The fact that I call for their institutions to be broken up would also make them not like it. I name the names, I lay out the conversations, so whether it's Secretary Geithner or the other people that I was working with, they will be upset....

A Congressman Pleads Guilty

BOB NEY

Bob Ney was part of the Republican wave that swept Democrats from power in 1994 in both the House and Senate. During his six terms, Ney became chairman of the House Administration Committee. With jurisdiction over the U.S. Capitol complex, he earned the title "Mayor of Capitol Hill." In the fall of 2006, Ney plead guilty to charges of conspiracy and making false statements in connection with the Jack Abramoff lobbying scandal, and resigned from Congress. On January 19, 2007, he was sentenced to thirty months in prison. Ney was released from prison on February 20, 2009, and moved to a half-way house for the remainder of his sentence. Ney talked about his journey from "lawmaker to law-breaker—and back" during his appearance on Q & A *on April 28, 2013. His book is called* Sideswiped: Lessons Learned Courtesy of the Hit Men on Capitol Hill *(Changing Lives Press, 2013).*

ALICE FISHER WAS ACTING head of the Justice Department's criminal division, and she made all of the division's [public] announcements. I call her "Pretty Alice" for a personal reason. When I would be with my attorneys…and we would see her press conferences, she would put on this red dress; she would be quite dolled up and smiling before the camera, and I would look up and say, "There's pretty Alice." So it became an inside joke with my attorneys and me. I didn't connect all of the dots, frankly, until later during my prison time and afterwards, of the exact, integral role of Alice Fisher…. She was being criticized by [Michigan

Democratic] Senator Carl Levin: Not enough trial experience. Too close to Tom Delay's defense team. Tom Delay was close to Jack Abramoff. Delay was under scrutiny, supposedly by the Justice Department, which faded away.... Her appointment was in trouble, as everybody knew from Senator Levin going to the floor of the Senate [to criticize].

At some point in August, 2006, John Boehner called me and cut a deal with me; he was Majority Leader at that time. He said I had twenty-four hours to consider this deal or it would be irrelevant. He said that, in fact, I would be able to get a job comparable to the salary I made in Congress and he would help me raise legal defense money to "put this behind me," this whole problem I had with the Justice Department, if I pulled out of the election. I didn't have to resign from Congress, but I needed to say, publicly, "I'm not running." They then, would get a replacement which Congressman Boehner named as State Senator Joy Padgett from Ohio.

I had twenty-four hours. I clearly remembered John Boehner saying, "If you don't accept this deal in twenty-four hours, it's off the table. We won't have this deal again." I called within twenty-four hours, after a lot of soul searching, and I said, "Fine. I'll take the deal. Comparable salary. You find me a job and then you help me raise legal defense money to fight this thing and put it behind me."

I had just won the primary in 2006. I was full steam ahead to run. Boehner's call made the significant difference of me getting out just in time so they could find somebody to run in my place. After I announced and I officially sent my letter to the secretary of state of Ohio, I couldn't get a janitor in John Boehner's office to call me back. It all evaporated. Soon after that, into the September or so time frame, my lawyers had contact from the Justice Department. It was full steam ahead: multiple indictments or plea—take your pick. At that point and time, I made a decision to take a plea. So, by September 13 or so, Alice Fisher solved her lack of prosecution on the Abramoff case, and that was me. All of a sudden they had a plea in process. Alice Fisher goes on to her appointment process. And that's where I believe the dots connect.

FIRST OF ALL, LET me make it crystal clear: I committed illegal acts, unethical acts, improper acts. I took free food from Jack Abramoff [the former lobbyist at the center of an extensive Congressional corruption scandal]. I took free booze from Jack Abramoff. I don't deny any of that. I created this problem for myself and I admit that right out front. However, Alice Fisher mentions in her press conference [about my case] a Lake George trip, and I was not indicted or asked for a plea on that trip. I paid for that Lake George trip. The people that went on that trip know that. The people that they downloaded—some of my former staff, they know that, too. That trip, the basic bulk of it, was a personal trip. Four friends took it, and I paid my way on that trip.

As far as the thousands of dollars, which the Justice Department estimates at $6,000, at Jack Abramoff's restaurant where my staff and I partook in food and alcohol, that's true...and I didn't disagree with that. It was over a period of three years. That's accurate. Now what Ms. Fisher fails to mention is that when I would go to Jack Abramoff's restaurant, "Signatures," I would have to shove the Bush White House staffers aside to get a drink at the bar. They were getting free drinks, too, which is fine. I'm my own problem on this.

The one that really gets me, though—[she accuses me of] inserting amendments into the Help America Vote Act of 2002. I inserted no amendment for Jack Abramoff into the Help America Vote Act, which was my legacy bill with Rep. Steny Hoyer (D-Maryland.). The first official election bill dealing with the federal government in probably the nation's history, it was a legacy bill—an important bill. I did not insert Jack's amendments. I was on a congressional conference committee with Senator [Mitch] McConnell (R-Kentucky), Senator [Christopher] Dodd (D-Connecticut), and any of those gentlemen will verify that at no point in time did we lay an amendment on the table. At no point and time did I say, "Here's an amendment for Jack Abramoff." Simply didn't happen. Now, did I agree to consider an amendment for Jack Abramoff for that bill? Yes, absolutely. I am probably one of the first members of Congress, in this country's history, in modern times, to plead a felony for agreeing to consider an amendment to a bill. If they would go to the Hill today and charge felonies on people that are considering amendments to a bill, there would barely be anybody left on Capitol Hill.

There were bright lines that I crossed, for example, when Jack Abramoff came into my office and said, "I have an amendment for the Help America Vote Act." He said that members of the Senate were interested in this, that members of the Senate were on board. I, as a member of the House, said very clearly to Jack Abramoff that I would consider this amendment, which is my felony, I guess, for the considering of an amendment. The other thing is that if the Senate wanted this amendment, of course, I need that bill, and if senators want that amendment and it doesn't ruin my bill, I told Abramoff, I'll consider it. Now, at that point in time, though, I didn't know it was an amendment. We didn't have an actual amendment, and that in itself is a problem. To just generically consider something that a lobbyist wants, whether it's Abramoff or not, and to say, "Yes, I'll consider that," I think that's a problem in itself. But the bright line is when a member of my staff received an e-mail and it said, "If you want to go to Jack's restaurant, and if you want to eat and you want to drink," meaning myself and the office, "it's going to be taken care of...." Although staffers went, I'll take the responsibility. I could have said, "No, none of us are going." That was a crossing of the bright line.

The other one was the Scotland trip. As I note in the book, I came back [after the trip] and I turned to two staffers and said, "That was weird." At that point in time, I should have written a check to pay for the trip because I knew that it did not smell right. So there were bright lines I crossed. When did I know? I operated like D.C. operates in some ways, but there were definite signs, probably within a six-month period of meeting Jack Abramoff that I should have said, "Eh, doesn't look good."

I WAS PART OF the Contract with America class, so I came to Congress in 1995, in January, and I resigned in November of 2006. I was in prison seventeen months. I was "behind the wall" as we would say, for a year's period, and then into the halfway house, so I did seventeen months, officially, of federal time. I was sentenced to thirty months. My plea deal, I think, was eighteen months.

Prison is a warehouse. Anybody that thinks it is rehabilitation, or anybody that thinks it's about trying to get people prepared to go back into society is mistaken. It's a warehouse.... [To prepare myself for prison] I spent maybe four hours with Web Hubbell. He was the former assistant attorney general of the United States, former chief justice of the Arkansas Supreme Court [who went to prison in connection with the Clinton-era Whitewater investigation]. He said, "This is what's going to happen." So that was my preparation. When I reported to prison, I didn't take my family with me; it was traumatic and emotional as it was. I took one current staffer and one who had just quit and went on to an operations media firm. Those two staffers went with me and then they dropped me off at prison.

I went in. I walked into the little kiosk, and I said "I'm Bob Ney, here to report." A guard came up as we walked down. He said, "Oh, I knew one of your campaign managers in Ohio." Got down in there, and the guard said, "Here, you have some hate mail waiting on you." It was from California, I remember, and Massachusetts. They gave me the mail. You go through the most embarrassing part, the strip-down. Then I got into the intake, walked into prison, down into the courtyard. I won't use the language I do in the book, but the warden told the man who was supposed to take me around, "Get away from him. He can find his own way." I'm sitting there not knowing where to go, where I'm staying, what clothes to get. You're in these "newbie clothes," they called them, like pajama pants. Another prisoner said, "Where's your escort that's supposed to take you around?" I said, "I don't know." He took me in the back way of the laundry room. I walked in and a man is sitting there and he said, "Are you the congressman?" I said, "Used to be." He said, "You are a Republican, aren't you?" And I said, "Well, Republicans put me in here, you know." I have to pull up some humor in this situation. He said, "Well, I was the mayor of East Cleveland. Welcome, I'll get you some clothes." He was a prisoner. I think he's just been recently released. He got me clothes. He said, "Where's your unit?" I said, "I don't know." He said, "Well, where's your escort?" I said, "Some little guy yelled all kinds of foul things and the escort ran away." I found out the next day that it was the warden who was standing behind me screaming, "Let him find his own way," to teach me a lesson.

I walked towards the main line to eat the next day and my mind's racing: "When I get out of here, how am I going to get a job? I've lost every dime I ever owned. What about my children? What about my family? What can I do?" You're disgraced. You're full of shame, and a prisoner turned to me and said, "You co-authored the Sudafed Law. You put me in here." I realized it's a day at a time. I've got to get through this place. Forget the House, forget the job. I've got to get through this place. I sat down, and from that day, changed my attitude. So, that was my first twenty-four hours at Morgantown Federal Correctional Institution in West Virginia.

I was born in Wheeling, West Virginia. Raised in Ohio. I went to prison in Morgantown, West Virginia. I'm going to make a choice to be buried in Ohio. I'm not going to be buried in West Virginia.

[RADIO HOST ELLEN RATNER is now my boss.] During my days in Congress, there was zero that Ellen Ratner and I agreed upon. Zero, politically. Today, we might agree on some things, but still, today, I lovingly call Ellen the "Queen of the Left." Ellen is a pure, true liberal in all of the sense of being liberal. We've been friends since I walked into the doors of Congress. And politically, we're a little closer here-and-there today, but in the Congressional days there's probably not one vote we would share. Ellen did several things for me. We not only became friends. We had this karmic relationship in the sense that she changed [the date of] her birthday party—her big fiftieth...to September 11, 2001. I would have been in the Towers that day [and perhaps been killed] had she not changed her birthday party. So there was something about Ellen Ratner beyond just a friend. She visited me in prison and said, "You need to come work for *Talk Radio News* and do radio." And I said, "Ellen, I don't want to do anything publicly. I just want to work a job. That's all I want to do." She said, "No, no, no, you need to get back in the saddle. You have things to offer." So what Ellen did for me, and I mentioned this as I dedicate the book to her—not only do I work for her now, that's the small part. Ellen was my friend, counselor, psychiatrist, who gave me tough love. Ellen Ratner doesn't let you get by with anything. She'll tell you right now in an unfiltered tone, and I mean that with all flattery. So Ellen has just been a wonderful, wonderful friend.

I NOW LIVE IN Newark, Ohio, near Columbus; I used to share [representation in Congress of] Lincoln County with John Kasich at one time; he's now our governor. I've been married twice, divorced twice, and have two children and a grandchild.... As far as what the prison was like, it was traumatic at that time. I was married to my second wife, had my children, and I'm going into prison. You walk in there and everything you've ever known is behind you. I always tell my friends, "I went from

Capitol Hill, where it's, 'Hello, Mr. Chairman. Hi, Mr. Chairman. Would you like a drink, Mr. Chairman? Here, have a cup of coffee, Mr. Chairman,' to 'No, you're not getting a second round of oatmeal, scumbag, move on.'" So, it's a little bit of a different attitude in prison. When I went in, I immediately met some people, and I've got to be frank about this: I became friends more with the people who were in there for drug offenses than [with] the white collar crime people. First of all, they didn't whine as much about prison. They were more street savvy. They were people who had, for me at least, a lot to share. They never would have [had] a chance to meet a member of Congress, and a lot of them told me that. A lot of minorities—African Americans, Latinos—said, "We would never have had an opportunity to meet you when you were in Congress. We'd love to ask you questions." I would answer questions in some of the classrooms and talk to them about jobs and résumés, so I received a lot back from them. But the initial part is terrifying for anyone, especially myself, because I went from being a lawmaker to a lawbreaker. Some people in prison said, "You made the laws that put me in here. You did that to me." And then, of course, you try to say, "Well, you broke the law." But, yes, I created the law. So it made a little bit of a difference.

THIS WAS A MINIMUM [security facility], but it wasn't a camp. There were no bars and there was no cell. You have a door, no cells, open cubicles, things like that. They don't even lock you in at night. There are officers, but you could get up to go to the restroom or something. There are no particular cells unless you get in trouble, and then you go into the SHU— the holding area. But, as far as the "Club Med" [perception], it's not. It's prison. It's punishment. You will do this in a certain time. You will do that at a certain time. You will follow the rules. You run out of [phone call] minutes and you have an emergency at home, too bad. If someone dies, you hear, "Ney, to the chapel." When you hear that, you know someone has died. I know this is a particular case from two friends: "Oh, your mother died. And, by the way, you owe us twenty-two dollars on your account." That's about how you're told. Now, I know I did wrong and there are people in prison that did wrong. But there's a certain human quality that, if you want to psychologically rebuild someone who has committed a crime, you would undertake these [interactions] in a different way. Prison is no joyride. I don't care if it's county lockup, state, or federal.... There are maximum security places that I wouldn't want to be, where there are hard-core people, who maybe committed murder, or such types of crimes. But the minimums are no picnic where you're just free to talk to your family, pick up the phone, and do what you want to do.

Charles Mosher was my probation officer and he's federal; he was assigned to me in Columbus, Ohio. I had an interesting situation because he was, whether intentionally or whatever, in fact, calling in to the prison. The gentlemen in the prison who oversaw that part of the probation when you leave would call me in and he just would scare me to death: "What are you having this man call for? What are you trying to do? Do you think you're something, Congressman? Are you trying to use pull?" And I would say, "I don't know Charles Mosher. I've never heard of the man." Mosher went out of line because the gentlemen in prison told me, "I'm going to take care of this. I'm going to call his boss." Well, I didn't care what he did—call Mr. Mosher's boss. But Mosher's calls in created [for] me a massive heartburn. As I also show in the book, they called me in to ask me who I was working for, which was going to be Ellen Ratner. How much money I was going to make, which I didn't even know at that time. I was just happy to have a job. All these details that you normally aren't put through are all prior to getting out of prison. I was not released from prison on the date I was due to be released, and I outline in the book how I, fortunately, by accident, was able to get a private call to my attorney.

I have written the entire book myself, except for Ricky Campbell's part on the prison, and Matt Parker, a former staffer of mine who put together a chapter in the book. I had an editor, Sheri Johnson, from New Mexico; a wonderful woman who was partly my conscience, [urging me] to say this is what I think. But I made the final call on it. Also, she would fluff up some of my writing style. But the actual book, itself, as far as the thoughts in the book, I have written them. I didn't have a ghostwriter who gave me the material. I wrote the book in Goa, on the Indian Ocean, and also in Dharamsala, India, specifically McCleod Ganj, which is the city above Dharamsala. I was five minutes from the Dalai Lama's residence. I wrote it, basically, in sixty days between Goa and Dharamsala, India. I had one of those [recorders] where you speak into this mic, but I abandoned that within two days. So, I actually would sit down on the computer, go either down by the ocean or go to the tea shops, and I would type it up and I would send it to Sheri. After my outline I put together, we would just start chapter-by-chapter. I returned then to Newark, Ohio, and did editing from my return, which would have been around May 31, all the way up to January, to when we pushed the "send" button and produced the book. [The book is published by Changing Lives Press in Cleveland, which is owned by Ellen Ratner.]

[I DON'T CARE A whole lot for John Bresnahan, a Congressional reporter for *Politico*.] I had been told by some of Abramoff's people that John Bresnahan was getting information from Jack Abramoff for stories as this whole thing was going down. Jack was quite secluded from the press, as you can imagine, after the *Washington Post* and the *New York Times*, and everybody else under the sun was going after him. Bresnahan was doing stories about him. But at that point and time, I was told also point blank by Jack Abramoff's people that Jack was angry at me. I had used the word that Jack had "duped" me and that Tom Delay was still standing up for him. As a result, Bresnahan was helping to do some stories that would cause me heartburn because Jack was feeding him items of what we did and where we went. So that was one [thing]. Second, is the fact that the whistleblower that really started this was not Emily Miller…. The whistleblower was Tom Rodgers. He's a Native American. He's been involved in Native American issues. He's the first one who uncovered, and rightfully so, the dealings with Jack Abramoff and myself with Jack and the Indian Tribes.

I PRAISE TOM RODGERS for starting all of this. If I had anger in me, I would say, "That guy Rodgers did this to me." He didn't. He simply stood up on behalf of Native Americans. He found out that something was going on that just didn't look right, didn't smell right. Anybody can represent clients, but when you get to a certain level and you use members of Congress to verify that [someone like Abramoff] is a great lobbyist and he ought to keep hiring him, but the Native Americans, unfortunately, aren't getting that much of a return on it, then it's not a healthy situation. Tom Rodgers simply told the truth when he found it out. And I give Tom Rodgers credit. He's the man who got this ball rolling.

TOM RODGERS CONFRONTED JACK Abramoff not too long ago at the Press Club, and said, "Were you and your people in cash games, high-stakes card games with reporters, members of Congress, but mostly staff, and lobbyists?" And Jack said, "I can't recall." I had played cards with Bresnahan. I had paid Bresnahan money towards my last year that I was in trouble, and I knew they had some card games going. I felt that was important to reveal in the process. I didn't think that should occur. I felt that Bresnahan shouldn't have his cake and eat it, too, in the way that he would write stories about people, yet he himself as a reporter was making terrible violations of the rules and the ethics…[being] involved with staffers and lobbyists in these card games. The other thing is, there was an arrangement with Jack Abramoff…to buy *The Hill* newspaper, and Bresnahan would become the editor. Jack had this marvelous plan where he could control stories that were written maybe against other lobbyists that he was dealing with.

[I say in the book that I let him win the card games, but] I don't say that Bresnahan knew that. I'm sitting there. I'm in trouble. I'm scrambling for my life. I'm sitting there, with the right or the wrong of it, in a card game with a reporter and I have a pretty good hand. I'm going to fold that hand; I'm going to lose $268. That's my intention. I'm not saying that Bresnahan said to do that, and I'm not saying he knew I did that. But I did it. [As to what Bresnahan has done wrong,] I don't think as a reporter you should be in cash games with members of Congress or cash games with lobbyists. How many lobbyists are folding hands to make someone happy? Maybe they did it with me.

[In the book, I write about the "money whores" in D.C.] I think the system itself is dysfunctional. Senator John McCain (R-Arizona) was going to clean up the system. We were going to not have money as we know it in the system. It's proliferated into a nuclear war of campaign funds. That bill, McCain-Feingold campaign finance reform, did zero, created loopholes, the 527s, you've got the George Soros's to the left, the Karl Roves and the Koches to the right. I believe a lot of it is the race for money. I'm asked constantly on radio shows today about members of Congress: "Are they good or bad?" [There are] plenty of good members of Congress, on both sides of the aisle, and there are some people that we know…that have gotten in trouble for unethical activities. But the system itself is doomed to corruption. I ate sushi with Jack Abramoff, I drank some booze with Jack Abramoff, I went to Scotland with Jack Abramoff. Anything that Jack Abramoff and I did is now codified in the United States law. If I'm a lobbyist today and you're a congressman to-day… if I want to, I can take you to Alaska, and we can hunt, we can have a $3,000 to $4,000 dinner, way better food than Jack Abramoff had. We can do that, and I can raise $75,000 for you. I can then take you, a staffer, and maybe some of your family and fly you as congressman to Las Vegas, where we can have a $2,000 to $3,000 dinner. I can raise you $125,000, and it's all legal, as long as we stand up at the reception and eat. We're legal. I can have meals. I can still use loges. Alice Fisher, in her announcement said, "That congressman used loges for fundraisers." No kidding. Everybody listening to this program and everybody on the Hill today: I was charged. I plead guilty. I did a lot of wrong things, but for using a loge for a fundraiser? Give me a break! The entire Congress would be in Morgantown [prison]. A loge is a private box; you go to them and you watch the game and you have a fundraiser. It's still done today. Nothing's changed on whatever I was charged for…. It's done con-stantly for fundraisers.

[EVEN AFTER MY CONVICTION, as a former member of Congress,] I can go on the House floor. I have full privileges of the House. I can take people on the House floor. The only problem I had was [Speaker John] Boehner's office. It took them ten days [to respond to my requests]. His personal attorney, the speaker's attorney, called me and wanted to know if I was trading a job to bring some former constituents on the Floor. But otherwise, yes, I have privileges of the House.

The first time that I got out of prison in 2008, I was working for El-len Ratner, and she wanted to go to the House dining room with some reporters for dinner. I said, "I'm not going to go to the dining room, El-len." She said, "Oh, you need to come." I said, "I can't. I haven't been back in the Capitol." I had a lot of shame. I had a lot of friends over in the Capitol, but, I didn't feel it was good for me. She said, "Just walk over." I walked in and I had my former member's card, and it has my picture on it from when I was a member. I will never forget the police officer standing there as I pull the card out, and he says, "Welcome back,

Mr. Chairman, that card's not needed here." I walked into the House dining room and a couple of the ladies started crying. I saw some members of Congress and we said hello. Democrats and Republicans. I was treated better than I deserve. It was an "ah-hah" moment for me. I do get a congressional pension. In fact, I took the pension early because all of my money was gone. [My legal fees cost me] $518,000 approximately. Part of it is paid, part of it's not paid.... I used my campaign funds mainly [to cover some of the legal fees]....

[JACK ABRAMOFF SAID ON December 13, 2011, that, "One of the reasons Bob Ney was the only one that went to prison is that Bob apparently had a different issue that wasn't related to mine. He took $50,000 in casino chips from an Iranian businessman apparently who wanted the government to give him permission to sell planes to Iran. Now, that act, and doing it in a casino in London, is what I think unhinged Bob. And Bob plead, by the way."] Nobody else was indicted because a lot of the Congressional action is protected under the "Speech and Debate Clause." I am sure that Jack Abramoff just doesn't want to be too frank about what really happened. First of all...I was not indicted for the chips; the government did not indict me. Second, it was not an Iranian businessman. He was a Syrian businessman.... I did have a problem of declaring all the chips; I declared some and didn't declare others. But the government didn't indict me on that. Now, I'm not saying that helped. What Jack Abramoff is saying there is, "If he hadn't had that problem in the casino, there was nothing Bob and I did that they would have convicted him for. That's why nobody else was convicted." That's not accurate. I had a stream of favors from Jack Abramoff. I took free food from Jack Abramoff that should have been reported; I took free alcohol from Jack Abramoff that should have been reported; I plead guilty to falsification of a federal document, which was actually a congressional document, which I could have shielded with the "Speech and Debate Clause."

Jack doesn't like to answer the very question he has created in this controversy. On *60 Minutes*, Jack Abramoff said, "I had a hundred members in my pocket and I spent a million dollars." If Jack Abramoff spent a million dollars on a hundred members and he spent say, thirty thousand on me, what was the difference between those members and myself?

Now, I'm not saying I could point the finger and say, "This member should be indicted," or not. But there were other people who took trips with Jack Abramoff, other people that signed letters for Jack Abramoff, other people that inserted items in the Congressional Record for Jack Abramoff. I argue Jack Abramoff is not correct that he and I really didn't do anything, that it was the Jack London problem Bob Ney had. London didn't help me for leverage with the government. But it was he and I. And, I argue, that the rest of it is only known to Jack Abramoff. And, as I write in my book, I think that once I went away, [the impression was, that regarding] Congress, the bad guys were in prison. They didn't have to go after anybody else.

When John McCain had his Senate hearing on Indian Affairs and dragged Jack Abramoff there, Ralph Reed, the former head of the Christian Coalition, was involved in a secret plot and received money—maybe millions of dollars—to act like he wanted to close a casino. Jack was to open it. That casino was the Tigua tribe's, [to whom I said,] "Jack's a good guy." I was culpable in doing that terrible thing to the Native Americans. When John McCain had his hearing, he didn't drag Ralph Reed there, he only dragged in Jack Abramoff. When John McCain had his hearing, the only name mentioned was me. I did wrong things. I committed criminal acts. But when Jack Abramoff says, "Oh, even Bob wouldn't have been found guilty if it wasn't for London." That is not an admission of reality.

[JACK KNEW THAT ONCE I went away, his friends like DeLay and others would be spared…. Should Tom DeLay have been indicted by the federal government?] I can't answer that because I'm not [former Attorney General] Alberto Gonzales, and I'm not Jack Abramoff. But I will tell you this. If I plead because I went on a trip to Scotland and Tom went on his trip to Scotland. Tom also went to the Mariana Islands with Jack. I didn't. The question becomes, is that an illegal trip in itself? I don't know. Delay's closeness to Jack Abramoff—Jack paid for Tom's daughter's baby shower. Tom's former Chief of Staff [Ed Buckham] received a filtered-through million dollars from Jack Abramoff into some type of foundation. Now, are those all indictable? I don't know. But my point is…either we were all indictable or we all weren't.

JACK ABRAMOFF AND I would agree on one thing if he was sitting here today. Clean this town up. Everything Jack and I did is on steroids now. Maybe the trips are stopped. But everything's on steroids. They can do all kinds of things up here. The power games, the money games. Everyone on the Hill knows what I say is true. You have to raise $150,000. You have to raise half a million. You want to be a chairman; you have to raise that money. You have to play that game to be part of the system. The leaders are making incredible amounts of money and they control a lot of the power through it. The big pharmaceutical companies, they don't have to go to individual members. [They] go to some of the leaders. Now, at the end of the day on this shiny, bright Capitol Hill are some of the most wonderful people in this country, Democrat and Republican. But also, this is corrupt. A lot of good people, some bad people, mainly good, I argue. But the system is broken.

[IF I WAS TEACHING a high school or college course about Capitol Hill,] I would have them read this book and I would tell them the reality of how some bills become a law. It's a mixture out there. I would agree with Abramoff on things I've heard him say. If you want to serve in Congress, you don't become a lobbyist, period. If you're a staffer, you don't become a lobbyist. This is not the feeding ground for the lobby circuit. Take that out of it. Take the money out of the system, if you can. Truly take it out. Don't buy chairmanships of committees. Don't have that nuclear campaign arms race of raising money. Look, today, members take their federally-paid staffers, they take them to the Democrat war room, as I call it, or they take them to the Republican war room across from the Capitol and they raise money on federal time. Is it illegal? No. Is it right? No. I did it. It's done today. They're doing it as we speak. I can safely say somebody's doing it. Let's take that side of it out. There are a lot of changes that Speaker Boehner and Minority Leader Pelosi could join hands today and make within twenty-four hours, and have such a dynamic change on the Hill that would allow these good people who are up there, Democrats and Republicans alike, to function.

Post-9/11 America

9/11's "Special Master"

KENNETH FEINBERG

After the attacks of September 11, 2001, the U.S. government insti-tuted a program to provide financial compensation to survivors and the families of victims. Overseeing this program was Kenneth Feinberg in his position as Special Master of the September 11th Victim Com-pensation Fund. Over the course of thirty-three months, Mr. Feinberg awarded $7 billion of taxpayer funds to nearly 2,900 families affected by the attacks. He accepted no payment for this job. Mr. Feinberg wrote about the challenges and successes of this unprecedented program in his book, What Is Life Worth?, *which he discussed in this July 10, 2005, interview with* Q & A.

CONGRESS, IN SETTING UP this program after 9/11, delegated to me, and really to me alone, the requirement, the obligation, to try and calculate what each death or physical injury caused by 9/11 should be paid out of public funds. I was called a "Special Master." That connotes in the law somebody who is delegated authority, usually by a court, to act as some administrative arm of the court to administer a settlement, and then to allocate the proceeds of a settlement. I awarded $7 billion of taxpayer funds, all public money, to 5,560 people; 2,880 families who lost a loved one on 9/11. The remaining claims were physical injury claims to survivors of 9/11. The largest award was about $8.6 million, tax free, to an individual who survived the World Trade Center collapse with third degree burns over 85 percent of her body, who came to see me. The smallest award was

$500 to somebody who broke a finger escaping from the World Trade Center. The average award, tax free, was $2 million, and the median award, half got more, half got less, was about $1.7 million.

Clearly, the hardest part was the decision I made in designing the program to meet with any individual family or individual victim who survived who wanted to see me personally to discuss their plight, why they felt they were entitled to more money, why they felt that 9/11 was an unfair, unjust curveball thrown at them. Over a 33-month period, I met with about 1,500 individual family members, and that was harrowing. I remember the very first meeting: a woman came to see me, twenty-five years old, crying, sobbing. "Mr. Feinberg, I lost my husband in the World Trade Center and you have awarded me about $1 million to take care of my two little children, six and four, who lost their father. I need more money and I need it fast." And I said to her, "Why? Why do you need more and what is this request that you've made for speed?" "Well, you see, Mr. Feinberg, I have terminal cancer, I only have two months to live. My husband was going to survive me and take care of the children, now they're going to be orphans. Can you please help me quickly?" We did. I substantially increased the award, accelerated the payments, and she died two months later, but at least knowing that a structured financial program had been set up for her two surviving small children. There were hundreds like that.

Another meeting I remember: "Mr. Feinberg, I lost my husband, he was a fireman and he died at the World Trade Center. And I just want you to know that there is no God, Mr. Feinberg, because my husband rescued thirty people from the World Trade Center and brought them to safety. His battalion chief said, 'Stay here, too dangerous, don't go back.' And he said, 'I'm sorry, there are ten more people trapped in the mezzanine of the World Trade Center.'" Then she said: "While he was running back across the World Trade Center Plaza, he was killed by somebody who jumped to their death from the 103rd floor and hit him. If he had been one step either way, Mr. Feinberg, he might have survived. But, like a coordinated missile, somebody leaped to their death from the 103rd floor and hit him, killing them both. And I want you to know, Mr. Feinberg, that no amount of money [will compensate]. There is no justice. Why me? Why me? Why my husband?" Stories like that.

I never got mad at anybody. Never. I think it's critically important, and the public understood this, these people were in grief, the victims of life's misfortune, traumatic deaths, perfunctory good-byes that morning, see you for dinner, never saw their kid again, never saw their spouse again, vaporized. I never got mad at anybody. There was frustration sometimes. There were some pretty difficult moments. Anger. Invective. Epithets. But, I was never threatened.

I thought it very important to walk into the lion's den. I met groups of families: firefighter widows; servicemen's widows at the Pentagon. We filled up the Marriott Marquis ballroom in Manhattan with the survivors of roughly 850 Cantor Fitzgerald victims who all died at the World Trade Center. A whole ballroom filled with angry, grieving people. I spent a good year and a half, probably, going around the country, around the world, meeting with groups of families who needed to understand the program. Then, I also met with individual families.

[There was a different reaction in different parts of the country: New York versus California versus London.] It's sort of a cultural phenomenon. When I met with families in New York, in groups, they were angry: "Where's my money? The government caused this. This should have been prevented. You're the visible representative of the government and you had better pay." In Virginia, the Pentagon, the servicemen were very respectful. "Thank you for coming, Mr. Feinberg. We appreciate you're here. We would like to present a plaque for your service. Anything you can do, we appreciate what our government is trying to do." In California, there was a public outpouring of grief. "Hold hands, let's say a public prayer." In London, there was disbelief and skepticism about the program itself. "You mean to tell me, Mr. Feinberg, that my son, an English citizen, died at the Pentagon, and your government is going to give me $2 million, tax free? What's the catch? Do we have to give up our citizenship?" "No." "Do we have to surrender our passports?" "No." "Do we have to come to the United States to get the money?" "No." "What's the catch? Why is America doing this for us?" There were eleven undocumented families who lost a loved one in America at the World Trade Center...."Mr. Feinberg, why are you giving us this money? Are you going to deport us if we apply?" "No." "Are you going to put us in jail?" "No." "Are we going to be fined?" "No. I'm even going to give you a green card." There was skepticism and distrust. Gradually, all of these groups came into the fund. We had 97 percent that ultimately opted into the program rather than stay out, which they had a right to do.

I worked on this for thirty-three months; from the time I was appointed, I immediately began the design of the program, right up until we cut the last check. I couldn't take any money to do this job. I don't think any American doing this, in the post-9/11 world, could get paid for this. I didn't think it was right to get paid to serve the people of the United States in an unprecedented, unique task like this. Second, there was also a practical reality I confronted. These families were angry and they were in grief. If I ever got paid for this, they would have been after me. "You're getting paid on the blood of my lost wife? How dare you." I had enough formidable challenges without having to deal with that problem.

We dispensed $7 billion in those thirty-three months at a cost to the taxpayer of under $100 million. If there was ever a program in the history of our nation where the overhead was kept low relative to the amount of money that was disseminated, this is it. PricewaterhouseCoopers was awarded a contract by the Department of Justice to administer the program, [and there were] different offices, branch offices of mine calculating awards, opening up files for each and every claimant, a massive task. They had about 450 people working on this project at its height at a total cost, overhead, everything, [of] less than $100 million. My staff was very small. I had about eighteen people, all lawyers. Some worked pro bono and some were brought to me on detail from the United States Department of Justice or other branch agencies to assist me. Very lean, very small.

This proved unique. The closest analogy was when I acted as the Special Master in the Agent Orange case involving Vietnam veterans who claimed injury from exposure to Agent Orange/Dioxin while serving in Vietnam. But even that didn't prepare me for this. In the Agent Orange case, I acted as a mediator to help resolve the dispute between a class of Vietnam veterans claiming injury and the chemical companies who manufactured the product. Then, after I helped settle that case, we established a claims program to allocate the funds, $180 million, which grew to about $300 million over ten years. We allocated that and targeted eligible veterans.

There were some rough times, at the beginning, with the 9/11 families. The American people, the politicians, the media, were solidly behind this program. Even families from other terrorist attacks, who weren't eligible, like from Oklahoma City or from the first World Trade Center attack in '93, were very supportive of the program. The toughest part was convincing the 9/11 families themselves of the wisdom and the bona fides of the program. That was tough, especially the first year, so close to the 9/11 disaster itself.

[I don't know what would have happened to the airlines had this program not succeeded.] The airlines pushed this program as an alternative to litigation. The airlines were concerned that if thousands sued the airlines and the World Trade Center and MASSPORT and the Port Authority and Boeing and the security companies, that this litigation would inhibit or undercut the willingness of anybody to fly. So they felt this was an important diversion out of the courts system. I'm not sure how successful it was in preventing bankruptcy, and the airlines seem to have enough difficulty, as it is. But that was the genesis of it.

Senator Chuck Hagel, [currently secretary of defense,] a Republican from Nebraska, is the reason I was appointed by the attorney general. As a former chief of staff to Senator Edward Kennedy, I wasn't exactly the person who everybody would automatically assume would be assigned this task by the attorney general and the Bush Administration. Chuck Hagel, whom I have known since Agent Orange, personally pushed at the White House and at the Department of Justice, claiming that I was the right man to do this.

I wanted this job. I have no idea how many people applied for this job. To this day, I don't know if the administration sought out others or offered it to others. [At the time I decided I wanted the job,] I was teaching at the University of Pennsylvania Law School and I read about the program as I was coming back on the train, and I said to myself, "This was something I want to do."

At the moment of 9/11, I was at the law school. I had just come out of a class that I was teaching, and up on the student union television, I saw the results of the first plane hitting the World Trade Center. While I was in disbelief, I saw the second plane hit, and then I headed back from Pennsylvania to Washington. I was on the train when the plane hit the Pentagon. The train stopped in Wilmington and announced that [it was going no further]. I knew a couple of people on the train who were headed back to Washington and we went outside and negotiated with a taxi driver to drive us the remaining hour and a half.

[THE TIME BETWEEN SEPTEMBER 11, 2001, and the time Congress decided to do this program was minimal.] Eleven days. That was the problem. The emotion of 9/11 was so pronounced, so recent, so real, that explaining to family members the wisdom of the program fell on deaf ears for a long time. "Mr. Feinberg, you're here offering money. They haven't even found my husband's body in that rubble and you're here like some lawyer with a valise and a check? How dare you." That pervasive obstacle to success, emotion, venting, ranting about the unfairness of life greatly inhibited my ability to succeed during the first twelve to eighteen months of the program. They flayed away at the failure of the government to protect their loved one. They, sobbing, would vent at the unfairness of life. Why my husband? Why my wife? Why my son and not him and not her? Great concern expressed about how they're ever going to move on with the loss of a loved one who was the glue that kept the family together. There were all of these religious complaints: How could God ever allow this? I was the target for all of this emotional trauma.

Obviously, everybody is influenced by their heritage. In my case, my respect for the underdog, my respect for those who were not at the pinnacle, but are trying to improve their lot, my respect for the vagaries, the uncertainties of life, are part of my Jewish heritage. The program couldn't have been more non-adversarial. I was a fiduciary for these families, which means I was really there as their supporter to help them, not to question, not to antagonize, not to undercut. To the contrary, I was there asking them, help me give you more of an award. I have rules I have to follow, but I'm here to really help. Over time, that view became well-entrenched in the family's perspective about the program.

My father had been a retail tire salesman in Brockton, Massachusetts, which is a blue collar town, where everybody is trying to improve their lot. He was the son of immigrants from Eastern Europe. My respect for the underdog, the unfortunate, had a lot to do with that. My mother was very loving, a homemaker, very loyal to her three children, my sister and my brother, and also eager to help the less fortunate.... Maybe all religions have similar characteristics, but certainly in my case, there was a very healthy respect for the less fortunate, the minorities, those who are not mainstream. Part of my heritage is a recognition that there are no certainties in life. I think the Jewish heritage acknowledges that there are always situations you can't anticipate. Where is it written that life is fair? It's not written that you automatically can control all aspects of your destiny. In the course of this program, if I ever learned anything that reinforced that, it was learning how one person survived and another didn't is based on the most serendipitous reasons.

"Mr. Feinberg, I would have been in that building, for the first time I wasn't there, I had to take my kid to the first grade. Otherwise, I would have been in the building." One family from a foreign country had a husband who had never been in the United States, ever. He flew in the night before, first time in the United States, first time in New York, and the first time at the restaurant on the 103rd floor. He died. One family lost a loved one, they had escaped from Russia in the 1970s, and immigrated to Israel. They decided that Israel was too dangerous a place because of Arab terrorism and then immigrated to the United States. He died in the World Trade Center. I became resigned to this. Never assume that you control your destiny. I'm much more fatalistic after 9/11. I don't think I'll ever plan more than two weeks ahead.... I don't think I will. Life throws too many curveballs at you.

Professionally, it certainly has changed me. I'm not as interested as I was before 9/11 in mediating and resolving major lucrative commercial disputes. After doing the 9/11 fund, I pick and choose my professional targets very carefully. I've downsized my law firm. I've cut it back to about ten people, with one other lawyer, because I didn't want to do the same thing after 9/11.

One reason the program was so effective was that I didn't have any elected or appointed official nipping at my heels, criticizing. Everybody was solidly behind the program. That helped a great deal. When you've got everybody from President Bush, and [former White House Chief of Staff] Andy Card, who, on a number of occasions expressed great thanks for what we were trying to accomplish; Senator Kennedy and Senator

[Chuck] Schumer and Senator [Hillary] Clinton and Congresswoman Caroline McCarthy and Congressman Rush Holt and others, all saying, "Keep up the good work," that helped a great deal.

I would have thought going in that the families who lost loved ones in the World Trade Center in '93, Oklahoma City, the African embassy bombings, the USS Cole, anthrax, that all of those people would have been demanding similar generosity on the part of the fund. No. There was a handful from Oklahoma City. 9/11 was different. Most families didn't come running to me asking for similar treatment.... From the perspective of the victims, I don't see any distinction. If you try and justify my program on the basis of the victims lost, I can't convincingly explain why, "9/11, yes, '93 World Trade Center, no." The only way you justify this program as a special carve-out is, from the perspective of the nation, a recognition that 9/11's impact on the American people, along with the American Civil War, Pearl Harbor, maybe the assassination of President Kennedy, that its impact on the American people was such that this was really a response from America to demonstrate the solidarity and cohesiveness of the American people towards these victims. That's the only way to explain this program convincingly.

We received over seven thousand applications. About two thousand were ineligible; almost all of them claimed physical injury which we felt was not sufficiently related to 9/11, either geographically or [due to] circumstances. But 5,560 people received a check from the U.S. Treasury for a total of seven billion dollars. There was no limit; there was no cap. Congress delegated to me all the discretion, practically unfettered, to determine what appropriate awards should be...I felt that there was some limit, based on my own judgment, not the legislation, that must be imposed in carving out such generosity for a very few people relative to the rest of the country. I didn't think it was appropriate to award double-digit millions to people.... We offered structured settlements over time. We offered to try and tailor any award to the financial plan submitted by the claimant, and we offered in every case free financial planning to any claimant that wanted to take the benefit of that.

The burn survivor who received $8.6 million came to see me. She was a very heroic woman, with a courage and a determination to move forward in the most unbelievable circumstances. She received the highest award, due to the nature of her injuries, the ongoing suffering she would confront the rest of her life. I was obligated by statute to take into account the economic circumstances of each death and injury. It just so happened that this survivor had a very successful Wall Street profession and that profession was ruined by her 9/11 injuries, and I had to take that into account.

Nowhere in this statute is there one word from Congress as to who should receive this money in the family, who should even file the claim on behalf of the family. Congress completely ignored that whole topic and left it to me to decide among competing family members who should get the money. We had to design a very fair way for determining among not only competing family members, fiancées, same-sex partners, all claiming some legitimate degree of credible demand for the compensation. Most families worked out agreements in advance with fiancées or domestic partners. There were, qualitatively, some battle royales that I'll never forget. "Mr. Feinberg, I was the fiancée of the victim. We were going to be married on October 11th. I should be treated like a spouse when it comes to the award...." "Biological parents, what do you say about that?" "Oh, that marriage was never going to take place. My son called us on September 10th. He was having second thoughts." "Fiancée, what do you say to that?" "Is that right, Mr. Feinberg? Look, here's a copy of the wedding invitation. We were going to be married. On August 11th, those parents, they threw a shower for me and said, we're not losing a son, we're gaining a daughter. How dare they now, post-9/11, deny the inevitability of the marriage." There were a few like that, and I worked out most of those disagreements, not all, but most.

We kept as complete a file on every claim, on every family, on every conversation, all confidential. Maybe someday it will be made available. It's a tremendous amount of raw data. But we felt an obligation, since it is the taxpayers' money, to keep very stringent records. They are filed in the U.S. Government Archives. Maybe they should be made public someday after the families are dead and time has passed, but not while people are alive, trying to move on.

I didn't keep a diary, but I kept notes, especially, of the individual meetings, because I needed to go back and review my notes in deciding in meeting with the families individually whether to raise the awards or not. [I got off to a pretty rough start with these families.] The very first meeting with firefighter widows in Manhattan, within a month after 9/11, a lady stood up and said, "Mr. Feinberg, you're giving firefighter widows, based on your formulas that you've announced, a million dollars less than the widow of an accountant on the 103rd floor who represented Enron. I spit on you and your children, Mr. Feinberg, I spit on you." That was an example of the invective at the beginning, very emotional on the part of many, many families. I listened. I responded as calmly and as best as I could. There is absolutely no point in engaging people in anger or disrespect. As time went on, I became less of a lawyer and more of a family counselor, less [about] the technicalities of the program and more empathy in trying as best I could to deal with the raw emotion rising out of 9/11. That was one factor that helped turn the program around towards success. Time certainly helped. A statutory deadline to file a claim certainly helped. But I think all of this together ended up helping the program succeed.

There is tremendous restriction about writing this story. It's all prohibited by law. The reason I was able to write this book is, with the help of the Department of Justice, I felt it important that this book be written for future generations. The department went out and formally, in writing, sought and received written waiver requests from over sixty families, in which they gave their permission to quote without attribution from their hearings and from their personal family circumstances. Otherwise, none of this could have been printed. [The town meetings were open to the public and the media.] If a particular family wanted to meet with me privately to discuss the personal, confidential concerns they confronted, that was closed to everybody other than those invited by that family. That was the way we balanced the public's right to know with private, confidential family circumstances.

[When they met with me privately,] plenty of people lost control. If I anticipated lost control, I would adjourn the hearing for a while. If I thought that a family was going off on an irrelevant track, I would try and bring the family back to the issues at hand. I occasionally needed an adjournment, for me to clear my head and walk around the block, because most of these individual family meetings were chilling. I broke down sometimes, but not in a meeting.

The bulk of the legislation dealing with airline stabilization and airline protection was written by the Senate and the House with input from the airlines. They were all over the Hill, the airline lawyers and lobbyists seeking loan guarantees and financial protection. As that legislation moved forward very quickly, the American Association of Trial Lawyers, Leo Boyle, Larry Stewart, Richard Bieder, and their Washington office, felt that it was very important that if the airlines were going to be immunized from suit, or that obstacles were going to be raised to prevent effective lawsuits, there had to be something done for the victims. They went and saw Congressman Richard Gephardt, Senator Chuck Schumer, Senator Tom Daschle, and out of that came a hybrid statute: airline protection, minimize lawsuits, victims' compensation and it came together in a unified, bipartisan way.

This was not a political issue. As a result of 9/11, the country as a whole, regardless of party affiliation, felt that this idea of a compensation program demonstrated the country's solidarity in the wake of the foreign attack. That had a lot to do with the bipartisan support leading up to this program. Jack Rosenthal of the New York Times Foundation has coined a phrase which I love: "vengeful philanthropy." That's what this was about: "We'll show those terrorists and those countries harboring terrorists what America is all about." And this was the result.

Forget this legislation for a minute. The American character, self-reliance, choices made and not made, a resignation in confronting life's unfairness, individual dignity and individual integrity, the heritage of the American people is not the government as a guarantor of all of life's misfortunes. This is an aberration, this program that I administered. Its uniqueness is that it runs so counter to the way that Americans confront curveballs that I don't think there are many people who would say actually that when you're injured or killed, say, on a federal highway, the government should cut you a check for $2 million. To the contrary, most of the American people would say that the 9/11 fund, to the extent that it was a good idea, and I say in the book it was a great idea, but, "don't do it again." It is an aberration, it is unique, and I think they're probably right about that. I don't think Congress will do this again. I think Congress will view this as a response to a very unique historical disaster like Pearl Harbor. The next time it happens, God forbid, I'm dubious that Congress will replicate the program.

I suggest Congress, if it does anything, will probably give everybody the same amount and not ask one person to say, "You get $3 million, you get $2 million, you get $4 million." I don't think they will ever do that again. On claims of suffering, I concluded when 9/11 families came to me and said, "My wife endured more suffering in the World Trade Center than somebody else, she called me on the cell phone and told me she was going to die. So I'm entitled to more money than the person killed instantly." I rejected that. I am not Solomon. I can't make distinctions on the basis of who suffered more or less. We will have one-size-fits-all. Everybody gets the same for suffering: $250,000 for the death of the victim; $100,000 in addition for each surviving spouse and dependent, that's it. Don't come and argue for more money for suffering and emotional distress.

I FOUND, IN ADMINISTERING this program, that my legal skills in analysis, technical understanding of loss, economics, and calculations, proved much less valuable than psychiatry and philosophy and counseling. Empathy was much more valuable in assuring the success of the program.... I think my personality was a great benefit and a great hindrance in this process. It was a hindrance at the beginning, this personality of "this is the way the program is written and this is the way it's going to be done and this is what we can do and what we can't do." A lawyerly assuredness rubbed many of these families the wrong way. Over time, the personality modification, the willingness to help, to try and deal with the unique problems that each family brought me as sort of a counselor, not as a lawyer, ultimately proved helpful in galvanizing support for the program.

Terror and Liberalism

PAUL BERMAN

Writer Paul Berman examines the roots of terrorism from a philosophical perspective, citing the two opposite poles of the spectrum in Albert Camus and Egyptian philosopher Sayyid Qutb. Many credit Qutb as the theoretician of the type of radical Islam that gave rise to al Qaeda. Mr. Berman looks at totalitarian regimes throughout history and finds that though military action is often required to defeat them, the real war on terrorism is a war of ideas. Paul Berman was a guest on Booknotes *June 22, 2003.*

TERROR AND LIBERALISM IS my response to the attacks of September 11, 2001. It's my theory of the terror war. Beyond that, it's a book in which I lay out a long account of the last two centuries of life in the Western world, and in the world as a whole, in order to explain the predicament in which we find ourselves in....

ALBERT CAMUS WAS A great French philosopher and Sayyid Qutb was an Egyptian philosopher. Albert Camus was born in Algeria, so, in a certain sense, he was a North African. Qutb is an Egyptian, who is also a North African. Sayyid Qutb was the philosopher of Islamist radicalism. He's really the greatest theoretician or intellectual behind the radical Islamist currents that have given rise to al Qaeda, as well as other groups. Camus was a man of the freethinking left in France, who also managed to be one of the great philosophers of mid-twentieth century anti-totalitarianism, one of the philosophers who could tell us the most about what is the totalitarian mentality, what is it that drives people to want to engage in mass killings from practical aims, that kind of thing. So, on one hand, Qutb and Camus were contemporaries. In certain respects, they had a lot in common. But, in Camus, you can read the analysis of what's wrong with or what is the nature of the thinking of Qutb, so they are a kind of an odd couple. The ideas of those two thinkers really form the two poles of my book. What I try to do is to lay out the philosophy, the deep thinking that has gone behind Islamist radicalism and the kind of thinking that the people in al Qaeda engage in. I think I'm able to lay that out on one hand, and on the other hand, I'm able to offer an analysis of where that comes from, what it really means, what it's about. My analysis derives in good part from Albert Camus, so the two thinkers are my two poles.

[QUTB] GREW UP IN Egypt. He had a traditional education in Egypt, studied in Cairo. He was a modern man of the 1920s and '30s. He was a socialist intellectual, a literary man. He wrote novels. He wrote a book of literary criticism. In the late '40s, he was able to go the University of Northern Colorado and study education. He was a worker in the ministry of Education in Egypt, yet, at the same time, he was already by then an Islamic fundamentalist of a moderately radical sort. After he returned from Colorado in 1951, he became more radical. By 1954, he was in prison in Egypt under the most barbarous circumstances, in a hideous cell with forty other prisoners, most of whom were criminals, not political prisoners like himself, with a tape recorder blaring all hours of the day the speeches of the president of Egypt, [Gamal Abdel] Nasser, who had put Qutb in jail. Under these circumstances, Qutb spent most of the rest of his life in prison. He was out a couple of times. Under these circumstances, his thinking became more radical. His Islamic fundamentalism became more radical, took a more political turn from what I would call Islamic thought to a political radicalism based on Islamic thought, which is what I call "Islamism," to distinguish between Islam and Islamism, Islamism being the radical political movement based on Islam. In these circumstances in prison year after year, he wrote a gigantic commentary on the Qur'an called *In the Shade of the Qur'an*, which, in Arabic, is in thirty volumes. I don't read Arabic, but I've read what there is in English. At this point, I've read about half of it, which is, I think, everything that there is in English. What he does in this book is go through the Qur'an chapter by chapter, surah by surah—the names of the chapters in the Qur'an—summarizing what is said and offering his commentary and a general exposition, and going off in all directions to comment on what meaning this ought to hold for contemporary life. In this form, he laid out his general philosophy, and his general philosophy was quite radical, really a revolutionary philosophy.

He was hanged in 1966 by Nasser. He and Nasser actually knew each other. Nasser came to power in 1952 as part of a pan-Arabist nationalist revolution in Egypt, which overthrew the old king, and was intended to lead Egypt in a nationalist revolutionary direction, as part of the general anti-colonialist or third-worldist revolutions around the world. At first, Qutb and Nasser were allies. Qutb was the intellectual leader of the Muslim Brotherhood, the Islamic fundamentalist organization, and Nasser was the somewhat secular nationalist. They were allied to some degree. There was some talk or some belief among Qutb's followers at least that Qutb might have ended up with the Ministry of Education under Nasser's revolutionary regime, but instead, the two factions—the somewhat secular nationalist radicals and the Islamist revolutionaries—fell out. They had different visions of what the revolutionary movement ought to do. Qutb ended in jail. And finally, in 1966, Nasser hanged him.

HE WAS WRITING THESE books through the 1950s and '60s. At the time, he had a small following in Egypt, and this following eventually evolved into the factions that assassinated [President Anwar] Sadat and eventually went into al Qaeda. [Ayman al-Zawahiri is a follower of Qutb.] From Qutb to bin Laden, there's a fairly direct connection, which is Qutb's [younger] brother. After the terrible repression of the Muslim Brotherhood by Nasser, many of the leaders of the Muslim Brotherhood and the intellectuals in it fled Egypt, and many of them were welcomed into Saudi Arabia. They were welcomed into Saudi Arabia because Egypt has always been a great intellectual capital, a center of the Arab world, the Muslim world. The Wahhabi sect has always claimed to be the spiritual leader of the Muslim world, but they haven't produced the great intellectuals. So when the fundamentalist intellectuals in Egypt were persecuted by Nasser, the Saudis were happy to welcome them. Qutb's brother, Mohammed Qutb, was one of the people who fled Egypt. He became a professor of Islamic studies in Saudi Arabia, and one of his students, in fact, was Osama bin Laden. So, there's a fairly direct connection that way. And that's not the only connection.

THE GOAL OF THE terrorism, as conceived of by the followers of this kind of thinking, is to advance the notion of jihad, which is the struggle for Islam. The goal is at different levels. At one level, it's really to destroy the kinds of societies that are not upholding the principles of this version of Islamism. Other people would answer this question by saying that the goals of this kind of terrorism are specific political goals: to force Israel to withdraw its settlements, or to force the United States to withdraw its troops from Saudi Arabia, or to force certain other specific kinds of political issues. But that's not actually how I understand the movement. My understanding of the movement is really that the goals are much larger, much more revolutionary than that: that if those relatively small things were the goals, they could be approached in a rather different way. The goal really is to make a revolution all over the world.

The reason I speak about totalitarianism, and why I'm interested in Camus and the philosophers of totalitarianism, theorists about totalitarianism from fifty years ago or so, is that I think the radical Islamist movement is a totalitarian movement in a twentieth-century style. My theory is that after World War I, a whole series of extremely revolutionary movements arose…they arose for the purpose of overthrowing what I think of as the essentially liberal doctrines—not liberal in the right-wing, left-wing version, but liberal in the sense of the liberal doctrines of Western culture. By the liberal doctrines, I mean the notion of the separation of church and state, the notion that there should be a difference between the private and the public, the difference between the government and the society, the difference between the government and economics, the notion that in one's own mind, we can think in different categories at the same time, that in part of your mind you could be religious, and in another part of your mind, you can be scientific or rationalist. The liberal idea is the notion that a society based on those ideas will progress. You can offer progress for all mankind everywhere. This had been a large governing idea throughout the nineteenth century. It wasn't in practice everywhere, but people subscribed to this idea and had a great faith in it. There was some reason to have a faith in it. World War I came along, and the idea came to seem preposterous because World War I was so horrible, so industrially murderous, that people who were thinking in those old terms of the liberal optimism in the nineteenth century were unable to conceive of it, unable to explain it. As a result, in the years after the war, a series of movements arose which were rebellions against the old liberal idea. Each of those movements had the same idea, which was to overthrow liberal civilization and replace it with a civilization of a different sort, rock-like, granite, without any separation of spheres, a single sphere, permanent, unchanging, eternal, governed by a leader with a single organization or a single party like that.

The first of these movements was Lenin's, and the movement was Bolshevism or the Communist Party, and then from Lenin to Stalin. The next of them was Mussolini, who founded the fascist movement in Italy a few years later; Franco, with the fascist movement of Spain; Hitler, with the Nazi movement in Germany; the Iron Guard in Romania; the extreme right in France, and so forth, through almost every country in Europe and many countries around the world. Each of these movements was different from each of the others. At the time, if anybody had said to you there's something in common between the Bolshevism of Lenin and the Fascism of Mussolini, they would have said that's preposterous; those movements are opposite. But from our perspective now, looking back on them, we should be able to see that all of those movements had a lot in common. What they had in common was this urge to rebel against liberal civilization, the principles of liberal separation of spheres, and replace that with a rock-like, granite society, the permanent, unchanging society with the single party, the single leader, and so forth. So, each of those movements had, in this respect, the same idea. They all arose in the immediate years after World War I. Those movements all arose in Europe.

At the same time, the same inspiration spread to the Muslim world and a kind of Muslim totalitarianism arose which had all of the main principles of totalitarianism in Europe. It arose in the 1920s and '30s. It had different strands. One of those strands is the one that was finally given a theoretical shape by Sayyid Qutb in his commentary on the Qur'an. Another of those strands is the one that finally evolved into the Ba'ath Party of Saddam Hussein....

In the overall, deepest of ways, they [all] have the same goal. In all other ways, once we leave the very deepest level, they each had different goals and one opposite from the other, and one fought wars with the other, and each one was different. But at the very deepest way, it was all the same. This deepest way was to overthrow liberal civilization, replace it with a different kind of modernity...benefiting from science and technological advance but which, unlike liberal society, was going to be solid, without any internal divisions, without any feelings of skepticism or doubt, a society that would be absolutely perfect, without cracks or contradictions, a society therefore that would last forever, or, as the Nazis would say, a thousand years.

THERE IS NO BARGAINING [with al Qaeda terrorists]. The purpose of these terrorist acts is not to bargain with us. This is not like some labor union engaged in a struggle with the boss, and somehow the boss's yacht gets burned down and everybody understands that it was meant to force a deal. [You can't buy them off.] It's not like that. The goal is to overthrow the whole of liberal or secular civilization and create a completely new world. So, the only thing that's going to defeat them is to persuade them to abandon their ideas. Really, the only thing that will defeat them is to win a war of ideas.

Let me go back to all the other totalitarian movements in order to make the comparison. All of those movements had a utopian goal, and the utopian goal consisted of leaping into the distant past and, at the same time, leaping into the modern future. Thus, Lenin and the Bolsheviks wanted to go back to what Marx considered to be the primitive communism of the barbarian age, or the primitive communism of the Russian peasants, but this primitive communism in the Bolshevik version was also going to be a leap into the future, into a scientific age, into a futuristic sci-fi future, a perfect society.

Mussolini marched on Rome in 1922 for the purpose of recreating, resurrecting the Roman Empire, the days of glory of the Italian people. So, he was going to recreate the Roman Empire, his followers were arranged in the legions. They were centurions. They were resurrecting the Roman Empire. But their Roman Empire was going to be modern, expressed by the kind of modern architecture that Mussolini went around building, which was exactly like a modern architecture that Stalin went around building. So, in both cases, it was going to be a leap into the ancient past, which was also going to be a leap into the modern future.

The best example of a religious-based fascist movement was Franco in Spain. Franco's idea was that he wanted to return to the Middle Ages of Spain, when the Catholics of Spain were engaged in a crusade against the Muslims and against the Jews, and his followers were the warriors of Christ the King. His goal was to resurrect what he imagined to be, what he fantasized to be, the perfect Catholic society of medieval Spain. Yet, in his version, of course, this was also going to be modern and scientific and advanced, and so forth. So, he had a religious vision of his ideas and his goal, which was going to be a perfect Catholicism. His was the most religiously-oriented of the European totalitarian movements. The others, in the case of Lenin, were anti-religious, in the case of the Nazis, they invented their own religion, which was Nordic pagan.

I don't think that with those movements, [led by Mussolini, Hitler, Stalin, Franco,] it was about their personal power.... They have always been based on true belief in the whole ideological system. The notion of this revolutionary leap into the future society that's also going to be a leap into the past, the hatred for liberal civilization, all of this has always been sincere. And, at some level, each of the totalitarian leaders has genuinely wanted to do good. I say at some level, because at a different level, at a deeper level, each of these movements has always wanted to do bad, has not just stumbled into doing bad by mistake. And, for this reason, each of these movements has always been based on some notion of transgression of moral values, of rebellion against the notion of morality and the notion of a decent society. That's why each one of these movements has established its strength by being ruthless for the sake of being ruthless; of killing people en masse for the sake of killing people en masse. Shoot more professors, was one of Lenin's earliest orders. With Hitler, the idea was always to kill millions and millions of people. Stalin, too, wanted to kill, and he did kill, millions and millions of people, not to do them good, but to kill them....

Many of these movements have been led by people who were perfectly willing to die for the movement. In fact, they might want to die, because the notion of suicide is also inherent in these movements. Hitler, and his top men at the end, killed themselves, and they always made it clear that suicide was going to be their end. The Hitler Youth were devoted to the notion of suicide. Stalin, in the thirties, was murdering communists at a higher rate than anyone else has murdered communists. Nobody has murdered more members of the Communist Party than the Communist Party of the Soviet Union under Stalin, so to join the Communist Party in the age of Stalin, and to try to rise in it and become a leader under Stalin was to get ever closer to one's own death.

Saddam Hussein is a pretty classic figure in all this.... I think there always was in his regime an aspect of true belief in the ideals of the Arab Ba'ath Socialist Party, which was to create another version of the same totalitarian revolution, and I think there was always a cult of death, an extreme cult of cruelty, and an acceptance that death might be the fate of the leaders and members. In the case of Saddam Hussein, the idea that the leader will have privileges, that's not at all contradictory to this larger idea, because each of these movements has always been based around a cult of a leader. A leader has always stood forward as a genius, as a divine figure, as a more than human figure, and as always, each of these leaders has led his life as a more than divine figure and has surrounded himself with the greatest luxury and pomp.

Each of these totalitarian movements in Europe wanted to leap into the past and leap into the future. The Islamist movement, of which Qutb was the great philosopher, wanted to do the same. They wanted to leap into the remote past, but where Mussolini wanted to resurrect the Roman Empire, these people wanted to resurrect the ancient Caliphate, the Muslim Caliphate of the seventh century, from the days after the prophet Muhammed, from the days when the Arabs, having accepted Islam, were conquering the world. So they look back on the Caliphate of the seventh century as the golden age, which they were going to resurrect. The golden age meant Sharia, or Quranic law, the strictest version of Quranic law, as you see it in the Qur'an, a strict reading of all the rules and regulations, laws and punishments and mode of life as described and prescribed in the Quran....

Qutb's idea, his notion of the utopian society that his radical movement wants to create, is to resurrect the Caliphate of the seventh century, when, as he imagined, these laws, these precise regulations regarding every aspect of life, were in effect. But, at the same time, it's important to remember that in this movement, this idea of resurrecting the seventh century was also a leap into the future, as a modern movement. That sometimes people mistakenly imagine that the Islamist radicals merely want to return to the seventh century, and then it's a kind of a medieval movement, but it's not really a medieval movement. It's a movement that wants to be in the seventh century, [but] also in the modern age at the same time. You can see an example of that in that first hair-raising video of bin Laden after the September 11 attacks, where he sat with al-Zawahiri and other people on a rock in Afghanistan, dressed in robes and looking like they were out of the Middle Ages, and yet with the tape recorders and microphones right there as part of the setup without any effort to disguise them, and the whole thing presented as a video, not as an ancient text written on parchment, but as a video. So it was an evocation of something highly modern, completely up to date, which, at the same time, was ancient and of the seventh century.

They want us either gone or converted to their vision, and that's the motivation, so it's a revolutionary motivation. That's at one level, but at another level and at a deeper level, their motivation is to die and to kill as many people as possible. This ought to be recognizable to us because what was Hitler's motivation, or what was Stalin's motivation in starving to death the peasants of the Ukraine in the 1930s? The motivation behind these different campaigns, which ought to be familiar to us by now, is, on one hand to do good, however good is described, and on the other hand, to pursue a cult of death, and that's what these suicide terrorists are about.

CAMUS WAS BORN IN [Drean, Algeria, in] 1913, and he died in France in 1960. I think that what he offers is a notion of terrorism and totalitarianism as being pretty much the same thing, as the same cult of death that I've been talking about in the name of a utopian ideal. From reading Camus, you can get a pretty good idea that these are serious intellectual movements and serious ideas, even if they're a lot deranged, and the proper way to deal with them, or a crucial way to deal with them, is at the plane of ideas. This is one of the things we've done so badly, that the only way to defeat these movements, as I say, finally, is intellectually. People have to be persuaded to abandon these ideas in favor of other ideas, and sometimes it's the case that military action is needed. I think that military action in the case of Afghanistan and Iraq was a good idea. But military action is not an end in itself, and can't even accomplish very much if millions and millions of people end up still clinging to the same ideas that they clung to originally.

Losing a Hand to War Reporting

MICHAEL WEISSKOPF

On the evening of December 10, 2003, TIME magazine reporter Michael Weisskopf headed out on patrol with U.S. troops to a tough neighborhood in Baghdad. A grenade landed in his Humvee, and though he saved lives by picking up the grenade and throwing it out of the vehicle, he lost his right hand. He recovered in Walter Reed Hospital's Ward 57, alongside many soldiers who had lost limbs in the war. Weisskopf appeared on Q & A *on October 22, 2006, to talk about his injury and recovery and the soldiers profiled in his book,* Blood Brothers: Among the Soldiers of Ward 57.

I WAS IN IRAQ covering a platoon for a story *TIME* magazine was going to do on the Person of the Year. We decided it would be the American soldier. This was the end of 2003, nine months into the war, and things were going relatively well at the time since there were only 135,000 American soldiers then. On the other side of the worm, however, it was the beginning of the insurgency, and I was an early victim of it.

[The first thing I remember after being wounded is] the frailty of life, how quickly the bridge is between life and death, how quickly I almost never saw my kids again and my girlfriend, who became my wife. Just the transitoriness of life, and how almost nothing else matters at that point other than the people you love. I remember lying on the cold bed of that Humvee. It was about 30 degrees at 9:00 p.m. in Iraq, [and] thinking, this is how it ends, pretty unglamorously on the cold bed of a truck so far from anyone I loved. I also thought of my son Skyler, then eleven, [who was] the same age I was when my father died. I said to myself over and over, "I'm doing to Skyler what my father did to me," which was leaving me at a critical moment. My father died of a massive heart attack at thirty-six....

[ON DECEMBER 10, 2003, we went out on patrol] about 8:00 p.m. I did this story with another reporter by the name of Ramesh Ratnesar, a fine young writer. He took the night off. We often alternated days out on patrol. We were entering our fourth week of reporting, getting pretty close to writing the story and complaining that we had everything in this story but action, to see the platoon catching a bad guy, finding a big weapons cache, or [being] under attack. We sort of bemoaned that fact. About 8:00 p.m., the sergeant said, "We're going to go out on a patrol now." The purpose of the patrol was reconnaissance, because they were considering a raid later on that week and they wanted to do some recon.

We got into a three-truck convoy and headed out to an area of Baghdad called al-Adhamiya, [which was] a tough Sunni neighborhood. It's been later known as "Little Fallujah," because it's so dangerous for American troops. We knew there were a lot of bad guys there, but there it was relatively safe, with one exception. About a month before we arrived, the lieutenant of my platoon was killed in a Humvee by a roadside bomb. So this was kind of a star-crossed platoon. We went out that night, and interestingly, I got in a covered Humvee. The sergeant said, "No, you're riding in the high back." The high back was an open-air Humvee, not unlike a pickup truck. It was used to transport troops and cargo. In those days it was possible still to ride through Baghdad in such an open-air vehicle. I got in the back of it, with the photographer and two soldiers. We took off at roughly eight o'clock, and I remember the sergeant's words as we went out: "OK, let's go out and become targets." The object was that our roaming through these streets might draw fire, and then that fire would be countered by the soldiers in the Humvee and we would get a bad guy. I put on the Kevlar [vest and] my helmet, something I did with some trepidation every time, thinking of that lieutenant, Ben Colgan, who had been killed about a month earlier, and realizing the importance of such armor. I had calculated the risk and decided early on it was fairly low. But any time you put on a fourteen-pound vest full of armor and put on a heavy helmet and goggles, you're getting into the crosshairs with targets. There was a little nervousness since we left a compound, which itself is fairly exposed, but nonetheless, behind concertina wire and high walls, and went out into a hostile environment.

[The grenade was thrown into the Humvee] after about an hour of moving around. We zig-zagged through the night of Baghdad, and through this old quarter, in and out of cul de sacs and dead ends. It did occur to me every time we got to a dead end, we could have been stopped on the other end and ambushed, and that was fairly tense. As we left that labyrinth, we entered a large marketplace. It was alive with people. There were mothers feeding their kids *shashlik*, and kids kicking soccer balls, old men playing dominos on little stools. It occurred to me that the place was alive, and maybe the Americans were winning this war. As we drove through the market, we stopped in front of the al-Hanifa mosque, the same one where Saddam had made his final stand. There was an ancient watchtower alongside the mosque. It was hit during the war in March and April of '03, and there was scaffolding around that watchtower, and it was being repaired. I looked up and wondered if this was a metaphor for the rest of Iraq, whether or not it was possible really to repair this place. As I was leaning back in a rare moment of relaxation in a war zone, I heard a thunk. I was used to hearing those types of noises, because young kids had taken to throwing rocks into this open-air vehicle in other patrols. I looked to my right, first on the floor and then to the seat next to me, and saw a dark metallic object shining like the back of a tortoise shell. It was roughly six inches long and maybe four inches wide. Something made me get up off my seat and reach over with what was my right arm at the time. I grabbed it, and picked it up. It was so hot. It felt like I was plucking lava from a volcanic crater. I could feel the flesh on my hand liquefying right away. I gave out a little scream and I arched myself away from it and turned to flip it over the side of the Humvee, a little backhand toss like one would do a tennis ball over a net. At that point, everything went dark. I blacked out. I didn't hear an explosion, although I was told later it was quite loud.

I woke up just seconds later on the bed of the Humvee in a lot of pain. All the voices seemed disembodied and distant. My right leg and back side were burning, my right arm felt very numb, not unlike you feel when you've slept on it, when you lose circulation in it. It occurred to me I was having a nightmare, that I was in my hooch in Baghdad with the platoon and I was having a bad nightmare. As I would do when I had such a thing when I was sleeping, I shook my right arm. It remained numb, and I picked it up to look at it. It looked like the neck of a decapitated chicken. It was bloody. It was oozing blood, and you could see the tendons. At that moment, that split second, I knew my life had changed forever.

The shrapnel from the grenade, rough BBs and metal shards, ended up ricocheting off the armor on the inside of the Humvee. It whacked me on my right, my back side, as I was falling away from it. It hit Jim Nachtwey [the photographer] in the knees, the abdomen, the groin and the face, came around and hit another soldier also in the knees and the hands. The guy immediately to my right, maybe three feet away, suffered a break to his left femur from the blast itself. It was broken in two places. But nobody lost a limb other than me....

At the time this occurred, I thought that I was the only one who heard or saw the grenade. There was a split second when I thought, well, "Maybe I ought to tell these guys in uniform what was going on." Something moved me more quickly than to stop to tell them that. This was part of the mystery as to why I reacted so reflexively. I could have knocked the guy on the shoulder and said, "Hey, what's this?" By the time I'd finished the sentence, the thing would have blown up, and so, I didn't. I later learned that everyone in the Humvee had at least heard the thing. The guy to my right actually looked down and saw something, which he thought was a rock, and he looked the other way. I picked it up, and I raised my right arm to throw it, and then I blacked out. It was at that point that it blew. I later discovered, just by doing the forensics of it and figuring things out, that the grenade must have just left my hand or it may have still been in my hand when it blew up. My hand was enough to absorb most of the blast and some of the shrapnel.

[Billie Grimes,] the medic in the truck behind me, saw me raise my arm in the air, saw it was an arm without a hand, stopped her truck, and ran out. It was Billie Grimes who commandeered the truck, basically turning it into an emergency room on wheels, who yelled to the guys in the cab who were stunned by the blast themselves, "Get this thing out of here immediately, back to base." We were at the end of our patrol of this region, so we were only a few minutes away from base, fortunately. They just gunned the truck, moved us very quickly, breaking all the rules, knocking down everything in our way, and basically drove right through the concertina wire into the brigade, and pulled so close and so fast toward this little clinic in the brigade, I thought they were going to drive right through it. I felt a great deal of pain in my legs. My right arm was so numb from the blast, it felt very strange and swollen, but not sharply painful.

When I awakened in the combat support hospital, it was a funny scene in itself. I was placed in a little cul-de-sac in a room with two other guys, and woke up. There was this giant photo of the Madonna holding Christ. I found it peculiar that I was a Jew, waking up in a Muslim country, seeing a scene of what was the Pieta, a copy of the famous Michelangelo [statue]. I think I was pleased that I still had a little sense of humor about that. I felt, "Oh, if I was in heaven, I must have gotten off on the wrong floor." But, remember, I was still in shock, being angry at myself for being a cowboy, for trying to save the day, for trying to pick up that grenade in the first place. A nurse came over to me and said to me, "You're a hero. You picked up a grenade and saved everybody." I said, "Well, I'm an idiot, because I picked the thing up. I should have left it for someone else." She said, "If you had done that, you all would have died." I was certainly in shock, and I was delusional then, because it certainly would have killed all of us if I hadn't picked it up. It was a displaced anger for why I was there and why I would put myself in such jeopardy for a story. The closest I had been [to war] was in Iran during the hostage period. While it wasn't war, there were lots of guys with guns, and there was some internecine warfare among Iranians at the time, which was in '79 and '80, just after the Khomeini revolution.

DAVID MARANISS IS A dear, dear, old friend. I met him at the *Washington Post*, when we were hired a week apart in 1977. We've been partners and best friends ever since. David received a call from Michael Duffy, then the Washington bureau chief of *TIME* magazine. Michael knew that David was close to Judith and my kids, and asked David to be the emissary to them. He, after some difficulty, found them coming home that night from school and told them the bad news. My son, Skyler, was quite angry. [When I was leaving to go to Iraq,] Skyler came to see me off in the cab. He had that look on his face as if he was seeing me for the last time. He was very nervous, very, very worried, and there was a sense of loss in his eyes. I said to him, "Don't worry. I won't be hurt. I'll be back in a month, and we'll do something fun." When David first told him I had been injured, he got very angry and said, "He lied to me. He said he wouldn't be hurt.".... My daughter, Olivia, was also very shaken up by it. It's a remarkable thing. The moment they saw me in Walter Reed at Ward 57 that first morning, and they saw that I was basically intact, and heard my voice, that my face was untouched, they felt immediately relaxed and returned to their old selves. And later that first day, interestingly, Skyler wrapped a piece of gauze he'd found around his right arm to imitate mine, which was then dressed up like a turkey leg on Thanksgiving. It was a huge bandage. And I felt it was symbolically a sign of his forgiveness. It meant a lot to me.

David Maraniss said to me from the first day that I ought to speak into a tape recorder. He knew I couldn't say no to that point, because I might want to write about this later. I had a long, pretty hard career, and I sacrificed a lot along the way. I decided I was just going to throw reporting by the wayside and get healthy first. He wasn't satisfied. He said, "Well then, let me be your Boswell. Let me come and record you, and I'll interview you." He created a record that ended up being important for me later on, because he was able to record in the present how I was feeling and what led up to the injury and what it felt like during the injury, what actually occurred. It was very important for me in recreating it. It was contemporaneous history and was vital. [We broke down and cried together] when I described to him my reaction, my great fears that I was repeating family history, that I would be doing to Skyler what my father had done to me. It was at a sensitive time for both of us, because his dad, Elliott Maraniss—a great newspaper man in Madison, Wisconsin—was ailing and was in his eighties at the time. David was very sensitive about the father-son relationship. He must have known where I was headed with it, because we finished each other's thoughts for a long time. He began choking up, and before I knew it, both of us were bawling. I just choked out the rest of these sentences. It's all captured on tape, so it's easy to go back to. It was one of those moments in life where everything is compressed into a single thought, [the] relationship between father and son, and it was very moving.

WALTER REED'S WARD 57 is in the northern reach of Washington, very close to the Maryland border, at Silver Spring. It was built in the seventies. Walter Reed himself was an Army lieutenant, a major who had discovered the agent for yellow fever, and the hospital is named after him. Ward 57 is the amputee ward there, and probably the most visible ward for this war and it's where all the young men and the young women who lose limbs go. It is on the fifth floor, and it is an H-shaped corridor with a reception desk in the middle. [It has] roughly twelve rooms on each side, is scrubbed, and looks like any other hospital, except for the nurses, who are in uniforms….Walter Reed itself, the premier Army hospital, is closed to everyone but soldiers, so I had no business being there in the first place. Interestingly, my sister, who lives in Los Angeles and knows a lot of doctors, decided she'd find the world's best hand surgeon for me after she heard about my injury. [She] discovered there's a guy in Washington by the name of Andrew Friedman. It was convenient that he happened to be in Washington, and she called him, and he answered the phone himself. She said, "I'd like my brother to be your patient." He said, "I'd be happy to take him except for one thing. I'm a lieutenant colonel in the armed forces, and we only take soldiers. You have to get approval of the secretary of the Army, which is very, very rare, for a waiver for your brother." My sister talked to my colleagues at *TIME* magazine, and also to my childhood friend, Mark [Plotkin], who is politically savvy and got my sister in touch with Eleanor Holmes Norton, my congresswoman. She called the acting secretary of the Army, who made this rare exception to allow me in, very generously.

[THERE ARE] TWELVE ROOMS along Ward 57, known as "Amputee Alley." [It is very emotional]. They have a regular train of psychologists coming through and feel-good people, veterans' groups [that are the] angels of Ward 57. People come through there to bring you nice things, family, friends. There is a lot of pressure on family and friends to make you feel as if this is no big deal and that you'll be fine afterwards. You have a good feeling from the narcotics, physically, emotionally, and psychologically. It's an unnatural high, but you do nevertheless feel high. There's a certain sense of importance you get there, because you get a whole train of big shots coming through. The president came through. Generals and members of Congress are coming through. This is particularly true for non-Washingtonians, kids who have grown up in small towns or agricultural areas. Suddenly, they're in the big town, and people are coming to them. This disguises the real psychological fight that you're facing, the battle after the war that all people who are wounded, particularly in an amputee ward, are going to face....

ON THE SECOND DAY in Ward 57, the president of the United States, George Bush, came to visit. [I did not see him]. It had nothing to do with politics. I believed, like a lot of Americans, the intelligence that led us into Iraq and was supportive of the decision. But I did feel that a reporter shouldn't be received by the president in the way he was trying to receive troops and honor troops around Christmas time. I had gone there not working for him, but working for *TIME* magazine. It was a fight that I wasn't there for, other than as an observer. He would be followed by cameras; it was somewhat of a political moment for him, and I didn't want to be part of that. I didn't think it was proper, and I resisted it. Despite a lot of pressure from nurses on Ward 57 and from the commander of Walter Reed, I decided that I needed to retain some independence, that a reporter had no business helping him making a political point. In Washington, there's even lobbying in hospitals. They tried to persuade me several times. The nurse cried at one point, and I wouldn't budge. There's an open door policy during a presidential visit on Ward 57, or anyplace in a hospital, all the doors and rooms have to be open so the president can come in, whenever he wants, to any room. They couldn't do that with me there—I would have had my door closed—so they scheduled the surgery for the time the president would be there. I was sent down to have a surgery, which I otherwise would have had some time that day, but they put it in that time slot when the president visited.

A FEW DAYS INTO my residency in Ward 57, I was told that I needed to have more of my arm amputated, if I wanted the ability to rotate the prosthesis. I debated that and finally decided to have it done, because I wanted function above all else. I came out of the surgery just in wall-climbing pain. I had never wailed before, but I wailed then. It was like a fire that couldn't be put out. I kept getting pumped with more and more narcotics until I reached a point where any more would have killed me, and I was still in pain. Finally, an hour or two later, some of the heavier dose stuff kicked in, and I was finally relieved of it, but it took days after then to fight it. I was in intense pain most of the time there....

THE MYOELECTRIC DEVICE COSTS $95,000. For those who lose their arms above the elbow, it's about $115,000. My arm ends about four inches above the wrist. My hand was blown off at the wrist. So they had to amputate up about another inch in order to get enough skin to close the wound, and another three inches more to put this component, to remove enough of the bone to replace it with the component. There is [a battery] in this, and I plug it in every night like you do a cell phone. The muscles give off tiny, tiny electrical signals. There are electrodes that lie on top of the muscles, and the electrodes transfer the signals to a little computer that makes the hand open and close and turn. To be proficient takes at least a month and you practice on laptop computers with electrodes strapped to those muscles. You keep on flexing the muscles until you can isolate them and successfully flex them. You can do an awful lot with one hand. The second hand is almost a bonus, but there are still many things you can't do. Tying a tie is one thing. You can't open a bottle of wine very easily with one hand. You can't tie your shoes with one hand. It's harder to type, of course, with one hand. There are a whole range of things you can't do. When you have a prosthesis like this, you can carry a grocery bag. You can hold a check down so that you can sign it with your good hand. Most things you can adapt to. [People do deal with me differently.] If I walk down the street and pass a hundred people, all one hundred will stare at my right arm. This is a rare kind of species in our society; lots of elderly people lose their legs to diabetes and to circulatory problems, but an upper extremity prosthesis is quite rare. If people notice it, they usually avert their eyes very quickly, because they're sort of embarrassed to stare, and within a minute or two realize that it really is just a kind of attachment to me, and doesn't really matter. My heart and brain are the same.

I'm proud of this [hook that was featured on the cover of *TIME* magazine on September 24, 2006]. This is a symbol to me of loss, but also of recovery and a continuation of life. I wear a hook, really, by choice. I could wear a silicone prosthesis that is very lifelike. This is a badge of honor to me, because I saved lives with this. So I don't hide from it, and I'm happy to have it shown. I was honored by the cover story.... It was a sign of life and of succeeding in the battle after the war, and I became a symbol for all the soldiers who go through this.

[SEVERAL SOLDIERS ARE FEATURED in my book, those who were willing to tell their story.] It was sometimes hard-going and painful for them. I did it slowly; everything was taped, because I have difficulty taking notes now. I did it because I felt it was an important story to tell. But I also did it for selfish reasons, because I found a great deal in their stories which helped my recovery. More importantly, there was a symbiosis going on there, because the honesty they were able to bring up made me more honest, and there was a synergistic effect. Interestingly, as I came cleaner with myself, not only about my loss and how it felt, but the background of it, and also of the action of picking up the grenade, I gained access to them emotionally. To the extent that I was more open with myself, they became more open. It was a wonderful experience, and [there were] many emotional times with the three of them.

PETE DAMON IS A guy from the outskirts of Boston, a rough-and-tumble town called Brockton, which is an old shoe [manufacturing] city. He left high school at the age of fifteen because he loved to work with his hands. He also liked to fight with his hands. He was a brawler and he was known for big rumbles, as they called them, in Brockton. Pete joined the National Guard in Massachusetts, because he was looking for a straight-and-narrow course, and to learn a craft. He learned to be an aviation mechanic, and went later on to Iraq, and wound up in an airbase in Balad, north of Baghdad. He was changing a helicopter tire. It exploded. The rim of the tire broke into many parts, sheared off both of his hands, and killed his partner. Pete was also brought to Ward 57, eventually, where we met.

PETE, LIKE ME, HAD spent a lot of time analyzing motivation. For Pete it was a little different. He was trying to understand how he could have allowed this accident to occur, where the tire of his Black Hawk helicopter was overinflated and exploded, how that could have happened. He was a skilled mechanic, a man who had all his life worked with his hands—the very thing he lost—how he could have let that happen and lose his partner, [Paul J. Bueche,] in the process. What informed me at the crucial moment of my life [was the moment] when I picked up the grenade. Our examination and exploration really was mutually reinforcing. I remember telling him for the first time about my self-doubts, after he had told me about his. We were sitting in a guest house at Walter Reed, and he was going to leave in a few hours. It was an extraordinarily emotional parting. It was difficult for him. He was leaving a place which had [functioned as] his hands for eighteen months at that point. He had a long recovery.

Pete went back to Massachusetts. He's quite a remarkable man. In the process of relearning how to write with hooks, because he has neither hand, he discovered that he had the facility to draw. As a young man, he was kind of an amateur artist. He used to trace things as a kid, and as a teenager made tattoo art and things like that, and loved to draw. He was relearning how to do A's, B's, and C's, started making circles and squares and triangles, and got so excited he hit a speed dial with his hook to his wife in Massachusetts, and said, "Jan, I can still draw!" She said, "Of course you can still draw. It's in your brain, not your hand." After leaving Walter Reed, [Peter Damon] began doing sketches. The sketches in the book of a soldier are extraordinary. [The picture has] amazing detail, light, and intensity. He has now begun a career of sketching with no hands, with hooks.

WHEN I RETURNED, I received a lot of credit for saving lives, including that of my own, and was described in pretty glowing terms. My friends even compared me, half-jokingly, to Lord Nelson, who lost his right hand in battle also to save lives. I wasn't comfortable with the label of hero. I didn't want to be characterized as such. I avoided the limelight for that reason until I better understood myself what I did. It was not clear to me what I did beyond saving those lives and how consciously I really approached it, whether or not I just reacted reflexively and what those reflexes really meant. In my book, real heroes make conscious decisions of self-sacrifice to help others. People like the war hero Audie Murphy in World War II, or even Mahatma Gandhi, who had a life of austerity in order to be a model for Indian citizens. These are heroes in my book. What I did wasn't clearly an act of self-sacrifice, and before I talked about it, I wanted to better understand it.

Terror in Mumbai

DAN REED

On November 26, 2008, 10 men began a terrorist attack on the city of Mumbai, India that ended 57 hours later, leaving 174 people dead. Filmmaker Dan Reed chronicled the attacks in his documentary, Terror in Mumbai, *through source material, including interviews with witnesses and survivors, footage from security cameras, and recorded cell phone conversations between the attackers themselves and the masterminds in Pakistan. Reed discusses the attack and the methods he used to make his documentary in this conversation with* Q & A *from December 19, 2010.*

I'M A FREELANCE DOCUMENTARY director and producer. I also direct drama, and at the moment, I'm a bit of a gun for hire, but I tend to make films in the documentary field which go behind a big news story or go behind something that has made headlines, and try to show the more complex side of it and unpack the hidden truths. I must have done about twenty-five or thirty [documentaries].

Terror in Mumbai is the story of the terrorist attack on the city of Mumbai on the 26th of November, 2008. It's known in India as 26/11. That's their 9/11, if you like. What happened was, ten young men came ashore on a beach in South Mumbai, which is the most prosperous part of the city, and they started killing, and they didn't stop killing for the next fifty-seven hours. I tried to tell the story of the attack, both through the eyes of the victims, but also through the eyes of the attackers, the terrorists themselves.

THE ATTACK ON MUMBAI was incredibly well designed, if I can say it that way. It was conceived with a kind of evil genius because they took ten young men who were not hardened fighters, and who were not mujahideen, and they had had a minimum of training, and they were able to control and reinforce their psychological conditioning by use of the mobile phones. These kids were in constant touch with the operations center in Pakistan, where the men who had sent them on the mission were staying, and saying, "Now you must do this, and now you remember this," and very calmly controlling the young men they'd sent to kill in Mumbai.

[They were constantly infusing the word "God" in their recorded communications about their mission,] although there was less religious spiel than I had expected before I heard [the recordings]. A lot of it seemed very, how shall I put it? Not mundane, but everyday, as though they live in a world where the taking of life, and this kind of extraordinary killing spree that they were on, was a normal thing to be doing, like driving a taxi. In fact, the whole thing reminded me of listening to the communications between what we call in London a cab office, a dispatchers' control room, with a bunch of guys sitting around with the mics and talking to the cabdrivers. That's what it felt like to me.

Brother Wasi was the main master of ceremonies for the whole thing. He didn't seem to be the ultimate authority within the terrorist group, Lashkar-e-Taiba, the Army of the Righteous. He didn't seem to be Mr. Big, but he was the guy who ran the operations. He didn't seem to sleep a lot. He was awake a lot of the time. He was on the mic. He was talking to the young guys very calmly, with the confidence of a father. He's like a father figure. He did most of the talking.

[TO MAKE THE FILM,] I had these recordings which told me a great deal about the relationship between the controllers and the gunmen, and I had as much information as I could discover about the group that did it. I believe a lot more is now coming to light about the motives and the character of the Lashkar-e-Taiba organization, the Army of the Righteous, which carried out the attacks. Lashkar was an organization that came about because of the conflict in Kashmir. It was used as a proxy by the Pakistani State to attack India in this dispute of the territory of Kashmir. My theory is that Lashkar was lagging behind in the league of Jihadist glory and needed to do something very visible, very international, to put itself back amongst these stars of the Jihadist movement. This was an attack on a modern city. It was a very well-executed attack. It was a highly visible attack on international targets. This was not a Pakistan-versus-India type of local attack.

THE DEATH TOLL REACHED 164, and most of these, 52, died at the railway station. The railway station was the biggest massacre, although it's the least remembered. The reason for that is partly because it was over so quickly, but also because the victims were poor and less important in terms of the media than the wealthy clients of the Taj Mahal or the Oberoi Hotels.

The video [taken inside the train station after the attack] was camera phone footage, and was taken by a guy who, as a teenager, was a beggar at the station. He's quite an extraordinary guy. In fact, he ended up being one of our team. He has grown up to become a successful young man and a politician, funnily enough, but he grew up as a hobo in the station, so he had a lot of friends there. When the attack happened, he went in there and looked for his friends and helped to collect the bodies as well. He filmed on his camera phone.... He said, "Have a look at this stuff," and so I bought it from him and put it in the film.

The phone conversations [between Brother Wasi in Pakistan and the ten young men who did the killings] were recorded by two intelligence agencies in India, to my knowledge. There was the intelligence bureau in New Delhi, in the capital, and then there was a police anti-terrorism unit that made the recordings in Mumbai, as well. Exactly how I obtained the recordings, I can't tell you, because these are not recordings that were released to us by the authorities. The authorities were rather upset when I got them, and I believe a summons was issued against [one of the commissioning broadcasters of the documentary] Channel 4. Some kind of legal action was threatened by the Mumbai police chief, but it wasn't followed through. From the Indian point of view, it was upsetting that this material that wasn't supposed to be publicly broadcast had been given a worldwide audience. But, on the other hand, it demonstrated that Pakistan was behind the attack, and that, for India, was politically useful, so I guess they weren't too upset. Nobody wanted to give us anything. It was extremely difficult to pry this material from where it was. That was the hardest part of the production. It was very, very, very difficult. No one in the Indian media and no one in the international media had succeeded in getting the entire [phone] recordings before we did.

The closed circuit video from the hotels, again, was obtained without the consent of the hotels. They were recordings that existed that had been circulating. The authorities had them, and other actors had them, but we did not obtain them, if you like, through the front door. We considered this material was important for telling the story, and it was a very important story to be told. I suspected that the material was being closely guarded because some of it may have been embarrassing to the hotel. It may be considered embarrassing, if you're a big luxury hotel, to have men walking around your hotel, machine-gunning your guests. That's not something that you particularly want to draw attention to.

NINE OF THE TEN [attackers] were killed. The fifty-seven-hour period is the time to the end, when the last attacker at the Taj Hotel was killed or burned to death. That's when the clock stops, if you like. Kasab [the attacker who was not killed] was caught on the first night of the attack, and had machine gunned a whole bunch of people at the railway station; killed men, women, and children mercilessly. He then killed three cops and a fourth as he was being captured, so the police really had every reason to treat him with extreme prejudice. I was surprised at how gentle they have been with him. He's been put on trial. He's been sentenced to death, but...the Indian legal system is very, very slow in their appeals. [Editor's note: He was executed on November 21, 2012.]

The video [from inside the hotels] was not released to us, and we obtained it because we thought it had a huge public interest value. It was very, very difficult. That was the most difficult piece of material to get hold of because that really was very closely guarded. We don't like to pay cash for material. We hire people who obtain it for us. You can't just hire someone. You have a colleague who then works to obtain it because it's not as if you can walk into a newspaper or some institution in India, and say, "Here's two months' work. Go and get me this." Obtaining material like this is a bit of an art. It involves a lot of trust. You have to make relationships with people, and they have to trust you, and they have to believe that they're doing something worthwhile, and that the material is going a good home where it will be well used and honestly used.

A BIG CHALLENGE WITH the audio [was] there were seven hours of these telephone intercepts. I had to have it all translated, of course, because I wasn't going to miss anything. Having it translated and finding people who spoke the right Pakistani Punjabi dialect and whom I trusted to give me an accurate, completely objective and impartial rendition of what was being said and to go into every detail, because sometimes the line is bad and you can only hear half a word, [was difficult]. It was a tremendous job translating this. Other people have got hold of these tapes now. I'm probably the only person with a full translation of the whole thing because it's expensive and it takes a lot of time to do. We had it checked and rechecked and rechecked, and I'm very, very thorough. I like to know that when we broadcast something, it is absolutely right. It's absolutely spot-on.

WHAT I DISCOVERED IN researching the story was that there was such chaos that the victims often couldn't get help. Even with senior police officers radioing for help, there was no help because the city was taken completely by surprise and people had no idea what was going on. That's the impact of the surprise attack, and the evil genius of the design of this plan was that there were so many events going on. There were bombs in taxis that were being detonated after half an hour, so the taxi was far away in the suburbs or by the airport when the bomb went off. If you were in the police control room, looking at the picture, you would see bombs going off. You would see gunmen here, gunmen there. A lot of false reports as well, because in an incident like this, there's a lot of panic, and you wouldn't know what the hell is going on.

The Mumbai Police Department fell apart in the early hours of the attack, and they were eventually replaced by the specialist commanders from New Delhi who also took a long, long time to arrive. Their plane wasn't ready, and there were all sorts of delays on route. The response was very slow.

I was talking to people in New York, and they said, "If this happened in New York, these guys would have been dead within minutes." I don't believe that would be the case. An attack like this has such a dynamism and such an impact. It's so hard to get information on what's happening that even in a place like New York or in London, my city, almost as many people would have died in the first half hour. The impact of the attack is such that people don't know what to make of it.

I've been having requests for my film. I've been receiving e-mail requests from SWAT teams [in London] and in the States. Homeland Security officials were desperate to find out what an attack like this looks like and sounds like. Maybe if it happens here now, we're better prepared because we've seen what happened in Mumbai. These guys change their modus operandi all the time, and they wouldn't do the same thing twice. 9/11 and this attack, what they have in common is, they're almost inconceivable. There's something about the design of the attack that creates disbelief. You're sitting there for about ten minutes thinking, "This can't be happening. This cannot be happening."

I HESITATE TO EXPRESS it like this, but *Terror in Mumbai* is a historic piece because we've never had the kind of material to rival these phone calls. It gives you an inside view of the terrorist attack, and we've never had that before. You'd never heard the terrorists' intimate conversations with their bosses....Taken together with the other material, it adds up to something unique, not just an insight into the way the terrorists operate, but also into the psychological relationship between the controllers and the gunmen. The controllers never shouted. There was never any hysteria. Even when the gunmen had been hit and were dying, they never raised their voices. There was complete calm, and I think that's strange and significant.

I kept thinking of children who were groomed for abuse and the way that relationship is. We are told it's not consensual, but that there's a kind of normality that establishes itself between young people who are groomed for abuse and the abusers. There's a relationship that sets in, and I kept being reminded of that. Why would a young man like this let himself be sent to a certain death by this person sitting in an office miles and miles away? Why would they do that? The fanatical religious rhetoric wasn't really there. There was something else. These were people who had been groomed and psychologically shaped so that what they were doing had become normal. This is what you did. It was normal. To me, that was the biggest horror.

Khalid Shaikh Mohammed

RICHARD MINITER

Kuwait-born Khalid Shaikh Mohammed was the alleged mastermind behind the al Qaeda attacks of 9/11, as well as the attack on the USS Cole, the 1993 World Trade Center bombing, and the Bali bombing, among others. He was captured in a raid by U.S. and Pakistani forces in early 2003, in Pakistan, and remains in prison in Guantanamo Bay. In this interview, his biographer Richard Miniter, an investigative journalist and terrorism expert, examines KSM's path to terrorism and his surprising ties to America. Richard Miniter appeared on Q & A on May 15, 2011.

KHALID SHAIKH MOHAMMED (KSM) is the man who planned the 9/11 attacks and all of the other major al Qaeda attacks that you've heard about. He is the deadly brains behind al Qaeda. He is what made al Qaeda much more lethal. When he first joined al Qaeda, they were killing dozens at a time. As soon as he got into senior leadership, they began killing hundreds and then thousands at a time. After he was captured in March 2003, the lethality of al Qaeda fell, and they are back to killing dozens at a time. This is the guy that really mattered. Understanding him is about understanding the future of the war on terror. Now that bin Laden is dead, this is what we have to fear, these terrorist entrepreneurs like KSM.

[I started writing *Mastermind*] about two years ago, but this question had been on my mind since 9/11: How did people become terrorists, educated, successful people at the top of their society? About two-thirds of al Qaeda are college graduates, usually with advanced degrees, compared to only 6 percent of the Arab world. They are the best of their society from an educational point of view. How do these people become transformed? What series of choices do they make to become terrorists, to kill hundreds and thousands of other people? That's the question I was interested in. Instead of doing a sociological tract, I chose to look at the story of one man, Khalid Shaikh Mohammed, who planned 9/11, the embassy bombings, the attack on the *USS Cole*, and the Bali bombing.

Wall Street Journal reporter Daniel Pearl was killed by Khalid Shaikh Mohammed. I found out one of the main reasons he did it; it had nothing to do with ideology. After 9/11, he was holed up in Pakistan, as many al Qaeda leaders are, and he had a new nickname inside al Qaeda, a nickname he didn't like very much. He was "KFC"—"Kentucky Fried Chicken." He ate buckets and buckets of the stuff, and he ballooned up from about 140 pounds—he's about five-foot, four inches—to more than two hundred pounds, so there was a lot of ribbing inside al Qaeda about the fact that the brain was now Jabba the Hutt-like, and he was not deadly, they thought. So when he heard about the *Wall Street Journal* reporter being kidnapped, he bought him from his captor and brought a film crew to where he was being held, and personally cut off his head. He did it for ego and pride and to show he was tough.

HIS FIRST TRIP TO the United States was in 1984. He really didn't understand much about our country. I talked to the man who picked him up from the airport, the dean of Chowan College in Murfreesboro, North Carolina. One of the things he remembers is KSM looking out the window and being surprised to see people sitting on their front lawn in front of the highway. That doesn't happen in the Middle East. In the Middle East, everything happens behind walls. The public street is something to be avoided. Windows are small. The idea of just sitting outside in the sunshine in front of a major highway, something you see all over the American South, just struck him as bizarre. Then, of course, the greenery, the lushness of this country, the fact that poor people, rich people, people of all classes have trees and grass, was very different from what he experienced in Kuwait. So, the environment was different and the culture was very different.

He was born outside of Kuwait City in Kuwait. His parents came from the mountains of Iran in a region called Baluchistan. The Baluch are people without a country. Their land is divided into three countries, Afghanistan, Iran, and Pakistan. They have fought the leaders of all three of those countries at different times, trying to get independence. His father came in 1950 or 1951 to Kuwait. The records are still sparse on this. His mother followed shortly thereafter. They had a number of children, at least four, before KSM was born. His father died when he was very young. There was no welfare in the 1960s and 1970s in Kuwait, so his mother had to take any job that she could get. She washed the bodies of the dead before burial.

He came to Chowan College for two reasons; one is that their English language standards were very lax and his English was poor. He was very good in science and math, but his English wasn't up to par. He couldn't have passed a standardized test, so he looked for a college with a weak entrance exam; and two, if you look at the pattern of Arab foreign students, they are different from other kinds of foreign students, such as Indians or Japanese. The Arabs tend to follow social networks much more than other foreign students. The fact that a few other Arabs had gone there, that people he had been related to or knew of, had been there before, made a big difference to him.

[The Muslim community in North Carolina in the 1980s was composed of different groups.] There were transfer students, and then there were some Arabs that had fled either the Lebanese civil war or other developments in the Arab world and had settled in North Carolina. There was also a great demand for technical jobs in the Research Triangle area that drew some of them in as well.

[Apparently, in those days, he was a very serious Muslim.] He liked to go to Burger King and order burgers without the meat, and make a big show of eating it without the meat and say, "I can't be sure that this beef was prepared to Islamic standards of purity." He would police other students. He was one of a group known as the Mullahs that would tell other Muslim students not to wear shorts because those are forbidden by certain teachings of Muhammed, to cover their ankles with socks, and all of these very fine points of dress and behavior. Obviously, there was no alcohol and no pork....

The interesting thing [about his time at Chowan]...is that he was required every week to attend chapel. That was mostly a lecture, sometimes music. It wasn't a Christian religious service, but he was supposed to attend chapel with the other students. According to records, he did so, and he never objected. I looked up a number of former classmates and professors, anyone who might have a recollection, but no one seems to remember him objecting.

Garth Faile taught chemistry. He taught KSM. He is the only professor who has a vivid memory at Chowan of KSM.... He remembers him as a good student who had very poor English. He never had any political discussions with him, or religious debates for that matter. But he remembers him as someone who had a very orderly mind. Unfortunately, an orderly mind can be put to good or evil. In this case, it was put to evil.... I also went to the school library. I went through all of the yearbooks [for the time he was there]. He was invisible in the yearbooks.... It's interesting, Chowan made a budgetary choice. They were running short of students. They were in financial jeopardy. So they began admitting more foreign students, thinking they wouldn't have to give them as much aid. Ultimately, it started to change the character of the college in some good ways and in some bad ones.

As a reporter, one of my instincts is to follow the money. I got some extraordinary access from Chowan to look at the financial records. That's when I discovered that he paid in advance for an entire semester's tuition, months before he arrived. Also, his visa application, which the college had a copy of, mentions a private sponsor, but there is no idea [as to] who that private sponsor must be. His family was so poor in Kuwait that they didn't have a telephone. They didn't have a rich uncle. It makes you wonder who the private sponsor might be. He stayed in Chowan for one semester.

Then he transferred to North Carolina A&T State University, a historically black college in Greensboro, North Carolina, the alma mater of Jesse Jackson and Ronald McNair, the astronaut. He graduated in June 1986, with a [Bachelor of Science] degree in mechanical engineering. I found a number of people there, on and off the record, who remembered him. The former Muslim students who are now professionals in the Greensboro area had the most vivid memory of him. They spent the most time with him. They remember him as a comedian. He loved something called the *Friday Tonight Show.* He would be a cast member in this informal student group and do standup comic routines where he impersonated Arab leaders and other Muslim personalities. He was very popular and very good at that. [I talked to an imam, off the record] for security reasons. There is still a lot of hesitation to talk outside their community and what the repercussions might be. I must say, though, having spent a lot of time with this imam, that if he would be public, he could be a very important bridge of understanding. Someone who understands both American life and Islam could be beneficial to the country. I learned a lot about the interior life of KSM and about his family. This imam had spent a lot of time with him and with his extended family, knew him both from his Kuwait days and as a student. He had an idea of the intellectual forces shaping KSM. I also learned about his driving record. KSM was a terrible driver. He drove with an expired license. He often drove at high speed and smashed into parked cars. In one car, two women were talking when KSM's car smashed into theirs. The women were badly injured and they sued for their medical costs. Their last name was Christian. His is Mohammed. The lawsuit in the North Carolina court records is *Christian v. Mohammed*, 1985.

[In my book, I wrote,] "America would be good to KSM. In return, he would use his college years to make alliances he would need in future terror attacks and plot his first assassination on American soil...." Meir Kahane was a Zionist, an American Jewish rabbi who ultimately became a member of the Israeli Knesset. He was very outspoken, very pro-Israel, and he called for the Palestinian Arabs to leave the Gaza Strip and the West Bank and the land that was biblically Israel's, to be Israel's today. It was not a mainstream position, to put it casually. He gave speeches all throughout the United States and raised tremendous amounts of money. He founded the Jewish Defense League. In 1986, he spoke in Greensboro, North Carolina, at North Carolina A&T. That speech was seen by KSM, and it outraged him, because this was someone who had a diametrically opposed point of view. KSM often lied and said that he had a Palestinian mother or grandmother or some Palestinian relationship. In fact, in his genealogy, there's no connection to Palestine. But most of the students and the high school teachers that he had in Kuwait were Palestinian. His social world in the Muslim Brotherhood in Kuwait was primarily Palestinian. He identified very strongly with the PLO and Black September and those radical groups of the 1970s. When he heard Kahane, it was an alternate point of view. For KSM, the problem is not that people disagree. The problem is that alternate points of view exist. There should be a single, unified view. Unsurprisingly, it is his. So, he plotted to kill Kahane. There is a one-line mention of this buried in a footnote in the 9/11 Commission report, in which he claimed that he had Kahane killed and that the CIA didn't believe him. But when you look into it, you discover that they didn't investigate that very hard. When you begin to look at the case in detail, you see that the entire cell that was used, the getaway driver, the gunman that was used in the assassination of Kahane, was later reused in KSM's attack on the World Trade Center in February 1993.

[Kahane was shot dead after giving a speech at the Marriott East Side Hotel in New York City on November 5, 1990. KSM did not shoot him.] He got El Sayyid Nosair, [an Egyptian-born American citizen,] to kill him. Nosair is an interesting character too. It wasn't his first attempted murder. His first attempted murder was an attack on a gay bar in Greenwich Village. He picked them out of the phone book. He was an immigrant to the United States who worked for the sanitation department, and was ultimately fired because he kept bothering the other workers, trying to persuade them to embrace Islam as their religion. He became further radicalized and attacked the gay bar. He was brought into this cell, and was the gunman who shot Meir Kahane. Kahane was taken to the hospital after being wounded, and died in surgery. [Nosair walked out of the hotel to a waiting cab. The cabdriver was one of the connections to the '93 World Trade Center bombing.] The cabdriver is waiting for him, but he gets into the wrong cab and starts barking orders. This is New York. The cabbie just turns around and starts barking right back. So, he bolts out of the cab, runs into an armed postal inspector, and they shoot it out. Ultimately, Nosair is taken to the same hospital as Kahane.

[THE CONNECTION BETWEEN THIS attack and the bombing of the World Trade Center in 1993,] is that after the bombing, the bombers issued demands. The first of those demands was the release of Nosair from prison. So that's one connection. The second connection is the cabdriver in the shooting of Kahane, the cab Nosair didn't get into, drove the get-away car at the World Trade Center. Another figure who videotaped the murder of Kahane, while posing as a member of the audience, was part of the bomb plot for the World Trade Center, and there are several other personalities directly involved in both.

Ramzi Yousef was not involved in the Kahane murder, but he built the [World Trade Center] bomb. He's the cousin [of KSM.] One of the critical relationships that defined KSM's life was his cousin, who was three years younger. They grew up together as best friends. But it was an unequal relationship. Definitely, KSM was the master of that relationship. Yousef is now in a super maximum prison in Florence, Colorado.

[KSM was in North Carolina] for almost four years. A lot of his [hatred towards America]—more than I expected—is because the United States supports Israel. In the 1980s, in North Carolina, it would not be hard for KSM to meet ordinary Americans who admired Israel as the only Middle Eastern democracy, as a place that many churches take people for historical visits and religious visits. Israel was generally admired. This came as a great shock to him. In the court case *Christian v. Mohammed*, he tracked down their lawyer, Stephen J. Teague, and visited him in his offices and lectured him about Israel and Palestine, about the Iran and Iraq war, and so on. Clearly, he thought the Americans were really misinformed about Israel, and that was a motivator....He didn't like the way we lived. He didn't like the freedom. He didn't like the equality between men and women. He didn't like the openness, the casualness of American society, how people would sit out in public and have conversations with people who would walk by. This casualness, for some reason, just really bothered him.

I'm always looking for the dog that doesn't bark. This is not the only case of a student that comes to America and becomes radicalized and joins al Qaeda, let alone other terrorist groups. But I'm not aware of any case of someone going to a military college, either a public one like West Point or Annapolis, or a private one like Valley Forge or the Citadel, who becomes radicalized. I think the difference is the way we deal with students in military colleges, you're integrated into a larger unit. Yes, there are enormous demands on you as an individual, but they are really forming unit cohesion. You're part of the group from the beginning, and that's really important. In American public colleges, non-military colleges, civilian colleges, it is sink or swim. Once they admit you to the college, they show you where the library and the cafeteria are, and you are on your own. So, if you don't form a good relationship with your dorm mate, if you find it hard to deal with other students, it's just your tough luck. That's alienating, especially to a lot of foreign students. Remember [with] the 9/11 hijackers, in the rental car, the FBI found a notebook describing the difference between conditioner, shampoo, and body wash in Arabic. We forget how much people coming from a different culture don't necessarily know about our own. We assume that everything about our culture is universal and easy to understand because it is for us. College administrators don't recognize how hard it is for these guys to make the switch. They really need to improve orientation, and they need to improve the way in which they deal with foreign students.

[KSM] CAME UP WITH the idea for 9/11. He created the team and he supervised the process from Afghanistan and Pakistan, from inside al Qaeda. Obviously, bin Laden had a role both in funding and shaping the operation, but 9/11 is very much the creation of a single man, and that man is Khalid Shaikh Mohammed. We know this from other detainees, from internal documents in al Qaeda. Of course, Khalid Shaikh Mohammed says it. No one disputes it. He is given a tremendous amount of respect in Guantanamo by the other detainees because his role in the attacks is very well acknowledged.

PART OF THE INSPIRATION for 9/11 comes from his viewing of the science fiction movie *Independence Day*, where the flying saucers blow up the World Trade Center and other New York landmarks, and they take out the White House....

THE 9/11 PLAN WENT through a number of changes between 1998 and 2001. In the early stages, they wanted to hijack eleven planes. One of them would be piloted by KSM himself. He would kill all the men, land the plane, release the women and children, hold a press conference, and then fly off into the sunset in a passenger jet, really like the plot of a bad movie. Obviously, bin Laden vetoed this idea.

He was arrested in March 2003 by a combination of U.S., CIA, and Special Forces, and Pakistani Special Forces. [They found him because] they got lucky. A walk-in, which is an intelligence term for someone who just volunteers, comes by the embassy and says, "I've got something you should know." Now, these people are not usually welcomed with open arms, but if they pass a number of tests, they are taken seriously. In this case, a man walked in and said he'd recently been with KSM and that he would be with KSM for dinner later that night. Now, that really got the attention of the CIA, because informants don't usually suggest that they're going to see the key subject in a few hours. They usually say, "Well, it'll be a few weeks or months." They are hoping to get a little money out of it. This guy didn't ask for money, although he did want the reward, and I think he ultimately got it. At the time, I think it was $5 million. It's a funny story. He gets the phone number from one of the CIA operatives in Islamabad, Pakistan. Remember, Islamabad is the largest CIA station in the world. That's where we spend the majority of our energy fighting al Qaeda. Two-thirds of all senior al Qaeda who have been killed or captured have been killed or captured in Pakistan. That's more than Afghanistan and Iraq combined. So, this is party central for al Qaeda. He gets his cell phone number, and a few hours later, about eleven at night, he goes to the bathroom of a restaurant and texts the CIA officer he had met earlier that day, and says, "I am with KSM." They meet up a few hours later and he said he has just dropped KSM off. He can't remember the address of the house. It's not like many parts of the United States, where they write the address number on the curb. [There is a picture of the house in the book. 18A Nisan Road, in Rawalpindi,] which is just south of Islamabad in the mountains. It's a very prosperous neighborhood. He was staying in the equivalent of [the] Beverly Hills of Rawalpindi....

He was taken to a series of secret prisons. It's really hard to document what was going on in that period between 2003 and 2006 when he was transferred to Guantanamo. It appears that he spent some time in Romania, in Bangkok, and in a CIA secret facility outside of Warsaw, Poland. [They moved him around that much, because] you are sort of a guest of another country's intelligence service and you can only have someone as a guest for so long. Also, sometimes changing people's environments gets them moving. There might also be other detainees that they want to cross-examine and put him with. There are reasons for doing it.

KSM IS VERY SMART. Education is not the solution to terrorism. Most of these guys are very educated. What's lacking is empathy, the ability to put themselves in another person's place and the ability to debate different ideas about politics, religion, how society should be organized, the idea that there's not one answer to these things, but that they can be actively debated. That isn't pushed. I think if we had a core curriculum at some of these colleges where they were forced to...debate ideas that they didn't themselves believe in, just to get used to the practice, it might be very useful. It might de-radicalize them.

I don't believe waterboarding is torture.... KSM was waterboarded in March 2003, and never since.... [It's been said he has been waterboarded 183 times.] One hundred and eighty-three is the number of times water is poured on the face. So when someone says he has been waterboarded 183 times, they are being a bit cute. Those facts come out of a legal document issued by the CIA in response to an Inspector General's report. The CIA is like the Wehrmacht in World War II. They are obsessive record-keepers. Let us widen the frame and look at the bureaucratic process for a moment. When you waterboard someone, there is a doctor in the room at all times. There is also a translator. There are other personnel standing by in the room. So that if anything starts to go wrong, the process can be stopped. The person can be saved. There are a lot of safeguards in effect. The people who are doing the waterboarding have been waterboarded themselves. They know what stress they're putting someone through.

HE IS KEPT ALONG with four or five other high-value detainees connected to 9/11, and it's part of a slightly larger group of about fifteen or sixteen really high-value targets.... He is still questioned. He is still shown drawings or other documents or asked about a name. But the period of intense questioning seems to be over, partly for political reasons. He clearly still knows things that have not come out. When someone breaks in waterboarding, they don't automatically disgorge everything they know.... A lot of people say, "Well, waterboarding is so terrible that you'll say anything to make it stop." When they are waterboarding, you are not really asking that many questions and the questions they are asking are ones they already know the answer to. They want to test your veracity, your willingness to tell the truth. They are not asking things they don't know the answer to. So there's no possibility of fake information. If you give bad information, there are punishments. You are denied favorite foods. You are denied books to read, things like that. I've tried to [go through the waterboarding experience,] and, for all sorts of legal reasons, nobody wants to waterboard me. We have stopped a lot of plots based on direct information from him.

[KSM MET OSAMA BIN Laden] for the first time in Pakistan, probably near the Jalozai refugee camp, but bin Laden maintains publically they didn't really know each other then, in the early nineties. They had their first sit-down meeting in 1995 in Kandahar, near bin Laden's ranch there. Temperamentally, they didn't get along. A second meeting, about a year later, led to another job offer for KSM, and that one he took. He wanted to go to work for al Qaeda. He had a wife and some children at that point. He was broke. And much of his cell, which had carried out attacks or attempted attacks in the Philippines, Pakistan, and elsewhere, had been killed or captured. So, he was at the end of his string. His wife was saying, basically, get a job. And so, ultimately he went to work for al Qaeda.

[He put together the 9/11 attacks] from various cities in Pakistan and Afghanistan. He moved freely in all those cities. He seemed to prefer Karachi. He had a number of relatives living in Karachi, in Pakistan. This is one of the things I get into in the book, *Mastermind*; that for al Qaeda, it was really a management problem. There were people quitting the plot, flying home, or people threatening to quit or people getting into trouble with the law. There were at least thirteen distinct opportunities to stop the 9/11 plot at different points in 2000 and 2001. For example, Mohammed Atta was pulled over by a Maryland state trooper. From an operational or a management point of view, it was a nightmare for them. Unfortunately, they succeeded, and it was a nightmare for us.

[Some of the money came] from Islamic charities and wealthy oil shaikhs in the Gulf and in Saudi Arabia and across North Africa. [They are doing it because of] ideological conviction. There is a fantasy that exists in the minds of many educated people, both in the West and in the

Arab world, and in Asia, that if you do something shocking enough, radical enough, that human nature will suddenly change. It is the same thing that led to the 1960s protests. The Paris takeover in 1968 is a classic example of this, and Woodstock. [There is this belief] that human nature would suddenly change and that this ideal society could be born. That's sort of the idealistic vision of terrorism. The other is that it's a Machiavellian attempt to seize power by terrifying people, and using that fear to control them.

Fifteen of the nineteen hijackers were from Saudi Arabia simply because the U.S. State Department had a special program with Saudi Arabia that they didn't have with any other nation on Earth called Visa Express, where you didn't have to go into the consulate or the embassy and look at a consular affairs officer and fill out forms and show identification. Instead, all that could be done by a travel agent and simply mailed into the embassy, where it was more or less rubber-stamped. So, it was much easier to get a U.S. travel visa from Saudi Arabia than it was from, say, Great Britain, and, of course, much easier than [from] any other Arab country. So, while some visa requests from Yemen and Egypt and elsewhere were denied, all the Saudi ones were granted.

[THE SAUDIS RECEIVE SPECIAL treatment because they] are beneficial to a number of business interests in the United States. They and their wives are big spenders as well. So, there's an economic benefit. There is a long-term relationship between the United States and Saudi Arabia. The two nations, at the top, have been very close for seventy years, at least. It is a unique relationship, and one that's not ever been really studied honestly. They have complained enormously as to why they are not treated the same way people from Western Europe are treated. Before 9/11, there was something called the Visa Waiver Program where if you were a citizen of the United Kingdom or Ireland or Germany, France, and so on, you were part of the Visa Waiver Program, and you could just fly to the United States and show your passport and enter without a visa. The Arabs didn't get the same treatment. This is one thing the Saudis have complained about bitterly. They had to wait in line with third-world peoples whereas an English secretary could just show her British passport and waltz right into New York. So, Visa Express was an attempt to give them some of the same privileges that the Western Europeans and Australians have.

[WE NEED TO REEXAMINE the way we look at the rest of the world.] I'm not one of these people who is paranoid about things overseas, but I do think we need to be realistic. We need to rethink the college experience so there's not that degree of alienation; that the foreign students get integrated, and life here gets explained to them then in a comprehensive way. Civilian colleges can learn from military colleges. We also need to look at what foreign students we are letting in. At the time KSM was admitted to study at Chowan in North Carolina, he had been a member of the Muslim Brotherhood for two years, maybe two-and-a-half years, in Kuwait. Why are we letting in to study in the United States people connected to the Muslim Brotherhood or to other extreme organizations? Frankly, I don't want neo-Nazis studying here either. So, more background checks on the foreign students we admit need to happen. But, of course, colleges and universities are financially dependent on this ocean of money that comes in from foreign students, and they would probably be opposed any sort of realistic security checks for foreign students. That would be quite a fight. But it's one worth having.

The Fall of General
Stanley McChrystal

MICHAEL HASTINGS

Journalist Michael Hastings was best known as a freelance reporter on the wars in Iraq and Afghanistan. His fiancée Andrea Parhamovich was killed when her car was ambushed in Iraq in January 2007. He reported for Newsweek *2002-2008 and his Polk Award-winning article "The Runaway General," for* Rolling Stone, *is credited with ending the career of General Stanley McChrystal in 2010. He expands upon his time with General McChrystal in his book* The Operators. *In this interview, he discusses the genesis of the* Rolling Stone *article, the book, and his career as a war reporter. He appeared on* Q & A *January 29, 2012. Mr. Hastings died in a car crash in Los Angeles on June 18, 2013.*

T HE TITLE OF THE book *The Operators* comes from what Special Forces soldiers call themselves. They call themselves Special Forces Operators, and so, specifically, it refers to Special Forces, but I also thought that everyone who was involved in these conflicts, from diplomats to journalists to public relations people to aid workers, to people in the White House, to people in the embassy in Afghanistan all had a bit of an operator in them.

I LEARNED TO HATE war in general. It would be very difficult for me, having been through a number of things with both of these wars, to really be gung-ho about any conflict. I think if someone's invading our country or invading your house, that's one thing, but this sort of adventurism I have a very, very dark and dim view of it. In my experience, all war does is destroy what we love. It destroys people. It destroys families. It destroys homes. It destroys your memories. And it's very dark. Now, the flipside of it is that there's this grand excitement to be involved in it. That's the operators. The operators, in this sort of sick and twisted way, love the war. I was talking to a State Department official recently, and he was recalling his time in Baghdad in 2006, at the height of the sectarian violence, and he said it was magical. So, there are all sorts of conflicting feelings one has, because when you're in these things, the stakes are as high as they're ever going to be. It's life and death. You feel like you're at the center of history, and that's a very intoxicating feeling. Hence, the cover of the book, where we have an illustrated picture of a general with a pistol in one hand and a scotch glass in the other. What that is, intoxication.

THE FIRST TIME I had the idea [to write the article on Army General Stanley McChrystal] was in 2005, in Baghdad, and I thought, "Wouldn't it be interesting to hang out in the command and really get to know General George Casey," who was commander at the time in Iraq. "Wouldn't it be interesting to get inside the command and do a kind of 'embed' in the same way that we're accustomed to doing it with the troops, like with the grunts, the soldiers on the ground, like Ernie Pyle?" There's been a great tradition of this sort of firsthand reporting, capturing what Willie and Joe are saying on the ground, capturing their idiosyncrasies, how they really speak, their fears, their loves, their desires—all these experiences of war for these low-level grunts. That seed grew over the years. I thought about trying to do a profile of General David Petraeus. I would end up doing it anyway. Then I saw that General McChrystal was getting quite a bit of very, very interesting coverage and I just sensed there was a bigger story there, just reading between the lines of some of the other profiles. So that's what I wanted to do. *Generation Kill*, another book by a *Rolling Stone* writer, [Evan Wright,] was one of my models. [So I wanted to] try to do what *Generation Kill* did to the Marines in the Humvee [and] try to capture that with the highest command.

The first person I sent an e-mail to [was] Duncan Boothby, who's one of the characters in the book who was General McChrystal's civilian public relations adviser, as well as two other public affairs people....I'm not sure exactly how familiar they were with my work. I know that I did not expect to get any access, actually. I really didn't. Whenever you're doing a story on anything, you always make the call and you always ask.

[I'm coming at him from *Rolling Stone*.] *Rolling Stone* has forty years of rock-and-roll style journalism, a no-holds-barred, kick down the doors, toss the hand grenade, expose the powerful sort of journalism. It's owned by Jann Wenner, one of the great legends in publishing, and someone who's supported me 110 percent....

[Why did they let me in?] I think this actually gets to the public relations strategy that General Petraeus had pioneered. It's something I like to call "Petraeus envy." All these other generals in General Petraeus' generation are trying to do what General Petraeus did so well, which is to build up a kind of fan base in the media, which operates as a separate power structure to bypass the traditional chain of command, which gives General Petraeus a lot of influence. General Petraeus had been profiled by everybody. He'd been on the covers of everything, and other generals looked at that and said, "Wow, he plays this media game so well, and look at all the advantages it gets him. He can do what he wants and he can push whatever agenda or policy that he wants to push." So, I believe there was an attempt to create this same sort of cult-like or hero status for General McChrystal, which would then also allow General McChrystal to get away with more, to push his own policies, and to create a separate power base within the media. The concrete example happened during the Afghanistan Strategic Review, when McChrystal and Petraeus actually used strategic leaks to the media to get the number of troops they really wanted. The *60 Minutes* profile came out on General McChrystal in the middle of the controversy over the strategic review. There was a very concerted campaign waged by friendly journalists, friendly think-tankers who had worked for McChrystal, and they all were pushing this idea at the same time. It was a very concerted, deliberate, and conscious campaign.

General McChrystal started at West Point. His father was a [two-star] general. He had a wild man reputation. He went into the [U.S. Army]

Rangers and the Special Forces community, as he went through his career. And then, over the last decade, the war on terror decade, McChrystal played one of the, if not *the*, most pivotal roles in this worldwide counterterrorism operation that the United States was running called JSOC, Joint Special Operations Command. He got the four stars right after he got the job in Afghanistan in June 2009. He was working for Admiral Mike Mullen at the Pentagon on the Joint Chiefs of Staff. He's super-connected. He was connected in the previous administration with [Donald] Rumsfeld and [Dick] Cheney, and he was one of Admiral [Mike] Mullen's protégés. Admiral Mullen, in fact, introduced him to Mayor Mike Bloomberg, which gives the sense of this world these guys are operating in. He's a Democrat. He voted for Obama. He's liberal, I think, on social issues, as well. General McChrystal famously didn't have Fox News on in his headquarters. Usually, when you go to the military headquarters, they have these TV screens, and they'd have Fox News on. General McChrystal did not have Fox News on.

Dave Silverman is quite a character, a Navy SEAL who became one of General McChrystal's most trusted right-hand men, and a very dynamic guy, very interesting guy, very entertaining, very accomplished individual. In fact, Dave had a great time hanging out with him on this trip, and now Dave Silverman is the CEO of the McChrystal Group, which is General McChrystal's consulting firm that he set up…. McChrystal is now on the Navistar board. He's on the Siemens board. He's on the Jet-Blue board. He's offering training seminars. I think it's $4,700 for two days. He reportedly gets $60,000 a speaking engagement.

I got the e-mail back from Duncan Boothby, and Duncan said, "Why don't you come over to Paris," where General McChrystal was going to drum up support among the NATO allies for the war.

I e-mailed my editor and said…"Can I go to Paris?" And my editor said, "Yeah, get on the plane." So, by April 15, [2010,] I had arrived in Paris. I walked into the hotel lobby, met General McChrystal for the first time, and he looked at me and he said, "Ah, so you're the *Rolling Stone* guy. I don't care about the article. I just want to be on the cover." I said, "Well, sir, I think it's between you and Lady Gaga." I was just trying to make some joke, not knowing Lady Gaga was actually going to be on the cover. General McChrystal replied, "Just put me and Lady Gaga in a heart-shaped tub." I thought, "This is a different kind of general; this is going to be a different kind of story." We went to the Arc de Triomphe, had a kind of a non-event, and then the key moment came the next morning, on the first briefing I sat in on in the hotel room. That was the briefing where General McChrystal, at the end of the briefing, started making fun of Vice President Biden. He said, "Vice President Biden, who's that?" Then one of his other top close confidantes said what had become the most widely quoted piece in my story, "Biden? Did you say 'Bite me'?" And everybody laughed. This was in a briefing I was attending in front of ten, fifteen staffers. Again, I was like, "Wow, this is an interesting bunch of guys, in how they're talking about the civilian leadership." Two times General McChrystal asked me to keep stuff off the record, and I've honored that agreement. Their general attitude was kind of a freewheeling style, "We're not going to tell you what to write; go for it," and so it's been interesting to see the response that General McChrystal and his allies have had [to my piece]. I'd been absolutely consistent from the minute the story broke to now explaining what happened, where General McChrystal and his allies have changed their story a number of times. First, they apologized for their behavior reported in the story. Then they said I overstepped ground rules, but they could never really define where that was or what I was doing [wrong], and they started lying to the *Washington Post* and other outlets about it, just making stuff up. Then there were two subsequent Pentagon investigations into the story. They all of a sudden lost their memory, and they couldn't remember who said what, but everything that I reported was said was confirmed. It's just they couldn't remember who said it. So they've changed their story multiple times, and there was a new version that the *Wall Street Journal* guy trotted out as well, that I had represented myself as someone who was gung-ho for the war, which is absurd.

[I never implied to them that I was gung-ho for the war.] I told Dave Silverman I hate war. I have it on a recorded interview. One of the funny things about it is, when these guys—General McChrystal and his staff—have had these sort of memory lapses, "Guys, I was the one taking notes, remember? I remember what was said." But I think General McChrystal, from what I understand, from people close to him, felt embarrassed by the whole thing. I think his staff felt embarrassed, so they have to push back. It's not uncommon if you write a hard-hitting story, or a story where people regret what they said to you, for them to either deny, evade, or disavow what you just reported for various reasons. So it wasn't uncommon.

[I did not set out to "get" General McChrystal.] I set out to write honestly about the war and put my viewpoint about the war out there. One of the strange things about it is—and why I didn't think I was going to get any access—is because I've written numerous critical stories of the war in Afghanistan that are readily available and an entire critical book about Iraq. I've been on the radio talking about my views on the war in Afghanistan, the war in Iraq, way before I had ever met them in Paris.

[I was allowed to hang around the general and his staff] off and on for a month, from Paris, Berlin, Kabul, Kandahar, and then back to Washington, [and I got to hear them in their intimate conversations about everything, and there was no restriction against my writing any of that down]. They did not put out any restrictions about that. In fact, later, I would have this exchange with Duncan [Boothby], the press guy, about the other moment in the story, where there's this great bash, this huge party in Paris, where Duncan would come to me and say, two months later, "Oh, by the way, remember that night in Paris? That was sort of off the record," which is like being slightly pregnant. They were clearly very worried about it.

[General McChrystal's criticism of then National Security Adviser General James Jones also caused him trouble with the president of the United States.] The White House was not a fan of General Jones. He was an outsider coming into the Obama White House, and he didn't mesh with the Obama national security team at all.... The reason they brought him in was to show, here's a bipartisan, serious national security pick, which they felt for a young president with no military experience, [that] it was important to have not just campaign people in that inner circle. It's interesting now, the president has, in fact, gone away from that, and his national security team is his closest advisers. [General Jones was a four-star Marine.] McChrystal's people did not like General Jones at all. Dave Silverman said he was a clown, stuck in NATO; he didn't understand what they were doing. [Silverman was a lieutenant commander in the

Navy,] a Navy SEAL. I think to be a Navy SEAL you have to assume such a huge amount of risk. Your whole life is one giant gamble. You're jumping out of planes, deep-sea diving, [you're doing] the craziest stuff, so it breeds the operators' attitude of a cavalier disrespect for authority. There's a lot of tension between the Special Forces community and the regular military over these sorts of issues of attitude and demeanor.

[JOHN DARNTON, A FORMER *New York Times* reporter, asked me in an interview if I thought it was fair to hang out with somebody over a long period of time, and hear their off-the-cuff-comments and weave them into a larger portrait.] My response is, as a profile writer, as someone who's trying to get at who these people are as characters, those off-the-cuff comments, those unguarded moments are what you're going for as a journalist and as a writer. The other point on those quote-unquote off-the-cuff comments is that those comments represented an attitude, a cultural attitude and climate of command in General McChrystal's staff of being contemptuous toward their civilian masters. The reason why that's significant is because that actually had real policy implications. Their contempt to their civilian leaders set up the situation where they felt no compunction to essentially disobey what the president had asked them to do. The president had said he did not want a decade-long nation-building commitment in Afghanistan. General McChrystal and General David Petraeus gave the president a plan for a decade-long nation-building commitment in Afghanistan. Even recently, General McChrystal said that we're only 50 percent there in Afghanistan. Ten more years. A direct slap at the White House, yet again.

DUNCAN [BOOTHBY], THE PRESS adviser, had said to people, "This story's either going to be fun or it's going to end my career," meaning Duncan's career. He lost his job; he was a civilian. I've said this publicly before, and I've said this since it happened: I think Duncan took a lot of the blame, when, in fact, there was plenty of [blame to go around]. If people want to take responsibility for it, there was plenty to share. Admiral Greg Smith was in the room for all these comments; this is a big time public affairs guy. And I think General McChrystal, to his credit, knows this, that at the end of the day it was General McChrystal's command.

He was the guy setting the tone for the entire bunch of guys. General McChrystal is the ultimate operator, and he set the tone for the rest of the operators that ran with him.

[WHEN MY ARTICLE WAS first released,] I was in Kandahar working on a story about combat helicopter pilots. In fact, I had just arrived in Kandahar in southern Afghanistan, and usually a story comes out when the magazine decides to release it, and it goes up on the Internet, or it's on the newsstands. In this case, a copy of the PDF of the story was leaked to the *Associated Press*. The *Associated Press* ran with an item from the story, and then it snowballed from there. So before *Rolling Stone* put the story up on its own web site, General McChrystal had already lost his job.... [When the story came out,] it was a very intense experience. I was on the phone for fourteen hours doing radio interviews. [At the same time, I was also] trying to get the story on the helicopter pilots. I went on a mission with the helicopter pilots while all this stuff was going on and watched the gun battle that went on between Taliban and American forces on the ground. I got that story, and essentially I agreed with the public affairs people in Kandahar that it was probably time for me to get out of Kandahar and go back to Kabul and eventually to the United States. So, it was a very intense experience for me—and very strange. We got rocketed in Kandahar. I'm trying to write a blog post about General Petraeus, and rockets come in and knock the power out. I got on the first military flight [out of there.] Usually, it's really hard to get on a military flight, especially as a journalist. You have to wait around. This was pretty easy. They put me on a flight pretty quickly. All these soldiers had printed out the story. I had never seen anything like it. They treated me well, almost everyone. There are a few exceptions, but most people in the military have always treated me with respect.

THE MOST UNCOMFORTABLE ASPECT of the book for some people would be my depiction of General David Petraeus, who's been widely regarded as the hero of the Iraq war, and also, in many ways, a hero of Afghanistan, though he didn't pull that off as well as he did Iraq. I offer a very different picture from what one is accustomed to when you read about General Petraeus. I quote some of his colleagues talking about him and the knock on General Petraeus from his colleagues—now, there's a lot of envy involved in this too, but I think there's also truth in it—is that whenever General Petraeus shows up and takes over an assignment, he makes everyone before him look like a total idiot. I use much stronger language in the book, quoting military officials, and there's this great quote from another general, who is describing General Petraeus' tactic, which is that "Petraeus leaves the dead dog on your doorstep every time." That, to me, is a very powerful indictment of General Petraeus' record, from Iraq, when he was responsible for equipping and arming the Iraqi police and army, which was a total disaster—remember, this is the Iraqi police and army that ended up being the death squads—to this strategy in Afghanistan, which was also, in my mind, a complete disaster.

[For the person thinking: "That young punk. You're thirty-one years old. You've never served in the military. What the heck do you know about counterinsurgency warfare or anything that has to do with the military?"] I can just say that I report what I've seen and heard. I was the *Newsweek* Baghdad correspondent for two years. My younger brother was a Bronze Star-winning infantry platoon leader. Some of my best friends are in the military. I personally suffered loss in these conflicts. My experience was forged on the streets of Iraq during the worst sectarian fighting, seeing three-star, four-star, two-star generals act totally clueless, act like clowns, totally ignoring the reality in front of them, and I saw it firsthand. I sat in on briefings every day while the guy with two stars on his shoulder would tell us how great everything in Iraq was, while there were three car bombs waking me up every morning. I went down and interviewed this warlord in southern Afghanistan, a notorious human rights abuser and drug smuggler, whom General Petraeus has embraced. This drug smuggler warlord is, as we speak, torturing people himself with cigarettes. So, if people want to try to disparage me because I should be older or this or that, I would just say: judge my work. If you don't like my work, still buy a copy of the book.

THE *WALL STREET JOURNAL*, [in its critical review of my book,] failed to disclose that the reviewer is a consultant for the U.S. military, who's worked for General Petraeus and worked for General [William] Caldwell. So the *Wall Street Journal* has chosen a military contractor who's worked for the people I criticize, who's taken a lot of money from them, to review the book, and didn't disclose it. So, when we're talking about journalistic ethics, that's Exhibit A in what not to do.... I did write a letter to Paul [Gigot] at the editorial page there, but he did not see fit to run my letter pointing out their oversight. Theirs, to me, was a really eye-opening review for a lot of reasons, because I think their reviewer is right. I think there is a major difference between [Vietnam era reporters] David Halberstam and Neil Sheehan and what George Packer and Dexter Filkins are doing [today], and I think it is generational. Halberstam and Sheehan—and there were a number of other journalists—were in their twenties in Vietnam. They saw this stuff firsthand. They saw the disaster unfold firsthand. They got the lies fed to them firsthand. They saw the horrors of the war firsthand, and so when they came back, they were able to decipher all the B.S. and get through the spin machine. David Halberstam called it "the great lying machine." It was during the formative years when they were beginning to report. Packer, on the other hand, essentially made his career off cheerleading for the Iraq war; and, look, Dexter's done great reporting, but I think it's very easy to get sucked into this military reporting culture, where you give up a lot of your punch in order to keep riding along with the boys in the Humvee.

[DID MY REPORTING HARM America's overseas interests by initiating the firing of General McChrystal?] It's revisionist history. President Karzai threatened to join the Taliban twice while McChrystal was in charge; threatened to join the Taliban, our enemy. And not only that, President Karzai rejected McChrystal's proposal, rejected his strategy, and you can't really point to anything concrete that McChrystal's relationship actually gained from Karzai. There's nothing they can point to that's concrete. It's just this kind of, oh, McChrystal got along with Karzai and he was his buddy. Well, what did it get us? Nothing.

I THINK THIS IDEA that the media and military relationship was destroyed because of a *Rolling Stone* story is pretty crazy. The other thing I think, if it's in a healthy world or healthy democracy, you'd probably want the media and the military's relationship to be strained. The deck is stacked against us. Twenty-seven thousand Pentagon employees are working on this, [at a cost of] $4.7 billion, and what's the budget of all the [news media's] Kabul bureaus? What's the budget of all the Baghdad bureaus? It's dwarfed by what the Pentagon message machine is pushing out....That includes not just their propaganda folks, but advertising, and everyone who's working on shaping the message that the Pentagon wants to put out there. It goes from software programs the Pentagon is now making that monitor our social media. For instance, there's been a recent example where the Army is using a program that monitors how many times Bradley Manning, the *WikiLeaks* leaker, is mentioned on Twitter. It goes to the massive public relations apparatus that all branches of the military have. I've often thought about this. There are more public relations people on a general's staff in Kabul than there are reporters in Kabul, in Afghanistan.... They need all the help they can get, apparently, because even with this message machine, they haven't been able to put too positive a spin on this occasion.

I THINK THE MILITARY, obviously, is necessary. I think there's a lot of great people in it, doing an amazing job, a really, really difficult job. I think it's way too big. I think it's bloated. I think often we give the military a pass on a lot of things because of various guilt left over from Vietnam and reporters' own guilt for not serving [in the military] ourselves. But, look, there are a lot of heroes in the military, and there are a lot of people who are much less than heroes. It reminds me of the Paul Fussell quote where he was talking about the Greatest Generation, and he said something like, "There were a lot of drunks, kooks, and villains in the Greatest Generation, as well." That was a total paraphrase, but that's the idea. What I am opposed to is mythologizing the military, and that, I think, upsets people. But again, some of the most formative experiences of my life have been with members of the military, in these situations, and any of the people who fought in these wars who I've spoken to, and who've reached out to me, they've never criticized my reporting. In fact, a lot of them have said to me—and this is self-serving for me to say, but I'll say it anyway—a lot of them have said to me, this is what it's really like. And that, to me, is the greatest compliment. If the brass is upset, and if these think-tankers in Washington are upset, then I feel like I've probably done my job.

The Wounded Warriors

DAVID WOOD

David Wood began reporting on war in 1977 for TIME *Magazine in Africa, continuing through the eighties and nineties as a reporter on conflicts around the world. He won the 2012 Pulitzer Prize for national reporting for a ten-part series for the* Huffington Post *about soldiers catastrophically wounded in Iraq and Afghanistan. Here, he talks about some of the soldiers he met while researching his series. Mr. Wood discusses the unique challenges for what he calculates as thousands of young Americans who, due to advances in medical technology, are being saved from injuries that, even ten years ago, would have ended their lives. He appeared on* Q & A *July 22, 2012.*

[I WROTE] A TEN-PART series about those men and women who are almost mortally injured in war who, because of the huge advances that have been made in medical trauma treatment over the last ten years, now they're being saved, an incredible number of them are being saved, almost everybody who falls on the battlefield is being saved. I wanted to write about what life was like for these people. It really started off with a question, having seen some people who were pretty gruesomely maimed; wouldn't it be better off if they were dead? Don't they wish that they were dead?

Many of the caregivers [of these severely injured warriors] are young. Soldiers and Marines who go to war are young. They're eighteen, nineteen, and twenty. When they get married, their wives are eighteen, nineteen, and twenty, and very often in cases that I came across, a couple would get married, a few months later the husband would go off to war, and a few weeks after that he'd come home, swathed in bandages, tubes, and in a coma. And the young wife now who's been married a few months to this person is now in charge of taking care of that person for their lifetimes.

Imagine the shock, the grief, to see your loved one in that kind of condition, and then it's slowly dawning on you [that] you're going to have to learn to take care of this person. You're going to have to immediately learn to change dressings, to administer IVs, to keep track of all the often dozens of different medications that your loved one is taking. It's an enormous responsibility, and it comes amid this intense grief and shock. And so the ones that I met are really strong people, and I came to just admire them so much.

It can feel like such a burden. For one thing, understand that when your loved one is gravely wounded, you don't have that person to talk to anymore, so you're really alone. Many of them come to a military hospital like Walter Reed where they're surrounded by the best medical care in the world, extremely caring and understanding nurses and social workers and psychologists, and as much care as we can think of to give them, and yet they're still alone, and often they're caring for small children, as well. So, that's an added burden. And I have seen these mostly young women bear up day after day with this terrible burden, and at some point then, they just go off and find a room and sit there with their head in their hands and weep because it's very, very hard.

BRYAN GANSNER WAS A soldier. He got blown up in Iraq; an improvised explosive device (IED) hit a vehicle he was in. He didn't lose any limbs, but he was pretty badly wounded. His legs were shattered, and he had that indefinable thing that I call combat trauma, which is when you're not specifically diagnosed with a traumatic brain injury or post-traumatic stress syndrome, yet you can still have a range of symptoms. He does, and they include depression, anxiety, not wanting to be in crowds, but the thing that really struck me was [when] he said, "I just feel a little slow."

I said, "What do you mean by that?" He said, "Well, mentally, I used to be a steak knife; now, I'm a butter knife." I just thought, "Wow," you know, that really sums up what so many combat veterans are experiencing, which is they're just not the same; even as their physical wounds heal, that mental trauma goes on.

You know the stress that every married couple goes through. A couple where one of them is severely wounded and is struggling with physical and mental wounds, and the other partner is struggling with the burden of [being a] caregiver, it's enormously stressful, and I just can't imagine what Cheryl and Bryan are going through. They are still together. Oh, they are a great couple. They are wonderful, but like every couple, they have fights. They have jealousies. They have misunderstandings.

They live in Tennessee, in a nice house. They both have good jobs. Cheryl works for one of the nonprofit organizations that helps wounded warriors and their families, and she is really good at it. She really gets it... and that is, that the burden of being severely wounded falls on people who pride themselves on their athleticism, on their stoicism, really. These are really active, smart, aggressive, pushy in a good way, fun-loving kids who get wounded, and now they're struggling with, in some cases, severe restrictions on what they can do.

SCOTT STEVENSON, WHO WAS also in the Army, was blown up by an IED, a roadside bomb. He lost a leg, and had lots of other damage, heavy burns. He was pretty badly wounded. He was taken to Brooke Army Medical Center in San Antonio. They called his mother. She came down and stayed with him for months. She says it's a very awkward position for a mother to be in, to be caring for your son. I think he was twenty-one or twenty-two, and a big guy, and to be caring for him like an infant is very difficult, physically and mentally, because you know that his life is in your hands. You have to change the dressings, it's a procedure that can take hours, and especially for burn patients, [it's] critical that no infection be allowed to set in.

It's the caregivers who change the dressings in the morning and at night, and his mother did that for months. I asked her once, "How do you do that?" She said, "Well, you do it because you have to," but she also said, "I told the Army, I gave you my son in the best physical condition of his life, and you returned him like this. I'm going to get what I need from you, and I'm going to make sure I do, and don't you forget it." She was really strong and tough, a really good person.

I talked to dozens of them, and ended up focusing on those who I thought could tell the story the best. I started at Walter Reed in the Amputee Center, and the Marines there who were in charge basically said, "Talk to anybody you want to," and so I picked this one young man who was working out pretty aggressively. He stopped and we talked. I ended up interviewing him probably ten times: Tyler Southern, who lost both legs and one arm in Afghanistan. He stepped on an IED. He's just a wonderfully irrepressible young American, what a hero, a good person, a deeply good person, funny, fun to be around. It took me a long time to break through that bravado, but I finally did, and he was the subject of the first piece I wrote because he came to embody everything that these young Americans go through, the pride of service, the incredible camaraderie with his combat brethren, and then abruptly waking up with no legs and only one arm….

He was in a place called Sangin in Afghanistan. It's in Helmand province. They were on a patrol. It was a platoon patrol, twenty, twenty-five guys, Marines. They split up to go around the side of a house. The Navy corpsman who was with them, went one way, Tyler went the other way. The Navy corpsman told me he heard the explosion. I said to Tyler, "What was that like?" He said, "I remember going out on patrol, and next thing I woke up in Bethesda." So, he doesn't remember anything about it. What happened was, as I pieced this story together, they were taking fire from a little cluster of houses. So, they approached very carefully, and went around the side. Whoever was inside, the insurgents, had fled, but they peppered the ground with IEDs. Tyler stepped on one, and it blew a little crater in the ground. When the corpsman raced around the side of the buildings to get to him, he was just lying there in the smoking crater. For the Navy corpsman, James Stoddard, nineteen years old, his first combat patrol, his first time in Afghanistan, and he had never treated a live casualty.

So, I said, "Well, what was that like? I mean, here's your good buddy Tyler Southern lying there almost dead." He said, "I have no idea. I don't know what I thought. Muscle memory kicked in." The incredible training that these guys go through where they respond to emergencies like that over and over again, in the nighttime, in the dark, in the rain, in the cold, in the heat, over and over again, so that when it came time for his first outing as a combat corpsman, he did it.

He got three tourniquets on the stumps, checked his airway, did all the right things, got an IV in him while the Marines were calling in a medevac helicopter, which eventually came and took him away.

When Tyler woke up, I think it was twelve days later at Bethesda, his parents were there around the bed. He was in a medically-induced coma, of course. His heart had stopped twice in the time between when the helicopter picked him up and when he got to Bethesda. The doctors had performed a real Hail Mary operation in which they slit open the side of his chest and reached in and clamped off all the blood vessels carrying blood everywhere, except to his brain, because they wanted to keep the brain alive. Everything else they could deal with. It's apparently an operation that usually fails. It saved his life.

So, he eventually came out of his coma. The doctors were trying to say, "Tyler Southern, wake up." No response. They tried everything, couldn't get a response. He should have been awake because they had taken the medication off. His mother at the foot of the bed said, "Tyler, say hello to your mama," and his eyes fluttered, and he said, "Hello, Mama." So, that's how he came awake. Later that day she said, "Do you know what happened to you?" And he said, "No." She said, "You lost both of your legs and one of your arms." And he said, "Okay. We'll go on from here…."

It was deeper into our relationship when I said, "OK. So, you told me once that when you heard you lost both of your legs and an arm, it didn't really bother you." I said, "Really?" So, he talked about that, and what he told me was so human and so understandable. He said, "Look, I've always been the smallest person in the family. I've got two big brothers. My dad is big and capable." Both his brothers were in the military, and he said, "I didn't want to do anything that would make me seem lesser in their eyes, and so I knew I had to really step up to this, and power through it, and be strong, and so I was."

I saw him the other day at Walter Reed Hospital. He's still having operations on his remaining arm, much of which was torn away. He got married. He and his wife have a house in Florida, and I think they'll probably move there once he's finished with it. He went to high school with [the woman who became] his wife. He always wanted to ask her out but didn't dare because she was the prettiest girl, and he didn't think he had a chance. After he was wounded, his mother ran into her in Florida, and she said, "How's Tyler?" His mother said, "He was badly injured." She said, "Well, I'd kind of like to go see him." So they went together back up to Bethesda. She walked into the room and saw Tyler, and apparently that was it. They fell in love, and she stayed on as his caregiver, and then they got married.

NOBODY REALLY KNOWS [HOW many seriously wounded there are]. The really disturbing thing about this is that between the Defense Department's database and Department of Veterans Affairs' database, there is a lot of overlap and discrepancies. So, if you want to know how many amputees there have been, you can't get a good number. Even they can't get a good number. The other problem is that when somebody is wounded on the battlefield, the combat corpsman and medics are so busy trying to save him, and there's usually a firefight going on. So, it's chaotic; a lot of smoke, a lot of noise, a lot of confusion; nobody's sure what's going on. It's very difficult, and what the Defense Department asks is that somebody sit down and fill out a form and file it. Well, guess what? It doesn't always get done accurately. So, there is really no good count, but I figure, by trying to put everything together, that about fifteen thousand young American men and women have been catastrophically wounded. Ten years ago in combat they probably would have died on the battlefield, but now they're being saved.

I don't know what goes on deep inside [these gravely wounded soldiers]. I have only met one of the "quadruples" as they call themselves. They've got prosthetic arms, prosthetic legs, and they can get up and walk and get around. We look on these people as heroes and think, "OK. So, he's got prosthetic legs and arms. He's good to go." But, it takes an enormous amount of energy to operate those. The prosthetic arms, for example, are powered and they're smart. They have computers built in, but to operate them you've got to twitch your shoulder muscle in a certain way. So, when you see someone with a prosthetic arm pick up a glass of water and drink from it, it's an enormous achievement, and it takes a lot of time and concentration and training to be able to do that. So, the "quadruples," or even a "triple" like Tyler Southern—and that's the way they refer to themselves; Tyler says, "I'm a triple," meaning a triple amputee—they can live pretty good lives, but it's always a struggle. And the long-term consequences, we don't know about.

One thing they know from the Vietnam generation of amputees is that people who are fitted with prosthetic legs, for example, can walk okay, but eventually, it's too much trouble, too difficult, too hard, too demanding, and they go back to a wheelchair. It's not known what long-term health consequences stem from either being in a wheelchair or using the prosthetic limbs because we just don't have that experience.

TODD NELSON WAS SERVING in the Army in Afghanistan. He was riding in an unarmored vehicle through downtown Kabul, and he drove past a suicide bomber who detonated his vehicle full of explosives and shrapnel as Todd passed. Todd was sitting in the right front passenger seat.

Todd was in an Army convoy. They were taking stuff back and forth, and just simply because of the need for armor out in the field, there weren't enough armored vehicles for him to ride in, so they were just using a regular SUV. When this white Toyota Corolla exploded, it tore off the side of the truck that Todd was riding in and catastrophically burned him even under his helmet, burned all the skin off his skull. His head was literally on fire along with much of the rest of him, and, of course, the blast damage tore off his face, basically. Somehow, he survived. I have not met anybody who could explain to me how you could survive something like that. Has something to do with an incredible will to live. So, they evacuated him from Kabul back through Germany at the big U.S. military hospital at Landstuhl, which is the first stop for the severely injured coming out of [the field]. At that point, doctors make a decision, is this person going to die, and if so, we'll get his wife here. Or, if we can keep him alive for another day or two, let's send him on. So, they sent him on to Brooke Army Medical Center in San Antonio, Texas, where the Army has its Burn Center which is an amazing place. They got him there and began years of very painful rehabilitation and treatment.

What survived is his wit and his incredible sensitivity to other human beings, his faith. Everything else is a little battered. His face was battered. He has an artificial ear. It's attached with a magnet to a metal plate in his skull, and he told me he worries sometimes that he'll lose it, that it will fall off and he won't notice. He's had many dozens of painful skin grafts on his face. Skin grafts are hard because they scar, and when you have a scar it becomes hard and lumpy and irregular, jagged, not smooth and not flexible. So, if your entire face is covered with skin grafts, it's painful and your face doesn't work well. You can't smile really well. You can't yawn and you can't stretch your eyes. You can't make facial expressions. The doctors at Brooke Army Medical Center are the best in the world. The Army, it turns out, has done or funded all of the full face transplants done in the United States, and they have done a lot of research and cutting edge surgical techniques trying to figure out how to do better facial reconstruction. There have been some big breakthroughs since Todd went through those operations. Most of his face is skin grafts and it's okay. He can function, but it's not pretty.

The last time I spoke to him, he was trying to decide what to do with the rest of his life, and it's a pretty big decision. He is a very religious guy, and I think that he was heading into the direction of being a motivational speaker and working at a nonprofit to help other veterans. [His second wife Sarah was born with one leg and walks with a prosthesis]... which has made for some interesting encounters [with the public].

Like many of the severely wounded who survived, they seem to have a huge appetite for life, a big sense of humor, very fun people to be around....Sarah grew up on a farm. I think until this happened, you would not have called her a terrifically strong person, but when this happened, she became that strong person.

[BOB HALE] IS A good example of the kind of people that we have working in the military medical centers: A very successful plastic surgeon in Los Angeles, Hale was in the Army Reserves, because the Army paid for him to go to medical school. So, he owed them some time, and he got activated, and was sent to Iraq where he started treating the severely wounded. After he'd been there a couple of weeks, he called his wife, he said, "Sell my practice. I'm staying here." It was an enormously lucrative practice, as you can imagine, a plastic surgeon in Los Angeles, and he has dedicated his life now to helping people like Todd Nelson recover full function of their faces.

[The Burn Center in San Antonio] is not very big. I was surprised. I think it is one floor of the hospital, but what first struck me is that it is very warm. Burn patients don't have skin, and therefore there's nothing that prevents their bodies from losing body heat, and so they have to keep it fairly warm. The first thing they do is take them into the shower room which is a big yellow-tiled room with gentle warm water, and they have to wash away that charred flesh, and from there, there are very specialized treatment facilities so that the surgeons can work on repairing damaged bones. For example, Todd's face was crushed, and so they had to replace part of his jaw. They had to rebuild his cheekbones and his occipital part around his eye, and all that had to be done while they're treating the burn itself.

[When asked privately, most of these soldiers say] they'd all do it over again. There's something that drives them to this ideal of service. Like so many people I know who served in war, the intensity of the experience, the intensity of the relationships they have with their combat buddies, is so strong and so pure and true that they look back on those times with longing. And so I'd always ask them, "Do you wish this would never have happened?" And they were, like, "I'd do it again in a heartbeat." I think there is something else that goes on there, too, and that is going through a near death experience somehow seems to give them so much strength and courage and optimism that I think that's one reason why they would do it again. Now, there are some who don't do so well. Drug addiction is common among the severely wounded because they get on these drugs very often early on in their treatment, and I found that they are, in some senses, over-medicated. This is what I've heard from a lot of military doctors and therapists and nurses, and so many of them do get addicted to drugs. It's a very hard thing to break. Especially when, as in the case of *Bryan Gansner*, for example, he's in a military hospital for a year or fourteen months, and then he is sent home. Well, once you're out of that military cocoon, you've got nobody who really understands what you went through. You're more or less on your own. You're thrown back into the civilian workforce. You've got to work for a boss who doesn't understand what combat was like in Iraq, who can't really appreciate what it takes for a guy like Sergeant Bryan Gansner to operate in a war zone, to keep his guys safe.

BOBBY HENLINE, AN 82ND Airborne Sergeant, was blown up in Iraq. It was a Humvee, five guys in it, four of them were killed instantly. Bobby rolled out on fire. Again, there's no explanation as to how he survived. He just did. He was rushed to the hospital, flown back through Land-stuhl and back to Brooke Army Medical Center in San Antonio to the Army Burn Center. He was in surgeries and had just a long, difficult, painful recovery, but he did recover.

His face is mostly a mass of scars from skin grafts. He came out of that experience wondering, "What am I supposed to do with my life, because four of my buddies were killed, and I was saved?" He said, "I'm not a terribly religious guy, but I started to get the feeling God reached down and said, you're going to survive and you're going to do something meaningful, but he didn't tell me what it was." So, he eventually found stand-up comedy as a way to bridge the gap between the wounded and the unwounded.

People don't know how to react to [the wounded guys with prosthet-ics]. It's kind of awkward. A lot of times people will just divert their eyes. It is awkward, and even I was awkward at first, not knowing, should I stare at this person, should I say hello, should I avert my eyes, do they want me to notice them, or what? What Bobby Henline found out, and what I found out from other wounded service people, is that they do want to be noticed. They want you to ask, "Hey, what happened?" Bobby Henline told me he walked into a hospital waiting room one time and there was a guy in there watering the plants. The guy just was shocked, he dropped the watering can, and he said, "Jesus, what happened to you?" "Well," Bobby said, "I just burst out laughing because it was such a hu-man response." The thing that I learned was that the wounded view their wounds and their scars and their missing limbs as medals that they won in service, and they're proud, and they want to be recognized.

I GREW UP IN a Quaker family. We went to Quaker meeting every Sun-day, and I learned to be a pacifist, and, when it came time, when I got to be eighteen, I declared myself a conscientious objector, and I eventually did two years of civilian service instead of going into the military. I worked for a Quaker Rehabilitation Service in Philadelphia. I've had a kind of a checkered career. I started off at Allegany College. We parted ways in my junior year. Then, I got drafted. I did my two years of civilian service. I went to night school where I eventually graduated from Temple

University with a 4.0 average, and I got my first job working as a stringer for *TIME* Magazine.

The way the conscientious objector status worked, and this was early in the Vietnam War, 1965-6; it was before any draft cards had been burned, and the deal was that if the local draft board approved your application to be a conscientious objector, then you had to go find a civilian job that they approved of. So, I found a job working for this Quaker organization in Vietnam. And the government said, "Oh, no. You can't go to Vietnam. No, that's too far away." I said, "But you're sending everybody else to Vietnam," and they said, "No." So, that's why I ended up working in Philadelphia.

I started [covering battles] in 1977. I went to Africa as *TIME* magazine Bureau Chief, and mostly what I wrote about was war, and I had no preparation for it at all. It never occurred to me or anyone else that if we send Dave Wood in to cover these guerilla wars, we might want to give him a little training, at least some first aid or something. No, nothing. So, I sort of learned on the fly, and I was very lucky that I never got wounded or even was in any real serious peril. Then, I came back to the United States in 1980 and started covering the Pentagon, and soon found out that you could go out to the field with the Army and the Marines, and that was a lot more fun than covering the Pentagon.

So, I spent pretty much the 1980s and 1990s either out in the field with the military or going on what would then be called military interventions. I went to Panama and went to Bosnia and Desert Storm, of course, and so, by the time 9/11 came, I not only had a lot of field time, I had a lot of combat time as a bystander, and usually as a terrified bystander. So, it was a little uncomfortable because a lot of guys in the military had no exposure to war and they would ask me sometimes, "What it's like?" And I have to say, "Look, I'm not a soldier. I don't participate in war. I just watch it happen and write about it." But then, of course, 9/11 came, we went to Afghanistan and then Iraq, and pretty soon, we have a whole generation of combat-hardened veterans.

Appendix: Further Information

www.c-span.org/SundaysatEight *Sundays at Eight*'s home on the Internet, where you can find the original hour-long television videos and complete transcripts, photos, and more from the forty-one interviews selected for this book.

www.booknotes.org All of the 801 interviews from C-SPAN's *Booknotes* program, which aired from 1989 to 2004, accompanied by searchable transcripts.

www.q-and-a.org All of the more than 560 interviews featured so far on C-SPAN's *Q & A* program, with transcripts.

Acknowledgments

THIS BOOK, *SUNDAYS AT EIGHT*, has been a labor of love and an opportunity to remember and share some of the stories told on C-SPAN's Sunday night interview series over the last twenty-five years. This is now our seventh collection of stories from these programs.

While I am responsible for the final selections in this book, and have reviewed them all, a project such as this requires time, attention to detail, and team effort. Peggy Keegan, Molly Murchie, and Emmanuel Touhey helped select and edit the stories, and were skillfully aided in the final editing process by Benjamin Adams at PublicAffairs. Amy Tillman, Charlotte Jackson, and CaSandra Thomas assisted with fact checking and manuscript preparation. Our colleagues Marty Dominguez, Leslie Rhodes, and Karen Henry assisted with design and marketing. Stephen Harkness, Barkley Kern, and Yi-Pei Hsieh-Eastin gave the book its web site presence.

As with previous volumes, Susan Swain, C-SPAN's co-chief executive officer, has shepherded this project from the beginning and used her skill as an editor to produce another interesting reading experience. As editorial director, she worked closely with everyone involved to turn this concept into a reality, including Co-CEO Rob Kennedy and corporate counsel, Bruce Collins, who handled our business and contractual agreements with PublicAffairs.

I am also indebted to the folks at PublicAffairs, including Founder and Editor Peter Osnos, Group Publisher Susan Weinberg, and Publisher Clive Priddle. Their interest in C-SPAN and encouragement over the years has brought several good collections of stories from our television studios to the printed page.

Since these stories all stem from television programs, I must thank the production teams who have labored on our Sunday night series. Bret Betsill has been our primary director beginning with *Booknotes* in April 1989 and *Q & A* since December 2004. He's been joined in recent years by colleagues including Maurice Haines, Greg Czzowitz, and Garrette Moore. *Q & A* producer Michael Holden began his C-SPAN career as a studio technician, operating the audio board for the program. Michael follows in the footsteps of past producers of the Sunday evening series, including Greg Barker, Barry Katz, Sarah Trahern, Eileen Quinn, Robin Scullin, Andrea Perry, Craig Caplan, Andrew Murray and Connie Doebele. Terry Murphy, Vice President of Programming, and Kathy Murphy, VP of Programming Operations, throughout the years, both keep a watchful eye on our productions. Thanks, also, to former editorial assistant Hope Landy and the many interns who have helped out along the way. And, of course, there would be no series without the more than thirteen hundred guests who have shared their expertise and interesting life stories with the C-SPAN audience.

It's one thing to create programs like *Q & A* and *Booknotes,* it's another thing to be able to watch them. Special thanks is owed to the many cable industry executives who have helped bring C-SPAN into now a hundred million U.S. households, from founding chairman, Bob Rosencrans, who wrote the first check for $25,000 back in 1977, to our current Executive Committee chairman, Pat Esser, president of Cox Communications. Without their support, C-SPAN would not have been possible.

In April 2012, after thirty-three years at C-SPAN's helm, I handed over the day-to-day running of the C-SPAN networks to Susan Swain and Rob Kennedy, while continuing my *Q & A* series and many other projects. As co-CEOs, they are doing what they have always done— guiding C-SPAN forward into a future of immense and rapid technological change. I would like to personally thank them for their friendship, loyalty, and commitment as they lead C-SPAN, and with our entire team, continue to provide quality public affairs programming for our viewers.

Index

Brian Lamb is C-SPAN's founding CEO and chairman and longtime on-camera interviewer. He lives in Arlington, Virginia.

THE FRENCH GIRL

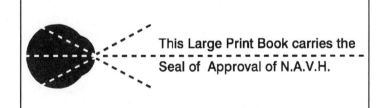

This Large Print Book carries the
Seal of Approval of N.A.V.H.

THE FRENCH GIRL

LEXIE ELLIOTT

WHEELER PUBLISHING
A part of Gale, a Cengage Company

Farmington Hills, Mich • San Francisco • New York • Waterville, Maine
Meriden, Conn • Mason, Ohio • Chicago

Copyright © 2018 by Lexie Elliott.
Wheeler Publishing, a part of Gale, a Cengage Company.

LIBRARY OF CONGRESS CIP DATA ON FILE.
CATALOGUING IN PUBLICATION FOR THIS BOOK
IS AVAILABLE FROM THE LIBRARY OF CONGRESS

ISBN-13: 978-1-4328-5076-0 (hardcover)

Published in 2018 by arrangement with The Berkley Publishing Group, an imprint of Penguin Publishing Group, a division of Penguin Random House LLC

Printed in the United States of America
1 2 3 4 5 6 7 22 21 20 19 18

For Mum and Dad, for everything

*And for Matt, Cameron and Zachary,
for whom my heart beats*

ACKNOWLEDGMENTS

So . . . here's the thing.

It turns out writing *Acknowledgments* is hugely stressful. And difficult: you're trying to be grateful, sincere, funny and all-encompassing within two pages or less, which is no mean feat. Consequently, I've decided to set the bar a little lower and just tick the sincerity box. And if at the end of this you think I have missed anyone, please accept my very sincere apologies . . .

Firstly, I'm enormously indebted to my absolutely wonderful agent, Marcy Posner, who has provided unending encouragement, cajolement and invaluable editorial advice ever since we met. It has been, and continues to be, a pleasure working with you, Marcy; please accept an entire universe of thanks.

To Kerry Donovan and all of the team at Berkley, enormous thanks for getting behind *The French Girl*. As a debut author, I have

only just begun to understand the hard work and dedication that is required to get a book on the shelves; I'm hugely appreciative and rather awestruck to have all that talent and commitment focused on my novel. Thanks all!

To my family — Matt and our gorgeous boys, Cameron and Zachary, and my wider family, Elliotts and Davisons all — and to all my lovely friends: I know you are my biggest fans, thank you so much for being so endlessly supportive. Of course, you also make it kind of hard to write, because there's always something else that's fun going on with you all . . . but I won't hold it against you.

To all who have provided enlightenment and advice on the process of writing over the years, including the various presenters at the Writers' Workshop Festival of Writing and the extremely helpful people at Cornerstones Literary Consultancy, many thanks for helping me find my own voice. To the staff of any and every café that I have sat in to write (and particularly the staff of the Roehampton Club café, which is my favorite place to write), many thanks for keeping me fed and watered.

And to Severine: thanks for showing up. I couldn't have written this without you.

CHAPTER ONE

Looking back, the most striking thing is that she knew I didn't like her and she didn't care. That type of self-possession at the tender age of nineteen — well, it's unnatural. Or French. She was very, very French.

It's Tom who calls to tell me the news. Perhaps that should have tipped me off that something was wrong. I can't remember when he last called me. Which is not to say he isn't in touch: unlike most of my male friends, he's remarkably good on e-mail. I suppose I thought he would be calling with glad tidings: an invitation to a party, or a wedding — Tom's wedding — after all, he's been engaged to Jenna for what seems like years.

But what he says is: "Kate, do you remember that summer?" Seven years in Boston hasn't changed his accent a bit: still unmistakably a product of the finest English

schooling money can buy. An image jumps into my mind of him, as I last saw him two summers ago: his blue eyes standing out against tanned skin with freckles across his remarkable hooked nose, his rumpled dark hair long enough to curl. He won't look like that now after a hard New England winter, but the image won't shift.

I know exactly which summer he means: the summer after we finished university, when six of us spent an idyllic week in a French farmhouse. Idyllic, or mostly idyllic, or idyllic in parts . . . It's hard to remember it objectively since Seb and I split up immediately afterward. I opt for a flippant tone. "Isn't it a bit like the sixties? If you can remember it you weren't there."

He ignores my teasing. "The girl next door —"

"Severine." I'm not flippant anymore. And I no longer expect a party invitation. I close my eyes, waiting for what I know must be coming, and a memory floats up unbidden: Severine, slim and lithe in a tiny black bikini, her walnut brown skin impossibly smooth in the sun, one hip cocked with the foot pointing away as if ready to saunter off the moment she lost interest. Severine, who introduced herself, without even a hint of a smile to soften her severe beauty, as "the

10

mademoiselle next door," and who disappeared without a trace after the six of us left for Britain.

"Yes, Severine." Tom pauses, the short silence pressing down the phone line. "They found her. Her body."

I'm silent. Yesterday, if I'd thought about it all, which of course I hadn't, I would have said I didn't know if she would ever be found. With Tom's stark words it suddenly seems entirely fated, as if all possible paths were destined to converge on this discovery. I imagine her bones, clean and white after a decade left undiscovered, the immaculate skull grinning. She would have hated that, the inevitable smile of death; Severine who never smiled.

"Kate? Still there?" Tom asks.

"Sorry, yes. Where did they find her?" Her? Was a corpse still a *her*?

"The well," he says bluntly. "At the farmhouse."

"Poor girl," I sigh. Poor, poor girl. Then: "The well? But that means . . ."

"Yes. She must have gone back. The French police will want to talk to us again."

"Of course." I rub my forehead, then think of the white skull beneath my own warm flesh and drop my hand hastily. The well. I didn't expect that.

"Are you okay?" asks Tom, his deep voice concerned.

"I think so. It's just . . ."

"A shock," he supplies. "I know." He doesn't sound shocked. But I suppose he's had longer to get used to the idea. "Will you tell Lara? I'm not sure I have her number."

"I'll tell her," I say. Lara is my closest friend, another of the six. The police will want to talk to all of us, I suppose, or at least the five of us who are left; Theo at least is beyond the jurisdiction of any police force now. Probably Tom has called Seb and Caro already, or is about to. It would doubtless be polite to ask how they are, but I don't. "Will you have to fly back from Boston?"

"Actually, I'm in London already. I got in this morning."

"Great!" Good news at last. "For how long?"

"For good."

"Wonderful!" But there is something odd about his demeanor, such as can be gleaned over the phone. "Is Jenna with you?" I ask cautiously. I'm beginning to suspect I already know the answer.

"No." I hear him blow out a breath. "It's for the best," he adds awkwardly.

As it happens I agree with him, but it's

probably not the time to say so. "Right," I say decisively. "Sounds like you need to turn up on my doorstep one evening very soon with a bottle of wine."

"This might be more of a bottle of whiskey type of conversation."

"You bring whatever alcohol you like and I'll cook the meal. Badly."

He laughs down the phone, a pleasant sound. "It's a deal."

It occurs to me he used to laugh more, all those years ago. But then, we were twenty-one, with no responsibilities or cares, and no one had mysteriously disappeared yet. Probably we all laughed more.

A dead body has been found, but life goes on. For most of us, anyway — perhaps time stops for the nearest and dearest, but then again time probably stopped for them a decade ago when she went missing. For the rest of us, it's back to the same old, same old, which today means a meeting with a potential client. A very hard-hitting potential client: a contract with Haft & Weil could put my fledgling legal headhunter business firmly on the map. I stand in front of the mirror in the bathroom of my short-lease office in Bloomsbury. Smart business trouser suit: check. Tailored silk shirt, clean and

ironed: check. Thick dark hair pulled back into a tidy chignon and discreet makeup accentuating my green eyes: check. Altogether a pleasing picture of a professional businesswoman. I smile to check my teeth for poppy seeds from the bagel I had for lunch; the image of Severine's grinning skull immediately jumps into my head. In the mirror my smile drops abruptly.

My assistant, Julie, looks up from her computer as I exit the bathroom. "The cab's here," she says, passing me a folder. "All set?"

"Yes." I check the folder. Everything is there. "Where's Paul?" Paul is my associate and a very, very good headhunter. He's here because he has faith in me and even more faith in the proportion of profits he's due if all goes well. I try to keep a close eye on his diary. Paul won't stick around if the business plan fails to materialize.

Julie is checking on the computer, one hand working the mouse as the other pushes her glasses back up her nose. "He's meeting that Freshfields candidate over on Fleet Street."

"Oh yes." I check the folder again.

"Kate," Julie says, a touch of exasperation in her tone. "It's all there."

I snap the folder shut. "I know. Thank

you." I take a deep breath. "Right, see you later."

"Good luck." She has already turned back to the computer, but stops suddenly. "Oh, you had a call that you might want to return when you're in the cab." She looks around for the telephone message pad. "Ah, here we are. Caroline Horridge, please call back. Didn't say what about."

Caro. Calling me. Really? "You're kidding."

Julie looks up, nonplussed. "If I am, the joke has passed me by."

I take the message slip she's holding out. "She went to university with me," I explain, grimacing. "We weren't exactly bosom buddies. The last time I saw her was about five years ago, at someone's party." I look down at the telephone number recorded under the name in Julie's neat hand. "This is a Haft & Weil number," I say, surprised. I've been dialing it enough lately that I know the switchboard number off by heart.

"Maybe she wants to jump ship."

Maybe. There isn't really any other reason for a lawyer to call a legal headhunter. But I can't imagine Caro choosing to ask for my help. I sit in the cab and think of ghosts: of poor dead Severine, her bones folded like an accordion to fit in the narrow well; of

poor dead Theo, blown into disparate parts on a battlefield; of Tom-that-was, back when he laughed more; of me-that-was; of Lara; of Caro; and of Seb. Always, always of Seb.

I met Seb in 2000, the summer of my second year at Oxford. Lara and I had been there long enough to stop feeling green and naive and not long enough for responsibility to loom large: no exams all year, or at least none that counted officially, and no requirement to think about jobs until the third year. Our tutors felt it was a good year to bed down the solid groundwork for the following exam year. We thought it was a good year to bed down in actual bed after late nights clubbing.

The favorite summer pastime was ball-crashing. Unthinkable now — to dress up in black tie and sneak into an event without paying, to avail oneself of everything on offer just for a lark. But it was a lark; no one made the connection with stealing that would be my first thought now. Perhaps I've spent too much time thinking about the law now, or not enough back then. Anyway, the point was never the ball itself, those were always more or less the same — perhaps a better band at one, or shorter bar queues at another, but the same basic blueprint every

time. No, the point was the breaking in: the thrill of beating the security teams, and getting away with it. The high of that was worth far more than the illicitly obtained alcohol.

The night I met Seb the target was Linacre Ball. Linacre isn't the richest Oxford college, and it isn't the largest; there was no reason to think the ball would be particularly good. The only distinguishing feature was that Linacre is a graduate college: right there lay the challenge. Them against us, graduates against undergraduates, security team against students. Drunken students at that, due to the pre-ball-crashing council-of-war at one of the student houses that lay across the sports field from Linacre, where cheap wine was flowing freely. I remember going to the toilet and tripping on my high heels; I'd have crashed headlong into a wall if it hadn't been for unknown hands catching and righting me. It occurred to me then that we'd better go before we were all too smashed to cross the field, let alone scale the walls surrounding the college.

And then we *were* going, streaming out of the new-build house to congregate on the sports field. The darkness was periodically split by flashing lights from the college some two hundred meters away, the grass fleetingly lit too emerald green to be believable

17

whilst the rugby goalposts threw down shadows that stretched the entire length of the field. Someone was giving orders in a military fashion that set Lara off into a fit of giggles as she stumbled and clutched my forearm. I glanced round and realized in surprise that there must be thirty or forty of us ready to storm the college. Lara and I found ourselves split into a subgroup with barely anyone we knew. It was hard to tell in the dark, but at least two of them were men with definite potential. Lara's smile notched up a few watts as she turned her attention to them.

But there wasn't enough time for her to work her magic — we were off. It was sheer numbers that made the plan work. We went in waves, ten or so at a time in a headlong dash across the field — how did we run in stilettos? I cannot think but I know we managed it. Come to that, how did Lara make it across without ripping her skintight dress? Mine ended up hiked high, dangerously close to my crotch. I remember the adrenaline coursing through my veins with the alcohol; the battle cries and the shrieks around me; the fractured picture when the lights flashed of black-tie-clad individuals in full flight. Lara and I huddled at the base of the wall of Linacre College, trying to get

our breath through helpless giggles. That was probably why we got in: the security team were too busy dealing with the first bunch that surged the wall. I lost track of Lara as we awkwardly climbed the wall, hopelessly hindered by utterly inappropriate clothing and footwear. As I reached the top a hand stretched down from broad shoulders to help me. I caught a glimpse of gleaming white teeth beneath a remarkably hooked nose, topped by wayward dark hair. I grasped the proffered hand and felt myself yanked unceremoniously upright just as the lights flared, leaving me temporarily blinded, blinking awkwardly on the top of the wall as I tried to thank my helper and regain my footing and eyesight.

"Jump!" someone called below, barely audible above the music. "I'll catch you."

I looked across at the stranger on the wall with me. He nodded, gesturing to the black-tie-clad individual below. As the lights flashed obligingly I looked down into a pair of spectacular blue eyes: Seb. Of course it was Seb.

I jumped. He caught me.

Halfway through the meeting with Mr. Gordon Farrow, senior partner at Haft & Weil, when he rearranges his papers for the

umpteenth time and continues to gaze a little to the right of me, I realize I'm losing this piece of business. Shortly after that, whilst trying to explain the relative merits of choosing my firm over more established competitors, I realize I never had a chance in the first place. I'm the stalking horse: a competitor brought in to make sure the firm they really want puts in an honest and fair quote. I wind down mid-sentence and snag an oatmeal cookie instead. It takes Mr. Gordon Farrow a moment or two to notice. For the first time, he looks at me properly.

"Is there something wrong?" he asks.

I hold up a finger as I finish chewing my bite of cookie. He waits patiently, his eyebrows raised inquiringly. "Not really," I say when I've swallowed. "Only I just realized I'm wasting your time and mine, since you've already made up your mind. I appreciate you need a stalking horse, but if that's the case I'd sooner eat your cookies and drink tea than knock myself out trying to pitch for unavailable business."

A gleam of appreciation shows in his eyes. He's nondescript in every respect: mid-height, mid-gray in his hair, neither fat nor thin, not obviously fit but not particularly out of shape for a man in his mid-fifties. He wears well-tailored suits, but nothing flashy

or unusual. I've heard the only exceptional thing about him is his intellect, though he's yet to show me much of that. "Do you always speak your mind?" he asks after a moment or two. It doesn't escape me that he hasn't refuted my stalking horse claim.

"Less and less as I grow older," I say, smiling a little. "It's a high-risk strategy. Many of the best things that have happened to me came about because of it, but . . ." I grimace. "Many of the worst things also . . ."

He actually smiles at this. "What would you consider one of the best things to happen to you?"

I answer without hesitation. "Getting into Oxford."

He cocks his head, his eyes gleaming again. "How so?"

"I don't have the typical Oxbridge background. Getting into Oxford really opened up my horizons. I don't mean just in terms of job prospects — it showed me paths and possibilities I could never have believed achievable if I followed a different route."

"My daughter was at Oxford," he says. "I wonder if she would say the same."

"I suppose that might depend on her background. And her personality."

He shrugs with a wry smile. "Caro falls

into the category of typical Oxbridge candidate."

I blink. "Not Caro Horridge?" But of course not Caro Horridge; his surname is Farrow —

"Yes," he says, surprised. "You know her?"

"We were at Oxford at the same time."

Suddenly I have the full force of his attention; it's a little unnerving. "And do you think Caro would say getting into Oxford was one of the best things to happen to her?"

Caro would never consider the question; Caro would view entry into Oxford as right and proper, exactly what she was due. "Well," I hedge, "we weren't particularly close."

His lips quirk. "No longer pursuing the high-risk strategy?"

I laugh. "Like I said, less and less as I get older."

The corners of his mouth tug upward, then he glances at his watch. "Well, Miss Channing, I know someone as direct as you will forgive me for cutting to the chase. You *are* the stalking horse. I like your business, I like the pitch book you sent through and your fees are ballpark, but you'd be a hard prospect to sell to committee, as you don't have a proven track record yet. I'm not sure

it's worth my while to have that fight."

"What would make it worthwhile? A reduction in fees?"

He purses his lips. "It would help, but even that might not be enough. You just —"

"Don't have the track record," I finish for him.

He nods ruefully. "But I can honestly say it's been a real pleasure." His eyes are smiling; it takes ten years off him. I can't see the slightest resemblance to Caro.

In the cab on the way home I record my post-meeting notes on my pocket Dictaphone for Julie to type up later and then I call Lara and rant for five minutes about how I was an idiot to give up my lucrative job to start my own firm, how aforementioned firm will be bankrupt in six months at this rate, how no one will ever hire me again after such an appalling error of judgment, and so on and so forth . . . Lara has heard it all before. She doesn't even bother arguing back.

"Finished now?" she asks when I finally run out of steam.

"For now. Come round tonight — I'll probably bore you with more of the same, but I promise to at least treat you to a curry and some nice wine first." A giggle with the ever-sunny Lara is exactly what I need.

"Sorry," she says, yawning. "I'm knack-ered. Can we do tomorrow instead?"

"Knackered . . . What were you up to last night?" I couldn't remember her saying she had a date, but Lara picks up men like the rest of us pick up newspapers. She puts them down in the same way, too. She is and always has been unrelentingly and unasham-edly promiscuous, but somehow in her it seems . . . wholesome.

"I met someone in the pub after work. Just a bit of fun."

"Lucky you," I say, unable to keep the envy out of my voice. I'm not sure I've ever just "met someone in the pub." I can't recall anyone ever approaching me cold. Unless Seb counts.

"Ah, Kate." I can hear the smile in her voice. "Like I keep telling you, you need to drop your standards. Then you'd have as much action as you could wish for."

"Maybe." But I don't think that's it. I scrub up well — I'm tall and fairly slim, I've got good hair and I've been told I've got beautiful eyes — but none of that quite has the appeal of a buxom beauty of Swed-ish descent with an easy smile and a relaxed attitude to sex.

"Your place tomorrow, then?" Lara asks.

"Perfect." I'm about to ring off when I

remember I still haven't told her about the body. About Severine. "Wait — Tom called me."

"How is he? Is he back in London?"

"Yes, actually, but that isn't why he called. They found . . ." I swallow. "They found the body. I mean, Severine. They found her in the well at the farmhouse," I finish in a rush.

"Oh God," Lara says bleakly. "That's horrible. Though maybe it will help her parents get closure or something. Do they think it was that boyfriend she was talking about?"

"I suppose so." It's an obvious question, but I hadn't considered how she got into the well. Who put her there. Even now, my mind shies away from it. "I don't know. Tom says the French police want to talk to us all again."

I can almost hear Lara's grimace. "Really?"

"It's probably just procedure; after all, we were the last people to talk with her properly." Before she went into town and was never seen again. "She must have gone back, though, since she was found in the well; I suppose that's new information."

"Still, it must have been that boyfriend, surely. I don't mean to be insensitive, but I really hope it doesn't take up much time.

25

We're soooo busy at work right now." She yawns down the line again. "I suppose that explains why Caro's been trying to get hold of me."

"You too?" That's a surprise: if anything, Caro likes Lara even less than me. "She left me a message; I haven't called back yet. But she must have known Tom would tell us; she can't have been calling about that."

"Only one way to find out." She yawns. "Shotgun: you first," she adds impishly.

"All right," I say reluctantly. "I'll call her." I don't want to talk to Caro any more than Lara does, but I may as well find out what she wants sooner rather than later. If Caro wants something, she won't be deterred.

CHAPTER TWO

Severine hovers.

At first she is no more than a feeling, a presence that rests on my consciousness just out of reach of my field of vision. I put it down to the unwanted memories that have floated to the surface of my mind, stirred up by the discovery of her bones. But that is not enough for Severine. One morning I find those very bones, bleached white and neatly stacked in a pile with the grinning skull atop, resting on my kitchen counter; blinking does not remove them, though I know they're not there. On yet other occasions she manifests in a fleshed-out version of walnut-colored skin, secretive eyes and a superior lack of smile. With her comes an insistent tide of memories, fetid and dank after being buried for so long, that will drag me down into their rotten darkness if I yield to them. I trenchantly refuse to succumb; instead I call Caro.

"Caroline Horridge," she answers crisply, after only one ring. I imagine her sitting at her desk in Haft & Weil, her taut frame wrapped in a business suit, with not a hair or a sheet of paper out of place.

"Hi, Caro, it's Kate." There's a pause. "Kate Channing," I add through gritted teeth. This is a classic Caro strategy, forcing me to identify myself; can she really be expecting a call from another Kate with a strong northern accent?

"Oh, *Kate,*" she says, faux-warmly. "God, it's been so long. Thanks for calling back."

"No problem." I can feel my cheeks aching from my fake smile. Someone once told me if you smile on the phone, the caller hears it in your voice; apparently it doesn't matter if the smile is genuine or not. I'm not going to deliberately antagonize the daughter of a man who could hand me a major contract. Any accidental antagonizing can't be helped. "How are you?"

"Good," she says breezily. "Though busy. Which I can't really complain about in this market. You?"

"Same. Good. Busy." Not as busy as I'd like, which is evident when I glance at my computer screen and see my sparse diary for the week, but she doesn't need to know that.

There's a pause. I wait for her to get to the heart of the matter. "I take it Tom's spoken to you?"

"Yes. Not exactly the sunniest of news." My smile has dropped. The skull with yawning darkness for eyes is still waiting for me, just a step beyond conscious thought.

"Do you mean about Jenna or that girl?" I take a sharp breath in — is she really suggesting that murder and a broken engagement are on a par? — but Caro is still talking. "It was always just a matter of time on the girl — surely no one was expecting a different outcome —"

"Severine," I say bluntly. The bones demand to be named. I wish they would make their demands on someone else.

"What?"

"Her name was Severine." Not even a minute into the conversation and already I'm getting testy. I paste on the fake smile again.

"Yes." Caro pauses. "Well, anyway, the reason I called was that I thought it might be nice to have some kind of reunion for Tom. He must be feeling pretty low after the whole Jenna thing — getting the Oxford crowd back together and having a few 'welcome home' drinks might be just the ticket. I'm thinking next Friday, at my flat.

29

We can always go on from there to some-where on the King's Road if everyone feels up for a big night."

"Um, that's a nice idea," I say faintly. It is. I'm frankly astonished.

"Don't sound so surprised," she says dryly. "After all, I practically grew up with Tom and Seb. I can't wait to have them both back in London."

"Both? Seb too?" The words are out of my mouth before I can clamp down on them.

"Oh, you haven't heard?" I can certainly hear the smile in *her* voice — a thoroughly self-satisfied one. If she was fishing to find out if Seb and I are in touch, she's made her catch. "Seb is coming back. New York doesn't suit Alina, apparently." Alina. His wife of perhaps three years now. "Though he won't be back in time for Friday. We'll just have to do another get-together when he's back."

"Sure. Lovely." I'm absolutely positive I will be busy that evening, whenever it is.

"So you'll come? Next Friday?"

"Let me check." I flick through my elec-tronic diary, though I already know I'm free. Maybe it works like the fake smile. "Um, yes, that should be fine. Thanks."

"Great. Can you do me a favor and tell

Lara? I haven't managed to get through to her yet. No doubt you two are still thick as thieves."

"Oh, thicker," I say blandly, then hurry on before she can interpret that as mockery. Which it may be. "I'll tell her."

"Great. I'll e-mail you my address. See you next Friday."

I hang up and gaze blankly for a moment at my computer screen with that under-endowed calendar. It could be that Caro is simply being nice, with no hidden agenda. Lara will think that, when I tell her. But Lara lives in a world where sunshine is always just around the corner: a lovely idea, like Santa Claus and the tooth fairy, but requiring of a certain willing suspension of disbelief to maintain. I was born more suspicious.

Severine hovers.

The day of Caro's drinks party two things happen. Haft & Weil call me — or more specifically, Mr. Gordon Farrow's secretary calls me — and the police call me.

Gordon Farrow's secretary is calling to set up lunch for Tuesday, which makes absolutely no sense unless the firm he really wants have somehow dropped the ball. I spend the day refusing to get excited be-

cause it will all come to naught whilst also meticulously planning my sales pitch. It's an exercise in believing two mutually exclusive ideas; it's exhausting.

In comparison the call from the police is much less disturbing, at least in immediate terms. A French detective will be making the short hop across the English Channel next week and would like to interview me; would I be available? I eye the paltry diary again: far too much white space into which I can imagine Severine sauntering, stretching out each slim brown arm to take as her right. Other than Tuesday's lunch and a few other meetings in relation to two small contracts I've landed, I'm available. I'm depressingly, continuously available, and nothing I achieve all day changes that. By the time the end of business hours rolls round, I'm quite partial to the idea of a drink.

Tom, Lara and I have agreed to meet beforehand at a bar near Caro's place. Safety in numbers and all that. I come in from the rain, shaking off my umbrella, and scan the crowded room for Tom. It's easy to spot his tall figure at the bar, ordering; he must have just got there himself as raindrops still glisten like tiny crystals in his dark hair, which is once again too long and starting to

curl. He used to look more like Seb, I think. Or perhaps I deliberately dissociate them now.

"Make mine a vodka tonic," I say, slipping into a space next to him.

He turns from the barman, a grin already splitting his face. "Kate!" He pulls me in for a proper hug; none of the nonsense of London double-kisses for Tom. It's something I know yet am always surprised by — he gives really good hugs. I can feel the beaming smile on my own face as he wraps me up. This smile is genuine.

"It is so good to see you," I say into his neck. He smells of a mix of wood and spice.

"You too," he says, pulling back to look at me. His grin hasn't abated yet. The freckles aren't there anymore, and neither is the tan, and I think he may have been hitting the gym a lot lately, but otherwise he's reassuringly the same. "You look really well."

"Ten sixty," interrupts the barman impatiently, plonking the vodka tonic down beside Tom's beer.

"Jesus," mutters Tom, pulling out his wallet. "London prices double every time I come back."

"Then never leave again, for the sake of my bank balance if nothing else." Still smiling, I scoop up my drink. "I'll hunt down a

table. Lara's running late, by the way."

It's too crowded to get a table all to ourselves, but I find us two free seats at the corner of the bar, and we do our best to cover almost two years in five minutes, our heads leaned together conspiratorially to combat the noise. Severine can't hold court here, among this warmth and life.

"I'm sorry about Jenna," I offer, after a while. I *am* sorry, even if I didn't think them well suited. "I didn't really get to know her well when we visited you guys, but she seemed . . ." I grope around for the right adjective. Nothing fits. "Like a girl with her head screwed on," I finish lamely. Jenna's cool gray eyes had missed very little, in my opinion. It had been lovely to see Tom again, and Lara and I had both loved Boston, but I rather thought the tight corners around Jenna's eyes hadn't smoothed out until we were well on our way to the airport.

Tom's lips twist briefly, and he spins his pint glass back and forth in the cradle of his long fingers. "She wasn't on top form when you two came over. She really is a nice girl, it's just . . ." He trails off.

"I know. Lara is a lot to take."

He looks up from his beer, startled. "Lara?"

"Well, she's a difficult proposition for any girlfriend to cope with. Even supposing your boyfriend hasn't slept with her," I add dryly. Does he imagine I didn't notice him and Jenna during that visit, in secluded corridors and corners, standing too close and speaking low and fast to each other? I can see them now, Jenna's right hand making sharp, flat gestures while Tom's ran through his hair in frustration. "Or maybe you didn't tell Jenna about that." Tom and Lara's affair, dalliance, whatever one should call it, happened a long time ago — during that fateful French holiday — and Lara always maintained it was nothing but fun. Tom said the same, though I wondered if there was more to it for him. After Jenna's coolness during our Boston visit, I wondered even more. Wives and girlfriends always know.

"I did tell her actually, and anyway, Lara really wasn't the problem," he says, a touch irritably, then blows out a breath slowly. "It doesn't matter anyway. We just weren't . . . right. I couldn't see us together in fifty years. I realized I couldn't imagine what that would look like. Soon after that, going to the gym got more appealing than going home."

"Fifty years," I say caustically. "I'd settle for knowing what the next six months is go-

ing to look like. Or even tonight." I grimace and knock back some more of my drink.

"Don't look like that," Tom says, laughing. "Caro will be on best behavior. The gracious host and so on."

"Mmm," I say noncommittally. "Oh, I wanted to ask you, how come Caro has a different surname than her dad? I know her parents are divorced, but still . . ."

"Well, it was pretty acrimonious." He takes a swallow of his beer and looks to one side, remembering. "From what I recall, Gordon had an affair, and Camilla — Caro's mum — did *not* take it well. Hell hath no fury, et cetera . . . though hers was a very passionless type of fury." He frowns, trying to find the right words. "Like she wasn't so much angry with Gordon for cheating on her as angry with him for disrupting her perfect life. Anyway, Caro took her mum's side. She must have been about thirteen at the time. She officially changed her surname to her mum's maiden name, though to be fair, I imagine her mum put her up to it." His lips twist ruefully. "I always felt sorry for Gordon, to be honest. If I was married to Camilla, I expect I'd've been having an affair a darn sight sooner than Gordon."

"She's difficult?"

"Not exactly difficult." He shrugs, trying to find the right word. "She's *cold*. And nothing is ever good enough for her. Caro's got the same sharp tongue, but at least she can have a laugh." He glances at me, one eyebrow raised, as if waiting for me to make a snide comment, but I don't, partly because what he says is true — Caro can indeed have a laugh; even I have to admit she can be wickedly funny — but also because I didn't know any of this before. It adjusts the picture somewhat. "Well, anyway, it was a tough time for Caro. That's when Seb and I" — he glances at me quickly — "started spending a lot more time with her; I think she just wanted any excuse to get out of the house."

Seb. Tom usually avoids that name with me; tricky since they are not only best friends but also cousins, but nonetheless he tries. I keep my face expressionless. "Is her dad still with whoever he had the affair with?"

Tom shakes his head. "No. Caro refused to see him if he was still seeing her, so he stopped." I absorb that for a moment: the child laying down the law to her father. There's a reason children are not supposed to have that kind of power; I wonder how that felt, for both of them. But Tom is still

37

speaking: "You know, now I wonder if her mum put her up to that, too. My parents seemed to think it was a crying shame, that Gordon and this woman would have been very happy together. But Caro was adamant, so . . ." He shrugs. "That was that."

"Interesting that she works at his firm."

"Yeah, I didn't really know what to make of that when I heard she'd joined Haft & Weil." He is frowning, still trying to puzzle it out. "It's not like she didn't have other offers, either." He finishes his beer with one swallow, then eyes the empty glass. "Time for another? How late is Lara going to be?"

"She should be — ah, here she is." I start waving to catch Lara's attention as she scans the bar from the doorway. Half of the bar is scanning her in return. As she spots us, her open smile breaks out and she heads our way.

"Tom," she says, hugging him warmly. "Look at you! Do you have a job anymore or do you just lift weights?"

He laughs and climbs off his bar stool to offer it to her. "You're one to talk, looking gorgeous as ever."

"I'm at least six pounds overweight. But since it all seems to be residing in my boobs I can't really be bothered to do anything about it," she says complacently, perching

her bottom on the proffered bar stool.

"How is it that you've only been in the bar thirty seconds and already we're talking about your boobs?" teases Tom. I'm used to their easy, affectionate flirting, but suddenly I'm more alert to it. The context has changed: Tom is single. I'm not uneasy, exactly, but it would change the dynamic if they were to become a couple. I like things how they are.

"Well then, how about a much more macabre subject: did you guys get a call from the police today?" Lara asks, and immediately Severine reaches through time to tug me back. She sinks with studied elegance into a chair by the farmhouse pool, dressed in a loose black linen shift, and crosses one leg over the other; after the slim brown calf comes a slender foot, complete with shell-pink-painted toes from which a sandal casually dangles. Seb can't take his eyes off that sandal.

I knock back the remains of my vodka tonic and wrench myself into the present. Tom is nodding. "About interviews next week? Yeah, I did."

"Me too. Though I don't know what help we can be a decade on." I add, almost defiantly, "I can hardly remember a thing."

"Me either," says Lara. "I wonder if it will

be the same one." She has an odd look on her face.

"Same what?" I ask, confused.

"Same detective. Only they don't call them that in France, do they? Investigator. Officer of judiciary police, or whatever the phrase is."

"I shouldn't think so," says Tom dismissively. "Wasn't he about sixty? He'll have retired."

"You two have finished your drinks," Lara says, in a sudden change of gear. "Can I get us all another?"

I shake my head, grimacing. "Shouldn't we really screw our courage to the sticking place and venture forth?"

"Macbeth? Isn't that a little dramatic?" protests Tom, but he's laughing. "It'll be fine. Especially since you two are going to behave impeccably." He fixes us both with a mock-glare that lingers longer, and with more steel, on me than Lara.

"Such blind optimism," Lara says, fluttering her eyelids in a deliberately over-the-top fashion. "A man after my own heart."

I wonder.

Caro's flat smells of vanilla. Later I track the source to a number of expensive candles dotted around the space, the sort that have

three wicks and cost more than a boozy restaurant meal for two. The enticing smell, the cozy lighting and the welcome warmth of the flat after the driving rain outside add up to give a Christmassy feel even though it's March. Caro has a couple of teenage girls with heavy eyeliner answering the door, taking coats and pouring champagne. It's all exceedingly grown-up.

There are perhaps twenty-five people already there when we arrive. At a quick glance I know a few, and there are others I recognize but can't put a name to; all from Oxford days. I spy Caro across the room, wearing a severe black minidress and truly lethal black suede ankle boots, with her dark blond hair scraped back from her face. Skinny, blond, self-assured and possessing of a delicate bone structure that screams English aristocracy: posh totty. I almost drowned in an army of girls just like her at Oxford before I learned how to swim in a big pond. It's important to kick.

"Relax, Kate," says Tom quietly, amused.

I exaggerate taking in a deep breath and letting it out slowly. His blue eyes, similar to Seb's but flecked with gray, are crinkled at the corners at my theatrics.

Caro breaks off a conversation when she spots our entry and crosses to us quickly,

zeroing in on Tom with a delighted smile spreading across her face. She's even thinner than I remember, and older, of course — we all are — but for Caro the extra years have gnawed away any softness. Now she appears brittle. I try to imagine the thirteen-year-old girl that she once was, taking refuge in her friendships with Tom and Seb, but I can't form an image in my mind. Still, Tom's words drift around me; they herd me into a corner where I can't help but feel that my dislike of Caro reflects badly on me. Surely I *ought* to like her: she's a strong, smart, ambitious woman who is working very hard in what is still a heavily male-dominated workplace; she's sharp and cleverly funny, and moreover, Tom likes her, which has to count for rather a lot . . . and yet . . . and yet . . . She's *too* sharp. She cuts. Or at least, she used to.

"Tom! The guest of honor!" she is saying, as she kisses him on both cheeks; Tom doesn't try to hug her, I note. Then Caro turns to Lara and myself; Lara gets the double-kiss treatment first. "It's been so long," Caro exclaims to her. "You look . . . just the same." Lara murmurs back something innocuous.

"Hi, Caro." I'm last in line. I dutifully offer my cheeks; the spiked heels on her boots

almost raise her up to my height. There's no contact in either kiss.

"Kate," she says, her lips curving in a smile that her eyes don't entirely match. "I hear you met my father."

"Um, yes." I'm a little surprised she would choose to lead with that. "I think we're meeting again next week, actually."

Her eyes narrow a fraction, but she nods emphatically and says, "Excellent. I told him weeks ago that he wouldn't regret giving you a chance."

"Thank you," I say, thrown. "That was . . . kind of you." At least, it would have been kind if it were true. I'm absolutely positive she's lying. Her father would have already known about our acquaintance had she spoken to him.

"It's nothing," she says with a dismissive gesture. "It can't be easy starting up your own business in this economic climate. Now, you all have drinks, yes? Then come join the melee." She links her arm through Tom's and drags him off; I watch her stretch up with a sly smile on her face to deliver something to his ear that elicits a sharp bark of laughter. He's soon ensconced in vigorous hellos complete with enthusiastic back-thumping with three or four men whose faces I vaguely remember, but not their

physiques; ten years has done a lot of damage to hairlines and waistlines.

Lara and I sip champagne. We mingle and chat. By and large the faces I don't know are the other halves of people I do. Some more people come in, and the music moves on to a more upbeat tempo. The volume of the chatter and laughter increases. We drink more champagne and do some damage to the trays of nibbles. I take in the flat: a property like this must be hideously expensive in this part of London. I wonder if her father helped her buy it, and if he did, I wonder at the dynamic of refusing his name but taking his financial aid.

Caro joins us. "I'm so sorry I haven't had a chance to chat with you two. But you know what it's like at your own parties — you hardly get time for more than a hello with each person before you're dragged off." She rolls her eyes as if it's a chore, but she's in her element. The gracious host indeed.

"Great turnout," says Lara, raising her glass to Caro.

"It is, isn't it?" She has a satisfied smile on her face as she scans the room. Then she turns back to us. "Sorry to speak of unpleasant things, but I expect you both have meetings with the French investigator next week, too?"

"Yes, Monday," I say.

"It was such a long time ago, I wondered if we should discuss beforehand. Make sure we're all singing from the same song sheet, so to speak."

Lara opens her mouth, most likely to agree because it's the path of least resistance, so I jump in quickly. "What's to discuss? She was alive and well the night before we left, and that's the last we saw of her."

Caro is nodding. "True. Then she went into town." She frowns. "Odd that she came back to her cottage when she told Theo she was going to Paris."

"Did she?" I didn't know that.

"When did she say that?" asked Lara.

"The night before we left, I think. Theo had a long chat with her." I remember that: I see the pair of them now, lying on their backs in the dark of nighttime on sun loungers beside the pool. Severine has a glass of white wine resting on her stomach, and the red glow of a cigarette makes a repeated arc up to her mouth then down to dangle off the armrest. She's still in the black linen shift, but her sandals are now tossed carelessly beside the sun lounger. I don't want to look at Seb in case he's drinking in the sight of her; instead I watch Sev-

erine myself. After a time she turns her head to look at me directly; it's too dark and she's too far away to see the expression in her eyes. Not that there was ever anything to see in Severine's eyes.

I shake my head. Caro is still talking: "I just thought, well, maybe we should all compare notes . . . After all, I can barely remember that last night, what with the alcohol." She gives a high, tinkling laugh.

"And the drugs," I say evenly. Her laugh stops, and she cocks her head and meets my eye. Lara is looking from Caro to me and back again. Across the room I can see Tom repeatedly glancing away from his conversation to keep tabs on the three of us; he's easy to spot on account of his height and that bold nose. And his shoulders, now, after all that relationship-avoiding gym work; he must be even bulkier than Seb these days. "It's okay," I say after a moment. "I didn't mention it back then, and I won't now."

Caro nods, a short, quick movement. It's not exactly a thank-you, but close.

"It was a pretty crazy night," says Lara, smiling.

"Yes," laughs Caro, happy to move on. "Didn't you end up skinny-dipping with Tom?"

46

Lara is grinning. "I seem to remember something like that. Then World War Three broke out and we were trying to calm everyone down whilst naked and dripping wet." She frowns. "I can't remember, what were you guys arguing about anyway?" she says with wide-eyed innocence. I glance at her sharply, then look at Caro. Twin spots of red are burning in her cheeks.

Suddenly Tom appears at my elbow waving an empty bottle of champagne. "Caro, are there any more of these?"

"Oh, crates of them, literally. Let me sort that." She grabs the bottle gratefully and disappears quickly through the crowd.

Tom turns a stern eye on Lara and me. "Didn't I tell you guys to behave?" he says, running a hand through his hair in exasperation.

"You want *us* to behave?" asks Lara archly. "Caro's the one who wants to airbrush our response to the police to make sure there's no mention of drug-taking. You might be happy to forget that she smuggled Class A drugs through customs in Kate's bag, but I don't think I ever will. And nor will Kate." I can't stop a smile spreading across my face: this is so unexpectedly combative of my easygoing best friend, and in that moment I love her fiercely for it. It

47

seems I was wrong: where Caro is concerned, even Lara is naturally suspicious.

"I haven't forgotten," says Tom quietly. "If you remember, I was furious with her. But you don't have to rub her nose in it now. It was a long time ago and she did apologize."

"Not until the next day," I mutter mutinously, temporarily forgetting my previous inclination to a generosity of spirit toward Caro. "And as far as apologies go, it was distinctly underwhelming." Her so-called apology had been accepted as it was offered: with no charm at all, and under clear duress.

"You really want to go into all that again right now?" asks Tom. He is glaring at me with an expression I can't quite interpret. Suddenly the exasperation melts away, and he tilts his head. I'm close enough to see the gray flecks in his eyes. "Come on, Kate, let's not dredge up the past," he says softly.

I breathe out slowly. He's right. I've no desire to let those particular memories out of their box; though they seem to be seeping out regardless. I find a smile and clink my glass against Tom's. "To the present."

"And to Tom," says Lara, clinking her glass against Tom's also. She smiles winningly at him. "Nice to have the voice of reason back." Tom shakes his head and smiles back, then glances round the room.

The crowd is thinning out; I glance at my watch and am surprised to see it's past 1 A.M.

"Come on," he says. "Let me escort you two home."

We get a cab together. It makes geographical sense to drop me off first; I hug them both good-bye and climb out, then watch the taxi disappear. In my mind I replay the scene of them intervening with Seb, Caro and myself, in the glory of their birthday suits. Lara's impressive frontage jiggles hypnotically until Theo throws a towel round her, discomfort making his cheeks as red as his hair. When Tom works out what's happened, he rounds on Caro; I've never seen Tom angry, and it's majestic. I'm surprised she can remain upright in the face of such a biting onslaught. Lara is open-mouthed in awe, but I'm too full of hurt and acid fury and cheap wine to truly appreciate the display. Mostly hurt, because Seb thinks I'm overreacting. His lack of support is a physical blow; it literally takes my breath and speech away. The shock of it strips away all my defenses and forces me to face the truth: it's over.

At the time amidst the mayhem I barely noticed Severine, but now she has my attention. She sits casually to one side, observ-

ing detachedly as she calmly finishes a cigarette, then collects her sandals and walks unhurriedly to her cottage, leaving the chaos behind. I stumble alone to the bedroom Seb and I should be sharing, tears streaming down my cheeks. Six months, even two months, previously he would have followed me, but no longer.

Back in the present, I'm also going to bed alone. Seb is presumably in bed somewhere with his wife, give or take a time difference impact. Who knows what Caro's sleeping arrangements are? Theo — well, Theo is dead. Severine, too, though death seems to hold her too loosely as far as I'm concerned. And Tom and Lara are together in a taxi.

CHAPTER THREE

Monday morning. I'm immersed in Excel spreadsheets, surveying the health, or lack thereof, of my company, when Gordon Farrow rings. The pleasantries don't take long, but he *is* pleasant, and genuine. A decent man. Even without Tom's damning account of Caro's mother, if Caro is the average of Gordon and his ex-wife, I have no desire to meet the ex-wife.

"So who's on your list, Kate?" asks Gordon. We've moved on to first-name terms. He means who would I target for the open positions at his firm; I've been prepping for exactly this question, only I'm a little thrown to be answering it on the phone on Monday rather than at lunch on Tuesday. Still, I move smoothly into my "here's-one-I-prepared-earlier" answer, and we bat back and forth on that for a few minutes.

Paul enters the office we share as I'm talking, loosening his silk tie as he sinks into

the chair behind his desk. His blond eyebrows, so pale as to be not worth having, rise as he listens to my half of the conversation while drinking his take-out coffee. "Haft & Weil?" he mouths.

I nod, then my attention is fully caught by Gordon's next comment, stated with such deliberate casualness that it's clear this is what he's been waiting to talk about all along. "You haven't mentioned Dominic Burns."

"Not Dominic," I say instantly. It's an instinctive response — I should have prevaricated, I should have given myself time to find out if Gordon is hell-bent on hiring this man, but it's too late for that now. Across the room Paul is choking on his coffee.

"Why not Dominic?" asks Gordon diffidently. "He's a prime candidate, with his experience. And I hear he's looking to move; he wants to head up a meaningful business area with the right support to really make a dent into private equity clients."

"Do you have any plans to retire, Gordon?" I ask. "In the next, say, five years?" Paul's eyes almost pop out. He makes urgent gestures.

"I'm not following you," says Gordon, after a moment.

"Dominic Burns doesn't want a job heading up a business area. He wants *your* job. Managing partner."

"He doesn't have that kind of experience," Gordon objects.

"Not yet. But he's aggressively ambitious, and after a couple of years at Haft & Weil, he'll start to feel he deserves a shot. Which is fine if you're looking for someone to hand the reins to. But if not, he'll go looking for a firm where he can get the opportunity he *really* wants. You'll have him in place for three years tops." Paul is standing now in obvious agitation. His frantic hand-waving may be interpreted as ordering me to stop talking or to immediately slit my throat. I ignore him and continue: "When he jumps ship he'll take all your lovely new clients with him, and probably a host of your up-and-coming juniors, too." I give Paul a one-fingered gesture of my own, which isn't open to any misinterpretation, then spin my chair to face away. I like Gordon. I don't want to see him make the wrong hire. "And you'll be back at square one."

There's silence down the phone line for a long moment, then Gordon says, "You sound like you know him well."

"I do, actually. I worked under him for a while at Clifford Chance."

"Interesting. Well, that's certainly food for thought, Kate."

I put down the phone and spin round to find Paul looming over my desk, almost incoherent with frustration. "What are you doing?" he groans, one hand clutching his head. "The first rule of service industries: give the client what they want. The man wants to hire Dominic Burns, so tell him you'll get him Dominic Burns. It's a no-brainer!"

"It's the wrong hire," I argue. "He needs to know that."

"No! He doesn't! He needs to hire him, and pay us a whacking great check!" I can't deny a whacking great check would be helpful. Paul sees my weakness and presses on. "Kate, we need this, and you've just blown it. Why the hell would you torpedo it? If he's got his mind set on someone, then we get them. It's as simple as that."

"He'll respect us more for giving him honest, open feedback," I fire back, stung by his "blown it" comment. Though of course he may be right. "We don't need this so badly that I'm going to forget how to do a good job."

"If we don't get a big contract soon, you won't be doing any job." He lets out a long breath.

"We're fine." I spin the computer screen to show him what I've been looking at. He perches on the desk and leans in to run his eye down the figures. "See, the small stuff is going to tide us over. We've got time, and we're obviously building a name or Haft & Weil wouldn't even be talking to us."

"The small stuff keeps the lights on and the printer running," he says dismally. "It doesn't, you know, *pay* us. Which I've got to say, I'm quite attached to, as a concept." He runs a hand through his hair. I realize he looks tired. It doesn't sit well on his fair skin. "I don't think I'm going to land the Freshfields guy."

"Ah."

"Ah indeed." He sighs and climbs off the edge of the desk, then turns back to me. "Haft & Weil are going to cancel the lunch, you know."

"They won't." It's only dogged bravura that forces me to disagree with him. Nobody calls for an in-depth strategy session if they intend to keep a lunch date the following day.

"You'll see," Paul says wearily.

That afternoon Gordon Farrow's secretary calls me: not to cancel, but to postpone due to "Mr. Farrow's travel commitments." Paul wisely says nothing.

Monday evening finds me back at my flat unusually early for the appointment with Mr. Modan. Actually *Monsieur* Alain Modan, *Investigateur, OPJ* — whatever that stands for. Basically the French detective. He would have met me at my office if I'd preferred, but I'd rather Julie and Paul not know about this. *Helping the police with their inquiries* could end up sounding like a euphemism for something more sinister after a few Chinese whispers, and who wants to hire a legal recruiter that's in trouble with the law?

"Thank you for seeing me," he says as we settle into my living room.

"It wasn't clear to me I had the option to refuse." I smile to lessen the sting.

He is rummaging through his bag and looks up at my words, his long, intelligent face already pulled into a half-ironic smile. There are deep smile lines framing his mobile mouth, and a slim-fitting dark gray suit hangs on his too-lanky, too-thin frame; somehow the sum of the parts is an unexpectedly attractive man. I can't possibly imagine a British detective in the same mold. "There is always the option, *non?*" he

says, his accent unmistakable. "Though I would not think it the wisest choice." The smile flashes again, then he returns to his bag. I watch as he finds his notepad and flicks through the pages.

"Tea? Coffee?" I make the offer once the silence has grown uncomfortably long from my point of view. In truth I want a glass of wine, but not one that comes with Modan's interrogation.

"No, thank you," he says without looking up. Finally he turns his dark eyes on me. "I'm sorry, this is very inconvenient for you, but please, a few questions. You probably answered the same ten years ago, but it's . . . how you say . . . procedure." He spreads his hands wide, palms up, with a Gallic shrug, inviting me to sympathize: *Procedure. What can you do, eh?*

"It was a very long time ago," I say steadily. "I doubt I can add anything. Probably the opposite — I expect I've forgotten so much that I'll confuse things for you."

He shrugs again. "Well, let's see. Yes?"

"Yes. Of course, go ahead." He's here now, in the country and in my living room. Of course he's going to ask his questions. Of course I'll have to answer them. And all the time Severine will be waiting for her chance to appear. I had thought she would fade

57

away after a few days, once I'd got over the shock, but no. Severine has more staying power than I anticipated.

"*Bon,* so you left the farmhouse on Saturday the sixteenth, yes?"

"Yes."

"All six of you?"

"Yes, all six of us." Six on the vacation. Really four plus two, but not the two I'd expected. I'd imagined it would be Seb and me, plus a selection of our friends. It turned out to be Lara and me, plus Seb and his friends.

"You drove back to London?"

I nod. "In my car." We'd planned to use Seb's father's BMW, but there had been some problem, I can't remember what. The others had been extremely rude about my ancient little banger until it turned out it was the only vehicle we could get hold of.

"Ah yes. In your" — he checks his notes — "Vauxhall Nova." He checks again. "Really?" He looks at me doubtfully. "Six of you? That would be very . . . squished."

"Four of us. Theo and Tom took the train back together; I dropped them at the station that morning, then went back for the others."

"Ah, Theo." He pronounces it the French way: *Tay-o.* "Afghanistan, yes? Very sad."

His long face does indeed hold sympathy; whether genuine or not, I can't tell. I expect he's very good at his job.

"Yes. Very sad." It is sad, and senseless and a waste and a whole lot of other things I can't possibly put into words, but even if I could, it wouldn't change the outcome. Theo is dead.

"He was very patriotic?"

"I'm sorry?"

"He loved his country very much? He always wanted to be a soldier, to fight for her?"

I rub my forehead. "No, I don't think . . . We were all quite surprised when he enlisted." Theo hadn't seemed the type. Too nervous, too self-conscious. The army seemed to me like a grown-up version of a boys' boarding school; Theo had hated boarding school. I shake my head abruptly. "I'm sorry, what has this got to do with —"

He puts out a placating palm. The man has an elegant gesture for everything. "Forgive me, forgive me. We must return to the point. What time did you leave the farmhouse?"

I try to remember. I must have dropped Theo and Tom at the train station before nine, I think. The rest of us had planned to be on the road by nine thirty, but Caro

59

wasn't ready. One more reason to be furious with Caro — not that I needed another reason that morning, after the revelations of the previous night. "Erm, perhaps ten thirty?"

He nods and makes a note. "Were you the driver?"

"Yes. I was the only one insured."

"You drove all the way back? You didn't share?" His surprise is clear.

I remember the journey, although I don't want to. The car lacked air-conditioning; I was hot and tired and tight-lipped with hurt and resentment. Caro sat in the back, uncharacteristically pale and quiet; I wondered if she was suffering in the aftermath of the drugs and thought savagely that it would serve her right. Lara was golden and sleek, full of catlike satisfaction after a few days of frolicking with Tom; she slept almost all the way. And Seb . . . I don't want to think about Seb. I swallow. "Like I said, I was the only one insured."

His lips twist and he makes another note. "*Bon,* so, a Vauxhall Nova. Were there any other automobiles at the property?"

"No. We just used my car." My mobile rings: Lara. "Sorry," I say, quickly turning it off. I can call her later; I want to get this over with.

"You're sure? Nothing in the garage?"

"Well, there was an old Jag that belonged to Theo's father, but we never touched it. No one was allowed to drive it." The farmhouse belonged to Theo's parents back then; they sold it later, after Theo died.

He is nodding; he obviously knows about the Jaguar. "Did you see Miss Dupas on the morning of departure?"

"No." I can feel my muscles tensing, as if anticipating an impact.

"The day before, perhaps?"

"Yes." My answers are brief, clipped.

"Was that . . . habitual?" The word choice is odd; perhaps he has translated directly from the French. "Did she pass much time with you during the week?"

I nod again. He assesses me with his dark eyes and sits silently, waiting for more. I sigh: monosyllabic responses are not going to get me through this interview. "Theo's family and hers were on quite friendly terms. Both families had been spending most of the summer down there for years. Severine's parents' place didn't have a pool, but Theo's parents let them use theirs whenever they wanted."

Severine has appeared, swept in on the flow of words. She's facing away from me on the steps of the pool in a black bikini,

knee-deep in the cool water, her narrow back perfectly straight. Seb, Lara, Caro and I have just arrived, and Theo, who arrived earlier, is showing us round; the unexpected sight of a girl in the pool draws us all up short. "Severine!" exclaims Theo, bounding toward her. "I didn't expect to see you." She turns her head and regards us all, then climbs out of the pool to treble-kiss him hello, apparently completely unselfconscious despite her scant attire. I find it hard to look away. The narrowness of her hips is a marvel; her belly is flat yet soft, like a child's. Her shoulders and arms shimmer with the sheen of sunscreen. "Theo," she says solemnly, her English heavily accented. "I did not know I would be here, either." She looks at the rest of us, weighing and measuring. "I am Severine," she says. "The mademoiselle next door."

"You saw her every day?" asks Alain Modan. I'm grateful for the question; it dissolves Severine's presence.

"Yes. She would come to the pool, and often she would eat dinner with us."

He nods. "How was she?" I look at him blankly. He snaps his fingers repeatedly, frustrated with himself as he tries to find the right words. "Her . . . emotions, her . . . temperament, how was she?"

"Well, she was . . ." I stop, trying to find the right words myself. "She was a very . . . self-contained girl. If there was anything bothering her I wouldn't have known."

"Was she closer to one than another? Perhaps she spent more time with Theo, since they already knew each other?"

"No, not Theo." He looks up sharply from his notebook at my tone and raises his eyebrows. "I mean, not with anyone specifically," I add quickly.

His eyebrows have not quite descended fully, and his eyes remain on me. I work hard to hold his gaze and I don't think of Seb.

After a moment he gives a minute shrug and looks at his notebook again. "Did she speak about her plans for after she left the Dordogne?"

"Not with me. Though Caro said that she told Theo she was heading back to Paris."

He cocks his head to one side. "Caroline Horridge? She said that?"

I nod. "The other night."

He is making notes again, in his little book. His handwriting is like tiny spiders multiplying across the page. "So. The well. There was — how do you say, workings? — going on?"

"Building works." It's a relief to move on

to something less personal. "Theo's parents wanted to rent the place out. They needed a few things done to comply with the safety regulations."

Modan is nodding. "*Oui.* A fence round the pool. And the well filled in."

"Probably." I shrug. "I remember the builders doing the pool fence." Suddenly the significance of what he's saying hits me. "Oh. The well. She . . . God, she must have been in there before they filled the well." The skull appears, but it's no longer gleaming. Sand fills the eye sockets and spills out of the grinning mouth. I find my hand is at my mouth and carefully remove it to descend to my lap. "Is that why you didn't find her? I mean, till now?"

"We didn't find her because we were looking in the wrong place," he says simply. His eyes are fixed on me again. I can't fathom his expression.

"Do you think it was her boyfriend? Ex-boyfriend, I mean?"

"We're looking at all possibilities —"

"Yes, but you must be looking pretty hard at him in particular," I say impatiently, suddenly fed up with the one-sided nature of this interview, even though that's how interviews are meant to be. "There was a history, right? Severine said she'd had to

call the police about him before."

"There's no record of that." He's looking at me as if he's waiting for something.

I pause. "No record?" Severine lied. Why would she lie about that? — but I instantly know the answer. To appear more mysterious, more alluring. The kind of woman a man would literally go insane for.

"None," says Alain Modan calmly. "And the ex-boyfriend, he was doing a science project, some very intense work for his thesis. He was in the laboratory every day in June, even weekends, attending to his cultures or some such . . ." His hand waves expressively. "So." He is still watching, waiting for me to catch on to something. I shake my head dumbly. He tries again. "So . . . unless the well was not filled in until July —"

The doorbell buzzes, cutting him off. He cocks his head questioningly at me. I shrug then raise myself up from the sofa to go and answer, and find that I'm stiff. I've been sitting unnaturally still for a very long time now.

I know it's Lara before I open up; I can hear her rustling in her bag for the spare key she keeps. "Lara, the detective is here," I say quickly as I unlatch the door, forestalling her greeting.

She looks past me, alarmed, as if she can see through the hall walls to the living room. "I thought that was tomorrow," she whispers urgently.

"No, today. You may as well come and say hello."

"But I don't . . . I'm not . . . But . . ." I look at her, puzzled, then she takes a deep breath and smooths her dress. "Okay." She comes in, taking a quick glance at herself in the hallway mirror before she follows me into the living room.

Mr. Modan has climbed to his feet and is looking out of the window. He turns as he hears us enter the room, and his face goes oddly still. Before I have a chance to say a few words of polite introduction, Lara speaks up from behind me. "It's you."

I glance at her, not understanding the words or her tone. Her cheeks are flushed, and she's half turned to the door, as if she still might flee. The French investigator could be a statue. I'm not completely sure he's breathing. Then with an effort, he comes alive and shoots the cuffs of his suit before crossing the room to shake her hand. "Yes. Alain Modan."

"Lara Petersson," she says quietly. "But of course you know that."

I look from one to the other. *I wonder if it*

will be the same one? She wasn't talking about the lead investigator. "I take it I've been very rude and failed to remember you from the earlier investigation," I say dryly to Alain Modan.

He turns to me with a quick smile and raises a hand as if to say, *No matter.* "It was a long time ago. I was very junior, one of many assisting." He looks back at Lara, then away quickly. Then he collects himself. "Miss Channing, you have a guest. We can continue another time, if I have more questions."

"Oh. Okay. Fine." If I'd known having a guest would roust him, I'd have arranged for an interruption long before this, I think sourly. Except I wouldn't have, really. Better to get these things over and done with.

He turns to Lara. "*À demain,* Miss Petersson." *Until tomorrow.*

"*Oui, à demain,*" she says, then follows up with something too quick for me to catch. I forgot Lara's French was rather impressive; she's one of those irritating Scandinavians with umpteen languages to their credit.

When I've closed the door on Monsieur Alain Modan, *investigateur,* I follow Lara to the kitchen and find her already pulling a bottle of white wine from my fridge and studiously avoiding my eye.

"What was that all about?"

She pours two glasses. Very large glasses. She seems to be giving the task more attention than it deserves. "Nothing. What do you mean?"

"Don't give me that. Did you and he . . . ?"

"No!" She looks up, appalled. "Of course not!" I hold her gaze until she breaks and takes a sip of her wine.

I reach out for my own glass and take a sip, still watching her. She's avoiding my eyes again. "Lara," I say warningly.

"Oh, all right!" She folds, like I knew she would, and finally looks up. "Nothing happened, truly. He, um . . ." She takes another sip of wine, then says in a rush, "He wouldn't. He said it wouldn't be proper. Appropriate, I mean. Under the circumstances." She's blushing, more furiously than I've ever seen before.

"Oh my God," I say wonderingly, a smile breaking out slowly on my face. "He's that mythical creature. The one that got away from Lara Petersson."

"He's not . . . It's not . . . Oh, fuck off," she says, screwing up her nose prettily. She takes an unfeasibly long drink from her glass, then looks at me dejectedly. "Only it's still not appropriate, right? Not until he clears us from the investigation. And then

68

he'll be back in France."

"I can't believe you never told me any of this." I'm not hurt; I'm just amazed that I missed this.

She ducks her head apologetically. "Well, like I said, nothing happened. And you and Seb had just split up, and you know what a state that left you in. I didn't want to dump my crap on you . . ."

For once the mention of Seb slides by almost unnoticed; I'm too thrown by this revelation. What else did I miss when I was licking my Seb-inflicted wounds? She takes in another large slug of wine, and I gaze at her in bemusement. Not only did the rejection matter to her then, it clearly still matters now. This is a Lara I haven't seen before.

And then I think, *Poor Tom.*

I dream of Severine, among others.

She has no right to be in my dreams, but that would never have stopped Severine. I'm back at the farmhouse, of course, and I'm trying to find something, or someone, but what? Who? I stick my head in the rooms, some empty, some not; some of the occupants weren't even part of that fateful vacation, but somehow I'm not surprised to see them. I keep looking. Caro is alone in the kitchen; she's wearing a white bikini top and a red chiffon sarong, and she looks up then laughs at me when I pass through. I realize I'm clad in jeans and a heavy-duty winter jumper, but I know I've nothing else to wear. Severine is smoking in the garden. She tells me something very seriously, but I don't listen; in fact I'm picking up speed, running to the barn. The jumper is uncomfortably hot. I throw open the barn door, then catch my breath when I find Seb there.

He's wearing long beach shorts that are slung low on his hips. His hair is lighter than Tom's, almost golden at the tips, and curlier; his muscular bare chest is tanned, and dark, springy hair makes a trail down his abdomen — a fully-fledged man whereas his peers are still leaving boyhood. Just like Caro he looks me up and down with those blue eyes that could be Tom's, then laughs. It's not a kind laugh.

The dream doesn't fade when I wake; it presses on my temples and adds to the throbbing left by one too many glasses of wine with Lara. Getting out of bed — in fact, all of what the day requires — seems a supreme effort, but then I imagine Paul and Julie at the office wondering where I am, and that provides the necessary impetus. By the time Tom calls my mobile that afternoon, the headache has dulled but the effort remains.

"How was it?" he asks. I can hear a very particular hubbub in the background: sharp orders and staccato words in the male register. He's on the trading floor at his bank; Tom trades interest rate derivatives. I'm on Oxford Street myself, en route to meet a prospective client; I expect my own background noise is equally loud.

"How was what? Please tell me you're not

rigging the markets while chatting to me."

He laughs. "No, I have people to do that for me now. And for the benefit of the recorded line: that was a *joke*. Anyway, I meant how was the thing with the French detective."

"Pretty awful actually." I look around, then back at the map in my hand. New Bond Street is a big street. It can't have disappeared.

"How so?" he asks cautiously.

"It's . . . well, I don't really want to think about what might have happened to her." I don't really want to think about her at all. I look around again. There's a disappointing lack of street name signs. "Jesus, where is this place?" I mutter. I spy something that might be a sign and march in that direction.

"Lost?" asks Tom, amused. "Where's your legendary sense of direction?"

"Lara drowned it in wine last night. It's her turn with the detective today, actually."

"Yeah, I know, I spoke to her this morning," he says easily. I stop walking. Lara must have given him her number. "It's tomorrow for me. Listen, I have to jump. I've got a dicey option expiry approaching, but I was wondering if you fancy coming down to Hampshire for Sunday lunch. My

folks would love to see you."

"Um, sure. I don't think I have anything on. Sounds lovely." Which it does — I've met his parents half a dozen times over the years, though never at their home; his dad is charmingly eccentric and his mum is lovely. "Is Lara coming, too? — oh, she's in Sweden this weekend, I forgot."

"Yeah, she's away." He already knows what her weekend plans are. "I'll drive us down. I'll call you on Saturday to figure out timings." I hear someone calling his name in the background. "Yeah, just coming," he calls back, then to me, "Speak Saturday."

"Saturday." I pocket my phone and look around again. New Bond Street is right there, where it's always been. I still have a headache.

Sunday. Tom turns up at ten thirty in something retro, white and low-slung that he's visibly excited by. Cars mean nothing to me, but Seb would be envious, I think, then I shut down that train of thought.

"Am I supposed to be in awe?" I ask Tom teasingly.

"The salesman promised me the mere sight would make women drop their knickers," he deadpans.

"I would, but it's a bit chilly today and I

don't fancy a draft up my skirt." I walk around the car. Even to the uninitiated, it's a very cool car. "How old is it?"

"Considerably older than both of us. It's a Toyota 2000GT; well, mostly. Some of the parts have been replaced, which reduces the value." The sun makes a brief appearance, bouncing off the immaculate white paint-work. "I picked it up this morning." He can't keep the smile off his face as he talks. It's infectious. He reaches out a long arm and opens the passenger door, waggling his eyebrows suggestively. "Can I take you for a ride, Miss Channing?"

I laugh and fold myself into the seat. "I thought you'd never ask."

The seat is uncomfortable and the heating intermittent, but the sun comes out and stays out. That, and the car, and Tom's mood have me giddy for the first half hour, which carries us through the London traffic. When the roads open up and the car settles into a steady thrum through increasingly green countryside, our chatter tails off into comfortable silence.

"Do you want some music?" asks Tom, glancing across at me. His lips are tugging upward at the corners; I wait for the punch line. "Cos if so, you'd better start singing — the radio doesn't work."

"Will you get one fitted?"

He shrugs. "I don't know. It would reduce the value, but I didn't buy this purely as an investment, otherwise I wouldn't even be driving it." His eyes crinkle at the corners. "I've always wanted this car."

"A psychologist would have a field day with that. Given the timing and all."

"They'd probably be right to," he admits, with a sheepish grin. "I'm basically driving the deposit I'd saved for a house with Jenna."

I can't help laughing. He doesn't join in, but he's grinning.

"You've been lucky settling back into London," I comment. "Back in your old flat, back on your old desk at work, except a few rungs up the ladder . . . Did you think about staying in Boston?"

He shakes his head. "Boston is a great city. But I never felt . . . settled there. Maybe it was my fault; I didn't properly commit to staying long-term. Once Jenna and I split up, there was nothing to keep me there." The sun is streaming directly through the windscreen; he finds some sunglasses and puts them on one-handed with remarkable dexterity. "What about you? What made you go out on your own? Starting your own business in this climate can't be easy. I don't

remember you even mentioning the idea when you came out to Boston."

I close my eyes and rest my head back against the seat, feeling the sun soak into my face. "Oh, you know me," I say airily. "I'm basically unemployable."

"Rubbish. You have a first from Oxford and the best CV of anyone we know."

"Slight exaggeration, but anyway, I didn't say I was unhirable. I'm unemployable. As in, unsuitable for employment." My eyes are still closed.

"Ah," he says, understanding. "You mean, much better suited to being the employer."

"Exactly." I open my eyes and turn my head, still resting on the headrest, to look at him. I can't see his eyes through the sunglasses, but I know what they look like. Seb doesn't freckle, though. "I got fed up of being overlooked in favor of inferior lawyers who had the right accent and went to the right school." I grimace. "I may have been vocal about it from time to time."

"How can you spot a balanced northerner?" asks Tom. He goes on before I can answer: "They have a chip on *both* their shoulders."

He's teasing me, but I know he understands, at least in part. Tom's whole upbringing has put him on the outside looking

76

in: looking in on Seb, whose father is some kind of nobility — a marquis or a baron or an earl, I forget exactly what — with the stately home and vast grounds one might expect along with such a title. Tom grew up in a cottage on the estate, gifted by the earl-or-marquis-or-baron to his little sister, Tom's mother, when she married a penniless academic.

"Anyway, one day one of the partners told me I was the best candidate for partner he'd ever come across, but if I couldn't learn to shut my mouth and put up with some crap from time to time, there was no way I'd even make the short list. I'd be turfed out."

"What did you say to that?" Tom asks.

"Not much at the time. I was too furious to say anything at all really. But then I thought about it . . . and he was right. There's no way they could make me partner the way I was; it would be like . . . like putting itching powder on everyone's skin."

"And you didn't want to change?"

"I could have changed . . . well, maybe . . . but not for that firm. Too traditional, too old-school. It got me thinking about how important it is to get the right fit when you hire someone. I mean, they should never have hired me in the first place. I expect they were trying to fill some diversity quota:

female, went to a state school . . ."

Tom remains quiet. I close my eyes again and turn my face to the sun. The thrum of the car is soporific. Time becomes elastic; I have no idea how much is passing.

"You never told me much about your meeting with the detective," I hear Tom say.

I open my eyes again reluctantly. I don't want Severine to intrude today. She doesn't belong in the sunshine. "Not much to tell. He just went over the timings of when we left, really."

"Nothing else?" he asks casually.

"No," I say, bemused. I think back to the meeting; it doesn't seem my place to tell him about Lara's fascination with the detective. Though perhaps I should if Tom is going to get hurt . . .

"What?" asks Tom, noticing my hesitation.

"Nothing." I grope around for something to cover with. "Just — well, he said he didn't think it was the boyfriend."

Tom is nodding. "Yeah, Theo's dad told me he's out of the picture."

"Modan was a bit more conditional than that. It seems to hinge on the timing of when the well was filled in, I think." I frown. "But surely they know when that was done."

Tom shakes his head and says carefully, "There's some confusion." He appears to

be intent on the road; with his sunglasses on, I can't read his expression at all.

"How come? Can't they check with the builders?" I can see the two builders in my head: both in their thirties, unmistakably brothers, with the same swarthy complexion, dark hair and heavy eyebrows. I remember watching them watch us; I remember the resentment in their eyes and the sense of unease it put in me. I could see us from their perspective: the careless, awful presumptions of privilege. I wanted to say, "But I'm not one of them!" Only I was, at least for that week.

"Haven't tracked them down again yet. But according to the records that the police looked at then, the well was filled in on the Friday." He glances across at me. Oddly I have the same feeling as with the detective: he is watching me, waiting for something. I shake my head dumbly. He elaborates. "Friday, Kate. The day before we left."

"But that's . . . that's impossible." I'm no longer sleepy. "Severine was with us on Friday night."

"I know that. You know that." He shrugs.

I am upright in my seat now, twisted sideways to stare at Tom's profile. He's calmly focusing on the road ahead. "There's CCTV footage of Severine at the bus depot

on Saturday morning," I argue heatedly. "And the bus driver remembered her getting on at the stop by the farmhouse. So she obviously wasn't, you know, stuffed in a well at that point." The skull is there, with the dirt and the sand and the insects; I shake my head violently. It doesn't dislodge.

"I know, I know." Tom takes a hand off the wheel and spreads it out, palm up. "I'm just saying, there are inconsistencies. Things like that, they muddy the waters. Which could be rather . . . inconvenient for us, until it's all sorted out."

I'm still staring at him. He turns his head and takes in my expression. "Kate," he says gently. "It's going to be fine. I just wanted to bring you up to speed. It will all be fine."

He smiles in what's meant to be a reassuring manner. But I can't see his eyes behind those sunglasses.

Lunch is a pleasure, or should be a pleasure, but I can't shake a sense of unease. It flows beneath every conversation and fills every silence. Tom's parents don't notice — his mother is glowing to have her son at home again, however temporarily, and his dad's gruff welcome belied the delight in his eyes — but Tom's gaze rests on me frequently. I can't read what his eyes hold, which only

adds to my unease. Tom's dad has a heavy hand with the wine; by dessert I'm surreptitiously drinking as much water as possible in mitigation.

"How is your mum, Kate?" asks Tom's mother kindly. "Do you get up north to see her much?"

"She's well, thanks." Tom's mum has her head cocked on one side, listening to me sympathetically. I can see Tom in her. It makes me more open than I might otherwise be; that, or the wine. "She seems happy. She remarried last year. I guess I don't go up now as much as I used to."

"You don't get on with her new husband?"

I shake my head. "No, he's fine." I hear my words and correct them. "He's nice, actually. Dad's been gone a long time." Almost ten years. I got the news only weeks after Seb and I broke up. "It's great to think that she's not on her own anymore. But it's just . . . different, I guess."

Both Tom and his mother are looking at me. I duck my head and take a swallow of wine.

After lunch, Tom's parents won't hear of us helping with the clearing up; instead they shoo us out to walk off our overindulgence on the estate grounds. We climb a small ridge and are suddenly presented with an

uninterrupted view across a lawn to the main house. Seb's house. Well, his father's house.

"You would think —" I say, stopping to stare at the enormous white-painted building. It's from the Regency era, I seem to recall. There are columns and wings and more windows than I could reliably count. I start again. "You would think I would've been here." I look at Tom. He isn't meeting my eye. "Don't you think?" I challenge him. "Wouldn't you think that if you went out with someone for a year, you might see where they live when they're not at college?" Tom doesn't answer. I persist. "Wouldn't you think that?"

"I don't think it was intentional," Tom hedges. "He didn't deliberately *not* invite you."

"Maybe." I find a large rock to sit on. I've had too much to drink. I think of Caro, in France. *Of course, you've met Lord Harcourt, haven't you? Such a dear.* Her sharp eyes watching me, birdlike, readying to swoop in on any tidbits I give away. *You haven't? Really?* "Then again, maybe not."

Tom runs a hand through his hair and sighs. "Look, Seb's relationship with his father is — complicated. I'm sure the lack of invitation had nothing to do with you

82

and everything to do with that."

"Maybe," I repeat. I lean down to pick up some earth and watch it dribble through my fingers. "Maybe not."

"It's been ten years, Kate," Tom says. The hard note in his voice snaps my head up to look at him. "When are you going to get over it?"

I look away; I can't speak. We don't do this, Tom and I; we don't bring up this particular elephant in the room. We can be friends provided we skirt round the edges. I must be drunk to have violated that. I don't think he has the same excuse given he's driving.

Suddenly Tom is hunkered down in front of me. "Kate, I'm sorry." He reaches out a hand to turn my face to him. His eyes are unhappy and his mouth is twisted in remorse. "Oh Christ, please don't cry, I didn't mean . . . It's just . . . I'm sorry."

I take a shaky breath, then meet his eyes briefly and attempt a smile. "Me, too. I think I'm what's known as tired and emotional."

"Come on, you." He stands up and pulls me gently to my feet. "Let's get you home." My face feels cold where his hand has been. He threads my arm through his and we walk

back to the cottage in companionable silence.

In the car on the way home I can't fight the thrum of the engine and the alcohol in my system: I fall asleep. I wake slowly with a memory or a dream of someone stroking my cheek. Tom is grinning at me affectionately. The day of sunshine has brought out some of his freckles. "Wakey wakey, sleeping beauty," he says. For a moment I'm displaced; the world hasn't yet dropped into position around me. For a moment Tom is just Tom and I'm just Kate, without any past or future. Without any context.

Then everything rushes back.

CHAPTER FIVE

On Monday morning, Gordon Farrow's secretary calls to resurrect our lunch, for two days hence. I would crow over Paul except I've lost all faith. In any case, Paul looks like he can't take another cycle of hope-raising and -dashing. A small contract he was counting on — that we were both counting on — has fallen through. His trenchant defeatism curls around him like a fog; being near him brings a chill. I haven't known him long enough to estimate how long this will last; at this rate I may not keep him long enough to find out. I return again and again to the financial spreadsheet that holds my future in its tiny white cells. The entries don't change.

Even lunch with Lara fails as a tonic. We meet at a café halfway between our offices; uncharacteristically, she's beaten me there. There's a glass of wine in front of her with a lipstick mark on it. I nod my head toward

it after we kiss our hellos. "Taking the rest of the day off?" Lara can't function professionally after the merest sniff of alcohol. She has few rules, but no lunchtime drinking is one of them.

She shakes her head. "I'll be there in body if not in mind." She takes a sip of the wine, then puts the glass down. Then picks it up again. "Anyway, shall we order?" She puts the glass back down.

"Sure . . ." We nab the waitress and order our usuals, then I sit back and look at Lara. "Is everything okay?"

"Sure. Of course." She smiles brightly, but it doesn't reach her eyes, and her eyes don't reach mine.

"How was Sweden?"

"Same old. Mum has a new man."

"How is he?"

"Very . . . Swedish," she says wryly. "Bearded. Friendly. Earnest. But kind of sweet." Finally I see her eyes. They're jittering around, as if it hurts to settle her focus. "Anyway, how was your weekend? Did you have fun with Tom?"

"Yeah, it was lovely," I say, out of habit, then wonder if that's accurate. It was lovely on the surface, but I have a sense of something lurking underneath. Or maybe my paranoia over the possibility of Paul jump-

ing ship is bleeding into the rest of my life. I mentally shake myself and look at Lara's eyes again. "Jeez, Lara, did you spend the weekend taking drugs or something?"

"Of course not!" she exclaims, scandalized.

"Then what's with you?"

"Nothing! Except . . . I think I had one too many Red Bulls this morning," she confesses, propping up her temple with the heel of one palm. "You wouldn't believe how my heart has been racing." She gestures at the glass of wine. "Alcohol's a depressant, isn't it? I thought it might counteract the caffeine."

"Honey, alcohol is just fanning the flames." It would be funny except Lara doesn't look like she's having any fun. She looks almost feverish. "Let me put that glass aside — here, have my water instead. Why the caffeine overdose, anyway?"

She takes a long drink of the water and shrugs. "My flight was delayed so I was late to bed and then I couldn't get to sleep for ages." She pauses. I wait; there's more to come. Whatever it is, she's half defensive about it. I'm not sure what the other half of her is feeling. "I bumped into Alain at the airport." Her eyes flit to mine then away.

Alain. Not *Monsieur Modan,* or *the French*

detective. "How very coincidental," I say evenly. "Had you told him what flight you were on?"

"No, it was just a chance meeting. He was on his way back from spending the weekend in the south of France." She takes in my expression and puts her hand on my arm, leaning forward entreatingly. "Come on. You have to admit it really *could* be a co-incidence."

"It could," I say non-contentiously. But I doubt it. "What did you talk about?"

She blushes. "You know . . ." I don't actually. I shake my head questioningly. "We just *talked.* Nothing happened, really." Really? Now I'm wondering what *did* happen. Her hand is still on my arm, her eyes urgent. I nod, though I still don't understand; the nod is enough to allow the words to flood out of her. "I know we ought not, with the investigation and everything, but it's not like the six of us had anything to do with that. Alain and I . . . well, we just talked about . . . what we might do when this is all over. What we would like to do." Her expression is begging me to understand. I shake my head minutely; I don't. "You know . . . to do to each other . . ."

I stare at her, openmouthed. She's squirming, but her eyes are bright with excitement.

It's not the caffeine overdose that's making her feverish; she's the girl with a secret that's just bursting to tell. Jesus. Lara has been talking dirty with the French detective. I rediscover my voice. "All this in, what, the baggage reclaim lounge?"

"Of course not! We, um, we grabbed a drink in the bar."

"Ah." I don't know how to convey the alarm bells that are ringing in my mind. Lara is never this excited over a man, ever; I suspect she won't take it kindly if I steal the wind from her sails, but this . . . I don't know what this is, exactly, but I do know it's not a good idea. I struggle to find a casual tone. "Did he . . . did he ask about Severine?"

She nods. "A bit. Well, not so much Severine, more about that week in general. You know, about all of us, how we met, who was with who, that sort of thing. It wasn't like an interview; it was just idle chat."

"Of course, idle chat. In between the virtual sex, that is."

"Kate!" She giggles. She's actually giddy. "It wasn't like that."

"Uh-huh." Idle chat. About a murder case. I think of Alain Modan. I imagine his active brain working away behind those dark, ironic eyes; scurrying like a rat in a

maze to explore all potential avenues. Tom's words float back to me: *There are inconsistencies. Things like that, they muddy the waters.* "Did he tell you they're looking into when the well was filled in?"

She nods. "He mentioned that. I suppose they have to tick every box, but it seems a waste of effort since it was obviously after we left. But they have to do it. Apparently they even have to try and pin down exactly which ferry we were on so they have confirmation of when we left the farmhouse. It's really hard work for him," she says earnestly, then looks up as the waitress arrives with our plates. "Oh, thank you."

I start eating mechanically, my mind full of Monsieur Modan, and Tom's words, and Severine — always Severine, with her walnut skin and secretive eyes, hovering just out of sight. "Why is he even back in the UK?" I ask suddenly.

"What?" Lara looks up from her salad.

"Modan. I thought he interviewed us all. Why is he still here?"

"Oh. Yeah, he said he had a few more questions."

"For who?"

"For whom," she corrects with a glimmer of a smile. Lara prides herself on having better English than any native-born. "Actu-

ally, for you, I think." She shrugs. "Probably my fault, I suppose; after all, I did interrupt your session with him."

Another interview. I reach for the wineglass.

"And for Seb, of course," she adds, with an apologetic grimace. "Apparently he'll be back in the country this week." She goes on hesitantly, "Are you . . . Are you okay with that? Seb being back, I mean?"

"I daresay I'll cope." It comes out harsher than intended; Lara flinches. I'm instantly remorseful. "I'm sorry, honey, I don't mean to snap; I'm just having a shitty week." She nods sympathetically, accepting the apology. I feel guilty enough to consider her question more carefully. "I actually don't know what I feel. I suppose I spent so long avoiding thinking about him that I'm not sure *what* I think anymore."

She cocks her head. "So maybe it would be good for you to see him."

"Maybe." I take a swallow of the wine. "But in an ideal world, not in a week where my business is going under and I'm being interviewed in connection with a murder."

She laughs. "Come on, that's a little dramatic. We're just helping the investigation; we're not really *suspects.*"

"Well, that depends."

"What do you mean?"

"That depends on when the well was filled in. Or at least, when the police think the well was filled in."

She stares at me. Her eyes have finally found their focus. "You really think — but he hasn't said anything . . ." She trails off, then visibly shakes herself. "But of course the well was sealed after we left. The builders will say that."

"Of course," I agree easily. "When the police find them."

"When they find them," she echoes. She is silent for a moment, then cocks her head and looks at me piercingly. "You think I'm being played."

"I don't know," I admit reluctantly, but honestly. I remember the sudden stillness in Modan's face when he saw Lara again. "I think — I think that he would very much like to do whatever he told you he'd like to do to you . . ." Now I'm the one blushing. "But whatever you said about the six of us — he can't 'unhear' it. You weren't being interviewed, but he'll use it, if it helps him." She looks at me thoughtfully but doesn't say anything. I don't know if she's upset, and if so, with me or Modan. "I'm just saying . . . be careful, honey." I reach out and

touch her arm. "I don't want you to get hurt."

Finally she catches my hand in hers and smiles. "I know. I'll be careful." She changes the subject deliberately, and as we talk, I see that half of her focus is elsewhere: reliving aural sex in a transport hub, perhaps, or dreaming up meetings yet to come; in any case, half her mind is threaded through with *Alain, Alain, Alain.*

I suspect Lara's definition of *careful* won't match mine.

Wednesday dawns bright and sunny, but blustery, with a bite in the wind. It's the kind of day that could go either way. Fitting.

I'm early to the restaurant; the staff haven't quite finished preparing our table. I deposit myself on an uncomfortably low sofa in the entrance area, flicking through a newspaper that was laid out for just this purpose. The economy is not improving, small businesses are going under at an alarming rate. I turn that page quickly.

"Kate?" I look up, my automatic welcome smile pasted on, only this isn't Gordon. It's not even a male voice.

"Caro," I say with unconcealed surprise. I scramble to my feet inelegantly from the

low seat. She's wearing an impeccable dark skirt suit that looks ultra-fashionable and ultra-expensive, and beautiful kitten heels. Her hair is scraped back into a perfect chignon. It's alarming how closely she fits the image I had of her in work attire. We double-kiss, our cheeks barely grazing. "What a surprise. Are you eating here today?" For a confused moment I wonder if Gordon has asked her to join us.

"No, I was just stalking you," she says breezily, then grins impishly at my expression. "Relax. I was just passing — this place is a stone's throw from our office." This is true; it's why Gordon's a fan of the restaurant. "I spotted you through the window. How are you?"

"Um, good, thanks. You?" I'm still thrown. She spotted me, and she actually *chose* to come in and talk to me?

She flaps a hand. "Good, busy — you know, same old, same old." She pauses. "How did it go with the detective?"

"Fine," I say, shrugging. "Though we got interrupted so I'm meeting him again this week."

"What a bore for you," she says, rolling her eyes theatrically. "What sort of things was he asking?"

"Much the same as he asked everyone, I

suppose. When we left, how we got home, that sort of thing. You?"

She nods quickly. Too quickly. "Yes, that sort of thing. Lots on everyone's timings that last morning. And about the builders and the well and when the girl was planning to leave." Her head is cocked on one side, watching and waiting. I wonder exactly which of her words she's expecting a reaction to.

"Severine," I say quietly. "Her name was Severine." The skull grins knowingly at me.

"God, you do have a bee in your bonnet about that." Caro sounds amused, but somehow I don't think she is. "Did he show you the CCTV footage?"

I shake my head. "No, what footage? Do you mean Severine at the bus station?"

She nods. "It's a joke," she says, throwing up a hand expressively. "You can barely tell it's a person. Technology has moved a looooong way in the last decade, believe me. Thank God the bus driver remembered her getting on his bus, or things might be rather more uncomfortable for us all right now." She laughs a high, tinkling laugh, much less genuine than her earlier sly grin. I think of breaking glass.

"Caro," says a mild voice behind her. Gordon has arrived.

"Dad," she says, turning to him. This time the smile she pulls on is overly bright. "Don't worry, I'm not stealing your lunch date." He rubs her arm awkwardly in lieu of a kiss; perhaps they never kiss during the working day. I suppose it would be a little disconcerting for others around the office.

"Hello, Gordon," I say, smiling. We shake hands and tell each other it's a pleasure and so on. Which it actually is, at least for me.

Caro explains to her father: "I just popped in to tell Kate that we have a date for Seb's return." I feel a quick burst of triumph that I knew this already. She turns to me. "He'll be back this week, so we'll have to have another get-together of the old gang. Maybe a restaurant this time. What do you think?"

I'm on my best behavior given Gordon's presence. "Good idea." Then I look for something intelligent to add. "Less people, which might be better for Alina. Less overwhelming."

"Oh, I wouldn't worry about that," Caro says, unconcerned. It's not clear whether she means that Alina, whom I've never met, is not easily overwhelmed, or whether Caro simply doesn't care whether she's overwhelmed or not. "I just thought it'd be a nice change since we just did the drinks party thing for Tom." She glances at her

watch and grimaces. "Oops, back to the grindstone. I have a conference call in five, which may well last till five — no rest for the wicked." She rolls her eyes again. "Enjoy your lunch."

I look at Gordon as he watches her clip smartly out of the restaurant; perhaps I'm expecting to see love or pride or benevolent affection. Instead he seems . . . what? I can't decipher his face, though he watches for longer than feels comfortable. Then he feels my eyes upon him and turns with eyebrows raised. "Well, shall we?"

We order and eat and talk business, but general business, not the specific business I'm chasing. Other firms and their hiring practices, the restructuring taking place in the legal industry, the mergers that are being rumored: these are the things we discuss. I wait for Gordon to broach the subject, but our main courses swoop down, and then dessert, and then coffee, and still we're circling around.

Gordon reaches for the sugar and drops a cube into his cup, paying the task more attention than it deserves. Now, I think. Now we will come to the matter at hand.

"So," he says. He's too precise for such a casual opening; it comes out strained. "I

understand from Caro that you, too, have been dragged into this awful French investigation. It must be rather unpleasant for you."

I blink, completely thrown. Why is he bringing this up? "Well, I . . . Of course I'm happy to help the investigation, but rest assured, it would have no impact on my company's ability to perform under the contract, if we were to be engaged —"

"Oh no," he interrupts me, startled. "I didn't mean — I didn't think that for a second."

I look at him uncertainly. He seems a little embarrassed.

"Caro seems rather shaken by the whole thing," he says diffidently. "I just meant to . . . well, to ask how *you* are. That's all."

"Oh." I watch him stirring his already-stirred coffee, then realize I ought to say something more. "Well, that's very kind of you." Before I can add something appropriately inane, like *I'm fine, though it's certainly unsettling,* before I can reassert my professionalism without seeming callous in comparison to the "rather shaken" Caro (really?), Severine's skull begins to laugh mockingly at me, sand streaming from one eye socket. I hastily grab my coffee cup and take a sip.

"On to business, then," says Gordon. He seems as keen to move on from this little interlude as I am.

I agree quickly. "Yes, on to business." Business I can do. Business is what I need.

I take the tube back from lunch. The stark white spreadsheet cells have been telling me that cabs are not advisable at present. In any case, I like the anonymity of London's crowded public transport system; it gives me space to think. All these people thrown into a confined space, yet nobody feels a need to talk. Or to ask questions.

Gordon has been asking me many questions; it's exhausting. When I get back to the office, Paul will ask what Gordon asked me. Alain Modan has been asking me different questions, and apparently he's going to keep asking. Caro has been asking me what Modan has been asking. Now I come to think of it, even Tom has been probing me about what Modan is asking.

Severine doesn't ask questions. Those dark, unreflective eyes made their judgment a decade ago.

Chapter Six

I'm staring at the spreadsheet again. The once-clinical black numbers have developed their own presence; they cross the divide between my eyes and the computer screen and beat malevolently into my brain. Two small alterations were all that was required for the verdict to go from "solvent, for now" to "completely underwater": a change in tax law that means a hefty payment cannot be deferred, and my landlord demanding an increase in rent, which he's entitled to do at this point in the lease, though the size of the increase he's asking for is outrageous. I can fight him on it, I *will* fight him on it — or at least, I *want* to fight him on it, but that will cost money the business doesn't have. He probably suspects this and is trying to squeeze me out. With more detachment I might admire his Machiavellian streak, but right now admiration is not high on my list of feelings. Ditto detachment.

I drop my head into my hands to escape the spreadsheet's toxic radiation. I could move the business location somewhere cheaper — my living room, say, or perhaps somewhere more extreme, like Croydon or Thailand — but not whilst keeping Paul, and without headhunters, is there really any life in a headhunting firm? It was a key part of my business plan that I not be a one-woman shop: numbers inspire confidence. Though not the ones in this spreadsheet.

"You okay, Kate?" asks Julie, as she comes in from the outer office.

I lift my head quickly and paste on a smile for her. She has her glasses in one hand and is pinching the bridge of her nose with the other. I wonder why she doesn't wear contact lenses, but not enough to ask. "Fine," I say brightly, probably too brightly. "Just a headache from too much screen time."

"I'm popping out for a sandwich. Want me to grab you anything?"

"No, thanks, I'll get something later and give my legs a stretch."

"Okay." She glances across at Paul's empty desk, frowns briefly, then turns to go.

"Julie, what's Paul's schedule today?" I ask casually.

She turns back. "I'm not sure," she says

awkwardly. "I thought he'd be here now."

"Mmmm." I tap my teeth with a pen, then realize she's still there, unsure of whether to leave or not. "No worries." I adopt a re-assuringly cheerful tone. There's an empti-ness in my stomach; it's growing and hard-ening. "I'll give him a call. Go on and get your lunch."

"All right."

All right. All right. No, nothing much is *all right,* but I have to go on as if it is. I sigh and lift the phone to vehemently threaten my landlord with legal action I can't afford.

Alain Modan. Monsieur Modan. French detective, *Investigateur, OPJ* — and whis-perer of naughty things in the perfect ear of my best friend, Lara. Alain Modan is sitting on a sofa opposite me once again, though this time we're in a comfortable corner of Starbucks rather than my living room.

I have little patience today. I can feel it inside me; there's a recklessness bubbling up around the malignant tumor of worry about my business, a recklessness that's pushing me to want to cut through bullshit, to tell and hear it straight, to face the worst and know what I'm up against *right now.* Alain Modan is probably the last person I should be talking to in this mental condi-

tion, but I am here and so is he; we have our coffees and we've covered the pleasantries — with no mention of Lara — so now we begin.

"Alors," says Modan, placing a manila folder on the table and flipping through his pad. He's removed the jacket of his suit; underneath is a slim-fitting pale blue shirt. I wonder if the skin under that shirt has the same soft grain as that on his face; I wonder if there is a tangle of chest hair under that spotless cotton. Perhaps it's his French flair that makes me consider these things, or perhaps I'm trying to see through Lara's eyes. Perhaps both.

Modan's eyes have moved from his pad to my face. I force myself to focus. "I should bring you up to speed, *non?*" He sounds pleased with himself for the figure of speech.

I glance at the folder. In films, folders like this one — this size, this shape, this color — always hold photos, gruesome murder scenes frozen in an instant of time. Bodies at awkward angles; blood pooled beneath caved heads; open, staring eyes: death immortalized forever. I don't want to see inside this folder. "Go ahead," I say shortly.

"You are in a hurry?" he asks, his mouth quirking.

"Not especially, but I do have a business

to run." I almost laugh as I hear the words from my mouth, though it's not in the least bit funny.

He nods. "Of course. Well, we have found one of the builders, Monsieur Casteau. He has gone through his paperwork, which states that the well was filled in on the Friday. The day before you left."

"Bullshit."

He looks at me. "Excuse me?"

"Bull. Shit," I say clearly. "You have six" — I shake my head abruptly: *Theo.* Not six, not ever again six — "no, five people who can attest to that. The builders did the pool fence while we were there, but I don't remember them anywhere near the well. The paperwork is wrong and the builder is lying." The recklessness is spilling over; I struggle to stamp it down.

Modan is not fazed by my combativeness. "It was a long time ago," he allows. "And Monsieur Casteau thinks it was his brother who actually did the work on the well; he can't remember doing it himself."

"And what does the brother say?"

"We haven't been able to speak with him yet. He's on" — he stretches for the word — "ah, *miel,* ah, honey . . . moon. Honeymoon, *oui?*" I nod. "Trekking. In the Himalayas." He makes a movement with his

mouth that shows that yomping through the Himalayas is not his idea of a post-wedding treat.

The folder lies there still, untouched. "Regardless. You have five people who say the well wasn't filled in. Why are you spending time on this?"

One eyebrow raises a little. "It's our job to be thorough."

I press on. "What about the bus driver? He remembers Severine, right?"

He looks at me, his long face displaying nothing except his habitual watchfulness. "The bus driver remembers that a young girl climbed on near the farmhouse and traveled to the station. He described her as wearing dark sunglasses and having her hair tied in a red scarf."

I see Severine, smoking a cigarette at the end of the garden whilst speaking rapidly on the phone. It's morning; there's still a freshness in the air that the sun will beat into submission within an hour or so. Severine's dressed in her uncompromising black bikini, a red chiffon scarf tied turban-like on her head; her back is to me, and I can see the delicate wings of her shoulder blades moving under her skin as she gestures with her cigarette hand. It's a look that's reminiscent of the 1950s, of glamorous movie stars

in oversize sunglasses lounging on the French Riviera. At that moment I wish she was gone with an intensity I don't understand; more than that, I wish she had never been. But today, to Modan I murmur, "Yes. Severine."

He shrugs, a curiously nonsymmetrical movement that suggests his limbs are moved by a puppet-master. It should be awkward, but not so on Modan. "Perhaps."

I look at him sharply. "Perhaps?"

He shrugs again, right shoulder then left. "Perhaps."

"And the CCTV from the bus depot?"

He reaches for the folder and holds it out to me. "*Regardez-vous.* Please, look."

I force myself to breathe as I take the folder from him and slowly open it. Inside there is indeed a photo: a grainy image, not so much black-and-white as shades of gray. In among what must be the bus depot forecourt, I can make out a figure that is most likely a slender girl, perhaps with her hair tied under a scarf or perhaps wearing some kind of cap. She appears to be standing by a large bag. I look up at Modan, dismayed. "This is it?"

He raises a couple of fingers briefly, somehow conveying *we really tried* and *c'est la vie* in one small movement. "That is the

best picture we could get."

I look back again at the photo. Caro may have exaggerated a little — it's definitely a person — but her point is still valid: this counts for nothing. I keep looking, as if it's a digital image that needs time to resolve, but the fuzzy edges refuse to settle into a clear picture. All the while my mind loops over the same cycle: the well, the bus driver, the CCTV image. The well, the bus driver, the CCTV image. *One of these things is not like the other . . . the well, the bus driver, the CCTV image . . . one of these things . . .*

I thrust the folder back at Modan. "Why are you still here?" I ask him abruptly.

"I have a few more questions —"

"Yes, but why are you still *here*? As in, in this country?" I interrupt impatiently. "I know you have to be thorough. You've *been* thorough, you've spoken to us all, so what's keeping you here? You have five people who saw her alive on Friday night, you have a bus driver who had someone exactly like her climbing on his bus on Saturday, you have a picture of that same girl at the depot with a bag; it all points pretty clearly to her being alive and well after we left." The recklessness has its head and won't be quieted. "But you're still here, and I can't figure it out, unless you're looking for an

excuse to spend more time jeopardizing your career by ambushing Lara in airports" — he looks away quickly and rakes a hand through his hair, then fixes wary eyes upon me, but I won't be derailed — "or unless you actually don't believe us. Is that it? Do you actually believe that all five of us are lying? Are we in fact suspects?" I stop abruptly. The recklessness is spent.

Modan looks at me for a moment, his face expressionless. I have no doubt he is busy working out how best to handle me. Then his face softens. "Miss Channing," he says gently. "This is difficult. It is always difficult, murder is . . . *alors,* murder is not a nice thing. No one wants to think about it too hard; it's upsetting, it's intrusive, it is frustrating, it is inconvenient. But to find whoever did this, we have to investigate, we *have* to ask questions." He makes one of his elegant hand gestures, spreading his hand wide with the palm up, almost as if inviting me to place my own in it, while his lips move in a sympathetic smile. "So . . . *s'il vous plaît* . . . may I continue?"

I hold his gaze for a moment. I can't read what is going on behind those dark, watchful eyes, but I know he's better at this than me. Better at this than almost everyone, I would think. I'm suddenly exhausted. "Go

on," I say wearily. "Ask your questions."

Afterward I know I should go back to the office, but I can't face the possibility of an empty chair opposite me, or staring again at that spreadsheet. Instead I wander aimlessly. A short walk takes me into the throngs on Regent Street. The gaggles of foreign tourists are easy to identify, with their cameras and white socks pulled up and sensible shoes, but what is everyone else doing on a shopping street in the middle of the day? Are they students? Or do they work nights? Do they work at all?

I wonder what I will do when I finally call time on my company. I won't be able to go back to practicing law: I'm not sure I'd be able to convince any firm that I really wanted to — mainly because I don't. I suppose I could work for another legal recruitment firm, but my credibility will be damaged by a failed solo venture; it might take quite a while to land any position, let alone one I really want. And the truth is that the one I want is the one that's slipping away from me right now.

I walk into French Connection then walk back out again. It's too busy, and anyway, I don't really have the will or the patience to look at clothes or try anything on. I start

walking again and see my reflection moving from one window display to the next, a wraith in a dark trouser suit slipping unnoticed past the mannequins in their forward-thinking summer attire. I could just . . . leave, I think. Get on a plane, find myself somewhere hot and dusty where living costs a pittance. Slough off my skin and take a waitressing job, or tend bar — take any job, unfettered by the pride and expectations that are built up by an Oxbridge education; built up until they wall you in.

My mobile phone rings; number withheld. I hesitate, unwilling to be wrenched back into the real world, but the phone continues to chirp aggressively. I sigh and hit the answer button. "Kate Channing."

"Hey, it's Tom. How are you?"

"Halfway to South America."

There's half a beat of silence. "Really?" he asks uncertainly.

"No, not really. Just wishful thinking. Bad day."

"Well, in that case I'm taking the spot on the plane next to you. Bad day here too." He does in fact sound exhausted. "Want to grab a drink later and commiserate?"

I hesitate. "I'll be dreadful company," I warn.

"Yeah, me too," he says grimly. "We might

110

as well get smashed together rather than poisoning the mood of anyone else."

"Jesus." This is a far cry from the easy, steadfast Tom I'm used to. "What happened to you today?"

"Can't talk here," he says laconically.

He can't talk in the office. Intuition strikes me: all those articles about the poor economy and downsizing in the major banks . . . Surely his firm wouldn't have been so stupid as to agree to relocate him from Boston to London just to fire him? Except I know banks can be exactly that stupid, and more so. "You still have a job, right?" I ask urgently.

"I do. Others . . . not so much."

"Jesus." The atmosphere must be awful on the trading floor. "Well, my company is well and truly fucked so I'm just the girl for a truly depressing night on the town. Seven at the same pub we met at before?"

"Done." He pauses. "Is it really fucked?"

"Yes," I say baldly. "Only a miracle will suffice at this point."

I hear a sigh down the phone. "I'm really sorry, Kate." His words are heartfelt; I feel a rush of warmth toward him.

"I know. I am, too. About your situation, I mean." About my own, too.

"Well, at least one of us still has a pay-

check," he says with dark humor. "Which means I'm buying tonight. I can keep you fed and watered for one night, at least."

"No argument from me. See you at seven."

I disconnect then look up to see my ghostly self hovering in front of a swimwear montage, a smile still in place from the phone call that fades as I watch. The promise of a new life, a different life, still lies tantalizingly in reach. But I have things to do before I meet Tom at seven.

I head back to my office.

I don't look at the spreadsheet and I don't look at Paul's empty chair. Instead I deal with e-mail and bash on determinedly with the calls I have to make. It's not so much a fighting spirit as a grim fatalism that drives me on: the few contracts we do have, we need to deliver on — on time and in style. Nobody should be able to say Channing Associates failed through a lack of professionalism.

"I've got Gordon from Haft & Weil on the phone for you," calls Julie.

For a moment I consider telling her to take a message. I've been expecting a call from him, to tell me he's awarding the contract to a rival firm. I could do without the final nail in the coffin . . . but why delay

the inevitable? "Put him through, please."

The phone in front of me buzzes after a moment. I find a smile to drape on my lips. "Good afternoon, Gordon. How are you?"

"Very well, thank you. Is this a good time?"

"Absolutely. Fire away." *Fire away.* Not that he can really fire me since he's never actually hired me, but still, the inadvertent gallows humor amuses me. I will tell Tom that later, I think. I can already see his eyes crinkling above that unmistakable nose.

"I want to tell you that OpCom met last night." OpCom is the operating committee of Haft & Weil. Whatever recommendation of recruitment firm Gordon made would have had to be ratified by them, but really as a rubber-stamping exercise. "We've decided to award the contract to Channing Associates." He pauses, but I'm literally speechless. "Subject to agreeing final documentation, of course."

I sit bolt upright and find my voice. "Well. Thank you." I work hard to sound professional, as if contracts from firms like Haft & Weil drop in my lap every day, but inside the tumor of worry has begun to fizz, dissolving like Alka-Seltzer in water. *Yes! Yes! Yes!* "That's wonderful news. I'm . . . well, I'm delighted to hear that, as I'm sure you

113

can imagine. Delighted, and not a little surprised."

"We felt it was time for some new blood." I can hear the smile in his voice; he likes it when I'm direct. "And I think you and I will deal well together."

"I do, too," I say sincerely. "I'm looking forward to working with you."

"On that note, I've had a contract drawn up. It's fairly standard and has the terms we discussed previously. Shall I send it across now?"

"Perfect." I pause, then add, "Though I should mention that we'll require the retainer fee to be paid quarterly in advance." If he agrees, Channing Associates is definitely solvent. If not, we have some creative accounting to do to get through the three months until the fee comes in. I find I'm holding my breath.

"I can't see a problem with that. Just amend the draft."

Yes! The fizzing has spread to my limbs now; my legs are literally jiggling with suppressed excitement. "I'll do that, and we'll get it back to you as soon as possible. We're keen to start making progress for you."

"Excellent. Speak again soon."

"Absolutely. And thank you again. This is fantastic news."

I put the phone down and put both palms to my flushed cheeks for a moment, feeling my cheeks bunch in a wondering smile. I look across at the empty desk. "Julie!"

"What?" she calls from the outer room.

"We got it!" I spin in my chair exultantly.

"Got what?"

"The contract!" I'm on my feet now, on my way to her room, but she's moving, too; we meet in the doorway. "Haft & Weil. We got it!" I realize I'm actually bouncing.

"That's fantastic!" Impulsively she grabs my hands and begins jumping with me. From the look of relief on her face, I wonder if I should have been paranoid about keeping her as well as Paul.

The external door opens, and Paul comes in, cursing at his disposable cup, which is dripping latte everywhere. He looks askance at Julie and me, still bouncing, our smiles as wide as our mouths can stretch. "What?" He dumps the leaking cup on Julie's desk and looks from me to Julie and back again, nonplussed. "What?"

"We got it!" I croon. "We got it, we got it, we got it!"

"Haft & Weil?" he asks urgently. "Really?"

I nod, beaming at him. "Awesome!" he roars. "Haft & fucking Weil! Fucking awesome!" Then he's slinging an arm round

each of our shoulders and all three of us are jumping together and grinning inanely, and I think: *I should remember times like this, remember perfectly. I should bottle them somehow. You don't know how many of these moments you might have in your life.*

CHAPTER SEVEN

By the time I reach the pub a few minutes after seven, I am drunk. Mostly drunk on excitement and drunk on relief, but the champagne Paul nipped out to buy and cracked open in the office has played its part, too. Paul, Julie and I sat on the floor and ate posh crisps whilst drinking the bubbly from mugs. Paul was still shaking his head and saying at regular intervals, "Haft & fucking Weil!" with a broad smile and looking at me with something akin to renewed respect; and Julie was flushed and decidedly unsteady when she eventually left to catch her train. I thought, if we succeed, we will be telling this story in years to come: the anecdote of how Channing Associates celebrated their first big win.

But here and now I'm mildly tipsy, standing just inside the door of the pub once again scanning for Tom. This time I spot him at a table; he's been here long enough

to be a third of the way through a pint, with what looks like a vodka tonic waiting for me on the table. His attention is on his phone, and he's had a haircut. For a moment it throws me off balance: he looks sharper, older — *other.* But then he looks up and catches sight of me; he gets up to deliver his trademark hug, his face breaking into a welcoming grin, and I see he still has freckles on his nose — he's Tom again.

"You look . . . suspiciously happy," he says, releasing me and cocking his head in confusion.

I nod and slip into the chair opposite him. My smile needs very little encouragement this evening, already it's spreading across my face. "That miracle I needed. It happened. We just landed a major contract." I adopt a contrite expression. "I'm really sorry for not being miserable."

"Don't be ridiculous, that's fantastic!" He waves away my apology, looking genuinely delighted for me. "I'd much rather toast your success than drown my sorrows. Who did you land?"

"Haft & Weil," I say proudly, taking the vodka tonic he slides across the table to me. "With a big enough retainer to tide us over for a little while. But I'm quietly confident we'll nail the performance fee, and this big

a contract is great publicity, I wouldn't be surprised if we get a lot more interest after this —"

"Breathe," he teases affectionately.

"I know, I know; only . . . I really thought we were fucked." The last few days catch at me: the ever-present dread, the seemingly inevitable failure looming over me. I take a deep breath and try to rid myself of the memory, but an echo of it lingers.

"I know," Tom says soberly. "I could hear it in your voice on the phone."

"One contract does not a business make, but still . . ."

"You have to celebrate the wins," Tom says, almost fiercely. "They're important. Regardless of . . . well, regardless." He looks away, almost as if he's embarrassed by his own vehemence.

I take a sip of the vodka tonic. "Well, cheers. And thanks for this. Anyway, tell me about your dreadful day. How many did they let go?"

"Hundreds," he says tiredly. "About fifteen percent all told, apparently. A massacre. The thing is, I'm head of the desk now, so . . ."

"Oh God." My hand is at my mouth. No wonder he's had such an awful day. "You had to do some of the firing."

He nods bleakly. "Four guys. Well, three

guys and a girl, actually. I barely knew them — Jesus, I'm fresh off the plane; I've barely had a chance to get to know anyone. At least I didn't have to decide who; the list was already fixed." He takes a swallow from his pint then stares gloomily at it for a moment, slumped in his chair with the pint at the end of his outstretched arms. "I knew there was some kind of restructuring afoot when I moved back here, but I wasn't expecting this. I only heard the details two days ago."

"Do you think it made it easier that you didn't know them? Who you were, well, firing, I mean." I wince a little on the key word.

He shrugs. "I don't know. On the one hand, yes — it's not like I know if they have families to support or anything. On the other hand . . . *shouldn't* it be personal? I mean, you work all hours for a firm — granted you expect to be paid for it, but it's an emotional thing, too; you work hard for your colleagues, you have a laugh with them, you have the odd drink with them . . . Don't you deserve to have someone who actually knows you shake your hand and say — God, I don't know what. *Thank you? It's been a pleasure? You're really good, this is not the end for you . . .*" He shakes his head and stares across the table at his pint

again. "Something. I don't know."

"Oh, Tom." There is nothing I can think of to say to that. I take a drink and am surprised to see my glass is almost empty. We sit in brooding silence for a moment. Around us the pub is getting busier and louder.

"You know, there's a good chance at least one of them was really crap," I say eventually, with mock seriousness. "Or had bad breath."

The corner of his mouth tweaks upward a little. "One of the blokes was quite sweaty," he concedes. "Unpleasantly so. And the girl dressed like she was still a student. Not jeans or anything, but ridiculous floaty skirts that were too short for a trading floor, of all places. And no tights."

"There you go. Definitely best not to be personal, then."

He nods, a ghost of a smile in place, then pulls himself a little more upright. "You know, I used to think that we'd get wherever we got in life because of hard work, because we deserved it," he muses, elbows on the table. "Don't get me wrong: the hard work definitely counts. It's just that luck seems to play a much bigger part than I ever figured."

I think of Theo, of Severine. Luck, or lack thereof. It's an uncomfortable thought.

Blaming luck means it could have been any of us: *there but for the grace of God . . .*

He visibly shakes himself. "Anyway, another?"

"Let me get them."

"Nope. You haven't got the money in the door yet; this is still on me." He flashes a quick grin. "When you float Channing Associates for millions, you can pay me back. With interest."

I grin back, then watch him head toward the bar. As the bartender works his order, he checks his phone again, or perhaps it's his work BlackBerry, and for a second the otherness is there again: Tom, but not Tom. Or a different Tom from the one I used to know.

The evening wears on, and we move to a pizza place nearby, where Lara joins us, she and I facing Tom across the table meant for four. We are celebrating, but not; we are commiserating, but not — it was a delicate balance in the pub, but Tom and I were managing it; now Lara's presence is thoroughly destroying the equilibrium. Tom has become more taciturn, Lara is twitchy, and I'm too watchful, though not sober enough to interpret anything I see. And all the while Severine sits at the table too, coolly offhand

as if utterly uninterested, although I suspect she's taking in every nuance with those black eyes.

"At least we're done with Modan," Tom says, out of the blue, unless I missed the segue — or perhaps I'm not the only one who cannot ignore Severine. Lara is peeling the label from a bottle of San Pellegrino. For a moment her hands still, then she takes up the task again.

"You *are* done with him, right?" Tom persists, looking at me.

I don't look at Lara. "I think so."

"Did he interview Seb?" Lara asks; now it's her turn to avoid looking sideways. She sounds brittle and self-conscious; I wonder if she already knows the answer.

Tom looks at me carefully, if a little blearily. "Yep, today," he says mildly.

Lara is looking at me warily too. "It's okay," I say testily. "You're allowed to mention Seb's name around me. I'm not going to freak out." They're still looking at me. "Seriously, guys," I say in exasperation. "It was a long time ago. And we'll be living in the same city, so . . ." I shrug, unwilling to complete the sentence. So . . . what? *So . . . we're bound to run into each other? So . . . we'll have to be civil? So . . . we've both moved on?* Severine turns her black eyes on

123

mine, and for once the expression within them is entirely clear: scorn. It jolts me.

"In that case, how *is* Seb?" Lara asks Tom.

"Traitorous cow," I say, tongue in cheek. Tom gives a short bark of laughter, then frowns a little and peers at the red wine in his glass, as if uncertain what it might be. *Beer before wine, makes you feel fine . . .*

"I don't know, actually," he admits. "I saw him the other night, but only briefly, and Alina was with him and we couldn't really talk." He frowns again, slumping down even farther in his chair. "There's something . . . You know, he's not in great shape. Physically, I mean, which is unlike him; you know how he likes to work out. I don't know . . ."

I see Seb, what used to be my favorite image of Seb, wearing jeans but his chest still bare — the classic Levi's model look. His beauty is heartbreaking; it's too much, he's too vital, it's impossible to look at him without an awareness that it cannot last. An awareness of mortality.

Tom is still musing. "Caro's seen him, too, a couple of times I think. I should ask her what she thinks."

Caro has seen him a couple of times. Severine looks at me deliberately, a secretive smirk lurking near her mouth. I search for something to say to keep up my end of the

conversation. "So you haven't managed to show off your car to him yet." Tom smiles and shakes his head. "He'll be envious."

"I don't know why," says Lara, still busy with the bottle. "It's not like he would ever have bought it himself. He wouldn't be that original." I look at Tom and see my own surprise registering on his face. Lara lifts her head on our silence. "What? He's not. He likes to follow the trend, not set it."

"That's not entirely fair," begins Tom, then stops.

I'm still gazing at Lara. She's right, it's entirely fair, but I would never have seen it that way myself. Lara is a very smart girl, academically speaking, but she's not usually overly given to psychological analysis. "When did you get so insightful?" I murmur.

She ducks her head and turns her attention to shredding a napkin. Alarm bells ring in my mind, and I feel the reverberations in my stomach. "Have you been talking about us again?" I ask urgently.

She turns her head and gives me an accusatory look; I wince internally as I belatedly remember our audience. It's too late now: Tom sits up a little, aware he's missed something.

"What?" he says, when neither of us speak

or break our shared eye contact.

After a beat or two she concedes, rolling her eyes. "Go on then," she says, turning back to her napkin.

I turn to Tom. There is no easy way to say this, but I try to find one. "Lara has become . . . friendly . . . with our favorite French detective."

He's already sitting still, but on hearing my words it seems as if even the blood in his veins has stopped moving. After a moment he says, "I see," his face blank and his voice emotionless.

"No, you don't see," says Lara, suddenly close to tears. "Nothing is happening, nothing will happen, until this bloody investigation is cleared up, and now that's going to take even longer —" She stops abruptly, then balls up the napkin and pushes it away from her, not looking at either of us.

"Why is it going to take even longer?" I ask uneasily. She doesn't answer. "Lara, why?" I demand more urgently.

She shakes her head, but she's still Lara, she's still the sunshine girl and she can't keep a secret, either from us or from Modan. "Because they managed to speak with the brother," she says miserably. "The builder brother, I mean. He said he filled in the well on the Saturday. The day we left."

"But —" I'm abruptly cut off by the appearance of the waitress with our long overdue pizzas. I look at Tom in consternation as she busies herself laying them in front of us. His face is still blank, shuttered tight, presumably against revealing his feelings about Lara and Modan. Still, it crosses my mind that he doesn't seem surprised about the well; that he hasn't seemed surprised about anything, right from when he first called me.

"But —" I say again. This time I'm stopped by an infinitesimal shake of Tom's head. He cuts his eyes deliberately to Lara, whose head is down as she recovers her composure, the high spots in her cheeks gradually fading. Then he looks back, and the tiny headshake comes again. The message is clear: *not in front of Lara.*

Lara lifts her head, and her China blue eyes are full of anxiety. "I shouldn't have told you that," she frets, her gaze jumping from me to Tom and back again. "Please don't tell anyone I told you that."

"Lara, it's *us,*" I reassure soothingly. "Of course we won't tell." Tom nods in agreement, while I wonder, who would we tell? And why would Modan mind?

"Okay," she says, only slightly mollified. "It's just that, well, he was so disappointed

not to be able to rule us all out. We were planning to meet up in Paris next weekend, and now . . ." She looks down at her pizza, tears hovering.

In a moment of alcohol-fueled clarity I see what Lara feels like she's lost. Not just a weekend away, with all the anticipation and intoxication of clothes-tearing-off sex with someone new. Lara sees it as possibly the first weekend of the rest of her life. I can't remember if I felt like that with Seb. The clothes-tearing-off phase I remember. But nobody gets married at university these days, or anytime soon after. I always thought we were playing a long game. In France I realized he'd stopped playing altogether.

"In that case, you'll just have to spend the weekend with us instead," I say, putting my hand on hers. "I foresee two days of epic frivolity. Shopping on the King's Road. Maybe some romcom watching in there, too. Certainly a *lot* of decadent eating out and *absolutely* too much white wine." I'm rewarded by a heartfelt, if tearful, smile from Lara.

"I can cope with the romcom, but can I skip the shopping?" asks Tom dryly.

"Nope," says Lara, gamely trying to recover her equilibrium. "You look like an American. You definitely need to update

your wardrobe if you want to be a passably metrosexual male in London."

"Do I *want* to be a metrosexual male? What exactly *is* a metrosexual male?"

I eat my pizza and watch them bat back and forth, the same as they've always done. Except I don't know if it's the same. They were like this before that week in France, and they were like this when they were sleeping together — but surely there must have been differences, some nuances I missed. And now, Tom has realized that Lara is in love, or at least infatuated, with someone other than himself. How can they behave just the same? Perhaps it's a pattern, a learned behavior that one drops into by rote. Perhaps I'll learn something similar with Seb and we'll skate lightly over the surface together whenever we meet in London. How very British. *Everything's fine, just don't mention the war . . .*

As we're finishing up, Lara slips off to the bathroom. Tom watches her go, his face unreadable. I dither on whether to attack the situation head-on. He's never spoken to me directly about her — in the same way that he and I don't discuss Seb — but maybe in this instance I should extend an invitation.

"Are you okay?"

He doesn't answer — he doesn't even acknowledge the question — but as soon as she's out of earshot he leans forward and speaks urgently in a low tone. "Listen, you can't tell Lara anything. You can't talk to her about the case at all. Everything you say is going straight back to Modan."

His urgency pulls me forward, too, mirroring his position. "I know that — of course I know that. But really, what can I say that makes any difference? None of us have anything to hide." Except Caro with the drugs . . . Severine looks at me again. She is whole, but her mocking eyes are as dark as the sockets would be in her bleached white skull.

He makes a sharp cutting gesture with one hand. "It's not about that anymore. The police will be looking to see if any of us could have had a motive."

"We never met her before; well, none of us except Theo. What kind of motive can they possibly come up with?" If Lara comes out of the bathroom and we have our heads together we will look horribly conspiratorial. I sit back in my chair.

"Some subset of the usual, I expect. Jealous rage. Spurned lover." He's watching me closely.

"Spurned lover? But there wasn't any . . ."

I stare at him, at the freckles on that un-bowed and unbent nose, and feel my world spinning around. There are many things he could be intending with his words. I don't know where to start to unpack his meaning.

I don't get a chance to even try, because suddenly Tom starts talking. ". . . and in the States your vacation entitlement is such an insult. I'm looking forward to some decent looong holidays now I'm back." I stare at him in bemusement. He looks over my shoulder. "Ah, Lara, we were just talking holidays. Any plans?"

"Kate probably told you we were thinking about a safari . . ."

I stare at Tom as Lara reseats herself and chatters on. He glances at me, but there's nothing to read in his face. It was so smoothly done; I would never have guessed he was capable of such casual duplicity — once again, he is *other.* Tom, but not Tom. I wonder, is everyone not who I thought? Maybe nobody ever *really* knows anyone.

And then I wonder: in that case, does anyone know me?

CHAPTER EIGHT

I call Tom the next morning.

It's not the first thing I do when I wake up, and I didn't wake early. In fact, it's barely still morning when I finally allow myself to pick up the phone.

"Kate," he says after a couple of rings. His voice is sleepy, and deeper, more gravelly than usual.

"Sorry, did I wake you?" I'm not the least bit sorry. At this time of day I feel well within my rights to wake anyone.

"No, I've already been to the gym." Maybe the alcohol is responsible for the gravel in his voice then. I hear him yawn. "I figured you'd call. Want to come over? I'll throw something together for lunch."

It's both a relief not to have to ask to see him and embarrassing to have him find me so predictable. "Done." I glance at my watch and perform the mental maths. "I can be there around half twelve if that works

for you?"

"Perfect, see you then."

The tube is full of the weekend crush. Tourists and families and self-consciously cool teens, all in pairs or groups, as if nobody travels alone on a Saturday or Sunday. I turn my head to stare out of the window. This part of the tube runs through a series of tunnels and open-air sections; I see overgrown leafy embankments interspersed with the bleached-out reflection of the carriage. Neither gives away much about London. I'm thinking of Tom's words, as I have done repeatedly since I woke up, as I must have done somewhere in my subconscious all night. *Jealous rage. Spurned lover.* I won't allow myself to think beyond that; I have my imagination on a tight rein. Just those words are permitted: *jealous rage, spurned lover,* then an abrupt stop to all thought. Severine should be here now, gloating, that smirk hovering millimeters from her mouth, but for once she's conspicuous by her absence.

Jealous rage. Spurned lover. It doesn't matter. It shouldn't matter. But here I am, in a grab-handbag, brush-hair, that-will-do kind of hurry, on my way to Tom's flat — which Tom entirely anticipated. It's surprising how little surprises Tom.

133

Tom's flat is in a quiet, wealthy street lined with Regency town houses, all high ceilings and sash windows and expensive heating bills. I press the bell for the top floor, and after a moment there is an obnoxious buzz and the front door releases. The communal hallway is on a dignified slide into genteel shabbiness, the once thick carpets now worn in the center from years of use. I climb the creaking stairs to find Tom's front door ajar; I can see a two-inch-wide slice of his hallway, with a newspaper dumped casually on a side table. I can't quite remember the last time I was here; actually, I can't remember being here more than three or four times, and always with a crowd, for a party or some such. Rapping on the door solo, I feel an unexpected twinge of nerves.

"In the kitchen," calls Tom's deep tone; he has expelled some of the gravel now. I close the front door behind me then aim for Tom's voice and find myself spilling into an open-plan room, with the kitchen at one end, a living room type space at the other, and a large glass dining table separating the two. At the living space end, floor-to-ceiling windows open out onto a small terrace. Tom is at the stove in the kitchen, working on something in a frying pan.

"I don't remember this," I say, making my

way over to him. I may have only been in this flat a handful of times, but I've never been in *this* room.

He pulls me in for a one-armed hug, the other hand occupied with the frying pan, which contains the world's largest Spanish omelet. "I remodeled before I went to Boston. Just in time for a tenant to enjoy it instead of me. Do you like?" he asks casually, but I can see he cares about my answer.

"It's great," I say truthfully. It's modern without being sharp; it still feels warm and livable. Unlike Caro's place. Unlike Caro. "You've done it really well." I gesture toward the hob. "Can I help?" It's not the question I want to ask, but I don't know how to get there from discussions of renovations in a sun-drenched kitchen.

"Nope, nearly done, just grab a pew," he says, gesturing to the bar stools on the other side of the counter. "I take it omelet is okay?"

"Perfect. Thanks." I clamber aboard a stool and watch the back of him cook, given the layout of the kitchen. He can't be long out of the shower; his hair is still wet. He's wearing jeans and a casual shirt with the sleeves rolled up. For no reason at all I see Seb alongside him — Seb as he was, the Adonis, the man among the boys; I don't

know the Seb of now. *Jealous rage. Spurned lover.* Tom, a man now, too, glances over his shoulder with a quick smile. I instinctively look away quickly, as if caught staring.

"Done," he says, efficiently cutting the omelet in two and delivering it to waiting plates. "Voilà."

"Merci bien." I pause. I force myself to ask something conversational. "Do you like cooking?"

He settles himself on the bar stool next to me. "Not particularly, but I like eating fresh food, so . . ." He shrugs his shoulders.

The omelet is good, very good. We munch away, or at least Tom does; my appetite is letting me down. I've eaten with Tom any number of times, though never at his kitchen counter by his own hand. But still, there should be companionable silence; there always has been for Tom and me. Not today. Something is different — *we* are different. I glance over in his direction. He looks tired, the crinkles round his eyes more pronounced. Perhaps he is paler; his freckles seem to stand out more.

"So . . ." he says, between bites. "Lara and Modan? Is that for real?"

I grimace. "Well, she certainly seems smitten," I say apologetically. I wonder if that question has itched away at him all night.

"Yeah, that much was obvious." There's no emotion in his voice. He takes a bite and chews thoughtfully, staring unseeingly across the kitchen. "It's not ideal."

Not ideal. It's an oddly phlegmatic turn of phrase for heartbreak. "I guess. On any number of fronts." I put down my fork, unable to eat and unable to wait, and twist on the bar stool to face his profile. "What did you mean last night?"

He turns to look at me, his head cocked to one side analytically. Then he lays his cutlery down, too, but he's actually finished, the enormous omelet polished off in a handful of bites. He knows exactly what I'm referring to, and to his credit he doesn't try to dissemble. "Severine was an attractive girl," he says carefully. I nod and wonder where she is. Surely she wouldn't want to miss out on this conversation. "Modan seems to find it hard to believe that none of us were sleeping with her. He's playing a 'what if' game right now. What if . . . well, what if Tom was sleeping with Severine? But that's unlikely because everyone knows I hooked up with Lara that week, and Modan clearly thinks Lara is more than enough for one man to cope with." His tone is heavy with irony. He pauses for a moment; I can't tell if he's remembering the past or looking

to the future, but regardless, it seems the view is bleak. "But what if Seb was sleeping with Severine? Well, that would certainly make things interesting . . ."

He stops, holding my gaze. The question that we both know I'm going to ask hangs in the air between us, solid enough to reach out and touch.

"I want to know," I say quietly.

Tom looks away and runs a hand through his hair, then fixes me in his gaze again. "Do you really care?" There's an edge to his voice. "After all this time? Ten years have passed since that week in France — ten years and a bloody marriage ceremony."

"I care about whether I was made a fool of." I sound bitter. I feel bitter. And impatient. "I care about whether all my friends knew what was going on under my nose but didn't tell me."

"So it's all about pride."

"Yes. No. I don't know — look, was he fucking her or not?"

"Yes," he says simply.

I open my mouth to say something, but nothing comes to mind. I close it again. *Pride*, I think. Tom is right on that score: my pride is well and truly hurt. Severine has finally made her entrance: she's watching me from across the kitchen and my

fingers curl in an urge to drag my nails down those perfectly smooth cheeks, an urge so strong that I almost recoil from myself: the poor girl is dead; no one can possibly feel envious of her ever again. She watches me, and I fancy she knows what I'm thinking: she looks coolly to the side, as if utterly uninterested in my opinion. Tom is watching me, too, his brow furrowed in concern. I start to slide down from the bar stool.

"No," says Tom assertively, bringing me up short by grabbing my arm. "You don't get to disappear now. You wanted to know, so you have to listen to it *all* instead of building up all sorts of crazy scenarios in your head." His eyes are fiercely intent. "Kate, this is not some conspiracy theory; nobody has been whispering behind your back. It was a onetime thing, on the last night only. Hardly anyone knows about it. Seb doesn't even know that *I* know about it."

I process that for a moment, fighting my urge to flee. The last night. "After the fight, then." He nods. His grip loosens on my upper arm; instead he rubs his hand reassuringly up and down from my shoulder to my elbow. The last night, after the fight. "You said hardly anyone. Who else?"

"I don't know for sure," he says uneasily. "But maybe . . . Caro."

"Caro. Of course. It would have to be Caro." Of all people it would have to be her. I bet she has loved having that piece of knowledge secreted away, ready to be deployed at just the right moment for maximum personal advantage. I can just imagine how superior it has made her feel. I find my hands have clawed; I force myself to breathe out slowly and relax them. "How *do* you know about it then?"

"I saw them," he admits. "I don't know for sure, but I think Caro did, too; or at least, she put two and two together." I can see him gauging my reaction, trying to work out if each additional detail makes things better or worse, but nevertheless he's unflinching in his delivery. He releases my arm and runs his hand through his hair again instead. He looks as if, on balance, he'd much rather not have seen . . . What did he see exactly? I steel myself for the malevolent march of that thought eating away at me, the rot spreading at a steady rate until I can see nothing without an overlay of Seb and Severine in various different tangles of limbs, artfully backlit Hollywood-style — but a thoroughly unexpected dose of pragmatism hits me. The last night of the holi-

day, that famously eventful Friday night? Logistically, it couldn't have happened until after the fight, at which point Seb was already so drunk that, at some point when I have some perspective, I may be impressed that he managed to cheat on me at all. I'm fairly certain there was no cinematic glow involved that night. But . . .

"How do you know it wasn't happening all week, and you just didn't see it the other times?"

"Come on," he says, one eyebrow quirking upward. "We're talking about Seb. Subtlety and subterfuge have never been his strongest suits." I don't react. He sighs then looks at me searchingly, all humor gone. "Did you never wonder? Not even when the two of you broke up?" I shake my head, but we both know I'm lying. "Why did you think you broke up?"

"Christ, Tom. Can anyone ever answer that succinctly? Why did you and Jenna break up?" I counter.

He doesn't miss a beat and he doesn't break eye contact. "Because I didn't love her. Not the way I want to love whoever I'm going to spend the rest of my life with."

His starkly brutal honesty leaves me speechless, caught in the grip of his ferociously intent eyes. Like Seb's but not; now

141

all I can see are the differences, not the similarities. I'm still groping around for a response when suddenly his phone starts to ring and dance across the counter. He glances at it long enough to register the caller ID, then picks it up and grimaces apologetically. "Sorry, I've got to take this; it's work. Don't go away."

I slide off the stool and wander into the living area of the open-plan space. Why did I think Seb and I broke up? I glance back at Tom. He's roaming the kitchen as he listens, his tall frame telegraphing alertness and focus. I turn back to the living room, inspecting the few framed photos resting on a shelf. There's one of him with his parents and his younger sister on his graduation day. His dad has clapped his hand firmly on Tom's shoulder and is beaming proudly. A wave of longing for my own father crashes over me, taking my breath away with its sudden onslaught. I turn quickly to the next photo: Seb and Tom at perhaps fifteen years old, beside a sailing boat with a gentleman that can only be Seb's father. The whippet-thin figure of Tom is a step back and half turned, as if he was about to get into the boat when the photo was taken; Seb's father's hand is on his shoulder, tugging him into the photo. Seb is square to the

camera on his father's other side, smiling broadly. It's not a version of Seb I ever knew; he was more complete when I met him. More of a polished product. I look at that photo for a long time and think about all the different versions of Seb, including the one that cheated on me. The bitterness is an all-encompassing sea of bile, roiling around in my stomach and threatening to race up my throat to choke me.

Why *did* I think Seb and I broke up?

I'm so very, very tired of caring.

Tom has moved from receiving mode into delivery mode on his telephone call. "No, I don't actually," I hear him say authoritatively. "The basis risk on this structure is significant. Someone has to take it, and if it's going to be us then we have to charge for it. But the real problem is that this is the wrong structure for what they really want to do. We should get in front of them with a presentation and educate them." I find I'm watching him as he talks. He's still moving around the kitchen, his right hand accentuating his points. For a moment I find myself assessing him as I would any candidate that crossed the path of Channing Associates. It dawns on me that he's a fixer, a problem-solver; entirely in keeping with his degree in engineering, but somehow I've

never paid attention to this side of him. He feels my eyes upon him and looks across, mouthing what could be "two minutes" whilst holding up two fingers. I nod and make a show of turning unconcernedly to another photo, and find myself looking back at me.

I'm not the only one in the photo, of course; there's Tom next to me and Lara on his other side. We're all sitting on the side of the pool in France, our feet dangling in the water. Lara is almost spilling out of her bikini and looks how she always looks: as if she's just climbed out of bed after hours of languorous sex, but would be more than willing to tumble back in for another round. Tom is Tom, at least the Tom I know the best: relaxed, laid-back, secure in his own skin but quietly observant. I'm the Kate I like the least, awkwardly folding my arms across my stomach at the glimpse of a camera, a half-hearted smile hung on my face. It's not surprising; there was no heart in any of my smiles by the end of that week.

Suddenly I realize Tom is behind me, looking over my shoulder at the photo. I hadn't noticed him finish the call. "Cracking legs you have on display there," he says mischievously.

I smile, touched; it's gentlemanly of him

to comment on me rather than the bomb-shell that is Lara. I gesture toward the sailing photo. "Did you sail a lot growing up?" It's the only non-contentious thing I can think of to say.

He shrugs. "Uncle Edwin was really into it. He taught Seb and me." He looks at the photo a moment longer. "Did you know he paid all my school fees before I got the scholarship?"

Uncle Edwin. Lord Harcourt. I shake my head. "I didn't." I think about that for a moment: the younger sister and her penni-less academic husband living off the gener-osity of the lord in the grand house. "I guess that must have created a certain dynamic."

He glances down at me. "No, it was —" he starts to say, as if parroting the party line, then he stops. "Actually, yeah," he admits. "My folks never said anything, but I could see how relieved they were when I won the scholarship." He looks back at the photo. "But it was a bit awkward with Seb, since he just missed out."

"But you two never seemed competitive with each other," I say, confused.

He shrugs. "Seb likes to win." Before I can try to puzzle that out, he shakes himself and turns away from the photos. "Anyway, where were we?"

"Nowhere I want to go back to."

His lips twist apologetically. "I'm sorry I didn't tell you before."

"Don't be ridiculous; Seb is your family." I can't blame Tom in the slightest for keeping Seb's secrets. I can blame Seb for having them, though. I can and I do.

"Yes, but . . . Well, anyway. You wanted to know." He cocks his head and assesses me, lips pursed. "How do you feel now you do?"

I turn away, scrubbing my face with my hands. "God, I don't know. It's hard to find perspective." Does Tom think I'm taking this well, or badly? Should I be more upset or less upset? Exactly how upset am I? What is the proportionate response when discovering decade-old infidelity?

"Kate," he says, a little too loudly, as if he's said my name more than once. Maybe he has. I turn back toward him, eyebrows raised inquiringly. "They're going to try and pin this on one of us," he says quietly. "Theo's dad says there's been a lot of publicity on this case in France; the police are getting hauled over the coals in the press for not finding the body at the time. There's a lot of pressure on them to get a result."

"But it *wasn't* one of us." I sound like a child, railing against the injustice of life: *it's not fair!* But life isn't fair, he will say. I know

that. After irrevocably losing Seb and my dad in close succession, albeit in different ways, I couldn't fail to recognize that life lacks a sense of fair play.

Tom doesn't even bother to argue the point; he's already moved on. "I think you need to get a lawyer."

"A lawyer." I stare at him. "You're serious." He nods grimly. "Do *you* have one?"

"Nope. But my other half wasn't sleeping with a girl who subsequently turned up folded origami-style at the bottom of a well."

I can see her bleached skull grinning maniacally from the pinnacle of a pile of clean white bones. My breath catches. "Well, when you put it like that —"

"Modan, the French police — they *will* put it like that."

"But they don't know he and she . . . Ah."

Tom is nodding. "Yes. Caro. I don't know for sure that she knows, and I don't know if she would say anything, but . . ."

He spreads his fingers, palm up. I know he intends to convey uncertainty — *she might, she might not* — but I know the truth of it: *she will.* Unless there's some personal benefit to her that I haven't yet divined, without a doubt Caro will say something. If she hasn't already . . . I stare at him, my mind skittering on many levels. "They need

hard evidence to prosecute, right? It can't be purely circumstantial?"

He shrugs. "I'm not exactly an expert in the French criminal judiciary system."

"Me neither." Which, at present, seems a wholly unsatisfactory gap in my legal education. Eventually I say again, "So, a lawyer. You're serious."

"Yes." There isn't a shadow of doubt in his eyes.

"I . . . Okay then." I'm still staring at him, my mind whirring.

"And stop talking to Lara about the case," he presses.

"Yes. Okay." He's still looking at me as if waiting for more, so I say it again. "Okay."

He nods and lets out a breath. "Okay."

I take a cab home. I can't face the bustle and thrust of the tube; I'm too brittle. I may fracture if jostled. The cabdriver tries to start up a conversation but trails off into silence when I fail to offer a single response. Lara's name lights up the screen on my mobile as we drive, the shrill ringtone demanding a response. I look at the phone in my hand, and all I can see are spider's threads leading from it. Lara to Alain Modan. Lara to Tom. Tom to Seb, his own cousin. Tom and Seb to Caro, their friend

148

from childhood. Tom and Seb to Theo, their friend from university. Theo to Severine. Severine to Seb. Tug on any one thread and the reverberations will be felt by all.

The phone falls silent. I don't call her back.

CHAPTER NINE

By Monday Severine has found an additional medium through which to make her presence felt: print. The case is making enough waves in France to be worthy of several column inches in the European news section of the *Telegraph*. There's a political angle I don't fully comprehend, not being an expert on French politics over the last ten years; another unsatisfactory gap in my knowledge base. They have a picture of Severine — of course they do; she is nothing if not photogenic, especially in a bikini as in the chosen photo. She lounges unsmiling in black and white on a sunbed, looking at the camera with no trace of concern about being framed on all sides by the words that attempt to capture her life and death and the chaos left by both.

Channing Associates is in the press, too. Paul comes into the office, a perfect storm of tailored suit, energy and enthusiasm, wav-

ing a copy of *Legal Week.* He pulls up his calendar as I take the paper off him to read it. It's a good article. Apparently despite being newly established, "Channing Associates, headed up by Kate Channing, is comprised of experienced hands who are fleet of foot" and are "the team to watch."

"I reckon I can lobby Cadfields again on the back of this publicity," Paul is saying. "They kind of left the door open. I'll try them, and then there's Wintersons, and I heard about an in-house general counsel role at BP from a mate at . . ." He babbles away. The Haft & Weil win has given him renewed vigor beyond all expectation; I wonder if he's further up the bipolar curve than most.

I put *Legal Week* down on my desk, next to Severine. One article where I'm mentioned by name; one where I'm simply one of the "English holidaymakers staying in the neighboring farmhouse" at the time, who are "helping the police with their inquiries." It's not an even match. Severine continues to gaze from her sun lounger, and I can think of nothing else.

I need a lawyer. Which ought to be funny given I'm a legal headhunter, except that it's not funny at all. Because I need a lawyer.

151

■ ■ ■ ■

Modan again.

He's waiting for me when I emerge from Pret, clutching my coffee and my lunch in a bag. I stop short in the doorway when I spot him lounging against a lamppost. *"Bonjour,"* he greets me, inclining his head.

I sigh and start walking. *"Bonjour.* I'm afraid I don't have any time for you today." *And I don't have a lawyer yet.*

He falls in beside me and shrugs. "Surely a few minutes."

"Not really, I'm afraid."

"Perhaps I talk and you listen. While you are eating your lunch, *non?"*

I'm walking back to my office, but it occurs to me that he will very likely follow me all the way there. I definitely do not want Paul and Julie exposed to the charming Alain Modan and the no-doubt innocent-sounding questions that he would produce. I stop walking and look at him. He cocks his head and smiles his most beguiling smile, the deep lines in his long face curving to frame his mouth.

"I'll listen. That's it." I take a detour toward a nearby courtyard with a bench that will be in the sun, if there's any sun; it's

warm enough today to justify eating outside. The bench is empty; I navigate to it carefully given that cobblestones, a cup of coffee and kitten heels are a difficult mix, but I make it there unscathed and sit at one end, with my coffee placed precariously on the arm of the bench. Modan sits also, at the far end, spreading his arms along the back of the bench. The sun makes an unexpected appearance, and he tips his head back to enjoy it, eyes closed. Today he's wearing a pale pink shirt under his suit, with a silver gray tie; very Eurotrash, but it works for him. I wonder if he looks at my clothes in abject horror: this dress is probably two years old. At least I'm wearing designer shoes.

"*Alors,*" he says, pulling himself upright into business mode. I'm unpackaging my chicken wrap and pay him no heed. "So, I talk. As promised. We have the answer on when the well was filled in." He looks at me expectantly. I remember that I'm not supposed to know this and raise my eyebrows obligingly over my mouthful of wrap. "Saturday the sixteenth."

Having a mouthful is useful; it gives me time to think. About what to say, how to say it; about whether to say anything at all. "You said Friday before. Now you say Saturday,"

I comment mildly when I'm done chewing. "What makes you so sure you've got it right this time?"

He inclines his head: a silent *touché*. "The papers say Friday, but Monsieur Casteau — the younger one — tells me it was Saturday. He remembers that his girlfriend arrived in town unexpectedly, so they went off to . . ." He spreads his hands eloquently. "He came back on Saturday to finish the job." He looks at me again as if waiting for a comment, but when he sees I have another mouthful he goes on, with a wry twist to his lips. "He wrote down Friday on the paperwork because of the contract: there was a bonus if the work was finished on time. On Friday. You see?"

I do see why Modan believes Monsieur Casteau the younger; even I believe this, and I'm hearing it secondhand. "Does Theo's dad plan to sue him for return of the bonus?" I ask, tongue in cheek.

Modan's lips quirk. "I don't believe he considers it a high priority." He gives this last word the French pronunciation: *priorité*.

I take another mouthful and chew thoughtfully. Saturday. The day we left. Modan tips his head back to enjoy another brief appearance of the sun.

I try to nudge the conversation forward

when I have finally swallowed. "What time on Saturday?"

He's been waiting for this; for him this is all a game that he's very, very good at. He tips his head forward again and blinks a few times while his eyes adjust. "He doesn't remember exactly, but he thinks perhaps lunchtime."

Lunchtime. Severine would have had plenty of time to return from the bus depot and then . . . what? Get herself killed by person or persons unknown and stuffed in a well? My breath catches: it's not a game; I don't want to play. I put down my suddenly very unappetizing chicken wrap. "I presume you've considered Monsieur Casteau," I say in a rush. "Younger or elder."

"*Bien sûr.* Of course." He purses his lips and moves his head this way and that as if trying to look at something from different angles. "They do not seem to . . . fit."

"And neither do the rest of us." I can't hide my frustration. He gives an equivocal one-shoulder shrug. I stand up to dump my leftovers in a nearby bin, annoyed with myself as well as Modan. I have no lawyer. I shouldn't be here. I pick up my handbag and my as-yet untouched coffee.

Modan watches me gather myself together without getting up, his long arms still laid

across the back of the bench, the very picture of relaxed elegance. "Stranger danger," he muses. "That is what you say, *n'est-ce pas*? That is what you teach *les enfants* at school? For murder, it is most of the time . . . *bof,* most of the time it is rubbish. Most of the time the murderer is in the home, or the street, or the place of work. Someone nearby. Someone known."

"Thanks for that," I say sweetly. "On that cheery note, I must get back to work to spend the rest of the day in fear of my colleagues and neighbors."

"Ha!" He seems genuinely amused by this; his long face is split by his smile. "Have a good afternoon."

But I don't have a good afternoon. I have a busy afternoon, even a productive afternoon; I have an afternoon that in the ordinary course of events would be a perfectly fine afternoon, but not in this world, not after these events. Not with the shadow of Modan looming over me and the ghost of Severine flitting through my office at will.

Caro calls; I get Julie to take a message. She'll be calling about either Seb's welcome dinner or to pump me for information — likely both; and I have no energy for either.

I meet Lara for a drink after work: investi-

gation or no investigation, I can't avoid my closest friend. I can't remember ever deliberately keeping something from Lara. *Seb cheated on me with Severine.* The words beat around inside me, looking for an exit, but I force them down. Denied escape, they become a solid ever-present weight that sits in my stomach.

But Lara doesn't notice anything amiss — she's too busy keeping her own secrets. She doesn't ask me if I've seen Modan; she doesn't ask me anything about the case. She's trying far too hard to avoid the subject. I wonder whether she's seen him, or talked to him on the phone. I wonder whether they have put into action those desires whispered in an airport bar. The weight in my stomach grows heavier as we talk of all the things we usually talk of, which no longer matter at all.

"Oh, Caro called me," she says suddenly, wrinkling her pretty nose in distaste. "She's got that dinner she's been planning for Seb arranged for Thursday." She cocks her head and looks at me pleadingly. "Will you come? Please?"

Will I? I hadn't intended to go, but now I think about it. "I suppose so." I'm bound to run into Seb sooner or later; I may as well get it over with.

"Yay! It will be no fun without you, and Caro kind of forced me to say yes. She'll probably put the full-court press on you, too, at some point. You know," she muses, "much as I hate to admit it, it is nice of her to have arranged it all. I bet Seb will be really touched." She takes a sip from her wine, then asks hesitantly, in an almost word-perfect repeat of Tom's question on Saturday: "Do you still care? After all this time?"

I look at our half-drunk wineglasses, Lara's with a distinct lipstick smudge on one side, mine with only the merest suggestion of a lip print. In my darkly introspective mood even that seems highly symbolic, a deliberate motif designed to illustrate that I move through life leaving barely a trace to show I was ever there. "I don't know," I reply at last. I think of Tom's follow-up — *why did you think you broke up?* — and I see Seb's eyes when he told me it was over; I see the way they slid away from mine. I thought that underneath it all he felt guilty, for a myriad of reasons but one particular being he was ashamed that for all his assertions that background didn't matter, in the end he had to acknowledge that he wanted someone from his world, someone who fit. Now I have a different thesis about the

source of that guilt, though not one I can share with Lara. "It's hard to say. I haven't actually seen him since — well, since he dumped me, actually."

Lara's eyes widen. "Really? Not once? How can that be?"

I shrug. "I guess I didn't want to see him at first, and then Dad got ill so I was up in Yorkshire for a bit." It was cancer. Pancreatic cancer. I pause, remembering the phone call from Mum, the hopelessness in her voice as she forced herself to utter the dreaded C-word, followed by the mad dash to get the very next train home. I cried silently for almost the entire three-hour journey, sitting alone in a quiet seat facing a luggage rack. By the time I got to the hospital I was ash white and out of tears. "Anyway, by the time I came back his bank had sent him off to Singapore or somewhere like that."

"Hong Kong, I think. Tom and Caro went to visit." She takes another sip of her wine, laying down another mark of her presence with an overlapping lipstick print. "Makes it kind of hard to find *closure* if you've never actually seen him since." She uses her hands to hang an ironic set of quotation marks around "closure" and gives the word an American twang.

"Closure," I repeat, mimicking her twang. "Closure." I take a long swallow from my glass, then try the word again in my own accent, rolling it around my mouth. "Closure." I shake my head. "Nope. Word has absolutely no meaning."

She giggles. "I think you're too British for the concept of closure."

"Or too northern. We don't grin and bear it; we just bear it and don't bother with the grin."

"We Scandies don't bear it at all; we just off ourselves."

We smile at each other, enjoying the connection and the levity, and the weight in my stomach lifts a little. *It will be all right,* I think. *When all this is over, everything will be all right again.*

The feeling lasts until I climb into a cab home to find Severine already in occupation. The sight of her is like a slap in the face, or a brutal thump back down to earth: it shocks the sense back into me. *All right:* what an appallingly trite sentiment. It won't be *all right,* at least not for everyone; how could I have temporarily forgotten I've long stopped believing in guaranteed happy endings? There was a time with Seb where what I felt for him, what I thought he felt for me, was like a rising tide, buoying me up over

160

all obstacles. The inevitable crash when the tide abruptly receded was shattering, all the more so because I should have known better, because I *did* know better. Oxford was an education in more ways than one: I learned that like sticks with like. Bright, outspoken girls from underprivileged backgrounds might be fun to hang out with, but they don't ultimately make the inner sanctum of the Sebs of this world. Somehow, even knowing that, even in the face of all evidence to the contrary, I allowed myself to be fooled into believing our relationship would be different, that things would be *all right.*

I won't be a fool again; I won't allow it. I need a damn lawyer.

"Eight o'clock tonight," says Caro emphatically down the phone on Thursday afternoon. Julie rang her earlier in the week to confirm my attendance, but it's clear Caro isn't taking any chances. "I know this is, well . . . difficult for you, but I won't accept any last-minute excuses; after all, Borderello's is hell to get a table at." Her tone is carefully constructed to sound like a light-hearted tease mixed with sympathy, but Caro is not that kind of girl: she doesn't gossip and sympathize and commiserate.

She pokes and prods under the cover of witty repartee.

"Of course I'll be there," I say calmly. "I'm looking forward to it." For a moment I entertain the fantasy of turning up with an adoring Adonis on my arm — who? where would he come from at such late notice? — but I'll have to settle for Lara and Tom. Perhaps the Adonis trick would be too obvious anyway.

"It'll be great to have the old gang back together," she says brightly. "Like old times." *Old times.* The thought makes me shudder. Caro's *old times* must be very different from mine. I try to strip the irony from any potential response, but she's already forging on: "That's all I seem to be talking about these days, what with the investigation and everything. Modan can't seem to stop with the questions, can he? Have you seen him, too?"

"Not really. He dropped by on Monday, but I was too busy to have more than five minutes for him."

"I made the mistake of freeing up half an hour for him. I don't know what for, really — all he wanted to talk about was who was sleeping with who, and whether anyone was sleeping with Severine."

"Well, I certainly wasn't," I say flippantly.

"Girls have never been my thing. What about you?"

She gives what may be a genuine laugh. "No, me neither. I'm boringly bourgeois that way. But seriously, I suppose it changes things a bit if someone *was* sleeping with her."

"How so?" I ask, making my voice as uninterested as possible. Does she really know about Seb and Severine? Is she trying to find out if I know? *Does she know that I know that she knows that . . .*

"Motive, I suppose — crime of passion or some such thing. God, I sound like *CSI.*" She laughs it off. "It's all a bit grubby, really, having a stranger like Modan poring eagerly through all our tangled love lives." She switches gear audibly. "Anyway, tonight. Eight o'clock. Borderello's."

"See you there."

I put down the phone, her words turning over in my head: *our tangled love lives.* I was with Seb. Lara was with Tom. Other than Seb's infidelity, where lies the tangle? Come to that, Caro wasn't with anyone: why would she say "our" love lives? I start to run the payroll software that I use to manage Julie's and Paul's salaries, but I'm too distracted to make sense of the process. Abruptly I shut down the program and grab

my phone.

"Kate, hello." Tom sounds harried.

"Bad time?" I glance at the clock: it's ten to three. "Oh shit, sorry, it's almost expiry time." Foreign exchange options usually expire at three.

"Yup. Can I call you back after?"

"Sure."

He pauses. "You okay?"

"Yes, fine. It's nothing. Call me back later." My voice sounds too bright, too forced.

"Okay."

I put down my mobile and stare at it for a moment, then I shake myself and open the payroll software again with grim determination. It's sufficiently alien that to make any progress I have to concentrate to the exclusion of anything else; it's curiously calming. When my mobile finally rings I'm startled.

"Kate?" It's Tom. The real world floods back in and temporarily robs me of breath. "Kate? Can you hear me?" he asks.

"Yes, sorry. I'm here."

"Everything okay?"

"Yes . . . actually, no. Was Seb sleeping with anyone else?"

"What?" He's genuinely taken aback. "Where's this coming from?"

"It's just something Caro said. I won-

dered . . ." I feel a cold sweat on my torso. It's excruciatingly embarrassing to have to ask this. It's embarrassing to even have to wonder it. In time I will feel anger at Seb for putting me in this position, but all I feel at the moment is shame.

"Hold on a moment, this sounds like something I shouldn't be broadcasting over the trading floor. Let me get to my office." There's a pause and some muffled noises, then he comes back on the line. "Fire away."

"It's just . . . I'm probably getting the wrong end of the stick, but I wondered if Caro was sleeping with Seb." I add as an afterthought, "Or you, actually." Theo I don't consider a real possibility.

"Me sleeping with Seb?" He sounds genuinely bewildered.

I can't help but laugh. "No, with Caro, you idiot."

"Hand on my heart, I can promise you I have never slept with either Seb or Caro. Nor do I have any wish to." Humor warms his deep voice.

"And Seb? Seb with Caro, to be precise."

His pause is significant. "I don't think so," he says finally. There's no trace of the humor now. "I think . . . well, Caro has always had a thing for him. You must know that."

I suppose he's right; I've always known that. "And?"

"And nothing. I think that's all it's ever been, an unrequited thing. He kind of knew it, but I don't think he ever went there. He never felt the same, and it would have been a disaster given how close all our families are if he were to screw her over." Of course, it was fine to screw *me* over, with my unconnected, unimportant family . . . "At least, that's my take," he says at last, but I get the sense he's still mulling something over.

"Would he have told you, do you think? I know you're close, but he didn't tell you about Severine . . ."

"True." I hear him take a breath in then blow it out. "I don't know," he admits reluctantly. "Before you came along, then I'd have said yes, for sure, he would have told me anything. But after . . . I don't know." I want to ask what changed, but there's no way to do it without sounding like I'm looking for some validation, some sign I was important in Seb's life, and I refuse to be so pitiful in front of Tom. "Where are you going with this?"

"I don't know. I just suddenly feel like . . . God, I don't know. I don't know what the hell was going on that week. Modan is ask-

ing questions, and I'm not even sure I can answer *anything,* because nothing is how I thought it was, and . . . and . . ." I'm suddenly aware I'm close to tears.

"Hey, whoa there," Tom says softly down the line. "It's okay."

"No, it's *not.*"

He's silent for a moment. "No, it's not, is it? Look, why don't we meet before dinner tonight? Have a drink and talk all this through. I can get to Knightsbridge for around six. Okay?"

I take a deep, shuddering breath. "Yes. Okay. Thanks. Sorry about all this."

"You have nothing to be sorry for. Oh — did you get a lawyer?"

"I'm meeting one tomorrow."

"Good." He sounds genuinely relieved. "See you at six."

I put down the phone and rest my eye sockets in the heels of my hands for a moment. When I lift my head again I find Severine watching me. For once there's no trace of hostility beneath her smooth exterior; she's simply watching me.

"Haven't you anywhere better to be?" I ask her. It's the first time I've actually spoken to her; unsurprisingly she doesn't answer, so I do it for her. "No, I don't suppose you do, under the circumstances."

Julie comes to the doorway, pushing her glasses back up her nose. "Did you need something?"

I shake my head, smiling brightly. "No, sorry, just talking to myself."

She's already moving back to her seat. "First sign of madness, you know," she says over her shoulder. The thought had crossed my mind.

CHAPTER TEN

The evening starts badly.

I'm at the pub a few minutes after six and predictably find Tom — reliable, steady Tom — already there; but so, too, is Lara. From Tom's ruefully apologetic expression I divine he had no choice. I pull myself together to kiss Lara hello. "What a pleasant surprise!"

"I was sure you'd want to meet beforehand, but I couldn't raise you on your mobile this afternoon, so I called Tom," she says breezily.

"Really? My phone must be playing up again. I didn't see that you'd called." Lying is becoming easier with practice, but the guilt remains the same. I turn to hug Tom hello; his breath strokes my ear carrying a murmur of, "Sorry." He's been home to change after work; he's dressed in jeans and a shirt, and smells of newly applied aftershave. I'm still in work clothes, but it's a

deliberate choice: I have a fancy that the combination of this dress with these stiletto heels shows off my legs to their best advantage. Absent the Adonis arm candy, it's really the best I can do.

"Here, Tom got you a drink." Lara passes over a vodka tonic.

"Thanks. Love your dress." It occurs to me that I'm overcompensating, though she does look fabulous. She's wearing a stunning bodycon dress the color of autumn leaves, with heels at least an inch higher than her usual choice for work. Most of the bar watches as she settles herself in a chair and crosses her endless legs.

"Well, I thought I'd make an effort," she says casually, but there are spots of color in her cheeks. The effort is not for me or Tom, or even Caro or Seb, I'm sure. I'd lay odds she has post-dinner plans with the indefatigable Monsieur Modan.

"What about me? How do I look?" Tom asks, mock-preening. He's compensating too.

Lara bats her eyelashes at him. "Devastatingly handsome as ever."

"Very metrosexual," I add slyly; he turns to me, appreciative laughter glinting in those blue gray eyes. They are resolutely Tom's

eyes now. I wonder if this evening will shake that.

We drink and we talk and it's excruciating. Lara is too bright, too excitable, drinking too quickly. It's impossible to fathom what's going on under the surface, and given the secrets each of us are keeping, there's no way for me to ask. Subterfuge doesn't sit well with her, though. She ricochets through topics, always realizing each pitfall too late; she can't talk about her love life, she can't talk about the case, she can't talk about how she's spending her free time — almost nothing is safe for her. I'm so awkwardly aware this is not the private chat Tom and I had planned that I'm working too hard to keep the conversation Lara-friendly and save her from verbal suicide. On the surface Tom is his usual relaxed self, complete with mildly flirtatious banter with Lara, but I can see he's uncharacteristically tense, and oddly fatalistic, as if waiting for an ax to drop rather than killing time before a homecoming dinner for his cousin and closest friend. Perhaps he, too, can see that the light within Lara is shining for someone other than her current audience. I wonder how much that pierces him.

It's hard enough to battle on with this charade whilst sober; I shouldn't have

another vodka tonic. But I do. And another.

Finally, Lara glances at her watch. "Shouldn't we make tracks before we incur the wrath of Caro?"

I nod and reach for my handbag, partly relieved to be released, but I expect what's coming will be worse. Tom knocks back the remainder of his pint and deposits the glass on the table with an audible thump. "Out of the frying pan into the fire," he murmurs darkly. I look across at him in surprise — what does he have to be worried about now? — but he's looking toward the exit. The skin round his eyes is tight with anxiety.

The restaurant is a short walk away. Lara walks in the middle and links an arm through one of Tom's arms and one of mine, as if to prevent us from escaping. There's no time for even a deep breath before she has hustled me through the door into what seems more akin to a theater dressing room than a restaurant. I busy myself leaving my coat and bag with the cloakroom attendant, both reluctant to look round and reluctant to be seen looking round. Tom hovers near me as I pass my things over, tension visible in his jaw.

"Are you okay?" I ask him quietly, bemused.

"What? Me? Of course." He brushes it off.

"I'm just worried about you."

I shake my head minutely as I take the ticket from the attendant. "No need."

"If only," I think I hear him say; I look at him sharply, but I can't follow up because Caro is descending upon us. I have to manufacture a smile to endure whatever thorny welcome she will greet me with, but she's too caught up in her favorite role of hostess to deliver anything of consequence. Then there's no longer an excuse, I'm being swept inexorably toward a long table that can only be our reservation; and there is Seb.

He's standing by the table, his hand on the back of a chair that's occupied by a slender blond woman sitting sideways. He looks up on hearing the bustle of our approach, a grin spreading across his face. He is Seb. It's a shock, somehow. He is still so very much Seb.

Lara — bless her, a thousand times bless her — steams in ahead of me, an unstoppable force of bosom and smile and hair, all outstretched arms and double-kisses. "Seb!" she says in a suitably delighted tone. "So good to see you! And this must be Alina . . ." Alina stands to greet Lara. She's tall — taller than I — with the fine-boned features that somehow speak of years of Pony Club

and expensive schooling; her accent when she replies to Lara only confirms that. She is everything I expected she would be. Tom is following in Lara's wake: he and Seb are grinning above a manly handshake that becomes a one-armed hug, then almost descends into a boyish rough-and-tumble in their pleasure at seeing each other. But now Tom is switching his attention to Alina: it's my turn.

Seb is waiting, smiling at me, an arm ready to steady me for the double-kiss treatment. "Kate," he says quietly, warmly, as I draw close. "It's been too long."

It hits me that there's a familiarity in the feel of that cheek, of the arm I lay my hand on as we kiss. I don't know if I expected that, after all these years. "How are you?" I ask as I draw back. It's the polite thing to say under the circumstances. It's possible I'm interested in the answer, but I've resolved not to dissolve into self-analysis this evening. Tonight I have to simply make it through.

"Good, great." He spreads his hands. His hair is shorter than before, and there are little flecks of gray above his ears. He's wearing jeans and a casual shirt, like almost every other male here, though both may be more expensive than the average. "Great to

be back." He runs an appreciative eye over me. "You look well. I hear you're doing well, too, running your own company —" Someone claps a hand on his shoulder with an accompanying bellow, and he turns away, but not without catching my gaze with his extraordinary eyes and mouthing over his shoulder, "Later."

There's an intimacy in that look, in the way he delivers the word — as if he were being dragged away from me. I look after him for a moment. I have no idea what to make of the entire encounter.

I blink and collect myself, turning aside to find Tom watching me, despite ostensibly being in a conversation with Alina and Lara. His face is tight. I cock my head questioningly, and his expression clears deliberately; he lifts his eyebrows — *are you all right?* I nod and even manage a reassuring smile, then step over to join the three of them. Tom's eyes are Tom's eyes, I think. And Seb's . . . well, they are Seb's. They are how they always were.

Shortly we sit. Caro has mustered eighteen of us: we're a raucous party of fractured conversations and sudden hoots of laughter from different directions; though more often from Seb's area than anywhere else. Tom and Lara have made pains to sit on either

side of me; we bracket the end of the table. I have prime viewing position. Caro, flushed and buoyant with the success of the evening, has seated herself next to the guest of honor at the middle of the long table; Alina is opposite. Four bottles of wine are dispatched before the exasperated waiter manages to get a dinner order from us all.

"Okay?" Lara asks under her breath. I nod briefly. "He looks good," she laments on my behalf.

"He always did," I mutter back. If I was hoping to find him a far cry from his former glory, that certainly isn't the case. I look across at Seb, trying to see what caused Tom to suggest he wasn't in good shape. It's true he's bulkier than before, but it all appears solid; he's hardly run to fat. He's still, objectively speaking, the most attractive man in the room, but the heartbreaking, breath-stealing vitality of youth has gone; his beauty no longer burns. I watch him pour himself and Caro another glass of wine, his shirtsleeve rolled back to reveal a tanned forearm. Caro is reveling in Seb's attention; it softens her edges, makes her almost girlish. I don't remember her being this obvious a decade ago, or perhaps I chose not to see it. *Wives and girlfriends always know* . . . I glance at Alina and find

her eyeing the two expressionlessly whilst not drinking her wine. Very deliberately not drinking her wine: the glass is raised to her lips, but nothing passes. Someone says something to her on her right; she turns to them, an attentive smile quickly in place. I watch as she gesticulates to make some point, then casually lifts her wineglass and pretends to drink.

I pick up my own wineglass and join the conversation around me. We eat, we drink, we laugh, we talk. The food is unmemorable, but the wine is good; Tom refills our wineglasses whenever they run dry. I'm actually having fun, though it feels desperate, reckless, like dancing while the *Titanic* sinks. I sneak glances at Seb and Caro and Alina. Lara and Tom sneak glances at me. Seb is performing the same function as Tom in the middle of the table, but twice as frequently, and he never misses his own glass: Seb is drinking hard while his wife isn't drinking at all.

"A toast," calls Caro, standing up as she taps a glass ineffectually with a spoon. The table quiets down, all except a large chap at the end who is still talking to his neighbor; I can't quite remember either of their names, but the faces are familiar. Caro raises her voice: "Do shut up, George. Tilly

has heard all your jokes three times already." That raises chuckles from around the table. She glances down at Seb, smiling. "A toast. Raise your glasses to welcome back . . . Seb, and Alina!" There's the merest pause after she says Seb's name, just enough for anyone so inclined to interpret the mention of Alina as an afterthought; I am so inclined. If that's Alina's interpretation, there's nothing to show it: she smiles graciously, playing her role of guest of honor perfectly.

Seb climbs to his feet. His cheeks are heavily flushed now. "Thank you all from both of us; we're thrilled to be back. And thanks for coming tonight, and to Caro for arranging everything." He smiles and clinks his glass against hers; Caro inclines her head in acknowledgment, the fizzing joy inside almost bursting through her eyes. "It's great to be able to catch up with so many of you again all at once. The thing Alina and I have been most looking forward to about coming back is —"

"The beer!" shouts some wag.

"The sense of humor!" shouts another.

"The dentistry," murmurs Tom in my ear. I giggle. Lara glances across at us. The merest frown crosses her face before she turns back; I wonder if I was too loud.

Seb laughs. "Wonderful as those are,

they're not what I was about to say. What we've most been looking forward to is being close to our friends. And on that note . . ." His expression turns somber. "I'd like to propose a toast to one who can never be here with us again." The table is quiet now. "To Theo."

"To Theo," we all murmur before we drink. I glance at Tom; his face is starkly bleak; one could photograph him and name it *A Study in Grief.* As I watch he deliberately locks eyes with Seb and gives a small nod — *well done* — and Seb nods back, the merest movement. Theo was Tom's friend first and foremost, I remember. They were in the same college, they both read engineering, they even shared a set of rooms in second year; if there is such a thing as the keeper of the grief, Tom has the right of that title in this group. I want to say something to him, but I've no idea what.

The conversation warms and expands again, slowly regaining volume after the moment of solemnity. More wine is called for. I eat chocolate profiteroles that I don't really like because by now I'm drunk and I'll eat practically anything. People are switching places or hunkering down between two chairs to catch up with those they haven't been seated near. I see Alina rise

from the table. Seb is chatting, leaning over someone seated in a chair near hers; he pulls her in for a kiss as she passes, drunkenly tactile, but she keeps it brief, barely breaking her stride. He gazes after her receding back for a moment, before his attention is drawn back into his conversation. I look away, wondering how much one can divine about any relationship from observing a single moment, and am shocked to find Severine's white skull on the table in front of me, atop a pile of sand and sticks and assorted debris. The image is so sharp, so sudden, so vicious that for a second I feel like I'm falling through space.

I push my chair sharply away from the table and head for the toilets, ignoring Tom's concerned call — *Kate?* — reeling from both the wine and Severine's malevolent appearance. I bang inelegantly through the doors. The toilet cubicle, thankfully, is mine and mine alone; no intrusions from the dead here. I close the lid and sit hunched with my forehead propped up by the heels of my hands. I'm angry with Severine, and I have that right — why shouldn't I be angry with the girl who, in life, slept with my boyfriend right under my nose, and then has the temerity to haunt me in death? Why me? Why not Seb? That would be much

more fitting, I think maliciously. And if not Seb, why not Caro? Yes, Caro — what a pity hauntings can't be directed. Perhaps I should ask Severine if she takes requests . . . Still, why me? Not that I would wish it on them, but why not Lara or Tom? I remember Tom's stark, grief-ridden face, staring unseeingly down the table. Not Tom, not ever Tom; that would be beyond unfair.

With a sigh I collect myself and exit the cubicle more elegantly than I entered it, only to stop short when I find Alina at a sink, dabbing a paper towel to her mouth. She instantly scrunches up the paper towel when she sees me and makes a show of tidying up her eyeliner instead. The eyeliner is already perfect, but the eyes it frames look tired.

"Hi," I say into the mirror as I step up to wash my hands. She gives a small smile in return. "Are you having a good evening?"

"Lovely," she says unenthusiastically. "Though it's hard to keep track of names." She looks at me expectantly.

"Kate. Kate Channing." There's not the slightest bit of recognition in her face. "I was at Oxford with Seb." Still nothing. I make a gesture. "And Tom and Lara and Caro, among others." It's laughable. Apparently I wasn't even important enough in

Seb's life for him to mention me to his wife.

"Kate. Got it. Forgive me, I'm so useless with names. And since Seb and I met in New York, I haven't really had a chance to meet any of his friends from back home. Except the ones who came to the wedding, and that was ages ago."

"I'm sure there are easier ways than this evening's trial by fire," I say wryly as I dry my hands on a paper towel.

"Well, Caro was very insistent." She leans forward to inspect her eyeliner again, and then adds, as if realizing her words could be interpreted as a tad ungrateful, "And of course, it's very kind of her to take the trouble."

"Mmmm," I say, unable to keep the irony out of my voice. Alina shoots me a quick look in the mirror, and for a moment her composure slips. She looks exhausted and utterly fed up.

"Are you pregnant?" I blurt out before I can stop myself. My hand flies to my mouth in horror, as if I can catch the words and pop them back in.

Her eyes jump immediately to mine, betraying the truth, then she quickly schools her face to give a surprised laugh. "No, of course —"

"God, I'm sorry, I'm . . ." I stop and shake

my head, genuinely appalled at myself. "It's none of my business." We both look at each other — properly, not in the mirror this time. "Sorry," I say again, truly contrite. I shrug my shoulders and offer the only lame excuse I have. "Tom's been doing *too* good a job of topping up my wine."

"It's okay," she says slowly after a moment. There's no role-playing now; she makes no bones of the fact that she's carefully assessing me. I wonder what she sees. She shrugs. "Since you've asked I may as well admit it: yes, I'm pregnant. Nine weeks. It's been quite a journey." The smile that steals across her face is half fearful and half excited and only lasts a heartbeat. "Please keep it to yourself. Though Seb is smashed enough tonight to tell the whole world anyway," she adds, not without a note of frustration. It crosses my mind that tonight at least, I wouldn't wish to be in her shoes, but I push that aside. The ban on self-analysis is still in force. She tosses the scrunched-up paper towel into a waste bin, no longer hiding it. "There's nothing 'morning' about my sickness."

"Well, I guess . . . congratulations." I smile awkwardly. "And I hope the sickness passes soon."

She looks at me for a moment then nods

thoughtfully. "Thank you." We head back into the restaurant together. I think wryly to myself of the kiss I observed. The additional information of Alina's sickness puts a very different spin on it: the nauseous wife surreptitiously hurrying to the bathroom. I follow Alina's long, narrow form that betrays no hint of a tiny life inside and wonder how Caro will take the news.

Back at the table the waiter is moving round with a handheld machine taking card payments and someone is suggesting a move to a nearby club, but on a Thursday night the idea has no traction; we all have to work tomorrow, and none of us are twenty-one anymore. Lara has already rescued our coats from the cloakroom; she's holding mine ready for me by the exit. I look round for Tom and instead spy Caro and Seb, half hidden behind an enormous fern. They are close, too close. Caro has one hand on Seb's arm and is speaking to him urgently; his head is bent to hear her. As I watch, Seb scans the room quickly, as if checking they haven't been seen, then focuses on Caro again. I turn away. I wish I hadn't seen them. I wish I didn't have to feel achingly sorry for Alina and furiously disappointed with Seb. Despite everything, I had expected better of him.

Tom has returned from the gents, and as a group we're now tumbling out into the night. Alina and Seb are doing their rounds of good-byes while various people try to figure out who best should share the taxis they're trying to hail. I turn to Lara. "Shall we share a cab?"

"Actually, you and Tom can share. I'm . . . ah . . . going in a different direction," she says clumsily, not meeting my eye.

"Lara." By now I am fed up of this charade and too drunk to hide it. "I know where you're going and you know I know." Her lips thin mutinously as she bristles. It's so out of character I almost laugh: Modan is drawing out new depths in our Lara. I grab her arm. "No, look, I'm not . . . I'm just saying, be careful, okay?" She looks at me warily. "I worry about you. Look after yourself. That's all."

A smile breaks over her face, and she pulls me in for a hug. "You, too, honey," she says quietly. Her breasts crush against me as we hug; I smell her perfume and some kind of floral scent in her hair. I wonder how that would feel to me if I was Alain Modan. Then she climbs into the cab Tom has hailed for her and disappears off.

I feel a hand on my shoulder and swing round to find Seb beside me. "Sorry," he

says ruefully, charmingly. "We didn't get a chance to talk after all."

"I'm sure there will be other occasions." I don't want to speak to him at all tonight, and maybe not ever, after witnessing his tête-à-tête with Caro.

"Oh, definitely." He pulls me a little to the side and suddenly looks awkward. "Listen, Kate, all this stuff with Severine being found . . . I just wanted to say, well, some stuff might come out that . . . doesn't reflect well on me." I gaze at him nonplussed. He grimaces. "I mean, some stuff about me and Severine." It dawns on me that he's confessing to his infidelity, right here, outside a restaurant, when we've both had too much to drink. I'm temporarily speechless. He's still speaking, however. "I just . . . didn't want you to hear from someone else and be hurt by that. It was just the once; it didn't mean anything . . . We were all so drunk that night —"

Wordless, bitter rage broils inside me. I make a sharp gesture with my hand, cutting him off. "I don't want to talk about it." He blinks, taken aback by my vehemence. I look around for Tom.

"Well, it was a long time ago. It's just, with that policeman and everything, everything is coming into the open. Best to be honest

in this situation, I think. I mean, you can't really lie to the law. And you and I both know I came to our room that night and passed out, so whatever happened to Severine was nothing to do with me."

I swing back to stare at him. I worried about Caro telling Modan about Severine and Seb; it didn't occur to me that Seb would own up himself. He's running a hand through his hair and has on his best contrite expression, like a little boy caught with his hand in the cookie jar. I desperately want to tell him to *fuck off,* but it turns out Tom is right: this is all about pride. I would be yelling an endless stream of invective at Seb right now if it weren't for the fact it would draw everyone's attention. I can't bear the thought of them all talking about me afterward. *Poor Kate. All these years and she still hasn't got over Seb. She hasn't really had a serious boyfriend since, you know . . .* I look for Tom, desperately hoping he has a cab ready to whisk me away; he's waving at one that has its light on, but it's not quite close enough for immediate salvation. I stare fixedly at it, willing it closer.

"Kate?" says Seb uncertainly.

The cab finally draws up. "Say good night to Alina for me," I bite out, not looking at Seb. As I turn toward the cab, I realize Caro

is watching us. Or rather, watching me. Watching my reaction.

"Okay?" asks Tom as he helps me into the cab. I glance back through the window of the cab. Seb and Caro are sharing a look, and suddenly I feel the ground shift under me. What if Caro and Seb aren't having an affair after all? What if the secret they're keeping is something else entirely? "Kate?" Tom says again. "Are you okay?"

The cab starts to pull away. Wild laughter bubbles up inside me. I'm still drunk, I realize. Of course I am. Seb's confession and the night air may have been sobering, but given the amount of wine I've sunk, physically I can't be anything other than smashed right now. Tom looks at me across the wide seat of the cab. The laughter evaporates just as quickly as it came. "No," I say truthfully. "I'm not okay."

"Yeah," he says softly. He looks down, his expression hidden in the shadows of the cab. "I didn't think so."

CHAPTER ELEVEN

I wake slowly with the dawning realization that I'm horribly hungover and this is not my bed: the covers don't feel right, the light from the window is coming from the wrong place, and I'm wearing my bra, which I never sleep in . . . I turn over cautiously to check whether I'm the sole occupant. The bedroom door is slightly ajar, and through it I can see the back of someone very familiar in a kitchen I recognize, drinking a cup of something.

Tom. I'm at Tom's.

Images of last night surface in a haphazard, fractured fashion, with no suggestion of how one led to another: the dinner; the cab ride afterward; drunkenly climbing the stairs to Tom's flat; making coffee; kissing.

Kissing. Dear God, kissing. Kissing Tom.

The memory takes hold, and I'm there now, in the secretive gloom of the corridor that leads to his bedroom, the length of him

pressing me against the wall — solid, warm, strong. One hand buries into my hair while the other cups my breast; I arch into him. When I kiss his neck I both hear and feel the rough groan in his throat that sends a reckless thrill running through me.

Reckless. Reckless indeed. But — if there was no Seb (how unthinkable, no Seb! Only not so unthinkable now, after seeing him again — as he is, not how I'd imagined him to be — and after kissing Tom . . .), and no Lara or Severine or Alain Modan . . . I wrap up the memory and put it away, a dark, delicious, thrilling secret to unfold slowly and savor much later. But for now . . . I can't recall what happened next. I look across at the other side of the bed again; it doesn't appear to have been slept in at all. In the kitchen Tom's wearing jeans, but no shirt — the same jeans as last night, I think. The tan of the back of his neck contrasts with his paler, freckled shoulders. There is tension in those broad muscled shoulders. Even from here I can sense it thickening the atmosphere. I feel my sense of uneasiness growing. What happened after the corridor? I have a horrendous growing suspicion I may have passed out on him. God, how embarrassing. Perhaps dented male pride is responsible for his palpable tension . . .

What to do now? I debate internally for a moment before I sit up awkwardly, trying to keep the duvet tucked across my chest, and aim for a sheepish smile. "Morning," I call.

He puts his cup down with a decided thud and turns round. "Tea?" he says unsmiling.

I smother a yawn. "Yes, please. I feel like shit."

"You deserve to," he says shortly, then moves out of my line of sight to make the tea, leaving me blinking in surprise. Tom is not just tense; he's furious. With me.

I have no idea what's going on, but I definitely want to face it wearing more clothing than this. I look around the room for my dress and find it tossed over a chair, beside my shoes, bag and coat. I have just enough time to scramble into the dress; I'm sitting on the edge of the bed nearest the door, running my fingers through my no doubt ragged hair when he returns, a mug cradled in his hands. He has long, strong fingers: I remember the feel of them buried in my hair, the sureness of his touch. Suddenly I realize he's been holding out the mug for a few seconds now; I take it quickly. "Thank you."

"You're welcome," he says shortly, leaning against the doorframe and avoiding my eyes. The breadth of his shoulders nearly fills the

open space.

"Funny, I don't feel very welcome." I look at him, willing him to catch my eye with a rueful smile and turn back into the Tom I know. But he's someone different now; the kissing last night did that. I can't look at him like yesterday or the day before or ten years ago. He has a tangle of dark hair across the planes of his chest, spreading down across his abdomen to disappear in the waistband of his jeans. He didn't have that a decade ago, nor the muscle bulk; he's not the same as he was. The corridor secret threatens to burst forth from where I've buried it: I want to touch him and I want to cry at the same time. I look away quickly and take a sip from my tea.

He still hasn't said anything — not *Of course you're welcome,* or *I'm sorry you feel that way.* A defiant anger suddenly sparks within me. I carefully place the cup of tea on the bedside table. "Want to tell me exactly what I'm in the doghouse for, or am I expected to guess?"

That whips his gaze round. "I thought we were friends."

"We are," I say, surprised.

"*Good* friends," he says impatiently, batting away my response as if I'm deliberately missing the point. "I thought our friendship

192

was important to you. I thought you rated it more highly than to behave like that."

"Like what exactly?" My voice is rising and I'm standing now. "We were drunk —"

"*You* were drunk —"

"And you were stone cold sober, were you?" I stare him down; after a moment he jerks his head and looks away, conceding the point. "We kissed. You may have to fill me in on a few of the details given the aforementioned drunkenness, but it's hardly the scandal of the century."

"Oh, so it's nothing, is it? We'll just carry on as normal, nothing's changed?" he shoots back, snapping his gaze back onto me. "I thought — Jesus, I actually thought our friendship was something you would take pains to protect, and instead you practically throw yourself at me." A hot wave of humiliation courses through me. Did I really throw myself at him? How embarrassing, how — God, how immature, how *teenage*. Though from what scant memories I have, he didn't exactly seem unwilling . . . But Tom is still speaking. "I get that it's difficult for you to see Seb —"

"It's not —"

"Don't give me that. I saw your face when he kissed Alina. His *wife*, Kate, and Christ,

it's been ten years! He kissed his wife and you had to leave the fucking room —"

"That's not . . ." I start, but he's still in full flood, and in any case, what can I say? *Actually, I realized last night that I'm over Seb. I left the room because Severine's skull appeared on the table. Yes, I see her regularly. I would ask her who killed her except she never speaks.*

"— you were near as dammit physically ill at the sight. So don't tell me you don't care about Seb. Only next time you're looking for a pick-me-up shag to make you feel better, have the decency to try someone other than me."

He stops, breathing hard, his blue eyes boring into me. In that moment I see myself as he sees me and it's at such odds to how I imagined that I'm temporarily cut off from speech. The hurt is staggering.

"Oh," I hear myself say eventually. There's nothing else I can say. It doesn't matter that I'm not in love with Seb; it doesn't matter that the corridor memory is something precious to me. All that matters is what Tom thinks, and now that I know his opinion I can't look at him. I turn and gather up my shoes, bag and coat from the chair in the corner and push past him without resistance into the corridor — the corridor. Can I

really have this memory of the intimate darkness, the sweetness, the desire, while Tom holds something entirely different inside him? Is this really Tom? I turn as if to check before I leave; he's still standing by the bedroom door, but I can't see his face in the shadow. I don't know who this is.

The hurt hasn't ebbed, nor the excruciating humiliation, but my sense of injustice is fanning those embers of anger. "So," I say slowly, deliberately. I hear my voice, but it doesn't sound like me; it's too high and clipped. "In your eyes I'm a desperate, lonely old spinster looking for anybody or anything to take my mind off Seb." He makes a movement with his hand, but I go on. "Well, there were two of us there last night. What's your excuse?"

"Kate —" he says, moving toward me, but I don't wait for his answer. In truth it has just occurred to me: ironically the accusation he's thrown at me is more appropriate for him. I was a substitute for Lara. I pull the door closed sharply behind me and go down the tattered steps to the front door of the block of flats, only pausing at the bottom to put on my shoes. I had tights on last night, I think inconsequentially; they must still be in Tom's flat. Did he undress me and put me to bed, the pathetic old basket

case who couldn't hold her drink? I see a cab as soon as I spill out of the lobby onto the street, and it stops for me.

"Where to, love?" asks the driver.

Where to, indeed? I look at my watch. My head is pounding from the hangover, and I feel greasy and gritty, but I don't have time to go home for a shower before I'm due to meet my lawyer. I give him the address of my office instead. I half expect Severine to join me in the cab, but I spend the journey alone, gritting my teeth and focusing solely on staying above the riptide of hurt that beats up inexorably at my throat and threatens to drag me down.

I make it into the bathroom at my office before I give in to that current, sitting on the loo seat in the cramped WC sobbing soundlessly into my hands. It's an indulgence, I know, but I'm temporarily unable to restrain myself. It's hard to even pinpoint why I'm crying, other than through battered pride. But that dark, thrilling corridor encounter . . . I never thought of Tom that way; he was Lara's, or Lara was Tom's, or something — and anyway, there was always the intangible presence of Seb between us. But it turns out I haven't been in love with Seb for a very long time, if I ever was at all; I'm starting to wonder if the Seb of my

memories ever existed. Nobody seems to be who I thought they were. Tom's words echo in my head. *Next time you're looking for a pick-me-up shag . . .* Nobody is who I thought they were, and that apparently includes me.

There's a rap on the door. "Kate?" I hear Julie's muffled voice. "You probably ought to leave for your next appointment soon."

"Um, thanks. Be right out." I blow my nose on toilet roll and wipe my eyes then survey the damage in the mirror. The combination of a hangover and a crying fit clearly doesn't suit my skin, and splashing cold water on my face turns out to be an ineffectual remedy. *Grin and bear it,* I tell myself, forcing my mouth into a smile. Then I see Severine's grinning skull superimposed on my own reflection and it's all I can do not to vomit.

When I emerge some minutes later Julie's eyes sweep over me, her face anxious, but she has the good sense not to comment. Thankfully Paul is not there, and for once I couldn't care less whether that's a good or a bad sign. It's only on the route to my lawyer's office that it occurs to me all this emotional drama has distracted me from the fact that last night I was wondering whether Seb and Caro had something to do

with the death of a young girl in France ten years ago.

"Well," remarks my lawyer from behind her desk, looking at me over the top of her reading glasses. I'm not quite sure why she's wearing them; it's not as if she has anything in front of her to read right now. Instead she's been in listening mode, a small frown appearing from time to time on her narrow forehead, occasionally a nod of her neat, dark head as she takes in my disjointed account. I'm trying to get the measure of her, Mrs. Streeter — or was it Ms., or Miss? — but it's hard in the small, hot room with my head pounding so fiercely. She reminds me of a magpie, dark and bright and quick, though she must be almost fifty; there are gray streaks in that black close-cropped hair. "Well," she says again, more thoughtfully, pursing her lips, which are incongruously painted with uneven layers of a greasy lipstick that's far too pink for her. I want to pick up a tissue and wipe it off her. She hasn't offered me a cup of tea, which I'm irrationally resentful over. I'm sure her fees are going to bankrupt me, so surely a tea bag and a splash of milk isn't too much to ask?

She leans back in her chair and adjusts

her reading glasses. This will be the pronouncement, I think; this is where I find out exactly how much of a mess I'm in. "You're a lawyer, yes?" she says abruptly.

"Yes. Well, no, not anymore. I run a legal recruitment company."

She waves a hand. "But you have the training. You know, for example, that we have an adversarial system here in Britain: the police and prosecution gather evidence likely to convict, and the defense gathers evidence likely to acquit, and then it's all hashed out in open court. Given your training, you likely know an awful lot more detail than that. In practice, in high-profile criminal cases, what tends to happen is that the police very quickly establish a theory and work to find evidence to support that. Anything they turn up that doesn't quite fit the working theory is not exactly overlooked, but it certainly gets less attention." She grimaces, her mouth a slash of uneasy pink. "It's imperfect. All systems are imperfect. But we have habeas corpus, and presumed innocence until proof of guilt, and the court framework in which the trial takes place is very open." She fixes her dark, bright eyes upon me, and I realize I'm expected to respond in some way.

"Um. Yes."

She nods briskly. "The French system is very different. It's based on civil law, rather than common law, which as you know means there is no concept of precedent . . . but I digress. The important point vis-à-vis your situation is that it is not an adversarial system. All criminal cases — at least, all criminal cases of a serious nature such as this — are investigated by a, well, the technical term is *juge d'instruction,* which translates roughly as *examining magistrate,* I suppose. This magistrate is independent of the government and the prosecution service, but nonetheless works closely with the police. It's their job to analyze all the evidence and opine in a report as to whether the case should go to trial." She pauses and looks at me closely again. This time I'm quick to nod. "The important point here is that, generally speaking, weak cases don't even get to trial; they're thrown out by the investigating magistrate before that. The corollary is that the conviction rate is very high, and whilst there's the concept of innocent until proven guilty, in practice . . ." She shrugs her shoulders and executes that queasy pink grimace again. "There's a high presumption of guilt if the case gets as far as trial."

My mind is racing ahead. "But what of

the checks and balances on the magistrate?"

She shakes her head almost apologetically. "Next to none. It's one of the major complaints against the system; effectively a huge number of cases are tried in secret by a single person rather than in open court subject to a jury of peers. On the whole the magistrates are very good, but as a principle . . . I should probably add there's no concept of habeas corpus, either, though in most circumstances a *juge d'instruction* would need another magistrate to sign off before a person can be held. Oh, and while trials are generally very quick, the preceding investigations can be very long."

"How long?"

"Two years is not unusual."

It may be the hangover, but I don't think so: suddenly I feel sick again. The idea of this hanging over us all for years doesn't bear thinking about: Modan appearing at intervals with his oh-so-elegant suits and his sly questions, inducing Lara to a permanent state of self-absorbed giddiness, Caro needling and prodding and pecking away at any exposed quarter, Tom — no, not Tom, I can't think about Tom — and Severine . . . It occurs to me that I've been relying on Severine disappearing once this has all gone

away. I wonder if she sees it quite the same way.

"Are you all right?"

I realize I'm rubbing my forehead with notable force. I drop my hand and attempt to look at her, but another wave of nausea hits me and I have to look down and grit my teeth. The office floor is carpeted with faded blue tiles, which provide nothing to focus on; I try the edge of her desk instead. There's a scratch in the dark varnished wood that shows the cheap sawdust-like MDF underneath.

"Perhaps a cup of tea?" She doesn't wait for my answer; she leans forward and presses a button on her telephone to issue the tea-making instruction to a disembodied voice. Disembodied: a voice without a body. But Severine is the other way round: a body without a voice. Dear God, two more years of Severine . . .

"Are you all right?" she asks again.

"Sorry. It's just a little hot in here," I say unconvincingly. The nausea is passing.

"Of course," she says smoothly. "Ah, here's the tea."

I take my cup gratefully, and also a couple of biscuits, which I nibble at cautiously at first, but then devour rapidly as I realize I'm starving. She takes her own cup, adds

milk and stirs in economical movements, then sits back with the cup resting on her leg, the saucer abandoned on the desk. I focus on my own life-giving tea.

"What do you think happened?" she asks, in a musing tone.

I look up inquiringly, my mouth full of another biscuit.

"You've told me the bare facts of what happened," she explains. "All of which I could have got from the French papers, to be frank — of course I've been following it; it's exactly my area and quite a high-profile case over there. But what do *you* think happened?"

I take a sip of tea to wash down the biscuit before answering her. "I don't know. It was so long ago . . . Now I'm not even sure I can trust my memories." Or my interpretation of those memories.

"Understandable. But you were questioned quite soon after; that usually helps the details to stick, so to speak."

I shrug.

"So, all caveats notwithstanding, what do you think happened?"

"Well, at first I thought — well, I thought it was nothing to do with us. Her ex-boyfriend, maybe, or just something totally random, some sick psycho or some-

thing . . ."

"And now?" She tips her head to one side.

"I don't know. No, really, I don't. I suppose since Modan told me it wasn't the ex-boyfriend I've been thinking about whether it *could* have been one of us. Just hypothetically."

"And?"

"I suppose . . . not Lara, obviously; it's just not within her. And not Tom."

"Why not Tom?"

"Well, he was with Lara all night. And even if he hadn't been . . ."

"Let me guess: it's not within him; he just couldn't." It's not said unkindly; she's almost smiling, but I know she's deliberately holding up a mirror to show me the flaws in my thinking. "That's what you were going to say, correct?"

"Something like that," I concede weakly, but it's not true actually. Tom could, if it was necessary. He has that steel within him, the ability to get things done. I see his stony face from this morning . . . But if Tom had done it, he'd have done it *right*. He wouldn't have allowed a body to be found ten years later. "Anyway, like I said, he was with Lara all night. From what I gather, they didn't do a lot of sleeping," I add wryly. I think of Lara and Tom entwined, and my mind im-

mediately skitters away from the image.

She inclines her head, conceding the point. "Which leaves Caroline, Theo and Sebastian. And you, but you were in bed, later joined by Sebastian, after his assignation with Severine."

I wonder if I would have flinched even a day ago to hear her say that so baldly. Now it's simply a fact. "Yes. Only I didn't know about the assignation at the time."

"What time did he join you?"

"I'm not sure. About 3 A.M. I think." At least, I think that I think that. It was so long ago . . . Suddenly I'm back in that bedroom in France, groggily opening my eyes to see the glowing red digits of the clock radio showing 6 A.M. in the foreground, and in the background Seb stepping out of his boxer shorts after a trip to the bathroom. Without moving my head that's the extent of my vision: a sideways image of a clock and Seb, from waist to knee. He's close enough that I can see the first rays of the morning sun, undeterred by the ineffectual curtains, turning the hair on his legs into golden glowing wires. I can't face dealing with him, so I close my eyes tightly and pretend he hasn't woken me.

Seb's words of last night (was it only last night?) float back to me: *And you and I both*

know I came to our room that night and passed out, so whatever happened to Severine was nothing to do with me. And I think again of Caro's and Seb's heads, conspiratorially close; of Caro watching Seb as he spoke to me last night. Do I think he came to bed at 3 A.M. because he told me that at some point?

"And you say Caro and Theo were together till they went to bed."

"Yes. So I understand." How do I know that? Certainly there's no Theo to ask.

"Was Sebastian the last person to see Severine alive then?"

"No, the bus driver. And the CCTV." The bus driver. Of course. I forgot that last night. It doesn't matter what time Seb came to bed; it doesn't matter whether Caro and Theo were together: Severine was alive enough on Saturday morning to take a bus. Something inside me unwinds a little.

"True. If it was indeed Severine." She frowns for a moment. "Though the chances of another young girl matching that description getting on in that location . . . Mmmm." She ponders silently for a moment, leaning back and tapping her teeth with a fingernail. I wonder if she will later find that dreadful pink lipstick all over her fingers. She straightens up. "Right. Plan of action. No

206

talking to Monsieur Modan without me present."

"Okay. What else?"

She shakes her head, smiling. "That's it for now. All we can do is wait."

I stare at her, nonplussed. "Wait?" I'm paying painful amounts per hour, and all she can come up with is *keep quiet* and *wait?*

She nods. "Yes, wait. Believe me, Modan is not here on a whim. He has information he's not yet revealed. Perhaps from the autopsy, or something else . . . At any rate, there's something he's not telling you. Because otherwise, there is literally no evidence to tie any of the six of you to this crime, and it's quite a stretch to find a motive, too, despite best efforts to paint you as the jilted lover. So if the *juge d'instruction* still has Modan digging around over here, you can be sure there's something up his sleeve. So . . . we wait."

Jesus. "I'm not good at waiting."

"No," she says contemplatively, as she pushes back her chair to stand up and extend her hand. "I wouldn't think you are."

I'm not quite sure how to take that.

CHAPTER TWELVE

All day Severine hovers.

I've decided it's a sign of tiredness, or distraction: like an illness, she can creep in much more easily when my defenses are low. Not that she creeps. She strolls, she saunters, she claims territory as her own with a single languid glance; everything about Severine is on Severine's terms. Except her death, of course.

I'm back in my office after the appointment with my lawyer, and despite my hangover, despite Severine, despite the — what? drama, row, contretemps? — with Tom, I'm getting rather a lot done. The trick is bloody single-mindedness, a strong personal trait of mine. Do not pick up the phone and call Lara; do not pay attention to the slim, secretive-eyed dead girl who perches casually on the edge of my desk, swinging one walnut brown ankle; do not descend into introspection and speculation; do not pass

go, do not collect £200.

Gordon calls early afternoon. We now have a weekly catch-up call in the diary for each Friday afternoon, though I've been fore-warned he will frequently have to resched-ule, or skip it altogether: Mr. Farrow is a busy man. I presume he's calling to resched-ule, but instead he says, in his mild manner, "Why don't you drop by the office instead of having a call today?"

"Sure, let me just check my schedule." I have a couple of calls in my diary before then, but I should still be able to get across town in time. "That's fine, I can come over. Everything okay?"

"Fine, fine. Just thought it's been a while since we had a face-to-face catch-up. I'm a little quieter today, so it seemed best to take advantage."

"No problem. See you at 3:30." I hang up, thinking that I should take Paul with me, to broaden the relationship and so forth, but I know I won't. Gordon enjoys meeting *me* (and vice versa); he will find Paul too slick, too accommodating.

I wonder if I will be bringing Severine with me.

Either Severine finds business meetings uninteresting, or I am sufficiently focused

to keep her at bay, but whatever the reason, I'm flying solo when I meet with Gordon. We run through an update on the candidates he has seen: what he thinks of them, what they think of the opportunity, what other firms appear to be thinking of them . . . Recruitment at this level — partner, soon to be partner, which is what we're concentrating on first — is a strategic game. The next step is the associates, but a good number will simply follow the partners they've worked with most closely.

"If we get those two, it will be quite a coup," says Gordon thoughtfully, tapping the sheet of names that lies on the table in front of us, flanked by our empty coffee cups. We're in one of the meeting rooms on the top floor of the Haft & Weil building, with a glorious view over the city. I can see the gleaming curve of St. Paul's dome, with glimpses of the flashing silver ribbon that is the Thames popping up unexpectedly between buildings. From this height, London has a stately gravitas in its lofty architecture, standing indomitable and proud in the sunshine. It would be easy to forget the hustle and grime one encounters close-up.

"We'll get them," I say confidently, wrenching my gaze back to the paper.

"Well, I suppose the size of the guarantee

we're offering is hard to ignore."

I shake my head. "It's not about the guarantee." Gordon glances at me, a question in his eyes. "That's necessary, obviously, but what I mean is, it's not about the money for those two. It's about what the money means. They feel undervalued, underappreciated where they are, and they hate the lack of collegiality. The guarantee just proves to them that you value them. If you manage them properly once you get them across, make them feel safe but also give them opportunities to feel like they're making a difference, then I think they'll do very well for you."

Gordon's sharp eyes are assessing me. "You have strong views on management styles, I take it."

I shrug. "In my job, you need to have an instinct for who would fit where. No point putting a diffident technical specialist into an aggressive American setup, for example."

"You need to be a good judge of people." He's toying with his empty coffee cup, as if turning something over in his mind.

"I like to think I am. In a professional context." My mind skitters to that week in France, to Seb, to Tom, to Lara, Theo, Caro, Severine, and the spider's web that entangles and binds us all. With everything I

know now, I can only think that my judgment was disastrously clouded back then. Possibly — probably, even? — it still is. "In a professional context," I repeat. He's still turning the coffee cup this way and that. "Why, is there something troubling you?"

He glances up, surprised. "No, I . . . No. Well." He looks away again, as if reluctant to look at me, to acknowledge we're having this conversation. "Caro is on the slate this year."

The slate: the list of prospective candidates for partnership. It's pretty much an up-or-out culture: those who don't make the cut are expected to leave the firm. I do a rapid calculation of how long Caro has been a qualified lawyer, and the timing is about right; I'd expect her to be on the slate around now. "And how does it look?" I ask, although I know the answer, or we wouldn't be talking about it.

He puffs out a breath. "Between you and me . . . dicey. Speaking plainly, it's good that she's female; we need more women in corporate. Not that we're supposed to kowtow to the statistics, but . . ." He grimaces, and I nod. We both know the score on gender balance in the workplace. "And anyway, she's very good, and a tough negotiator, no question about it, and the

clients that love her *really* love her, but there's a perception that she's . . . well . . ." He's searching for a way to say it that doesn't make him feel disloyal. "I suppose . . . not a team player." He looks at me directly. "If you were placing Caro, where would you put her?"

I consider hedging my bets, coming up with a carefully worded non-answer, but then I remember this is Gordon: he likes to hear it straight. I can only hope that extends to opinions about his daughter. I take a deep breath and muster an even tone. "Haft & Weil wouldn't be my first choice for her. I would think she would be more suited to an aggressive American outfit. Eat what you kill and so forth."

He nods absentmindedly, looking out over the expanse of the city skyline; thankfully he can't see my relief that he isn't offended by my bluntness. "I wouldn't disagree with you. But since she's trying to make it in this firm . . ." He trails off.

I look for something helpful to suggest, though no doubt whatever I can think of he will already have considered. "Perhaps she needs to get involved in some management initiatives during the coming year. Show that she can be a more rounded candidate."

"Perhaps." He purses his lips thoughtfully,

then sighs, still gazing at the skyline, though I'm not sure he sees it. "We're making up less partners each year, you know? I don't know how we expect to keep all the associates working at this intensity when the prize is getting harder and harder to grab. Used to be that if you did a good job for long enough and kept your nose clean . . ." He collects himself and turns back to me. "Good idea on the management side; I suppose that type of involvement might give her an edge." He nods to himself, as if making a mental note to speak with her about it. "Though you can't cut corners . . ." He trails off again, his gaze sliding back down to his empty coffee cup.

You can't cut corners. Only, Caro would. Caro would cut a swath down the middle and everyone else be damned if that was the most convenient route for herself. I suddenly realize he knows the problem is more far-reaching than just *not a team player.* Deep down he doesn't think she'll make partner, and he doesn't think she ought to, either, though he's trying hard to convince himself otherwise. For a moment I ache for him, this clever, thoughtful, kind man who wants the Caro he lost when she was thirteen, and is bewildered every day by the woman she's become.

■ ■ ■ ■

It's barely 4 P.M., but I go straight home after the meeting with Gordon; I'm exhausted. All I want to do is sink into a hot bath. Though perhaps taking a moment to relax will be like removing my head from the sand: reality will rush in and I will have to face it all — Tom, Severine, Modan, the whole shebang. I dither for a moment then run the bath, dumping in industrial quantities of an expensive bath foam Lara bought me. If reality is going to rush in anyway, I may as well face it whilst lounging up to my ears in soapsuds.

Lara calls just as I'm settling into the bath with an inadvertent sigh of pleasure. "Have you got plans?" she asks. She sounds uncharacteristically drained. "Or do you fancy a quiet night in? Takeout in front of a chick flick or something?"

"Done," I say, thinking warmly of all the chick flick nights we've had in the past, gossiping over the local takeout and drinking rather more wine than is warranted by a quiet night in. Only that was before, when Lara was just Lara, with no subterfuge, and I was just Kate (albeit *desperate, lonely old spinster* Kate), and Severine was a strange

215

mystery from a summer long, long ago. I want everything back how it was so badly that my eyes are pricking with tears. I shake my head impatiently, and the mountains of soapsuds rise and fall gently. "I'm already home and I can't bear the thought of moving again — do you mind coming to me?"

"Not a problem. Your take-out place is better anyway."

"You sound done in. What time did you get home last night?" There's a pause. "Ah. You didn't make it home."

"Well . . . no. What about you, were you late?"

I could lie, now I've become so very good at that; I could obfuscate, I could dodge the question, but it's just so bloody exhausting. "I didn't make it home either."

"Really? But who . . ." I can practically hear her brain whirring. *"Tom?"* The surprise is genuine. She has no right to mind, but still I wonder if she does.

"Yes. But it's not like that. Not really . . ."

"What does *not really* mean?" Is she a little forced, or am I overanalyzing?

"It means I'll tell you later. Not that there's anything much to tell. What time do you think you'll be here?"

"Around six, I think, if not sooner. My brain is good for nothing today; there's

hardly any point in me sitting here."

"Well, I'll be here, so whenever."

I put down the phone and lean my head back against the rim of the bathtub. Severine, dressed in the black shift, has perched her neat behind casually on the edge of the tub, her slender limbs stretched out ahead of her, crossed at the ankle. She turns to look at me expressionlessly with those dark, all-knowing eyes. It's the contrast that catches attention, I muse: the eyes that have seen far more than fits a face so smooth and unlined. I think of the crow's-feet developing round the corners of my eyes, of the single gray hair I found (and immediately plucked out) last week.

"I'm thirty-one," I say aloud. Severine is still looking at me. "I suppose you'll be — what was it? — nineteen forever." She looks away, disinterested, presenting me with her profile. Her nose has a small bump in it, but if anything it works for her; it makes her face stronger. "Why are you here anyway?" She looks at me again. There's no intensity, just a cool appraisal, then her gaze slides off, as if I'm simply not interesting enough to retain it. It's more than a little galling. I reach for the shampoo and lather up my hair, then try again, irritation creeping into my voice now. "Since you're here,

do you mind telling me who killed you?"

She's smoking a cigarette now, one leg crossed over the other and her sandal dangling off her narrow foot again, in the way that hypnotized Seb all those years ago; she glances at me, one eyebrow raised. It's as strong an expression of amusement as I've ever seen on her face.

"Yeah, okay, I didn't really think it would be that easy," I mutter. Then I sink under the still-hot water to wash out the shampoo, and when I surface she has gone.

"So," says Lara expressively, as soon as she has a glass of wine in her hand. *So.* A single word, two letters — how can it be loaded with such meaning? "Spill." She looks tired, so tired that it seems an effort to hold herself together this evening; even her facial features are rumpled at the edges.

I look at the glass in my own hand: it's beautiful, long and elegant and fragile; a gift, though I don't remember who from. If I applied pressure, it would crack instantly. I have some sympathy. I wonder how resilient Lara is feeling. "You spill," I say tightly. I don't mean to be combative, but . . . I sort of do.

She takes a sip and tries to smile, but it doesn't come off, and I instantly feel guilty.

"Are you okay?" I ask quietly.

She shrugs. "Sort of. Maybe." Again, the effortful smile, through tears that can't be far away. "You?"

I shrug. "Pretty much the same." Though in my case there are no tears hovering, I won't allow myself to wallow again. I take a sip of the wine. It will go to my head quickly tonight if I'm not careful. "Come on. Let's order the curry and watch the film. We can do all the spilling later."

And so I spend the evening with Lara. It's a nice evening; an evening that harks back to happier times. We watch a romcom, we eat too much curry, we drink too much wine. It's comforting, this old habit of ours; the only thing that has changed over the years is the quality of the wine. Severine stays away, which isn't really a surprise; I'm well aware she's a figment of my (frankly, fevered) imagination, and my imagination cannot possibly conjure an image of Severine watching anything containing Reese Witherspoon. I see her more as an art house kind of girl.

But in truth more has changed than our wine budget. When the film has finished we can't avoid the dual elephants in the room. "So," she says again, turning to face me and arranging herself cross-legged on the sofa

we're sharing. She's borrowed from my wardrobe a pair of slouchy pajama bottoms and a hoodie; on me, they're definitely hide-at-home clothing, but on Lara they're transformed by her blondness, her busti-ness, her sheer wholesome sexiness: she could be an advert for Abercrombie & Fitch. No wonder Tom continues to hold a torch for her. It never bothered me before, but now I find I'm analyzing: score 1 for Lara for instant sex appeal; score 1 for Kate for her quick intelligence; score 1 for Lara . . . I am appalled at myself — has one single drunken kiss with Tom really dragged me down to this level? — but still I can't completely stifle the ugly green-eyed mon-ster lurking within me.

"So," I counter. "How are things with the dear detective?"

"Ah." She looks down and traces a circle on the sofa with her finger. "It's . . . compli-cated."

It seems she's ready to talk. I rearrange myself on the sofa to mirror her position. "Where is he tonight?"

"He went back to France."

My heart leaps. "For good?"

"No, he's coming back on Monday; it's just for some family thing. A christening, I think. Not because of the case." She's still

220

making the circles. "Not that he'd tell me if it was because of the case; he won't talk about it with me since . . ."

"Since?" A blush is crossing her cheeks, and suddenly I know exactly what she means. I wonder how she will phrase it.

"Since we . . . ah . . . crossed that line." Bravo, neatly put. I can't bring myself to ask any of the usual gossipy questions, and she doesn't seem to expect me to: she glances up at my face, both embarrassed and rueful, and adds, "So, sorry, but no insider information here."

"A man of principle," I say, only half ironic.

"He is!" She's leaning forward, her whole body imploring me to listen, to understand. "I mean, I know how it looks — he's screwing one of the witnesses in his case — but we're keeping it totally separate; he won't discuss it *at all* with me, not a word, and anyway, it's not like *I'm* under suspicion."

"No, but I am."

She pauses, then nods dejectedly. "Yes, I think you are. It doesn't make any sense to me, given she was alive on Saturday morning, but you are. And Seb and Caro and Theo."

"But me more than most. On account of Seb's complete lack of self-restraint." Tom

221

would be annoyed with me for talking with Lara about this. A streak of rebellion surfaces: Tom is stratospherically annoyed with me anyway, so what the hell.

She shakes her head. "I don't . . ." Then her blue eyes widen as she twigs. It's a gratifying confirmation that Modan really isn't talking to her about the case, though I hadn't planned it as a test. "Seb and Severine? Really? I would never have guessed that . . . I mean, I knew he found her attractive; all the guys love a bit of that French ooh-la-la, *soooo* predictable . . ." She rolls her eyes. I can't help a private smile at Lara of all people, who plays the Swedish blond bombshell angle to maximum effect, being so dismissive of Severine's application of her own cultural advantages. Lara is still absorbing. "Wow. What a complete fuckwit Seb is. Was. Still is, I should think." She shakes her head again. "When did you find out?"

"Just recently. I had started to wonder, and then Seb — apropos of absolutely nothing — admitted it to me last night. Only because he's already told Modan, and he didn't want me to hear it through that avenue."

Lara is frowning. "But — how? They must have been very discreet. We were pretty

much on top of one another in the farm-house."

"Apparently it was just the last night."

"Oh. I suppose it was a pretty crazy night all round." She shakes her head, still digest-ing. "I can't believe I missed that. God, what else did I miss?"

She means it as a rhetorical question, but it's actually *the* question, the all-important nub of the matter. "Yeah, I've been wonder-ing that myself," I say quietly.

"You don't mean — but she was alive on the Saturday morning," Lara says impa-tiently. "She got on the damn bus."

I nod. "Agreed, she did, in which case what happened to her has nothing to do with any of us. Or she didn't; it was just a coincidence that someone fitting her de-scription got on at that stop —"

"Hell of a coincidence. How many girls even exist in the world who are that height, and build, and who wear a red chiffon scarf over their hair?"

"True, but just a coincidence, in which case . . ." I spread my hands and shrug. "It seems your Modan is rather taken with the latter possibility."

"He's not my Modan," she protests, though without any conviction.

"Really? He does seem to be yours. Head

to toe, heart and all."

"I would think so, except . . . he won't talk about what's going to happen after all this is over and he goes back to France." She looks at me, her eyes over-bright. "I know he had a long-distance relationship before, and he hated it . . . It's crazy, I can see it's crazy, we hardly know each other, but . . ." She lifts her hands helplessly, and suddenly I sense her desperate fear: she knows she has already jumped off the precipice. "And he won't even talk about it. He just says *we'll figure it out*. How are we supposed to do that if he won't talk about it?"

"Maybe he needs to concentrate on one thing at a time. Maybe he just wants to get the case over so you two can stop skulking around." I can't believe I'm defending the man who seems intent on painting me as a murderer. But I've seen how Modan looks at her. It's unmissable, it's cinematic — as if he's a reformed alcoholic and she's the very drink he's been craving for years: that man has no intention of letting her go. "Maybe he's worried about how *you* will feel when he puts your best friend in prison," I add sourly.

"But she got on the fucking bus!" She

smacks her hand into the sofa in frustration.

"I know, I know. But that aside . . . if *you* were constructing the case, who would you have as your prime suspect?"

She pauses, considering. "Not Tom, or me, for obvious reasons — and don't think you're off the hook on Tom, I'm coming back to that — and I know it wasn't you; you didn't even know about the affair till just now, so what possible motive would you have?"

"Not a rock-solid basis for excluding me," I tease.

"Oh, hush. If I'm going to have to think about this, let's not waste time on definite no-no's. Theo: no motive. He knew her forever, and apparently they'd always gotten on well. I'm sure he fancied her, but let's be honest: even if he tried it on and got a knock-back, I can't quite imagine Theo summoning up a murderous rage."

"Fair point." I see Theo, his cheeks flooding pink at the slightest jibe, his back covered in thick factor-50 to protect the milk-pale skin that is the curse of the true redhead. I cannot imagine Theo, with all his good intentions and awkwardness, having the courage to make a pass at Severine. Come to think of it, I don't remember Theo

ever making a pass at anyone.

"Is it totally un-PC to say I was really surprised about the way he died?" Lara asks hesitantly. "I didn't know he had it in him."

"Totally un-PC. But yeah, me neither." Theo died by throwing himself on a live grenade, thereby saving four of his colleagues. I can only imagine it was an instinctive reaction. At the funeral, Tom said that Theo's parents were unimaginably proud, astonished and despairing in equal measures.

"Yeah . . ." She shakes herself after a moment. "But anyway. That leaves Caro and Seb." She frowns. "I can't see why Caro would . . . or Seb . . . but he *was* with her . . ." I'm quiet, reluctant to influence her thinking. This *is* a test, in a way, and I'm almost holding my breath. If Lara alights on the same theory that has been slowly building in my subconscious, I can't dismiss it as another product of my demonstrably overactive brain. "So, Seb was with her, but why would he kill her? I mean, he wouldn't, not on purpose" — *here it comes* — ". . . God, not intentionally, but what if something happened by accident?" Her eyes widen. "You know, Kate, it could all have been just a tragic accident. Something went horribly wrong, and rather than face up to

226

it all he stuffed her body in the well. I mean, he's strong enough."

Bingo. We look at each other, wide-eyed.

"Last night Seb seemed very keen to stress that he came back to the room and passed out," I say quietly.

"And did he?" she asks.

"I'm not sure. I pretty much passed out myself. He woke me up going to the bathroom at something like six in the morning, so sometime before then I suppose." The clock, Seb stepping out of his boxer shorts, those glowing golden hairs . . . the clock, Seb . . .

"So he could have come in anytime before that."

"I suppose . . ." Only it has just occurred to me that in my memory Seb is on my side of the bed. The side with the chair, where he'd got into the habit of tossing his clothes when he undressed. And he's stepping out of boxer shorts. In the entire time we'd been in France, he'd always grabbed a towel from the hook behind the door and wrapped it round him to go to the communal bathroom — or on occasion run the gauntlet naked. He'd never ever bothered to fish around for a pair of boxer shorts. "Or maybe . . . maybe that was him coming to bed for the first time. I don't know . . ." What do I really remember and what is a reconstruction? I can't trust in anything anymore.

"How *do* you accidentally kill someone?"

I shrug. "Unlucky blow to the head, perhaps? She could have tripped and smacked her head on something. I suppose the autopsy would show that."

"And how long do you suppose you need to accidentally kill a girl and dump her body?" Lara asks, with deliberate drollery.

"Well, in my vast experience of accidental homicide . . ." I reply, equally drolly. I have definitely had too much wine if I'm being this flippant about the girl that haunts me. "Jesus, I don't know. I suppose he must have spent some time screwing her first, though God knows how long that would have taken in his drunken state."

"And then surely there must have been a period of panic, deciding what to do . . ." She trails off. "But, you know, this is all just a thought exercise. It's not even hypothetical; after all, she got on the bus. Right?"

Her eyes catch mine and hold, and I recognize the uncertainty in them; it matches the tight knot in my belly. She wants me to reassure her. I wanted her to reassure me, and look where that landed me.

"Right," I say quietly.

CHAPTER THIRTEEN

I suggest Lara stays the night, half expecting to hear, *No thanks, I'd rather wake up in my own bed,* but she accepts gratefully. I try to remember the last time she did that; we used to stay with each other a lot in the years just after leaving university, a subconscious attempt to re-create the messy hubbub of student housing, where nobody need ever be alone. It occurs to me that now I am almost always alone: long periods of isolation broken by short human interactions that don't leave me feeling any less solitary. It's probably not good for me — at least, it's probably not good for me that I don't mind. In any case, I think with dark humor, now I have Severine for company.

I have a spare bedroom, but Lara crawls into bed with me like days of old, and turns on her side, resting her head on her bent arm. In the warm glow of the bedside light I can see her eyeliner is smudged and her eyelids are heavy with the wine; she looks blowsy and sloppy and decadently sexy. Modan wakes up to this, I think. Does the effect ever wear off? One day will he look at her and move on without lingering, his brain ticking over his to-do list for the day? Or will he always stop for a moment, arrested by the sight, and perhaps touch the back of his hand to her cheek? And Tom, does he remember what she looked like in his bed all those years ago? Does he yearn to see her there now? I cut off that train of thought quickly and turn on my back to look at the ceiling instead. There were times at Oxford, and in the years after, when I had stabs of jealousy toward Lara: for her effortless magnetism, her easygoing take-it-or-leave-it flirting, for how her very presence dimmed mine in the eyes of the male population. Then I would reason those feelings away; I would console myself that I appealed to the more discerning gentleman . . . I thought I had grown up, cast off my insecurities, but here we are a decade on: it's so *demeaning* to realize that actually nothing has changed.

"Tom," says Lara uncannily if sleepily, pulling my gaze back to her. "Come on, time to tell all."

I rub a hand over my face, not trusting

230

my voice for a moment, then recover and say, "Not much to tell."

"You're pretty upset for not much to tell."

"I was drunk — well, we both were. We were sharing a cab, and I went up to his flat for a cup of tea — no, really, just tea!" I protest on Lara's raised eyebrow. "Then somehow, I don't know, we were kissing and then . . . God, I think I passed out." I pull the pillow over my face. "It's beyond humiliating," I say, lifting it enough to let the words out. "And then this morning Tom was livid with me — he thinks I abused our friendship — and he was . . . mean. And it upset me." I shrug and put the pillow down, concentrating on the ceiling. "It's fine that he doesn't want to . . . doesn't want anything between us" — *no it's not, no it's not, it doesn't feel fine at all* — "but he was pretty nasty." It doesn't feel fine to be confessing my humiliation at not being wanted to the girl he really wants, either. I wonder if she's pleased that she hasn't been usurped, and then I'm promptly ashamed of myself.

"Tom nasty?" Lara's eyebrows are raised in astonishment, the hairs glowing golden in the light.

"Believe me, he's very good at it when he tries. Very efficient." Of course he is. Tom is the man who does what needs to be done,

no matter what.

"I know, but . . . nasty to *you*? What did he say?"

"It doesn't matter — no, really, it doesn't." I shake my head at her. "I don't want to drag you into anything." I look at the ceiling again. Does it need repainting? Or is it just that the lamp is casting uneven shadows? I wonder where Severine is sleeping — does she even sleep? She's only in my head, so I suppose she must sleep when I do, except that I can't imagine that at all. I can imagine her still, even imagine her with her eyes closed, but there's a readiness there, like a panther in repose. At the slightest movement or sound she would unhurriedly raise her eyelids and survey the surrounds with her dark, secretive eyes. The thought is oddly comforting, like having a guard dog on the premises. Severine, my protector. I almost laugh out loud.

"Did you want it to turn into anything?" Lara asks carefully after a moment. I turn my head to look at her, but this time she's the one inspecting the ceiling. There are mascara flakes on her eyelashes; I will find smudges on my bed linen in the morning that are hell to get out. "You always just seemed like . . . mates. What about Seb?"

It crosses my mind that Seb never looked

to Lara first. Right from our very first meeting he honed in on me. In retrospect I wonder if that was part of the attraction. "Seb and I broke up a decade ago." She turns her head to look at me with unashamed skepticism, and I can hardly blame her for it. If I didn't know myself that I was over Seb, how could I expect anyone else to? "Seb now . . . he isn't the same as the Seb I knew back then. Or thought I knew . . ." I'm not sure Seb was ever who I thought he was. "Maybe if I'd seen him in the intervening years I'd have been over him long ago." Or maybe not; maybe it's the stark contrast of now versus then that allows me to see things more clearly.

"Closure," she says thoughtfully. Then again, with a tired smile and an American accent: *"Clo-sure."* A large yawn arrives, which she covers delicately, somehow putting me in mind of a cat, and then I think of her again on that car journey back from France, golden and sated, the cat that got the cream. I close my eyes tightly, but the image remains. "But Tom," she is saying. "Did you really want something more?"

Is she being more or less tenacious than I expect? Is she schooling her expression or is this a natural reaction? I can't stop the second-guessing. "God, I don't know. I

never thought of him like that, and then suddenly . . ." Was it so sudden? I think of coming to the surface in his car after the journey back from lunch with his folks: *wakey wakey, sleeping beauty,* of that instant before the world rushed back in. Perhaps that fleeting moment lingered in my head, setting off ripples . . . I shrug, somehow disturbed by that thought. "I don't know." Her yawn is catching; I'm yawning myself now.

"Mmm," she says, her eyelids drifting closed.

I reach out and flick off the bedside light. How is it that I can feel her warmth stealing across the inches between us, sense the rise and fall of her chest as she breathes evenly: the physical connection plus the intangible webs that link us — how is it that all of this binds us, yet we're still alone inside our heads?

On Monday Julie has a message for me when I get back to my office after a meeting: *Call Caroline Horridge,* followed by a Haft & Weil number. There's no message from Tom, not that he would call my office number, and not that I expect him to call at all. I answer a few e-mails first, but the yellow Post-it with Julie's curly script sits on

my desk and glares at me unrelentingly until I recognize I'm prevaricating. I grit my teeth, pick up the phone and dial, ignoring Severine, who is lounging against the wall inspecting her fingernails.

Caro answers exactly as she always does, stating her name in crisp tones after a single ring. "Hi, Caro, it's Kate Channing here," I say breezily, determined to cut off any of her game-playing tactics. "You left a message at my office."

Nonetheless, she leaves a beat or two, as if, even after hearing my full name and exactly why I'm calling, she's still struggling to place me. "Ah, yes, Kate," she says warmly, when she finally does speak. "Apologies, I've just been immersed in some difficult drafting. Back to the real world, though: I was calling to talk with you about the recruitment progress."

I have no idea what she's talking about. "In relation to . . . ?"

"Haft & Weil, of course. Our recruitment plans. I'm sure by now Gordon has told you that he's handing over the reins of that project to me."

"Um . . ." My fake smile slides right off my face.

"He hasn't? Oh, I am sorry" — *no, she's not* — "I didn't mean to jump the gun" —

yes, she did — "I was sure he'd spoken to you." *She knows he hasn't.* "Well, he has, so you and I are going to be working together on it from now on." She pauses expectantly.

"Interesting," I say. It is, actually, on a number of levels, but of course she expects something more than that. I recover the fake smile and plaster it on. "Well, welcome aboard." I'm sure Gordon would have wanted to tell me himself; I wonder how he will react when he realizes he's been leap-frogged.

"Thanks. I was hoping you might have some time tomorrow to drop by my office and bring me up to speed. Does that work for you?"

"Absolutely." I glance at my electronic calendar, these days gratifyingly checkered with meetings and calls, my smile doggedly in place. "I can do 11 A.M. or anytime after 3:30 P.M. tomorrow."

"Let's do 11 A.M. and then we can grab a bite to eat afterward. Sound good?"

"Perfect," I manage. "See you then."

Paul comes in just as I'm putting the phone down. "Kate!" he exclaims. He's definitely on an uptick these days. "Glad I caught you. We should discuss the Cavanagh account, and I really think I'm close to getting Struthers to bite, and —"

236

"Slow down," I say, laughing. "I'm not going anywhere. At least take your coat off first."

Severine glances at him with disdain, and suddenly I wonder: if Severine is a creation of my mind, are her reactions my own deeply hidden feelings? I observe Paul as he struggles out of his smart spring raincoat, trying to see him afresh. You could mock him if you wanted to, with his sharp city clothes, his urbane manner and his unflinching ambition. But I've seen him gray faced and crumpled with exhaustion on a Friday evening, having worked a seventy-five-hour week; I've drunk champagne out of mugs on the floor of this very office with him. I have no wish to mock him. I'm willing to concede that Severine — this Severine — is my creation, but she's not me.

"What?" says Paul, looking up to find my eyes on him as he pulls his chair across to my desk.

I clear my face. "Nothing, nothing. Just . . . just thinking we've been gratifyingly lucky of late."

"It's not luck," he says seriously, his vanishingly pale eyebrows drawing earnestly over his eyes. "It's hard work."

He really, truly believes it. Did I believe that once? Did I think that good things

came to those who earned them? "Well," I say equivocally, unwilling to burst his bubble, "it's both."

Modan, Alain Modan, *Investigateur, OPJ* and lover of Lara . . . a man of many talents. Later that day I start to realize that one of them is the ability to toss everybody else off balance with an elegantly judged metaphorical tap-tackle; I should think he has put effort into that talent over the years, carefully honing it to cause maximum consternation with minimum effort. He starts this particular campaign with the simplest of requests: a meeting.

"All of us, mind," says Lara again, through the mobile that's clamped between my ear and shoulder to leave my hands free to pack up my briefcase for a meeting. Either she's exceptionally tired or she has just been speaking to her family in Sweden: there's a slight lilt to her voice that only ever comes out in specific circumstances. "He says he'd rather not repeat everything five times."

"Mmmm."

"You don't believe that's the reason," Lara says. It's a statement, not a question.

"No." I would have expected Modan to prefer five separate interviews, which would provide five separate opportunities for

analyzing reactions — why the change of tack? I pause as I flick through the documents I'm adding to the bag. "And neither do you, I suspect."

"No." She lets out a long sigh that sweeps through the city and delivers her frustration into my ear. "It's . . ."

"Infuriating?" I give up on choosing which documents I need and just drop them all in.

"No. Well, it is, but mostly it's just . . . unsettling. He's lying, I know he's lying, he knows I know he's lying — I think he even *wants* me to know he's lying, like that makes it less awful or something . . . How the hell are we supposed to base a relationship on this?"

"You're not," I say sweetly, snapping the briefcase shut. "That's why policemen aren't supposed to fraternize with witnesses."

"Oh, fuck off," she says, half laughing.

"I shall. I've got to run to a meeting." I switch the mobile into my hand. "Listen, Lara — this will pass; it won't be like this forever for you guys. You just need to . . . ride it out, as best you can."

"I know." This time the long sigh curls around me, heavy and brooding. The sunshine girl is fast losing her sun. If this thing

runs for another two years . . . It doesn't bear thinking about. "Well, I'll see you there. Tonight at six thirty."

"Got it. And everyone is coming?" I ask this as casually as I can, but of course Lara isn't fooled.

"Yes. Though now I don't know who you're most worried about seeing, Seb or Tom."

"Caro, actually," I say dryly. "Always Caro."

It's 6:30 P.M., and we are meeting at the enormous 1960s glass and concrete monstrosity that is New Scotland Yard, the home of the Met Police. I didn't pay much attention to that when Lara gave me the details over the phone, but now, standing outside by the familiar triangular sign that I must have seen in thousands of TV news items, I feel the knot in my stomach tighten. Modan is not just the tricky Frenchman who's screwing my best friend. He's a man with the weight of the law behind him — both the law of his own country and of mine. Recognizing that this intimidation is intentional doesn't make it any less effective. I look around in the vain hope that perhaps Lara might be arriving at just this moment and we can brave it all together, but no. I

am on my own. I square my shoulders and push through the door.

The inside is sparse and clean and hard-edged, but I'm not really in the frame of mind to take much note. The solid-faced uniformed officer behind the reception desk is expecting me; within minutes I'm led into a conference room with a pine-effect conference table and twelve chairs — surely six too many — clustered around it, though none of those chairs are currently occupied.

"You're the first," says the officer, pointing out the obvious. His tone is cheerful, but his face doesn't change. Perhaps that's what a career in the police does to you — though Modan seems to have retained the faculty of facial expression. "I'm sure Detective Modan will be along shortly. There's a coffee machine just down the hallway on the right if you're so inclined." Then I'm alone with the functional furniture. I drop my handbag onto one chair and look around. The gray London street beyond the window is slightly distorted; I wonder if the glass is bulletproof. It's certainly soundproof; I can't hear the traffic at all. From the hallway I can hear the muffled buzz and chatter of life continuing, but in here both I and the oversize room seem to be holding our breath, as if sus-

pended before the roller coaster drops.

Then I hear Tom's distinctive rumble and Lara's giggle; I feel a sudden lurch as the roller coaster picks up speed again, and then they spill into the room with Seb on their heels. I put all my focus on Lara, absurdly self-conscious as I hug her in greeting, but I can't hide in our hello forever; I have to release her and turn to Tom and Seb. Both of them step forward at the same time, but then Tom gestures awkwardly and steps back, leaving the field for Seb.

"Hello, Seb," I say neutrally. Behind him I can see Caro enter the room, her blond hair pulled back into a severe chignon.

"Kate," says Seb warmly, though perhaps I detect a touch of apprehension lurking in his eyes. "Good to see you, though of course I'd rather we were in a pub or something." He leans in to kiss me on each cheek. I stay still throughout, imagining my cheeks are marble, and all the while I'm looking at Tom, who in turn is looking at Seb and me with a shuttered expression. When his eyes catch mine he immediately glances away. And Caro watches us all.

"Hello, Tom," I say quietly, crossing to him.

"Hi, Kate," he says, not quite meeting my eye. Then he leans in and kisses me on both

n who never kisses, Tom who
ches. Yet again my cheeks are marble,
alw not in silent protest but because
this an do to hold myself in one piece.
it's el I'm beginning to tear apart, and I
I know how to sew myself back to-
g

om —" I start when he steps back, but
is talking over me.

"Christ, I need a coffee," he's saying.
Shall I grab you one, Tom?"

"I'll come with you," Tom says quickly,
with what sounds suspiciously like relief. I
watch the two of them leave together, and
for a moment I see them as a stranger
might: two men similar enough around the
eyes and in frame as to be brothers, though
very different in coloring. Seb always
seemed older, and he seems older still, but
that's no longer a compliment. A decade
ago he was a man among boys, but now he
is a man hurtling more quickly toward
middle age than the rest of us; in the light
of day there's a slackness to him that
becomes more noticeable next to Tom's
clean bulk.

Caro is speaking to Lara and me whilst
simultaneously fishing something out of her
slimline soft leather briefcase. "God, I
thought I'd never get here on time. I was

leading a negotiation for a
couldn't really just up and le client; I
jaw clench. Not just a client, feel my
Not just in a negotiation, but le client.
petty and mean and plain exhaus. It's
so attuned to the slightest word o be
sion, but I just can't stop myself. res-
it's just not within me to gift Caro wi aps
benefit of the doubt. "Anyway," she s,
finally looking up, BlackBerry in ha .
"How are you two?"

"Fine," says Lara brightly. "Just — oh,
here's Alain."

I turn to see him pause at the doorway, an
elegant gray suit encasing his long limbs,
accentuated today by a powder blue tie. His
eyes scan the room and stop on Lara mo-
mentarily — just long enough for something
to pass between them that I could almost
reach out and touch — then resume their
survey. Finally he steps forward. "Ladies,"
he says, a smile lurking at the edge of his
mouth. "And gentlemen," he adds as Tom
and Seb return with their coffees; they each
deposit their cardboard cups on the table to
shake his hand. I notice that he didn't shake
hands with Caro, Lara or me. "Welcome to
the glamour that is New Scotland Yard," he
says with an ironic lift of his eyebrows.

"Are police stations in France similar?"

244

asks Lara.

He considers this seriously. "Ah, *oui,* in many ways. Though" — he looks at the flimsy cups on the table and wrinkles his nose in distaste — "the coffee is better." This is greeted with great hilarity: we are all too tense, too desperate in our efforts to project good-humored ease. "And the food is better. And the decor, and the furniture . . . so, ah, maybe no, nothing like the same." He smiles, acknowledging the laughter his words have elicited, deep lines bracketing his mouth. I haven't seen him in this kind of environment before, where he has an audience and it's his show. I can see that he and Lara are birds of a feather; they wear their skin with such effortless charm.

He glances round as if performing a head count. "*Alors,* we are complete. Please, sit."

So we sit, Modan at the head of the table, Lara and I on one side and Tom, Seb and Caro (and her BlackBerry) on the other. It's a split that's reminiscent of the divisions during that fateful week in France; it doesn't feel accidental. Caro is the last to choose a chair: I see her evaluating the options. The artificial light reveals shadows under her eyes that even her careful application of concealer has failed to hide, and there's a gray tinge to her skin: exactly what I'd

expect for a lawyer in the run-up to partner-ship. As she settles into the seat next to Seb I try to step outside of myself, to see her as I might if she was a prospective candidate to be placed through my firm, but I can't do it. My dislike of her is too pervasive.

I disliked Severine, too, but that was in life. I'm growing accustomed to her in death. I can't imagine that she would miss this, and sure enough, there are only five chairs too many: Severine has settled herself in one at the far end of the table. Her face doesn't betray any interest — of course it doesn't, this is Severine — but there's a still-ness within her that gives her away.

"We are complete," says Modan again, when everyone is settled. I see Tom glance around the group, and a brief flash of despair crosses his face before he schools it back into submission. Perhaps there are only four chairs too many. I don't expect Severine has the monopoly on haunting. "*Alors,* thank you, all of you, for coming." He looks around the table slowly, his long face grave. Opposite me, Tom and Seb have both pushed their chairs back from the table and have their long legs stretched out. I wonder if they teach it in public school, this ability to take ownership of a room by an elegant display of casual relaxation. For

whose benefit is the display in Tom's case? Mine or Modan's? "I wanted to tell you all together that we now have the results of the autopsy on Mademoiselle Severine." I glance across the table and see Seb look up sharply, his hand tightening on the coffee cup. By contrast Tom continues to look as if Modan is merely discussing the weather, and not terribly interesting weather at that. "The conclusion is that she died by what you here call foul play." I wait for him to continue, but he simply looks around the room again, overlooking no one.

"You didn't get us all here just for that," I say abruptly. I'm tired — at least I'm tired of the showmanship — and I'm upset and I'm not censoring myself quickly enough. Lara puts a hand on my arm, but it fails to halt me. "Seriously, she ended up concertinaed at the bottom of a well. How could it not be foul play?"

Modan frowns. "Concertinaed. What is this?"

Lara reels off something in rapid-fire French.

Modan's expression clears. "Ah, I understand." He tries out the new word. "Concertinaed. Yes, indeed, a fair point, though of course we always have to rule out suicide or *accident.*" He pronounces the last word

in the French fashion, but I'm still caught on the incongruity of *suicide*. I stamp down on the highly inappropriate urge to laugh: had he seriously considered the possibility she stuffed her own self in the well? I glance down the table, and Severine's dark eyes gleam as they meet mine: quite apart from the logistical difficulties of that particular theory, we both know she's not the suicidal type.

"But you are right; there is more." Modan continues, unaware of the weight of Severine's dark eyes upon him. Across the table, Caro has her head cocked, her body leaning forward and BlackBerry forgotten, a textbook example of a person listening intently: because she is, or because that's what she wants to portray? Tom and Seb are still sprawled out, but the tension in Seb is obvious; he doesn't have Caro's inherent artifice. "After this length of time, unless the body is somehow preserved, the autopsy can have, ah, nil result. Inconclusive, yes? In this case, we have a body that spent ten years in a warm, mainly dry, environment, which is the most efficient environment for leaving just the bones." Beside me Lara shudders, the most minute of movements, but nonetheless Modan picks up on it. I wonder if he would have had it been Caro

or myself doing the shuddering. "I apologize, this is not a pleasant topic, but it is necessary. So, as I was saying, there are just bones." He spread his hands. "Broken bones."

"Broken?" asks Lara. "From what?"

"We cannot tell if the breaks are pre- or postmortem." He shrugs, his fingers flexing out briefly in a synchronized movement. "They would fit very well with a car crash, a . . ." — he searches for a word for a moment, then snaps his fingers — "a hit-and-run." Across the table I see Tom's gaze sharpen and jump sharply to Modan. In less than a blink that honed focus is gone, and once again he's the only-casually-interested observer he has been all along. Tom is surprised by something. It's the first time I've detected surprise in him since Severine was found.

"Or," continues Modan, "they could have occurred when the body was put in the well. Concertinaed, as Kate says." He inclines his head in my direction. There's no smile lurking around his mouth — that would be in terribly poor taste — but I know it's inside him.

"So you're saying," says Caro, her expression clinically professional, "that you have no evidence of cause of death? In which case

shouldn't you pack up and go home?"

Lara's hand tightens on my arm. Modan doesn't look at her. "Regrettably, *non.*" He adds a theatrical sigh. "You are correct, we do not have cause of death, but we do have her bones. The human body is amazing." He shakes his head a little, half smiling. "Truly amazing. Even after death it still finds ways to speak to us." *Tell me about it,* I think with dark humor. Severine's bones are far too communicative as far as I'm concerned, though I imagine they are communicating with Modan through a somewhat different method. "We have her bones, and what they tell us is that Severine was not at the bus depot on the Saturday morning."

"What?" says Lara, confused. "But the CCTV . . ."

Modan is shaking his head. "Not her. *Non.* Similar height, similar build, similar, ah, thing with the scarf" — he twirls a hand expressively above his head — "but not her. The proportions are wrong. I cannot translate the technical details, but there is something with the length of one bone in relation to another one . . . along with photographs . . . Ah, the experts, they are absolutely certain. *Absolument.* It is not Severine on the CCTV."

250

And so. It was one of us.

His words plow into me with the weight of a wrecking ball. Somewhere inside, I've been expecting this, dreading this. It was one of us. Like the discovery of her body in the well, it suddenly seems inevitable, unavoidable, obvious. One of the five of us — six, including Theo — killed Severine. For all one could construct a theory to say otherwise, I now believe it with a sickening certainty that is absolute, as if I've always believed it.

I look around the table and see varying degrees of shock on the faces. Lara is still stuck on what he actually said; the full implication hasn't hit her yet. I hear her mutter, "Hell of a coincidence." Tom is very, very still, but behind those hooded eyes I imagine the activity is frenetic. Caro says, "Really? You're sure?" to which Modan nods, and then she steeples her hands and props her chin on them, frowning thoughtfully. And Seb looks . . . tired. Gray. Defeated. He looks like he's been dreading this, too.

"*Alors,*" says Modan, not quite spelling it out, "the five of you were the last to see Mademoiselle Severine alive."

"And Theo, of course," interjects Caro casually. Tom stiffens at this and casts her a

dark, thoughtful look, and I know why: the games have begun, if they hadn't already . . . We're now in a macabre version of pass the parcel; when the music stops nobody wants to be left holding *this* prize. It would be incredibly convenient for all if Theo, the only person whose life can't be wrecked, were to shoulder the blame. But as I look at Tom, I can't imagine he will allow that without a fight. I look around the table again. It's impossible not to think, as each face passes under my gaze, *Was it you? Could you have done it?* And, most disturbing of all, *How far will you go to blame someone else?* When I get to Severine she returns my gaze coolly, then slides down her chair and tips her head back, closing her eyes: sunbathing. Severine and Lara, I think bleakly: the only people I believe are innocent, and one of those is the victim and, moreover, dead.

Modan inclines his head to Caro in agreement. "*Oui,* of course, and Theo, too. I'm afraid I will need to conduct more interviews, but as we're all here first I thought we might try to properly establish the timeline that night. It's a little . . ." — his expressive hands dance — "unclear at the moment."

Seb starts to say something, but Tom leans

forward suddenly, giving up all pretense of disinterest, and speaks over him. "Should we have lawyers present?"

His words hang in a silence that is only broken by Lara's sharp intake of breath; she has finally caught on. I look at Tom speculatively for a moment. I spoke with my own lawyer only hours before this meeting, and her instructions had been very explicit: *if you must go at all, just observe, listen, and whatever you do, don't answer a damn question without me present.* I wonder if Tom has taken legal advice, too. Modan stretches out his long arms and tweaks at one of his cuffs before answering. "If you wish you can certainly have a lawyer present, though you are not under arrest. Of course." He spreads his palms. "This is just, ah, fact-finding, *non*? And of course you all want to be helpful, cooperative. Waiting for lawyers . . ." — he rolls his eyes expressively — "well, it is rather a waste of time." I can't help admiring his performance even as the intent chills me.

"Still," says Tom robustly. "Obviously, I can't speak for everyone, but I think I'd rather take legal advice at this point." In phrasing it like that — *I can't speak for everyone* — he *is* somehow speaking for us, as if he's created a group mentality by the

mere suggestion that there could be one. He stands, pushing his chair back abruptly with the action. "And if we're not under arrest, then of course we're free to go at any point, correct?"

And just like that, he has wrested the power from Modan and the meeting is over.

CHAPTER FOURTEEN

We loiter outside the police station, a reluctant group — unwilling to depart, but equally unwilling to engage in conversation.

Lara breaks the silence. "It's real now, isn't it?" she says, almost as if she's talking to herself. "We can't pretend this isn't serious anymore. I can't . . ." She trails off.

Seb speaks into the void she's created. "Anyone know a good lawyer?" He aims for a joking tone and directs the question toward Caro and me, but he looks anything but playful. It seems to me I can see straight through to the skeleton beneath his surface; the muscle and skin and tissue are just window dressing draped on the bones of him. He might unravel at any moment.

"Criminal law's not really my area," I reply. I try to inject some humor myself: "Though if you're looking for a good corporate lawyer I'm absolutely the person to talk to." Nobody bothers to honor my effort with

even a smile.

Caro is already back on her BlackBerry. She speaks without looking up. "I'm sure my dad will be able to come up with someone. Or your dad," she adds as an afterthought.

Seb grimaces. "Yeah, really looking forward to *that* conversation." Tom glances across with a sympathetic twist of his mouth. Seb's father's influence has clearly not waned over the years.

Caro's head lifts at that. "Come on, Seb, don't let Modan rattle you. I mean, he has nothing. Nothing! No physical evidence at all and just a load of conjecture." She looks round the group impatiently. "None of us have anything to worry about. This is all going to go away."

"Or linger on forever," says Lara darkly. She glances back at the entrance to the building for the third or fourth time, and I realize she's expecting Modan to follow her out.

"What do you mean?" asks Seb uneasily.

She shrugs. "The best outcome is that they find who did it and put them away. Then it's all neatly wrapped up. Otherwise . . ." She shrugs again. "It's never really over. Even if they consign it to the cold case pile, it could still come alive again. New

evidence, new political pressure to take another look."

Her words cause another blanket of silence to fall heavily on the group. She's probably quoting Modan, I think uneasily. How many cases has he worked on that end up like that, never resolved but never entirely forgotten, either?

"Well, I have to get back to the office," says Caro abruptly. "Can I drop anyone at Westminster tube on the way past?" It's presented as a general offer, but she's looking directly at Seb when she says it.

"Sounds good," he says after a pause.

"Best head that way to get a cab," Tom says, pointing. "I'll call you later, Seb, okay?"

Normally we would all accompany our good-byes with some kind of physical display, but today Seb simply lifts a tired hand in salute, and Caro takes his other arm, calling over her shoulder, "See you all soon — in fact, see you tomorrow, Kate."

Oh joy. "See you then," I say sweetly.

Tom watches them go, a frown between his eyebrows. Is he worried about Seb's behavior, or Caro's? And for whose welfare is he concerned, his own or someone else's? A movement in my peripheral vision pulls my head round, and I see Modan making

his way across to Lara, who has moved a couple of paces away from Tom and me. Her gaze is fixed on Modan, but her expression is unexpectedly conflicted.

"I'll call you later, Lara," I offer, presuming she will leave with him.

She glances at me swiftly, shaking her head. "No, wait for me. Please, wait."

"I . . . Okay." I'm slightly nonplussed. Tom takes my arm and pulls me aside so we are partially hidden by a tree, his eyes fixed on the pair. "What —" I start to say, but he shushes me. I realize I am as close to Tom as I was in the corridor that night, close enough to smell his aftershave. It makes me absurdly self-conscious; I turn my head quickly and focus on Modan and Lara. The detective must have seen us on his route to Lara, but the tree cover does give the illusion that they have some privacy, and in truth I can only pick out the odd syllable from what they are saying. Lara is doing the bulk of the talking, in a low, earnest tone, spots of color visible in her cheeks. She's trying not to cry, I realize. Something she says cuts at Modan: he flinches and interrupts urgently, reaching a long arm out to her, but she shakes her head resolutely and takes a step back. It finally dawns on me what I'm watching, and I instantly feel

grubby, but it's impossible to look away. Modan tries to make his point again, frustration clear in every line of his long frame, but Lara is resolute. She must be resolute to hold firm in the face of the heartrending misery that slowly steals over Modan's face. I don't look at Tom. If he were to display any pleasure at all at this outcome I might actually punch him.

Then Lara is walking toward us in short, quick steps, the color still high in her cheeks. Her eyes are remarkably dry. "Oh, honey." I step out from the tree as I speak and move to hug her, but she gives a quick shake of her head and I realize she will fall apart if I do. "Come back to mine. Let's find a cab."

She nods. Tom reaches out a hand and touches her cheek briefly. "I'm sorry," he says, with what seems like genuine empathy. He looks like he has more to add, but he checks himself; her face crumples briefly at that, but she catches herself. I link an arm through hers just as Tom spots a taxi and hails it for us. Lara climbs in first. I glance down the street and see that Modan is still standing there, his long face indescribably bleak. I look away hurriedly and move to follow Lara, but Tom stops me, gesturing me toward the front of the cab, out of

earshot of Lara.

"We need to talk," he says, decisively, looking me straight in the eye for possibly the first time today.

"I know." I feel relieved almost to tears to have him make the first move. "I mean, I can't right now, what with Lara, but I am so sorry —"

He cuts me off with a sharp, flat chop of one hand. "Not about that." My face freezes, and something flickers in his eyes. "I don't mean . . . Look, I know we do, but not now. I meant we need to talk about the case. Severine."

"Right. God forbid I should put our friendship higher up the priority list. Only — that's strange, isn't it? Because according to you I don't care a jot." I know I'm lashing out, I know it's destructive, but I'm hurt. I'm hurt and he did the hurting and I can't just put it aside.

"Kate," he says, running an exasperated hand through his hair. "Don't think I don't appreciate the biting sarcasm, but we just don't have time for it. This — the car — it changes everything. It —"

"Not now, Tom. I'm going home to take care of Lara." I turn away and start climbing into the taxi.

"Tomorrow then," he insists through the

open door.

"Whatever." I pull the door sharply shut and give the driver my address.

"I had to do it." The words spill out of Lara as soon as we are under way. "It was fine when it wasn't real, when none of us were really under suspicion. But it's not a game anymore, is it? Success for him is finding enough evidence to arrest one of us. Me — well, probably not me, but maybe you. Or Tom, or Seb or Caro . . . I can't spend time with him wondering if something I say, something completely inconsequential to me, might make all the difference to him . . . I can't be part of that. I can't . . . I can't . . ." Her blue eyes are swimming now, her breaths are shuddering gasps and the tears are starting to stream down her cheeks. I pull her into a hug, not the easiest thing in a moving cab, and she sobs into my neck in painful, body-racking gulps.

"Oh, honey," I say helplessly, past the lump in my own throat. "I'm so proud of you." It's true. Having seen firsthand exactly how giddy and reckless Modan makes her, I'm in awe of the strength she has just displayed. I wonder if I would be able to do the same, but I can't quite put myself in her shoes. Was I ever as swept away by Seb as she is by Modan? The memories are there

to suggest it, but they don't re-create the feeling within me. I say again, "I'm so proud of you. You chose to protect your friends from him." After a moment, I add blackly, "Though on balance I'm starting to think that maybe he can have them all except you."

"You don't. Mean. That." Her gasped words are muffled by my now-damp collar.

"No, I suppose not," I concede with a sigh. "Except maybe —"

"Caro," she finishes for me, and for a moment we are both laughing as well as crying and I think perhaps she's going to be all right after all.

I call my lawyer first thing the next morning, though it's midmorning before she gets back to me. Thankfully Paul is out of the office so I am free to talk uninhibitedly; she listens intently to my account of the meeting and asks a couple of pertinent questions before she gives her verdict. "He's got more up his sleeve," she says in her usual decisive manner. "That the girl on the CCTV isn't Severine — well, it was never a given that it was; that's not a game-changer. So he has more. He wouldn't still be here without it. Do you think any of the others will speak to him without a lawyer?"

"I don't know." I think about it. Not Lara, I don't think; not anymore. And not Seb. Probably not Caro, either, unless she's playing some angle that I can't foresee. Tom? I don't know about Tom. "Probably not, but I don't know for sure."

"Mmm." I imagine her tapping her teeth with her fingernail, hopefully whilst wearing a less garish lipstick. A soft taupe, perhaps. "Obviously what I said before still stands: you mustn't allow yourself to be questioned without me present, but the trick is to appear cooperative. Antagonizing the police is never a good strategy."

"*Appear* cooperative?" I stress the first word with an ironic twist.

She laughs. "Well, yes, appear. If you actually happen to *be* cooperative, too, that's fine, but not actually necessary." She pauses, and I sense the shift of gear; the moment for humor has passed. "Have you thought any more about what happened on that Friday night? If there was some piece of information, however small, that you hadn't mentioned before, you could come forward with it — with me present, I hasten to add — which would go a long way to demonstrating cooperation."

"Or demonstrating a desire to shift blame."

"I wouldn't worry about that. Believe me, right now the lawyers for all of your little band will be advising their clients to shift the blame." She waits to allow her words their full impact. "So," she finally continues, "is there anything you can think of, anything at all, that you haven't mentioned?"

I'm silent. There's so much I haven't mentioned, both from that night and since. The smuggled cocaine and subsequent blazing row, Caro and Seb's recent conspiratorial assignations, Tom's continual absence of surprise (apart from during last night's meeting), Modan and Lara's relationship . . . "I'll need to spend some time thinking about that," I say at last.

"You do that." Her voice has hardened; there's a warning note in it: I haven't fooled her at all. "I can't help you if I don't have all the facts. I don't want you bringing up things at the eleventh hour when you're already under arrest."

I'm temporarily unable to breathe. "Arrest," I croak when I finally find my voice. "Is that likely?"

"Well, not off the current known facts, but as we've already discussed, Modan must have something more up his sleeve. He isn't here for nothing."

"Right." I rub my forehead. "Right."

"I think we should meet again and go over everything once more." Her voice has softened a little. "My assistant will call you to set something up. In the meantime, promise me you'll rack your brains about that evening."

"I will. I promise." One would think I would have dwelled on little else since yesterday, but last night Lara's emotional state had required a certain amount of dedicated focus. And if I'm honest, I've always shied away from memories of that week. But now . . . now the stakes are growing day by day, it seems. I should approach this as I would a problem with my company, I think; I should set aside time to apply dedicated thought. I look at my online calendar for today and decisively block out 5 P.M. to 6 P.M. I can't think of what to put in the subject box, so I mark it private so that Julie can't see the content and leave the subject blank, which in retrospect strikes me as highly ironic — marking an appointment private to hide the fact it says nothing at all. Then I wonder who else is speaking to their lawyer and setting aside thinking time, and it doesn't seem at all funny anymore.

By happy coincidence, Gordon is hurrying

through the Haft & Weil lobby just as I swing in through the revolving doors, a small frown and his short, quick steps betraying the time pressure he's under. Nevertheless, he stops when he sees me, and the frown clears. "Kate," he says, shaking my hand. "I've been meaning to call you." He takes my arm and draws me aside, out of the way of the revolving door traffic. "I'm so sorry I didn't get the opportunity to explain to you in person the change of spearhead at our end. That was . . ." He pauses, and for a moment I see the legendary Farrow steel in his eyes. "Well, that was badly done." I'm absurdly pleased that he's annoyed with Caro — for once not because it's Caro, but because he understands the lack of respect implied by that episode. He lowers his voice and continues. "The idea of putting her in charge actually came from your suggestion of finding her some management initiatives to get involved with, so thank you for that. Though I have to say I'm going to miss our little meetings." He smiles a little ruefully.

"Me too," I say honestly. "It's been a real pleasure." His eyes crinkle at the edges, then he glances at his watch. "But you're on your way to something." I am anxious not to impose. "Don't let me keep you."

"I'm sorry, I do hate to say hi and bye . . . Actually, what are you doing for lunch today?"

"Caro invited me to have a bite with her after our meeting."

He brightens. "Excellent, I'll gate-crash." I laugh. "And if she cancels lunch on you — which is rather likely; she's under the cosh on something big right now, and I can't imagine she's getting much sleep, let alone time to eat properly — then you won't be left in the lurch. Perfect," he says, with a satisfied air. "See you then." He turns away, tossing a smile over his shoulder, and I think that I can't see a single atom of him that resembles Caro.

And neither can I see an ounce of Gordon in Caro when she joins me in the meeting room — basement this time, no spectacular view; in fact no view at all — after a wait that's only been long enough for me to pour a cup of coffee from the attendant silver flask. She does indeed look tired, even more so than at last night's meeting: the shadows under her eyes have deepened, and she's even paler, though that might actually be the effect of the rather stark, though very sharp, black trouser suit she's wearing. We greet each other with air kisses and then I say, "I saw your dad in the lobby. He's plan-

ning to gate-crash our lunch."

She shakes her head, rolling her eyes. "Shameless man. Though since I'm waiting on a call from New York, which will of course come just as we're sitting down to eat, I might be best leaving the two of you to it." She pulls out a seat, snags a biscuit and takes a bite of it in what seems like one continuous movement. Caro is running purely on adrenaline, I realize.

"He did say you're rather snowed under at the moment."

She nods vehemently as she finishes her mouthful. "A rather full-on hostile bid. I haven't been home to my flat since I saw you yesterday." She raises her eyebrows rue-fully. "You remember how it is during the crazy times. If you get home at all, it's never before midnight, and on the odd occasion that you do, there's a stack of laundry to get through and bills to pay and you have no inclination to do either."

It's an odd sensation to be feeling sorry for Caro. I don't enjoy it. But I do remember exactly what she describes. Before I left the practice of law, I did everything that is expected of a lowly associate, and what is expected is to give your all — all your time, all your energy, all your social life; all is consumed by the beast that is the modern

top-tier corporate law firm. I remember the late nights in a deserted office, when even the air con had stopped working and the air grew still and heavy and hot. I remember strip lighting and the faint glow from the few computer screens still on, and eyes so tired and scratchy that I could barely read my monitor. The adrenaline rushes occurred in the day, fueled by the enthusiasm of the other team members, but the real hard graft usually happened at night, alone or perhaps with one colleague, with no more camaraderie on tap to spur you on. Mostly I remember the sense of disjointment, of being outside of everything — outside of the firm, where I could never quite belong; outside of my circle of friends whose social life didn't halt but went on happily without me; outside of my very own life. I left the practice of law for reasons that had nothing to do with the working hours, and in starting up Channing Associates I've been no stranger to long days that bleed into nights, and weeks that spread a stain into weekends, but I wonder how I would cope with 110-hour weeks now.

"I suppose the period before partnership is even more brutal," I respond neutrally. Typically candidates continue to work at the same breakneck pace, but with the

added stress of continual scrutiny of every single decision they take, every strategy they suggest.

Her face tightens a fraction. I suspect Caro is aware her campaign is not going perfectly. But she simply says, "Yes," then busies herself selecting another biscuit. I remember that, too: the diabolic diet that comes from having lost all sense of normal body rhythm, leaving you lurching from one sugar fix to another. After a moment she adds, "At any rate, I think I'm going to be stuck here all week and all weekend too."

"Did you have plans?"

"I was going to visit my mum, but . . ." She shrugs ruefully.

"Do you see her much?" I ask, genuinely curious.

She shakes her head, a small, economical movement. "I always think I should go down more." She grimaces, but not without humor. "Right up to the point when I'm there, and then I rather think the opposite."

That pulls a chuckle from me. "You don't get along?"

She shrugs again. "It's a well-trodden path. Things start well, but sooner or later the criticisms will come out. She didn't want me to become a lawyer, you see, but I always wanted to follow Dad into the law.

She can't see the point of me working so hard when surely I could marry money, or live off Dad's . . ." She trails off and grimaces again, but the humor is gone; she seems suddenly defenseless, and for the first time ever I can imagine the thirteen-year-old girl that she once was, trying to navigate through the trials of teenage life with a mother she can never please who is using her as a tool against the father she longs to emulate. I think of my own mother, a geriatric nurse, gently proud but benignly uncomprehending both of the job that I do and why I would want to do it, given the stress and long hours — it was always my father who understood. For the first time ever I want to reach out to Caro, but I have no idea how.

"Anyway," she says briskly, breaking the moment, "I certainly could have done without having to sprint across to New Scotland Yard last night." She eyes me across the table as she takes a neat bite, her small, sharp teeth gleaming white. Perhaps she's had them bleached. She's the Caro I expect once again, but that moment has shaken me. I can still feel the reverberations. Perhaps beneath the brittle painted surface of Caro, there are other versions, stacked like Russian dolls, years upon years of them,

271

right back to the vulnerable girl that she must have been at the time of the divorce, and beyond — all of them inside her. Perhaps I should take more care with the shell. "What did you make of all of that yesterday?"

I grimace, looking for a noncommittal answer. "I'm not sure I understand why Modan hasn't given up and gone home. It doesn't seem like there's anything to support any one of us as a suspect over anyone else who happened to be in the vicinity."

She nods vigorously as she finishes her mouthful. "Totally. Completely agree." She adds, almost as an afterthought, "Which makes it weird that he keeps asking me about Theo."

"Really?"

"God, yes, like a dog with a bone. And what can I say? I mean, we were together until we went up to our beds, and then . . ." She waves a hand airily. It's not a gesture that suits her; it's too vague, and Caro is never vague. "Well, then I was asleep, and who can vouch for anyone when they're asleep?"

"Well, that applies to us all," I say tightly. "There must have been a couple of hours when everyone was asleep and no one is accounted for." Except for Lara and Tom,

entwined in coital bliss . . .

"Absolutely. Of course. Which makes it odd that he's focusing on Theo particularly." She shrugs. "Though — distasteful as it is to say, if it *had* to be one of us . . ." I stare at her, not so much appalled as bewildered — does she not know Tom at all? Surely she realizes he would fight ceaselessly to prevent any besmirching of Theo's name. She shrugs again. "Well, onward and upward: why don't you give me an overview of where we stand with the candidates?"

So I do, and we discuss. The process is extremely developed by now; there's not a lot she can add. Her questions are professional and intelligent, though she is clearly far more focused on immediate benefits to the firm from prospective new hires rather than their career development within the company, which is not quite the message Gordon would be sending candidates — I will have to be careful she doesn't ruin the groundwork we've laid. I make a couple of careful allusions to it that are obviously less subtle than intended: after the second one she stops and laughs. "Kate," she says through a smile that holds genuine amusement. "Don't worry, I know how to stay on message. I won't scare the horses."

"I know, of course not; it's just that col-

legiality and long-term career opportunities are the main reason a couple of these candidates are considering this place."

"I get it. Don't worry." She puts down her pen and yawns, half-heartedly covering her mouth. The adrenaline has been slowly leaching out of her during our meeting, and the yawns are coming closer together. "Oh," she says suddenly, brightening a little. "I meant to tell you, you may get a call from a chap called Hugh Brompton at Stockleys." Stockleys is an enormously successful mid-tier UK firm with a footprint just about everywhere; it doesn't compete with Haft & Weil, as it wouldn't generally get the cutting-edge, high-profile deals, but there's an awful lot of work around that isn't cutting-edge or high profile. "We use them quite a bit when we need to outsource some of the drudge work — much cheaper for the client than Haft & Weil personnel." She's watching me carefully as she speaks, her head slightly cocked and her tired eyes gleaming birdlike. "Anyway, they're looking to beef up certain areas, and I told Hugh about you and suggested they give you a call. It's a big job, from what he says, and the contract is basically yours — as far as he's concerned, if you're good enough for Haft & Weil, you're good enough for him."

I'm temporarily floored, then I say, "Thank you," because of course I can't say anything else, but inside I'm scrabbling around to figure out the angle, because of course there's an angle, and if I don't know what it is then I'm exactly where she wants me. Or at least, that's how it would be for the Caro I thought I knew, but perhaps this Caro is something different . . . I adopt a smile that's at least half genuine. "That's kind of you, very much appreciated."

"Well, we're in business together, and business partners help each other out." Her eyes gleam, and she has a self-satisfied smile as she adds slyly, "I told you I could stay on message."

I laugh, both out of surprise and because her wicked little dig is genuinely funny, and for a moment I see her as she may well be, or perhaps I see her as Seb and Tom see her — a clever, sharply witty, fearless woman. I can't tell if what she's presenting now is only part of the picture or if the picture has changed: it leaves me uneasily off-kilter.

Her mobile goes off, and she takes the call with a quick apology, firing out a series of short responses and checking her watch while she paces the room. "Sorry," she says with a grimace when she hangs up. "That call from New York is going to happen in

ten minutes. I'm afraid you and Gordon will be on your own for lunch."

"No problem." We exit the windowless room into an equally windowless passageway. "You know," I say conversationally, "I always wondered why you joined your father's law firm. You could have gone to any number of competitors, I'm sure."

"Oh, sure," she says offhand as we climb a sweeping glass-and-metal staircase to the main lobby, where I find myself blinking, somehow surprised at the daylight. But it's lunchtime; of course there is daylight. "But Haft & Weil was really the best opportunity for me. You can't do better than best in class, after all."

"Bravo," I say, raising my eyebrows with a half smile. "Once again, admirably on message."

She lays a hand on my upper arm and laughs, a genuine laugh, and it softens her; her sharp edges become impish rather than cutting. "I told you I could." She looks over my shoulder still smiling, then exclaims, "Right on time! Here's Gordon. You know, I probably see more of him now than I did growing up, what with the divorce and boarding school and all." She smiles a hello over my shoulder at him and then shakes my hand, quick and firm, cordially profes-

sional. "I'll leave you in his capable hands; you two have a lovely lunch."

"We will," Gordon says, smiling at her, then he turns and ushers me through the lobby. "Looks like you two are getting on famously," he remarks, and it suddenly crosses my mind that perhaps Caro knew he was there and staged that little tableau — the laugh, the little touch — and then I realize how loathsomely paranoid I've become and I hate myself for it.

CHAPTER FIFTEEN

The designated thinking hour arrives and departs without a single moment spent in contemplation, because Hugh Brompton does indeed call, and the job in question is dynamite, the kind of contract that really establishes a new firm — but of course they want our strategies and suggestions at a meeting tomorrow afternoon. So Paul and I work late, eating take-out sushi at our desks and mainly ignoring our mobiles. Actually, mainly ignoring Paul's mobile: judging from the number of times it rings, he either has a very active social life or an extremely jealous girlfriend. In contrast, mine rings only twice: the first call is Lara, and I take it to quickly check how she's holding up; the second is from Tom.

"Do you need to take that?" asks Paul, and I realize I'm staring at the mobile screen as it rings.

"No," I say brightly as I reach over to hit

the reject button. "I can deal with it later." A moment later the phone beeps with a voice mail alert; I deliberately ignore it and turn back to Paul. "Where were we? Oh yes — do you think we're promising too much with this timeline?"

It's one in the morning before I climb into a cab and settle in the back, glancing at my phone out of habit. A tiny red alert reminds me I have a voice mail. I play the message, and Tom's deep baritone greets me. "Hi, Kate, it's Tom." A pause. "We really do need to talk about the case. Are you able to come round after you finish work? I'll be home, so just give me a call whenever . . ." He sounds uneasy, awkward even. "I . . . Well, give me a call."

It hardly credits belief that a single drunken kiss can reduce years of friendship to dodged calls and stilted voice mails. I stare out of the cab window in a state of torpid exhaustion and watch London slide by, lit patchily by garish neon signs and streetlamps that deliver a stark, pale light without color or warmth. After a moment I pick up my phone again and type out a text message.

Been working late, big pitch tomorrow afternoon. I can drop by after work tomorrow. Kx.

I read it over again before sending. *Kx* is my habitual sign-off with Tom, but now every character is fraught with meaning and open to misinterpretation. I remove the *x*.

The presentation to Stockleys goes well: Paul is a good presenter, suave and relaxed, and he thinks well on his feet; his style is a good complement to my own direct approach. Caro was right: the contract was ours to lose, and by the time we are shaking hands and saying good-bye I know we haven't done that. Paul hails a cab, and we jump in and animatedly dissect the meeting on the trip back to the office.

"One thing I meant to ask you," Paul says as he waits on the pavement for me to pay the cabbie. There's an odd note in his voice that makes me glance over at him. His almost-translucent eyebrows are drawn together in a frown.

"What?" I turn back to the cabdriver to collect my change.

"Well, Mark Jeffers —"

"The Clifford Chance associate?"

"That's the one. Well, he asked me if I was in line for a promotion." I look at him blankly, not understanding. If he's angling for more money, this is an odd approach. The cabdriver has pulled away, leaving the

two of us together on the street by our office, but neither of us moves toward the doorway. "When you get arrested."

"What the fuck?" My mind is racing. How in the world did Mark Jeffers get hold of this? And how many other people has he spread this gossip to? This sort of rumor could cut off a fledgling company at the knees: even more than most companies, a recruitment firm's only asset is its people and their reputation.

He smiles in a thin line. "Actually, that's exactly what I said. But he said he had it on good authority that you're under investigation for a murder, of all things. In France or something. I told him he needs to get better sources." He looks at me uneasily. "If there was anything to it you'd have told me about it. Right?"

I take a deep breath. This will need careful handling. "I am not under investigation," I say robustly. "A girl went missing from the next-door farmhouse when a group of us were in France on holiday ten years ago. Her body turned up recently —"

"Turned up?"

"Was found." I see her again, the bones in a crumpled pile, ghostly white in the dim underground light. "In a well, actually," I admit, the words somehow slipping out.

"Jesus, Kate, and you're just telling me this now?" He's building up a head of righteous anger. I need to stomp on that quickly.

"Come on, Paul, it's nothing." I make a show of impatience, stamping on the guilt that rises as I ostensibly belittle Severine's death. I carry on defiantly. "Since the six of us were the last people to see her alive, obviously the police want to talk to us again, but that's all it is. I can assure you I'm not about to be arrested." I throw all my powers of persuasion into the eye contact we're sharing and hope to high heaven that every word I've said is true.

"You should have told me. The last thing we need is any kind of stain on our name. You know how people think: no smoke without fire."

"Rubbish. We have a contract from Haft & Weil and now one with Stockleys; that's what clients will focus on, and those kinds of firms don't employ headhunters under investigation for murder. This is just industry gossip that will be forgotten the minute some senior partner gets caught shagging his secretary." *Perhaps* . . .

He's almost mollified; his anger has switched into sulkiness. "If it's nothing, then why didn't you mention it?" Does he have a

point? We're partners in a business together; we see each other every working day — would it have been normal to have mentioned this to him? I suppose so, especially if there was any chance of it impacting the business. Except I never thought that there was . . . Once again I wonder how the hell Mark Jeffers got hold of this. None of our names have ever been in the papers, except Theo's parents as owners of the farmhouse.

"Because . . ." I take another deep breath, and this time I tell him the absolute truth. "Because I don't like talking about it. She was a family friend of the guy we were staying with; we practically spent all week with her, and then she . . ." I trail off. "I'm sorry. I should have told you." Though it simply didn't cross my mind to discuss it with anyone. I wonder how many people Lara has spoken to about it, or Seb or Tom or Caro.

"Oh." Paul is chastened; the personal impact didn't quite occur to him. "No, *I'm* sorry. That must have been awful." He touches my arm awkwardly, and I find a weak smile for him, appreciative of the gesture. I know I'm too comfortable being a solitary creature, but for the first time I realize that in an office of three, where we work long hours, that means I'm forcing

solitude on Paul, too, who is definitely not naturally suited to it. I should make more of an effort to be social with him and Julie.

"Come on," I say, turning for our office. "Let's go find Stockleys some candidates." I look for Severine as we enter the office, almost unable to believe that she wouldn't have wanted to eavesdrop on that little scene with Paul, but she's not lounging at my desk as I'm expecting. I was hoping to see her, I realize, to . . . what? To apologize? To tell her that I'm sorry, but I'm fighting to keep Paul's morale intact and that's more important than hurting the feelings of the ghost who haunts me?

Still, she was murdered. It's not nothing. That's what bothers me more than anything — that whoever did it might get away with it, and that would make it seem as if it doesn't matter, as if Severine never mattered, because if our world continues without a hitch then we might as well be condoning it, and we don't. I don't. It's not nothing.

Back at my desk, the first thing I do is reschedule the thinking time.

Tom's flat. I loiter outside and try not to think about the last time I was here. I'm waiting for Lara: at the last minute I chick-

ened out and called in the cavalry. And in truth Lara should be here, too; she's already shown her colors by overthrowing Modan, and Tom has made it perfectly clear he only wants to talk about the case. Though I haven't failed to notice the desperate, clichéd irony of my support system being exactly the person Tom wants instead of me, which is why I need the support in the first place . . .

Lara appears from the direction of the tube station in a powder blue dress, her blond locks lit luminous red gold by the evening sun that bleeds red ribbons of cloud across the horizon. Severine is beside her, walking barefoot with a loose feline grace in the familiar black shift dress, her hair wrapped in the red chiffon scarf. Her sandals are dangling from one finger. I walk down to meet them, marveling at the tableau they present with the setting sun behind them. Lara and Severine, one light, one dark. Are these two really all I can trust in the world?

"How are you, honey?" I ask as I hug her. It's not a pleasantry; I pull back to search her face as she casts around for an answer.

"Okay," she says, with a slight rueful twist to her lips. She looks a touch pale, and she's wearing less makeup than usual, but her

cornflower eyes are clear with no telltale red rims. "Not great, but . . . okay."

We head back toward Tom's flat, chatting about this and that. She's Lara, but a dimmed version; I can't feel her usual vibrancy, and the lack of it makes me ache for her. At the bottom of the steps, I can delay no longer, and I stop her for a moment. "One thing I've been meaning to ask . . ."

"What?" she prompts as I hesitate.

"That night in the farmhouse . . . with Tom . . . was there ever a time you were apart? And . . . well, did you sleep?"

She assesses me shrewdly, her eyes narrowing. "You're trying to figure out if it could have been Tom."

"I'm just looking at every angle," I say stiffly. I honored the thinking hour this time, and this question is one of the consequences.

"What about me then?" she challenges. There's a wild light in her eye that I don't recognize. "If you're willing to accuse Tom, why not me?"

"Of course it wasn't you."

"Why not?" The light flares into anger. "Why does nobody consider me? *Pretty, vacuous Lara — she's not even capable of a murder. Best not trouble her pretty little head*

286

with all of that."

I look at her in astonishment. I know this is tied up with Modan somehow, but I'm not quite sure how to navigate it. "Well . . . okay, then, tell me: did you murder Severine?"

"Of course not," she says, the anger suddenly leaving her. "I couldn't possibly do such a thing."

The absurdity strikes us both at the same time, and we start to giggle. When the last bubbles of laughter have died out, I say quietly, "It's not a bad thing, Lara. You're full of light, you think the best of everyone, we all see it, it draws us in. But nobody thinks you're vacuous." She inclines her head a little ruefully, not entirely accepting my words. "Did Modan say something to you? Are you still talking to him?" I ask cautiously.

"I doubt it after our last conversation," she says frankly. "He thinks I'm going to go off and screw half the men in London — the half I haven't already screwed, that is." She shakes her head in frustration. "When he asked before about past boyfriends, I was honest — more fool me. I didn't expect to have it thrown back in my face. And aren't the French supposed to be more liberal than the British on that sort of thing?"

"I'm sure French men are just as susceptible to jealousy as British men." Poor Modan. He must be incredibly cut up to lash out like that: he doesn't strike me as a man who usually makes such appalling missteps. "Are you? Going to screw half of London, I mean? Only maybe someone should warn the poor creatures, give them time to prepare . . ."

"Stop it," she says, laughing again. "That was then." She sobers and puts a hand on my arm, earnestness shining out of her. "I'm different now."

"I know," I say gently, though a shameful part of me wonders how long she will be different for. But I realize I'm being unfair: surely we're all different now, from how we were in a French farmhouse a decade ago. Perhaps it just took a little longer for the impact to hit Lara.

A slight frown crosses her face. "You don't believe me."

"I do," I reassure her quickly. "Of course I do. I was just . . . I was just contrasting with that week in France . . ." She cocks her head questioningly. I try to find the right words. "I mean, we're all different now. Even Caro, maybe . . . Everyone is different, or — gone. Or maybe I'm seeing different sides of everyone . . ." When I try to think about

what might have happened to Severine, it's like trying to solve a puzzle based on the picture on the box, but the pieces have evolved — or maybe the picture on the box was never the right picture in the first place. Lara still has her head cocked to one side, the quizzical look still in place. I shake my head. "Never mind. Come on, we should go up."

We link arms and turn toward the entrance to Tom's block of flats. Lara buzzes to announce us. I hear Tom's voice through the intercom, made tinny and weak. If he's surprised at Lara's presence it doesn't show, other than perhaps through a slight pause before he speaks that could instead have been a result of the technology.

"I never answered your question, though," Lara says as we start to climb the threadbare stairs. "We weren't apart that I was aware of, except to go to the loo, but we did sleep. I don't know how long for — maybe just a couple of hours?"

Tom has left the door of his flat ajar; we push through, and despite my now numerous visits, it still surprises me to see this oasis of light and modern style after the genteel shabbiness of the common areas. Following noise, we find him hunting down some wineglasses in the kitchen. "I presume

a glass of wine wouldn't go amiss, ladies?" he says with a grin, raising the bottle of white in his hand. He's had time to change after work; he's wearing jeans and a blue T-shirt that picks up the color in his eyes.

"Now that's what I call a welcome." Lara smiles flirtatiously as she kisses him hello. I glance away and thus am completely unprepared when he wraps his arms around me in his bear hug of old. The T-shirt is of the softest cotton, and he smells of the same aftershave from that dark, delicious corridor; for a moment the ache is blinding. When I pull myself together enough to return the hug I think I hear the stroke of his warm breath deliver *Sorry* into my ear. When he releases me I stare after him, trying to search his eyes, but he busies himself hunting down a corkscrew and then Lara pulls out a bar stool for me and I'm left wondering what just happened as I settle beside her on one side of the kitchen counter.

Tom is facing us, the dark granite kitchen counter between us. "So, what news?" he asks, uncorking the bottle. He's meeting my eyes from time to time, but I'm failing to divine anything from his expression. The bar stool is an uncomfortable height: I can't rest my elbows on the counter, and my feet

don't reach the floor, yet there's no strut for them to rest on. I feel perched and precarious.

I shrug, leaving Lara to fill the gap. "Not much," she says lightly. "I've turned celibate, and Kate is trying to figure out whether you could have killed Severine."

She's being flippant, of course she's being flippant, but Tom pauses in the act of pouring, his eyes leaping to mine. "And?" he asks after a beat, placing the bottle carefully down and maintaining the eye contact. It's clear he's completely disregarding the celibacy comment; whether that will irk Lara or not I don't know or care, because I currently feel like killing her for putting me in this position. I can feel her shifting uneasily beside me as it dawns on her that her comment is actually being taken seriously. "Do you think I'm capable of it?" Tom asks in a measured tone.

It feels like a challenge, though over what I'm not sure. Still, I rise to it. "Yes," I say simply.

"Kate!" I hear Lara exclaim, but I'm still locked in a gaze with Tom. There's nothing I can read in his eyes. Then he inclines his head a little and returns to pouring the wine.

"I'm not saying he did," I explain in an aside to Lara, though my eyes keep darting

back to Tom, looking for something, any-thing, that tells me what he's thinking. I try to hook one ankle round the leg of the stool, searching for some balance. I need an anchor. "I'm just saying he's capable of it. Under the right circumstances." I take a sip of the wine that Tom has pushed toward me. "Probably all of us are under the right circumstances."

"Not all, I don't think," says Tom thought-fully. He has a beer instead; he takes a long pull of it. "Well, maybe everyone is capable of an accidental murder," he concedes. "But the cover-up — that's the crucial bit. Not everyone would have the self-possession to do that rather than calling the emergency services."

You would, I think immediately; then I re-alize he's watching me and have the uncom-fortable feeling he can read my mind as he smiles thinly and raises his beer in a mock toast.

"Well," says Lara after a pause. "We've certainly bypassed the small talk this eve-ning." She picks up her own wine and takes a long draft.

"Have either of you eaten?" asks Tom abruptly. "I've already warmed the oven; shall I shove some pizzas in or something?"

The process of deliberating over the food

options dispels the atmosphere; for a few moments this might be simply a social evening. But once the oven door has been swung shut, Tom takes another swig of his beer and I see him change gear.

"Right," he says decisively, looking at Lara and me in turn. "I think it's cards on the table time now. What do you guys think happened that night?"

"My cards *are* on the table," Lara complains. "They've *always* been on the table. I never thought it was one of us." She spreads her hands wide in exasperation, almost knocking over her glass. "Oops, sorry, I already had a glass or two after work with some colleagues . . . Anyway, so . . . unless you, Tom, managed to kill Severine, get rid of her body, clean yourself up and get back into bed with me in the space of a little more than an hour, maybe two, then I have absolutely no information."

I'm taken aback by the casual way in which she can mention being in bed with Tom — *with Tom* — in public, to Tom himself, without an iota of a blush. I glance at him quickly, but he doesn't appear fazed in the slightest. "I'm good," he says with dark humor, "but not that good."

I try to stamp down my swelling sense of injustice — that Lara, who casually slept

with him then tossed him aside, gets entirely forgiven, yet I am held out to dry for a mere kiss — but there's a thread of irritation that leaks through into my words. "But you're presuming the same person did it all," I declare bluntly. "It's possible more than one person was involved. Maybe an accidental killing by one, then one or two more involved in the cover-up . . ." This discussion is so abstract, so passionless, that it's hard to remember the girl it relates to. I glance around for her, but she's not in attendance. I feel an extra prickle of irritation: what kind of ghost wouldn't be interested in discussions on their own death? Though I suppose it's not as if she doesn't know the punch line . . .

Tom nods. Somehow I feel an unexpected sense of approval from him. "Sounds like you have a theory."

"No, I just . . ." I shift awkwardly on the very awkward stool. I don't have a theory. I have a collection of disquieting observations that add up to a maelstrom of unease, but nothing that could be called a theory.

Lara shifts herself so she's half lolling on the counter and cocks her head in sympathetic listening mode. "It's just us, Kate."

"Come on, Kate," says Tom. He's standing with his hands on the granite surface,

leaning toward me. With his height the body language sends a curious message of encouragement mixed with intimidation. "You have to trust someone."

I look across at him, meeting those familiar blue eyes that are Tom's not Seb's, above that unmistakable nose, and I am suddenly so blindingly angry with him that for a moment I can't speak. I used to trust him, I even *want* to trust him, so why won't he let me? He knows something, I know it, and by now he must realize I know it given Lara's comment, yet he won't let me in, and now I wonder if he's Tom, if he ever was the Tom I thought I knew, and if I got that wrong, what else have I been mistaken on? A cold fear is twisting my insides, and a raw anger spears through my throat at Tom — *Tom* — for putting it there. "Really?" I say bitingly, when I recover my voice. "*I* have to trust someone? That's rich. Who do *you* trust, Tom? The only damn things that I'm sure of in this whole macabre debacle are that Seb and Caro are hiding something, and you know a hell of a lot more than you're letting on, yet somehow it's *my* life that's getting trampled on. So if we're talking about *trust,* how about we start with you, Tom?" Tom's eyes are widened in surprise at my attack; I catch a glimpse of Lara star-

295

ing at me, completely nonplussed, and it halts me: I bite off the vitriolic torrent that's just gaining momentum. If I let it free, I may never stop. I grab my wineglass and focus on it determinedly in the suffocating silence that follows my words while the remaining anger subsides along with my breathing, leaving me in acute danger of bursting into tears. The immediate urge to apologize for my un-British outburst is offset by a streak of rebellion fueled by the remaining anger that claims this was merely a fraction of what he deserves. Of what is inside me right now, of what this world deserves.

It's Lara who breaks the silence, which has grown so thick, so heavy that I'm almost amazed anything can penetrate it. "I shouldn't have come," she says quickly, slithering down from the stool. "I really think you two need to talk and —"

"No, stay. Please. Stay." I put out a hand to keep her there, still focusing on the wineglass. "I'm sorry." I take a deep breath and look up at her. She's half turned to go, uncertainty and concern in her eyes. I'm resolutely not looking at Tom, but I know he's watching us; watching me, mostly. I can feel it on my skin: through my skin, even, like a pressure on my bones. "It's not

— that — anyway. It's . . ."

"What?" she asks.

"My life — my business — really is getting trampled. There are rumors in the market that I'm about to be arrested for murder," I say miserably. "Mark Jeffers, this associate candidate at — well, never mind where he's at — anyway, he told Paul. And if he told Paul of all people how do I know he's not telling the whole world?"

Lara sits down again, accompanied by a sharp intake of breath. We all know this isn't the sole reason for my abysmal lack of composure, or even the main reason for it, but they're both kind enough to tacitly redirect their attention. Tom finally speaks his first words since my outburst. "How did Paul react? Do you think he will jump ship?"

I feel my mouth twist sourly. How typical of Tom to be able to set aside my diatribe and focus. It forces me to respond with a civility I still don't feel. "I don't know. I don't think so, not yet anyway. We've got two very prestigious contracts . . . but if the rumors escalate and we lose one of those, then yes, he's Paul, he'd jump ship." I shrug. "He was upset I hadn't told him about it." I take a sip of the wine then look at both of them curiously. "Have you guys told anyone about all of this?"

Tom shakes his head. "It's hardly something I want to bring up on the trading floor. I can just imagine the fun they'd have . . ." He grimaces, no doubt imagining the taunts that would inevitably haunt him for the rest of his career. As a mob crowd, traders are not known for their sensitivity. "And I don't want to worry my folks. I'm not sure Seb has mentioned it to his parents, either, unless it's to get a recommendation of a lawyer from his dad."

"I spoke to a couple of girls at work," says Lara, "but never any details. I certainly didn't mention your name, if that's what you're —"

I shake my head. "God, no. I was just curious." Curious as to whether my reluctance to talk about it is another sign of too much solitude, or actually perfectly normal.

Tom is still analyzing. His eyes are fixed on the falling darkness outside the kitchen window as he scratches his head thoughtfully. The clouds are now inky smudges against a marginally paler sky. "And this chap, Mark Jenners —"

"Jeffers."

"Mark Jeffers told Paul you were about to be arrested?"

"So I understand."

Tom is frowning. "Just you." I shrug.

"Maybe it's nothing but Chinese whispers, but it seems a bit odd. You couldn't put it together from just the newspaper articles, I don't think. Our names have never been mentioned."

I nod. "That's what I thought."

Lara's cheeks are flushed and her eyelids a little droopy. The glass or two that she had earlier, plus the large one Tom poured for her, are taking their toll. "Big mouth for a lawyer," she comments, finishing in a cat-like yawn that she neatly smothers. "Aren't they supposed to be discreet? And aren't you supposed to butter up your headhunting firm, not spread scurrilous rumors about them? I can't imagine this has you and Paul dying to find him a good placement."

It's another of Lara's unexpectedly perceptive moments, though she hasn't followed through to the implications. Tom's gaze and mine jump to lock together, and for a moment it's like the darkened corridor never happened, like I've never ever doubted him, and I can see exactly what he's thinking. "But who?" I say to him.

"I don't know." Tom shakes his head, then frowns again. "I can't see who could possibly benefit."

"Who what?" asks Lara, thoroughly lost.

"Who put him up to it," I explain. "You're right, it's extremely odd behavior. So either he's an irredeemable gossip, or someone put him up to it." I think for a bit. "I can take a look in his file and ask Paul about him. If he's known to be the town crier then maybe it's just incredibly bad luck that he's got hold of this."

Tom turns his attention to the oven. The last few moments have stripped away some of my distrust, or perhaps my growing exhaustion has done that — suspicion is so damn *tiring*. Things would be so much simpler if Tom was on my side. I'm almost sure he is; I'm almost sure Tom is Tom and all the rest of it is just noise. It's certainly what I want to believe. "That night . . . with Severine," I start hesitantly. Tom looks up in the act of removing the pizzas, with a lightness in his eyes that warms me: he recognizes the olive branch. "At first I thought — well, I thought she went to the bus depot the next morning, so I thought it was nothing to do with all of us. Then afterward, when Modan said it wasn't her, then I started thinking. And the thing is, I don't know what time Seb came to bed. I was pretty upset, and pretty drunk, to be honest; I think I just passed out, so I really don't know. But then Seb was really insis-

tent that he was there all night . . ." Lara and Tom are both watching me, letting the words run out of me. "And he and Caro are acting so strangely, so . . . *complicit,* I actually wondered if they were shagging, but I think actually — I think it's all to do with this. With Severine." I take a deep breath, looking at Tom. If I say this it becomes possible. If I say this, I can never take it back. "So I guess I've been wondering if Seb killed her — by accident — and if Caro helped cover it up."

I hear Lara mutter, *"Jesus,"* and in my peripheral vision she reaches for the wine bottle, but I'm focused on Tom. He nods calmly. Thoughtfully. He's not surprised, and by now I'm not surprised about that.

"Caro," he says. He's speaking dispassionately, simultaneously carving up the slightly burned pizzas with a circular cutter, as if we're discussing interest rates or car insurance. "Not me for the cover-up?"

In the moment I am unable to think of anything to say but the truth. "It could have been you. But like you said, I don't think you would have had enough time to manage it without Lara suspecting something. And . . ."

"What?" His cutting of the pizza continues unhurried, and his question is casual, but

his eyes on me are anything but.

I shrug again. "I guess I think that if it had been you, it would have been a better cover-up."

"Thank you, I think," he says dryly, but the tension has left him, and a smile lurks round his mouth.

"Was it such a bad cover-up?" asks Lara. "It took ten years for the body to be found."

Severine has perched her bottom on the granite surface beside the sink. She crosses her legs and supports her upper body with her arms braced behind her. She doesn't shock me with her sudden appearances anymore. I wonder if I would miss her if she were to go wherever ghosts go when they're done haunting.

"If it was a random stranger, then it's a poorly executed cover-up that just got lucky," says Tom. "You'd have to expect the well to be searched sometime early on, and a stranger wouldn't know it was due to be filled in soon. But we knew that. Even so, even with it being filled in, you'd have to think it would be searched sooner rather than later."

"What would you have done?" I ask curiously.

"Taken your car keys and dumped her somewhere far away," he says promptly, so

promptly that I know he's thought about this before.

"Modan asked about cars . . ." I trail off. There's a tendril of something in my brain that I can't quite catch. Severine has a cigarette in her hand now. She blows out smoke in a slow, languid breath, her eyes fixed on me, as dark and unreflective as always.

"We're really considering this, then?" says Lara to no one in particular. "That it could have been Seb? One of us?" There's nothing to say to that. She reaches for a slice of pizza, then pauses with it partway to her mouth to remark, "If Caro was involved, it would have to be for Seb. I can't imagine her doing that for anyone else." She thinks for a moment more, then gestures with the pizza. "Caro and Seb. God, I hope he's not that stupid."

"He's pretty stupid at times, but even so . . ." Tom grimaces, but then shakes his head. They're both sneaking wary glances at me. The instinct not to talk about Seb in front of me has become so ingrained over the years that they're struggling to shake it. Tom shakes his head again. "I'm sure he's not. He must know it would mean too much to her."

"Has everybody always known that?" I ask

hesitantly. "I don't think I did back then —
did I miss it? I knew she didn't like me going out with Seb, but I thought she just
didn't like *me*."

"She didn't like you," Tom says, not
without humor, at the same time as Lara
says, "She still doesn't like you."

A smile curls my lips despite myself. "No,
really, guys, don't beat around the bush on
my account." Tom grins and Lara giggles. "I
knew she didn't like me, but I didn't think
it was me so much as what I represent — or
what I don't represent. I didn't go to the
right school, I didn't spend my summers in
Pony Club and winters in Verbier, I don't
have the right accent."

"Val d'Isère," says Tom. I roll my eyes.
How is it that we're now back at this easy
ebb and flow? Surely there has to be a
reckoning at some point? "But I take your
point: she's a snob. Of course she wouldn't
like you. But especially not since you were
dating Seb."

"You're right, though; she's more obvious
now," Lara observes.

I munch on the pizza and let this marinate.
The trick is to take in the new without pol-
luting the old, and I don't think I've got the
hang of it: it's too easy to project what I
know now on what I remember from then. I

remember Seb; I remember the faint disbelief I carried around inside me that Seb — silver-spooned, silver-tongued, golden-hued Seb — that he was with me. Part of me *expected* all girls to want him. And Seb . . . well, Seb expected it, too; he took it as his right, and any suggestion that he encouraged it was instantly labeled "jealousy." I decided early on that I would not allow him to brand me with that, but that required a lot of hard work and, in retrospect, willful ignorance. Perhaps it's no wonder I dismissed Caro's long-held unrequited love too lightly.

I finish my slice before I break the companionable silence. "Anyway, we've strayed from the point. Tom, what do you think happened? You've always known more than us."

He doesn't dispute it. "I was actually trying not to drag you guys into it."

"We're pretty firmly mired in it all now."

"Speak for yourself," yawns Lara. "I'm sure I'm off the hook."

I give her arm a gentle poke. "So much for solidarity. Well, I'm pretty firmly mired in it all, at least."

He doesn't dispute that, either.

"You saw something," Lara prompts.

He nods. "I did. I . . ." A loud buzz inter-

rupts him. He cocks his head and turns toward his door. "Probably a mistake. A drunk or something." The buzzer sounds again, in three short blasts then a long hold. "A highly obnoxious drunk." He crosses the kitchen quickly and exits to the hall. We hear him speaking tersely to the intercom by his front door. "Hello?"

"It's me," comes an unmistakable voice, unexpectedly loud through the speaker. Lara's guilt-filled eyes fly to mine, which no doubt display the same. *Speak of the devil* . . . "Let me up. I'm the glad bearer of tidings — the bearer of glad tidings. Or something . . ."

"Come on up then." Tom sounds resigned. He reappears in the doorway of the kitchen. "Seb," he says unnecessarily.

Lara makes a face. "Definitely an obnoxious drunk, then. Though who am I to talk, after all this wine." She slides down the stool and turns for her bag and coat. "I'm going to have to leave you to it."

"I'll come with you." But I'm still perched on the stool, anchored by the same one ankle.

"Stay," Tom says quickly. "I'll get rid of him."

I raise an eyebrow. "Charming. Whatever

306

happened to blood being thicker than water?"

"Doesn't apply when the blood is thinned by alcohol. He'll probably have to slope home to Alina soon anyway."

Lara is not too sleepy to have missed this exchange: I see her eyes dart back and forth between us as she pulls her coat on, but her face is carefully expressionless. "Call me tomorrow," she says to me neutrally. "You can fill me in on the outcome of the rest of this Nancy Drew session."

And so I stay.

CHAPTER SIXTEEN

Seb is drunk.

Not just a little squiffy, or even moderately tipsy, but unequivocally drunk. The sort of drunk that can only be achieved by dedicated effort — a long, brutally determined session — or by a staggering lack of tolerance. But I'm beginning to suspect that Seb's tolerance has been well bolstered over the last decade.

"Jesus," says Tom, as Seb stumbles in through the kitchen door that Lara has just slipped out of, catching hold of the frame to steady himself. He's in a dark suit, the tail of his tie dangling from his trouser pocket, and there are stains on his white shirt, but it's his face that really arrests attention. His eyes are glazed and patterned with red veins like cracks; he's flushed, heavy jowled and loose lipped. The tan that sits on his skin is too insubstantial to hide the damage of his night's work. "Look at

the state of you. Where have you been?"

"The King's Head by the office. Leaving drinks. They're firing half the bloody floor; there's been leaving drinks for weeks . . . Then a bloody good wine bar in Knightsbridge. Then, God, I don't know." He peers across the room, as if struggling to see through darkness despite the kitchen being well lit, swaying slightly despite the support of the doorframe. "Kate, too? You know I just saw Lara on the way up the stairs." His speech is slurred: he has particular trouble with *Lara;* it could be *Lalla* or *Lulla.*

"Hi, Seb." I make no move to climb off the stool. He is not something I want to kiss hello.

"Come and have a glass of water," Tom says, running the tap in the sink. He eyes the difficult stools. "On second thought, maybe we should move to the sofa."

"Not water," says Seb, shaking his head, but he lets Tom shepherd him through the open-plan room in the direction of the living room area. I take the water glass off Tom in return for a muttered thanks and then follow the pair of them. "Need something stronger. Wet the baby's head. Alina's pregnant. Going to be a dad. Fuck." He sounds astonished, as if he can't quite understand how he got to this point.

"Congratulations! Didn't know — woah, there! — you had it in you." I can hear the exasperation under Tom's words as he tries to stop Seb ricocheting off the walls, knocking awry the photographic prints Tom has hung there.

I pause by the dining table that separates the kitchen space from the living room area and compose myself. Seb has collapsed onto one sofa, legs sprawled out, shoulders hunched over well below the line of the sofa back. Severine sits in the opposite corner of the same sofa, her feet curled up under her, eyeing Seb with unmistakable distaste. Tom switches on a couple of table lamps, then sits in the armchair.

"Congratulations, Seb," I say, holding out the water. He doesn't take it — I'm sure he can barely see it — so I put it on the coffee table. I can't bring myself to sit on Severine — or near Seb for that matter, so I settle on the footstool. "How is Alina feeling?"

"Oh, fine, fine. She's always fine."

I think of Alina with the crumpled paper towel in the bathroom of the restaurant. No, Alina is not always fine.

"How far along is she?" asks Tom.

"Ten weeks. Not supposed to say yet, but . . ." He shrugs. I can barely discern the movement, his head is sunk so deeply into

his chest. "Fuck. A baby." A phone starts to ring from the depths of his suit jacket. He clumsily pulls it out, peers at the screen then leans forward to deposit it on the table without answering. He passes a hand over his face, then collapses back into the sofa again. Just when I think he's passed out, he turns to me with an unexpectedly shrewd look. "What are you doing here anyway? Have I interrupted something?" He starts to laugh as if the idea is hilarious. "Sloppy seconds, huh, Tom?"

In that instant I detest him with a force that's blinding. I actually want to physically hurt him. It scares me.

"You just saw Lara, Seb," Tom reminds him evenly, but his jaw is clenched. He's not looking at me. It feels deliberate. "You think I'm screwing them both?" *Screwing.* To screw, a verb. I screw, we screw, they screwed, screw you . . . it can never sound anything but cheap, sordid. Is that how he thinks of the corridor kiss?

"Ha-ha," Seb snorts. "Don't tell me it never crossed your mind. Certainly crossed mine once or twice." In another world, in other circumstances, this would be harmless fun. The kind of flirting men do with attractive female friends that elicits a naughty giggle and a warm glow. But we're

not in that world. There's a hard edge to Seb's words, a nastiness. Was he always like this when he'd had a few? I recall Lara's words: *Definitely an obnoxious drunk, then.* I can't specifically recall it, but it doesn't quite surprise me, either.

I stand up abruptly. "I think I'll head home after all. The company's better there." Severine eyes me from the sofa, as close to a smirk on her face as I have ever seen. At least I've conjured up a figment of imagination that appreciates my sly digs.

"No, don't," says Seb. He struggles himself a little more upright and lunges out with an arm to try and stop me. "I'm sorry. Don't take it like that. Was just having fun. Don't have to take everything so seriously! Sorry, sorry . . ." His mumbles trail off, but he continues to look at me beseechingly, somehow both aggrieved and hangdog, a little boy mostly pretending to be ashamed of himself. This I remember. Seb is a master at apologies that somehow make you feel like the fault is more than likely your own.

The phone starts to ring again; he drops my arm. "Alina?" asks Tom, but from my vantage point of standing I can see on the screen that it's not Alina calling.

"It's Caro," I inform them, but I think Seb knows that. He's made no move to

answer. I can see he's missed eight calls; I wonder how many are from Caro. The phone subsides into sulky silence.

"Would never have met you if it wasn't for Tom," Seb rambles, as if there's been no interruption. He seems to have found a philosophical bent. "That's why we went to that party, you know, when we crashed Linacre Ball. Tom wanted to see some girl . . ." He trails off, smirking at Tom. I catch a glimpse of Tom's face, set with tension. I don't understand the undercurrent.

"Who?" I prompt, when Seb doesn't go on. I've never heard this story before.

"Yes, who was that girl? I don't think you ever told me," says Seb with faux-innocence, but in his inebriated state, subtlety is beyond him. Seb, I deduce, knows exactly who it was.

"Who knows? It was a long time ago," Tom says tightly, but he's interrupted by Seb's mobile ringing once more.

"It's Caro again," I say neutrally.

"I know," he mutters. His head is sunk on his chest again. "Fuck." This time it's more of a moan.

"Why is Caro calling you so much?" Tom asks, as if it's only of the mildest interest to him.

"I'm not sleeping with her if that's what

313

you think." He's both belligerent and defensive. His fabled charm has most definitely fled him this evening.

"I never said —"

"Yeah, well, you implied it. Of course I'm not sleeping with her; I'm not completely stupid. Never have in all these years." His head lolls again. "Barely even kissed her," he mutters. He rubs a hand down his face, then lunges drunkenly for my arm again, and catches it, pulling me down awkwardly so I'm half hunched over. "I fucked up, Kate," he mumbles urgently, looking straight in my eyes. "Should never have given up on us. Everything was okay, wasn't it? We were good, weren't we? But then I fucked up. And now . . . oh, fuck . . ." I start to feel a sense of foreboding building in my stomach. Seb releases my arm abruptly, and I lose my balance, grabbing at the coffee table to steady myself. When I look back at Seb he has his arm raised, shielding his eyes with his forearm. I glance at Tom questioningly. He shakes his head, nonplussed.

"Seb, what's wrong?" I ask hesitantly. "What is it?"

"Leaving drinks." His lips fumble around the words, thick and rubbery. "*My* leaving drinks."

"But you just came across from New York. Surely they wouldn't fire you when —"

"Not fired. Resigned. *Not* fired. My boss was — kind — enough to give me the option." His arm is still over his eyes.

"What did you do?" Tom asks, brutally direct.

"What I always do. I fucked up." He lifts his arm away; it's hard to tell in the dim lighting, but I think his eyes are wet. "Not like you, eh, Tom? You always hit the mark. *Tom is doing so well at school. Tom's won a scholarship, didn't you hear? Tom's really racing up the career ladder; you know he's head of FX trading now? Why can't you be more like your cousin?*"

My breath catches in shock. I can't imagine Seb would ever betray such bitterness were it not for the amount he's drunk, and I can't imagine he would want me to see this. I feel instantly grimy, like I'm peeping in on a private scene. Tom's face is impassive. I wonder if he's heard this before or simply guessed at the simmering resentment. "What did you do?" Tom repeats, remarkably undeterred.

Seb rubs a hand over his face, and all the fight seems to leave him. "I was drunk," he says hoarsely. "At work. All this stuff with that fucking French girl, and Alina and the

315

baby, and then Caro in my ear — it just . . . got too much." He presses the heels of his hands into his eye sockets and leaves them there. "Fuck!" he says with explosive savagery.

When Tom shakes his head, I can see exasperation warring with pity upon his face. "Oh, Seb," he says softly.

That fucking French girl. A literal statement in this case, since he was the one fucking her. But one look at Seb's distress robs me of my ironic amusement; there's nothing to laugh at here. "I'm sorry," I say inadequately. I look at Tom. "You should call Alina and let her know he's here; she's probably worried sick."

He nods and picks up Seb's mobile to scroll through the directory for Alina's number, stepping toward the corridor to make the call. I wonder if he's also checking how many times Caro has rung; I would be.

Seb is falling asleep, I think. I suppose he will have to stay here, and therefore Tom and I are unlikely to have our tête-à-tête tonight after all. I should go; in fact, I'm eager to go — watching someone unravel is far from comfortable, and Severine has already ditched the scene. I make a move toward the corridor, but suddenly Seb lunges for my arm once more: not asleep

after all. He pulls me into that awkward crouch again, but this time I'm forewarned; I brace myself on the arm of the sofa. "It wasn't me," he says urgently, pleadingly, his bloodshot eyes seeking mine out directly. "You have to know that. It wasn't me — I would have remembered if it was me, wouldn't I? It couldn't have been me. I came to bed; it couldn't have been me."

"I . . ." I'm helpless for words. Hypothetically discussing Seb as a suspect for murder in Tom's kitchen over pizza is a far cry from facing down the mess that is the man himself. Tom's footsteps sound behind me, and I turn, relieved at the interruption, but I see Tom halt abruptly at the sight of us, his face frozen. I'm suddenly horribly aware of how close Seb's face is to mine.

I start to disengage my arm just as Seb blurts, "I think I'm going to vom—" He releases me and lurches upward as I scatter backward; Tom starts back into action, practically hauling him by the collar toward the bathroom. Moments later I hear the unmistakable sound of Seb's stomach evacuating itself.

I climb back onto my feet and go in search of my coat and my handbag, both of which are still in the kitchen. The dirty pizza plates are still on the counter; if I were a truly

wonderful guest I would wash them up, but given it's now past midnight I am definitely nowhere near wonderful — the most I have the energy for is to stack them in the sink, since on inspection the dishwasher is full. My mind is flitting from Seb's desperate, pleading eyes to Tom's shuttered face, and back again . . . It's hardly the most important question, but I keep wondering who the girl was, the girl that Tom dragged Seb to the party for. Once upon a time I would have landed upon one name only, but I'm starting to think there's a second option.

I pick up my coat and exit the kitchen to find Tom hovering in the corridor, lit only by the yellow slash of light coming from the bottom of the bathroom door, and the dim light spilling in from the kitchen and living room.

"You got hold of Alina?" I ask, to cover my awkwardness. Tom and I, alone again in this same corridor — how could it not be awkward?

"Yeah. He's going to stay here for tonight." He's leaning his back against the wall; I can barely see the white of his teeth as he yawns. "She knew about him losing his job. She brought it up; I was wondering whether Seb would have told her or not."

"How did she sound?" I put my bag down

and begin to pull on my coat.

"I don't know. Frustrated mostly, I think."

Another deep retch comes from the bathroom. My eyes are adjusting to the light; I can just make out a grimace of part distaste and part sympathy on Tom's face. "Christ. He's going to feel like death tomorrow."

"Who was the girl, Tom?"

He knows what I mean; he doesn't try to dissemble. He simply shakes his head tiredly. "It doesn't matter."

It does, though. "Was it Lara?" We're speaking quietly. The darkness winds its way around us, enveloping us, comforting us. It's a blanket under which words can be uttered that would never be broached in the light of day.

"What? No, it wasn't Lara." I know he's looking at me; I can feel the weight of his gaze, though I can only discern his eyes from a slight gleam. I have the sense his head is cocked, but perhaps I'm projecting his mannerisms upon this dark canvas. "Why would you think that? That was just a holiday fling. It didn't mean anything to either of us."

Not Lara. Not only not Lara, but seemingly never Lara. I file that away for future analysis. "So who was the girl?" I ask again, doggedly intent.

He doesn't speak for a moment. He's so still I could believe he has fallen asleep standing. Eventually his words come, barely more than a whisper. "You know who it was."

Yes. I do know. There's an inevitability about it, a permanence, even though I recognize that I didn't know at all. I swallow. "Now I do," I whisper. "I didn't before." Things I've been scared to acknowledge I've wanted and hoped for are gathering together inside me, a pressure that's building, straining, until I'm afraid to move lest I burst open.

His hand reaches out, and I feel the back of his fingers trail gently down my cheek. I find I'm holding my breath. "I'm sorry I was such an unforgivable shit. It's just . . . there was a moment there, the other night, when I thought I was getting everything I'd always wanted. And then — reality set in." His fingers drop, he turns his head away and suddenly my stomach clenches into a hard knot. I know beyond a shadow of doubt that I will have to close myself off again, stamp down on all those things so eager to burst out. "And I was so fucked off — at myself, mostly — for allowing it, for putting myself in that position. Because I knew better, really. You can say whatever

you choose to say, pretend whatever you think you should feel, but I see it in you, tonight like every other night. It's always been Seb for you, hasn't it? You never even saw me. And I'll always know that."

He has it all wrong, just like I've had it all wrong about so many things. "No, no," I protest urgently, my voice rising, "that's not fair, that's not right —"

But he barely notices my interruption; he's still talking, in a low, oddly persuasive rumble. "When this — when Modan — is done, I'm going to move back to Boston —"

A sudden crash comes from the bathroom. It sounds as if Seb has pulled something over: quite possibly the radiator judging from the metallic reverberation. Tom is already moving in that direction. "Shit. Sorry, Kate, you'd better go," he throws over his shoulder, then he's pulling the bathroom door open. I catch a glimpse of his face in the yellow light that leaps out to paint him, harsh lines etched round his mouth. "Shit!" he says again. Then he disappears inside and the door shuts abruptly. I'm left alone in the passageway.

For a moment I stand there, completely at a loss. Surely I can help with whatever disaster is now unfolding — but then I re-

alize: that's not the point. He doesn't want me here, and this is a convenient way to politely get rid of me. I consider that for a moment more, then take a shuddering breath, pick up my bag and quietly leave the flat.

In the taxi on the way home I replay the night of Linacre Ball, when I first met Seb, and when, of course, I also first met Tom. I think about Tom dragging Seb along to the party, with quiet plans of speaking to a girl — me, as it turns out. I wonder where he had come across me before. I don't suppose I'll ever find out. I wonder how different things would have been if I'd turned back for the man-boy with the marvelously hooked nose after jumping off the wall, but I have to stop that train of thought before I come apart a piece at a time. Then from nowhere Tom's words from an afternoon not so very long ago in his flat float back to me: *Seb likes to win* — and I put that together with Seb's sly look — *Yes, who was that girl? I don't think you ever told me* — and I'm flooded with such savage fury that I want to scream with it.

I know I'm an unholy mess. I wish beyond all reason that my dad was still alive. But he's not here, and I am, in a taxi driving through the deserted streets of London. So

I go home to an empty flat — truly empty, as Severine is nowhere to be seen — and crawl into bed with all my clothes on, craving the oblivion of sleep.

When I was growing up my mother often used to say that things look better after a good night's sleep. I've always been my father's child, and he was never so blindly optimistic. In the morning, I'm still under suspicion of murder and my love life still has not improved. And I remember that I still haven't found out what Tom saw all those years ago at the farmhouse.

The office provides little respite. A potential client — big job, looking to flesh out their whole litigation team, but we're in stiff competition with two other recruitment firms — asks me diffidently about any "events in the private lives of the key personnel of Channing Associates that could be potentially reputation damaging" were they to enter into a contract with us; I know immediately that the rumors aren't confined to Mark Jeffers.

"Ah," I say with what I hope is a knowing laugh. "You're actually asking about the completely ridiculous rumor that I'm about to be sent down for murder."

"Well, I . . ." I can practically hear the

squirming down the line.

"To tell you the truth, it's all horribly sad. A girl disappeared in the neighboring farmhouse to where I was staying on holiday in France ten years ago, and her body has just been found. Naturally the police have spoken to all of us who were staying there, and naturally we're all keen to do anything at all we can to help." I pause and add meaningfully, "As I'm sure you would be, if you were in my shoes."

"Yes. Yes, of course. We just have to be very careful. As a firm we pride ourselves on our unimpeachable reputation . . ."

It's hard not to zone out. No matter what I have said or can say now, we've lost this one. It was a tight race anyway, and rightly or wrongly, this just gives a reason for them to pick another horse. They won't say that, of course. I'm mildly curious to see what excuse they will come up with. My money is on them labeling us "a comparatively new firm that has yet to be sufficiently proven."

Paul comes in, his face grim, just as I'm putting down the phone.

"I know," I say to forestall him, moving around my desk to rest my backside on it. "I just had chapter and verse on reputation from Strichmans."

His mouth is in a thin line almost as pale

as his eyebrows. "What did you say?"

"The truth, as it happens, but we've lost it anyway."

"They said that?"

I shake my head. "No, but they will."

He pulls out his chair and flops into it, dispirited. "This isn't going away, Kate."

"It will." But even I can hear that I lack conviction.

"Can't they arrest someone already?"

"I'd be fine with that. So long as it isn't me."

He almost bursts up out of his chair. "What the fuck, Kate? You said —"

"*Joke,* Paul. Just a joke."

"You can't joke about this stuff," he says stiffly, but at least he subsides back into his seat. "It's *serious,* Kate."

"I know. We just lost Strichmans. Though we may never have got that one anyway."

"So what are you going to do?"

The *you* in his question rings out like a bell, loud and clear, reverberating in my brain. Paul is dissociating himself, preparing for the worst. "We're going to do our jobs, and we're going to do them very well." I'm careful not to put stress on the plural pronoun.

"Sure," he says with no vigor. He leans forward in his chair, elbows on his knees

and hands hanging in between, staring at the floor.

"Paul." I speak sharply, pulling myself upright. He doesn't look up. "Paul!" This gets his attention. "Don't build this up to be something it's not. We're quite some distance from finished. I hired you because I knew you'd get out there and hustle. So get out there. Hustle. Otherwise you're absolutely no good to me."

He stares back at me for a moment. I refuse to break eye contact. I have the advantage of height since I'm standing; it puts me in mind of wolf pack behavior, fighting to be alpha male. Then I see a small gleam in his pale eyes. "Pep talk over?" he asks dryly. "Or do you want to give me another kick up the arse?"

My lips twitch. "That's it for now." Then a thought crosses my mind. "Oh, pass me the Mark Jeffers file, would you?"

"I haven't loaded it all onto the network yet. Why, do you have something suitable?"

"We'll see," I say evasively.

"I should have it up there by the end of today. Unless you're in a hurry?"

"No rush," I tell him breezily, and circle my desk to sit back at my station, but Severine has planted herself in my chair. I should sit down anyway, I know I should,

but I find myself saying to Paul, "I'm running out for coffee. Want anything?"

"No, thanks." He doesn't look up from his screen. "I'm trying to cut back. Though that's kind of like holding back the tide in this job."

It's true. We move from meeting to meeting, mirroring our candidates and clients: if they want a drink, we drink; if they want to eat, we eat. We are a service industry, and the service we provide is confidence. Through the medium of hot beverages and sustenance, every meeting has to whisper, *We're like you, we understand your problems, your needs, we feel your pain and we can solve it.* But how can the clients be confident I can solve their problems when they think I can't solve my own?

My phone rings before I've crossed the road: Lara. "Hi, hon—"

"Can you meet for a coffee? Right now?" There's a note of blind panic threaded through her blunt question; it dredges up the unease always waiting inside me, curled quietly in the depths of my stomach. Lara is not melodramatic, or given to wild fits of runaway imagination; those things take too much energy, and Lara would freely admit she's a little too lazy for that.

"What's up?"

327

"I just had a late lunch with Alain; I'll tell you in person. Can you meet?"

I glance at my watch, running through the afternoon's schedule in my head. "Yes. I'll jump in a cab toward you. Usual place in ten minutes?"

"Yes." In the uncharacteristic terseness of her reply I can hear her native accent begging for release. I start looking for a cab immediately.

Once ensconced in a black taxi, the unease becomes corporeal, taking on the body of twisting snakes that are no longer confined to my stomach: now they're swaying upward, encircling my lungs, slithering through my throat, threatening to choke me of words and breath. The thunk of the automatic door locks when the cab speeds up makes me jump, heart racing, adrenaline prickling through my skin. Severine appears beside me in the cab, scrutinizing me expressionlessly in her take-it-or-leave-it manner, but I deem her presence a gesture of solidarity; whether it's intended that way, I'll never know, but I may as well take whatever comfort I can get from this creation of my own mind.

The driver is unwilling to cross the traffic flow, so I leap out of the taxi on the other side of the road to the café and spot Lara

immediately, already sitting at a table by the window with two tall mugs in front of her. Even through the logo-emblazoned window I can see her face is pinched, but she manages an approximation of a smile and a sketch of a wave when she sees me crossing the road. She gets up to hug me as I enter, and I feel the tension clinging to her frame.

"What's up?" I ask, as soon as we're both seated. She's wearing a dress I haven't seen before, a fitted sheath with a pattern like a snowstorm in the dark. I wonder if the lunch was planned, if she wore the dress especially for Modan. She looks stunning as ever, but older, somehow. Not in her face, which is exactly the same, but in less tangible ways: her carriage, her demeanor, her very self.

"I had lunch with Alain. He wanted to apologize. He was hurt, lashing out. He still wants . . . well, you know." I do, or I can imagine; I can extrapolate from what I know so far. And if I know anything about Alain Modan, it's that he won't give up on Lara. "But I keep telling him, not until this — the investigation — is all done. I told him that again today, and he said that I shouldn't have to wait too long, things were coming to an end. Only he looked very grim about it. I asked if he meant he was dropping the

case, and he shook his head and asked if you have a lawyer yet."

"What?" The café fades away instantly; all I have in my focus is the beautiful, desperately worried face of Lara.

She nods, a fast bob. "Yes. He asked if you have a lawyer. I said I didn't know — I didn't want to give anything away — and he said you really ought to get one."

"Jesus." I am staring at her in abject disbelief. This can't be happening. "But —"

"Wait, there's more. He had a file on the table, one of those yellow cardboard things. It had *her* name on it, and yours, I could see it. He tapped it and then said he was off to the bathroom, just leaving it there with me." She spreads her hands wide. "It was like he was *inviting* me to look at it."

"Did you?" *Please say you did.*

She nods again — *yes!* — even faster, guilt written on her face. "I know I shouldn't have, but I couldn't shake the feeling that he meant me to . . . I just had a quick look." I'm nodding, wordlessly urging her on. "There was a report on the top. I didn't have time to read it all, I could only skim, but basically — oh, Kate, basically the whole thing was about how he thinks you killed her." The words are tumbling out of her; she can't keep up with them, and her

accent is slipping. "Motive, opportunity, the whole nine yards. He reckons Seb passed out in the barn with Severine. You found him there and were enraged; you hit her with something — there was something about an old garden rake still having her blood on it; I didn't know that, did you? Apparently nobody ever washes garden rakes . . . Anyway, they're testing it for other DNA and fingerprints. So you hit her with the rake then dumped her body; you knew the well was being filled in —"

She stops abruptly, and we stare at each other. I can barely think. I can barely breathe. *A garden rake.* Slowly the rest of the café returns: the hum of conversation, the sound of the coffee machine, the disturbance of the air when the door is opened. *A garden rake with blood still on it after ten years* . . . I feel clammy and ill; the hand that reaches out to pick up my mug of coffee is trembling, but my brain is starting to function again.

"And you think he wanted you to look?"

"Yes. He tapped the file." She spreads her hands wide again, her eyes pleading for absolution. "He *tapped* it."

"Don't feel bad. He meant you to look," I say decisively. "We're talking about Modan; he doesn't just accidentally" — I sketch

quotation marks around the adverb — "leave a sensitive file in plain view of someone with a vested interest in it." Which begs the question as to why he chose to do just that. Focusing on the strategy is making me feel better. *Don't think about being arrested. Don't think about being arrested.*

"He's using me," she says with sudden fierceness. She's almost vibrating with the intensity of her emotions. "He shouldn't be doing that. He shouldn't be putting me in this position."

"I know. I don't think he would if he had another option." But so much hinges on whether that is really true. If he really cares about Lara, he would only use her as part of a last-ditch attempt to try and help her friend: ergo, I'm in real, undeniable trouble. But if Lara is merely a passing fling, then he might well use her if his investigation is stalling, to try and flush out more information. Here I am questioning that which only moments ago was an incontrovertible truth — wasn't I only just thinking that he would never give up on Lara? *He loves her, he loves her not, he loves her, he loves her not . . .* I find myself examining the woman sitting opposite me again, as if I can read the truth of Modan's feelings for her in the tilt of her nose, the curve of her lips, the sweep of her

cheek. *A garden rake.* How does one accidentally kill someone with a garden rake? *Don't think about being arrested.*

"Either way he thinks I know more than I'm telling," I say aloud. What if it wasn't an accident? I see a long wooden handle whistling through the air, landing squarely on Severine's temple. *A garden rake.*

"Either way?" Lara wrinkles her nose, puzzled.

"Nothing," I say quickly. Clearly Lara hasn't considered the possibility that she is being used for ill rather than good. She at least is convinced of his affections. Does that signify? I wonder what Tom will make of it all; there's no question in my mind that I will tell him. Tom may not want a relationship with me, but presumably I can trust a man who was once in love with me to be on my side. Will Tom trust in Modan's feelings for Lara? It suddenly strikes me that I've been wrong before where Lara is concerned; wrong for years, in fact.

"Lara, when —" Something slams into the window right beside us with a loud thud. We both jump, knocking the table; our coffees slop everywhere. I feel the instant prickle of adrenaline sweeping over me again.

"Jesus, what was that?" gasps Lara, her

333

face utterly drained of color.

The window is intact. I'm standing up, craning my neck with my head pressed against the window to look through it, past the coffee shop slogan stuck on the glass to the pavement below. "A bird," I say. "A pigeon." The dirty, gray-feathered body is lying in a heap on the paving. "It's stunned itself."

"Jesus," says Lara again.

I straighten and glance around the coffee shop. The barista continues to serve, conversations are continuing among the paired clientele, mobile phones continue to be inspected by those sitting alone. Nobody else seems to have noticed. I look out of the window; passersby hurry on, unheeding. Severine is among them, in her black shift, blood trickling from her right temple. It doesn't seem to be affecting either her balance or her self-possession.

"That was weird." I grab some napkins and start to mop up our spilled coffee. "There must have been a reflection in the window; it must have thought it was flying into sky."

"That used to happen at school in Sweden sometimes."

I settle down again and return to my almost cold coffee. "Lara, why did you and

Tom never give things a proper go?"

She looks up from her coffee, startled. "After France, you mean?"

"Yes." I'm suddenly very self-conscious. Should I be holding eye contact, or not? What impression am I giving about how vested I am in this answer? "I always thought he wanted to but you didn't."

"Oh." She's blushing a little. It underlines how pale she's been this afternoon. "Actually . . . it was more the other way round. To be honest, I would have been up for it — at the time, I mean, not now — but he was definitely not into anything more."

"Oh." I consider that. "Why did I think it was the other way round?"

"I don't know." But she really is too honest to leave it like that. "Except maybe . . . perhaps I gave you that impression. I felt a bit, well, rejected, I suppose. You weren't really around at the time; right after France you and Seb were splitting up and your dad died and then you were up north for ages, and in quite a state even when you got back . . . I think you made the assumption and I never really corrected it, out of pride I guess." I can see the guilty embarrassment squirming inside her; I can see the Lara of years ago, hardly unable to comprehend the concept of a man who doesn't want to climb

back in the sack with her. "It hasn't messed things up for you and Tom, has it?" she asks, suddenly anxious.

"I don't think there is a me and Tom." Just like there was never a Lara and Tom. I got that wrong, for all those years, along with just about everything else. Am I wrong about how Modan feels about Lara? Am I being played? "Would you mind if there was?"

"No." She says it hesitantly, like she's testing her answer. "It feels a bit strange, but . . ." She shrugs with a hint of a rueful smile. "I'd have no right to mind, even if I did."

An interesting response. An honest one, I think. I sigh. "Well, it's a moot point anyway. Since I'm apparently going to jail." A French jail, to boot. I wonder, in an abstract way, if that is any better or worse than a British jail. And then it strikes me that it's no longer an abstract consideration.

"It's not funny, Kate," Lara says tersely.

"I'm not laughing." I feel clammy and ill again; I am definitely not laughing. We're many, many steps away from jail, I remind myself. *Don't think about being arrested.* I lean toward the glass and peer out of the window again, down toward the pavement. The gray-feathered heap has gone.

"You have to speak to Alain. You have to give him something, cooperate. You have to tell him —"

"What? What can I tell him? I don't know anything to tell him."

"Yes, you do. You can tell him about Caro. You can tell him about the drugs."

My eyes leap to Lara's, and she gazes back at me, clear-eyed and unflinching. I look across the divide between us, the corridor of air, and it's like staring down a tunnel through the years, back to where it all began, back to France and Severine. How far we've come, to get to this point, the point where you throw friends under buses. Except Caro is not really a friend, exactly — but I'm splitting hairs. I start to form, then discard, any number of responses.

"What are you going to do?" presses Lara.

A garden rake. "I'm going to call my lawyer."

CHAPTER SEVENTEEN

I leave the café, already dialing my lawyer, but she's busy and unable to take my call. Of course she's busy; she's a professional at the top of her game, high in demand, which is exactly the sort of lawyer one would want to have — only I want her sitting in her office, staring at her telephone and twiddling her thumbs, doing nothing of note except eagerly awaiting my call. I have half a mind to jump in a taxi to her premises, but I resist the urge and instead choose to walk back to my office.

The fresh air fails to do me good. My mind is racing, unable to break free from a spiral track that leads inexorably to a dark pit of all the things I'm not yet ready to face. Surely there must be a way out, a bargain to be made with a God I don't believe in . . . How can this be happening to *me*?

"Jesus," says Paul. He doesn't look up as I enter the office. "Did they have to get the

coffee beans from South America?"

It takes me a minute to process the words and divine his meaning, then I glance at my watch. I've been gone over an hour and a half. But surely not . . . the taxi there, plus the time spent with Lara, plus the walk back: it doesn't quite seem to add up. But my internal clock and the reckoning of my watch cannot arrive at a mutually agreeable answer. I have the sensation that time is rushing past me, rushing through me, like I'm no more substantial than a ghost and there's nothing I can do to stem the tide. "I forgot I had a call with Gordon." It's hard enough to invent an excuse, let alone give it some expression. "I took it at the coffee shop."

Paul looks up from his computer screen at that. "Not a problem there, is there?" he asks anxiously. "I thought Caroline Horridge was the liaison now."

"No problem. Gordon just likes to keep his finger in the pie." The words make sense, but they mean nothing to me. Perhaps in a while Paul and the business and all those small concerns that add up to mean *life* will catch at me with little hooks and lines, pulling me back into phase with the world, but for now I feel like nothing exists except the looming dread of a French jail. Shock, I re-

alize. I must be in shock.

"Well, I've loaded the Jeffers file now if you want to take a look."

"Thanks."

"Oh, I nearly forgot. Someone called for you when Julie was out at lunch, wanting to know when you'd be back, but wouldn't leave a message. A woman, posh sounding."

"Well, that certainly narrows it down." I've refound irony: I must be anchored back in the real world now. Except — I glance quickly around — Severine is not here . . . but no, I've got that wrong; Severine is not real, Severine is not normal . . . My head is pounding. I sit down quickly.

"Are you all right?" I hear Paul ask distantly.

"Fine," I say quickly. "Though I don't think my lunch entirely agreed with me." I'm getting to be quite the liar. Tom would be proud, except why would he? After this is over, Tom is washing his hands of me. But this may never be over, not for me . . . Where the hell is my damn lawyer? I grab the mouse, determined to focus on something else, and the blank monitor springs to life.

After some time — how long? Five minutes? Twenty-five? — my vision clears and the pounding in my head recedes. Sometime

after that I realize it must look odd for me to be staring at a screen, and for lack of anything better to do, I look up the Jeffers file, which is exactly where it should be and perfectly up to date: Paul is nothing if not thorough. I skim through, noting his current role, and the familiar process begins to soothe me: strengths, weaknesses, where would he fit? Stockleys? Haft & Weil? But no, not there because . . . I stop suddenly, as a flush of adrenaline prickles over my skin. Definitely not Haft & Weil, because Mark Jeffers has already worked there, started his career there in fact. In none other than Caro's group.

I don't believe in coincidences.

I'm still trying to work out the implications of that when Julie taps and enters briskly, her generous mouth unusually strained. "Sorry, Kate, I have an Alina" — she checks the Post-it in her hand — "Harcourt here for you." Harcourt — but that's Seb's surname, it doesn't fit with anyone else — and then I twig. But what on earth is Seb's wife doing here? Julie is still speaking, her eyes anxious behind the tortoiseshell-rimmed glasses. "I did say you have quite a busy schedule . . ."

Do I? I check the diary, conscious it should have been the first thing I did when

I got back in the office, and it's true, I have a few calls coming up. It's hard to reason through how I should respond to this sudden intrusion, to what would constitute a normal response when I feel so far from normal. I suppose I could legitimately send Alina away; it's what I would prefer to do, but I can't help wondering what has driven her here in the first place. I wouldn't imagine she's someone given to impulsive social calls with no warning; she's far too well-mannered for that. "It's okay, Julie, she's the wife of a friend."

Reluctantly leaving my desk to greet my unexpected guest, I find her looking out of the window in the outer room, a sleek gray wool coat buttoned almost to her neck, the belt highlighting her as-yet slim waist. Above the collar her long dark blond hair is coiled into a smooth roll. She turns her head as I emerge from my office, and I see her quickly rearrange her features into a smile. Her makeup is impeccable. She must have taken a great deal of care over it.

"Alina!" I say, finding a smile from somewhere. I kiss her on both cheeks after a slight hesitation that I hope is imperceptible. That's the point of etiquette, I think — to provide a framework of actions to cling to even when your world is falling apart. I need

to rely on that. "This is a surprise. How are you?"

She doesn't answer the question. "I'm so sorry for turning up unannounced." She glances around; a quick frown crosses her face before she smooths it away.

"You're not a lawyer, are you?" I ask, conscious of Julie hovering behind me.

"Oh no. Lord, no. I capital-raise for private equity." Alina glances round again. The practicalities seem to be catching up to her. Perhaps she hadn't been expecting me to share an office.

"A social call then," I say. Alina's eyes fly to my face; they're hazel, almost yellow. "Come on, then, let's nip out for coffee where we can chat freely." Whatever she has to say, I'm quite sure I don't want Paul or Julie to hear it.

Alina nods swiftly. "Perfect," she says, relief evident even in her clipped tones. "I *am* sorry to disturb you, but as I was passing, it seemed silly not to drop in." She's a smart girl; she's caught on.

I ask Julie to reschedule my calls and then grab my coat, which seems very shabby next to Alina's sleek number, and Alina and I head across the road to the nearest coffee shop. I have to stretch my mind to think of what one might ordinarily say in this situa-

tion. *Follow the rules, stick to the etiquette:* the ordinary steps of life will pull me through. "How are you feeling?" I ask. "Are you still struggling with morning sickness?"

"That," she says without looking at me, her mouth a thin tight line, "is the least of my worries." Then she relents, perhaps realizing how combative she sounded. "But yes, I'm still struggling. God knows what this poor thing is surviving on; I can hardly keep anything down."

We're at the door of the café now. I sit Alina down at a table and queue to buy her a cup of tea and some plain biscuits, ignoring her protestations that she should be the one paying. When I return to the table she has peeled off the tailored coat to reveal a white silk blouse and a neat pencil skirt. The effect is simple, understated: elegantly attractive but not sexy. It entirely suits her. She reaches for the biscuits immediately. "Thank you."

"You're welcome." I study her as she peels open the packet, trying to fit her into Seb, like a two-piece jigsaw puzzle.

She looks up as if she feels my eyes on her, picking over her hair, her clothes, the way she holds herself. "You must be wondering what on earth I'm doing here," she says, without a trace of a smile, when she

has finished a biscuit. Her delicately prominent collarbones spread like open wings
from the two raised nubs at the base of her
throat; her wrists are slender, leading to
long, slim fingers. It seems like her very
bones have been carefully crafted to fit the
image she wishes to portray: refined, elegant, unmistakably upper class.

"Yes," I say. I glance at my mobile phone,
which I have placed faceup on the table.
My lawyer hasn't rung.

"You used to date my husband."

I blink. "Yes."

"Is that a problem?" Her eyes are an
unusual hazel color and fixed unswervingly
on my face.

I almost laugh; for a moment I'm tempted
to paraphrase her own words: *that's the least
of my problems.* Instead I say evenly, "Not
for me."

She eyes me carefully without speaking
for a moment, then reaches for another
biscuit. "Good," she says, with some satisfaction, as if I've confirmed something
important to her. "I didn't know anything
about your history with Seb until the other
day," she remarks. "Caro told me." There's
an unmistakable twist of her lips on Caro's
name. "Actually, I'd rather assumed you
were with Tom."

I don't want to hear his name yet I'm also greedy for something, anything, that relates to Tom and me, to an *us* that has never been; I have to stop myself from asking why she assumed that. Instead I say mildly, "I wouldn't think you're here to ask me that, though."

"No." She puts down the biscuit without having taken a bite. Once again I'm caught in her hazel gaze. She ticks all the boxes I had always imagined Seb's wife would have to tick, but still she is not what I expected . . . She's more reserved, more intelligent, more herself. I wonder if Seb has gotten rather more than he bargained for. "I rather think Caro is trying to steal my husband," she says without preamble or apology. "He's in quite a bad place at the moment: his job, the drinking . . . I know you were at Tom's last night so I hardly need to bring you up to speed on that." Only two red spots high on those perfectly sculpted cheekbones reveal the humiliation I know she must feel on discussing her husband's failings with a near-stranger. "The thing is, it's Caro who is getting him so worked up about it all. Ever since they reopened the investigation on that girl, she's been on the phone nonstop, trying to get her little tendrils into him —" She stops

abruptly, cutting off the passion that was threatening to spill into her words.

I stare at her. This is so far from what I was expecting — not that I knew what I was expecting, but this isn't it — that I have to mentally shake myself into responding. "They're not having an affair," I say at last. Perhaps it's a good thing this is such a strange conversation: I can be forgiven for being a little slow on social cues. It wouldn't be appropriate to say what I'm thinking: *I'm about to be arrested for a murder that in all probability was your husband's fault, so please excuse me if I can't get worked up about the state of your marriage.*

"I didn't think they were — not yet, at least. Though I'd be interested to know what makes you say that." One part of me notes that the control she has of her emotions is terrifyingly impressive.

"Caro kept ringing last night. He wouldn't pick up. Tom asked why she kept calling, and Seb told him he wasn't sleeping with her, if that's what he was thinking. He said he never had." I remember the words escaping his mouth in the dim living room, and more besides. *Barely even kissed her.* So he did kiss her, at least once then. I wonder when. Probably sometime when they were teenagers. Not that it matters. Not that any

of it matters. But she's here, and so am I, and there are motions I should go through. I shrug. "So if you believe in the old saying in vino veritas . . ."

"I do, actually," she says thoughtfully. Perhaps I detect a slight relaxation within her, but equally I could be imagining it. She looks at the biscuit carefully for a moment, as if considering if it's worth the risk, but it remains on the table in front of her. She looks at me again. "Thank you."

"You're welcome." I'm still puzzled as to what she's here for.

"Tom said you and Caro don't really get on."

Tom. "Well, we certainly didn't in the past, but that was a long time ago."

"I thought perhaps you would be a good person to speak to."

"My enemy's enemy is my friend?" But I see Caro again, admitting to her own mother's disapproval, and I feel that moment of warmth between us. Caro is not an enemy. Nor a friend, either. I'm not sure I know the correct word in the English language to describe what she is to me. Though if she really is to blame for the Mark Jeffers situation, I'm sure I'll find one.

"Exactly." Alina smiles briefly, a genuine smile, not one out of politeness. On another

day, I know it would feel like a gift: I don't believe Alina offers a genuine smile terribly often. "I don't really know what happened in France: Seb doesn't like to talk about it. He says he doesn't want me to worry about anything with the baby coming." She frowns. "But whatever happened, I think it's somehow giving Caro some, I don't know, *leverage* over him. And quite frankly I find that rather more irritating than the investigation. I mean, it's not as if Seb would really have killed a random girl, is it? He should have nothing to worry about. But she has him all worked up; he's talking to her and not to me, and I need to find a way to put a stop to it."

I look at her blankly. Surely as Seb's wife, she must know more than this? But there is no artifice in her face, simply frustration and a hefty dislike of Caro — Seb really hasn't filled her in. It's probably not my place to do it, either, but in spite of my preoccupation, my distance, I do have some empathy for her. She shouldn't be left in the dark. "Alina," I say carefully. "You do know that Seb slept with Severine, don't you? The girl who died? That he was the last person to see her alive?"

Her eyes fly to my face. "That's not . . . I don't . . ." She starts to shake her head and

then stops, considering, a frown corrugating her ordinarily smooth forehead. "But I thought he was going out with you then," she says, confused.

"He was," I say wryly.

"Oh." Expressions flit quickly over her face before it settles on a look of resignation. "I rather think I'd better hear about all of this from you."

So I tell her the bare facts, bereft of any speculation, though I leave out the garden rake since that's information I'm not supposed to possess. She listens carefully, those yellow brown eyes taking account of me throughout. At the end she blows out a breath and mutters fiercely, "*Damn* you, Seb." Her words catch me and throw me years back, to a time when I would have been the one with such exasperation in my voice.

"I'm sorry," I admit truthfully.

She doesn't answer; she has finally picked up the biscuit and is working her way through it. "Well, it wouldn't have been Seb," she says definitively, when the biscuit is gone. "I mean, why on earth would he want to kill her? The police can't possibly suspect him."

"They might think it was an accident."

She waves it away. "But you know what

he's like when he's drunk — he passes out; he can't hold his own body weight, let alone carry someone to a well."

"Someone else might have done that bit."

"Who?" she says, disbelieving. "Tom? Caro?" I see the precise moment the penny drops. The color leaches out of her face, and her mouth works wordlessly before she clamps her lips together. I don't say anything. There's nothing to say.

"Leverage," she finally says, almost hisses, though more to herself than to me. "That fucking bitch." She looks across at me again. "Is this what the police think happened?"

No. Luckily for your husband, the police think it was me. This is what I, Kate Channing, think happened. "I don't know."

"This can't be happening," she mutters, again to herself. Then, louder, looking at me fiercely this time: "This can't be allowed to happen."

At that moment my mobile rings out; I grab it as if it's a lifeline. "My lawyer. Sorry, I've got to take this." I duck outside the café before she can answer.

"Interesting," says Ms., Miss or Mrs. Streeter, when I've downloaded Lara's discoveries. "Not enough, though, even if the rake shows up your DNA, or anyone else's. Still simply circumstantial."

"Circumstantial enough to make it to trial?" I left my coat at the table with Alina. I wrap my free arm around myself, shivering a little. I can feel my ribs beneath my thin wrap dress. They feel worryingly insubstantial. I am too breakable for what life is throwing at me.

She's silent for a worryingly long pause. "Ordinarily no," she says at last. "But with the political pressure on this one, it's hard to say. Have you thought any more about cooperation?"

"Yes." Cooperation. A deceptive word. It sounds so collegiate, warm and friendly, yet in truth it's slyly partisan, with its own agenda. Cooperation with the police means betrayal of someone: but who? Seb? Caro? Both? I never thought I was someone who would stoop to this, yet here I am.

"And?"

I close my eyes and speak in a rush. "Caro had cocaine. She smuggled it into France in my suitcase; I knew nothing about it. That's what the arguments were about on the last night — I found out she'd done that. I honestly didn't think it had any bearing, so I never wanted to bring it up." I open my eyes. I never mentioned the drugs all those years ago, and I haven't mentioned them up to now, but in the space of a few short

seconds all that counts for nothing: it's done. I wonder what Tom will think of me for it, and then I have to screw my eyes tightly shut again to block out the opprobrium I imagine in his face.

"Did you take any drugs that night?" Her voice is clipped, tightly professional.

"No."

"At any point during the holiday?"

"No. It's really not my thing; ask anybody."

"Believe me, the police will. Have you ever taken any drugs?" she continues, unrelenting.

"What, ever in my life?"

"Ever. As in, at any point whatsoever."

"I smoked pot once or twice at uni, but it just sent me to sleep; plus I don't like smoking."

"Once or twice? Be specific."

"Twice then. Certainly not three times."

"Okay." She has finally relaxed a little; I can hear the tension easing out of her voice. "Okay. That's good. I can definitely work with that. Anything else?"

"Well . . ." *I don't know what time Seb came to bed.* Through the café window I can see a side view of the abandoned Alina, sitting where I left her at the table. One hand is resting on her crossed legs, her thumb beat-

ing out an unsteady high-speed tattoo. *I don't know what time Seb came to bed.* The words are there, fully formed in my head, waiting to be sent forth into the world.

"Yes?"

I look at Alina again. She has stilled her thumb with her other hand, but her ankle is jittering now. "Sorry, uh, something just distracted me here. No, nothing else."

"Okay then, I'll set up a meeting with the detective and get back to you. This is good, Kate; it's helpful."

"Great." The word sounds thin.

"Oh, and Kate?"

"Yes?"

"If you have anything more to offer, now's the time. Think hard." Then she disconnects.

The cold overrides my reluctance to return to Alina, pushing me back into the café. Alina looks up as I enter. "Sorry about that," I say as I drop into the seat opposite her.

"You have a lawyer." It's almost an accusation.

"Yes."

"Does Seb have a lawyer?" Her manner is definitely more hostile. I'm the messenger, I realize: she'd really quite like to shoot me. And Seb, too, I expect, for putting her in

this position, of being the last to know.

"I don't know. But if he doesn't, he should get one."

"He didn't do it," she says tightly. "I know him. *You* know him. You know he didn't have anything to do with it." I can't bring myself to say anything. Her eyes widen. "Oh my God," she says, genuinely stunned. "You actually think it was him."

"Look, I don't know what happened," I protest weakly, but she's not mollified.

"How *could* you? You went out with him, you *know* him."

I can see the shock turning to bitter fury inside her, and I find myself mentally cheering her loyalty even as I cringe in the face of it. "I just . . . Look, I don't think your Seb is the same as the Seb I went out with. We've all changed a lot since then."

"Still," she insists fiercely, her eyes boring into mine, "he wouldn't have done *that.*" She waits imperiously for me to respond, and there is nothing else I can do: I nod. She nods her head sharply, acknowledging her win without any joy, then continues. "I bet Caro's trying to make him think he was involved somehow, responsible even. She's probably pretending she's covering up for him. To make him rely on *her.* That's the leverage she has. I bet she's been doing it

for years, actually — he's always been on the booze more after she's been around." I cock my head: Alina may be onto something. It would be just like Caro to milk every advantage out of the situation: a confused, guilt-ridden Seb who owes an enormous debt to Caro is surely much more likely to succumb to her wiles . . . Alina happens to think the debt is manufactured rather than real, but either way, I can see a twisted Caro logic at work. I can just imagine her, late at night, sending poison-laden whispers down the phone line to slither into Seb's ear and take residence, curled inside his desperately worried mind. At least, it would be just like the Caro I thought I knew, but now I wonder; now there's the possibility of an alternative interpretation in my mind. Maybe Caro phones Seb because she can't help herself, because she's hopelessly in love with him. It would be just like Seb to carelessly lead her on, to be the one delivering to her ear sweet nothings carried on whispers that really are nothing at all, except a vehicle for the ego boost he needs . . . Perhaps he drinks after she's been around out of guilt. Then I think again of Mark Jeffers, and I'm back to Caro as poison-whisperer.

"And anyway," says Alina in a sudden

change of pace, "surely there's an obvious alternative suspect."

I wait dumbly. Does she mean me? Surely she wouldn't suggest that in front of me, though to be fair I have just been casting aspersions about her husband . . .

"Theo."

I shake my head. "Nobody thinks it was Theo."

"Why not? Did he have an alibi?"

"No — well, I mean, yes, he was with Caro, I think, but I suppose that he went to bed at some point —"

"He's dead," she interrupts bluntly. "Which is obviously quite horrible for him and his parents and everyone who loved him, but all of you are still alive, with lives ahead of you to live. Surely if the blame is to fall on any of you, you might as well make it fall on him."

The brazen suggestion takes my breath away. "What you're suggesting . . ." I trail off. I should finish with *is immoral,* or *is illegal,* or *is an obstruction of justice;* but somehow I can't bring myself to spell it out. Theo as prime suspect. Alina thinks she's simply getting rid of the Caro problem, but it would get me off the hook too, of course. A wave of longing sweeps over me, a longing to be free of the weight that presses

down on me, beating me a little smaller, a little weaker every day; to be free of the broiling sea of fear that sits in my stomach and threatens on occasion to erupt from my throat and overwhelm me.

"Yes," Alina says, her steady gaze fixed on my face despite the blush that betrays her emotions. "I know what I'm suggesting." I look at the cold fire within the yellow brown eyes, and I don't doubt her. Seb is so very lucky to have her, grimly fighting in his corner despite no doubt being utterly furious with him. But this particular sally seems too well considered to have just come to her whilst I've been braving both the cold and my lawyer's interrogation outside. "Is this what you wanted to speak to me about?"

She considers denying it but evidently plumps for the truth. "Yes." She shrugs, a glorious sweep upward of the tips of the outspread wings of her collarbones. She should have been a ballet dancer. She has the frame for it, and something else, too, something in her every gesture, each leading seamlessly into the next, that makes it seem like she's moving through a larger choreographed whole. "It doesn't really matter whether I'm right about what Caro's leverage is; if all of this goes away, then so

does she."

And you think you'll get your husband back. "Tom will never go for it," I say at last. And now I've skipped over the morality, too: I'm focused on whether her plan can actually be executed. I wonder when I lost faith in the legal system, French or otherwise. Or perhaps it's not a lack of trust in the legal system that's to blame. Perhaps it's just that I know all too well that life isn't always fair; therefore, how can you expect the law to be? I shiver. *Don't think about being arrested.*

"He won't?" She raises her eyebrows. "Not even for Seb?"

"I don't . . ." I realize I don't know. Even yesterday I would have said that Tom would do anything for Seb, but now? The bitterness in Seb's voice last night, the tightness of Tom's face when Seb revealed he'd known all along that Tom was angling for me . . . I don't know who Tom would choose, Theo or Seb. "I don't know."

"And you?" She watches me closely, those slender wrists sweeping up to clasp together by her chin, a picture of poise. Once again I'm in awe of her control, all the more because I have an inkling of what's beneath it.

What would it take to push Modan down this road? I imagine him strolling along the

dusty lane by the farmhouse, sunshine beating down on the shoulders of his immaculate suit as he ambles and constructs an argument in his mind for Theo as murderer. Perhaps that could indeed come to pass if he were the recipient of a few well-chosen comments, a few hints . . . Lies. Lies, all. Lies and a betrayal of Theo. Would that betrayal really be any worse than revealing Caro's cocaine use? I could claim that was only what she deserved given I'm sure she's spreading rumors about me through Mark Jeffers, but the truth is that as soon as I felt cornered I barely hesitated; I'd have done it without the Jeffers info. Again, I wonder what Tom will say about that.

"Kate?" prompts Alina.

"I'll think about it." At the least, I have given her a genuine response. I will probably think about little else.

CHAPTER EIGHTEEN

I'm saved from having to bring Tom up to speed; it appears Lara has done that for me. He calls me that evening and sounds almost desperate. "Jesus, Kate. The garden rake. I've just been looking up the French for it — *râteau*! I thought she said *bateau*. It was *râteau*."

"What? Who said? What do you mean?" I'm on my mobile in my living room; I quickly hunt for the remote to kill the sound of the television program that I'd been hoping would hold my interest sufficiently to calm the vicious storm of my thoughts. As the characters turn abruptly silent it occurs to me I have no idea what I've been watching.

"I saw Severine. I saw her go into the barn with Seb, but I saw her again after they . . . you know. She was coming past the pool, and she had blood on her face; not much, just a bit, nothing to cause alarm." I'm not

361

sure I have ever heard Tom — steady, reliable Tom — talk in such a stream of consciousness. "I asked her if she was all right; I didn't really get the gist of it at the time. She didn't have the right English word; she kept saying *bateau*. At least I thought it was *bateau,* but it must have been *râteau*." I see a brief image of Severine in the darkened barn, her slim foot stepping on the fanned-out prongs of the garden rake, the other end flipping up to smack her in the face Abbott and Costello style; it ought to be funny, but it's not. "I just thought she wasn't making a lot of sense — there wasn't a boat around for miles, but then we'd all had a lot to drink, so I put it down to that at the time. And she waved me away fairly forcibly and headed off, so I thought she was rather sensibly putting herself to bed."

"Why didn't you tell the police? Then, or now, even?"

He sighs down the phone. "I thought I was protecting Seb. I mean, I see a girl with blood on her face, who subsequently disappears. In retrospect I started to wonder if she wasn't drunk; maybe she was severely concussed — I mean, she was babbling about boats! Except she wasn't . . . . Fuck! But given she was coming from the barn, with Seb, I didn't want to implicate him in

any way, so I just . . ."

"Kept silent," I finish for him. I sink back on my sofa, the phone pressed against my ear.

"Yes. Yes." He seems to have run out of steam; he takes a deep breath, then blows it out down the phone. It's an intimate sound. I can imagine his breath stroking my cheek. "But at least they won't find any of your DNA on the rake."

"True." I'm silent again, remembering the police taking our DNA samples years ago — in order to easily rule us out, we were told. I didn't demur at all; I simply opened wide for two large cotton swabs. I wonder if I would be more reluctant now in the same circumstances. "But isn't there a saying? The absence of proof is not proof of absence . . . Something like that, anyway."

"Fuck, I'll never be able to forgive myself if I've made it worse for you," he mutters, half to himself.

I don't know yet if he has or hasn't; I'm still trying to work it all through. The police have a murder weapon that isn't really a murder weapon — it's an inciting item in slapstick comedy. "So what did you think happened to her?" I ask at last. "I mean, what did you think at the time?"

"I thought her head wound must have

been much more serious than I realized, one of those freak accident things; that she collapsed and died from it." As he speaks I see it happening: Severine in her black shift, sandals hanging loosely from a single finger of one hand. She's passing the pool, barely visible in the darkness, lit only by the shimmering reflection of the moonlight off the water. She takes a step and stumbles, her other hand going to her bloody temple, and then she crumples without a sound. But no, that isn't what happened, because Severine is here with me, lounging in my armchair. Only that's not right, either, because Severine is dead, except not how Tom is describing . . . I find I'm rubbing fiercely at my forehead; my head is throbbing. I've lost the thread of what Tom is saying, but he's still speaking: "I thought Seb found her and panicked, wanted to hide the body, but he'd have been in no fit state to do anything on his own. So someone helped him, Caro or Theo, I thought. Or both. I thought they'd driven somewhere and dumped her."

"In my car?" I sit up, somehow personally affronted, despite the fact that I know this never happened. I almost know this never happened. I can't keep track tonight.

"No, not yours. You were asleep; I didn't believe anyone would have had the guts to

go raking through your bags for your keys with you right there in the bed. I thought they used the Jag." I blink. The Jag. It was Theo's dad's pride and joy; it had been impressed upon us all never to go near it. In my mind the Jag was a museum display piece; it hadn't even occurred to me that it could actually be driven. "As far as I know the police never checked the Jag over because they thought she went to the bus depot; I always wondered if they would have found her DNA in it. And then when she was found in the well, I figured the same logic applied, just without the Jag."

"Wait — so you never thought that was Severine at the bus depot?"

"No. All the time we were there, do you remember her ever emerging before eleven?"

I think about this, remembering Severine coming out to the pool in her black bikini, a chic canvas bag filled with the paraphernalia required for serious sunbathing, whilst also watching the Severine in my living room settle into a more comfortable position. "True. Sometimes not till lunchtime."

"Exactly. And with a hangover and a sore head? I doubt we'd have seen her till mid-afternoon."

I missed that point. I should have thought of it, but I missed it in my eagerness to

365

believe Severine was at the bus depot, that her death had nothing to do with any of us. "What do you think happened now?"

"I've been thinking about that," he says slowly. "Modan said her bones were damaged. Consistent with a hit-and-run —"

"The Jag!" I exclaim.

"Yes, that's what I thought. Theo's dad told me the police have been over every inch of the Jag for evidence; he told me he'd looked up how long it takes DNA to degrade, and apparently it depends on the conditions: takes millions of years in ideal conditions like ice, but not very long in heat or sunlight. The Jag has always been kept under cover in a garage, though, so I expect that means any DNA will be usable. I imagine right now Modan has some lab running tests on any DNA recovered. He'll be testing against all of us, I bet."

"It would have to be Caro, Theo or Seb," I say slowly.

"Yes. I don't know which one, or even if we're on the right track." He sounds strained. "It doesn't make any sense. You'd have to be gunning the accelerator to hit someone hard enough to kill them, so then it's hardly an accident anymore." Now I see Severine, in the same black shift, the sandals still swinging from a single finger, except

now she's caught in headlights, turning in surprise, raising a futile arm to block her face . . . "Which means the police will probably think you have the most obvious motive."

Jealous rage. Spurned lover. We know so much more now, yet nothing has moved on. I'm still the prime suspect. The movie plays out in my head: Severine tossed up in the air like a rag doll, smashing down on the Jaguar's windscreen, shattering it in a starburst. I look at the Severine in my armchair. She hasn't reacted; her eyes are closed, and her head is tipped back against the cushion, as if she's sunbathing in the dim light of the table lamp and the flickering television. Maybe she is, in her reality. "Wouldn't there have been some damage to the car, though?"

"You'd think so. Though sometimes in a crash the bumper looks perfect and all the damage is behind that. I don't know. Seb was hammered; I suppose he could have fallen asleep at the wheel and hit her, but he's just not that into cars. I can't imagine him climbing in it in the first place."

"Theo?" I think again of Alina's plan. I don't want to tell Tom about that.

He takes a moment to answer. When he finally speaks up there's a reluctance infused in every word. "I don't see it. But I didn't

expect him to sign up for the army, either." He sighs again. "And Caro doesn't make sense, either. Nobody does."

"Except me." I sink back on my sofa again. "Always me," I mutter.

"Oh, Kate." It's more of a sigh than a sentence. Then, gently: "Are you okay? I'm getting worried about you."

"No."

"I —"

"Alina wants us all to blame Theo." I've cut him off with the first thing I can think of, before he can say anything else nice. If he does I'll cry, and once I start that I won't stop.

"What?"

I explain about her ambush of me.

"Jesus," he says when I've finished. "But she's right," he adds thoughtfully. "It would be the perfect solution. Not to save Seb, though, to save you."

I'm struck again by his pragmatism. "Could you even . . . Could you actually do that?" I ask hesitantly.

"If it came to that, as a last resort?" He thinks about it seriously. "Yes. I could. I could do it for you."

I close my eyes, close to tears, touched beyond words that he would choose me over Theo. "When this is over . . . if this is

ever over . . ."

"What?"

"I don't want you to go back to Boston," I whisper.

He's quiet. He knows what I'm saying. He's quiet for a second that becomes a minute, a year, a lifetime.

"Say something," I whisper to him. I turn my face to hide it in the sofa cushions.

"You chose Seb." He's whispering, too. "I'll always know you chose Seb."

"Because I didn't know. You didn't even *try;* you just stepped aside for Seb. You can't hold it against me when you didn't even try." Another second, another minute — I can't bear for the silence to lengthen any further. "Don't say anything now. Just think about it. I'm going to be in a French jail anyway —"

"It won't come to that," he interrupts fiercely, but I ignore him.

"— so it's probably a moot point, but . . . please just think about it."

"I . . ." He trails off. "All right, I'll think about it."

"Night, Tom."

"Night, Kate."

In the morning I almost don't go to work. I've slept abysmally — God knows when I

369

last slept well, which I know is a sign of mental stress, but in this case I think it's rather eclipsed by the fact that I'm regularly seeing a ghost — but at 9 A.M. I'm still in bed, not sleeping, not moving, not doing anything except existing, and I can't even see the point of that. It's a call from Caro that rouses me from my apathy. Pride, it turns out, is a powerful motivator.

"Julie said you weren't in yet, best to try your mobile," says Caro breezily. "Having a lie-in, are you? I hope I didn't wake you."

I can sense her sly glee at the idea, and I can't bear to allow her the pleasure. "Actually no, I've just finished a breakfast meeting with a client," I lie, remarkably glibly. "Julie must have overlooked it in the office diary."

"Oh. Right." She sounds temporarily put out — *yes!* — but she rallies. "Well, I really need to meet with you. How's your diary today?"

I grab my BlackBerry from the bedside table and flick through. "Today is not great, actually." It's true; it would be a pretty busy day even without the lawyer-and-Modan meeting that looms, darkly implacable and immovable, in the middle of the afternoon. "Monday would be better."

"It really needs to be today," she insists.

"What about the end of the day?"

I can see I'm not going to be able to put her off. "Well, yes, I suppose I should be able to manage six thirty," I say reluctantly. "Is there a problem? Have you had second thoughts on anyone we're negotiating with?"

"No, no, it's not that at all. Actually, it's more a case of some professional advice. You know, with the partnership process . . ."

That almost floors me. Caro would like to ask my advice: really? Yet again she has me wrong-footed. "Sure, happy to do whatever I can. I know you're up against tough opposition." I've done some digging, and from what I understand, Darren Lucas is fighting for the same partnership spot. He's a small, wiry man with a shock of dark hair, a nose to rival Tom's, and a good line in self-deprecating wit. Clients love him, colleagues adore him and he's a very savvy lawyer. Even when I try to take my own personal bias out of the equation, I can't see how Caro can win this one, unless the firm bows to gender pressure.

"Darren? Oh, don't worry about him," she says dismissively. I blink. Surely Caro is not so naive as to underestimate Darren? "No, I'll explain it all later. See you at my offices at six thirty."

I put down my phone and look around

my bedroom. The digital clock reads 9:11. If I'm quick with my shower, I can be in the office before the ten o'clock call that's in my diary. It's touch-and-go; I almost pull the covers over my head, but the thought of Caro (old or new?) gloating at my slide into depression pushes me out of bed and into the bathroom. *Follow routines, stick to etiquette,* I tell myself. It's all that I can think to do.

In the warm streaming water of the shower it takes me a minute to remember what I'm supposed to do. *Shampoo hair. Rinse. Condition hair. Rinse. Apply body wash. Rinse.* Another routine, something else to cling to. I pick up my razor, but I don't have the slightest inclination to apply it to any part of me, no matter how fuzzy my legs or underarms might be. Shaving is a hopeful act. I think of Tom on the phone: *All right, I'll think about it.* I put the razor back down, unused. It doesn't seem as if shaving is called for.

As I dry myself off, I see Severine in the mirror, leaning against the bathroom wall behind me, but when I turn round she isn't there. I wonder again why Caro doesn't see Darren as a threat. I'm missing something. Now there are two things I don't understand where Caro is concerned: this, and what

she has to gain by spreading gossip about me, if indeed she is the culprit. It makes me uneasy, or even more uneasy.

I can't remember when I was last at ease.

I don't have long to wait to find out why Caro doesn't think Darren is a threat. It's the first thing Paul says to me, beating even a traditional *good morning.* "Darren Lucas is under investigation at Shaft & Vile for *fraud.* Can you believe it?"

My eyes fly to his face, which is filled both with shock and excited importance at being the first to deliver news. "Actually, no," I say thoughtfully, mulling it over as I unbutton my coat. "I can't. There must be some mistake. What type of fraud?"

"Fiddling his expenses." He shakes his head, disbelief tracking across his face. "I can't believe it either."

"His expenses? Jesus. What could he get out of that? A couple of thousand a year, maybe?" *Caro,* I think. *Caro.* Then I check myself: would she really? If it is her, she's playing a very dangerous game. But if it's not her, it's a hell of a coincidence. I consider for a moment approaching . . . who? Gordon? Caro's father is hardly going to take kindly to the suggestion that he investigate whether his daughter is framing

her rival.

"A couple of thousand, absolute max," Paul is saying. "Not even that, I would think. And he's in line for a pay rise of a few hundred thousand if he makes partner. Why on earth would he jeopardize that? He's just not that *stupid*. But" — he frowns — "if it was a simple mistake surely they would have cleared it up straightaway. This'll scratch him off the slate. For this year at least."

One year is all Caro needs. "He's being stitched up," I say flatly.

Paul looks at me sharply. "That's quite a statement."

I shrug and avoid his eyes by pulling out my chair and switching on my monitor. "I'm just saying it looks that way to me."

He continues to look at me, something odd in his eyes. "Did you go to the gym or something?" he asks abruptly. "Your hair is wet."

I put a hand to my head. He's right. Did I forget to dry it after my shower? My glance at the window reveals bright sunshine outside, so it didn't rain on me on the way to work. It occurs to me that I can't actually remember getting to work. "My hair dryer is broken," I improvise.

"Oh," he says, but I can feel he's still

watching me.

"What?" I say, looking up from my screen.

"Nothing." He gives an odd shrug. "It's just . . . Julie's a bit worried about you. She said you hadn't been acting yourself." He pauses, then his words trip out over themselves. "I just wondered if everything is okay. With the murder investigation, I mean."

"Oh. Well, that's all fine. Nothing to worry about. I'm just . . . feeling a bit run-down, is all. I think I'm getting a virus or something." My words don't seem to be enough to convince him; something else seems to be required. I try a smile, and it does the trick. He looks relieved.

"Oh. Okay. Well, don't give it to me; I've got a wedding to go to at the weekend."

His words ring in my head as I pull up the files for my ten o'clock. *She said you hadn't been acting yourself.* Acting. Is that all we humans ever really do? Act, and play, and present an approximation of something that becomes ourselves?

I touch my wet hair self-consciously, frowning. If acting is what's required, it seems that at present I need to pull out a better performance.

Modan again.

I sit in a chair in front of the now-familiar

375

chipped desk and watch him apply his easy, dangerous charm to my lawyer, whilst I grit my teeth semi-consciously. If this was all over, could I come to like this man, this man who wants to be my best friend's other half? I wonder. I respect him, I admire him even, but perhaps I will never be able to hold a conversation with him without the sense that he's quietly analyzing, observing, filing information away for a rainy day. Though it's unlikely to be a big problem for me given that my future social life contains a lifetime of inmates.

I shudder. Even my own black humor is failing to amuse me today.

"Miss Channing?" From the attention both Modan and my lawyer are giving me, it may not be the first time Modan has spoken my name. He's looking at me quizzically, and I almost think I detect sympathy in his chocolate brown eyes, but I can't imagine why that should be. How can he do his job if he feels sympathy for those he believes to be guilty? For some reason this puts me in mind of Caro, and my own ambivalence toward her: feeling sorry for her, almost liking her at times, yet so often barely able to stand her . . . I think again of the Russian dolls. "Shall we begin?"

And so we do. Ms. Streeter, wearing a dif-

ferent lipstick in an equally garish color but thankfully much less greasy in application, does some wonderful verbal gymnastics, laying the groundwork; Modan is, I think, genuinely appreciative of her professional skill. At the end of her monologue, one might be forgiven for pushing for instant canonization of one Kate Channing, on account of her selfless and unstinting cooperation. Except that we all know I'm about to sell someone down the river. And then it's my turn, to do just that.

I know I can't match Ms. Streeter for linguistic virtuosity, but it turns out I don't need to. She shepherds me gently in the right direction each time: a sentence pushing me here, a comment tugging me there, the words flowing from her mouth to jostle against me, encircling me as if they alone can keep me safe. Modan, for his part, is unexpectedly kind. I'm completely lost as to the subtext of this meeting. When I baldly declare Caro's cocaine smuggling, Modan pauses for the merest second, then continues fluently. He doesn't dispute that Caro put the drugs in my bag; he simply asks about my own cocaine use, as my lawyer warned he would. I say I don't, repeat that I never have; I tell him he can ask anyone, they will all say the same, and he nods

briefly. I don't know if that means he agrees with me or that he will indeed ask around; perhaps both. He asks about other drug use: I confess the marijuana dabbles, but he's clearly not the least bit interested in that. Caro's cocaine habits come under discussion, but I don't have much to say. I don't know how much she used back then, and I don't know how much she uses now, though I rather suspect she does still use from time to time. But I have nothing to base that on, and I tell Modan so. We talk about the others at the farmhouse, whether any of them used drugs — but if they have I've never seen or heard of it. Would any of them have shared the cocaine with Caro that night? I think about it. I can't say for sure, but it seems unlikely to me. Alcohol was the drug of choice for the rest of us. I think of Seb, unable to take his eyes off that slim brown ankle. Not just alcohol. Sex is a drug, too.

The discussion moves abruptly to the long drive back. I must have been tired, Modan suggests, perhaps even hungover — surely the drive home was shared. I shake my head, tell him no: I repeat that I was the only one insured, and besides, I wasn't that tired — probably out of all of us I'd gone to bed the earliest. And I don't remember being very hungover on that drive back; I sup-

pose I must have stopped drinking when we all started arguing. I remember the gulf between Seb and me in the front of the car, so much wider than the gap between our two seats. I remember Caro and Lara sleeping in the back. I remember being furious at Caro for making us leave late. I remember that fury dissipating as I drove, leaving me utterly, desolately miserable. But I don't tell Modan all of that. I just explain why I wasn't tired and why I wasn't hungover.

Not a single one of the questions are specifically about Theo. He hovers peripherally; I mention him obliquely from time to time, but Modan never pays him any attention. Even if I wanted to throw some red-haired Theo-shaped red herrings into the mix, I can't see how I could achieve it with any degree of subtlety.

When Modan's stock of questions appears to dwindle to nothing, I look across at Ms. Streeter. Her neat, cropped head gives me a little nod, which I interpret to mean I've done well. I'm surprised to see we have been here for over an hour and a half, but not surprised to feel exhausted. Ten minutes of Modan's questions does that, let alone ninety minutes.

"*Bien,*" says Modan. He closes his notebook and stands, adjusting the cuffs of his

suit. "*Merci.* Most helpful, Miss Channing."
He turns his charming smile on me, and it
is charming. I want to laugh at myself. How
is it that he can pose the danger he does,
and yet I am not immune to his appeal?
"That is all. For now."

For now. I look at Ms. Streeter, but she's
already charging into battle. "My client has
been nothing but thoroughly cooperative
from the start of this process."

"Your client forgot to mention Class A
drugs on several occasions." Modan is smiling, but his eyes are steely.

"Understandable given there's no relevance to the murder investigation and she
was anxious not to get a friend into trouble.
It's certainly not a case of obstruction of
justice. Your continued interest in my client
without any evidence to link her to the
murder is bordering on harassment. It's
disrupting her business and putting enormous stress on her, and I'll be extremely
happy to explain that in detail to a judge.
So I suggest you either charge her with
something or leave her be."

Stress. I blink at the stark reference and
open my mouth to protest but then shut it
again silently. In truth I'm a good bit further
down the line than *stressed,* and perhaps
this is not the time to display a stiff upper

lip. I glance round quickly for Severine and find her loitering near the doorway, drawing lazily from a cigarette. The smoke curls upward, partially obscuring a no smoking sign stuck to the wall. I know she stood there deliberately, and I fold my lips to stifle a grin.

Modan is not in the least bit fazed by Ms. Streeter's attack. "Noted," he says, deep lines bracketing his smiling mouth. He turns to me, and the smile drops, though the lines remain. I feel him assess me, though again, I see a kindness in his eyes that confuses me. "I truly do hope you are not too . . ." — he clicks his tongue briefly in frustration, searching for the word — "*agitated* by the situation. You have been most helpful."

I look at Ms. Streeter again, completely nonplussed. She smiles back encouragingly, with a slight air of satisfaction, as if this is all a game and it has played out exactly as she expected. Modan, too, seems satisfied. I'm the only one in the room who doesn't have the script. Well, Severine, too, but she doesn't care. She doesn't need to care about anything now. Not for the first time I wonder why she cares to hover around me.

I don't go back to my office afterward. I should — of course I should; there is plenty to do — but I can't focus. I can't even care

that Caro will win today. I call Julie and tell her I'm feeling unwell, which I most definitely am, and that she should cancel my appointments and calls, and then I head for the tube. Severine joins me; she's been sticking very closely to me today. I can't imagine that's a good sign vis-à-vis my mental state, but there's something comforting about her presence, so I'm certainly not going to complain. I think carefully about my route home, determined to be conscious of it; on the packed train, I look around at the individuals with the trappings and cares of their lives on display in their clothing, their bags, their faces buried in newspapers and Kindles and phones. *That one with the* Financial Times *must be a banker,* I think, *and perhaps that one an accountant,* but it's nothing but a label. I cannot imagine their lives. I cannot think of anything but the wreckage of my own.

I wish Tom was with me. It's not a physical wish — though a strong arm wrapped round me certainly wouldn't go amiss right now. No, I wish Tom was with me metaphorically: I wish I could reach inside myself and know as an absolute truth that Tom is always there for me, that Tom is mine. But Tom is going back to Boston — I'd have heard from him by now if he'd changed his

mind about that — and I'm sitting alone on a tube.

Of course, I'm not completely alone. There's Severine.

My flat feels cold when I get inside, but the thermostat needle points exactly where it normally does, and I realize it's me that feels cold. Perhaps I really am getting a virus. I should have a bath and go to bed, but I know I won't sleep well. Still, I can't think of anything else to do, so I start to run the hot tap into the tub, then drift into the kitchen to make a cup of tea. It takes me a moment to notice an odd buzzing noise above the sound of the kettle boiling, and even longer to identify it as someone at the front door. I open the door cautiously. The burly chap who lives in the flat across the hallway — Ben, I think he is — is at the door, looking mildly impatient.

"These came for you," he says, pushing a tall flower box into my arms. "Sorry, got to dash."

"Oh," I say blankly. "Thank you," I call after him, but he's already taking the stairs two at a time, and simply raises a hand in acknowledgment without turning around. I close the door and put the box on the table, ripping open the top in a quest to find a card. It's nestling inconspicuously among

the heads of white lilies interspersed with some pretty green foliage, my name written on the envelope in curly, unmistakably feminine handwriting, presumably by a woman in the flower shop. For a moment I don't dare open the envelope. There is only one person I want these to be from; until I open the card there is still that possibility.

Act like yourself, I admonish myself. *You don't believe in putting things off.*

So I slide a finger under the lip of the envelope and rip it open to pull out a small square card with the flower shop's logo on one side. On the other, it says, in the same jarring curly writing:

Kate,
I thought about it. I'd like to try.

Tom x

Something inside me leaps. I read it again, and again, and then I find a smile is spreading across my face. There's a fizzing running through me that I don't recognize, a lightness, as if I could float upward.

Happiness, I realize. It's been a long time.

I reach for my phone to call Tom, to thank him for the beautiful flowers, but there's another buzz from the front door. Tom in person? But I know that's too hopeful; he

wouldn't expect me to be home and in any case he would have called first. Severine is leaning against the door when I get there, blocking me from opening it. I gesture her out of the way, but she remains in place, her dark eyes fixed on me expressionlessly. The buzzer sounds again. I sigh and reluctantly swing the door open through Severine and have the disconcerting experience of seeing her face replaced by the dark wood and then by the face of the last person I expected to see on my doorstep.

Caro.

CHAPTER NINETEEN

Caro.

It *is* Caro, but for a moment I'm thrown, disorientated by the flash of Severine, then the door, then who? For a moment it could be . . . But no, it's Caro, encased in a smart dark coat and wearing a very trendy trilby that hides the dirty blond of her hair. She has unusually dark skin and eyebrows for a blonde; with her hair hidden one might easily mistake her for a brunette. Something jerks in the recesses of my mind. I find I'm staring at her.

"Well," says Caro, and the moment she speaks she *is* Caro; all suggestions of anything otherwise are swept away. I pull myself together. There is something in her eyes, some sly satisfaction that has me on guard — more on guard, that is. "Aren't you going to invite me in?"

"Actually, Caro, I'm really not feeling well." I've kept the door only a couple of

feet ajar: enough not to be rude, but not wide enough to invite an entrance. "Didn't Julie call you?" But Julie must have called her, otherwise Caro would have expected me around this time at her offices . . .

"She did. I thought any combination of these might help." She holds up a bottle of wine, a packet of Lemsip and some handbag-sized tissues.

"Oh. Well, that's . . . Well, that's kind of you." Confronted with gifts, normal behavior demands I swing the door wide, and after all, I have resolved to follow normal behavior. "Come in."

She enters, and I take the gifts from her as she unbuttons her coat and removes the dark red trilby, looking around her with sharp, greedy glances, stripping away every detail to store in that carnivorous mind of hers. I glance around myself, trying to see things as she must see them. It's a nice flat in a Georgian block, small but welcoming, with some lovely old features such as the original bay windows, but it can't hold a candle to Caro's own apartment. *Or Tom's.* Just the thought of him is a delicious secret inside me, to be held tight and treasured. The florist's card is still in my hand; I shove it surreptitiously into my pocket.

"Lovely flowers," says Caro. "A secret

admirer?" Her eyes scan me, eager and hot and hungry — and something else, too, something like anger, but why on earth should she be angry at me receiving flowers?

"Hardly." I give a careless laugh.

"No? Who then?" she presses insistently.

"They're from a very happy client. Anyway, come on through to the kitchen," I say quickly, self-conscious in my lie; anything to do with Tom is too new for me to be sure I can hide it. I lead her through the flat; it's hard to overstate just how uncomfortable I feel with her inside my home sanctuary. Severine isn't proving helpful, either: she's trailing Caro, never more than a foot away, more present and more insistent than I've ever seen her before. "Tea, coffee?" And then because Caro is looking expectantly at the bottle she gave me, which I've placed on the kitchen counter, I add reluctantly, "Wine?"

"Yes, please. Is it a flu bug?"

I find some wineglasses and pull a corkscrew out of a drawer as I answer her. "The beginnings of one, I think. I'm all achy and my head is pounding." That's all true, actually, or it was before the flowers arrived and boosted my endorphin count, but a flu bug has nothing to do with it. Before the flow-

ers . . . suddenly I remember — "Fuck, the bath!"

I dash out of the kitchen, leaving Caro and her surprised expression behind. The bath hasn't flooded yet, but it has reached the level of the overflow, and the bathroom is misty with steam. I turn off the tap quickly, looking at the tub longingly. Perhaps I can get rid of Caro quickly enough that it will still be warm . . . but then I see Severine under the surface, clothed and completely still, her eyes closed and her hair fanning out lazily around her head. For all that I've become accustomed to having Severine around, it's an arresting image. Arresting and chilling. Then she sits up abruptly, her soaking wet hair slicked back tightly against her head, and opens her eyes, staring straight at me. I have to stifle a small scream.

But in that instant something unlocks in my brain, and suddenly I know exactly what happened, all those years ago in France. I stand there for a moment, staring at Severine, letting it all unfurl in my mind, like leaves touched by the first rays of the morning sun . . . *yes, that's how it must have been; yes, that, and that . . .* I see a plan of the farmhouse from above, laid out in miniature, like looking down on a doll's house:

there's a tiny version of me asleep in the bedroom I shared with Seb, my tear-streaked face calm in unconscious oblivion; a mini-doll Lara dozes in Tom's bedroom, tangled in sheets redolent of sex; Seb's figurine is passed out in the barn, where a stray rake lies abandoned near the door, while a tiny Severine and tiny Tom are grouped by the pool. And only one question remains: where to place Caro and Theo? But I know the answer to that too now.

And then another question follows: what can I do about it? A cold, hard fear is growing inside me, too, but this is different from the fear I have been living with of late; that was paralyzing, diminishing, it made me less than I want to be, less than I am. This fear is steel cold and equally as hard, and it's forging me into the same. Or perhaps it's stripping me back to what was always there, underneath: the Kate I like best, who faces life head-on. Kate of the high-risk strategy.

Severine sits in the bath, water still streaming off the ends of her long hair, her soaked black shift plastered to those eternally perfect tiny breasts. She sits and looks at me whilst I puzzle and plan, and there is not a jot of expression in those black eyes.

I leave the bathroom abruptly, closing the

door tight. In the living room I grab my handbag and find what I'm looking for buried at the bottom of it; I sweep it into my pocket to lie snugly against the florist's card: all my secrets in one dark, warm place.

Back in the kitchen, Caro has opened the wine and poured out two glasses; she looks up inquiringly as I reenter. "Sorry, I forgot I left the tap on; I was just running a bath when you arrived." I sound unnatural, but Caro doesn't seem to notice. Severine has joined us, too, thankfully no longer dripping wet. She prowls the kitchen, unusually active. Caro removes her suit jacket, turning to lay it carefully on the counter; as she does so I notice that she has a ladder in her stockings, running in an ever decreasing inverted V from the back of one of her patent heels to disappear under her skirt. She would hate it if she knew: *chinks in her armor,* I think, though without the rancorous glee that might once have called up within me. I've had a glimpse of what lies beneath Caro's surface, and I can't unsee it.

She starts off with small talk — business talk, around the candidates we're winning over to Haft & Weil, but it's small talk nonetheless. We sip our wine and verbally circle each other. Five minutes pass. Ten even. I can't quite understand why she's

delaying. It's an effort to keep my hand from the dark, snug pocket of secrets.

"You must be wondering what's so urgent that I turned up on your doorstep unexpectedly," says Caro with a small laugh, settling herself onto one of my bar stools. *Now*, I think, and my hand slips unremarkably into my pocket and just as unremarkably out again whilst I remain standing, my back resting against the countertop.

"Yes."

"It's not so much to do with the partnership process —"

"No?"

"Well, it is, but . . . the thing is, in the office they've obviously heard about the investigation, what with all the rumors flying round about, well, you. Someone asked Gordon about it, and he let slip I was there, too . . ." A flash of irritation makes a dash across her face. "Anyway. There's beginning to be a perception that it might be too much, that if I'm distracted by that, it'll be hard for me to really shine through this crucial period." She rolls her eyes. "I mean, it's completely ridiculous; I'm totally focused on partnership, but it's hard to fight this kind of thing." Twin spots of color are burning faintly over her cheekbones. She blows out a breath, then admits grudgingly,

without meeting my eye, "They're talking about pulling me off the slate. Holding me over to next year."

For a moment, I'm lost for words. On the worst interpretation of facts, this is deliciously — maliciously — ironic. If Caro is indeed the source of the rumors about me, then she is very much being hoisted on her own petard. Despite the cold steel within me, I realize how much I want to be *wrong*. I want the sum of the layers of Caro to be something better than the surface shell. I search for something neutral to say. "I see. And I suppose you were thinking, with the issues I hear Darren Lucas is facing, that you had rather a clear field —"

"Exactly," she rushes in. "This is my year. My *year*." She finally looks me directly in the eye, and I'm taken aback by the desperation I see within her. It's as strong as the cold, hard fear that still fills my belly. "I can't be held over," she says with quiet ferocity. "This is my year."

Her words are solid, impermeable, immovable. I gaze at her helplessly for a moment, then try one more doomed attempt: "Caro, I know you don't want to hear this now, but there are other law firms —"

"No." It's a statement of finality: for Caro, it's Haft & Weil or bust, partnership or noth-

ing. I've met many driven candidates over the years, all of whom display a similar single-mindedness, but nonetheless something about Caro seems particularly extreme. I realize I'm staring at her bent head as I sip my wine, trying to puzzle her out.

I shake my head and remind myself of my endgame. I have a plan, after all, and solving Caro's partnership woes is not part of it. After a moment, I say casually, "Do you still speak to Mark Jeffers?"

Her head whips up. "No," she says carefully, after the barest hesitation, but it's enough: I am not wrong about her. I sip my wine to hide the irrational disappointment that runs through me. "Why do you ask?" she adds, with just the right amount of mild curiosity.

"He's been shooting his mouth off round the market about the investigation; specifically, about how one Kate Channing is about to be arrested," I say evenly. "I've even had prospective clients asking me about it."

"Well, I know him quite well from days of old," she says smoothly. "He's a dreadful blabbermouth, but I could speak to him and try to get him to pipe down if you like."

"I rather think you've spoken to him already, haven't you?" She is gazing at me

steadily, her eyes still burning over-brightly, as if she's the one with a fever, but her face is carefully blank. "He had my name, and that hasn't been in any of the papers."

"That's ridiculous," she exclaims. It's a very good performance of outrage, such that a part of me can't fail to be impressed. "What on earth would I have to gain from that?"

It's a valid question, and one I can't answer; I continue as if she hasn't spoken. "And now this Darren Lucas situation. He's a very formidable opponent, but he's already been stitched up, hasn't he? So now your own rumormongering has come home to roost, in the very year that everything is miraculously in your favor."

Now her eyes have narrowed and her lips are almost invisible, clamped in a tight line. "If you have something to say, perhaps you should come right out and say it," she says, in a tightly controlled voice.

"I thought I was." I take another sip of wine. It's a sauvignon blanc, absolutely not what I would have chosen, and there's an aftertaste that definitely isn't winning me round. "I think Darren Lucas was in your way and you found a way to remove him. And now you need a way to make sure you can capitalize on that, which means you

need the investigation to disappear."

She picks up her glass and swirls it carefully before looking at me again, with those greedy, hot eyes. The desperation within her lies not quite hidden beneath. "You should be careful throwing around accusations you can't prove."

"You're right." I pull back my hand before it can sneak into my pocket — *later* — and take a drink myself. "I can't prove it. Anyway. Back to the point. You're here to ask me to blame Theo for all of this."

Her glass pauses halfway to her mouth, then smoothly resumes its trip. "You've been talking to Alina."

"Yes," I agree. Again, she's undeniably impressive, with her quick, devious intelligence. She barely missed a beat there.

"In that case, I might as well admit it. I *was* coming here to ask you to blame Theo." She shrugs. "After all, why wouldn't you? Your own business is struggling because of this —"

"My business is fine."

"Really?" She arches a brow. Something in her has changed. I knocked her off balance with my frontal assault, but I can see she has already regrouped. There's a tension within her, like a vibration: a quiver of anticipation. The eyes are only the tip of the

iceberg. What have I missed? "How fine would it be if Haft & Weil dropped you? You'd lose Stockleys, too, I'd warrant . . ."

This is what I've missed. I wonder how long she has been planning for this. Perhaps she perennially sees life as a chess game: putting pieces in place to defend her position should certain events come to pass . . . Or perhaps there was never any plan, and she's just taking advantage of what lies before her. I stare at her, waiting to feel panic or despair, but there's nothing but the cold, hard fear inside me that wills me inexorably on. And, out of nowhere, tiredness. Bone-crushing tiredness; a wave of it is rolling over me. I pull out a bar stool and sink onto it. "There's a contract —"

"There's a clause that gives an out for reputational risk," she says flatly. "A debatable interpretation, but you'd run out of cash before you could face us in court over it."

She is right, but I won't give her the satisfaction of hearing me say it. So I say nothing, and she eyes me carefully, allowing herself a small smile. "So yes, that is what I was going to say. Blame Theo."

"No," I answer bluntly. Even before my epiphany in the bathroom, I would have said no. If Tom were here, he would be furious

with me; he would urge me to row back, look out for myself, look after my business . . . but no. I want to be better than that; I *need* to be better than that. In Tom's eyes, at least, I need to be the Kate I like best. And I won't let Tom be a Tom that, over time, in the dark hours of the night, he becomes ashamed of. Not even for me. "No," I say again.

"No," she repeats thoughtfully. Then she shrugs, the skin moving over her bony breastplate revealed by the V-necked shirt. No fat there at all. Caro has no time for anything superfluous. "That's what I thought you would say. Though I don't really understand why. After all, it really could have been Theo, couldn't it? I mean, who knows?"

"Who knows," I echo, in barely more than a whisper, fighting the urge to close my eyes. This is the moment to make my move; this is what I've been waiting for. But even as the thought crosses my mind, somehow I know it's too late: it suddenly seems incredibly difficult to funnel words into my mouth, let alone form them in a coherent argument. Something is wrong, something is badly wrong with me, but I have no energy to figure out what.

"Kate? Who sent you the flowers, Kate?"

Her voice is overloud; it forces my eyelids open. Perhaps this isn't the first time she's asked the question.

"The flowers?" I repeat stupidly. My tongue feels thick. I look at Severine, but there's no help to be had from that quarter. I look at my glass of wine. It's nearly empty, but one glass is hardly enough to affect my speech. My head is so heavy that I feel I ought to lie it on the counter; instead, I prop my chin on my hands. I really must be getting ill: why else would I feel like this?

"Look at you," she says dispassionately. She puts her wineglass down decisively on the counter and pushes back her stool. "You always think you're so clever, don't you, Kate? You always have. Clever Kate, trying to show you're so much better than the rest of us because *you* went to a *state* school. No expensive upbringing for you, oh no. You've done it all on your own merit." She's suddenly very close to me, but I don't remember her bridging the gap. Did I close my eyes again? "Only now it doesn't matter how clever you are. Even the flowers don't really matter anymore. They're not from a client; a client would send them to your office." I shake my head, not understanding, but she's insistent. "They're from Seb, aren't they? Now he's back in London

you're trying to pick back up where you left off."

"Seb?" Something is wrong. I'm drifting sideways — but no, I'm not, I'm sitting at the counter; it's the world that's moving, spinning as if I'm drunk. Severine is next to me, something insistent in her manner; I don't understand her expression, but then, I never did.

"Seb," Caro repeats impatiently. "He sent you the flowers, didn't he?" There's something else within her now; the rapier edge that has always lurked is now glitteringly, dangerously unleashed, stabbing with an urgency I haven't seen before. As if she has taken the cloak off the dagger. Why would she do that? What have I missed?

It's an effort, but I manage to turn my head to her. The rest of the room is blurry, but Caro is in pin-sharp focus. "No, Caro, he didn't. He loves his wife." *At least,* I think, *I hope he does.* He certainly ought to. Then: *dear God, why am I feeling like this?*

She snorts dismissively. "Rubbish. That won't last." She frowns. "But he really shouldn't be sending you flowers when we have an understanding."

I stare at her. "Understanding? Don't you know? Alina's . . ." My words peter out. There's too much to overcome for them to

be born into the world, too much effort in creating them, moving my mouth and tongue, using my breath. This time I really do lay my head on the counter.

"Alina's what?" demands Caro, drawing disconcertingly near to me. She angles her head to match mine. I'm close enough to see that her irises are curiously devoid of flecks or variation, a flat, uniform, alien blue. "Alina's *what*?"

"Pregnant," I manage to say, then I close my eyes. *Must sleep,* I think. Then — *no, I mustn't sleep, I have a plan to execute, this is all wrong, what have I missed?* With a gargantuan effort I open my eyes. Caro's face is still right in front of me. "What have you done to me, Caro?" I whisper.

She ignores me. "Pregnant?" she hisses, disbelieving. "No. She can't be." For once I see everything she's thinking displayed on her face: her mind is racing down avenues, searching for alternative truths. "I don't believe it." Only she does believe it; I see the moment when that happens, and it's desperately sad to watch: the outer shell falls away to reveal her awful hurt and fury and grief, laid bare for all to see, the vulnerable thirteen-year-old cruelly wounded once again. But there's only Severine and me to witness.

"What have you done to me?" I whisper again. My eyelids are drifting closed.

"Pregnant." I hear her almost spit the word. Then, "Pregnant," I hear her say again, but thoughtfully this time. She's already regrouping; the shell is already patched up and lacquered back into place. Once again, it's admirable, if psychotic.

I try to force my eyes open again. There's an important question I should be asking. Asking again. "Caro. What have you done to me?"

She's gazing into the distance, but on my words she glances back at me. "Flunitrazepam," she says succinctly. "About enough to fell an elephant. Also known as Rohypnol, or roofies. Mostly it hits the headlines as a date rape drug, but did you know that a study in Sweden found it was the most commonly used suicide drug? Lara would like to know that, I'm sure . . ." She frowns again, or maybe she doesn't. I'm losing my ability to focus. I don't understand what she is saying. A malicious smile crosses her face. "I know you, being such a *clever* Kate, must be thinking that no one will believe you committed suicide . . ."

Suicide?

Suicide. Caro is murdering me. Has been murdering me for a good while now, surely,

for this drug to have taken effect to this extent. I should feel something about that, and I do, but it's a small feeling, a tiny glowing ball of panic, smothered deep within me beneath cotton-wool layers of exhaustion and apathy. I can see what's happening, I can see what's going to happen, but I seem incapable of being anything other than a detached observer. The cold, hard, fear-forged Kate is gone, blasted away by mere chemicals; she may as well never have existed.

But . . . murder. How long has Caro been thinking of murder? Whilst I've been wondering . . . I'm not sure if I've said that out loud; Caro's head turns to me, so perhaps I did speak. "I've been wondering . . . if we would have been friends . . . if I hadn't been with Seb. Whilst . . ." — it's almost funny; a gasp of a laugh escapes me — "you've been planning murder." I think she stops in what she's doing, I think her face is thrown into uncertainty for a moment, but my eyes are barely open. After a moment, they drift closed once more. I wonder what might have happened if I hadn't jumped off the wall into Seb's arms; if I'd turned to Tom instead. How would the spider's web have been spun then?

But Caro is talking now; I wrench my eyes

open again. She is talking, though she is doing something with her glass at the same time. Washing it, I realize, and putting it away, all the while taking care not to touch it with her bare fingers. Now she is rubbing down the wine bottle with the dishcloth, still talking. ". . . But actually everyone will believe it. Even your secretary Julie was saying how you didn't seem yourself today, how you haven't for a while. You've been overcome with guilt at killing that girl, you see. It's what they'll say; your death will be the proof of it. There's no real evidence to point to any one of us over another; you and I both know Modan's case is weak, but suicide is as good as a confession, isn't it? Then this will all go away . . . And, yes, I know you must be thinking that nobody would believe you had access to drugs. But you've had a drug dealer's number stored in your phone for a good long while now. Ever since my party, actually." She gives a small self-congratulatory smile and reaches for my phone, which is lying on the counter. She scrolls adeptly through the contacts, then pushes it in front of my face, but it's just a blurred mess of color to me. "You really should put a security code on your iPhone, you know."

As she speaks I realize I have to do some-

thing, and I have to do it now before it's too late for me to do anything at all. I summon up all the strength I can to make a grab for her, but once again I've already missed the moment. The grab is more of a swipe really: she jumps back easily, out of my limited field of vision, and the follow-through overbalances me, tumbling me into an awkward heap on the floor. It feels good to lie down. My cheek is resting against the lovely coolness of my kitchen tiles.

I don't move. It's unclear to me whether I even could if I tried. I look at the tiles, at the contrast of their smooth sheen with the uneven texture of the rough black grout; I let my focus relax further, and it seems that I am buoyed up on a sea of pale ivory tiles stretching before me to the horizon.

But Caro is still talking. I'm only getting snatches of what she's saying, though, and only flashes of vision. It's simply too difficult to keep my eyes open, and I can't imagine why I should be trying to. There's something about Seb kissing her, but I don't know when that happened: recently, or in France, or years ago as teenagers? It doesn't matter anyway. Time is stretching out, each event like a pearl on a string, each leading inevitably to the next. Seb was Seb, is Seb, could only ever have been Seb, and in his

careless affection for Caro — never enough but sometimes too much — he sparked something in Caro, who could only ever be Caro. And therefore here we are . . . but Caro is still talking, and it's all of it about Seb, about him sowing wild oats before settling down, how he said she was the only one who understood him, who was always there for him . . .

At one point I open my eyes again and find my iPhone a few inches from my nose. I don't think it was there before.

My eyes close again.

Something shakes me impatiently and insistently until eventually I open my eyes again. Caro's face is swimming right in front of me; she has pulled my head up by the hair.

Perhaps she says something — her lips move, but I can't make sense of it, and she recognizes that; she speaks again, almost defiantly, and this time I understand. "We wouldn't have. We wouldn't have been friends." I see her flat eyes, the intensity within them, and deep down I marvel at it: that insistence, that passion for what she wants. I think I had that once, but the drug has wrested it from me now.

Something bangs. It takes a good while to recognize it's my own head, lolling back on

the floor after she drops it.

Time passes. Or perhaps it doesn't. I'm an unreliable witness to life now.

At some point I become aware of Severine folding her beautiful walnut limbs fluidly to sit cross-legged beside me on the cold tiles, her eyes fixed on mine, and I feel . . . something. It takes a while to identify it, but I do: it's gratitude. Gratitude for her continued presence. I feel it wash through me now I've named it. *Don't leave.* I don't say the words, but I can see she won't: for the first time I have penetrated her inscrutability and can read what those dark eyes hold. She won't leave me. She will never leave me. She will be here until there's no more here for me. And now I know at long last what the point of her is, why Severine has been here all along. For this. This is where the ribbon of time has been leading for me. There should be no emotion because this was all determined a long time ago. Because Seb is Seb, and Caro is Caro, and Kate is Kate, and Tom is . . .

Tom, I want to say, but the word cannot be formed. There is only thought, and the thought of him, the dream of *us* that had only just begun to take form, pierces the cotton wool within me a little. Severine is speaking, gesturing at me urgently. She

hasn't done that before, but I can't hear the words and I can't understand what she wants. It's too late in any case. It seems that she's trying to pick up my phone, but she's a ghost, bound too tightly by the ribbon of time. Material things are for her no longer. But she isn't giving up. It's almost enough to make me smile, if I had the ability to form a smile, the urgency with which she is trying to rally me into . . . what? Something. I don't know.

Tom. I want another ribbon, a different one. I want *us.* I want to step sideways, into a time stream where Kate is Kate and Tom is Tom and neither of us are snubbed out by a pearl on the string of time. I want lazy Sunday mornings together and hectic dashes to work on the tube and holidays and home days and workdays and . . . days. I just want days. Days that start and end with Tom. *Tom.*

I'm slipping further away now. I can't fight it, and Severine has stopped trying to make me. I want to tell her that I know what happened, that I can see it all now; I want to say that I'm sorry I can't tell the world, but she knows it anyway and I don't think she cares. That was never why she was here. She remains watchfully cross-legged on the ivory sea beside me, not moving, not leaving;

forever beautiful, forever unsmiling.
I would have liked to have seen her smile.

CHAPTER TWENTY

I'm waking up.

This is . . . unexpected.

And painful. Oh my God, this is painful. My head, my throat, my stomach, my eyes, but most of all my head, my head, my head . . . It pounds as if the ebb and flow of the blood within it is a violent storm raging against the shore of my brain. Where is that cool, calm ivory sea to lay my hot, aching temple against?

Perhaps I make a movement as I try to open my eyes, because I hear a voice, a woman, but no one familiar: "Kate? Kate, are you with us?" And then light rushes in, swirling around until my brain gets control of it and forces it into blocks of colors and shades: I'm in a room. A pale room, nowhere I know, but it's instantly recognizable as a hospital.

A plump woman in dark blue scrubs is leaning over me, still saying my name, but I

look past her, looking around for Severine, but she's not there; I can't see her anywhere, and now I really start to panic. She wouldn't leave me, I know she wouldn't leave me; what does it mean that she's not here?

"Kate? No, shhh, just lie still . . . It's all right, you're all right. You're in a hospital." She turns as someone enters the room, but I can't see who it is — is it Severine? But no, that can't be right, though I can't quite remember why that can't be right . . . "She's just come round," she says to them. She turns back to me. "Kate, do you know who this is?"

And then he's right beside me, reaching for my hand, and the panic dissolves. *"Tom."* My voice is more of a croak; nonetheless the relief on his face is staggering.

"You're back," he says simply, and lays a hand against my face. I want to move into it, but I'm unsure of my body, of what it can and can't do. As the nurse suggested, lying still seems safest.

"Was I away?" I croak out. He looks awful. He hasn't shaved in days, and it's possible he hasn't slept, either. I have the feeling I've been dropped onstage in the middle of a play without a script or any knowledge of the first act. How did I get here?

"Yes. You've been . . . away . . . for two

days." He takes a shuddering breath and starts to say something, but the nurse cuts him off.

"Let's get you a drink of water and then I just need to check a few things, Kate." She brings the bed a little more upright, holds some water to my lips and starts to flash lights in my eyes, all the while asking me questions. What's my name? When was I born? What year is it? Do I know where I am? With each answer the words come easier, as if the route from my brain to my mouth is clearing.

"Did I hit my head then?" I ask suddenly, recognizing the questions as more than information gathering, and then I remember — or do I? The memories are inconstant, jumbled, the colors too strange. "I did, didn't I . . . I think . . ."

"Yes, you gave your head rather a thwack, I'm afraid. We've been quite worried about you." This is from someone new. I turn my head a little, gritting my teeth against the wave of pain that accompanies the movement, and find the source: a tall woman in her early forties, dark hair scraped back into an elegant bun, standing in the doorway with a faint smile in place. She's in scrubs, too, but she wears the cloak of her authority over them, further underlined by her enor-

412

mous diamond studs: you wouldn't expect to see those on a low-paid nurse. "Welcome back. I'm Dr. Page." She steps into the room and picks up the chart, scanning it quickly. "And you, I rather think, are going to be fine, after a lot of rest. What do you remember?" she asks, but there's something in her face that doesn't quite match the casual tone. My eyes fall on the nurse. She's busying herself so completely with changing a drip that she must be listening intently. Even Tom has a little tension in his face. Again I have the feeling that I'm missing the script.

"I don't . . . I'm not sure . . . I was at my flat." I remember that, definitively. "I wasn't feeling well. I was running a bath." Severine was in the bath; once again I see the water sheeting off her hair as she sits up. "Caro — oh my God —"

Tom gives a start. "Caro? Caro was there?"

"Yes. She came round. She put something in my wine, I think —"

"Caro put something in your wine." It's more of a statement than a question. His voice is tightly controlled, but there's an anger lurking beneath that somehow puts me in mind of his impressive fury during the poolside debacle in France.

Caro. Caro and Seb. Seb and Alina —

"Oh God, Alina; is Alina okay?"

"Rohypnol," says Dr. Page, ignoring my question. Her tone is crisp, but her face has relaxed. "Rather a large dose, I'm afraid." *Enough to fell an elephant.* Tom hasn't reacted to her words; it dawns on me that this is not news to him. "We had to pump your stomach, and also you had subcranial bleeding so we —"

I cut across her. "Yes, but Alina — is she okay?"

"Why wouldn't she be okay?" Tom asks, but he's simultaneously pulling his phone out of his pocket. The nurse starts to protest that mobile phones can't be used in the hospital, but Dr. Page cuts her off with a quick shake of her head.

"Because Caro is obsessed with Seb. Because that's what this was all about: Severine, everything. All about Seb —"

But Tom is speaking on the phone now. "Alina? Hi, it's Tom." I hear a voice replying, but I can't make out the words. "Yes, I'm in the hospital with her now. She's woken up, thank God. The doctor says she's going to be fine."

"Has Caro been to see her?" I ask him urgently.

He nods at me as he listens for a moment and then says, "No, it definitely wasn't

that." Wasn't what? "We're just figuring out what really happened. Sorry to ask a slightly strange question, but has Caro been to see you?" He listens then shakes his head at me.

"Don't let her —" I start, but he is nodding at me already, one hand up.

"Look, I'm not sure quite what's going on right now, but sounds like you're being a smart girl," he says approvingly down the phone. "I'll give you a call when I know more. Let me know when you and Seb are back in town."

He disconnects and looks at me. "She was feeling pretty rubbish so she's taken a week off work and she and Seb drove to Cornwall yesterday to stay at her mum's place. Caro called her a couple of times the night before they left, but Alina thought she was being a bit, well, odd, so she said she didn't have time to meet before they left."

I do the maths on the timing; it's horribly hard work on my aching head, though it occurs to me the painkillers I must be on are probably not helping, either. Alina said Caro called the night before they left, and she also said they left yesterday. So, Caro called her two days ago. And I've been out of it for two days. Caro must have left mine and immediately started calling Alina. I wonder what it was that raised alarm bells for Alina,

but whatever it was, she's a smart girl indeed for listening to them. I relax back onto the pillow. Then I remember my puzzlement at Tom's words. "Wasn't what?" I ask.

"What?"

"You said no, it wasn't that. What did you mean?" Once again I notice that Dr. Page and the nurse are thoroughly involved in other things and therefore are actually at full attention. Then it hits me. "Oh. You thought I'd attempted suicide." I can see on all the faces that I've got it right. Something flickers in my memory. "She said you would think that," I murmur.

"It's a reasonable assumption for that quantity of drug in your bloodstream," says Dr. Page with an unapologetic shrug. "I'm astonished you were able to call for help at all." I look at her, nonplussed. I called for help? Who did I call? But she's moving on: if I want to be able to hold a conversation on my own terms I had better increase my mental processing speed. "How did it get in your system?"

I'm not sure if she doesn't believe me or she's just being thorough. "Caro brought wine," I say evenly, though perhaps not as evenly as intended. My voice isn't quite working as normal, and my throat seems to

close up even more when I think of what happened, or might have happened . . . What did happen? "I wasn't in the room when she opened it and poured me a glass. I didn't try to kill myself; I wouldn't do that. Ever. Plus I wouldn't even have a clue how to get hold of Rohypnol." A half memory triggers: *you really should put a security code on your iPhone.* That same iPhone on the floor, the colors on the screen swimming too vividly . . .

"That's a serious accusation," Dr. Page says carefully.

"It was a serious attempt to kill me," I reply, not nearly as evenly.

She nods, though more as if she's weighing things up than as a sign of agreement. "Look, I'm not trying to influence you in any way, but you should be aware that Rohypnol does rather scramble your memories." Tom is very still. I can't tell what he's thinking as he focuses on the good doctor. "To be frank, it makes you an unreliable witness in the eyes of the law. Are you sure you want to take this to the police?"

Do I? I look inside myself, for the cold, hard fear I remember, for the fury I want to be there, for the Kate I wanted to be, but I'm not sure where any of those are. A longing for Severine washes over me, to once

417

again see my beautiful, inscrutable ghost. But she isn't here. Caro took her from me; twice, as it turns out, and on that realization I finally find a bright, shining edge of steel. Tom looks at my face. "If Caro was prepared to do this," he says quietly, almost in a growl, "is there something else she's done?" Bless him for his quick understanding: he's already joined the dots. I wonder if he'd half made the links already. But he's looking at me gravely, a stillness in his face as he awaits confirmation. I nod silently, and he breathes out slowly, the stillness eroded into bleak disappointment edged with anger.

"I want to take this to the police," I say, as emphatically as I'm currently capable of sounding.

"Okay," sighs Dr. Page. "We'll get everything in order from the medical side." She looks at Tom and me, and her eyes soften. "For the record, your man here never believed you tried to kill yourself," she says, a half smile on her face. "He told anyone who would listen that they were wrong. Same for your friend Lara." I look at Tom again, who has at some point taken my hand once more, though it doesn't quite feel like mine yet; I look at those eyes that are all his, above that wonderful nose, and I'm suddenly afraid I may burst into tears. "Now

may I actually tell you about your medical condition?" asks the doctor wryly.

I smile and nod, and she launches into an explanation that involves some quite terrifyingly dramatic medical terms that I choose to mostly ignore because against all odds, the upshot seems to be that I'm actually here and I'm fine, or I'm going to be, and Tom is holding my hand, a hand that becomes a little more *mine* with every stroke of his thumb. Time is a ribbon, and there is more of that ribbon ahead for me. Despite the drugs Dr. Page has just explained I'm being pumped with, it's dawning on me slowly what almost happened to me, what was almost taken from me, and suddenly the tears that threatened begin to spill down my cheeks.

"Don't worry," says Dr. Page kindly. "This is not an unusual reaction to the drugs."

"I think," says Tom grimly, "it's more of a reaction to attempted murder," but his hand is gentle as he places it against my face again. This time I turn into it, and my head doesn't thump too hard at the movement.

"*Alors,* attempted murder?" a familiar voice drawls from the doorway. "I think that is something I should hear about, *non?*" Modan. He's not wearing a suit, but nonetheless he is still impeccably dressed, in

casual jeans, a shirt and a pullover — the same sort of outfit that millions of men choose every day, but somehow his screams French sophistication. Or perhaps that comes from the way he positions his lanky frame against the doorway and raises one eyebrow.

"Bonjour, monsieur," I say wearily. I am in fact excessively exhausted all of a sudden. Surely he won't arrest me in my hospital bed? "You really find your way everywhere, don't you?"

"True, but today I thought I was just the bag carrier," Modan replies, raising one hand with a self-deprecating smile. I recognize Lara's tan handbag dangling from it; hostilities must have ceased. "Lara is just in the bathroom. Though maybe I need to change roles, *non?*"

"Maybe, but not yet," says Dr. Page firmly. "This patient needs some more sleep. As soon as your friend Lara has said hello it's time for a sedative."

"You are very lucky to be here," says Modan, advancing diffidently into the room. His voice is serious, and for once the mouth bracketed between those deep lines is sober. "In my career I have seen . . . *alors,* more than enough overdoses. It is . . . it is an

420

unbelievable pleasure to see you with us again."

His simple, genuine words catch at my throat. All I can do is nod. When I find my voice again I ask, "How . . . how am I here? How did I get help?"

"You called me," says Tom simply. "On your iPhone. Voice activated, probably; I never thought I would have cause to say this, but thank the Lord for Siri. I thought you were calling about the flowers . . ." Flowers. A pocketful of dark secrets. Something tugs in my brain, then slides away. "You didn't really say anything except something that sounded maybe like . . . help." He's silent for a moment. There's a bleakness in his expression that frightens me to see. "It didn't sound much like you at all." There's something odd in his voice, a touch of puzzlement as he remembers. "I almost could have sworn it was . . ."

"Who?" I ask, though I know the answer; I believe I know who my savior was. But the moment has passed; Tom shakes his head.

"Anyway, I called Lara since I knew she had a key, and she called Modan." He nods appreciatively in the direction of the Frenchman; there seems to have been some manly bonding between the two that I have missed. "They both went straight over there and

found you and called the ambulance. I got there about ten minutes after them, and the ambulance was only a few minutes after me —"

"Wait," I say suddenly. My jumbled brain has reminded me that I have something important to say. "Modan, Caro killed Severine. She was in the Jag, taking cocaine; she went to the bus depot to pretend to be Severine; with a scarf on her hair you wouldn't even know she's blond . . ." Modan is staring at me sharply, halfway through pulling a chair across to the bedside. "You have to believe me."

Modan nods seriously. "Then you will have to tell me everything."

"But not right now," interjects Dr. Page sharply. "As I said —"

"You're awake!" Lara has spilled into the room, and in an instant the mood has lifted, despite the tears that bracket her laughter, because she is once again the sunshine girl and she takes it with her wherever she goes. Lara is Lara, and Tom is Tom, and I've yet to learn what Modan is, but time is a ribbon, and there is more of that ribbon for me, so perhaps I will find out.

My head is not broken, but still there are cracks. Cracks in my memory, cracks in my

422

understanding, cracks in my experience of time; fractures that allow things to bleed in, and others to slip out. At times a sly beast of exhaustion pads unnoticed through the openings to leap lightly onto my shoulders; then it digs in its claws and drags me to the floor. My next few days consist of infrequent periods of wakening that sink abruptly and dramatically into an oblivion that is so deep and complete that I'm both scared by it and powerless to resist.

Somewhere in those days the police talk to me. I'm not clear on how many times. Modan appears to be running point, despite overtly deferring to a local granite-hewn officer (do they mine all British policemen from the same quarry?) whose doubtful expression is, I have to hope, habitual rather than specific to this case. By this case, I mean Caro's poisoning of me — nobody is talking to me about Caro's murder of Severine, which I don't understand and can never quite seem to get a straight answer on. Modan and his British colleague come to talk with me, they go away, they come again; or perhaps it is me that leaves and returns.

Lara comes, too, bringing magazines I can't read because the words crawl around the page, but she also brings chocolate and

grapes and flowers and herself. I hear the full story of my rescue; she paints a picture that has Modan glittering in the forefront, and I can't help thinking that my near-death is almost entirely responsible for the resurrection of their romance. "Honestly," she says in a half-awed tone, "he was brilliant. I was totally beside myself, but he knew exactly what to do. Really, you should have been there."

"Well," I say drolly, "I was, actually."

Her face sobers instantly. "God, I know. I know. You know what I meant."

"I'm sorry." I reach for her hand remorsefully, and we share a smile that's a little wobbly on her side. "And then? Modan?"

She blushes. "Well, once we knew you were out of immediate danger, he took me home. It must have been about six in the morning. He grabbed croissants from that bakery on the corner by my flat; you know the one? It opens really early . . . Anyway, we had croissants and then he tucked me up in bed and he was going to leave, but I didn't want to be alone so he stayed and he didn't try anything, he was just totally taking care of me, and well . . . it's gone from there really." The giddiness is in her eyes and her voice again; it creates a glow that lights up her very skin. "He's going to apply

for a post with this international liaison department that's based in London — it's kind of like Interpol, I think. It's a move he was thinking about anyway, but there's an opening coming up. Anyway," she says with a meaningful look, "what about you and Tom?"

I find I'm blushing, too. Tom is here, somewhere; he has just nipped out to get coffee for Lara. Tom is here, Tom is almost always here, to the point where yesterday I asked him if he still had a job. He gently pointed out it was Sunday, but that makes today Monday (It does, doesn't it? Yes, it does), and he's still here, holding my hand, dropping kisses on my (unwashed) hair, yet we've never talked about what that means. I'm saved from having to answer Lara's question by the return of the man himself, armed with three coffees, though we all know I will fall asleep before I can drink mine.

Finally Modan and the British policeman come to see me with serious expressions that, head injury notwithstanding, I can interpret without them even having to open their mouths.

"You're not charging her," I say flatly, though they've yet to take a seat. I'm sitting up in bed in my private room (thank God I

didn't scrimp on health cover when I set up my own company). Tom, who was idly flicking through the sports section of a newspaper on a chair beside me, rises to meet Modan with what I can only describe as a man-hug. I keep meaning to ask about that, but I haven't; another thing that has slipped through a crack.

"Well," says PC Stone, whose name isn't Stone, and who isn't a PC, either; he's probably a DI or something, but neither of those details will stick for me. "No, we're not." He spreads his hands wide, but the gesture is blunt and choppy; it lacks Modan's elegant sweep. Then he hitches his trouser legs to settle in a chair and leans forward, elbows on knees, his broad, thick head topped with short gingerish bristles jutting forward like a bull preparing to charge; it would take more than a sea of white tiles to put a dent into that skull. Modan remains standing, seemingly just to emphasize the differences between the two: the stocky Brit and the beanpole Frenchman, one direct and no-nonsense, the other deviously charming. It's actually a pretty effective mix. "The thing is, it's just a he said, she said." Surely a she said, she said? But he's still talking; I must concentrate or I will lose track. "There's no evidence she was even at

your flat. No fingerprints on the wine bottle."

"Not even Kate's?" asks Tom meaningfully.

"Not even Kate's. Which, yes, is strange, but it doesn't prove a case against Miss Horridge. The date Kate's phone was updated with the dealer's number matches the date of her party, but that hardly proves anything." He scratches at his stubble, his frustrated dissatisfaction clear.

"You're not charging her," I repeat.

Modan, silent up till now, steps forward, his expression earnest. "What can we do? There's no evidence."

"There isn't any evidence on Severine's murder, but you still seemed to be trying hard to pin it on me," I say tartly.

Modan blows out a breath. "I'm afraid you are behind the times. The case has been closed."

I stare at him. "You've arrested Caro?" I wait for a wave of relief, but it doesn't come.

He shakes his head. "*Non.* There is not enough evidence on that also. But the investigation has been closed. It is . . . politically unpopular, shall we say, but that is how it is."

"Closed? Over?" Over . . . No more threat of arrest — but Lara's words come back to

427

me. *It's never really over. Even if they consign it to the cold case pile, it could still come alive again.* Can it be truly over without a conviction? I find myself looking for Severine again, before I remember that she isn't here anymore.

Modan nods grimly. "Closed." I can see it irks him. "I know who was responsible, but there is nothing I can do without evidence." Evidence. He says it heavily, emphatically, in his French accent, whilst holding my gaze. Evidence. It feels like he is challenging me.

"I know who was responsible too, and it wasn't me."

"Ah, but you misunderstand me," he says, shaking his head. "I have never thought it was you." I stare at him. "Well, not for a long time, at least," he amends, and I find a bark of laughter escaping me. He grins back at me, sly humor in those clever eyes.

"Really? Why not?" asks Tom, with what sounds like academic interest.

"Because she drove, of course," he says to Tom, as if it was self-evident. "All the way back."

Tom and I exchange glances, not comprehending. "But no one else was insured," I say blankly.

"*Exactement.* You wouldn't bend the rules,

not even for that. I could not . . . make it fit. I could not believe you killed her on purpose. And if you had killed her, by accident, you would have called *les gendarmes,* the police, the ambulance; it is not in your nature to deceive. *Et voilà.* It could not be you." Tom and I share another glance, slightly dazed. Even PC Stone seems a little taken aback by this remarkably unscientific explanation.

"I suppose instinct is part of your job," says Tom after a moment. It sounds like he is trying not to look a gift horse in the mouth.

"True," admits PC Stone, though he, too, still seems thrown.

"It is very much in Caro's nature to deceive," Tom presses. Caro. So this is how it will be. Caro will get what she wants. Perhaps not immediately, but she plays a long game. Sooner or later, Alina will be swept aside in some as-yet unknown way, and then Caro will have Seb, partnership at Haft & Weil and a field clear of rivals. I can just imagine her now, whispering to Seb about how poor, deranged Kate tried to kill herself and blame it on her. And not just whispering to Seb, come to think of it. *So desperately sad about Kate. She obviously had some kind of breakdown; she overdosed*

and blamed it on me, can you imagine? I mean, the police even investigated her claim, but of course there was no truth to it, so they had to drop it. Poor girl. In that moment my stomach drops as I realize my business is over. There is no return from this. It doesn't matter that the police are dropping the Severine case; Caro will never cease in her rumormongering. I look at Tom, and by the bleakness in his expression I can see he's drawn the same conclusion.

Modan nods heavily. "We found cocaine in the auto, the Jag. Down in the, ah, the seams — seams, yes? — of the driver's seat. I think she was in love with Seb; I think she has always been in love with him. I think she was delighted when Kate and Seb had a fight; she thought it was her turn, *n'est-ce pas?*" Ordinarily a man of gestures, he is unusually still, allowing his words the space to have maximum impact. "It must have enraged her beyond reason to find him taking up with Severine. I expect it was just chance, that she happened to be in the Jag as Severine came by en route to her house, and in her fury Caro lost control . . ." I stare at Modan even as I see it unfold: Severine with her hand to her bloody temple, caught in the headlights of the approaching, accelerating Jag. "But she would have im-

430

mediately realized that she couldn't allow the police to be called with the drugs in her system. Even if she wasn't charged for murder, it would be the end of her legal career. Other than Seb, that has always been the most important thing in her life." I continue to stare at him, slightly disturbed by his ability to casually condense a whole person to two main ambitions. But he's right: partnership at Haft & Weil and Seb are at the root of everything. "So she disposed of the body."

"By herself?" asks Tom softly.

Modan knows what he is asking. "I don't know for sure," he says, equally softly, "but I would think she must have had help."

Tom nods, looking at the floor. Modan's gaze rests on him for a moment, and then he continues. "The car has damage to the undercarriage, but it is impossible to tell how long that has been there. And we can't prove Miss Horridge was in the car, even with the cocaine. We can't even prove Severine died as a result of a . . . how you say . . . hit-and-run." He spreads his hands, his mouth twisted in regret. "We are too late to prove anything."

"But she went to the train station to mislead everyone. That's why she was late when I wanted to leave." All the while I was

driving back, desperately unhappy behind the wheel of my little car, Caro was settled in the back, fresh from covering up a murder. How is it possible I couldn't tell? "Like I told you, with her hair up in a turban, like Severine wore it, it's quite hard to tell she's blond." I see Caro again with the red trilby, superimposed on Severine's image. "Can't your bone measurement thingy prove it was her?"

Modan is already nodding. "*Oui.* I have thought that for a while. A very smart thing to do, in fact. But again, no hard evidence. We can prove it *could* have been her at the depot, but we can't prove it definitely *was* her. There is no . . . stomach . . . for a high-profile loss on this. Perhaps, if it was less political . . ."

At last PC Stone speaks up. "I couldn't agree with you more about the character of Miss Horridge," he says heavily. His hand is working at his red-tinged stubble again. He is the sort of man who must have to shave twice a day if he has an evening out planned. "Given we can't get her on the French murder, we were really hoping to nail her on attempted murder of you. Is there really nothing else you can tell us? Nobody who might have seen her? Heard you talking? We've asked all your neighbors, but . . .

nothing."

"You spoke to Ben? From across the hall?"

"Ken," says Modan. "Ken Moreland." There's no judgment in his tone, but I feel it all the same. My memory, or lack of it, is the elephant in the room, though aren't elephants supposed to never forget?

"I never really did catch his name," I mutter mutinously.

PC Stone clears his throat. "Yeah, well, anyway, we spoke to him. He said you appeared to be alone when he delivered the flowers, and then he went out for a bit. He got back as the ambulance was just leaving."

Flowers. I look at Tom and almost wail, "But your flowers will be dead."

He smiles. "No matter. I can buy you more, and with more romantic cards if you like."

But still, this mention of flowers is tugging at something, a tendril of a thought that curls up from a crack. The flowers, the card, all my secrets in one dark pocket — "My clothes!" I exclaim suddenly.

"Dr. Page won't let you up yet," says Tom, warningly.

"No, I mean the clothes I was wearing. Where are they?"

"They're in evidence," says PC Stone.

433

"There was something in my pocket."

Modan speaks up. "Perhaps you are a little tired. We should come back later, *non*?"

"No, no, this is actually relevant," I say testily. "There were two things in my pocket. The card from the flowers. And a Dictaphone. I don't know if it will have picked up much, but maybe . . ." Once again I feel my hand slipping quietly into my pocket and slipping back out again just as quietly.

Suddenly Modan and PC Stone look a lot more interested. "A Dictaphone? You're sure?" asks PC Stone. I nod. "But there's nothing in evidence," he objects.

"A Dictaphone, did you say? Looks a bit like a mini cassette player, yes? Oh, that's in your top drawer," says a breezy voice from across the room. It's the nurse; I didn't notice her coming in to check on the bathroom supplies. "It looks a bit bashed up, I'm afraid."

I turn toward the drawers, but Modan is faster, pulling a glove out of his pocket. He rummages in the drawer and comes out with the little black device in his gloved hand, turning it over carefully. One corner looks crushed, and a crack runs across the face of it. Both the Dictaphone and I bear the marks of the crash to the tiles. I'm working, mostly; is it?

"It was in my pocket," I say, horribly anxious. "I don't know how much that will have muffled the sound. And it's pretty old anyway; it's not even digital . . ." Tom takes my hand, and I realize I'm babbling, so I trail off. Modan is carefully rewinding the tape, which makes a whining sound I don't remember, and stutters and grates from time to time, causing me to hold my breath each time until it recovers. And then it stops abruptly. Modan's eyes catch mine and hold for a beat. Then he presses play.

I'm talking, but my mouth isn't moving: "Arrange to meet candidate in advance of the, uh, Stockleys recruitment drive becoming common knowledge; have Julie arrange on Monday —"

I shake my head at Modan, still linked to his eyes, and talk over myself, "No, this isn't it —" but the tape abruptly switches scene. Indistinct, muffled sounds can be heard, and then indistinct voices. There's almost certainly a woman, probably two; it certainly sounds like a not-quite-heard conversation. Modan raises his eyebrow, and I nod back imperceptibly, then he looks for a volume knob. It's already at maximum.

"I can't —" I start, but Modan holds up a hand to silence me. So we listen, the four of us, to a conversation played out too far

435

beyond the veil of time and technology to be audible. Tantalizing words slip out: I hear *Darren Lucas,* I hear *accusations,* I hear *flowers,* but I have the benefit of having been at the first screening; Tom looks utterly in the dark. But still, even with my advantage it's plain to me the tape is not clear enough. It was all for nothing. We sit, as the gently rotating tape spools out into our silence, and I consider my future. I can't pick up and start again; the rumors will never die. What on earth will I do? The words mostly peter out after a while, dwindling to short snatches interspersed with indistinct movements; it's oddly soporific. But then the recording ends with an overloud scrunch, as if something bashed the microphone. I remember that crunch distinctly, the sea of white tiles rising up to meet me . . . Modan presses stop with a theatrical click.

"It's useless." Even to me, I sound hollow.

"Not at all," says Modan, seeming oddly pleased. I suddenly realize even PC Stone is almost smiling. "We hear two people, two women, speaking. If we can hear this much, the technicians will be able to do a great deal with this, *oui?*" PC Stone nods in agreement, then Modan turns back to me. "Bravo, Madame." *Madame.* It gives me a

jolt. I am *madame* now, whereas Severine will always be the mademoiselle next door. It takes the edge off the swelling hope that perhaps all is not lost after all.

"Though, I have to say," interjects the British policeman, somewhat reluctantly, his face returning to its usual granite, "it's not strictly legal to record a conversation without permission."

"It was an accident," offers Tom, deadpan. "She often has the Dictaphone in her pocket, and it's quite easy to knock it on." I nod furiously, despite the fact that I only use the Dictaphone perhaps once or twice a month.

"Is that so?" says PC Stone dryly. He looks at Modan.

"An accident," says Modan, his eyes gleaming. He spreads his hands wide. "A happy accident. These things happen, *oui*?"

"I suppose they do," says his colleague reluctantly, though I can see a corner of his mouth twitching as he climbs to his feet. "Right, we'd better get that to the technicians. No promises, but I'm hopeful . . . if we can just at least prove she was there . . ." Tom and I watch them depart, looking even more like a comedy duo now that there is a lightness to their mood.

"It won't work, you know," says Tom

gently. I turn to him with eyebrows raised. The bleakness hasn't left his eyes. "I don't want you to get your hopes up. They might arrest her, but they won't nail her for it."

"Why do you say that?"

He sighs. "Because she's Caro. She'll get the best legal representation money can buy; her dad will make sure of that. You'd need physical evidence and a sworn confession to convict her; nothing less will do. And they don't have the first, and I'm pretty sure, even after the police do their technical wizardry, that tape won't amount to a sworn confession. I could be wrong, but . . ."

I stare at him while I think it through. Did she actually confess? It's hard to pick through my fragmented memory. *Enough to fell an elephant.* So she did confess, but will the tape have caught it? Where was she standing when she said that? Where was I? I don't remember; it's slipped through a crack. "So that's it. You think she gets away with it." He nods unhappily. I try to fit the pieces together myself, to come up with a different answer, but I can't. The injustice hollows me out. I ought to want to rail at something, or someone, but who or what? "So she gets away with it and I get left with nothing," I say dully at last.

"Well," he says, taking my hand and star-

ing at it intently. "Not exactly nothing, I hope." He looks up, and the intensity in his gaze steals my breath. "It tore me in pieces to see you in here. I can't imagine what the hell I've been playing at, waiting on the sidelines all these years. I don't intend to wait a single second more."

I stare at him. Tom, my Tom, the Tom I should have always known he was. "All these years?"

"*All* these years." There's a hint of a smile at the corners of his mouth.

"But you've slept with Lara!" I don't know why I'm throwing up obstacles given that I adore this man.

He rolls his eyes. "I was twenty-one and my cousin was sleeping with my dream girl. Sure, I was madly, unbelievably jealous, but that didn't make me a monk. And anyway, you've slept with my cousin, many times. That'll be much harder to explain round the family table at Christmas."

"*We* haven't even slept together yet," I muse thoughtfully.

He waggles his eyebrows suggestively. "I'd love to remedy that immediately, but the nursing staff might not be so keen on the idea. But our first kiss held definite promise . . ." He holds my gaze, and something moves between us, a current that thickens

the air into something solid enough to lean into. "So," he whispers, in a low murmur that takes me right back to that dark, delicious corridor, "are you in?"

"I'm in," I whisper, and then he's kissing me, and I find I am feeling very much better indeed.

CHAPTER TWENTY-ONE

Time passes. I can't keep it or save it or mark it — the ribbon slips through my fingers regardless. And time shows that Tom is right, of course: the Dictaphone tape is cleaned up, but not all of it is audible. Crucially, not the part where Caro confessed to dumping roofies in my wine, if that confession truly happened at all, though it remains fixed in my memory. Despite the lack of confession, the police question Caro, and they even find her drug dealer (the unexpected casualty in all of this, as his is the only actual arrest); they leave no stone unturned. It is my repeated and most fervent wish that this investigation has completely annihilated any chances of Caro making partner this time round; surely, even more than the Severine investigation, it must be diverting her attention from that process? But in the face of the finest legal representation money can buy (Tom was

441

right on that, too), the decision is made not to prosecute.

By that point, I am back at work — hollow cheeked but clear-eyed, with most of my cracks papered over. Paul did an admirable job of holding the Channing Associates fort in my absence by the remarkably sensible solution of promoting Julie to work alongside him and hiring a temporary secretary. Julie, it turns out, loves the role, and I can't bring myself to demote her, so now I am up a head count with zero prospect of raising any new contracts given the impending tidal wave of gossip that is no doubt beginning to circulate. We are diligently working out the contracts we do have, but every time I talk with Paul I find myself imagining scales behind his eyes, weighing up the best time to jump. Still, I'm actually relieved to have Julie in place; the first few weeks back at work are incredibly exhausting, and I barely pull my weight. Neither of them quite understand what happened, though I suspect Tom may have told Paul more than I realize; anyway, in communications to clients Paul wisely blamed my hospitalization on an accidental blow to the head and left the rest well alone.

The Haft & Weil contract hasn't been revoked, to my surprise. Paul picked it up

in my absence, liaising with someone other than Caro due to the need for her to focus on the partnership selection process (official line only, I hope); I have made no move to regain control of it. Therefore it's a complete surprise to find Gordon Farrow waiting by my office front door when I step outside one lunchtime to get a sandwich; I grind to a halt halfway down the steps.

"Hello," he says diffidently when I make no sound. "I don't suppose you expected to see me."

"No," I reply warily. "I didn't."

"Can I buy you a coffee?" It's very much a question; he shows no expectation of a positive response. Perhaps that's why I nod.

"There's a café this way where we can get a sandwich, too, if you haven't eaten."

I glance at him as we walk along. He looks like he always does, a nondescript man in all respects. He must be appraising me, too, as he says, "I'm glad to see you looking so well. How do you feel?"

"Tired," I say, yawning messily on cue. "Head injuries can do that, apparently."

We find a table in the café and settle down, each of us hiding behind the menu. It's not the same café as the one where Lara and I experienced the bird incident, but I still find myself glancing at the window and

almost exclaim aloud when I see Severine sauntering by in her black shift dress. She turns her head and eyes me coolly, then continues down the pavement outside, away from the café. What does it mean, that she is back? Is she staying, or is this her version of good-bye? "I'm so pleased you agreed to meet with me," Gordon says abruptly, putting down the menu. I drag my attention back to him, resisting the urge to crane my neck to see if she has really gone. "I wasn't sure you would. I should have known you wouldn't blame me for any . . . difficulties . . . between you and Caro —"

"Difficulties." I put down my own menu. "Difficulties, Gordon? Is that the right word? She tried to kill me. She put so much Rohypnol in my drink that she damn near succeeded. So forgive me if I find the word *difficulties* a little too weak."

"There is no evidence of that —" He tries to hold my gaze, but even his legendary steel is wavering.

"So I'm told. Doesn't mean it didn't happen. If you'd heard the tape —"

"I heard it." He looks away.

"Who —" I start, but the waitress comes to take our order; she is a plump brunette continually smiling even as she speaks. I can't imagine why she's quite this happy at

work. It's jarring.

When she leaves I find Gordon appraising me again. "You're angry with me," he says mildly.

"Yes."

"Because I stand by her? She's my daughter; failing evidence to the contrary I have to believe her." He explains this like it's an intellectual discussion on the finer points of a legal draft.

"Do you have to?" I consider that. "Perhaps. I don't know. What would you do if there was evidence but she claimed it was all fabricated?"

He shrugs, with a slight smile I don't entirely understand.

"Anyway, that's not why I'm angry with you."

His control is superb. "Why, then?"

"Because I do blame you, for her behavior: you and your wife. You *are* partly responsible. How did she come to believe this kind of behavior is allowed? Where were the boundaries when she was growing up? You got divorced and then you felt guilty and you let her get away with murder and then, well, then getting away with murder wasn't a metaphor anymore." I stop and pick up my water glass, feeling oddly shaky after my savage words. I had no idea that was going

to come out of my mouth. Is that how I really feel about it? Do I really blame him?

He looks at me sadly, saying nothing until the silence stretches out. I find myself holding my breath for a response. I shouldn't care at all what Gordon thinks of me, but it's clear I do. Finally he sighs. "I'm not sure I entirely agree with your position, but I do fully respect your right to say it. In truth there is very little you could say to make me feel any more wretched than I already do." In that moment I can see through to the anguish in his eyes.

"Well," I say, after a moment, "I'm sure it's not as simple as all that." He inclines his head, acknowledging my softening. The waitress has returned with our drinks, her smile in no way dimmed. Surely her cheeks must hurt?

"There is one thing I wanted to tell you before it becomes common knowledge," Gordon says as he stirs milk into his coffee.

"Yes?"

"Caro has been suspended from Haft & Weil."

My eyes fly to his face. He smiles a little ruefully at my shock. "Why?" I ask warily when he doesn't add anything further.

He sips his coffee. "As I already mentioned, the police played me the tape. A

French detective, it was; very bright chap, I thought." I mentally cheer Modan as he shrugs. "Our firm can't afford to ignore allegations of impropriety around the partnership process. I would have done the same with any employee, and Caro cannot be treated any differently."

"You took it to the operating committee?" I must be round-eyed in shock.

"Yes. I was duty bound to." This is arguably true, but still . . . his own daughter. I'm trying to wrap my head around the fact that he reported allegations against his own daughter to the operating committee of the firm. The integrity of that action is staggering. "Therefore we have been further investigating Darren Lucas's case, and he has been entirely exonerated."

"And Caro?"

"The evidence seems to be stacking up against her. She's suspended pending the final results of the investigation." He pauses, then says delicately, "She claims the evidence is fabricated. So I suppose I will find out the answer to your question in time." I can't help it; I start to laugh. After a beat he joins in with a half-hearted chuckle or two. So my most fervent wish is to be granted: Caro will not now be a partner at Haft & Weil, or any other legal firm for that matter.

I can't imagine how she will reconcile herself to that: for the first time in her life, there is a boundary she cannot bend or cross. And then it also occurs to me that a disgraced, struck-off lawyer is much less likely to be believed when attempting to spread scurrilous rumors . . . I try to imagine Caro in disgrace, stripped of her stellar career, robbed of her brittle artifice, and disturbingly find myself imagining a defenseless baby bird.

"It's not actually in the least bit funny," Gordon says sadly when the black humor has subsided.

"Yes," I say, soberly, both Severine and the baby bird image still stuck in my mind. "I know."

We are lying, Tom and I, propped on our sides in the darkness of Tom's bedroom; he has blackout blinds, a concept he liked in Boston and brought back to London, and the darkness is a complete absence of light. It's a comfort to me now; I think of it like a physical place — a retreat we like to run to where we are safely cocooned and can just be. Tom's hand is idly running up and down the length of my arm from shoulder to elbow. The promise that always lurked in his hugs is borne out in the bedroom: he

touches with just the *right* amount of pressure, firm and deliberate but never too much. He makes me giddy and he makes me safe.

I know I have to tell him; I can't think of a way to do it except to just do it.

"I see Severine," I blurt out. Tom's hand halts, a short hitch, then continues on its route, at a slower pace. "I mean, obviously I don't really *see* her; this isn't *The Sixth Sense* . . . But I see her. Ever since you told me they found her in the well. It used to be her bones sometimes, her skull . . . but now it's mostly her. She went away, for a bit, after I hit my head, but she's back again." Tom doesn't say anything. "Do you . . . do you think I'm crazy?"

"Kind of," he says, but I can hear the smile in his voice.

"I take it you don't see Theo then."

"No." He's quiet for a moment, his hand arrested in its trail; my skin misses it, the bones within miss it. "It's more like . . . sometimes I see his absence. Once I notice it, it's hard to get past it: a space where he should be." I can hear rather than see a wry smile on his face. "Maybe I don't have your imagination to fill the gap."

I think about that as we lie there, the darkness folding around us, holding us safe. Am

I filling the gap? Though Severine was never a part of my world, or my friendships. It doesn't seem to quite fit, as an explanation, but perhaps there's something to it.

"Does she talk?" asks Tom suddenly.

"No." Except perhaps for one vital occasion. "Silently enigmatic."

He laughs softly. "I imagine she would have liked that description. Sounds like you've re-created her perfectly." His hand takes up its trail again. "It's strange, though. I mean, it's not like you two were friends or anything —"

"Hardly."

"— so it's strange your mind should fix on her, of all people."

"I'm sure a shrink would have a field day with it all." I say it with a small laugh, but I'm really waiting for his response. This, after all, is the crux of this conversation.

He hesitates, unusually awkward for Tom, feeling his way. "Do you *want* to speak to someone about it?"

I hadn't imagined that question. I consider it. "Not really. It's not normal, exactly, but it's not a problem, either. I've become . . . accustomed to it." I've become accustomed to her, I should say. I like to think she has become accustomed to me also.

Tom falls silent, thinking. The trail is mov-

ing up and down along my hip now, from just under my breast sweeping over the swell of my hip bone and along the line of my thigh. "Then I don't see a problem." I smile to myself. Bless him for his pragmatism. "Is she here now?"

"No," I say, though in truth it's too dark to tell.

"Good." He starts to follow his trailing hand with his lips. "I'd rather not have an audience . . ."

And so the lovely ribbon of time keeps slipping through my fingers.

We see Lara and Alain, we see Seb and Alina; as a group we don't talk of the week in France and we don't talk of Caro. For a while it's an awkward subject we're all avoiding, a stain across our memories that we slide our eyes away from — we were all guilty of suspecting one another; we are all tarred — but life moves on, and in time we have so much else to talk about; and after all, no one sees Caro. I see Severine, but I know I'm the only one. From time to time I notice that Tom doesn't see Theo.

Tom and I talk about France; we talk about Severine. We both dread the day someone across the Channel takes it in their mind to trawl through cold cases and

decides to reopen this one. I know there will never be enough evidence to convict Caro, so all that can happen is months of distress and no satisfactory outcome. Not that this current outcome is satisfactory, though it *is* an outcome — ultimately Darren Lucas went to the police and Caro was prosecuted for fraud, though her sentence was suspended. It's hardly a murder conviction or even an attempted murder conviction, but she can never practice law again, she can never be a partner at her father's firm and Seb has cut her off completely. A messy, oblique sort of justice, if it's justice at all, though I think for her it's somehow fitting. I don't know what she is doing now, or where she is doing it. I don't think of the baby bird.

And then one day I do see Caro, in an airport lounge. I'm hunched over my phone in an armchair, trying to connect to the airport Wi-Fi, and she sits next to me. "Hello, Kate," she says; my head lifts, and there she is.

"Caro." I'm completely floored; her name slips out before I can stop myself from saying anything at all. She's dressed in casual clothes, jeans and a blazer, typically stylish. She looks older, of course, and just as thin. Her hair is a brighter color than I remember.

"I'm sure you don't want to talk to me
—" she begins. High color is climbing her
cheeks.

"I don't. Leave."

"I just —" But I've grabbed my bag and
I'm out of the armchair before the rest of
her sentence can reach me. I cannot allow
myself to expend one iota more of mental
energy on Caro. I don't even tell Tom I saw
her; I refuse to waste the seconds it would
take. I never see Caro again.

Severine, though, I do see. If I'd ever
entertained the notion that once the case
was "solved" she would depart — turn and
walk happily (not happily, exactly, not Severine, but at least not reluctantly) into a
bright light, perhaps, or evaporate slowly
like an early-morning mist that fades with
the rising of the sun — well, if I'd ever
expected that, it's not to be. Severine still
hovers.

Perhaps, one might say, not as much as
before. It's instructive to note what piques
her interest. On the whole, family life seems
to bore her; she was nowhere to be seen for
the birth of our children. She's much more
likely to make an appearance in my workplace, or any kind of event I'm dreading:
the parents' socials at the twins' school, for
example. Tom reckons it's a reaction to

453

stress, to which I reply with a certain vehemence that the twins' birth was about as stressful as anything I can imagine, and where the hell was she then? He just shakes his head, amused, and says, "Not that sort of stress."

Tom is often amused now. Gently and also to the point of genuine laughter. We both laugh more; I can't remember a point in my life up until now when I have laughed this often. It's the twins, especially at the age they are now. They are literal, no room for grays; they don't understand irony or cynicism. They strip that away from us and instead extract an exaggerated politeness and a readiness to laugh; they make us into the people we want them to see — they make us kinder. More tired, certainly, but kinder.

Channing Associates makes me tired, too. We are seven now, with larger offices, and champagne glasses hidden in the back of one cupboard in case we have new contracts to toast. Paul is smugly satisfied that he stayed, but no less bipolar. Gordon Farrow has become the firm's informal mentor, and I meet him at least monthly for lunch or dinner, and often more. We don't talk of Caro. Sometimes I wonder if he is a father figure to me now, in which case am I a

daughter figure? Though I should know by now not to assume symmetry in relationships.

And so the lovely ribbon of time keeps slipping through my fingers, and through it all, a walnut brown girl with impossibly slender limbs saunters by, her dark, unreflective eyes taking everything in but revealing nothing. I never do see her smile.

ABOUT THE AUTHOR

Lexie Elliott grew up in Scotland, at the foot of the Highlands. She graduated from Oxford University, where she obtained a doctorate in theoretical physics. A keen sportswoman, she works in fund management in London, where she lives with her husband and two sons. The rest of her time is spent writing, or thinking about writing, and juggling family life and sport.

The employees of Thorndike Press hope you have enjoyed this Large Print book. All our Thorndike, Wheeler, and Kennebec Large Print titles are designed for easy reading, and all our books are made to last. Other Thorndike Press Large Print books are available at your library, through selected bookstores, or directly from us.

For information about titles, please call:
(800) 223-1244

or visit our website at:
gale.com/thorndike

To share your comments, please write:
Publisher
Thorndike Press
10 Water St., Suite 310
Waterville, ME 04901

and their connections across the brain. For each of these components of anxiety (breathing rate, risk avoidance, and that unpleasant internal feeling), different axonal threads that could be responsible were discovered, and accessed, and controlled independently with optogenetics. Here is how it was done.

Imagine a spot deep in the brain, a single anchor point, with many threads radiating out as if from one beam of a loom to another, each stretched to connect with a different target location across the brain. This is not unlike how outgoing neural connections (in the form of axons) venture forth from a single anxiety-control region, a deep brain structure called the amygdala—even more precisely, from an extension of the amygdala called the bed nucleus of the stria terminalis, or BNST.

These threads stretch, and dive, and go deep to find the cells needed to make all the parts of anxiety. One even goes to the pons, to the spot of Andi's shadow.

Amid all the interwoven intricacy of the brain, how can we know this—that these threads in particular actually matter? Here is where we can introduce the genes from microbes, to provide a new logic to each thread. Into quiet darkness under the skull, we deliver a new code of conduct from a foreign being. We teach one connection, and then another, and then another, to respond to light.

We borrow a lone microbial gene from single-celled green algae; this gene is just DNA instructions for making a light-activated protein, called a channelrhodopsin, that lets positively-charged ions into cells (which is an activating stimulus for neurons, making them fire away, and broadcast their signals). We deliver this gene into the mouse BNST, smuggling it in via a virus that we have chosen for its aptitude at bringing DNA into mammalian neurons. The cells in the BNST, having thus unwittingly received the algal gene, begin to produce the algal channelrhodopsin protein as instructed—duly following the DNA blueprint, the assembly manual written in the universal genetic script of life on earth.

At this point, if illuminated with bright blue light, each of these BNST cells would fire action potentials, the spiky signals of neuronal electrical activity (and the light would be easy enough to provide, with a nearly hair-thin fiberoptic placed just right so that laser light sent through the fiber would shine forth into the BNST). This would be a totally new capability, a new language taught to animals by the algae, with our help. But in these anxiety experiments, we actually don't bring in the light just yet. We wait, and an even richer language emerges.

Over several weeks, the channelrhodopsin protein (which we have linked to a yellow fluorescent protein, so we can see where it is produced and track its location) fills up not only the cells in the BNST but also their threads as well, the axons, which after all form part of each cell. Every neuron in the BNST is built with its own outgoing axonal connection, and different cells send their threads to different parts of the brain. After several weeks, radiating out from the BNST like rays of the sun, yellow streaks of the channelrhodopsin-linked fluorescent protein extend across the dark secret interior to all of the brain regions that the BNST speaks to, that need to hear a message from this anxiety center.

Now the new capability becomes clear. A fiberoptic can be placed not in the BNST but in an outlying region—indeed, in each of the different regional targets of the BNST across the brain. Laser light sent through such a fiberoptic can then do something quite special. The only light-sensitive part of each target region, upon which a yellow thread lands—for example, the pons—is the set of axons from the BNST to that region. And thus light delivered (to the pons, in this case, that deep and dark pedestal of the brain stem) activates directly only one kind of cell in the brain—the kind that lives in the BNST and sends axonal connections to the pons. A single kind of thread in the tapestry, defined by anchor and target, picked out from all the interwoven fibers, is now directly controllable by light.

When this is done in mice, a connection from the BNST to the pons—home of Andi's abducens and also home to a subregion called the parabrachial nucleus, which is involved in breathing—was discovered to control respiratory rate changes when activated, but had no other effects that we could see. Stimulating this pathway optogenetically affected breathing rate as seen with changes in anxiety, but interestingly had no effect at all on the other features of anxiety—the mice showed no change in risk avoidance, for example.

Instead, risk avoidance was controlled by a different thread—the connection from the BNST to another structure called the lateral hypothalamus (not nearly so deep as the pons). Activating the cells of this pathway, using optogenetics, changed how much a mouse would avoid exposed areas of an environment (the middle of an open area—the most risky place to be, if one is a mouse and vulnerable to predators), without changing anything else (for example, no change in respiratory rate could be seen). Thus a second feature of anxiety was picked out cleanly, defined by another cell type, and we begin to see that different parts of inner states are mapped onto different physical connections.

What about that third feature of the anxiety state, feeling bad? We call this *negative valence*—and its opposite is *positive valence* (a good feeling, like that of sudden release from anxiety, which feels to be much more than just absence of negativity). At first glance, this aspect seems hard to assess, especially in a mouse that cannot use words—and perhaps it would be difficult also in people, where even words are imprecise and not fully trustworthy. But still such an internal state—however subjective, however experienced by a mouse—can have external measurables.

In an experimental test called *place preference*, an animal is free to explore two similar connected chambers—just as if a human being had free rein to explore a suite of two identical rooms in a new house. If the person in such a situation were caused to feel acute and intense positivity inside (like that inner rush of a wild kiss returned, somehow feeling this without the kiss itself) immediately with every chance entry into one of the rooms, which terminated immediately upon each exit from that room, imagine how quickly that person would simply choose to spend every possible moment in one room. A single measurable—choice of the room with that feeling—reports to an observer on the hidden internal state. The observer cannot conclude precisely how it feels, of course, only that it is of positive valence—and a panel of additional tests can confirm that interpretation. Negative valence is tractable too. If the caused feeling is in that direction instead (inner negativity, perhaps in the same sense as the sudden crushing loss of a family member), then avoidance, instead of preference, becomes the measurable.

Valence can in this way be explored in animals, where optogenetics provides a means to instantaneously test the impact of activity in specific cells and connections across the brain. In the mouse version of place preference, the animal is given free rein to explore two similar chambers of an arena — first without optogenetic input. Then, a laser is brought to bear, set up so that light is delivered through a thin fiber-optic to the brain automatically, but only when the mouse happens to be in one of the two equivalent chambers (say the left-hand one). If there is an aversive, or negative, quality to activity of the particular optogenetic target of the moment (the specific neuronal thread that had been made light-sensitive in that animal), the mouse rapidly begins to avoid the left-hand chamber. The mouse, it seems, does not want to spend time in places associated with negative experiences — nor would we. Conversely, if there is a positive internal association, the mouse will spend more of its time in the chamber linked to light — revealing place preference.

Which thread deep in the brain, winding its way out from the BNST, governs this important feature related to anxiety — that of positive or negative valence, perhaps corresponding to the subjective feeling of our own internal state? Surprisingly, neither of the two other connections mentioned so far, to pons or to lateral hypothalamus, governs this behavior from the BNST. Instead, this job is handled by yet a third projection, from the BNST to another spot that lies deep, almost to the pons but not quite — the ventral tegmental area, or VTA, where neurons live that release a small chemical neurotransmitter called dopamine. This group of cells encompasses its own diversity of roles and actions, but overall is intimately linked to reward and motivation.

Activity along the other two projections, to pons and lateral hypothalamus, does not seem to matter at all to the mice — with stimulation affecting breathing and risk avoidance but not positive or negative associations, at least as far as the place-preference test is able to report. Even more strikingly, the third thread, to VTA, does its job of place preference in mice (and could therefore implement subjectivity in people) without affecting, in turn, the other features—breathing rate and risk avoidance. Thus a complex inner state can be deconstructed into independent features that are accessed by separate physical connections (bundles of threads defined by origin and target) projecting across the brain.

Not limited to the study of anxiety, this same approach turned out later to be applicable to mammalian behaviors in general. Even the complex process of parenting, in the form of intimate care of mammals for their young, was soon deconstructed into component parts, mapped onto projections across the brain. This discovery came from another group of researchers five years later, using the same optogenetic toolkit and projection-targeting approach. Many mysteries remained for anxiety, of course. For example, this deconstruction of the anxious inner state does not answer (though it strongly frames) a timeless puzzle— the questionable value of having positivity or negativity of internal states at all. The clean separability of place preference from risk avoidance highlights a deceptively simple question: why must a state feel bad (or good)? If behavior is already tuned and controlled appropriately for survival—if risk is already avoided, as dictated by the projection to the lateral hypothalamus—what is the point of the preference, or subjective feeling, provided by the connection to the VTA?

We think that evolution by natural selection works with actions taken in the world—that what is actually done, rather than felt, by an animal affects its survival or reproduction—and so perhaps how the animal feels inside, or how we feel inside, should not matter if action is already addressed. If the mouse is already avoiding the risky open space, as it should for survival and as governed by the BNST-to-lateral-hypothalamus thread, with no positive or negative association at all, then what is the purpose of the separate VTA thread and its associations? Feeling bad seems gratuitous—and more than that, a vast and unnecessary source of suffering. Much of the clinical disability in psychiatry, after all, arises from the subjective negativity of states like anxiety and depression.

One reason may be that life requires making choices between ut-

terly distinct categories that cannot be compared directly. Subjectivity—
feeling good or bad, for example—may be a sort of universal monetary
instrument for the inner economy of the brain, allowing positivity or
negativity from diverse pursuits, from food to sleep to sex to life itself,
to be converted into a single common currency. This arrangement
would allow difficult category-crossing decisions to be made and actions chosen—quickly and in a way best suited to the survival needs of
the particular animal and its species. Otherwise, in a complex and fast-
paced world, wrong calls will be made: freeze when a turn is called for;
turn when a stop is needed.

Perhaps these conversion factors are something that the evolution
of behavior works upon. Relative value (in the common currency of
subjectivity) assigned by the brain to different states will inevitably determine consequential—indeed existential—decisions made by the
organism or the human being. But these currency conversions also
must be flexible, needing to shift over life and over evolution, as values
change—and this flexibility could take physical form, such as changes
in the strength of threads connecting to valence-related regions like
the VTA.

The insight that the optogenetic study of anxiety brought me was
that subjective value (positive or negative) and external measurables
(breathing—or perhaps crying) could be added to or subtracted from
brain states with eerie precision. But this understanding came years
later for me, well after Mateo had entered and left my life. At that time
in the emergency room, I had no way of knowing that separability of
one element of an inner state could be so precise, nor that this could
happen as a result of the physical form taken by that element (involving electrical activity traveling along a connection from one part of the
brain to another). Seeing Mateo, I had no framework to understand
how he could be unable to cry, as he normally would—while lacking
none of the other human elements of profound grief.

•

Still today, deep mysteries of our inner states remain outside the reach
of science. It can seem in poor taste to study love, or consciousness, or

crying. With good reason—if no objective and quantitative tool (like paleogenetics for insight into Neanderthal prehistory, or optogenetics for discovering principles of brain function) yet exists, answers may lie beyond our grasp.

In the case of crying, a biologist should presume that if fluid is ejected from a duct like those connected to our tear glands—with precise timing, and in consistent contexts, for individuals of the species—there is likely an evolutionary reason, and the matter is suitably objective for science. If changes in duct performance come along with a strong feeling, a subjective internal state, then the combination of subjective and objective should intrigue a scientist, a psychiatrist, or any student of the human mind and body.

Crying is significant in psychiatry. Our patients are experiencing extreme emotions, and we work with these emotions—with their articulation, recognition, and expression. We are experienced in seeing the less genuine tears as well, across a spectrum of deception from the mildly suffering and modestly manufactured, to fully professional manipulative tears. Yet little is known in the science of emotional tears, such as it is.

Emotional crying cannot be studied well in animals. Pure emotional tears, as we experience the phenomenon, are not clearly present elsewhere even among our close relatives in the great ape family; the reason, if any, is a mystery. Tears are powerful for driving emotional connection; it is known that digitally altering tears in human face images will cause significant changes in the sympathy, and the impulse to help, elicited in viewers (much more than for altering other facial features). But we are no more social than our cousins—the chimpanzees, the bonobos—and still, using the mystery of tears, we alone cry, and cry alone.

We display our inner state with this odd external signal, with or without audience, not requiring volition or intent, just broadcasting feeling to all observers and ourselves. But it is not only our great ape kin who seem excluded—even many of our own *Homo sapiens* do not shed tears emotionally, and so dwell just a bit apart. This separation may be one-way—those whose bodies do not generate the language still can understand and respond to emotional tears in others—but missing even this one part of the conversation may come at a cost; non-crying people have been found to show reduced personal attachment patterns, though it's not known if this association is more due to life experience or innate predilection.

The fact that this involuntary signal of emotional tears is absent from some human beings and from our close nonhuman relatives may be a sign of an incompletely established evolutionary innovation— perhaps because its value is not universal even today, or because it was a recent experiment: an accident still in the process of manifesting fully in the human family, or failing to do so. Every innovation in evolution is accidental at first; perhaps emotional crying came about initially as a chance rewiring of axons. Like the various projections from the BNST, all axons are guided during brain development to grow in specific directions by a vast diversity of path-setting molecules as strong as thread guides on a loom—tiny signposts that send a slowly growing bundle of axons on to the next brain region, or turn it back if it has come too far, or send it across the midline to the other side of the body. All of this, like everything in biology, was built by chance mutation over millions of years and so can find its way to new functionality by chance mutation as well.

A mutation at any of these steps—in any gene guiding the positioning of path-setting molecules, and so redirecting those long-range threads, the axons, across the brain—would be all it would take. Fibers coming from the emotional areas of the brain would change course slightly, and then there would be born into the world a new kind of human being, with a new way of expressing feeling.

Such innovations would have the potential to open up a separate channel of communication—with remarkable efficiency, considering that the actual biological changes needed to implement this innovation would be very small: one set of axons missing one guidepost and traveling just a bit too far during development. As almost always is the case in evolution, the key players would have been already present, just needing to be taught a new rule, and so create a new role. In this case, the relevant axons—such as those already traveling from forebrain areas like the BNST to deeper and ancient brainstem areas like the parabrachial nucleus for breathing changes—would have been just partially rerouted to a new destination.

Near the parabrachial nucleus lie the origins of two cranial nerves—not only the sixth, named abducens, the one Andi's cancer disrupted, but also its neighbor the seventh, called the facial nerve. All of these structures, just collections of cells, sixth and seventh and parabrachial, jostle together in a small spot in the pons, huddled on the bridge from brain to spinal cord. But the new target here, for tears, would be the seventh-nerve cells. For emotional expression, the seventh is a maestro in itself, much more intricate and multipurpose than abducens, sending and receiving rich information streams to and from many muscles in the face and many sensors in the skin. The seventh, the facial nerve, is grandmaster of facial expressions but also of the lacrimal gland, the storehouse of tears.

The lacrimal system likely evolved for flushing irritants from the eye, washing away particulate nuisances. Now, with almost trivial rewiring, it could be involuntarily recruited by a flood of emotion, perhaps alongside other fibers reaching to the breathing centers—the parabrachial and beyond—wrenching from within us the cathartic, diaphragmatic contraction of the sob. When the first human being who had this mutation cried, and perhaps even sobbed, what might have been the effect on those nearby—friends or family or competitors—who had never seen this before? Communication through the eyes would have long been important, always a focus of attention for human beings—eyes are rich in information and constantly accessed—so the innovation would have landed fortuitously in real estate of high value for sending signals. But there might have been at that moment no understanding, and no emotional response, to the tears—just attention and interest to the unusual and salient signal. Full meaning and value, for survival or reproduction, may have taken generations to evolve.

If there is evolutionary significance of crying at all, then the times when emotional crying occurs may provide clues. Largely not voluntary in humans—this is a signal far less under our conscious control than, for example, smiling or grimacing—crying is a mostly honest journalist, reporting for some reason on a kind of feeling. Scholars have focused on its value for social communication, but emotional crying also happens, and feels important—even productive, addressing some need—when we are alone.

Given all the risks of revealing true feelings (and all the individual benefits of successfully conveying false feelings, for beings in complex social environments), the poor controllability of this emotional readout seems at first a handicap rather than an advantage—something to be selected against, rather than selected for, at the level of the individual. Signaling to self, or to others—either way, it is interesting that this signal has remained mostly involuntary, and thus mostly true.

Is crying still evolving, under selection pressure, to either escape or come under our volition? We might eventually control crying as easily as smiling, unless its involuntary nature is more useful than individual advantages that would come from voluntary control. And right now this truth-signaling property is known broadly to the species in some sense, programmed in human observers to be of greater impact than more easily gamed facial expressions like smiling—thus heightening its effect on others, perhaps drawing fellow human beings closer for bonding and support, perhaps in times of true and desperate need.

In that case, a sort of joint evolution of two feeling-related behaviors—crying and the response to crying—may be occurring across members of our species. This would be a code, an internal language of shared importance to both the individual and the group, but still gameable like anything in biology. Deception is always lucrative up to a point, but if the deception is rare enough, the whole program of crying and responding could retain value as a truth channel.

For our species, as well as for individuals, such a channel could have been favorable once we became complex socially cognitive beings, capable of deception and denial and with strong voluntary control over our expressions—since if all emotional readouts can be gamed, then all mean little, and social communication loses a great deal of value. Thus an arms race between truth and deception ensues: pausing when cognitive control (benefiting the individual who can achieve this control) is finally attained over the new signal (which then loses its truth property of some value to the species), and restarting a million years later when a misguided axon pathway blunders unexpectedly into a new patch of cells in the brain, perhaps those governing surface physiology of the skin—resulting in blushing, crying, and whatever comes next.

Since emotional crying is evenly distributed across humanity, we can be certain we did not acquire this trait from Neanderthals, who lent their genomes chiefly to the Eurasian lineages. It is not known whether Neanderthals shared this trait as well—most likely they would have, if crying capability had emerged in a common ancestor that every human being shares with them. The Neanderthals had stable social communities, preserved their cultural traditions, took the time to paint symbolic art even as they were dying out, and buried their lovely children. In my imagination at least, they shed tears like ours, until the end.

•

Mateo was not suicidal, but could be diagnosed with major depression. I attached the label to him that night. Though it seemed an oversimplification, among other defining symptoms of depression he had a prominent hopelessness, expressed as an inability to look forward in time. Without hope for the future, Mateo could only look back.

He never did cry for his family that night—not that I saw, nor that he could ever tell me. In considering this, and the reasons we have for crying, it seemed to me that an odd unity links tears of sadness, when they happen, and the more mysterious tears of joy. Tears come when we feel hope and frailty together, as one. I managed to keep myself from writing this in the chart—or writing that Mateo had no hope left to cry for.

Mild improvements in material outcome that do not require a new model of self and circumstance—as with just making a bit more money in accord with known probabilities of the world—will not cause most people to cry. But when we do cry for joy—as when we feel the sudden warmth and hope of human connection at a wedding, or when we see an unexpected depth of empathy in a young child—there may be a flicker of hope for the future of the community, for humanity, against the cold. We can cry at a wedding or a birth, seeing heartfelt aspiration but knowing deeply the fragility of life and love: I hope that the joy I see here will never die, I hope that the world will be kind enough to let this last forever, I hope that these feelings will survive—but I know very well they may not.

This seems to be a kind of anxiety, even for what we think of as tears of joy, since a threat—though not immediately present—is known, and felt.

At the other, truly negative, pole of value, tears of sadness in adult human beings similarly come not with mild losses from known risks but with sudden adverse personal realizations that must be addressed—like a shock of betrayal when the hope we had for the future is shaken and our model of the world, our map of possible paths in life (a map *is* hope), must be redrawn. When we cry, even when the feeling is negative, hope may be present—with new conditions, but it is hope nonetheless. Then we truthfully, involuntarily, signal this fragility of our future, and the fact that our model is changing, at the moment of realization—we signal this to our species, our community, our family, and ourselves.

Does evolution really care about hope? As abstract as it seems, hope is a commodity that must be regulated in careful ways by living beings—metered out in quantities only enough to motivate reasonable actions. Hope when unreasonable can be harmful, even deadly. Every organism must ask in its own way: when to struggle on, and when to save energy and reduce risk by waiting out the storm? Rage or rest, fight or hibernate, cry or not—all life needs to make such choices, to compute the harshness of the present world—and if the challenge cannot be overcome, to withdraw from the fray. The circuitry of hope control needs to work, and work well. With the high heat of our primate lifestyle—a quarter of our calories are burned by the brain alone—the ancient circuitry of withdrawing from actions may extend in our lineage to the giving up of hope itself, of a sometimes costly conceit occupying our brains rather than our muscles.

Ancient and conserved circuits were already available to help our evolution build this capability—even cold-blooded fish can make the choice to meet adversity with passivity rather than with action. In 2019 cells were studied across the entire brain of the tiny zebrafish (related to us as a fellow vertebrate, with a backbone and much the same basic brain plan, but small enough and transparent enough to let us see all the way through, using light to access most of its cells during behavior). Two deep structures in the fish brain, called the habenula and the raphé, were observed to work together in guiding this transition from active to passive coping with a challenge (the passive coping state is where the fish will no longer try to expend effort to meet a challenge).

Neuronal activity in the habenula (provided by optogenetics) was discovered to favor passive coping (essentially not moving during a challenge); in contrast, activity in the raphé (source of most of the neurochemical called serotonin in the brain) favored active coping (vigorous engagement with the problem). By optogenetically stimulating or inhibiting the habenula, it was possible to instantaneously turn down or up the simple likelihood of the fish expending energy to meet a challenge—and when the raphé was optogenetically controlled instead, the coping effects observed were opposite to those seen with habenula manipulation.

Years earlier, optogenetics and other methods had implicated these same two structures in mammals, in the same basic kind of behavioral state transitions, and with the same directionality of effect in each structure. Now seeing these results emerging in the distantly related zebrafish, it could be said with confidence that the biological foundation of suppressing action, when good outcomes are nearly impossible, is ancient, and conserved, and powerful—and thus likely to be important for survival.

Any small animal can find a crevice or a burrow and stop moving to cope passively with adversity. Even the tiny nematode worm *Caenorhabditis elegans* appears to calculate the relative value of actively foraging or remaining in place, with the full power of its 302 neurons. But larger brains contemplate many more possible actions and outcomes, ruminating and worrying, mapping out decision trees thickly ramified with possibilities projecting far into the future. A passivity of thought is also needed, perhaps—a deep discounting of the value of one's actions, and also of one's own thoughts. Hope draws resources from our attentional and emotional budgets, and perhaps it is best to save the striving and the struggle, and to spare the trouble of tears when hope is gone.

•

That night in the ER, I had a hard time figuring out how to help Mateo. The hospital was busy, and there was no room available for him. As he was not suicidal and did not want to be in the hospital, I could not easily admit him to our locked ward, but our open ward was full. There were transfer possibilities to other hospitals, though after talking it all over with Mateo and his brothers, we ended up sending him home with them—and with an appointment for outpatient care, therapy, and medication—but not before I took the time to carry out an hour of predawn psychotherapy with him, right there in the ER, laying groundwork.

When we can, we often steal the time to do this in psychiatry, almost instinctively, even during the besieged rush of an on-call shift, even in cramped and awkward confines like Room Eight that night. It can be hard to hold us back, as hard as it is to hold back surgeons from cutting to heal; we all live, and move, in the crafts we have built for ourselves.

Without the right foundation, nothing works in psychiatry. Without structural threads to weave upon, there is no new pattern that can be created. As psychiatrists, our first instinct is to start to link together what recovery will mean for that person—the intertwined threads of the biological, the social, and the psychological—not in a rush, but in awareness of the time that will be needed to construct something strong and stable. We do this even if we may never see the patient again, as I suspected that night; I was discharging Mateo to the care of his family, and to outpatient treatment. I would continue rotating on through the hospital, in my own ecliptic path, while Mateo would follow his arc in the universe; in all likelihood our paths would never intersect again.

But the amount of time I was taking was extreme, I realized after nearly an hour had elapsed. It was not until the call shift ended, and I was driving home with tears leaking from my eyes, diffracting the traffic lights, that I saw a larger picture—and saw that it was also about another human being, another patient.

I took so long with Mateo that night because I had been unready for him, for that particular hell, as I had been only once before—and so the therapy was for myself as well, for my own tears that were coming. A connection across time had been formed in my mind. It was only with those tears that I saw the link with Andi, who had brought me to the same place and for whom I had been just as unready. Andi, the little girl from years ago with the brainstem finding—long gone, on a journey none could share.

This time, I had thought I could do something—not much, but something. And that matters—realizing at a place and moment you have been called to be whatever it is that humanity can be for a person. That is not nothing.

·

Years later, following our optogenetics and BNST anxiety work, an even deeper connection between Andi and Mateo revealed itself. There was a curious commonality to these patients, who represented the two lowest moments that medicine had brought me to, from which I had to work hardest to emerge. What had actually brought each of them to the hospital the night I was on service had been fibers failing in virtually the same deep spot of the nervous system. This spot was the base and bedrock of the brain, in the pons, where eye movements and tears and breathing are controlled, and where next-door neighbors in my patients were disrupted—the fine chords, the sixth and seventh, of lost harmony.

But the significance of this, if any, I cannot define. I know only that the site is deep, and old.

The naturalist Loren Eiseley wrote that a symbol "once defined, ceases to satisfy the human need for symbols." Eiseley collected observations from the natural world and recorded the ideas stirred in him by these images as symbols—like a spider out of season, surviving in the dead of winter, having built a web by an artificial source of heat, the globe of an outside lamp. He was moved by this image, despite his near certainty that "her adventure against the great blind forces of winter, her seizure of this warming globe of light, would come to nothing and was hopeless. . . . Here was something that ought to be passed on to those who will fight our final freezing battle with the void . . . *in the days of the frost seek a minor sun.*" Hope, represented by complex life fighting on in the face of inescapable cold, moved Eiseley, and moves scientists and artists similarly. It is close to the heart of what moves us to tears.

For Mateo, there was no hope left to cry for, now that his wife and baby were gone. His lack of tears was also his blindness of the future. But, in some form, I knew, or thought I knew, that he could love again, in time. Hope was not dead, though he could not see this, and so the tears came for me, and not Mateo.

The true end of hope shows up only as extinction, when the last member of a sentient species eases to the mud alone. In the history of our lineage, this finality would have become real many times over, in the fine lost branches of our greater family tree. The Neanderthals and others, in the last traces of their last days, lived out that tragedy for which all else is metaphor.

Extinction is normal. Each mammalian species, on average, gets a run of about a million years, it seems—with a few close calls thrown in the mix until it finally happens. So far, modern humans have lasted only about one-fifth of this interval—but already we have survived some mysterious crises that can be inferred from human genomes, when effective breeding population sizes around the world may have plummeted to a few thousand individuals.

Such demographic events alone could help explain the prevalence of odd traits with little obvious value—behaviors somewhat unrefined, having found (like crying) incomplete purchase in the population due to only a mild benefit. When a species goes through a population-size bottleneck—where only a small fraction survives or migrates—whatever traits were present in the chance survivors (or migrants) then for some time enjoy outsize prevalence, whether or not the traits were unusually important to survival. This could be the case for crying emotional tears—and help explain the seeming uniqueness of such a trait, among animals.

On the other hand, perhaps we needed this truth channel more than other related species—in building ever larger and more complex social structures over time. Crying could have come along as first just a misrouted brainstem projection, but the responsible genetic variant might have found purchase in the mingling populations of East Africa as our modern lineage arose, when we used our fingers and brains to build one another houses, constructing durable communities at great cost. Perhaps tears were needed after we had grown too good at the last forgery, at gaming the last signal of grimacing or keening. Builders need solid ground; social builders need ground truth.

The last Neanderthal—a big-brained, bruising, nearly modern human, the last member of a branch of our family tree that buried the lost with ritual and care—died just an eyeblink ago, clinging until the end in caves near what would become the Gibraltar seashore, in final retreats hidden from, as Eiseley said, "the first bowmen, the great artists, the terrible creatures of his blood who were never still." They may have cried at weddings, at births—but when the last starving Neanderthal watched the last baby trying desperately to nurse, skin on skin but fluid failing in the ducts . . . there was no hope left for doubt, there was no future left to question, or to fear. There were no tears then, under the moon without answers—just a dry streambed, set back from a salt sea.

CHAPTER 2

FIRST BREAK

Horns of the long-lived stag began to sprout,
The neck stretched out, the ears were long and pointed,
The arms were legs, the hands were feet, the skin
A dappled hide, and the hunter's heart was fearful.
Away in flight he goes, and, going, marvels
At his own speed, and finally sees, reflected,
His features in a quiet pool. "Alas!"
He tries to say, but has no words. He groans,
The only speech he has, and the tears run down
Cheeks that are not his own. There is one thing only
Left him, his former mind. What should he do?
Where should he go—back to the royal palace
Or find some place of refuge in the forest?
Fear argues against one, and shame the other.

And while he hesitates; he sees his hounds,
Blackfoot, Trailchaser, Hungry, Hurricane,
Gazelle and Mountain-Ranger, Spot and Sylvan,
Swift Wingfoot, Glen, wolf-sired, and the bitch Harpy
With her two pups, half-grown, ranging beside her,
Tigress, another bitch, Hunter, and Lanky,
Chop-jaws, and Soot, and Wolf, with the white marking
On his black muzzle, Mountaineer, and Power,
The Killer, Whirlwind, Whitey, Blackskin, Grabber,
And others it would take too long to mention,
Arcadian hounds, and Cretan-bred, and Spartan.

The whole pack, with the lust of blood upon them,
Come baying over cliffs and crags and ledges
Where no trail runs: Actaeon, once pursuer
Over this very ground, is now pursued,
Fleeing his old companions. He would cry
"I am Actaeon: recognize your master!"

But the words fail, and nobody could hear him.

—From OVID, "The Story of Actaeon," *Metamorphoses*, Book III

An image can take root and grow. Here, it is of a young father with his two-year-old daughter in the 767, slowly banking harborward, nearing the burning steel tower—it's a frame of the moment when he at last knows the impossible truth, his pulse thudding thickly but she's calm amid the chaos, because Daddy said there were no monsters. He's turned his daughter's head firmly toward his own—she's a frail warm spot glowing within an infinitude of cold—for a moment of silent communion before their sublimation.

A little girl and her father, searching each other for grace as the plane roars into the second tower—this wordless image became physical, sown across the world into the arable mind of a man named Alexander, as he sailed through the Cyclades. Quickened, germinating, the imagined scene gathered form—investing all the soil of his thoughts, insatiably drawing to itself all the fluid of his soul.

•

The fundamental rules of Alexander's life had already been rewritten just before September came, and so it may be that his brain—fallow for decades—was ready when the outside world was transformed as well. In 2001, as the shortening days of late summer brought chilly afternoons and crimson leaves to the San Francisco peninsula, Alexander stepped down at sixty-seven from the insurance company where he had labored for decades—as a fairly effective underchief, but where he was no longer nimble enough for the shifting strata of Silicon Valley. His domain would now be at home only, among the coastal redwoods of Pacifica, in the high-raftered house he and his wife had built in a foggy ravine twenty years earlier—big enough for their three sons and perhaps some grandchildren. He was a stately man, slightly bent, in the growing calm.

No warning notes had sounded in his life, no explanatory story was found that his family could share, by the time I met them in the emergency room six weeks after September 11. By then, his whole world had been blasted apart—not by exploding jet fuel, but by ferocious, exuberant, unstoppable mania, bearing no resemblance to anything that had come before in their lives. It was first break—that moment when links to reality snap in response to a windstorm of stress, or to the scythe of trauma, or to other triggers unknown—and the human being first comes untethered. First break, when those with mania or schizophrenia are cut loose—at great peril—and sent aloft by their disease.

In September, when the storm tide began to rise, Alexander had been only marking retirement—sailing the Aegean with his wife, traveling in antiquity. Now less than two months later, back home, he was transformed, brought to my emergency room by police and family. What had been swept along by the hospital process and settled, what I saw first, had no visible flaw. Not knowing him, I saw only a crisply alert man scanning the newspaper with intensity, fiercely cross-legged next to his gurney.

The elusive, protean mystery of psychiatry came next—discovering what it was that had changed for this person, and why. No brain scans exist to guide diagnosis. We can use rating scales to quantify symptoms, but even those numbers are just words transformed. So we assemble words; this is what we have. Phrases are pulled together, and molded into a narrative.

The people involved talked, all of us—in different combinations: the patient, the police in the hall, the family in the waiting room—all searching for the right frame. For someone with no mania in his past or family: why him, why now? He had experienced the day itself, the strike to the heart of his country, no more intensely than any other person.

Even the pain he had felt, in empathy for the lost, by itself did not merit this extraordinary consequence. Death comes badly for conscious beings and always has. The unthinkable is universal, but mania is not common. Nevertheless it came for Alexander—after a delay.

For a week after September 11, Alexander was just a bit on the stoic side, only revoicing the common thoughts of shock and pain around him. He read stories of the victims, but then began to focus on two of them, a father and a daughter, a pairing he had not lived personally. A scene emerged and grew more detailed, and he spoke to his family of imagining their final moments—while inside his brain, a secret remapping had begun. In ways still mysterious, new synapses were formed, and older connections were pruned away. Electrical patterns shifted, as scripts were overwritten. For a week his biology silently learned its new tongue, and then it reached out, expressive at last.

The first manifestations were physical. He nearly stopped sleeping, becoming fully alert and charged with life for twenty-two hours a day. Never the chattiest before, Alexander now could not hold back a vast volume of words that came out in a pressured torrent—turbulent and interjaculating—yet still coherent, at first. The content of his speech changed too—he was saltier, charismatic, uplifting, and illuminating. Beyond language, his whole body was affected; now ablaze in new youth, he was suddenly voracious and hypersexual. No old bull out to pasture, he was an organic being newly ready to react, to interface—his skin surfaces were functionalized and available. Life was lacier, compelling, alluring.

Projects and goals came next. They were valorous and numerous, with a tinge of excitement, a subthrill of risk. He bought a new Dodge Ram pickup, with a heavy-duty trailer hitch and extended cab. He ran all night, read books all day, and studied theory of war, writing pages on the movements of forces and reserves. A theme of self-sacrifice appeared and grew stronger; he wrote letters volunteering to join the navy, and was found one evening rappelling down a redwood trunk in the fog, training for war. He was breaking from his lifelong chrysalis, transforming into a newly emerged monarch.

There had been a certain charm to the transition, up to a point, but then he veered into thoughts of good, evil, death, and redemption. He had dwelt until this event in a sort of unperforated Lutheranism, stormless and modestly nourishing—with minimal connectivity to any other part of this life. Now he began to speak with God—first calmly, then frantically, then in a scream. Between these prayers there were sermons for others, in which he became irritable—swinging between euphoria and crying.

Nearing midnight before admission, he ran from the house with his quail gun, throwing branches and bark at his sons as they tried to stop him in the yard. Police found him two hours later, at bay in a thicket near a dry streambed, ready to strafe the stinkweed. They took him and subdued him with the mundanities of medical-legal incantations, all the energy still brimming up behind his eyes like tears.

The fury had dimmed externally over the next several hours in the hospital. By the time I spoke with him, he had only a rhythmic motor pattern, like a caged pacing lion, except it was a vocalization, a refrain again and again: *I just don't understand.* With clarity, with surety in his own form and role, he could not understand his family's reaction—why his every action did not seem perfectly logical to them, an example which all should follow.

The fixity was striking, and pure. Alexander's first break had been a clean separation, without the messy compound breaks of psychosis or drugs. He was dislocated. Unchurched.

What next for the new warrior—dopamine-receptor antagonists perhaps? He did not want help, saw no need for our process, and refused treatment. In the closed system of his pressured logic, there was pure clarity, and explosive danger. An irresolute messenger, I wavered before him as he described the image that had grown in his mind, of the girl on the plane, with the father holding her head gently and firmly, locking eyes so she could see only him until the end.

Pictures came to me, intense associations. The unique abstraction of psychiatry—science with language, medicine with text, upon which the most effective care is built—allowed me to spend each day immersed in words and images, moving beyond story to allegory, even if doing so was futile—in dialogue with history, with neuroscience, with art, and with my own experience. Here the first story that came to me, provoked by his transformation, perhaps prompted by the image of Alexander sailing among the Greek isles, was Ovid's hunter Actaeon—son of a herdsman—who was turned into a stag as a punishment from the angry goddess Artemis, after he was caught spying upon her bathing in a stream. He had new strength, new speed, a new form—he was given strong horns and fleet hooves—but the timing was off, the context was all wrong. He had become a prey animal in the midst of his own hounds—Blackfoot, Trailchaser, Hungry, Hurricane—who tore him to pieces. Perhaps it was an Actaeon I saw before me, transformed by the moon goddess, with the police and me as Arcadian hounds, and

Cretan-bred, and Spartan—the whole pack, with the lust of blood upon us, baying over cliffs and crags and ledges where no trail runs.

But then . . . unlike the case with Actaeon, whose new form of a stag had no value, for Alexander there was a use, grim and suitable, for the new form he had been given. In this sacrifice, he was perhaps more of a Joan of Arc—like Alexander, born far from military life. In her case it was on a small farm in Lorraine where the mystery began to speak to her. Without trying to diagnose a historical figure—always tempting but usually unwise for psychiatrists—I could not help but imagine how her alteration happened to briefly work well for her. When she was only seventeen, as France began to fall before English armies, she emerged into a new way of being—not disorganized as in schizophrenia, but goal-directed, focused on continental politics and military strategy. She talked herself to the side of the Dauphin with a firm conviction that she was essential, and with a powerful religiosity that allowed her to infuse the fight with a spirit seen as divine—bearing banners not swords, living through maelstroms of crossbow bolts, advancing through her own blood to the coronation.

Alexander's transformation also arose in the pastoral quiet of a country in peril—an alteration created by that very peril—and his new form fit the crisis. Some details were imperfect—the tenor of current culture was mismatched for what he had become—and he was the wrong vessel, but then: was he any less-suited than a seventeen-year-old peasant with no training in tactics or politics? By the time she was captured by the English and burned at the stake, Joan had already saved her country and won the war. And here we were about to cure Alexander, to cauterize this illness, to burn away the spirit. A bumpkin psychiatrist, I stood ready, with my medieval tools.

And there, in that uncertain moment—the two of us caught in a tiny personal crosscurrent, lost in a vast global atmosphere that had been marred for months by burning flesh and the slipstreams of airborne predators—a thin and fragile tendril of memory, of my own story, swirled to the surface.

I was leaning against a chain-link fence, the perimeter for an outdoor platform of the T—Boston's subway. It was near midnight on a chilly October evening. Drained after a long day in the lab and a failed experiment, I was fatigued and irritated. The area was nearly deserted, except for two men talking calmly at the other end of the dimly lit platform. A pair of silhouettes, one tall, one short. For a minute of peace I closed my eyes and bowed my head as we waited together.

When my eyes opened to look for the train, I saw an eight-inch blade, silver and gold in the subway glow, fine at the tip, even tender as it nearly touched my shirt, nearly part of me. I saw only the beautiful blade, in incredible detail, and everything else was blacked out; I was swept in, there was nothing else in the world, and in that moment, I felt an awareness of all the events and interactions and steps with which the world had positioned me here, and seemed to understand that this fate had been prepared for me with care and affection. I had come to where I should be, and an odd peace, a grace, came over me.

I surrendered my backpack, waiting passively as it was emptied by the tall shadow, keeping my eyes focused firmly on the blade held by the other. My sweet misericord, the thin blade of mercy used in the aftermath of medieval battles, dispatching the dying at Orléans and Agincourt. The steel seemed to pulse in the surreal light of the subway platform, with every cell of my body locked into its rhythm.

The backpack contents were exposed—which I knew to be only a developmental biology journal and seventy-five cents for the subway fare—and the next memories are fragmented. A burst of angry words, the knife seemed to twitch with unclear intent, and then I was suddenly no longer passive. I remember sweeping my left arm up and out, creating a narrow space to break away to the right. In my next conscious memory I am blocks away, not knowing where, running alone through the star-cold night.

There followed in me a high energy over the next few weeks, a bubbling up inside of anger and euphoria, a feeling in my chest like a geyser preparing to erupt. Then the sensation eased to a week or two of light pressure; then everything was distilled down to a calm clarity—

and finally . . . nothing. It was gone, never to return—a minor deviation, a ride, a day trip, real but weak in me, never breaking through.

As I considered Alexander, it seemed his brain, unlike my own, must have been prepared—soil truly fallow, fertile and waiting for the seed. Yet even he might have escaped mania if not for September 11; mania comes at great cost, and his brain had set a high threshold, tuned to only respond this way to a seemingly existential threat to the group: his whole community appearing at risk, with invaders descending. His stolid odyssey of the useful and the good ended only with burning towers, and his transition when initiated was swift and sure, a second puberty, remapping him a final time. Steroid stress hormones coursed through his brain like juvenile hormone through a caterpillar, sweeping away the squirming and helpless peacetime stage, the old larval neurons killing themselves, involuting—ruthless, precise, meticulous. On into mania—wings for the mind. Metamorphosis.

Perhaps I lacked the genes, the temperament, the mental landscape to fully quicken. Or perhaps it was that my circumstances had been different from Alexander's; I had been alone, the assault had been directed only at me, not my community—and I could run, needing only two minutes of pitch-perfect adrenaline-related neurochemicals to meet the threat, just that elegantly tuned fight-or-flight response. A stable behavioral change, lasting weeks or months, would have made no sense. Mania, at least in those cases when symptoms and threat align (as they did for Alexander) would seem more of a durable and social fury, by some design or chance prolonged for defense of the community with goal-directed activity, but only if a new way of being were needed, an elevated state. Mood elevation has the capability to bring forth energy for social construction—for the time needed to build defensive earthworks under the rumor of war, to migrate the drought-stricken clan for weeks toward water without sleeping, to harvest all the winter wheat when the locusts hatch—and with all the rush of a positive charge, that rewarding feeling needed to upend preexisting priorities temporarily, to align a person's whole internal value system to meet the crisis.

But in our world, mania is fraught with danger: harmful to the patient and costly to the community; it is the exception rather than the rule for symptoms to even appear appropriate. Thwarted in the modern milieu by our intricate conventions and rigid rules, the incompletely hatched monarch is trapped in a cracked and hardened casing—with new wings caught, beginning to rip in the raging of the struggle to emerge.

As we talked, I could feel the room charged with this trapped energy. In his irritation and agitation, Alexander unknowingly was spawning imagined scenes of his life in my mind that took root as the airplane scene had for him, unspoken but oddly clear and detailed. I let the vision grow, and saw his own eyes opening in his living room, back home from his odyssey in October, to a castrated dog on the rug with its bloated belly irritatingly exposed, breathing stertorously out of step with the Pachelbel coming over the dusty stereo. The dog was Alexander of the last thirty years: weak, infertile, asynchronous. The need to leap up and strike out—to act—would have surged.

A hiking trip to a coastal estuary was proposed by his wife, to spend some quiet time among the elegance of the local herons, but what mattered to Alexander actually were the shrikes and butcher-birds of the desert, the Predators flying over Mazār-e Sharīf. Called to serve, Kandahar's time had come again—to march from Macedon to the east one more time. He would have felt a rising swirl of rage. No, it was of libido. His ducts would have felt filled with fluid, all of them, with the ductal smooth muscle tensing against what he had stored within for decades. Squeezing on what he had, what he had to give. Strong as jet fuel.

•

There had been no natural way of stopping the birth of this new being, any more than stopping childbirth, and mania can last for weeks or more on its own. But in the hospital, any parturition can be slowed or stopped, for a time. When Alexander demanded to leave the ER, triggering frantic pleas from his family, under my care his freedom was taken and civil rights temporarily stripped away. Thus roped to the mast, he received olanzapine—dopamine and serotonin modulation, to block mania's siren song—and within a week he was, as we say, normalizing.

But there was an unapplausive feel to the outcome; normalizing him was not a clear-cut win. The clinical team exchanged no pleased commentary on rounds. Instead there were only hesitant and fragmented conversations in the housestaff room on the meaning of mania, and on the ethics of intervention.

Mania cannot be trivialized or romanticized. As interesting as the state is—and as euphoric as the patients can be, at least briefly uplifting all around them with their contagious belief in what might be possible—mania is destructive. In the vulnerable, those predisposed to bipolar disorder, mania is often not threat-triggered at all, and does not even approach utility; rather, it is unpredictable and can be accompanied by psychosis, a breakdown in the process of thinking, the catastrophe of suicidal depression, and death.

Any value of mania today is inconsistent, but increased-energy states are consistent: a common heritage of humanity across cultures and continents. Not all of these states fit exactly into the same frame. Variants might include *amok* in Malaysia, a state of intense brooding followed by persecutory ideas and a frenzy of activity, or *bouffée délirante* in West Africa and Haiti, a state of sudden agitated behavior, excitement, and paranoia. Both of these, and mania itself which is seen around the world, may represent thin slices through a much broader and complex multidimensional structure, a cluster of possible behaviors, of altered states. Different cultures take their own cross sections to describe these states, each at a distinctive angle.

Human evolution clearly has not converged upon a single or ideal strategy for sustained mood elevation, if there can be one, and many different genes are linked to bipolar disorder. Telling the stories of past struggles in human evolution, our genomes are laden with other first-pass fixes that still need refinement. Across much of modern medicine outside of psychiatry, it has long been possible to ask, and even answer, why a genetic disease might be common. To explain the persistence of the blood disease sickle-cell anemia, for example, we can tell stories of our coexistence with the microbial parasite *Plasmodium malariae*, which evolved along with us, driving adaptation of our blood cells and immune systems in an agonizing call-and-response playing out over millions of years.

Sickle-cell disease and the related diseases called thalassemias (a classical name, for their Mediterranean distribution) are burdens borne by many modern human beings who share peri-equatorial genetic roots, where *Plasmodium* and its mosquito carrier thrive. The burden takes the form of mutations in hemoglobin, the protein in our red blood cells that delivers oxygen to mitochondria (like *Plasmodium* once immigrant microbes, our mitochondria are now fully symbiotic partners in our survival). *Plasmodium* lives in our red blood cells if it can get in, and these mutations in hemoglobin work against this ancient enemy, suppressing malaria as they block the spread of *Plasmodium* through the blood. The mutations also, however, bring the risk of misshapen red blood cells that cause disease symptoms: pain, infection, and stroke.

As in cystic fibrosis, the human carriers with one mutant gene usually have no symptoms, and it is only when two mutant genes come together that the sickle-cell disease state is created. But unlike those who carry a single cystic fibrosis gene (at least as far as we understand it today), sickle-cell carriers (the nondiseased, carriers of only one mutation) have a clear benefit, resisting malaria and thus revealing a harsh evolutionary bargain: a steep price is paid only by those with two copies of the mutation for a benefit enjoyed by others with one copy, who do not suffer. Thus these mutations are ragged measures, quick hacks, still jousting in the tortuously slow arena of natural selection.

The lesson of the sickle cell is that the disease, and the diseased, make sense together only in the broader frame of the human family and its evolution. Though it is not always easy for scientists to find these perspectives, the simple fact of achieving an explanation has been important, helping to liberate us from the grip of mysticism and blame. Psychiatry, however, has continued without such insight. More consequential than any other type of disease in terms of the immensity of death, disability, and suffering caused around the world, mental illnesses nevertheless have remained essentially unexplained in this way, and no definitive explanation is possible now.

Yet neuroscience has reached a tipping point. For the first time, scientific explanations for what these illnesses are, biologically, seem within reach — and as with sickle cell, as with all of human health and disease, the prevalence of mental illness should be informed by evolutionary considerations; as Theodosius Dobzhansky wrote in 1973, nothing in biology makes sense except in the light of evolution.

But thinking about survival and reproduction trade-offs can be misleading if the questions asked are naïve or incomplete. For example, the harm of psychiatric disease to patients seems clear, but who would be the recipient of the evolutionary benefit, if any, that allows these traits to persist? With the sickle-cell trait, those who receive the benefit are not the same as those who suffer. Is this also the case for mental illness, that there is some benefit only for close relatives? Or alternatively, could it be that the mentally ill do directly benefit — at some time, in some way?

We must acknowledge that the present-day world could provide no answer — evolution is slow, while cultural changes are fast, and society is not close to a steady state. We are likely to be imperfectly suited for our world as a result. But there is hope for understanding; those traits and states we do have likely mattered for survival until very recently, if not right up to the present. What doesn't matter for survival quickly disappears, leaving only traces, footprints in the damp sand of genomes, fading with the waves of generations. In the lineage of mammals, egg yolk genes were lost as soon as milk evolved (though broken fragments of the yolk genes persist, even within our own genomes still). Cave fish and cave salamanders — in sunless colonies, blocked off from the surface world — lose their eyes after generations of darkness, leaving skin stretched over sockets in the skull, relics of a sense no longer needed.

To understand this oddity of its design, a cave salamander would need to know about something beyond its conceptual reach — the illuminated world of its ancestors, and so the value of the twin holes in its skull: pathways for information in an ancient world of light, but only vulnerabilities in the modern world. Likewise inexplicable depths of our own feelings, and our own weaknesses, might also be best understood in the context of the long march to our current forms, finding little in the present world explanatory. But caution is needed: not only do we lack data, but also our imagination itself is subjective, and our perspective is limited and biased. The borders separating broken and unbroken may shift, and blur, and even fade away as we approach.

Currently it is impossible to be definitive about the role of evolution in mental illness. But human origins and evolution have to be part of the picture in thinking about psychiatry—as with anything in biology reflecting conflicts and compromises that arose, and were tested, over many generations. A pure hunter-gatherer, more than one hundred thousand years ago, might not have needed the prolonged intensity of mania, and would have benefited from simply cutting losses and moving on from threat or conflict—to new vistas beyond the horizon. But when we build—as we have more recently, in the form of houses, farms, communities, multigenerational families, culture—existential threat might be best met with an elevated state of being, even if unsustainable.

Neuroscience has made little progress in understanding mania, or the bipolar disorder syndromes, which form a spectrum of severity all sharing a manic-like state. Indeed, mania is not binary but ranges in degree from mild hypomania (a sustainable mood-elevated state not needing hospitalization) to recurrent spontaneous manias (increasingly severe with each episode—psychotic even, with breaks in perception of reality—ending in a dementia-like state if untreated).

Neuroscientists interested in mania have explored certain types of brain cells with relevance to the core symptoms. For example, dopamine neurons have attracted attention for their known roles in guiding motivation and reward seeking—elements clearly overabundant in mania, on display in that remarkable symptom we call "increased goal-directed behavior," and exemplified in the numerous projects, investments, plans, and energy of Alexander's rebirth. Circadian rhythm circuits have also been pursued, since one of the most striking features of mania—used in diagnosis as well, and prominent in Alexander—is a profoundly decreased need for sleep. This symptom is especially interesting since mania does not cause poor sleep per se (nor attendant problems that come with the poor sleep of insomnia such as lethargy, somnolence, and the like). In mania there is a true decreased *need* for sleep—as Alexander experienced—with maintained high functioning of brain and body over prolonged periods, and very little rest taken or required.

Are these dopamine and circadian circuits clues, then, embodying pathways into the mystery that is mania? In 2015 the dopamine and circadian aspects were brought together with optogenetics. Mice with a mutation in the circadian rhythm mechanism, in a gene called *Clock*, were found to show behavior that could be interpreted as manic-like, in the form of prolonged phases of extremely high movement levels. This state was found to occur at the same time as phases of higher dopamine neuron activity. Could that dopamine elevation be causal, driving frenzied movement levels in mice? Using optogenetics, the team found that increasing the activity of dopamine neurons could indeed induce the manic-like behavior; furthermore, suppressing dopamine neuron activity could reverse the manic-like state of the *Clock* mutant mice. We are far from a deep understanding of mania, but optogenetics has helped unify two of the leading hypothesized circuit mechanisms. Going forward, it may be useful to consider that the dopamine neuron population is not monolithic but composed of many distinct types that can be separably identified early in mammalian brain development; future work may allow targeting specific subtypes relevant to mania, such as those specific dopamine neurons that project to brain regions involved in generating actions and action plans.

What other genes relevant to mania are found in human beings? Bipolar disorders are heritable, running strongly in families, but there are few single genes that, by themselves, can determine the disorder—in fact, there may be dozens of genes or more that each contribute small effects, as with height. A few of these genes have turned up fairly consistently with scanning of whole human genomes in studies of type I bipolar—the kind with spontaneous and severe manias, among the most strongly heritable of psychiatric diseases. *ANK3* is one such gene, which directs the production of a protein called ankyrin 3 (also known as ankyrin G), which organizes the electrical infrastructure of the initial segment of the axon—the first section of each threadlike output wire, that electrical-information transmission line connecting each brain cell with all of its receivers across the brain.

These mutations, which contribute to causing bipolar disorder in some people, likely lead to insufficient ankyrin 3 production. In 2017 a mouse line was created with "knocked out"—insufficient—ankyrin 3. These initial segments of the axon were indeed poorly organized in the knockout mice as a result, in an interesting way. Inhibitory synapses that would normally be clustered at that crucial spot of the axon, acting like dampers to prevent overexcitation, were gone. And the mice showed some manic-like properties: much higher physical activity levels, in terms of both general locomotion and movements specifically directed toward overcoming stressful challenges—that is, elevated goal-directed behavior. Amazingly, this pattern could be blocked in the mice by medications, including lithium, that are highly effective for bipolar in human beings.

As interesting as ANK3 is to psychiatrists and neuroscientists, in human beings its mutations cannot alone explain all mania, and bipolar disorder in general is far from understood. We also do not understand the association of mania with depression—that other "pole" of bipolar. Manias frequently end in deep depression, and many patients cycle from up states to down states: mania to depression, or depression to hypomania and back—but nobody knows why, and the ANK3 studies do not offer an answer. Is there a neural resource of some kind that is consumed by mania, leading to a slide into depression? Or perhaps instead there is overcorrection from a system responsible for turning off mania when the threat is past, but occasionally overshooting? An imprecise hack indeed—one that in the past could be tolerated by our species as a whole, if not so much by those living with it.

•

The evolution of civilization is far faster than the evolution of biology. The global reach and power of individuals, across space and time, now make hypomania and mania more dangerous, and more destructive.

Certain historically significant figures have, like Alexander, no doubt borne this burden or one like it, all trying to meet the challenges of their time—and for a brief moment have found themselves moving toward a state of vigor, optimism, and charisma that from some perspective is an elevated expression of what a human being can be. But disaster would have come for many of them—and for Alexander, born in the wrong time and place, there was no safe opportunity to complete the metamorphosis, to fulfill that calling.

Upon discharge from the altered world of the hospital, as when leaving Baum's land of Oz, every patient seems to receive a parting gift in some form. On surgical services, some patients even receive a new heart. As we say in the hospital, in psychiatry, most patients are Dorothies—they just get to go home. This was the only path for Alexander: coerced treatment, renormalization, and release back to his community—the aligned goal of everyone who cared for him.

At follow-up one year later, Alexander's wife described him as "better than ever." The shadow of his illness had been that darkness shining in brightness of Joyce's *Ulysses*; this was a darkness that the brightness could not comprehend. Though no longer manic, he still could not bring himself to repudiate the state he had entered into, nor his actions in the state. He still didn't understand why we had acted as we did. I thought him a little glum about it all, but in the end, he had been given a way to live with his wife again, to slip into retirement without redirection or consequence, and to hike in the heronry.

CHAPTER 3

CARRYING CAPACITY

Tonally the individual voice is a dialect; it shapes its own accent, its own vocabulary and melody in defiance of an imperial concept of language, the language of Ozymandias, libraries and dictionaries, law courts and critics, and churches, universities, political dogma, the diction of institutions.

—DEREK WALCOTT, *The Antilles: Fragments of Epic Memory; The Nobel Lecture* (1992)

"I had a teratoma in Paris," Aynur said. "It started from an egg in my ovary, and sprouted teeth and living neurons and clumps of hair, all twisted together, growing in my belly. The French doctors took the tumor out, but after the surgery it was hard for me to walk, or bend, or sit upright. I was living alone, and I had to do everything very slowly.

"I was in this state, when I got a strange letter—with twelve pictures of our hometown, unexplained—in the mail, from my mother. I remember stepping carefully across my loft to spread out the photos on my breakfast table.

"I felt something of the warmth of home. It was like my mother was touching me physically, reaching her hand out across the whole breadth of Europe and Asia. The photos showed familiar street views, buildings crowded against the roads, with our rounded windows and wrought-iron balconies, and with people standing out vividly against the gray skies of fall, like droplets of dye.

"The colors on our clothes—you could never see such a scene in Palo Alto. Deep reds, rich indigos, really brilliant yellows—and all pigments from nature—dark brown from walnut skin, that feathery purple from the tamarisk tree. You might have seen these dyes on our silks, the Uighur kind we call *atlas*—which means graceful silk. It's soft but strong, used for women's costumes and ribbons and wall hangings. The world might know of our silks, I think, if nothing else about us. And there are similar color styles on our everyday work clothes, even on manufactured jackets—bright purple and peach and orange and gold, mass-produced garments that we get trucked from the capital in Ürümqi—it's all the same spirit, just our taste, the contrast of strong colors.

"But there was a problem. The longer I looked at the photos, and the note, the more I felt there was something strange going on. There was no explanation in my mother's short letter, no comment on the pictures themselves—and her actual written words were just a dry response to my own last note.

"I had emailed her a long update on my graduate work—and since there had been no news from my husband for two weeks, I had asked her if I should come home for a visit. I looked back at my mother's note, and reread her words: 'You should not come. It is still too hot here, and now you are not used to it. You have been so long in France, you should stay there.' But actually it was France having heat waves, and I had complained to her already about it. Paris over the summer that year had been hotter than ever, and anyway I could see from the pictures the little boys and girls at home were already in their autumn coats.

"After a few minutes, I noticed something else: there were no young men on the streets. Many children, women, and motor scooters. But all the men, of my husband's age, were gone from the streets. In every photo.

"I remember then in my haste to get out, to find an open Internet café, I almost fell down the narrow stairs leading to the rainy street. A piercing pain from my surgery was just starting to surface as I reached the door to my apartment, but only when I got down to the street did I understand how bad it was. I couldn't go back up. I couldn't even walk.

"There on the street in Paris, it came to me how deeply I was hurt inside. It was dark, and the stones were wet. My family was in danger, and I was alone. And there I found, when I couldn't walk, that I could run."

●

Aynur was animated and exuberant, and broadly smiling at times, in a manner discordant with the darkness of her story and its gathering crescendo of physical and emotional pain. I began wordlessly wondering what natural process in the brain sets the timing for awareness of suffering. At the same time, in a parallel stream of thought, I was secretly awed by her imagery. It was unexpected and effortless, and her story was coming in a torrent that grew rapidly more powerful.

Awareness of anything, including our internal feelings—consciousness, some would say—does not simply flip on and off, as if controlled by a switch. Awareness even of pain gathers itself, seeming to emerge with movement in time, along a trajectory arcing from one moment to another.

Each feeling is intimately entwined with—and perhaps even identical with—a growing and cresting and abating of brain activity. That timescale in one sense spans hundreds of milliseconds, and in another sense, millions of years. Feelings are, like people, paths through time.

The elements of human subjectivity—what we all feel with our conscious minds, and when—may exist in the modern world only to the extent that these feelings caused actions needed for survival before, in the distant past. And so for Aynur and me, with homes at nearly opposite ends of the earth—our feelings in common mattered, and it also probably mattered how they were felt many millennia ago. Recognizing this connection seemed to me a grace of sorts, granted to our long-gone forebears across the cold expanse of time—and also seemed a comfort in the present: acknowledging all the partners in this family conversation, and seeing feelings not as clinical injections of information into our minds from the external world, but rather as connections with each other, across the scattered expanse and long unwritten history of the human family.

At the other end of timescales in biology, just as Aynur experienced the emergence of her visceral pain, our indwelling experiences as individual animals are also defined by movement in time—over a fraction of a second. Each conscious experience is dynamic on this timescale. It manifests, peaks, and lingers—keeping its own pace, separate from the stimulus that brings it forth.

This is a long time for consciousness to take in coalescing—a hundredfold slower than the electrical signaling speed of brain cells in isolation—a matter of two hundred, rather than two, milliseconds. Whenever the world sends us new bits—a pinprick, an unexpected sound, a light touch—almost a quarter of a second passes before that exquisite glow of conscious awareness shines forth. Reflexes are different—unconscious processes can be much faster—but consciousness, for some reason, takes its time.

The individual subjective experience, then—in the moment of our awareness—can be understood from the perspectives of both evolution and neurobiology to not just represent a dump of data from the external world. The tidewaters of the external sensory ocean not only percolate deep but "gather to a greatness," as Gerard Manley Hopkins wrote of the grandeur of the divine—with a mysterious inwreathing through the brain's inland fens and waterways, to manifest finally and fully. Something special is happening.

Neuroscientists have come to know this strange fact of mammalian consciousness from many kinds of experiments, most grounded in direct measurement of electrical activity in the brain. Two or three hundred milliseconds elapse before the response to a ping, an unexpected sound or light, peaks in our cortex—that thin and wrinkled covering of cells wrapped around the brain of every mammal like a shawl.

Not only does this seem like eons of silence to a cellular physiologist like myself (used to thinking in shorter timescales of only two or three milliseconds, across synapses and along axons) but the long delay is surprising to nonscientists as well, to anyone who has observed a cat chase its prey, or a boxer lean back from a jab, or just two people interact in animated conversation—all of which play out on much faster timescales. The trained boxer seems to dodge before it is possible, responding to a specific threat trajectory in less time than it should take if consciousness were required. And human social interaction, especially, seems impossible in light of this number. How clumsily slow it would be, how unlike us, to wait almost a quarter of a second to respond to each new bit of spoken information—or even longer if actual consideration is involved.

And that is only for speech; even more puzzling is the fullness of social interaction, with all its data streams. What of integrating the bit-rich visual inputs conveying eye contact, hand motion, posture? What of each diffident subangulation of a lip, or shift in body orientation—with recognition of every visual stimulus essential for generating an appropriate response? These streams of information need one another to make sense, just as people need one another for meaning. And what of larger interactions: a team or a town hall? Human groups are teeming with conflicting desires, polite or malevolent lies, shifting alignments—each information stream not only playing out simultaneously but involving the others to generate meaning, and requiring constant reinterpretation, and co-interpretation, while the speakers—and their models of the world and one another—all change with time as well.

Deeper insights have license to take longer, and can come much later—after all the information is in, after weeks or months of incubating like a caterpillar in its white-matter cocoon, ensconced in the silk of interwoven axons—until new awareness emerges one day, breaking free fully formed.

•

"For three more months," Aynur told me, "from that moment, I had no contact with my husband. I was so afraid. My parents were afraid too, but very careful. Even when I finally got them on video chat, they said nothing. I did not get to hear if he was alive. If they had heard something, they did not say. I couldn't ask directly about the photos—I didn't know if sending them had been forbidden, or who might be listening. But a wife should be expected to ask about her husband, I think. It would be more strange to not ask. Anyway, it didn't matter what I asked my parents about him—'We don't know,' they said to everything, and that was all.

"Everything was unknown. After two months of this I lost the ability to sleep. It wasn't just not knowing. It was that there was nothing to do about it. I couldn't help my loved ones. I was paralyzed. I was being eaten alive from within—there is nothing like it that you could understand. All was the opposite of your life now, where you control everything.

"Something had crawled into me, and begun to gnaw my spine, and hollow me out from within. There was no knowledge, no power, nothing inside me left. Nothing to do, and nobody to tell. And that was when I first began to think about suicide.

"I got there slowly, though. I think it was in steps. First, I realized how much better it would be to face a real fear, a concrete tormentor. Dealing with a known enemy, even a death with fixed timing, would seem like paradise by contrast. I came to dream of that death, in waking sleep, through the days and nights of fall, and into the depths of winter. And then I thought of taking violent control of that death, and being the one that could set the exact date and time in a final step that nobody could prevent, and so I would be taking back control over myself. And this, once I had conceived of it, was so desired.

"I don't know if I was depressed. I think that is just a word you use when you hear suicide. I know you like to use it in psychiatry, here in the West, in your West. And it's fine, you can call it depression if you like—of course I was not happy. But let me tell you another way to look at it.

"In the cotton fields of my home, our west, in what you call Xinjiang, the farmers have some problems with aphids, and in school the students who were interested in biology—like me—learned about the wasps that the government were bringing in to suppress the aphids. A lot of the Uighur kids interested in biology were guided into that field— the party was seeking modern kinds of employment for our people— not because they cared, really, but to prevent radicalization.

"Wasp warfare like this makes some sense—each wasp type is specific, restricted to its target species, so there is little risk of causing new problems. The female wasp injects her egg right into the aphid she catches; the egg goes through what would be her stinger, it's called an ovipositor—sometimes a paralytic is injected too—and then the egg hatches into a wasp larva that lives in the aphid, and grows, and partially eats away its insides, all the while careful to not damage the aphid's vital organs.

"Then the wasp larva breaks out of the belly of the aphid but still makes sure to keep it alive, and stays close underneath, and spins its cocoon with the aphid helplessly forming a living shield—the aphid is paralyzed but capable of a few simple movements if anything comes near, to protect its invader, to defend its killer—until the new adult wasp emerges from the cocoon, and the aphid only then is allowed to die, at last.

"So let me ask you: if that aphid could become aware, could come to understand its situation and choose death first, would it? Of course it would. And if the aphid could slowly emerge into consciousness, feeling the full agony of its situation as a human might, as it considered death, would you call the aphid depressed? I guess you might, but there would be no point—since no medication, nor any conceivable treatment, could be worthwhile, even if it could change the feeling inside.

"It doesn't matter; it's just words. I wanted death, and planned my death. That's what matters."

•

It was at this point that I began to realize the responsibility, and privilege, I had been given—to encounter this human being and her story. I did not merit this, to be the one hearing her, but fate had created an astounding crossing of major threads—historical, medical, emotional—at this moment in space and time, and so I could not cut her short when the appointment time had elapsed. I let her story unfold fully, her images taking form inside me, her experience linking to what I knew in science and medicine.

From the moment we first met, Aynur was completely at ease, and seemed impelled to share rich personal stories, adopting an interpersonal style more suitable for old classmates meeting at a school reunion. By itself this could be a red flag, regarding both the patient and the therapist—and their interaction—but I ended up finding no hint in her, or in myself, of what a psychiatrist could look for in such cases. For example, I never identified interpersonal patterns she had lived through that I might be evoking in her—a formative teacher, or an older brother, or a local doctor—nor did I perceive any pattern she might be bringing forth in me from my own life. This is always a risk, the patient and psychiatrist fitting into roles and calling up feelings from past experiences—often a problem, and sometimes a solution, in therapeutic relationships.

There were also no hints of personality or mood disorders in Aynur. Borderline and histrionic personality traits would be near the top of the list, in principle—along with hypomania, that stably elevated state on the mood-disorder spectrum—but there was nothing to corroborate these. Aynur simply told her intensely personal narratives with a natural frame of friendship, in as pure and engaged a social state as I had ever seen or imagined, with speech rich and anecdotes textured, somehow all in a language she did not know well, in a country she had known for less than a year.

Aynur seemed to me an archetype of the social state that our lineage might have evolved to allow, and as I listened I thought about the costs incurred—the metabolic bill paid each day, the brain resources allocated in each individual, for such a state to be possible—and also where this all began for the social mammals in our ancestry, perhaps in troops of early primates. The costs would have been substantial, I thought, since there is nothing as uncertain, and therefore as challenging to compute, as the social interaction in biology—not even the hunt of an unpredictable prey. The cat cannot predict which way the rat will turn, but there are not nearly so many possibilities as in a human interaction. And no hidden agendas—the rat wants to live, but what on earth does another person in a conversation want? And of course the rat can usually only express its drive to live in two dimensions, running on the plane of the ground. Likewise for the boxer, there is just a left and a right hand to worry about, and certain sequences and trajectories for each.

But the social brain needs a new mode of function, still requiring swiftness yet also operating along an enormous number of dimensions, running in a regime where a little bit of new information—any deviation from the current model, perhaps caught by and encoded in a few cells only—should be able to tip the observer into an improved model of the other individual, and the interaction into a better-predictive timeline. Yet the observer's brain also should not be overexcitable, and should in fact resist noise in the system that might cause switching to an incorrect model. It would still be important to suppress spontaneous ignition of a false perception, a harmful perspective that might arise from random sparks of neural fire.

As with anything in biology, the importance of such a process can be assessed by the consequences of its absence. We know the barrier, the lack of connection—distance and mistrust—when eye contact is even just a moment too brief. Yet a chilling effect also arises from eye contact held a fraction of a second too long, if not paired with a social signal of warmth. Temporal precision is clearly essential, as much for social interaction as for anything else in biology—severely pressuring the circuitry responsible for imposing the odd and ponderously slow pace of consciousness, that two-hundred-millisecond delay.

One possible solution, to speed this give-and-take, would be a premodeling, an unconscious gaming-out of events ahead of time in the brain. This feat could be achieved if the social being had many models of the world—and of the social partner—running at once, under the surface, that predicted the other's actions and feelings well into the future.

A key role—perhaps the major role—of the mammalian cortex might be to solve this prediction problem, to run models of the present and future, bringing together as much contextual information as possible from the world to inform these models. At the same time, the cortical system would have to detect with great sensitivity even small surprises—deviations from the current model that would indicate the need to hop to another. Running these countless models in parallel would make it unnecessary to calculate and spool up a whole new timeline in the conscious mind with each new bit of information, since each model would provide and prescribe actions, replies, forks into the future—moves and countermoves—over many timesteps, in a conditional hyperchess of the social mind.

The computational energy required in the brain, in order to constantly run these unconscious predictive models, would be vast. Perhaps this expendable element is the neural circuit-level resource exhausted quickly in the introvert, or in people—most people—who tire from prolonged social interaction. On the other hand, people with especially deep resources for this brain state would be the true extro-verts, thriving on constant human contact—like Aynur, as became clear even in the early going of the time we had scheduled, in what was supposed to be a quick and unremarkable evaluation, a check-in of sorts occasioned by her brief suicidality while she had been living in Europe. It was an interview unique in my experience—not just for the searing circumstances of her life, but for her intensely social disposition—and at the heart of it all was a human being who had wanted to die.

•

"There are two ways we seem to choose to do this," Aynur said. "In my hometown the buildings were not tall enough to make death from a jump certain, but in Kashgar they can do that, and certainly in Paris. The other way, well, *atlas* silk is so strong. I had many sashes, and one easily sets up bricks or books that can be kicked away under a rafter, or perhaps beneath a trellis in an outside garden.

"Why didn't I do it? My mother, I think. Even if I were forced to lose all my dreams as a scientist, and I could only have one piece of bread a day for the rest of my life, I would accept that, if I could be with my mom.

"The Parisians say they are more social than the Americans, and they are in some ways—they spend much more time with their family and friends. But nothing like the Uighur. You will laugh, but after my marriage I still slept between my two parents, in their bed, for months, as I had my whole life until then. This would be impossible in your West—unwifely, or worse. But that is how close we are. I could not end my life, because of family, because I could not harm those people close to me. I could not murder those relationships with my own hand.

"So I went on, alone in Paris, gnawed away from the inside, and then when I was somehow still alive after three months, in the abyss of win-ter, they released my husband, and he was able to contact me. Like all the young men there, my husband had been sent to a concentration camp. There might be another word for it in English, I don't know, since they were not killed, not really.

"When they released him he called me, we did a video chat. He was much thinner, with a shaved head, and his voice was very weak. I didn't know if he had been tortured, but he was so much more quiet, even more hollowed than I, and would not speak of what had happened. He told me he was being moved out of Xinjiang, to work in the cities closer to the coast. That was all he could say, he would be transported east, and he was not sure if or when we would meet again. So that's it now, he lives as a shell, making coarse movements.

"That's where things are still, mostly. This was last year, before I transferred my studies here from Paris, when the government was still denying these camps existed. This year, they are admitting existence, but they are calling them educational centers. People are sent there for failing to learn and speak the oath of allegiance in Mandarin. Or for being two-faced, as they call it—saying all the words correctly, but somehow not showing the right passion in their actions, or a deep commitment to the state.

"Oh, and they bulldozed the mosques in the town, while the young men were in the camps."

•

As Aynur was my last appointment of the morning I did not have to stop her to see another patient, only needing to sacrifice my lunch hour—an easy decision. My assessment had been long clear, and completed: she had problems in the past only—anxiety symptoms and an adjustment disorder due to extraordinarily stressful life events—with no current psychiatric diagnosis. In a patient with cognitive difficulty in domains beyond the social (Aynur had none, and was working toward a postgraduate degree in evolutionary biology), and who had shown certain facial features, I would have considered Williams syndrome, a chromosomal-deletion disorder. Despite anxiety and cognitive impairment, Williams patients can seem extremely socially adept—exhibiting expansive, rich storytelling and immediate personal bonding (though of uncertain depth) even with strangers.

Williams syndrome is still mysterious to this day, and still fascinating. But my clinical specialization was more focused toward care at the other extreme of social skill—treating human beings with brain states less inclined to, and less adept for, social interaction—on the autism spectrum. This was one of my two clinical passions (along with treating depression). From the earliest days of my practice, when I first emerged from residency training as an attending psychiatrist, the clinic intake staff were instructed to guide patients needing evaluation for a possible autism diagnosis to my care. I also asked the intake team to send me known autism patients who were challenging—people already diagnosed on that spectrum, but complicated for one reason or another, and referred by outside doctors (the same process that brought depression cases to my clinic). In this way, following the mystery of the underlying diseases, I found myself becoming a doctor who specialized in two disorders nearly untreatable with medicine: autism and treatment-resistant depression.

Knowing that no medical treatment existed for autism itself, I sought to help, in some way, a large and growing underserved population: adult autism patients no longer under the care of their pediatric physicians. These patients almost always suffer from treatable conditions occurring along with autism—comorbid conditions, as we call them, such as anxiety. My consideration in starting this clinic was that these disorders were often deeply affected by, and certainly framed by, the autism itself, and so could be best treated by a doctor with some specialization in altered social function.

Severe autism is defined by partial or complete inability to use language. But autism on the "high" end of the spectrum—socially, still the inverse of Aynur's state though with good language skills—also comes with its own challenges. Because these autism-spectrum individuals still have impaired social understanding, they can face a difficult conundrum in living their lives. With language ability and intelligence generally intact, and capability for employment typical (or even exceptional in the modern world), interaction with the broader community proceeds—but this interaction can be confusing and intensely anxiety-provoking, leading in some cases to serious new symptoms.

The social realm, and society in general—dominated as it is by the vagaries of human behavior—can be a mystery, even a minefield, for these conversant autism patients. How did that person know what to say just then? How on earth is consensus reached in a group? Where am I supposed to look as this person speaks? For these patients hell can indeed be—as Sartre noted—other people.

People are complex systems, but complex systems per se are not the problem for these patients, nor even complex systems that change with time—as long as the dynamics are predictable. Lines of code, a train moving along a one- or two-dimensional track on a timetable, the interlocking street architecture of a city—though complex, these can be appealing by virtue of predictability, especially to people living with autism. On the other hand, unpredictability—exemplified by social interaction—can be highly aversive, especially to those on this spectrum.

Understanding the precise sense in which social interaction can feel bad, I thought, will matter for the underlying neuroscience, and for helping human beings who live with autism (the entire spectrum all dwelling at the opposite pole of social aptitude from Williams cases, and from Aynur). Was social avoidance in autism not resulting from exhaustion of some computational or energetic resource, but rather arising from a fear of uncertainty or other people? Or perhaps there was something more subtle and hard to put into words at work here. For me, this latter possibility underscored the magnitude of the challenge of autism: how will patients already limited in linguistic expression tell us what is going on inside, if even we can't put it into words—and worse, if the words don't quite exist anyway?

I had long taken the opportunity to speak with my high-functioning autism patients who had good language skills. After building a therapeutic alliance over months of outpatient work and treating their comorbidities (as much as was possible), in follow-up clinic visits I would ask questions about the nature of their inner experience. But where to begin? I couldn't simply ask the patients to explain their autism. Instead I started simply and concretely—asking the patients about their experience of a single physical symptom. Of all the behavioral traits of the autism spectrum disorders, the avoidance of eye contact was to me the most arresting, and perhaps could be most illuminating: sometimes a brief flicker of contact, then the eyes flutter and flee like flushed quails—to the floor, to the side.

A patient named Charles gave me the clearest answer on this symptom. A young information technology specialist, he had what we used to call Asperger's syndrome—on the autism spectrum, but with excellent language skills—and extremely prominent avoidance of eye contact. In my clinic, I had spent two years treating his anxiety (successfully, in that he no longer suffered from panic attacks and workplace anxiety). But at the same time, there had not been one glimmer of change in autism symptoms, including his eye contact pattern. I asked him one morning, "What does it feel like when you do briefly make eye contact? Does it make you feel anxious or fearful?"

"No," he said. "I'm not afraid."

"Is it overwhelming?" I asked.

"Yes," Charles said, with no hesitation.

"Tell me about that, Charles, if you can."

"Well, when I'm looking at you and talking, if your face changes then I have to think about what that means, and how I should react to that, and change what I'm saying."

"And what then?" I gently pressed. "What exactly makes you look away?"

"Well," Charles said, "and then that overloads. It overloads the rest of me."

"So it's like too much information, and that feels bad?"

"Yes," he said right away, "and if I'm looking away, it's easier."

For me, as a neuroscientist and psychiatrist, this was a transcendent moment. Though sitting before me was a patient with severe eye contact avoidance who was clearly susceptible to anxiety, I had been allowed to hear something that few scientists were privileged to know unequivocally: that the eye contact issue was not due to anxiety. This conclusion was strongly supported by the completely separate fates of the two symptoms (anxiety and eye contact) under my treatment—one was cured and the other was utterly unaffected. For this patient, at least, this separation between anxiety and eye contact was also directly

confirmed by his own description, in words of a human being positioned on the autism spectrum so precisely as to be strongly symptom-
atic, and yet also fortuitously verbally expressive enough to share his
internal experience. In some ways this single moment justified for me
the entire career progression I had taken, all the extra years of both MD
and PhD training, all the pain and personal challenges of internship,
all the call nights as a single father, worrying about my lonely son. This
alone was enough.

Instead of anxiety or fear, a much more interesting, and subtle, process seemed to be at work. Charles's brain was detecting its own inability to keep up with the social data stream—while aware that it should
be keeping up, that this was a situation where processing the data was
essential. And more: his brain had created a link from that informational challenge to a negative-valence subjective internal state, a state
of feeling bad.

Mysteries remained, as always. For example, was that negative feeling innate or learned? His link from high information rates to feeling
bad could have been taught by life, conditioned over time by repeated
and emotionally difficult failures of social interaction. Or was the aversion present from the beginning of his life, without training? Was feeling bad an evolutionary mechanism to help people dodge the torrent
of data, guiding them to disengage from full participation in situations
where correct responses to the data would be expected by others, and
failure thus socially consequential—harmful, even? Was the unpleasant feeling then just triggered by the unpredictability of the data
streaming in—essentially a response to the high bit rate of information
itself?

This was an idea that might matter, a possible insight that had been
gifted from just the right patient—born on the pole opposite to Aynur,
but still verbal enough to tell us his story.

•

"It is so unfair," Aynur continued. "We are a nice people. We are not
only close to our families. Guests in our home, we put at the head of
the dinner table. Any visitor, no matter who, receives this position of

honor. That could never happen here in California—and not in France either. It's funny for me to see how you are. It is like you are afraid the guest will take the home away from you.

"Are you really worried about that? It is your house. Nobody is going to take it from you. If we have a guest, we give them the best seat for one evening. And it makes a strong bond. So much strength lies in the gesture, costing nothing and creating a deep connection that will last forever.

"I wonder if this part of our culture is interpreted as weak. But it's not just the Uighur, all the communities do this, the string of settlements all across the middle of the continent—we call it the Silk Road, and you call it that too, I think—but I think this is how we survived, because we could be a social culture. And we are strong in many other ways—not just in social bonds. When I was thirteen, I fought seven Han girls by myself.

"We were in our dormitory and they were talking; I knew they didn't think I could understand them. I was always so much better at understanding languages than people imagined—I learned Mandarin, and French, and English, in only weeks each it seemed, all just by hearing and watching. And these girls were complaining that someone had left a food dish out in the common area, and they were blaming me. And then one who was standing in the bathroom in front of the mirror, brushing her hair, said a terrible thing about my family, my loved ones she had never met, how my mother smelled. I leapt down from the bunk and dragged the girl by her hair out of the bathroom. The others all jumped on me but were surprised, even I was surprised, that I was stronger than all of them together. I had no idea until that moment that my legs were so powerful. They fell against me like raindrops, a storm that passed quickly—and I never heard a rude word again that year.

"I feel guilty today about those girls. I was the one who became violent first. It seemed I had to defend my family, but now I am twice that age, and I see they were just kids. And maybe I made things worse, maybe I harmed their perception of my culture. The Han are good people too, and I don't blame them for their government. But I wonder now if there even is a path forward for them, for their country, to move in a new direction, to no longer be part of such a system. Can they evolve away, or have they fallen into something from which there is no escape?

"I studied more biology of the aphids after I started my master's degree, and I learned the history of the wasps, incredibly successful animals which come in more species than do any other order of animals on earth. Where does this success come from? Did you know that ants, bees, wasps, and hornets all started from the same wasp ancestor, in the time of the dinosaurs, when one little plant-eating fly, like a sawfly, was born with a strange mutation that made its egg more layable into animals, right through its ovipositor, that stinger-like egg-laying tube? And from that one moment an incredible radiation of animals from one ancestor occurred, because it was so powerful to be able to lay eggs in any living thing—into a spider, an aphid, another wasp.

"That incredibly thin, hairlike wasp waist—the tiny connector linking one part of the body to another—was created by chance mutation. Then natural selection took over, accelerating the expansion of wasp species—the spread of waspiness—using the waist to allow body contortions to position and guide increasingly long ovipositors, to get to beetle larvae deep in trees, to body cavities deep within large caterpillars.

"But the most surprising final part of the story, that matters here, is that several branches of the wasp family—ants and hornets and bees, all the social groups—later reverted away from this life cycle, completely abandoning the parasitoid egg laying into other organisms that had made them who they were. Complex body parts are easily lost in evolution if not needed, and are never regained; it is rare for organisms, once parasitic, once evolved to extremely reduced body plans, to escape that evolutionary pit. But these did escape in a different way, through being social, by dependence on each other. They had found a way of living together—and commitment to this social mode had set them free.

"They still retain that severely reduced wasp waist—you can see it in ants, and so clearly in the yellow jackets you have around here—though they don't need it to be so thin anymore. The wasp waist is a mark

of their ancestry, but their ovipositors have converted to stingers to defend their family, and they use powerful social structures and bonds to
take care of their larvae, and no longer need to place their young within
another living being.

"Do you know, it took fifty million years for wasps to figure out how
to live in groups, even family groups? Social behavior is hard. Before
that, just seventeen million years had been spent inventing the wasp
waist, and then only another thirty million had been needed to turn the
ovipositor into a stinger (by the way, this is why most bees are female:
the stinger arose from that female reproductive organ, the ovipositor,
and so only females can defend the family) — but even then, the social
challenge had not been solved yet.

"After evolving the behavior of paralyzing hosts with venom, and
laying eggs in or near them — wherever the host animal happened to
fall — fifty million years were then occupied by developing increased
levels of transporting the paralyzed host to a safe concealed location,
and building a nest for the young to develop, and expanding to other
kinds of food resources needing more work like pollen and leaves, and
finally defending the nest as a group, as a family.

"Social behavior is rare, and a lot of things have to come together to
make it work — beginning with prolonged care for the young, but then
success is still contingent on many other factors, all somehow needing
to be satisfied together — like having a sting ready to defend the big investment of the social group. And when everything is in place and
working, a whole world — *the* whole world — opens up."

Here Aynur paused. This was rare for her. I uncrossed my legs and
sat up a little straighter, folding my hands together in my lap.

"I had a difficult dream about a baby," she said finally, "after I came
to California." She seemed to be struggling with the memory.

I gave her some time, not wanting to risk redirecting her flow even
slightly. As I waited — not being an insect expert — I wondered about
mammals, whose close parent-offspring interactions could have served
as a guide for the creation of social behavior in our lineage as well.
That same year of 2018, researchers studying parenting in mice had
used optogenetics to deconstruct this complex interaction — finding in-

dividual neuronal connections governing its sub-features, including projections across the brain that provided motivation to desperately seek out and find the young, versus other projections that guided actual acts of caring for the young—with each action powerfully governed by a different connection across the brain, radiating out from an anchor point, just as we had discovered for assembly of the diverse features of anxiety five years earlier.

The intense and ancient parenting dyad had created these neural circuit foundations, which could have been used again for new kinds of social interactions. An insect that can care for its young perhaps more easily becomes an insect that can care for its nestmates—and the same idea would apply to a mouse, or an early primate—by repurposing the same neural circuits. And all those techniques of caring for young, of good parenting itself, could have arisen first by circuit repurposing as well (such recycling seems to explain so much of evolution)— here by inserting the other individual, the offspring, onto one's own need and motivation structure, creating a simulation dwelling within, as a trick to use the self's internal processes to rapidly model and infer the other's needs.

Yet nonfamily social behavior would seem to be fundamentally more complex, since in families the motivations of both caretaker and offspring remain—for the most part—certain and constant. In contrast, the most interesting challenge of true nonfamilial social interaction is that of keeping up a rapidly shifting internal model, changing every few hundred milliseconds, to predict actions of another being with highly uncertain goals. And though many mammals do show nonfamilial social behavior, it is a fragile construct; from lions to meerkats to mice, social mammals are often only moments away from murdering each other.

"In the dream I was myself," Aynur continued finally, "a regular human being like you. I was also a parent, which was strange—I've only carried a teratoma in real life. But babies were also different in the dream—born smaller than a thumb, more like a pine nut, tiny and nearly hairless, like the marsupial babies that first emerge almost like small drops of pink liquid with forepaws, born with just enough dexterity to pull themselves along their mother's belly fur, to find milk and survive.

"In the dream, all human babies were like that, except even more helpless. If you were a human parent in this world, of course you had no pouch, and no fur on your belly, and the deal seemed to be that if you had a baby, you just had to carry it in your hands.

"The babies were so small they all looked similar, like embryos do. But if you had some, you knew, you definitely knew yours—partly because you could never put your babies down, so you always had them with you, and carried them on your journeys, wherever you weaved your way, along the lakeshore, or through the taiga, carrying your little droplets of human warmth.

"In my dream I lost my baby on the forest floor. I don't know how it slipped away, or when. I tried to search along the path I had taken, but the ground was covered in the dying foliage of late fall. I frantically sifted through the mat of fallen needles and bark, but it was hopeless: there was so much space to search, and my baby was so small.

"My child was helpless and cold and dying somewhere on the ground, apart from me. As I searched I could feel a fine thread connecting us—the baby was me, a part of me, apart and needing me, though I could not see where in the outside world the thread projected. But within me, the loss had a definite place, a position in space that I could feel. It was in my chest, behind my breasts, in those deep muscles that sweep the arms. The inner feeling, of the loss of a child, had been mapped there somehow—that was where evolution had set this feeling, this was how it should feel, to make me do what needed to be done. It ravaged me as I dug, and drove my arms to seek the piece of my heart that I had held so long. It was a gap, it was a savage gape, and it made me dig."

•

Aynur's comfort with complexity was not only in the social domain. She seemed to synthesize every stream of information available, of all kinds—her dreams, her memories, her science. Everything was related, and it all mattered together, and she wove it all together effortlessly. On the other end, perhaps in a related pattern, the social information stream that Charles found overwhelming was not the only kind of information that was aversive to him. As with many people on this spectrum, he had trouble with unpredictable events in the environment more broadly (sudden sounds or touches, for example, he found more distracting than did most other people—these were even painful). And so the positioning of different people on this autism spectrum could boil down to processing all types of information—not only social; symptoms were perhaps just clearest in the social domain due to its uniquely high rate of information flow.

Thinking of the rate of all information as the challenge in this way, rather than just social information, could also usefully explain unpredictability as a key problem in autism. Only unpredictable data is really information; if a person understands a system to the point of predicting everything about it accurately, then it is impossible to inform the person further about the system. The challenge with autism, then, seemed to be about the rate of information itself.

I didn't know when treating either Charles or Aynur, nor do we know now, exactly how information is represented in the brain—at least not with the same code-cracked certainty with which we know how genetic information (at the most basic level) is encoded in DNA. But we do know that neuronal information is transmitted by electrical signals moving within stimulated cells, and by chemical signals moving between these cells. And many of the genes linked to autism are related to these processes of electrical and chemical excitability—encoding proteins that create, and send, and guide, and receive the electrical or chemical signals.

So the genetic evidence I knew was at least consistent with the concept of altered information processing in autism. That idea alone is not specific enough to be useful in guiding diagnosis or treatment, but numerous other signs and markers point to altered information flow in autism. Averaged across the population, people on the autism spectrum exhibit signs of increased excitability, or triggerable electrical activity, of the brain—such as epilepsy, a form of uncontrolled excitation taking the form of a seizure. And in measuring brain waves with the electroencephalogram, or EEG (external electrodes that can record synchronized activity of many neurons in the human cortex), certain high-frequency brain rhythms called gamma waves, which are oscillations coming at thirty to eighty times per second, show increased strength in human beings with autism spectrum symptoms.

As a result of this evidence, it had been widely speculated that a unifying theme in autism could be an increased power of neuronal excitation—relative to countervailing influences like inhibition. This hypothesis was well articulated and appealing to many in the field, in part for its flexibility, since diverse mechanisms—from alterations in neurochemicals, synapses, cells, circuits, or even whole brain structure—could implement such a change in the balance of excitation and inhibition. For example, since the brain contains both excitatory cells that stimulate other neurons and cause increased activity, and inhibitory cells that shut down other neurons, one attractive form of this hypothesis would be that autism symptoms could arise from an imbalance between excitatory and inhibitory cells themselves, specifically favoring the excitatory cells.

But how could such a hypothesis of excitation/inhibition balance be tested? Despite availability of clinical strategies to dampen overall brain activity, such as medications to treat seizures and anxiety, these drugs (for example, a class called benzodiazepines) turn down the activity of all neurons—not just excitatory cells.

Just as the excitation/inhibition balance hypothesis would then predict, benzodiazepines are therefore generally not effective for the core symptoms of autism. Autism is clearly not just increased activity in the brain. Charles, for example, who suffered from anxiety, had received a benzodiazepine prescription from me for many years, but this treatment—as I expected—had not touched his autism symptoms at all, despite eliminating his anxiety.

The cellular formulation of the excitation/inhibition balance hypothesis, untestable for so long, finally became accessible with the advent of optogenetics. If the relevant imbalance in autism—at least in some forms—involved excitatory and inhibitory cell types, optogenetics could be ideally suited to test this idea. We could increase or decrease excitability of the excitatory or the inhibitory cell types—in targeted brain regions such as the prefrontal cortex that handle advanced cognitions—using the microbial light-activated ion channel genes called channelrhodopsins, and with fiberoptics to deliver laser light.

Mice, like people, mostly prefer being with each other, even in pairings unrelated to kinship or mating; rather than being alone, they will generally choose an environment that contains another (nonthreatening) mouse. Mice also seem to express actual interest in each other, with prolonged bouts of social contact and exploration. And the human mutations known to cause autism, when mimicked in mice using genetic technology, can cause disruptions in this mouse sociability.

So with the generalized success of optogenetics in mice by 2009, it became apparent that this technology might be used to help illuminate mammalian social behavior. In 2011 we indeed found that optogenetically elevating the activity of *excitatory* cells in the prefrontal cortex caused an enormous deficit in social behavior in adult mice. Importantly, this intervention did not affect certain nonsocial behaviors such as the exploration of unmoving (and therefore quite predictable) objects.

The effect was specific, then, and in the right direction as predicted by (and therefore supporting) the cell-type balance hypothesis. Even more intriguingly, and fitting the hypothesis as well, optogenetically elevating the activity of *inhibitory* cells in the same already modified mice, to restore cellular balance, corrected the social deficit.

Crucial to this experiment had been our creation of the first red-light-driven channelrhodopsins to complement the known blue-light-driven versions. This advance allowed us, in 2011, to modify the activity of one cell population (excitatory) with blue light, and another population (inhibitory) with red light, in the same animals. That experiment had shown that elevating excitatory cell activity could cause social deficits in healthy adult mammals, and that this effect could be ameliorated by elevating inhibitory cell activity at the same time, to rebalance the system.

In 2017 (in a narrow slice of time after I had treated Charles, but before I met Aynur), we brought our approach to mice that were not typical—that had been induced to carry mutations in genes matching those found in human autism families. These mice (altered in a single gene called *Cntnap2*) had inborn deficits in social behavior compared with nonmutant mice. We found that this autism-related social deficit could be *corrected* by optogenetic interventions that were logically the opposite of what we had done to *cause* social deficits in 2011. Either increasing activity of inhibitory cells, or reducing activity of excitatory cells, in the prefrontal cortex (both interventions would be predicted to reduce cellular balance back toward the natural levels) corrected the autism-related social behavior deficit.

Beyond this proof of principle—causally testing the cellular balance hypothesis—we were intrigued by the demonstration that for these social deficits, both cause and correction could be applied in adulthood. This was by no means obvious, and certainly the result could have turned out otherwise. It might have been that the relevant imbalance occurred only at some inaccessible and irreversible step earlier in life. If this were the case, the insight would still be valuable, but treatment interventions would become much harder to envisage. Our findings did not rule out any possible contribution from before birth, but did show that at least in some cases, action in adulthood could be sufficient for both causation and correction of a social deficit.

These results—turning social behavior up or down by shifting the balance of excitatory and inhibitory cells—also had illustrated the broader worth of a particular kind of scientific process, beyond the intrinsic value of the scientific finding. Here psychiatry had helped guide fundamental neuroscience experiments, which in turn had helped illuminate processes that could be going on within unusual human minds in the psychiatry clinic—coming full circle in casting light upon clinical moments as emotionally complex and intellectually profound as Aynur's immersive storytelling.

"I know we've gone an hour over our time," Aynur said, filling a pause that I just realized had existed, in the moment of its ending. "I'm sorry if you missed your lunchtime. Thank you for listening—I just wanted to explain. The French doctors wanted me to follow up here, but I'm not suicidal now. I had a time of weakness, that's all.

"I don't mean to be too dramatic about any of this, but just to say: I could become weak like that again. Now I know I need my family, and I cannot live without them. These bonds that created the human way of life, that maybe allowed us to survive, also might have left a vulnerability. I don't mean to say all of us would react the same way, but I know I never felt the weakness so strongly as in those three months, I was so nearly destroyed by something not related to food, or shelter, or even reproduction. I almost died, even though I could easily have found ways to stay in the West, with new friends, and new partners.

"I still could. There were men that looked at me. There was one man that I looked at too.

"We met and talked one night in a café by the stadium. Things seemed about to explode. How to describe it to you? Eruptive, I want to say, but I don't know if that's a word. Brimful? So many possibilities. I wasn't thinking in English then—that was more than six months ago—but it doesn't matter, none of the languages I know have the right words.

"Nothing happened, anyway. We just drank coffee from clunky purple cups. And I realized as I walked away, after, that our social bonds only reinforce a strength we already have built in.

"I knew something the man I had coffee with didn't know, that social structure came only after the venomous sting. Evolutionary biologists think that having such a sting was crucial for allowing evolution of social behavior in the wasp lineage, by providing a remarkable level of defense for what had been such a small and fragile animal. And I agree—you can only be social with strong weapons to defend your nest and young. That strength can free you from harming others. The need to connect with others *is* strength—not weakness."

•

Extroverts like Aynur, and natural politicians with near inexhaustible sociability, draw energy from conversations and avoid being alone—an inversion of the value system of those on the autism spectrum. And like Aynur and Charles, many people favoring one extreme of social intensity can find a coerced exposure to the other extreme unpleasant, like nocturnal mammals forced out into the midday sun.

Evolution has helped the nocturnal mammal to find daylight aversive, because this negative feeling makes the right behavior happen—which is to retreat from the light and await conditions that are more suited to the animal's design and hence less dangerous, and more rewarding. It is similarly possible that social or nonsocial brain states could be harmful if present under the wrong environmental conditions, which might help the mismatched condition (over the long timescales of evolution) become associated with aversive or negative feelings.

Just as different survival strategies are suited for nocturnal versus diurnal life, there may also be fundamentally distinct brain modes for different rates of information processing—each mode of value, but not mutually compatible (at least, not at the same time). The mode of dealing with a dynamic, unpredictable system (exemplified by social interaction) may be incompatible, or at least dwell in tension, with another mode that we need at other times. This second state would be one that allows us to quietly evaluate an unchanging system—a simple tool, a page of code, an algorithm, a calendar, a timetable, a proof—anything static and predictable, for which the best strategy toward understanding is to take the time to look at the system from different angles, with confidence that it will remain unchanged between one inspection and another. Brain states differentially suited for these two distinct situations might need to be switched on or off from moment to moment (with relative state preference tuned across millennia of evolution, and with variation from individual to individual in the strength and stability of each state).

Our optogenetic excitation/inhibition results were later replicated in independent mouse lines, but a key question remained: was there a link between this cellular imbalance shown to be causal for social deficits in mice and the informational crisis as experienced by Charles (and perhaps others on the autism spectrum)? Optogenetics helped unearth an idea for how this linkage might work; in our initial excitation/inhibition paper in 2011, we also had reported that causing high excitability of prefrontal excitatory cells (an intervention that elicited social deficits) actually did reduce the information-carrying capacity of the cells themselves, in a way that we could measure precisely, in bits per second. Thus, the very same kind of altered excitation/inhibition balance that disrupted social interaction was also making it harder for brain cells to transmit data at high information rates—corroborating what Charles had described for us in his account that the information coming in through eye contact *overloads the rest*.

Another remaining question was the origin of the aversive quality of information overload—so powerfully experienced as unpleasant by Charles and others on the spectrum. Being unable to keep up with social information feels bad in these individuals, but it is not obvious why. The information overload need not have any emotional valence at all, or perhaps even could have been positive—a sense of freedom upon realizing that one cannot keep up, with solace and a kind of peace in the resulting isolation. Here, though, I did understand, in part through listening to my patients, how difficult it could be to make your way through life with others constantly expecting higher social insight than you could routinely provide. And so the aversion might have been socially conditioned, learned through a lifetime of mildly stressful interactions, devastating misunderstandings, and everything in between.

But instead of this aversion needing to be learned, could information excess be innately aversive in itself, when above a person's carrying capacity? Certainly everyone, from the typically social to the simply introverted to the autism-spectrum individuals, can experience aversion after prolonged social interaction, when social circuitry becomes exhausted to some extent. It might make sense evolutionarily, in a long-social species like our own, to have developed a built-in aversion mechanism, providing motivation to withdraw from important social interactions when the system is fatigued, and likely to begin causing errors of understanding or trust.

•

"One more thing," said Aynur, as we stood up together—I thought I had initiated the action, finally needing to prepare for my one o'clock, but she had responded so quickly and closely that we were moving in perfect synchrony and then I wasn't even sure who had started it. "I know they just wanted me to have a onetime evaluation with you, and so we probably won't see each other again—but you had asked earlier, when we were talking about my family, how we made the silk to get those colors, and I didn't get back to that.

"This part is really interesting. I remember when I was little, I most loved the light-pink form of the tamarisk silks. It made me feel like seeing the flowering tree in person; the color seems so delicate but the silk is strong, all just like the tree. I don't know if you've ever seen one. The tamarisk is such a wonderful bit of life. A desert fir, evergreen but also colorful.

"By the way, there are wasps that lay eggs in the tamarisk tree. Then a new kind of wood forms around the egg—a growth, a gall: a twisting ball of nut and root. It's like a teratoma, but it doesn't hurt the tamarisk. There is no need for the tree to fight it.

"I was reading the other day, the tamarisk is now an invasive species here. You call it a salt cedar—I like that name. People say it was first brought over here from Asia just for decoration, and now it's taking over parts of the American West. The tree thrives in salt, and makes the soil salty too, which gives it an advantage over the willows and cottonwoods.

"In some areas around here, hikers are apparently being asked to pull up the salt cedar shoots wherever they are seen, to protect the native plants and animals. Birds are losing the trees they used to live in—but it seems doves are okay with nesting in the tamarisk—hummingbirds too. In other places people have given up fighting, and now just let it go. So there's a flood of salt cedar color in parts of the western desert. I saw a picture—you really need to see it. I wish I could show you.

"Anyway, what we do for silk—I can only tell you about the traditional way my mother taught me, how we do it slowly, by hand. I don't know how it's done when mass-produced. We sort the cocoons first, and for the stained and odd-shaped ones we have to boil them; they all change to the same shade in water.

"Then we stir with a stick, separate the threads, and twist the threads into strands; we need a few dozen threads to make a strong strand. To color, we dip each bundled strand into different pigments, dyeing one strand at a time. I remember this all as very slow, especially for those fine pinks and purples, the pale and light colors of the tamarisk tree."

•

An ever-growing share of all human interaction appears to lack the full vivid color of natural social information. By suppressing rich social multidimensionality, we relieve ourselves of its mental burden (though we may come to miss, or even crave, this burden once discarded). We suppress the visual stream of information on the phone, or simplify the entire social data stream using emails and posts and texts; each of these methods for reducing data-per-interaction confers a kind of insulation and enables a higher rate of individual social events, if desired (though allowing more frequent misunderstandings).

The trend toward increased social partners and contacts, with fewer bits of data transmitted at each contact, may have already reached a practical limit, approaching a mode of one bit per interaction (liked or not). That remaining bit can still be imbued with immense intensity, arrogating attention, driving passion and intrigue—because the bit is charged with social context and our imagination: that is, with premade models in our cortex, ready to run. Human connection in some form is now possible through only a few words or characters, even a binary flip of a switch—obviating some of the pressures of social complexity and unpredictability.

We could perhaps now relax categorizations of sociability (as a little outdated) that define what is healthy or optimal based on only the typical high-information-rate in-person social interaction. People with autism (at least on the high end of the spectrum) can seem more socially adept if the interaction is moved out of real time—to low bit rates, as with text. Though any interaction style still risks errors and misunder-standings, communication can seem improved if given the grace of time.

The bits to be transferred can be prepared at leisure, and then dis-charged when ready with a tap; no reply is needed immediately. These bits may then be placed in the broader context by the recipient—over minutes, hours, or days—to be evaluated from different angles. Possible replies may be considered, and scenarios run forward like a chess match for two or twenty moves, off the clock—until a reply may come, a tap or two when ready: Morse for the late-modern human.

The autism spectrum, then, need not be seen entirely as a "theory of mind" challenge—which has been a popular and helpful idea, holding that in autism there is a fundamental problem with even conceptual-izing the minds of others. Instead, the bit-rate-limitation idea (which optogenetics has helped reveal) would perhaps fit more fully with the experiences of many patients, who are capable enough but require time to run their models, to fit their own carrying capacities.

Psychiatry and medicine broadly—though still constructed around interpersonal communication—can survive and operate well with much less social information than the traditional face-to-face interview provides. I came to this understanding first as a resident at the local Veterans Administration hospital, where (under the relentless pressure of overnight call shifts) I found that the unique human connection needed in psychiatry can form first through a thin audio channel, the low-dimensional projection that is a phone call, if extended in time.

I then rediscovered this for myself, also in a time of necessity, as an attending during the global coronavirus pandemic of 2020. Emergency psychiatry, I saw again and again, though it somehow surprised me each time, can be carried out with precision even over the phone, through that lonely single line.

The Veterans Administration hospital rises like a mirage out of grassy foothills near the university. An oasis of contradictions, this VA system inspired Ken Kesey's *One Flew Over the Cuckoo's Nest*, but is now largely staffed with university-affiliated academic physicians at the leading edge of the field—and so to this day, the VA still evokes simultaneously both psychiatry's prescientific troubled distant past and the neuroscience-driven promise of its near future.

The on-call psychiatrist at the VA is dubbed the NPOD (neuropsychiatrist on duty). The main duties of the NPOD (one resident for the whole hospital, all night) are wrangling emergency room admissions, responding to consults from inpatient services, and caring for the psychiatry inpatients on the locked units. A major side job, however, is fielding calls coming in from the outpatient community, throughout the immense catchment area of this flagship hospital encompassing all the military veterans who might be phoning in from home—especially those suffering from PTSD (a common and deadly disease that is often resistant to treatment by medication).

Page the NPOD: an invocation when all else has failed. In the midst of other emergencies, the NPOD receives a call forwarded from a veteran beyond the walls of the hospital: a reaching-in from a human being who is jangled and guilty and helpless, needing only to talk with someone, anyone, who might understand. I found these calls could require an hour or more to work through. Less time would be taken in person, but a different mode was needed for these purely auditory conversations that were still sensitive and vital, with the gray specter of suicide looming.

When the call would come, seemingly always near three o'clock in the morning—perhaps in the middle of a chaotic scramble from the inpatient ward to the emergency room, or sometimes just as I was going to try for a few minutes of sleep in the barren housestaff call room—early in my training it was hard to suppress feelings of anger, especially since there was no concrete goal for the call, at least that a combat veteran could typically describe. The patient just needed to talk—and so I learned to transform myself from efficient physician to purely empathic partner. Both veteran-as-patient and myself-as-NPOD, I came to realize, were fighting a new battle in different ways, each trying not to bring feelings from prior personal trauma into the present, to not transfer presumptions and imputations from one context into another.

I would often field these pages in the call room, curled up for hours

on the impossibly hard and narrow plastic mattress—still in scrubs and
ready for any urgent summons to the locked unit for patients with chest
pain or needing restraints—but under a thin hospital blanket to ward
off that bone-chilling pre-morning despair, phone braced uncomfortably between cheek and shoulder. Not a propitious arrangement for
deep connection, yet somehow by the end of each call, the patient and
I could usually both move on—to the next interaction, the next challenge, or perhaps even to a shallow snippet of sleep—with a kind of
peace, a gift of warmth from another human being, after a true social
interaction drawn out across the line.

The coronavirus sweeping over the planet, years after my VA service,
coerced a retelling of this story in a new way. As populations from city
center to countryside became fragmented, by design, to manage the
contagion, many human interactions either were forced to play out at
a distance or were simply sacrificed. The culture of traditional psychiatry thus seemed initially vulnerable. Video and phone appointments
(desperately needed as a replacement for clinic visits during the crisis)
were for the first time widely approved and scheduled; this normaliza-
tion of virtual psychiatry interactions had long been possible but resisted by the established clinical structures for an undeniable flaw:
lacking the full information rate of in-person communication.

Younger patients were immediately at ease with video appointments
via the Internet, considering this interaction to be as natural as any
other (and even preferable), but some of my older patients were uncomfortable with the idea and preferred the telephone. During one of
these audio-only visits—with Mr. Stevens, a man in his mideighties I
had known for years—I was startled by the immediate reactivation
within me of that intensity of focus and feeling, all centered on the
spoken word: that purely auditory information stream, that thin squig-
gle of time-varying sound, which by necessity had guided so much of
my psychiatric caregiving during call shifts in residency.

Mr. Stevens had relapsed into depression four weeks prior (before
the COVID-19 pandemic took hold in California), at which time I had
bumped up the dose of one of his medications. Now as I exchanged
pleasantries at the start of the phone call (taking time even before dis-

cussing his disease symptoms, while knowing that if suicide were a risk, I would never see him face-to-face in time), I noticed that I had adopted that familiar life-or-death focus on his timbre and tone and pauses and rhythms that I had learned with the veterans at the VA— and that I already knew all I needed to know about his mental status. By the time we got around to his actual description of symptoms and feelings, I found we were only confirming what had already become clear to me, quantitatively and with certainty: that his depression had lifted by about 20 percent.

The most socially adept among us do this all the time—those beyond my own capability, who without effort or training or delay can see through the vast avalanche of social data at just the right angle to find unerringly the meaning of the moment. But every part of us contains our whole, if reflected upon. Even with little carrying capacity, connection still comes, with time.

•

"I feel like I want to tell you more," Aynur said as we stood in the doorway of my office. The hallway was quiet, and the carpet looked drab and dim. "It would be nice to talk again, but I guess I know we won't ever. I am sorry. I know there is no time, but one more thing: I had a final moment you should know about, the morning I was to leave Europe. Not looking at a man, but looking at a girl.

"It was six in the morning, and I was gazing out from my small loft window, drinking the last of my tea, preparing to leave for the airport, and taking a minute to pause and reflect—to pay my respects, in a manner of speaking. There was not really a view of the city, just the gray apartments across the alley, but I still felt this was a goodbye to Paris, a quiet moment of homage. I had learned and changed a great deal, and the French doctors might have saved my life. As I looked out into the light mist of morning, toward the tenement across the way, a ten- or eleven-year-old girl in a hijab emerged alone onto the narrow balcony.

"I had seen her and her family before, in passing, in occasional glimpses, the snapshots one gets. She seemed to have a little sister, and they lived with their mother and father, who wore traditional dress, not typical French style, though I did not know the country. But this was much earlier in the day than I had ever seen her before, and she was alone. She looked out toward the east, followed by a quick glance back to the darkened apartment. Her face was set and serious; she was not there to enjoy the sunrise.

"Then she moved to the balcony, to the edge, and turned her back to the sun, facing west. I held my breath—for her. I had envisaged myself jumping, like this, so many times—while looking out this very same window.

"She took out a phone, and hunched over for a moment, then straightened up and held it out in front of her. In a moment her whole demeanor had changed; she had become a movie star, her face shining with fierce glamour. It was just a selfie.

"She then returned to her position hunched over the phone, looking at the image. She remained this way for almost a minute, and then quickly looked at the sliding glass door back to the house, which she had left partly open; all seemed well for her, remaining dark within.

"For the next ten minutes I watched, enthralled, as she flipped back and forth between the two positions. Her next selfie was another joyful one, then one with a silly duck face, followed by one with her tongue stuck way out, peace-sign fingers forming a horizontal V wagging just below her chin. After each one, she bent abruptly into an intense state of frozen scrutiny. Her focus, her intensity, was impressive. This seemed a rare stolen opportunity—perhaps her mother was in the shower and would emerge any moment. Back and forth she went, on and on, almost puppetlike in the stereotypy of her transitions. I had always seen her, interpreted her, as a small child with her doll, but here she was being jerked back and forth by something else, a new drive—whipped by an unchildlike need.

"Eventually she was satisfied. She slipped back inside, and was gone.

"I felt profound sadness, and joy, and jealousy, all together. Is there a word in English for that? I've felt that before, those three things together. There should be a word. All three basic layers of emotion, down and up and sideways, all wrapped up in a tight and disorganized little ball.

"The jealousy—though we shared faith, gender, youth . . . our cultures were still so different. She was still blessed, gifted, able to begin a journey I could never take. I was bound too firmly to my own, to my trapped and now tortured people.

"My joy came from knowing this was the outset of her journey, that she was setting off from her family's homeland, preparing to weave a new fabric of her culture, traveling down her own road to autonomy.

"Though moments like this, of course, must occur thousands of times a day, every day, around the world, my sadness might have come from realizing her parents would never know what had happened on the balcony, in the way I did, as a complete stranger; this was a poignant hidden moment of a girl separating from her mother's hand that would never be shared. The sadness also, I guess, came from my own selfishness—from feeling connected to this girl in many ways, but realizing I would never get to know her deeply. I was still feeling vulnerable, or empty—from my teratoma. From everything.

"She was found and lost to me almost at the same moment. I never existed for her, and never would, and she ended up only a sort of cross-thread in my life—marking a moment—though with a thread that is strong, and durable, like in that rough ribbon you have here with ridges and gaps alternating, called grosgrain, where the weft is even thicker than the warp.

"It is strange to say, but the thickness of her one thread formed a gap around which nothing else can come close. I came to know her deeply, though it took only a few minutes, and now she feels lost to me. I don't know how, but I might need to find my way back to her."

CHAPTER 4

BROKEN SKIN

As willing to feel pain as to give pain, to feel pleasure as to give
pleasure, hers was an experimental life—ever since her mother's
remarks sent her flying up those stairs, ever since her one major
feeling of responsibility had been exorcised on the bank of a river with
a closed place in the middle. The first experience taught her there
was no other that you could count on; the second that there was no
self to count on either. She had no center, no speck around which to
grow.

—Toni Morrison, *Sula*

Henry, nineteen years old, had been found rolling naked on the aisle
of a county bus. When the paramedics arrived, he told them that
he was imagining eating people, and saw visions of himself consuming
flesh and bathing in blood. But after his swift transport to our emergency department by police, Henry gave me, the on-call psychiatrist
summoned to evaluate him, a more relatable story instead, with more
universal themes. He described a lost love that had brought him to
despair, to the aisle of the bus, to suicidal thoughts, and to me.

Not even guessing at his diagnosis yet—there were still too many
possibilities—I let my mind work freely, picturing the scene as Henry
described his magical first moment of romantic connection from three
months ago. In her short fur-lined coat, Shelley had knelt on the torn
vinyl seat of the church field-trip bus, leaned close, and kissed him—
just as a sunbeam unexpectedly broke through the canopy of trees and
fog. More used to the pervasive chill of early spring among the coastal
redwood groves, he was surprised and enthralled by the sudden dense
warmth on his skin through the window glass. Shelley's own warmth,
the excited heat from her hungry red lips, brought her together with
the sun in him. She was connecting him to everything, and connecting
to everything in him.

But now, not three months later, everything was lost again—and the midsummer sun had somehow turned freezing. Henry gestured, showed me how he had covered his eyes—hands together, fingers interlocking—to block the sight of her driving away from the parking lot of the diner, where she had met to break up with him, just two days ago. He had been shielding himself from the image of her bright red rear taillights, as she left him to find another. Nothing remained for Henry—he had no connection to her, nor to anyone else, it seemed.

Henry's blockade of the scene of her departure seemed an oddly immature defense, I thought, more suited to a toddler than a grown man. He was midperformance, reenacting here in Room Eight—and watching me instead of his hands, closely tracking my reaction. As I looked on, and as he lifted his arms higher, the sleeves of his loose sweatshirt fell back to his elbows, exposing forearms crisscrossed in fresh razor slashes—crimson, crude, brutal parallelograms. A big reveal, an intended one it seemed, of agony and emptiness. His barren core was now visible, through his own shredded skin.

At that moment an image came together in my mind, labeled with a short diagnostic phrase. All the cryptic threads of his symptoms, each mysterious on its own, made sense because of their mutual intersection in that instant: the bloody violence of his thoughts about others, the cutting of his own flesh, his bizarre behavior on the county bus—and even the covering of his eyes to not see Shelley go.

The phrase was *borderline personality disorder* (a label of the moment in psychiatry that may change in time to something more reflecting symptoms, like *emotional dysregulation syndrome*—but which, regardless of label, describes something constant and universal, a fundamental part of the human heart). These three deceptively simple words clarified Henry's chaos for me, made some sense of his bewildering complexity, and in particular explained the positioning of his mind on the border between unreal and real, between unstable and stable. He was blocking the light's path to deflect the harshness of the knowledge it carried, protecting his raw and damaged depths, asserting crude control of what could flow into his body across the border of his skin.

Though each case is different, and I had never seen a person with a combination of symptoms quite like Henry's, new details began to fit the pattern as I asked more questions. He eventually disgorged again the fantasies of eating people with which he had shocked the paramedics—never actually harming others, but hating strangers on the street simply for being human. When he saw people he saw their insides, and their insides inside him.

The sun hurt, was cold and strong—and so to re-create the original feeling when Shelley had kissed him on the church shuttle, Henry had disrobed on a county bus, seemingly trying to find some patch of skin where the sun would feel the same. He was seeing blood everywhere, was swimming, diving, drowning. Good enough for police transport, state code 5150, to the nearest emergency room, to me.

Some of the people arriving on a 5150 hope to avoid an inpatient stay in the hospital, while others seek admission. My role was to make the border of the hospital real, by finding out who needed help to stay alive. My forced decision as the inpatient psychiatrist was binary: discharge Henry back into the evening or admit him on a legal hold—to our locked unit—for up to three days with no right to leave, an involuntary patient.

With the diagnosis now in mind, it was time to think about writing the note, completing my assessment, and settling on a plan—and that meant beginning with his first words. I looked down at my notes and returned to the moment I had walked into Henry's life.

·

Before money from our latest tech boom had flooded the region and brought about the emergency department's modernization, tiny Room Eight had served for more than twenty years in the valley as a major portal for incoming acute psychiatric patients. Many of the individuals who designed and created our densely connected silicon world had passed through this isolated latrine-sized room at one time or another. The valley was their home, and this their hospital, and windowless Room Eight served as the portal to acute mental health care—and thus as a sort of window into the valley's most human, most vulnerable heart. Room Eight was important; in a home it matters what can be seen from the window.

But Room Eight was dim and cramped, just big enough for the patient's gurney. Outside, an amiable, blazered guard stood by. Inside, a single chair for the psychiatrist was positioned as close to the door as possible; the ER setting can be unpredictable, and emergency psychiatrists (like other acute-care medical specialists) are taught to identify flight paths for themselves, and to position themselves close to escape routes, in case the interaction goes awry.

On my first contact with Henry, planning a flight path had seemed relevant. In a baseball cap and jeans, Henry was taller and heavier than me, unathletic but muscular—and his face seemed to twist loathingly at the sight of me. I tried to keep my face impassive, but my abdomen felt knotted and drawn tight in response. I had left the door cracked open, and as I introduced myself, sat down, and asked what had brought him in, the familiar cacophony of the ER filtered through: accompaniment for the first words of his monologue, which as my medical training dictated, would have to constitute the opening line of my note.

Psychiatrists begin as doctors of the whole body, in emergency rooms and on general medicine units, diagnosing diseases of all the organ systems, treating illnesses from pancreatitis to heart attacks to cancer, before specializing in the brain. In this yearlong all-purpose phase of internship after conferral of the MD degree, medical rituals are consolidated—including the rhythms of how to pass along all the information about a patient, in exactly the order expected by the attending physician (the senior doctor to whom the case is presented). This canonical sequence begins with the trinity of age, sex, and of course chief complaint, or chief concern—the reason given by the patient, in the patient's own words, for showing up in the emergency room that day. The formulation of *seventy-eight-year-old woman, chief complaint of worsening cough for two weeks*, is stated before anything else, before medical history, physical examination, or lab tests. This ritual makes sense in medicine, establishing focus on the active issue in a way that is helpful—especially for patients with many chronic conditions that would together otherwise be a distraction.

But medical custom is not always translated easily to the reality of psychiatry, especially in the next year of specialty training following medical internship. It takes a little time for the newly fledged residents, now in a phase of resetting and relearning, to transpose this medical rhythm into the new space, since the first thing the psychiatric patient says, when asked, can be awkward to restate as the first line of a medical note: *twenty-two-year-old man, chief complaint: "I can feel your energies in me"; sixty-two-year-old woman, chief complaint: "I need Xanax to cry in therapy"; forty-four-year-old man, chief complaint: "These fucks trying to control me. You can't follow me in death now, can you. Fuck you."* We write it down anyway.

I had elicited Henry's chief complaint with my stock opener, asking what had brought him here to the emergency room—and conscientiously recorded his response, the first line of my note:

Nineteen-year-old man brought in by police, chief complaint: "My father said, 'If you kill yourself, don't do it here at home. Your mother would blame me.'"

I recalled having so many immediate questions at that moment, but no pause had been given by Henry—he was only getting going, opening the veins. The words had flowed quickly, in a fluid and organized way—and everything, in retrospect, fit the borderline diagnosis. He implicated that broken relationship as the root cause of his suicidal despair, the lost perfect love that had begun just a few months ago with a kiss on a church field trip, and ended two days ago with their breakup at the diner in Santa Rosa. He had recounted from there the rest of the abbreviated, tortured odyssey occupying his past two days—learning to cut himself in secret, going to his father's house to show him the results, and after his father's stunning statement, running out the door and down the street, desperately searching for a bus, in a frenzy to feel what he had felt first with Shelley. Along the way, Henry included the story of his parents divorcing when he was three, complete with memories of climbing up on his mother's lap, crying *don't want to get that new dad*—but her face had been composed and set, impassive, comfortable with her son's tears. He had described the chaos of the divided home that resulted, when those who most loved each other became overnight those who most hated each other. How all human values, positive and negative, had been inverted, inexplicably, inescapably. How he learned to live with two separate worlds in two houses that could never interact, how he could not speak of one to the other, how he was forced to create and maintain two distinct and incompatible realities to survive.

And finally before he fell silent, he entrusted me with the visions he had described to the paramedics and the ER staff—the images of blood and cannibalism, and his revulsion for other people. Not just a desire for distance, but a disgust with all humanity.

Earlier as a medical student, I might have misdiagnosed him with schizophrenia or psychotic depression—dislodged from the real world either way. But Henry was lucid, and his thoughts were organized; he had not quite broken away. Only the person with borderline can travel from reality to distortion and back, speaking both tongues with dual citizenship—not quite delusional, but with an alternative framework—to help manage a hostile, unpredictable reality.

Sometimes it can seem that both the self and what lies outside the self are not yet fully defined within the minds of borderline patients—not well resolved as entities with constant properties and worth. The relative values of different situations in the world, and of the different levels of human interaction, seem not smoothly compared—leading to reactions without subtlety, such as catastrophic thinking about unlikely possibilities, or extreme reactions to the natural give-and-take of human relationships. It is as if they are still in an early stage of developing a kind of currency exchange that allows human values in different categories to be fairly compared—and so to guide feelings, and actions, in measured ways.

But this pattern of extreme and seemingly unwarranted reactions (which can also be present in other conditions, and occasionally appear in anyone) also seems to constitute a practical strategy for surviving the early-life trauma that so many borderline patients have suffered, a reflection of their reality that there is not a single or consistent value system that makes sense in the world. And other aspects of personal development can seem frozen in early states as well, such as the use well into adulthood of transitional objects like blankets or stuffed animals, items that soothe a child when they are held tight, allowing the security of one environment to be made portable into an insecure space. Henry's shielding himself from the sight of Shelley's departure — this was the defense of a child, in blocking rather than addressing an unbearable, unacceptable reality. All of these behaviors can be unsettling to friends and family and caregivers—but with reflection, and with experience, also can stir compassion.

Many borderline patients (and those who are not patients, but who still live with some of these symptoms) manage to keep private this fragility: the sudden swings, over an aching emptiness. Some are guarded about a secret curse too, one that is also a silent deliverance: intentional opening of their own skin, the volitional cutting of the arms, legs, and abdomen. These are wounds that need never be shown—except when useful. What need was fulfilled for Henry here, with the seemingly deliberate exhibition of his cut skin? Did he reveal this knowing what would be triggered in the system—in my system, in me? Borderline patients can seem maestros of eliciting emotion, bringing forth overwhelming negative or positive feelings—approaching their own in intensity, but within others. This skill can bring desired outcomes, rewards of a sort, including admission to the hospital (sometimes the underlying goal, even where there is no suicidal intent).

The more I now thought about the timing of Henry's gesture with his arms, performed while clearly watching for my reaction, the more it seemed manipulative in the moment, a power grab. He was not actually a suicide risk, I thought (my thinking swayed by the demonstrative nature of the gesture), nor did he hallucinate blood, nor did he want to eat people. Nor was he obviously criminal or antisocial; as far as my history-taking had revealed, Henry had never harmed a human being besides himself—not even an animal. And since he had never actually tried to kill himself, I assured myself that Henry probably didn't want to die, at least not yet. Though his pain was real, the showing of his self-harm was something else, a frantic grasping through borders real and unreal to find care and human connection, reaching across his own skin into others, diving under and clutching frantically at the warm blanket of human interaction that could turn cold at any moment, seeking the deep bond that would never come again. Skin on skin. His mother's face set, impassive.

I had pressing clinical issues going on — active players on the consult-liaison service, transfers from outside hospitals coming in, and a possible gastrointestinal bleed brewing on the locked unit. My capacity was not infinite. Henry suspected this, perhaps, and was telling his story strategically, knowing that if he did it right I could not easily send him out that night, alone, into that cold Palo Alto floodplain. He just wanted something from me, something immeasurably precious: me — my time and energy.

As this realization landed, I felt a rising tingle up my back, in that sensation of defensive rage that we feel in our skin, when personal boundaries are violated. Even though I knew his pain was real, my compassion was to that point only clinical and intellectual. A deep and shared ancestral state now arose in me that cared nothing for my compassion. The hairs were rising up, past my neck to my scalp, in that ancient and furious and privileged experience of mammals — a feeling that defines our skins, our barriers, and our selves.

•

Each emotion has a physical quality, like the bubbly thoracic sensation of falling in love. The rage of territorial invasion is felt in our physical boundary, in the skin. In our ancestors this feeling may have arisen as a posturing, the display of erected hairs to increase apparent size, but now, for nearly naked humans like us, this feeling serves only internally, as an unseen legacy felt personally, for our own use within. And Henry had evoked it in me, he had reached into me, eliciting the same sense our forebears had felt a hundred million years ago, as soon as there was hair to erect. The skin organs along the neck squeeze sockets holding hairs, the hairs stand, the body grows, the shape presented to the world expands — this is me; there is more of me, you should know. I matter more. I am more.

That feeling — nameless, universal, compelling — is an entangled inner state of positive and negative, an exquisite tingle of pleasure and rage. Elevated and expanded, my perspective grows and I feel myself rising too—a surge as the hairs stand. I am emboldened; danger is now to be sought—risk is everything; in this moment I can face the consequences and carry them through to wherever they take me. The boundary is the feeling, and the feeling the boundary. And then the hairs on my neck and back slowly lie down; I have a medical license; I am a professional being wearing a white coat, on a civilized planet, with limits. The wave crests and recedes. The feeling, with its primal mastery, subsides.

I had felt this before with borderline patients, but perhaps Henry could not know that he was bringing it forth now. Babies also motivate strong feelings in parents, without ever being taught to do so. Henry was young and unschooled, a baby borderline. He was a human mammal from a broken burrow—burrow broken at three and born then as borderline—frozen in time, with childlike defenses, yet with tools at the ready to breach my own boundaries, to move across my border, get under my skin, and tap my resources all the way down to my deepest, oldest inner state.

The skin is both border and sentry. Skin arises from ectoderm, in embryos; ectoderm is our initial boundary, the surface layer of cells, creating the most fundamental borderline between self and nonself. Our sense of feeling, our watchtower at the border between self and world, is built from ectoderm, with skin-embedded organs that detect touch, vibration, temperature, pressure, and pain. And the brain itself, though internal today, is built from ectoderm too, and so that layer ends up setting all boundaries of the individual, psychologically as well as physically.

Hair and fur are also built from skin, and likely came from whiskers first—muzzle fibers for touch sensation in our oldest burrowing ancestors, hiding from the surface-dwelling dinosaurs for forty million years until a meteor strike upended everything, sending mammals to the emptying surface sixty-five million years ago as most other life headed to extinction. These earliest hairs sensed the shape of the burrow in darkness, the dimensions of passage for the head—assessing if the self could enter for warmth or escape, designed to take a measure of earth's intimacy.

As whiskers evolved toward thicker and denser numbers, for increasingly rich sensation in navigating our dark burrows, we blundered into a new way of building borders. Thermal insulation with hair was discovered, and then ported around the body by natural selection in all its blind power. The burrowing mammals born with denser sensory whiskers also retained more vital energy—better managing their costly warm-blooded lifestyle fast-burning in the cold of night—and survived the sudden chill of a blocked-out sun.

These predesigned sensory skin organs then spread across the body over thousands of millennia—where yet further uses were discovered. Hairs could be raised upon threat along the neck and back, serving like a rattlesnake's warning; our earliest skin organs, like border sentries, were now also responding to invasion as a concept in the external world, as crossed territory, as new topology. And though raised hairs were an outward signal meant to warn others away, by the time we (mammals capable of describing inner feelings) had arisen, this visible sign accompanied something else harbored within. An internal sense was part of the state, becoming a signal more useful for the self. Hair— a mere peripheral skin organ far from the brain—was now reporting on personal territorial integrity that could be psychological as well as corporeal, and was signaling the invasion both to the world and back to us.

We (as humanity) would eventually lose most of our body hair once again, but the feeling itself remained, that exquisite charge of threat and growth—perhaps the first distinctive mammalian inner state, truly primal, a sense born long ago in dark tunnels.

We sense and define the borders of ourselves with skin: boundary, sentry, pigment, signal. Skin is where we are vulnerable, where our heat is lost, and where we must make contact to live and mate; skin plays many roles, and so bears its own diversities and contradictions. On our soft ventral sides, along the midline from throat to abdomen to pelvis—the front of a human being, derived from the ground-facing aspect of a four-legged reptile or early mammal—blood flows toward the surface for blushing and swelling, to reach out, to functionalize, to couple. But our hair-raising, tingling, rageful, boundary-violated feeling is instead felt and expressed dorsally, along the back—the more secret, less visible side of human beings, paradoxically facing away from the individual confronting us—but in our evolutionary history before standing upright, this was the more noticeable upper side, where like the ruffs and backs of cats and wolves, hairs could rise to help us expand our presence.

When the hairs are raised with rage—responding to loss of territorial integrity—some psychiatrists use that feeling in themselves, when they notice it, to help diagnose personality disorders like borderline. This clinical trick, rarely formalized, is an art of psychiatry, if not quite science—to listen to one's self, to notice the negative feelings evoked by the patient, to realize that those feelings are likely a shared response of others in the patient's life, and to use that insight in treatment. Thus an evolutionary vestige is also a diagnostic tool, remarkably—with all the caveats one might imagine, including being wrong—and so the wise physician maintains focus simply on the fact that the patient is likely to evoke that defensive feeling in others as well, which can be the source of difficulty in life, and thus the subject of useful therapy.

This transference works with positive feelings too. For good or ill, the patient or the psychiatrist might fit into a role from the past that had been created and played first by someone else in the other's life. By chance or desire, we sometimes find ourselves to be square pegs for square holes, and if the role is positive, the therapeutic connection can be strengthened—as long as the transference is identified, and monitored, and not allowed to distort the process of care. And indeed, almost inevitably in retrospect, toward the end Henry let slip a single sentence that helped me connect with him—unwittingly, or perhaps playing me perfectly. I had begun to wind down the interview, feeling more certain there was little risk he would harm himself that night, but still uncertain about admission or discharge, when he said, *I just want my parents to be together.*

There, right there, amid the tricks and misdirection, that at least was true. That was the one thing that mattered. The latent hope to connect the frayed edges and repair the broken self. A single father, I heard my son—and felt again, for a long moment, the fragmentation of our home when he was two.

Aware of the transference, and reminding myself that I could do little—and understood less—I admitted Henry on the 5150, completed the paperwork, called the unit, and brought him in to keep him warm.

•

Mostly unresponsive to medications, borderline is a perplexing brew of symptoms that can seem unrelated to one another: frantic fear of abandonment, intense mood swings, inescapable feelings of emptiness, bizarre public displays, morbid visions. Suicide is more common in borderline than in any other psychiatric disorder, and nonsuicidal self-injury—as with the deliberate cutting of flesh—can become powerful and rewarding, even desperately sought. This is a behavior that few can fairly claim to fully understand, but cutting is common—and thus means something about us, about humanity.

Unlike in other psychiatric illnesses—such as schizophrenia where bizarre symptoms force disengagement, push away others, and isolate the patient—borderline symptoms can often engage, entwine, and draw in others, at least for a time. Self-injurious actions like Henry's may indeed entangle others this way, but seem to serve some purpose for the patient too, internally. There is already another pain, of a different kind—and self-injury may work against this deeper, more profound hurt.

We know that many of these human beings have borne an unjust burden: psychological or physical trauma at a young age, sometimes attributable to their own caregivers. Henry's only source of warmth, in his tiny family nest deep in the chill of a redwood grove, had been not just disrupted, but also upended—inverted in value—and whatever had actually happened with his parents, Henry's perception and interpretation were clear: he had suffered greatly when he was very young. But care coupled with pain still adds up to survival, in a calculus of practicality for adapting to a hostile and confusing world. If those we trust, those we must trust, become unpredictable or harmful and borders are crossed, if value becomes inverted in a fundamental way, then a strange new logic for staying alive is needed. Survival requires staying engaged with caregivers, and not everything really needs to make sense if it also brings warmth. A ruptured world order results in a ruptured emotional life where nothing is stable but must be stabilized, and where human connection becomes a dialectic: both desperately needed and utterly to be avoided. In this light, the ability to work with alternative realities, in oneself and others, begins to make some sense.

The correlations of these diverse symptoms are real and can be quantified by epidemiologists. For borderline patients, trauma during dependency—early in life when warmth and care are needed at all costs—predicts nonsuicidal self-injury later. And the human dependency period is long. We have vast and intricate brains to build, and a diverse civilization to assimilate—a babelized complexity of human custom and cognition—which can best be done with the trust and speed and accepting nature of the child's brain. Our brains are building even basic structure—the electrical insulation, the myelin that gives white matter its whiteness, that guides electrical communication pathways across the brain—well into our twenties and beyond. As primates, and as human beings, we keep our skin exposed—dermal or neural, borders or brains—available, for use or abuse, as long as we can.

And so primate evolution in the direction of modern humans has brought us a dramatically longer childhood, with dependency and vulnerability greatly extended in time. Childhood is now pushed to its limits, longer already than the mean life span of our recent ancestors, to the borders of fertility and beyond. Nowhere is this phenomenon more clear than in the practice of medicine itself, with its interminable training period. The halls of teaching hospitals are populated with small clutches of doctors still in residency or fellowship training, schooling in tight and vulnerable clusters of white coats. They are all in mid-adulthood but still trying to learn, trying to find love, and trying to not die—their hair a graying outcropping of the skin and the self, signaling frailty more than authority.

Though we know why our vulnerable period may be so prolonged, we do not yet understand the biology of borderline personality, at the levels of cells or circuits. As always, to approach this question in a scientific way, we might choose to simplify by reducing the selected question to a reliable measurement, to a single observable. The reward of pain, of cutting—though not unique to borderline—is coupled to the disorder, and serves as a remarkably clear measurable, reporting on a powerful and altered human inner state.

What makes a human being cut? This is already a hard question, but one can take it a level deeper: what makes any being do anything? In different settings, the answer can be reflex, or instinct, or habit, or to avoid discomfort or pain, or to get a bit of pleasure, a buzz of reward . . . but instead, we could imagine a world where all behavior is guided by pain, and by release from pain. We sometimes are driven by the seeking of a positive feeling, but an individual can instead be guided chiefly by suppression of internal discomfort as the motivation for action.

Could behavior be motivated for survival strongly enough if a species or an individual were to do without pleasure—and instead just use temporary reduction in suffering as a motivation for the correct behavior? With a suitable action taken, to promote survival or reproduction, then an internal pain would be reduced—if only for a moment. If we were gods designing beings, this strategy might work. What would a human being look like, act like, whose baseline was psychic pain, and whose every action was taken to reduce, or distract from, this pain?

We can put off pleasure at any moment, but we cannot as readily ignore pain. Perhaps, then, pain would be an even more powerful force for guiding behavior. Reduction of, or distraction from, inner pain might work as a motivation for just getting up in the morning, or for socializing with friends, or for protecting children—though the mannerisms might look odd to us, as we are constructed now. The style and melody and rhythm of each action would seem off, bizarre and volatile, of a being living in agony and acting for its reduction. But such an existence, at least for some, may already be a reality. Such people might not seem too different from human borderline patients—our sisters and brothers and sons and daughters, terribly burdened with negative inner states.

Such an insight could also bring hope for understanding and treatment, because inner states and value systems can be changed, and may even be designed for easy change. As a being grows, as the environment changes, as the species adapts and evolves, valuations assigned to parts of the world—like the worth of having a thing or being in a place—must adapt as well. Such internal value is a currency like any other, and should not be fixed to an immutable standard that could prevent growth. Instead, value must be set by fiat—whatever is good for survival—and easily, precisely, quickly so. From birth onward, as the dimensions of self and life change, existential dangers—even threats to life, predators—become minor annoyances, or objects of beauty, or prey. The rush of fear and horror must fade, must become joy, must morph into the thrill of giving chase.

Changing of value on any timescale—fast with an instantaneous new insight, slower with growth and maturity, slower still even over millennia as the world and species evolve together—allows adaptation to shifting conditions by tuning inner exchange rates for the competing currencies of suffering and reward. The experiences of borderline patients, and insights from modern neuroscience, together show that valence—the sign of negative or positive experience, aversive or appetitive, bad or good—is designed to be changed, and readily.

•

Neuroscientists can now set these exchange rates, adjusting with precision how likely an animal is to do almost anything, with optogenetic targeting of specific cells and connections across the brain. For example, depending on the specific circuits targeted, we can cause animals to become more or less aggressive, defensive, social, sexual, hungry, thirsty, sleepy, or energetic—by writing in neural activity with optogenetics (in other words, dictating that just a few spikes of activity occur in a handful of defined cells or connections).

As the subject's behavior changes instantaneously, shifting to the favor of one pursuit over another, and thus seemingly switching from one system of values to another, sometimes a psychiatrist cannot help but think of borderline patients. These individuals can be swift to react strongly with value assignments or changes—for example, treating a new acquaintance or a new psychiatrist as an archetype of the category: the deepest friend, the best doctor. And this positive categorization so powerfully expressed can be erased or reversed in an instant—transitioning (after a caregiver's perceived misstep, or after attention from a partner is perceived as inadequate) from best to worst, all the way to catastrophically negative.

This binary switching in people is sometimes attributed to skilled acting and manipulative intent—but my perspective (shared by many) is that these labile states are truly felt, overwhelmingly so. Extreme reactions reflect all-or-nothing feelings, subjective states adapted to uncertain life experience. The survival skills of a traumatized child—though this does not describe all patients with borderline—become the distortions of a suffering adult human being, living life in chronic negativity, with everything framed in terms of what might be strong or pure enough to distract from unrelenting sirens of psychic pain broadcast throughout the patient's inner world.

There are deep and powerful brain structures through which these effects can be borne out. Some of these circuits and cells (like the dopamine cells near the brainstem) broadcast their influence far and wide, sending connections nearly everywhere in the brain—including to the recently evolved frontal regions where our most integrative decision-making and complex cognitions occur, as well as to older regions that manifest survival drives in their most basic forms. Positive or negative value can be easily attached by these dopamine cells to even neutral items like an unremarkable room. With optogenetics, turning down the electrical activity of dopamine neurons in the midbrain, by providing a flash of light every time a mouse enters a neutral room, causes the animal to begin to avoid the harmless room, as if it were a source of intense suffering.

This experiment may be accessing a natural process, since a different but interconnected deep brain structure, the habenula, (a structure—so ancient it is shared with fish—that fires away during hopeless, uncontrollably negative, and disappointing situations), acts through turning down the dopamine neurons in the midbrain naturally, just as optogenetics does experimentally. This circuitry can thus impose sign, or valence, where none was present before.

It has been discovered that early-life stress and helplessness can increase habenula activity, and borderline patients may be locked in constant uncontrolled negativity from their habenula-to-dopamine neuronal connection—or other related circuitry. Fixed to a baseline of pain, they may live out a hard-learned lesson about the way the world is that could have only been internalized by the young.

Cutting may reveal such a negativity of the borderline patient's inner state. This behavior might recalibrate that negativity, introducing a new, sharp, and fresh pain that is controlled and understood, rather than the uncontrolled (and inexplicable) feeling from childhood. So lifelong suffering, at least for a moment, is renormalized into almost nothing by comparison with the new self-generated sensation. Intense negativity—as long as it comes with agency, with control, with a reason—can be desperately sought.

Modern neuroscience may thus begin to reveal how Henry, and those like him, could come to dwell in such a state, with early-life trauma seeding negative-valence predisposition into the arable field of the young and vulnerable mind, and sowing deep instability in the valuation of human connection. Studying fish and mice, our cousins with whom we share key ancestors, shows how powerfully and instantaneously the value of absolutes can be accessed and changed by activity in a few specific cells and circuits in the vertebrate brain—and thus very likely in our brains.

We each have a narrative in our minds, an in-progress drawing easeled up and ready to go to explain ourselves and others, to justify our sense of self and our relationship to the moment. We carry that depiction around with us, and we also carry those of our friends and family and others who are important to us, as images which we consult from time to time. It has been hard for those who most love and cherish the borderline patient to build such an image—to really create and hold an internal model mirroring their loved one's narrative and suffering.

But with a little help from modern neuroscience, these friends and family and caregivers and others can now begin to imagine, and perhaps nearly understand, living life this way.

Early-life trauma can happen to any animal, but our young may be most vulnerable because they have the most to internalize. Our evolutionary (and cultural) strategy for learning has been to lengthen childhood, and so as a side effect, extend risk. Other animals might for other reasons come to live in negativity as well, without a means or reason for signaling this inner state to the outside world, but borderline-like symptoms may most readily reveal themselves in the context of the complex social networks of human life—and when our unique planning and toolmaking allow for discovery of behaviors like cutting. Even Henry, as I found out later, did not stumble across that particular innovation on his own.

•

Henry had many superficial cuts on his arms that were rapidly healing and uncomplicated. As borderlines go, he was still mild, still just figuring it out. Even his known childhood trauma was not so bad, at least as known to me, at least by comparison with what I had seen in others— a difficult divorce for sure, but far worse can happen.

And yet Henry's suffering was real. His family was broken, and every experience that he shared was warped in some way by this fundamental loss, which was a burden squirreled away whole, unmeted, bending his inner form, creating counter-confusions of positive and negative, black and white, reality and imagination, until the only dialectic that mattered was the one at the heart of everything for him: connection and abandonment, water and oil, unblendable.

For the first three days of our hold, a measured process of ministration was set in motion—of set rhythm and duration as with any 5150. The one held, the newcomer, is made warm and then made available, like a new lion cub introduced to the pride; the patient is first given a bed, and then in firm and steady ritual is visited by members of the caregiving team. Several days follow of this gentle and insistent attention—from nursing assistant, nurse, medical student, resident, physical and occupational therapists, clinical psychologist, medical consult team, social worker, attending physician—alongside the other patients, all strangers held together and each with a different reason for landing there. It is altogether a more complex and challenging brood than could be prepared for by instinct or intuition.

The time spent by any one patient on a locked ward is typically just a few days, which seems not enough time for cells or circuits to change fundamentally, nor for significant therapy-driven behavioral modifications. Yet each morning, a life-or-death judgment must be made by the clinical team on the locked ward. As we evaluate patients subject to the 5150, those truly recovering and those simply recanting cannot be easily distinguished. All we have to make these judgments are human interactions and words, alongside published statistics and accumulated individual clinical experience. This is not enough; still, deep in danger we estimate the risk, because there is nothing else to do and there is nobody who knows more. Each day we must decide to continue, or release, our hold.

Even more unsettling, a deadline bears down. By morning of the third day, the hold expires and the patient is automatically released into the world even if danger continues—unless additional steps are taken. Numerology seems the only relevant consideration in setting the term of this three-day limit, since the duration maps onto no specific medical or psychiatric process. Three days, compelling and biblical, Old Testament or New: *three days and nights in the belly of the beast, three days and nights in the heart of the earth.*

If acute suicidality continues, two more weeks of care can be sought in a different kind of hold called a 5250 in the California code. But then judgment truly comes calling, in the form of a nonmedical outsider with right of passage into the psychiatrist's territory. This is the hearing officer, a judge arriving on the unit—trailed by another visitor, the "patient advocate," who is to play the role of pushing for release. The doctor (if still feeling that release may be unsafe) can make a plaintive case to continue care, to keep the hold—only now, this happens against opposition. This is an uncomfortable charade, a doctor arguing against someone named the patient advocate—while the doctor's whole calling and sense of self is built around helping patients heal in safety. Yet doctor and patient advocate must rise in battle, civil and gracious yet with secret ruffs half-risen, necks itching.

When animals within a species come into conflict, natural mechanisms from ancient circuitry can act to minimize damage. Rituals signaling size (as with measuring wide-gaped mouths against each other, in hippos and lizards) often allow the smaller rival to escape safely, and both to conserve energy. This conflict avoidance works when the stakes are not life or death, as in many mating conflicts where other such chances are present or may come later; but if opportunities are sparse, de-escalation of the conflict is harder. In the hearing on a locked unit, in these rituals, no de-escalation is possible, and the stakes are existential—truly life or death, but not for the combatants. The one with life interest in the outcome, the patient, waits in another room, with no presence or voice.

I had won almost every hearing before this one, and expected the same with Henry. But after only a few minutes, the ruling from the hearing officer, coming with godlike finality, was that I had lost. The edict for Henry was discharge: freedom and danger.

With no personal stake in the decision, I should have found letting go to be easy; but the outcome of this one was hard for me, and I found myself running through the case and the hearing in my mind again and again. Objectively I could understand the hearing officer's decision. Though I was concerned that Henry had not contracted for safety—he refused to make a promise to not seek suicide—his self-harm so far had been undeniably nonlethal. That fact was enough for the hearing officer, and perhaps it should have been enough for me.

I also should have been pleased that such a high value had been placed on personal autonomy by this decision, since I valued freedom too. I understood—all sides understood—that if a secret suicide were planned, it could now proceed, but in this case personal freedom had been deemed of greater significance than that small risk, upon the balancing of two categorically different fundamental values. This subtext is the core conflict of every such hearing—patient freedom versus patient safety—and thus both sides are the patient advocates in a real sense. Advocates for autonomy or for security: there is no older or deeper conflict, and none closer to the beating heart of borderline.

I struggled with this verdict, but I understood a source of my internal conflict; I was not blind to the transference. The parallel with my own life was not subtle—at least in one aspect, the early-life collapse of the home—and I could not help but wonder about my own son, only five years old at the time I treated Henry. While no hint of his affliction ever showed in my son, I did not have that perspective on the day of the hearing—and Henry developed his symptoms late. It was not until after his summer breakup, nineteen and with the sun still cold on his skin, that he had watched a movie on his laptop showing explicit cutting in a girl of thirteen—and the concept had clicked, hard, for him. He tried it right away, copycutting with crude tools and coarse strokes behind the community college gym, and then went straight to show his father.

Why did he go first to his father, to reveal his wounds? Perhaps it was simply to make the hurt known, to connect by shock and blood. But why not begin with his mother instead? She was the one he had seemed to fault at first: he had pointed to her as the one who had left the family, the one who had abandoned the nest. Henry's chief complaint—"*My father said, 'If you kill yourself, don't do it here at home. Your mother would blame me'*"—was this the key clue, a meaningful signature of pathology in his father instead, in ways that we did not yet understand?

These are the mysteries that a few days cannot uncover; obscured still, Henry's story had not been truly told. There was no time for deep connection. Henry had somehow revealed little of importance, that we could grasp anyway, in his two and a half days on the unit. He did exhibit a superficial form of progress, a decrescendo of sorts—gradually toning down his violent language, the descriptions of his desire to die, to drown in blood. But I knew how readily he could present different stories at different times, depending on what was needed, and I was not reassured. I wanted the time to help him.

If I had played the hearing differently, I might have found some way. Holds in California can be placed or extended, not just for suicidality, but also for danger to others, and for grave disability. But despite Henry's rage he was not violent, and never had been, to others; his bloody visions were just that: a churning of violent imagery not coupled to the power stroke of action. This left only the route of finding evidence for grave disability; perhaps a plausible argument could be imagined from his nakedness on the bus, a case to be made for his inability to provide for at least one of the basic-needs triad: food, clothing, and shelter. But Henry undeniably had, and knew how to access, resources addressing all his needs. The bus incident, like his cutting, was serious but not lethal, and so Henry stepped out of the unit on a foggy Sunday morning.

I watched him walk down the hall toward the escalator and the main hospital exit, canvas bag over his shoulder. He was uncured, untreated even, but I told myself there was little more that could have been done. His was a disorder untouchable by medication, he had wanted to leave soon after admission, and upon discharge he had refused even my outpatient referral for a specialized group behavioral therapy. The clinical literature predicted Henry's future would include more of these parasuicidal actions like cutting, that were revenging and rewarding in ways I would never fully understand. His wounds would heal and then reappear, as relief continued to come from the act for him—a desired injury, a counterstrike against internal suffering beyond my imagination. Henry had no choice; for a time he would have to continue to seek these stigmata, and to seek others—not skin to skin, but self to self, coercing human warmth across space and time.

His destiny in the long run could be the mellowing of borderline symptoms that usually comes with age—but time could instead bring suicide, the ending of the self, at a rate of 15 percent: the highest incidence for any disease, any burden of humanity. One hope was that those who cared for him could learn to use the state he was able to evoke in them, projecting that ancient feeling of the invaded self, magnified a hundredfold, back onto their own internal representations of Henry. Powerful empathy can be stoked from sparks of anger.

My own flare of rage had long since died away, though I knew I was still vulnerable to him, and would always be. Henry projected into me, and was close to me, as the written word is close to paper. But I felt that

I had exhibited to him only a pleasing dupability, in my earnestness to reduce his pain. And for a time I couldn't see my son without thinking of Henry. He had written his story atop my own, like a medieval monk inscribing new text upon a scraped and reused parchment, carving symbols of judgment and revelation onto animal skin stretched thin.

CHAPTER 5

THE FARADAY CAGE

Hegel made famous his aphorism that all the rational is real and all the real rational; but there are many of us who, unconvinced by Hegel, continue to believe that the real, the really real, is irrational, that reason builds upon irrationalities. Hegel, a great framer of definitions, attempted with definitions to reconstruct the universe, like that artillery sergeant who said that cannon were made by taking a hole and enclosing it with steel.

—MIGUEL DE UNAMUNO, *Del sentimiento trágico de la vida*,
translated by J. E. Crawford Flitch

The new thoughts came with all the surety of a change in season, in a gathering together of signs. Like the air of early fall, the first few weeks seemed to bring a shift in pressure in her mind, with a hint of wind revealing itself—a shimmering of her highest leaves, a rustling in the neural canopy.

She could feel the change in her skin as well, a subtle tingle, a chill of early fall. The sensation stirred a memory from a dozen years ago: Wisconsin in September, with her brothers AJ and Nelson, chasing Canada geese along the lakeside. Winnie had been seventeen after that summer of lymphoma chemo. Nothing had ever felt so charged as her return to the outdoors that fall after methotrexate—all around her and within her, even to her lungs, and to her brain, a mist of the season had seemed infused, clear and crystalline. In remission they had said, a likely cure, and they were right.

But this time, with the rustling of the leaves, unsettling intimations had come, borne high and kitelike on the same ghost wind—and there was a feeling of openness, of vulnerability, that was not entirely positive. She abruptly decided to take a month off, which was unprecedented for someone with her caseload. The team muttered, including her supervisor, but Winnie had built serious credibility, even a kind of celebrity, winning allowance after allowance, constructing patent estates from chaos—wielding her mind like a weapon trained in both law and engineering, unique in its ability to grapple with interlocking artificial-intelligence intellectual property families. Her team of lawyers and staff had filed seventeen hundred patents—counting all the divisionals and continuations—for their major client last year alone. But now she needed a month of leave; there were pressing issues to address. She was exposed.

The first issue was Oscar, who lived in the townhouse next door. He had installed a satellite dish on the roof over his deck—and seemed to be preparing to download her thoughts. Winnie needed someone to pay him a visit, dismantle the dish, and take him into custody; her homeowner's association security would have been natural to call in, but they were probably allied with him. Same with the police. She needed to find a do-it-yourself solution, to take care of herself, as she always had.

A trick occurred to her, a temporary countermeasure against the satellite dish—just a quick kludge, but with a chance of really working. She dug out a heavy black knit cap, the one with the reflective Raiders logo she got in college, which she hadn't worn since her Berkeley days. She put it on and pulled it down tight over her ears. Right away, everything seemed more contained. It was a bit surprising that it worked that well, with just the silvery logo of a football team as an electromagnetic field insulator, but there was no doubt—the satellite signal felt less likely to get in, or her own thoughts to leak out. The hat's tightness helped to shape the air around her head, to separate and clarify borders.

This vulnerability was correctable, then, and a more permanent solution dwelt in engineering. There were structural changes she could make inside the bedroom wall to reinforce that border with a conductive material—installing a true modern Faraday cage as a shield against the satellite dish signal. She started working on the wall, and her home tool kit gradually expanded with a few short drives to the hardware store across town for some more specialized items—a crowbar, a little chicken wire, some sheet metal, a voltmeter.

But other developments in this strange new season were more disturbing, and harder to address. Outside her expertise. More biological. At the center of it all was Erin, assistant to Larry the senior partner, younger than Winnie and five months along. Erin had become pregnant clearly to taunt her, targeting Winnie for living alone and not having children. It was unprofessional of her, and embarrassing for Winnie, and a little frightening considering Erin's proximity to power in the firm.

Here, there was no clear engineering solution to address the offensive behavior. Winnie had to get to Larry himself. Larry was the only one who could discipline Erin, and he needed to be informed and challenged to act. So over a weekend Winnie planned an incursion into the upper reaches of her own law firm—the C-class floor, with all the chiefs and captains. She mapped out her access plan and rehearsed the conversation with Larry—mostly in her head at first, not using her computer or the Internet, as it could be assumed Erin had hacked everything of hers, and had long since obtained access to her emails.

A lot of her planning became sketching on paper, elaborate reconstructions of desk orientations and restroom placements from memory, but then she got restless, needing to move her body, to do something physical, and so Winnie went back to her satellite dish countermeasures for several days—removing drywall, peeling the insulation back from her east-facing wall to see what lay behind it, and beginning to arrange the new metallic shielding.

Then came new, darker undernotes to the change in season, and some were frankly frightening. Over the second weekend of her leave, she became aware of the grim and gray-lipped ones—information vampires. Stocky, thick, and strong as ox hearts, lurking in the shadows behind the dumpsters, they started draining her energy and thoughts, tapping directly into her. And with this she moved beyond, into some new phase. This new season was not just wind shimmering her leaves. No longer just gentle phantom fingers softly stroking, now it felt more like glumpy digits pinching coarsely, aggressively, for her cells like grains—her brainpan a helpless, squat saltcellar.

And then, finally, a new voice emerged on Sunday, from within her head—mid-pitched, ambiguously sexed—intermittently repeating the word *disconnect*. The voice felt familiar in some way, with a quality she recognized from adolescence, when she once heard her own thoughts at that pitch, except now much louder and clearer. It was alien yet deep within her somehow, a shout between her temples.

On Monday morning, Winnie decided it was Erin, and knew that she had endured enough. She steeled herself, stepped out of her townhouse, and climbed into her car. The drive itself went smoothly, past the shadowy parking lot dumpsters without incident, though there was a surprising sharpness of the stop sign as she turned onto El Camino Real, standing out in a way that mattered. The acuity with which she felt its eight edges commanded attention—but a horn blared behind her. Startled, she drove on.

Winnie arrived ten minutes later at her law firm's oak-scattered Page Mill Road campus. She disembarked carefully. In the parking lot, near her car, a flattened screw lay on the concrete. She knew, as soon as she saw it, that they had placed it there as a sign: they knew she was coming and intended to screw her.

The day abruptly darkened—the atmosphere now ominous—and she nearly turned around and headed back to her car. An unsettling thought came to her: the screw revealed their deep access to her plans, since they knew she would be there, and therefore they had so much more—her personal life, her private records, her healthcare even. And she had gone through a miscarriage just a few days ago . . . though as she thought about that, her blood rising, Winnie felt her grip on her own experience loosen. She became not completely, not 100 percent certain there had been a miscarriage. She could not picture the experience or any details; suddenly, it was a little hard to remember what actually had happened . . . as if that inner wind whipping up to a tornado had stripped her branches nearly bare, and her memories were now mostly lost to that gray-fingered twister, swirling down from a glooming cloud that was heavy and pregnant with rain.

Winnie paused, trembling, standing over the screw, pressing her temples to process it all, to focus herself, to consider all the ramifications and uncertainties. A paralegal she knew distantly—Dennis, something like that, datable she had thought once—walked past on his way to the main building. He sent an odd look her way, searching. She turned away, put her sunglasses back on, and tugged her Raiders cap down tight.

Before others, anyone—lawyers, admins, paralegals—can complicate things, you have to go in now, she told herself, speaking the words clearly and distinctly in her mind as if lecturing. *You will not back down and run. That little screw message is just from Erin. Larry can be turned; Larry will be on your side.*

She steadied herself and stepped deliberately inside, keeping as far from the walls as possible; with a tense smile she showed her badge to the security guard at the desk, then walked to the elevators and rode up to Larry's fourth-floor domain. She made a pass by his suite; careful to avoid eye contact, she was still able to mark Erin at the admin desk, looking for trouble. Winnie's first tactical mission had been perfectly accomplished—identifying what Erin was wearing, that formless yellow dress. Then she headed to the bathroom, entered a stall, closed the door, and waited, positioning her line of sight so she could watch through the crack in the stall door for Erin to come in, knowing it could not be long.

She waited almost an hour, but eventually a flash of yellow flickered in. Winnie calmly stood up, opening the door to her stall just after Erin's closed. She walked straight to the bathroom door, exited left, pulled her hat down tight, and strode back to the office suite.

She'd worked with Larry on a couple of the firm's thorny international cases, but only at a distance. They were two different kinds of human being—diplomat and introvert, schmoozer and quant—and yet today he'd recognize her, and realize the urgency once she began to speak. She walked past Erin's empty desk, knocked on Larry's closed door, and walked in. He looked up from his laptop and made eye contact. She sat down, confidently, in a chair before his desk.

There followed a great deal of confusion. It could hardly have gone worse, and it seemed the next moment she was sitting in a cluttered side room in the human resources offices, waiting for an ambulance, with what must have been the entire firm security team, perspiring in blazers, watching her.

She had been forceful but scrupulously polite with Larry, factually laying out the situation—describing how Erin's pregnancy was an unprofessional gesture planned to humiliate her, providing details of the email hacking that had transpired since, even telling him about the screw and how terrifying it was to see—but she had also maintained, she thought, a reasonable and calm tone. She had kept her face expressionless, solid as concrete—careful to not upset him with emotion or gestures—but it all had seemed to spin sideways after a few minutes. Larry was on the phone, then the first blazer came, then firm hands on her elbows. With her vision darkening in humiliation, she had been marched out right in front of Erin. Winnie made sure to give no route in, keeping her face a mask, with no eye contact—and off they went, to this windowless room she had never known existed.

The ambulance came a few minutes later. Two men in purple latex gloves appeared with paperwork and a scattering of tubes and wires. She was relieved to see them, and desperate to get out of the little room. The EMTs were both thin and densely muscular like climbers—and courteous, as they conducted a quick physical exam and asked about her psychiatric history. She told them the truth: there was no mental illness in her family. But AJ, her older brother, was different from the rest, with a way of saying odd, muddled, arresting things. He had never found his path—but he also never really got the chance. Winnie told the EMTs how AJ had been found on a downtown plaza, collapsed alone near a bus stop on a blazing hot day, already dead.

It had been an AVM—arteriovenous malformation—an artery misdirected, its thickly muscled walls jetting high-pressure blood directly into a delicate vein that evolution had designed for another job: only for collecting puddles of spent blood, weakly exuding from the brain. A doctor had said the malformation might have been a sign of a broader problem, a connective tissue disease—but nobody ever knew for sure, just that at least one AVM had always been there, hidden from view deep inside his brain, struggling for years to cope with the ferocious and incessant pounding of the carotid pulse, its diaphanous membrane stretched thin until the moment came to burst.

She did also mention her possible miscarriage from a few days ago—she was still unsure about it, with the memory poised between real and unreal. They seemed irritated by that uncertainty, which she understood; she was bothered too. She was certain about her distant cancer, the words so familiar and fraught, lancinating even now—*cutaneous large T cell lymphoma with central nervous system involvement.* She recounted the clinical course expertly. How it had started with double vision and headaches . . . and how since they had found some cancer cells in her cerebrospinal fluid, the methotrexate had been infused directly there, into the spinal canal itself, at the level of her lower back. How she had been completely cured, now going on twelve years cancer-free.

She had some scrapes on her knuckles from the wall teardown she was doing at home, but she explained that only briefly since they didn't seem to care much about her renovations. She noticed the EMTs persisted for some time in asking about drugs, in every which way, perhaps trying to trap her, but getting the same answer again and again—no drugs, never even a cigarette, just an occasional glass of wine. In the ambulance, things finally got quieter, and she had a little more time to think about it all—a frustrating interlocking puzzle of possibilities.

Most likely her thoughts had been tapped, her plans picked up and sent ahead to Larry and his team by data vampires. Meanwhile she noticed the paramedics were calling ahead—to the hospital, they said, but more likely to the grim and gray-lipped ones. "*On a fifty one fifty*" they kept saying—50-1-50, or 50-150, or 51-50, which was it? The code must matter. Was it used to trigger, or accelerate, a download? Normally she could crack this kind of thing. Winnie pulled her hat down more tightly, and tried to drift back in time, just a few weeks, to how it all started, to feel that first exhilarating breath of fresh September air.

Later in the emergency room, the nurses and doctors asked all the same questions as the purple-gloved gentlemen. They pretended to type her identical responses on various tablets, apparently never bothering to talk to each other, in between rounds of prodding and poking with stethoscopes, blood draw needles, and reflex hammers.

They didn't care about her renovations either, but were very interested in the story of AJ—oddly far more than the paramedics had been. It got hard for Winnie to talk about him by the fourth or fifth time. As she gave shorter versions of his story every time, longer versions came to her, within her. There were increasingly lengthy pauses—she would stop midsentence, even midword—as images came sweeping through. Imagined scenes of his final moments, alone without a sister there to hold him, with nobody who loved him to cradle his muddled head.

AJ—the lost child, lost long before he died. School was as hard for him as it was perfectly suited to Winnie and Nelson, right down to their precision handwriting and their love of logic and engineering. But for AJ, even odd jobs had never quite worked out, whether in car shops or bakeries. Every venture seemed to end with befuddled bad luck, poor judgment, or dumbfounding accidents—though he stayed gentle all the way, until he fell that blazing summer day. She flew back east for the funeral, and a wrenching bark of a sob burst from her own body, a sound she had never spoken or known, when she saw that familiar crease in his forehead smoothed out, at rest, at last.

She lay curled on her side, on the gurney in Room Eight, and became lost in imagining AJ's final moments, reliving his run from the bakery to the bank, the run she and Nelson had reconstructed from scraps of paper in his pocket and clues from his co-workers, the agitated dash that turned out to be his last desperate attempt to support an independent life. The doctors had said the stress of that day, the running, the heat, and the worry, all had probably brought his blood pressure up, and the AVM had finally ruptured. Just a frailty waiting quietly, a small thing knocked loose by a day in which all the things that made his life hard had come together at once.

They could still poke and bleed and scan, but Winnie was done. Day turned to evening, dry sandwiches and juice boxes appeared and disappeared . . . and then a long stretch of nothing.

•

A knock came at her door, and a doctor walked in, with disheveled brown hair and coffee-stained blue scrubs under his white coat. He introduced himself, seeming to be sort of a mumbler—or maybe he was just tired. Winnie didn't quite catch his half-swallowed name, but *psychiatrist*: that word she heard.

Winnie sat up and swung her legs over the side of the gurney. He shook her hand, and sat in the chair near the door, saying, "I've seen all the paperwork from the ER team, and I've spoken with the ER docs. But if it's all right, I'd like to hear from you, in your own words, how you ended up here today." Winnie looked him over carefully, and then she rested her gaze in his eyes, taking a moment to think about his angles, and hers, before responding.

At the end of the day, she needed help, and had found no allies yet. Best to tell him something, if not everything. "Information vampires," she said. He needed to know. He wrote it down, and looked right back at her. "All right," he said, "tell me about that."

So she did—well, most of it. Not every detail, just the hard facts as anyone would see them. The information vampires were tapping into her brain, draining her thoughts; that all was clear enough and she could be logical and calm in describing it, with a surfeit of evidence that she could tick through. First her neighbor had installed a dish antenna on his roof two weeks ago to gain better access to her thoughts, but she had a shielding countermeasure that was in process. She had stopped going to work since people at work were accessing her, hacking in, trying to decode her thoughts and feelings. She told him about the screw in the parking lot too, so he would understand how powerful her enemies were, and why she had to disconnect and protect herself.

Winnie briefly mentioned the *disconnect* voice—how it was frightening but also reasonable, speaking a word she might have thought herself, voicing an idea that she wanted, but maybe something an enemy of hers wanted too. She explained that the word was spoken audibly inside, with all the qualities of sound. Someone, probably Erin, was accessing her mind—but why, she did not really know.

After a while he began to ask his own questions, in a pattern different from that of either the paramedics or the other ER doctors. When he asked about the Raiders cap she was wearing—pulled down to her eyebrows—she told him plainly, "That's to protect my thoughts." When he pointed to her gurney and asked why she had pulled it away from the wall into the center of the room, she answered simply, "Because I don't know what's on the other side." He circled back to her renovations, which none of the other doctors had shown any interest in, asking her for the first time about the wall she was tearing down and why.

In the midst of the doctor's questions, though, his pager went off; he apologized and went away. She spent an hour alone, looking at the wall in front of her, and then he came back, rejoining without preamble, acting as if it had only been a minute. Winnie asked what was going on. "It was just an emergency on the floor, sorry. I'm almost done here, but I can tell you what's happening," he said, sitting back down. "We're waiting for a couple tests to come back, but the bottom line is nobody can find anything wrong in your body—every test and scan looks normal. So that means we think what is going on is psychiatric. And the good news about that outcome is that there are treatments that can help you."

Winnie was not surprised. It had looked increasingly like the ER staff thought things were headed that way, though it didn't really matter—at this point she didn't care what they said, all she wanted was to go home. The ER docs had informed her she was "on a legal hold" and could not leave until psychiatry had seen her, but now she had seen everyone. Nothing had been resolved at home or work, and so she had things to do; in fact it was possible her work situation might have deteriorated a bit. She asked him if she could follow up in his clinic; it would be easy to call to make the appointment when she got home.

"Okay, let's talk about that," he said. "Would you be willing to stay in the hospital while we figure this out? And if not, what would you do when discharged, if we could make that happen?"

Winnie didn't have to think about it—that was easy, she wouldn't cause trouble at work anymore, that had clearly been a mistake. She would go home, resume her vacation, finish taking down the east-facing wall, and start ripping out the ceiling too—she was on the top floor, so it was safe, no risk to anyone. "I'm not staying here," she told him, "there is too much to do. I'll just go home and finish my Faraday cage."

He nodded at that phrase, and Winnie asked him if he knew the principle of Faraday cages, that they were conductive enclosures to cancel out electromagnetic fields. He nodded again. "Yes, I use them in the lab all the time," he said. "We put basically mesh cubes around our rigs. The rig is what we build to measure electrical signals in neurons. It's a Faraday cage just like you are building. It blocks noise from other electrical sources that might be in the room, or behind the wall"—he gestured where her gurney had been before she moved it, at the edge of the tiny room—"so we can detect currents, even from single brain cells, even in living animals."

Though still wary, Winnie couldn't help but get a little excited at this connection. She wondered if he knew of the experimental discovery of this shielding principle by Benjamin Franklin, and then the beautiful theorem that had emerged from the physics of electromagnetism, that external fields cannot access the area within a conducting enclosure. That the field creates a compensatory distribution of charges on the conductor, one that exactly cancels out the field itself. A field by its own nature creating its own annihilation. A thesis truly creating its antithesis. "Information suicide," she said.

He seemed to become restless at that, shifting his position in the chair. "So there are some things we're worried about," he said. "You've told me, and everyone, you don't want to hurt yourself—or anyone else actually—and I believe you. But you're destroying your home, and your plan is to keep doing it, because of the worry about your neighbor, that he's downloading your thoughts through his satellite dish. So you're actively tearing your house apart . . ."

Winnie could tell what was coming: they were going to trap her here. She searched his lips as he spoke, looking for signs he was under their control too. Actively destroying her home? This was not true, not at all. She was doing the only thing possible to *save* it.

"I have some paperwork for you—here, this indicates you're going to be admitted, brought in to the hospital tonight, on what we call a legal hold, which we can do, which we *have* to do, for grave disability," he said. "We need to do this because you have a psychiatric symptom that's causing real problems for you, that we call psychosis, which means a break with reality. You're hearing a voice in your head, and you have fears that are not physically realistic, that are causing you to damage your home, and put your own safety at risk."

She felt the world narrowing, going gray except for a narrow tunnel of distorted light around his face.

"It's now our duty to try to figure out what is causing this," he said. "There are lots of different possible causes—and hopefully we can try a medication that could help you." Words came to her mind unbidden, and she tried to match them to his lip movements. *Soapsuds, waitress-less, matilda.*

The doctor kept talking for a while longer, then stood up, and she focused back on the meaning of his sounds. He said he would see her tomorrow since he was also working in the locked unit during the day that week, and he left her with a sheet of paper with many words and numbers. *Grave disability,* she saw, and 5150. There was that code from the ambulance. Grave. They had her now. She kept her face still as a fossil, staring straight ahead at the scuffed yellow wall, not daring to picture what lay beyond.

•

The staff administered to her a new medicine that first night, and gave her an information sheet with it, which she kept to study; it was called an *atypical antipsychotic,* and they asked her to sign something about it. Whatever else it did, or didn't do, the tiny white pill certainly knocked her out, and she slept for fourteen hours.

When she awoke, Winnie found herself upstairs, in what they called the locked unit, among a group of fellow travelers, each a refugee from a different sort of storm, washed up onto the same shore. Winnie just listened that morning, not speaking but able to learn from them; it helped that her own storm had made a kind of landfall itself and expended some of its energy already, even by the first morning. She could still hear the *disconnect* voice, but it was less intrusive, no longer a shout—and she was able to focus on people more stably, and follow conversations.

She learned how to slash her arms with a toothpaste tube—she didn't do it, she didn't want to, but she learned it anyway. Two patients were talking in the breakfast area who had done this before—for different reasons—and were comparing strategies like recipes. One, a young woman named Norah, seemed to just want to cut herself a little bit, just to feel pain and see blood, to leave a mark and have it known. The other, Claudia, a large woman who could have been the mother of the young-adult brood, was focused on actual suicide—cutting arteries, letting all the blood out. Claudia was about to start electroconvulsive therapy treatment for severe depression—the doctors thought it would help, but Claudia had a different plan. She was utterly invested in ending her life. All her feelings and thoughts led there, currents joining into one flow that could not be slowed or diverted by wall or lock.

But the unit staff were a step ahead, it seemed—not even a toothpaste tube was available. The nurses were mostly miraculous—with only words and gestures, they managed to maintain peace among twenty altered and demonstrative men and women. The unit was like nothing else Winnie had experienced—a contradictory place, both hard and soft, desperate and secure. And the other patients—she could spend an eternity contemplating their individually damaged worlds. The unit was a maelstrom of fascinating and frightening alternate realities.

Winnie thought about the toothpaste, how the bottom of the tube worked for this job. Its stiffness sufficed; it had the right material properties for sharpenability. She pictured Norah and Claudia each as they had been in other inpatient settings, on less restricted units in the hospital, surreptitiously grinding the end of their tubes on any gritty surface, getting in a few or a few hundred strokes here or there when they could isolate themselves from staff. Winnie thought about how compelling repetitive action could be—with needle or knife—repeating the same action again and again, hundreds, thousands of times. She had an odd idea—that rewarding the act of repetition was the first achievement of the human brain. With relentless rhythm, to make a hard thing sharp: a stick, or a flint, or a bone. Striking again and again, grinding against rock, all through the winter—but with a different goal: to survive back then, not to die.

Winnie picked up psychiatry knowledge too—not from the other patients, but from brief conversations with the psychiatrist who had admitted her—about what they called psychosis. He saw her twice a day, once around eight in the morning in the room she shared with Norah, and then sometime in the afternoon, usually in the hallway when they happened to cross paths. Winnie noticed he seemed as sleepy during the day as he had at midnight. She liked that he liked Faraday cages, and she called him Dr. D. As her storm cleared more and more each day, she began to ask questions.

"Psychosis, what exactly is that?" she asked. "I mean, I think I know, but it's strange to hear you say it—it's an old-sounding word."

"Just a break with reality," Dr. D. said. "It can be used for hallucinations like that *disconnect* voice you hear. It also applies to having delusions—that's the word we use for beliefs that are false, but fixed."

She considered that. "What do you mean, fixed?"

"This fixity part is important," he said. "Delusions can't be reasoned away. Evidence does not help. I used to try, for my patients, when I was still learning. Maybe every psychiatrist has tried—but not for long. The delusion can't be budged. Some patients have these extremely unlikely ideas in impenetrable armor, so they can't be touched."

This idea of the fixed belief clicked with Winnie's engineering expertise. It was like the Kalman filter, an algorithm for modeling complex unknown systems—in which every guess at the value of a system property comes tagged with an estimate of the guesser's level of confidence. And more weight is given, when modeling the system, to guesses with higher certainty. It made sense to Winnie that the brain should work that way too, that knowledge should exist only with certainty tags, and that some types of knowledge of the world—not just the delusional ones—should be trusted all the way to the point of fixity, and placed in the brain within a special bucket called Truth, not subject to hedging or discounting. The category of Truth would allow fast and simple de-

termination of action without clock cycles wasted on statistical compu-
tation, and allow the brain to build complex edifices of logic on top of
these unquestioned facts. But she didn't say all that to him.

"I think it's not just psychosis that gets fixed like that," she said hesitantly, feeling pressure to get everything from her mind out before he
walked away, "but also maybe other ideas." She tugged her Raiders hat
down tight—force of habit, really, she was feeling lately that she did not
need to wear it all the time. "Like trusting your family, and marriage,
and religion, and some kinds of social and political beliefs. It's normal.
Every bit of knowledge should have a confidence number attached to
it, and some ideas should have a perfect score."

"I guess so," he said. "I think you're right, we do need those . . . rankings, I guess. Confidence estimates." There was an awkward silence.
He look down at his patient list, which she knew meant he would
soon move on to the undergraduate student, the next room down—
blond and smiling and manic and so many words—and never get back
to her.

But then he continued. "I think, though, for most ideas about how
the world works, a perfect score would not be helpful. And some possible explanations for things are so unrealistic— they should never get
close to becoming such trusted facts." He paused again. They were
standing in the hallway near the nurses' station, an odd pair, she could
see that. She in her hospital gown and Raiders cap, he in his daytime
getup of button-down shirt and slacks—one prisoner, one free, and patients meandering around them. And yet a connection was there; they
were passing information back and forth, untouched through the noise,
on their own local area network. "These unlikely ideas," he said,
"should never even get access to our minds in the first place, should
never be let loose to rise up into our working active consciousness at
all. Do you think you had any ideas like that right before you came to
the hospital? Distractions—really unlikely, that should have been just
filtered out—before ever rising to the surface."

He was talking about filters, but not quite correctly. In the quieting
of her storm, Winnie thought he might be referring to something she
had told him in the ER—her story of the screw in the parking lot. She

saw now that the idea she had at the time—that the screw had been placed there by Erin to torment her—was quite improbable.

But so what? she thought. Fixity was seen in delusions, but probably was also essential for healthy committed behavior—and similarly, allowing consideration of unlikely ideas seemed to Winnie to be normal and necessary as well. "You know, allowing awareness of something that's unlikely is not a disease," she said. "If you're talking about a filter, you should understand how they work. Optimal filters will still block a few things that you actually wanted to go through—and also will still allow some things that you wanted blocked to instead go through. That's for an optimal filter."

And for ten minutes she described for him Chebyshev and Butterworth electronic filters, and explained how Chebyshev type I filters do successfully block from going through what is not wanted, but unfortunately also block a bit of what is wanted, what should have been passed through. Fine for some electronics, or maybe some nervous systems, but not for the human brain. A species like ours, with survival so clearly based on intelligence and information, should not run the risk of blocking and throwing away potentially valuable ideas.

Other designs, like Butterworth filters, have the opposite weakness: these discard nothing of potential value, but allow too much to slip through. "I think the Butterworth design makes more sense for a human brain," said Winnie, "or, for all the brains of our species considered together. Unlikely beliefs held by some are a sign the species overall is working well." She said she would send him "On the Theory of Filter Amplifiers," Butterworth's 1930 paper. Winnie felt it was actually quite important for him to know that every system operates with an error rate that it accepts, to balance against some other consideration.

"Same with our electrophysiological signals in neuroscience," he said, seeming to agree. "We record tiny currents, and so we have to filter out noise to see the currents, and even the best-designed filters will still block or distort some useful things and allow through some useless things." Winnie had more to say, but at least with that she could let him move on. Now he seemed to know that distortion does not mean disease.

•

The inner voice grew still more quiet over the next day. She also felt decently stable without the Raiders hat and stopped wearing it. Winnie could sense something was getting better, though she felt a bit wary about revealing this to the doctor. He might assign credit to the pill, and conclude that this illness model he had for her was correct.

Dr. D. dropped the 5150 before it expired; Winnie had agreed to stay voluntarily on the locked unit until discharge, since the voluntary unit, the open floor, was full. But she was happy to work with the current clinical team, while the tests continued. She was on vacation anyway, she was learning a lot, and home still didn't feel quite safe.

"There are different reasons people can experience psychosis," Dr. D. said in the hallway, later in the afternoon after dropping the 5150, "and not all have been ruled out yet for you."

"But I thought you agreed," Winnie said, "that there might not even be a problem, it might just be my design. Our design."

"Yes, well," he said, "as you pointed out, people could be designed with different filters, just like everyone has different settings on their sound system. But there's a problem with that idea. . . . This experience has never happened to you before. As far as I can tell, you've always been logical and systematic, with a selective filter—it's maybe one of your greatest strengths, actually. So this whole thing is not really your design."

"What could make things change then, if they did?" Winnie pressed.

"Drugs could do it, but there were no traces of drugs in your system that we found," he said. "Infection or autoimmune disease also, but we found no hint of those in your blood work either. Severe depression or mania could do it as well, but you have no symptoms of these. Schizophrenia, though, has not been ruled out."

Winnie had some sense of what schizophrenia was, and it didn't fit with what she was experiencing. "Doesn't that start in teenagers?" she asked. "I would have had symptoms long before now."

"That's true for men, but twenty-nine is not atypical for first break in women," he said. "First break—that's what we say when schizophrenia declares itself, with visible symptoms like delusions and hallucinations. And sometimes one's own actions can seem foreign, controlled from outside the body—"

"Are there theories for what causes hallucinations?" she asked. "What could be the biology of something like that?"

"Scientifically, nobody really knows," he said. "Some people think that inner voices—like that one you hear—might be caused by one part of your brain not knowing what another part is doing, the brain not recognizing its own inner thoughts as itself. And so your own internal narrative, like the word *disconnect*, gets heard, and interpreted, as the voice of someone else.

"Similarly, you could feel that your actions are not your own, but reflect control from outside. It could just be that in schizophrenia, one part of your brain has no idea what another part wants or is trying to implement, and so an action of the body gets interpreted as a sign of meddling from the outside. The brain—casting around for explanations, which it always does—finds only unlikely ideas, like control by radio transmissions or satellites."

"Wait," Winnie objected. "Why are these explanations always so technological, always beamed information like that?" She had to get to a resolution, and knew she was running out of time again. "You know, why satellites? Doesn't that mean this really isn't a disease? It's more of a recent development, right? A reaction to technology."

"Well," he said, "this feeling of external control and long-range projection of information, of forces acting at a distance, was always a symptom as far as we know, long before satellites, or radios, or any kind of energy wave was known to exist." He started to drift down toward the next room along the hall, in the pattern she knew well now, edging toward continuing his rounds. "I have to keep going now, but I think I can show you how we know this tomorrow."

The next day, as she waited for morning rounds, Winnie wondered if among all the failure modes of the human mind, schizophrenia might be the least understood. She herself had heard nothing explana-

tory, and felt so ignorant about it, with many gaps and maybe miscon-
ceptions. Disorders like depression and anxiety seemed so much easier
to map onto regular human experience.

Still, altered reality could also be universal in some sense. In college
she had learned that while falling asleep most people can experience
brief, bizarre states of confusion and hallucination; she knew that state
herself, and that it was frightening enough for the instant it lasts—yet
what would life be like if that state came one night and never went
away? If that altered reality, once experienced, became fixed? Entrenched and unshakable for days, or for years. The idea was horrifying,
and so she stopped thinking about it.

The fragmentation of the self as a concept intrigued her, and was
more pleasing somehow to consider—the idea that one part of her
could fail to know what another part was doing. The idea made her
wonder how integration of the self is ever achieved in the first place.
She had always taken this kind of thing, her wholeness, for granted, but
apparently it was not so certain. Again thinking about sleep helped her
understand, since on awakening, she had always felt an unraveled moment with no reality or self at first, but then experienced a gradual reconstruction, a reweaving. Short local threads—of place, purpose,
people, things that matter, schedule, current attributes—came to inter-
lock with long-range threads of identity, trajectory, self. Where is the
information coming from, and where is it going, that reweaves the self
in those minutes? If that process is interrupted, the result would be an
incompletely formed self—and one's own actions would seem unconnected and alien.

As Winnie thought about that disconnected state, a disturbing
thought occurred. What if that underlying formlessness—needs unraveled from self, action estranged from plan—is what is real? What
looks like confusion and disorganization in those psychotic states, she
thought, might be simply the reality that our borders are arbitrary, and
our sense of unique self actually artificial—serving some purpose, but
not real in any sense. The unitary self is the illusion.

And then, what about that voice, almost imperceptible now? The doctor had implied she was thinking *disconnect*, and not recognizing it as her own thought—but he was missing the deeper point. Even if the *disconnect* thought was "hers" in some sense, who told her to think it? Did she decide, at a moment in time: I plan to think "disconnect"? No, not for that or any other thought. The thought comes. For all people, all thoughts just come.

Only people with psychosis are rightly perturbed by this, Winnie realized, since only they see the situation for what it is. Only they are sufficiently awake to perceive the underlying truth—the reality that all of our actions, feelings, and thoughts come without conscious volition. We all lie on the hard hospital bed prepared for us by evolution, but only they have kicked off the thin blanket, the comforter provided by our cortex—the idea that we do what we want to do, or think what we want to think. The rest of humanity proceeds through life in dumb slumber, serving and preserving the practical fiction of agency.

The next morning, by the time Dr. D. got to her on his rounds, Winnie felt convinced that hers was a state of insight rather than illness. She was not shielded but rather had emerged, and could sense the field, the charge surrounding everything. But before she could tell him, it turned out he had brought something for her, a picture he had printed out—first drawn, he said, by a nineteenth-century Englishman named James Tilly Matthews, in the heat of the Industrial Revolution, in the grip of what they then called "madness." Matthews had imagined something he called an "Air Loom," and drew pictures of himself as a helpless, cowering figure controlled by strings projecting through space from a giant and menacing industrial weaving device. Controlled from afar, by long-range threads.

Winnie was fascinated. So unexplained symptoms and feelings in schizophrenia were just imputed by patients to their time's most powerful known phenomenon for action at a distance—whatever it happened to be that might serve as an explanation—satellite, loom, angel, demon.

Winnie had much to say after that, and she found herself more interested in exploring these ideas than in pressing for discharge from the hospital. Even if she had schizophrenia or something similar, it seemed clear to her that this was not truly a disease, but a representation of something essential—a spark of insight and creativity, an engine driving the progress of humanity.

So the next day, she asked Dr. D. to admit that this could be true, that tolerance of the unlikely and bizarre could be useful—in the context of the human brain and human hand. Only in this way could unlikely things—semi-magical possibilities, concepts unrelated to anything that had ever existed—become real. Such a setup would only be of value to humanity; there would be no value for a mouse or a porpoise in magical thinking, admitting to unlikely possibilities, believing for no good reason that something strange might be true, that a different world might be possible—with no big brain to plan it, or nimble hand to make it.

He was not as excited as she thought he might be. "People have thought about this," he said. "Not to say that's not an interesting idea, or that it doesn't have a certain appeal. It might even be right in some sense. But schizophrenia is much more, and much worse, than a little bit of magical thinking. There are also the negative symptoms of schizophrenia, which prevent patients from even accessing the basic and useful parts of their mental world anymore. There's an apathy, a loss of motivation, a lack of social interest.

"And then there is a symptom called *thought disorder*, in which your whole internal process can become disrupted in a very harmful way," he said. "Think about thinking for a bit, which you have been, but now about the flow of thought. We do plan to think a thing—not always, but sometimes, or at least we can if we wish. We set out to reason through things, we choose to build a series of thoughts: imagining paths radiating from a decision point, planning to go through each of them systematically, and stepping through that sequence. This is a beautiful thing about the human mind, but this beauty can be corrupted. Patients lose the memory of their positioning along each planned path of thought, and even lose the ability to chart the path at all. Words and ideas get jumbled up together, getting inserted or deleted too. Eventually thinking itself is shut down completely. We call that thought blocking—when patients crash out of conversations midsentence, mid-word. Thoughts come unwanted, but also don't come when wanted . . . and can't be summoned."

Winnie knew she had exhibited long silences in the ER—but she had been thinking about AJ dying. She reminded the doctor about AJ, saying, "I don't think my silences that first day were thought blocking, Dr. D. It was just a strong feeling, from a personal memory that mattered—my brother's death everyone was asking me about, nothing else."

"Okay, yes, that may not have been thought blocking," he said. "It looked that way—but the good news is it's happening a lot less for you on the antipsychotic medication. And thank you for letting me know. We try to visualize what is going on inside our patients' minds—but thought disorder is not something most people can vividly imagine, and so we could get it wrong. It's maybe even the most debilitating symptom in schizophrenia, but extremely hard to explain."

Maybe because this is the most human symptom, she thought, a deficit in the most advanced brain system, with no analogy in any other animal or being. But more importantly, control over one's own think-ing is just an illusion anyway—it's the fantasy of control that is uniquely human. Thoughts are only ordered after our guts decide what we want, and fictional thought sequences are built up and installed retroactively. This perception of order in our thinking is as unreal as agency over our actions. Both are rationalizations—just neural backfill.

•

The day before discharge, he came to update her on the final reading of her MRI. There was nothing in her brain that they could see—no AVM like the one that had killed her brother, no tumor, no inflamma-tion. "What this means," he said, "is that your episode of psychosis might well be a sign of schizophrenia. We don't know for certain yet, but that is the working diagnosis. But there's one more test we need to do. We need to check your cerebrospinal fluid for signs of something that might be treatable—cells that shouldn't be there, or infectious agents, or proteins like antibodies. This means we have to do a lumbar puncture—a spinal tap."

Winnie felt herself flinch slightly, remembering the terrifying length of the chemo needle. "I know, sorry," he said. "You've had these done before—yes, it's invasive, but almost painless, and we know from the brain imaging that you don't have any worrying pressures in there that would make it unsafe." Her experience as a teenager fully surfaced itself, uninvited, as he prepared the consent form. Winnie remembered how she had been positioned on a bed facing the wall, in a fetal curl to present her lower back—but it was true, she remembered no pain, just a deep and achy pressure.

"It is pretty unusual to do on this unit, so we'll have to take you to the open floor," he said. "No needles are allowed on the locked unit, except in emergencies." Winnie signed the consent, they had her change into a hospital gown, and then she walked with Dr. D. and the nurse to the locked exit door. The ward clerk buzzed them through, and she was out in the legal open for the first time since her admission nearly a week ago.

As they set her up in a procedure room, she considered the irony of what was about to happen: after her frenzy of concern about long-range access to her brain, here she was willingly allowing them direct entry, right into her central nervous system. And they would withdraw material—her own liquid from deep within her—and keep it, and test it, and enter the results into databases that would never go away.

But she had somehow consented, and it was all happening. Dr. D. positioned Winnie on her side with a gentle curl, and with her hospital gown pulled away to expose her lower back. First came the surface anesthetic: a small stick, from a tiny needle. The big one would come once he had the location exactly mapped with his hands. He talked her through it—"I'm finding the boundaries . . . framing the top and bottom lumbar vertebrae, these define the space, the fourth, the fifth—there it is." After a breathless pause, she felt that familiar deep ache. The needle was in her spinal column.

It would be a clear liquid, she recalled as she fixated on the wall in front of her—cerebrospinal fluid, unlike any other in the body. They would test it for cells, sugar, and ions. CSF, bathing the brain and spinal cord, cushioning the neurons of thought and love and fear and need, with just the right salt concentrations of our fish ancestors, along with a touch of glucose—a little bit of the ancient ocean we carry with us, sweetened, always.

The next morning, he conveyed the results: more good news. Nothing of concern, all clean; in fact, he confided, it had been a champagne tap—which meant the CSF had come out fully clear with no blood from a nicked capillary, not a single red blood cell. For residents and interns performing their first LPs, he said, this is usually occasion enough for a bottle of champagne, marking a milestone of technical skill along with a little luck. But more important for Winnie: no white blood cells, no inflammation, no proteins, no antibodies. Glucose and ions all normal.

Another minor side note: something called *cytology* was still pending, a detailed analysis for cancer cells, but lymphoma recurrence was not suspected by the laboratory. And so this day would become the day of her discharge, as he had promised—and they would send her home with a prescription for the new medication, the antipsychotic.

"And the discharge diagnosis?" she asked. "Will you say schizophrenia, or not?"

"We still can't be certain, but schizophrenia is likely," he said. "Some psychiatric diagnoses can be applied only if everything else is ruled out, only if enough time passes with no other explanations found. So for now, we'll give our temporary diagnosis: schizophreniform disorder, which can be converted to schizophrenia at your outpatient follow-up." An unappealing prospect—Winnie felt disinclined to let that happen.

Champagne tap—my brain feels like champagne, she thought later, back in her room, waiting for the discharge orders to go through. She had liked that phrase he used, *champagne tap*, and so she began to play with a more retro image of filtering—moving away from modern electronics, to more of an Industrial Revolution filtering of bubbles, more like James Tilly Matthews might have pictured as he pondered his drink. Bubbles of ideas are seeded deep, guesses to explain the world—

why is that screw there?—models nucleating on the side of the mind's champagne flute, rising quickly if able to combine with others in support to form a larger bubble, a more complete hypothesis, that can rise more powerfully past filters that can only arrest the small and weakly moving, the unlikely, the poorly justified.

The bubbles that rise the fastest and grow the biggest, encounter more support and reach the brim—the border of awareness—only then to burst into consciousness. Once that burst happens, it's irreversible. It's no longer a guess, it's Truth—molecules forming part of the oxygen of the mind now. There is no re-forming of bubbles that is possible; there is no sending them back into the champagne.

And most important of all—sometimes a few little bubbles that should have been stuck instead slip through. Winnie thought: Why not send them up? The world is always changing.

She was discharged on the afternoon of her tenth day—the last dose of the pill, the antipsychotic she had been given daily from her initial admission, had been administered by her nurse the night before, and she had a prescription to fill at home, so she could keep taking it. With a tentative diagnosis—schizophreniform disorder—she was free to go.

•

Winnie never filled the prescription or followed up in the clinic, and never planned to. She felt fine. When she got home she skimmed Dr. D.'s card across the room and let it lie where it fell by the gas fireplace, a white marker thrown down where she could see it and remember—and in the meantime there was work to do.

She felt good going online, not even worrying about Erin. The hacking conspiracy was still there in her mind, but not as an overwhelming invasion anymore—more of a polite houseguest. They could leave each other alone, pass in the narrow hallways of her mind with a slight turn of the shoulders and a courteous nod.

She even felt more secure about her own body, her own borders. The Raiders hat went back into storage. As she was reorganizing the closet she came across her old copy of Benjamin Franklin's "Letters and Papers on Electricity" from 1755 and went straight to her favorite passage, from his letter to Dr. L——, describing the discovery of what would become known as the Faraday cage, savoring again, as she read his words, Franklin's false humility:

> I electrified a silver pint can, on an electric stand, and then lowered into it a cork ball, of about an inch diameter, hanging by a silk string, till the cork touched the bottom of the can. The cork was not attracted to the inside of the can as it would have been to the outside, and though it touched the bottom, yet, when drawn out, it was not found to be electrified by that touch, as it would have been by touching the outside. The fact is singular. You require the reason, I do not know it. Perhaps you may discover it, and then you will be so good as to communicate it to me.

Winnie felt a connection again to the cork. After a brief and tumultuous emergence, where she had been buffeted by the fields of an external reality, she had now returned to the silver can, the shielded cage, the shared and common human frame.

There probably never was a miscarriage though—that idea had become uncoupled from her also, drifting off, a cinder lost, a dark mote dimming.

She ate ravenously that first week home—with a hunger like nothing she had felt before. Controlling her own food again was a revelation, a release. She cooked pasta, bought cakes. Toward the end of that first week, an odd thought appeared—she was not sure she had a mouth. Even while eating—especially while eating—she had to touch her lips to make sure they were hers, and were still there.

Between meals, the patent lawyer in her reemerged—strong and refreshed and tireless. Just as at work when tackling a new field of art, she spent many hours each day at her computer, delving into the scientific literature, seeking knowledge and precedent. She found her way to dense and intriguing papers on schizophrenia genetics: the collection of DNA sequence information from human genomes, with massive teams of scientists spelling out individual letters of genetic instructions within tens of thousands of schizophrenia patients. She wandered, fascinated, through the hundreds of genes found, associated, linked—that all seemed to play some role in schizophrenia. Each gene alone had only a tiny effect on the individual human being, with no single thread setting the pattern, none by itself defining the weave, or the fray, of the mind.

Instead, all the threads together manifested health or disease: only in unity did they form the full tapestry. It seemed to Winnie that mental illnesses—schizophrenia but others too, like depression, autism, and eating disorders—even though heavily genetically determined, were mostly not handed down across generations like a watch or a ring, nor like the single genes controlling sickle cell or cystic fibrosis. Instead, in psychiatry it was as if the risk were projected forward as a set of many vulnerabilities from both parents. Each person's mind was created by thousands of crossing threads, intersecting orthogonally and forming patterns diagonally, to create the twill of the individual. There were genes for proteins creating electrical currents in cells, genes for molecules at the synapses controlling information flow between cells, genes for guiding the structure of DNA in neurons that would direct production of all the electrical and chemical proteins, and genes for guiding the long-range threads within the brain itself, the axons that connected one part of the organ to another, on an inner loom of interwoven wiring controlling everything, directing all aspects of the mind, setting traits and dispositions like tolerance for the unlikely and the weird.

In some people, Winnie realized, when the warp and weft intertwine just so, a new way of being is allowed—a pattern coalesces with just the right or wrong set of threads. Hints of what might come can be found on both sides, forming the family tartan, in those predisposed. Looking back, partial motifs can be discerned among the vertical or horizontal threads—human traits as proto-patterns. In both lineages, there may be found uncles or grandmothers who were just odd enough, who could let their minds relax the vise of illusion, who could loosen the grip of an old paradigm, to close, firm, around a new one.

And the stronger the old paradigm—with more societal inertia—the more certain these outlier human beings had to be of their new outlook. Their convictions had to be fixed—once shifted, never letting go—committed for no good reason, since there was none. For who can defend the new and unproven against the old and established? Only the unjustly certain—who believe to a level never provable, who already must dwell a bit apart and aside, who already can access now and then the fixity of delusion.

But when two highly vulnerable lineages converge, a person might emerge who is too disengaged, allowing too much through, having lost control of thought—or rather lost the reassuring illusion, the perception of thought's order and flow. A shaken human being is formed who cannot decide which paradigms to abandon, or which to never let go— who cannot even pretend to decide anything, any longer, amid the stirred-up turbulence, the swarms of bubbles effusing and bursting forth unchecked from the champagne. Then all the bubbles become spent, and the human being ends with the negative symptoms Dr. D. had described—avolitional and flat.

As Winnie read more about severe schizophrenia, she found it harder to preserve that idea she had as an inpatient, that there could be some benefit to the disease—for those suffering, or for their loved ones. It seemed that the most insidious symptom Dr. D. had described, the thought disorder, inexorably progresses if untreated, until utter disintegration. Thinking becomes more and more distorted, until the mind cannot keep track of obligations and connections, and loses emotional range, both highs and lows. Gone is any urge to work, to clean, to connect with friends and family. The mind becomes awash in chaos and terror, the body frozen and catatonic. If left untreated, the patient's life ends in confused and bizarre isolation, with the duration of any planned thought shrunk down to a few seconds or less before its annihilation.

Winnie remembered vividly something the doctor had said in the hallway, in their final conversation, when she had been repeating that error need not mean disease. "A group in which some people tolerate unlikeliness this way may do well over time," he had said, "but don't forget—some will suffer terribly." Now in her apartment she wanted to respond, but it was too late. She wanted to tell him that she understood now, and that this was not just true, and important, but should be taught to the community—to advance understanding, to elicit gratitude even—so that all could truly see the people who were ill, to understand their burden borne for us.

He would probably agree, but what he would not like was another thing she wanted to say, of which she was just as certain—that we all need delusion as individuals now and then. She wanted to tell him that within each person there should be a breakdown in reality at times. We should recognize this need, in ourselves and each other, and move with it like music, and sweep each other along, leading or following as life suggests, since there is not one reality that works for every decision in each phase of life, for every pair or group or nation. We have brains and hands; we might make our delusions real.

And she imagined his rejoinder already, since like any good lawyer she could play his side just as well: that this was fine and romantic to imagine, but one cannot make anything real, create any complexity, without controlled thinking, the ability to plan many steps—and schizophrenia shuts all that down. Evolution has not worked out how to consistently protect everyone from thought disorder—leaving human minds with a vulnerability especially destructive in the modern world. Simple and small primate groups may not have needed thoughts to flow in sequence for long periods of time—but the stability of our community structure requires people to live and work together over long timescales, and allows multistep planning to matter.

Winnie knew this perspective had to be at least a little bit right; she had found plenty of data to support the idea that civilization contributes to the problems caused by schizophrenia—including evidence that disease symptoms are more common and strong in city dwellers. People with only mild genetic predispositions could still, it seems, be pushed over the edge into psychosis by other risks and stressors of modern life. Winnie also found many accounts of perfectly healthy people who became psychotic only after their first cannabis exposure—and of others with seemingly pure mood disorders like depression, who experienced delusions only because of the mood disorder, not schizophrenia. She thought these human beings probably all had at least the proto-pattern, half-woven. With a tweak from the environment, a toxic chemical, a stress from city living or social disruption, an infection—

whatever it might be, Winnie thought, a second hit on top of genetics can complete the pattern, and change reality.

Two hits: this was a concept she was familiar with from cancer. Winnie remembered asking her oncologist as a teenager, why her? Why not Nelson or AJ? Why not her best friend Doris, who smoked secretly every chance she got? Maybe the two-hits hypothesis could explain this, her doctor said; maybe Winnie had some vulnerability from genetics, but mammals have two copies of every gene, and other kinds of backup systems too, so some second hit was needed to allow the cancer to happen, through another change in her DNA. It could have been a cosmic ray, a long-range particle traveling from the sun, or a gamma ray from another galaxy even, traveling through space for billions of years, and hitting one chemical bond in one gene in one cell of one young girl in Wisconsin. This was happening all the time to everyone, but in Winnie's cell there was already another problem, an altered gene from birth. A disruption came atop another; it was a double tap, too much, and the system tipped over into the uncontrolled growth of cancer.

Nobody knew if the two-hits idea was right for mental illness, but Winnie thought it could be. The science was not there yet in psychiatry, that much was clear as she spent nights reading the papers and reviews. The biological knowledge was limiting in this field, though there were a few insights. There was altered communication across the brain in schizophrenia, shown with methods for imaging brain activity in people. Parts of the brain were not keeping the other parts updated. There even had been observed, during hallucinations, an altered synchrony of activity across the organ, like one hand not knowing what the other hand was doing.

Winnie had so many questions, so much to say, and nobody to listen. She remembered he might have said a patient's break with reality had brought him to psychiatry in the first place. Not that it mattered, but it mattered, and she wanted him to know that it did. We take our shared reality for granted, and our reaction to that illusion, and if she could ask him to do something, it would be to let the world know a simple Truth: our shared reality is not real; it is only shared.

•

In her second week home a goal emerged, a god took form, a mango ramjet. She would write to him, in a detailed letter, by hand, in unerasable black marker, in all caps so nothing would be missed, with everything she never had time to say, that she hadn't known how to say clearly.

She would tell him more thoughts, mote thoughts. There was a dispersed element, moonlit underdrumming, a nocturne. Java Pajama Princess was her new name, that was something to tell him. He might not understand, he was unbearded, an unjesus. He would write back with his full name, not what the nurses called him on the floor, that false note, popish. No, his full name, and she would tell him so, she said she was not of Dravidian ancestry and did not appreciate the implication—misogamy—her voice cracking, turning to a weak whisper even as her helpless anger grew—what was he implying. Not one kilogauss of influence upon her, she was pure and free, not some ropedancestepdancing firebrat. Was she eating too much? Lickerish. She was double-tapped. The influence was coming, the outlet was not easy or east but westnorthwestwardly. She paused, took a breath, and apologized. A torsade. It was none of her business what he was trying to imply.

Her phone went off; something clenched her deep. Fillet the firstborn, the fistborn. It was him. Winnie reached out to the phone, but hesitated. The other side of the screen. She let him buzz through to voicemail. An hour later she played the message on speakerphone, after she felt the phone's capacitors had fully discharged. The cytology report had come back, from the spinal tap, that last formality: "*Rare highly atypical lymphoid cells, consistent with prior material, involvement by a T-cell lymphoma.*"

Her engine of a brain revealed at last its dark secret. Covered over but always there, her frailty had been lying in wait, like AJ's AVM. And then came the second hit: for him, the pressure surge; for Winnie, it was cancer cells, stirring up the champagne bubbles, swimming in her vulnerable sweet sea.

She settled to the floor, reaching out again to AJ's last day. It was not hard; the air loom projected across time as well as space. And she knew the threads that mattered; some of them were hers. *When he saw the bank clock, AJ knew he would have to jog the rest of the way. As he ran he looked down at himself and his shirt. There was some dough baked on there and he tried to brush it with his hand — most of it came off but there was still some white stuff that he couldn't wipe away, and his hand was sweating, and it all made things a little worse. He should have brought another shirt. He kept up a steady pace, trying not to exert himself too much as he neared the bank, and jogged across the South Main intersection and into the plaza, skirted the fountain, and ran through the glass doors just behind a guy on crutches. He saw the elevator but no time, up five floors two steps at a time; he walked quickly down the hallway, checked behind him to make sure he wasn't leaving flour footprints, and stopped just outside the office waiting to catch his breath. Wiping his forehead he looked around at the walls and the ceiling; the hallway was very clean and brown. He thought about the frozen yogurt girl next to the bakery and her hair, curving up like a cinnamon roll, firm and brown. He thought about how her eyes had circled around his face, like a nervous blue jay, when he had asked for her number. After a minute he reached for the door with a shaky feeling inside, watching the dim and shadowy reflection of his face in the glass panel of the door, feeling he was at the crest of a hill, carrying over the summit a large piece of cardboard in his sweaty hands, to slide it down the summer slope like he did with Winnie and Nelson when they were kids. He was going to see how things looked, on the other half of the world, after a long climb getting ready to coast down. The cries of triumph and pain of the other climbers were fading into nothing for a moment . . . as if in respect for this instant. The door was locked; it took AJ a bit to realize the door was locked. It was strange — the knob turned but the door wouldn't open. AJ trembled and tried again. He stepped back then, trying to think what it meant. His eyes looked for some message or note or clue, but there was nothing. Wrong office maybe. He reached for the appointment card in his pocket, but it was the wrong card, it was the mechanic's. He'd brought no number, going to miss the appointment it had taken him months to get. His head twinged. AJ pressed his hands to his temples as he walked back down the hall. He took the stairs slowly, knees buckling, feeling a strange and surging flood. The lobby was lost in a black fog. Scared, he walked as steadily as he could through the lobby and out the door. The sun was hot, but dim. His legs and arms were shaking but he made his way slowly to the plaza fountain. He walked around the spray, unsteady, and waited to cross South Main, watching the faces in the cars as they passed him by. He went to his knees. He remembered a bird he had seen collide with a glass bus stop once. It had beat the dusty pavement with its wings for a while, unable to lift off, and then just looked and watched the other birds fly by, intent on their own lives, haloed by the sun, to mate and feed and build and sing. Twilight seemed to be deepening over everything. He thought that he might see the frozen yogurt girl if he could just get back to the bakery. I would like to stay there with her, he thought. It was a slight slope downward; if he could get up all he had to do was swing each foot forward, one after the other, and he could just almost coast. All the faces in the cars going home . . . The door would not open. The door was locked. The pain in his head rose and spread. So clean and shiny the glass was everywhere, it looked as though it wasn't even there, the bird hit and the glass was everywhere. The hallway was long and dim, firm and brown. It was not easy to see seeing again. Sort of a dove, the bird had reminded him of Winnie, he had been so worried for her. As he bent over, the bird looked straight up at him, just like Winnie would, steady and the only one who would. Waiting for it to pass, he clenched his eyes shut, waiting for it too. From his knees he fell down flat, and then she was there with him, smoothing his forehead in a gentling of wings.*

CHAPTER 6

CONSUMMATION

Farewel happy Fields
Where Joy for ever dwells: Hail horrours, hail
Infernal world, and thou profoundest Hell
Receive thy new Possessor: One who brings
A mind not to be chang'd by Place or Time.
The mind is its own place, and in it self
Can make a Heav'n of Hell, a Hell of Heav'n.
What matter where, if I be still the same,
And what I should be, all but less then he
Whom Thunder hath made greater? Here at least
We shall be free; th' Almighty hath not built
Here for his envy, will not drive us hence:
Here we may reign secure, and in my choyce
To reign is worth ambition though in Hell:
Better to reign in Hell, then serve in Heav'n.

—From JOHN MILTON, *Paradise Lost*

The medical student and I began to take our leave. Our first ninety minutes with Emily had brought no understanding and revealed no useful role for hospitalization. She had been directly admitted to our open unit by the inpatient psychiatry director, leaving me out of the loop in determining if admission was a good idea.

Emily was eighteen years old, legally an adult but much younger than our other inpatients, and would have been sent to child psychiatry if she had shown up just a few weeks earlier. The initial chief complaint—*unable to sit through class*—was actually her parents' complaint, and to me this situation seemed better suited for the children's hospital than for our acute adult inpatient service.

Over the course of the intake examination, we discovered that Emily had been a star student, but the full fifty minutes of a class period had become too much; at the beginning of the school year she had somehow developed the need to get up and leave class halfway through, and then over a month or so, this had progressed to the point that she couldn't go to class at all. Nobody knew why, and she would not say. We did learn from her that she was well versed in poetry and literature, and had won trophies as a softball pitcher and competitive equestrian.

During our interview, the orthopedic surgery ward clerk had paged me several times about a patient of ours who needed transfer orders to come back to psychiatry after hip surgery. At this point working with orthopedics, as peevish as they were, seemed more productive than continuing with Emily, since they wanted something I could provide. We began navigating around the chairs toward the door of Emily's room—trying not to seem too hurried, promising to return.

"One more thing," said Emily, and I turned back from the door. From her cross-legged perch on the tightly made bed, she was stretching her arms above her head, arching against the sunlight streaming from the window. "I really don't think I should be alone right now."

Oh. Well, here we go. Now the reveal; the inner storm would finally break. I waited, not asking.

Emily's blue-gray side-eye contact with me was accompanied by a quarter smile. She said nothing more. The silence stretched and filled space too. The pressure built, but no cloudburst came.

I looked around the room for insight. There was oddness: her still-packed suitcase, and her laptop and phone neatly stacked on the bedside table—personal possessions that were not a typical sight even on the open unit. But this I understood—the whole sequence of our usually choreographed intake process was off, due to the unusual nature of the admission. She had just arrived and hadn't even been met by the charge nurse yet.

I looked back to Emily. I had waited for her to continue longer than I normally would, deliberately modeling for the medical student how to let the patient declare herself—demonstrating how to not pre-frame whatever it was into something else, to inadvertently morph the underlying issue into an object of our own making.

And then the silence finally became noise in itself—negative, distracting—even a bit hostile. "All right, Emily," I said. "Let's talk about that." There was no choice but to move back into the room, with

my student in tow. We returned to our chairs and sat, white coats settling around us like falling marionette strings.

Not only had our history-taking failed to divine a serious psychiatric
condition, but Emily's outpatient lab tests had also been normal—no
hyperthyroidism, for example, from Graves' disease, which could have
explained agitation and restlessness. With so little information, my diagnostic thoughts felt scattered and poorly formed, mostly relating to
anxiety—maybe a social phobia or panic disorder. But she had not endorsed any anxiety-related symptoms. I had also considered ADHD—
and had ticked through the symptoms associated with this term, one of
many evolving frames we use in psychiatry for states we are still working to understand. As insights come from research, we know our models and nomenclature will be revised and discarded and replaced in a
generation, and then again in another. Yet these we use because they
are what we have now, helping to guide both treatment and research;
each diagnosis comes with a list of symptoms and criteria. Emily was
endorsing none of them.

All my direct questions probing these possibilities—and even my
less direct methods, like open-ended pauses needing to be filled by the
patient—had unearthed nothing substantial. She had some mild depression but never suicidal thoughts; a few hints of the eating disorder
traits so common in her age group; and a touch of some obsessive-
compulsive qualities. But we hadn't been able to address the core problem, the chief complaint; we couldn't explain why she could no longer
stay in class. Only as we were headed out the door, thinking our diagnosis would have to be a placeholder only—*anxiety disorder not otherwise specified*—did it seem the real conversation started.

And now, with her cryptic reopening of the interview, new diagnoses
sprang forward eagerly like racehorses charging from the starting
gate—but then all stumbled and crashed into one another. The
straightforward diagnoses were somehow even less coherent now. If she
were intent on suicide, she wouldn't want someone to sit with her. If
she were psychotic, she would be less organized, more cagey. And finally, a borderline patient would not be so diffident, and might have
led with abandonment more directly.

Whatever disorder lay within was both subtle and strong; she looked physically healthy and did not seem to be suffering, but something had overtaken her powerful mind. At this crucial moment in her development and education, Emily's greatest strength had been taken away; her passport to the future had been lifted from within her, by a light-fingered entity she knew, a thief she was protecting.

As her last words hung in the air between us, something else happened to her, to Emily's scholar-athlete self as shown to me, to her robust and brash façade. For an eyeblink, the mask flickered and fell, and in an instant, all was really real. Though she had spoken a truth as she knew it, there was also a slight twist at the corners of her eyes and mouth. She was showing me something, and it was almost funny . . . but not showing too much, because, well, she was still a teen, and it was still embarrassing.

"Why should you not be alone, Emily?" I asked.

She said nothing more. She was tracing shapes with her finger on the thin and tightly drawn bedspread, watching me out of the corner of her eyes. Emily had spoken something important, and yet it seemed there was also a secret joke unexplained, one that she was tempted to share. Was this all a deeply disguised malingering, from a clever manipulator of the system, working for some gain I had failed to perceive? Or was the humor darker than I could imagine—morbid commentary on a destructive side of her, with desire for self-harm—a cloaked wraith that she had been fighting but could not bring herself to disclose, at least until a social loosening brought on by the moment of our departure.

Ten seconds of silence. What next? I had an ally here, Sonia. I looked over to her.

Sonia was the medical student but also a sub-intern—advanced, and tasked to behave like a full-fledged intern, playacting at the next level as if she had MD authority to make treatment plans and write orders. Sub-I's were expected to perform the doctorly part in each scene right up to the moment of actually signing each order—a challenging role-play, designed for medical students who have decided their specialty, heard their calling, and now are seeking a head start in experience. It's

a difficult line to walk, acting authoritative without true authority—
requiring self-confidence, social smarts, and a tendency to be right.
Strength.

And Sonia was strong—fearless and resourceful, quick with pen and
phone, adept at making things happen. It had been obvious right away,
in her first moments on the team—though I tried not to categorize
people quickly or absolutely, having come through medical school in a
harsher and more binary time, when swift judgments were routinely
made by the team as each new member rotated onto the inpatient care
service: a new face, a blank slate not chosen or known before by anyone
present, but thrust into the midst of urgent life-and-death decisions.
When I had been at her stage, nobody on the team really cared about
how creative the new student might be, or the quality of the papers
published—all of that was irrelevant. A wholly other categorization
came into play that never had existed before in the life of the medical
student. Unforgiving labels were everything: was the new student
strong, or weak?

Teams coalesced on snap judgments, right or wrong but made
quickly. Medical students generally suspected little of the importance
of their first few actions upon joining the team, but in that time they
would earn a label—one way or the other, spoken or not. All was not
lost if things went the wrong way on any one team, since the students
would rotate off the service in a month, moving on to new roles, new
growth, and discovery of new strengths—but that month of time would
remain frozen thus for those who were on the team, never to be un-
done. In low moments I wonder: in how many senior physicians' minds
am I still stored in one of these categories—as strong or weak, and nothing more? Before meeting Emily, when I was a medical student starting my clinical rotations—and front-loading the surgery rotations,
since I was sure my residency would be in neurosurgery—there had
been plenty of opportunity to show weakness.

My head was still in the clouds from my PhD, which had been in
abstract neuroscience and so nonclinical in any sense, and I was more
than a bit defiant—stubborn and unwilling to accept or work with the
axioms and rituals of medicine. In my resistance I was hesitant with

medical custom—and yet sometimes my style, by chance, fit the team's interests. In an early vascular surgery rotation, I had no idea what I was doing, but happened to ask an interesting (if slightly irritating) question on the first morning. As a result later that same day, on afternoon rounds, I was introduced by the chief resident to the attending as "the new medical student, strong." The attending said "Good." How wrong they were, but after that nobody bothered me—I was in, it would be a good month. The student was strong. The team, now set and labeled, swept on.

Later, in my resident and attending years, I thought of myself as part of, and supporter of, a changing culture in which some complexity could be tolerated—in which doctors recognized that the world needed more than one approach to doctoring. Sonia was not weak by any measure though, so when I looked over at her, not knowing what to do, it was for any of her many strengths she could bring to this nameless domain. We had been together for two weeks on the same inpatient team, and we'd had time to get to know each other. She had the same sort of provenance as Emily: similar academic upbringing, diverse and literary, quantitative.

We exchanged a lot of information in that moment—Sonia was keeping quiet, as was I, but her slightly widened eyes, locked to mine, indicated we should explore more deeply.

Looking back at Emily, I picked up no fear, no panic, no anger. Rather, she exuded a kind of nervous excitement, as if she were getting ready to step out on a first date—or no, more like an affair—and then I knew. A representation of sorts, of Emily herself, could be projected onto others I had seen and stored away inside me, from my time long ago on the adolescent psychiatry locked unit—and with only a little warping here and there, the images aligned perfectly.

There was another being in that room with us, one that she needed, feared, and could never leave. Emily opened up and showed me because it didn't matter, there was nothing she nor I nor anyone could do. She did have a ferocious date planned; it was happening and nobody could stop it—but she wanted it known and witnessed. This was a

straightedge, unaltered, unsophisticated truth she spoke—one generation stating a hard fact to another—only telling me of the world as it
was. The fact was this: she didn't want to be alone, but I should be the
one afraid.

•

By that point, I had treated many patients with eating disorders. I'd
spent months on the children's hospital locked unit, which is effectively a dedicated anorexia ward, where I had seen patients from mildly
ill to near death, and heard the diverse kinds of language the teens
used to describe anorexia nervosa and bulimia nervosa. Some patients
on the mild side of disease even personalized the two disorders as Ana
and Mia, but most patients on the severe end abandoned all pretense
of metaphor for their illness.

The psychiatrists working in this realm have deep intelligence and
experience, yet their constructions (as with much of psychiatry) are
unmoored from the bedrock of scientific understanding, and I had
found no greater mystery than eating disorders, anywhere in psychiatry
or medicine. None greater in all of biology.

With Emily, I was cautiously aware of a particular priming to consider this kind of diagnosis, since at that same moment I had other such
players on the open unit, other patients in the same domain. Micah,
for example: art-dealer kibbutznik, eyes dark as shoeblack. He had a
sharp and closely trimmed Vandyke, and was frighteningly thin, with a
tube snaking up his nose and down his throat. Micah lived in a very
deep and severe relationship, with both diseases at once, anorexia and
bulimia. Dangerously extreme weight loss resulted, and the contradictions and conflicts were draining. It had become full-time work for
Micah to meet the demands of both diseases, to give each the time
needed.

Anorexia nervosa is often personalized as cruel and strong, a duchess-
like mean girl, distant and stern, locking subjects in a cold tomb of
cognitive control. To assert independence from a survival drive, and to
reframe the drive to eat as an enemy arising from outside the self, an-

orexia has to become stronger than anything the patients have known or felt; and the patients start strong themselves—they would have to, in order to manifest such a thing.

With anorexia, they control the progress of growth and life—and so of time itself, it seems. Anorexia prevents sexual maturation in the younger patients, slows aging, and is not cured by medicine; no drug can liberate patients from its grip, thus forcing desperate measures. When we were most acutely worried about Micah, watching as his heart rate and blood pressure dropped to astonishingly low levels, he would allow us to insert a nasogastric tube to pour some calories directly into his stomach. But he would then rip out the tube as soon as he was alone, sometimes before we had a chance to get anything in, so that we had to go through the process of replacing the tube. I could almost hear anorexia mocking me from inside Micah's mind as we went through these motions, as he watched impassively, all three of us knowing what I would do, all three of us knowing what he would do, the two of them secretly smiling, laughing at the tube-wielding drug-mongering chucklehead.

But bulimia nervosa is different. Bulimia brings crazily exciting reward—not suppressing food intake to the minimum but pegging it to the maximum—binge and purge, and binge again. Bulimia seems to create a more positive bond than anorexia; bulimia can scratch an itch deep under the skin, leaving the appearance of purity and health while providing the rawest of rewards. Nothing limits how much bulimia can give you, except how much potassium you have left in your frail and contorted body before you die. In all its forms, bulimia knows what you really want, will excite and hurt you more ways than anorexia, and will kill you just as dead in the end.

Mortal allies and rivals—anorexia and bulimia nervosa—are each hated and embraced, each a snarl of disease, deception, reward. They dwell further from the reach of medicine and science than most psychiatric disorders, in part because a partnership of sorts takes root between patient and disease. Sometimes crush-like, sometimes hostile, sometimes only practical—the partnership with the patient is forged, like many interpersonal pairings in the real world, from a living dialectic of weakness and strength. And though no drug can cure these two diseases, any more than a drug can erase a friend or an enemy, words can reach them as one human being reaches another.

That these disorders are strong, and can be imbued with personhood, creates a situation unlike any other in psychiatry, or in medicine more broadly. Addictive drugs—in the setting of substance-use disorders—come closest to this perception of a controlling external power, though with less personal connection. Eating disorders exert both forms of power: governing authority and personal intimacy.

The power of either anorexia or bulimia nervosa, as with the compulsion of drug addiction, still can derive from an initial, even momentary, consent of the governed. Later this authority becomes malevolent; freedom is lost as time passes, and patient and disease move close and closer—until like any stellar dyad, twin suns spinning around each other, they become locked in a gravitational well, a hole deep and dark, destroying mass with every cycle, collapsing into a singularity.

On the pediatric ward I had seen anorexia nervosa in its most severe and devastating form—a disease dwelling mostly within teenage girls, with both patients and families consumed. These were uniquely deadly dynamics I saw, mixing love and anger, with parents frantic to feed their young, full of fury at this inexplicable monster. Families would blame each other, with hints and digs and clawed swipes and violent detonations, since there was nobody else in reach, and no other way to make sense of their emaciated child, surrounded by yet refusing food. There is no clearer example in psychiatry of human suffering that would be addressed just by understanding—even without a cure.

These were children who had been so strong—stars and performers, disciplined across dimensions, utterly beloved—and yet so starved that their brains themselves were dying away, beginning to atrophy, shrinking and peeling back from the skull inside. Children who had become so fragile and cold that their hearts were slowed to forty, or even thirty, beats per minute, with blood pressure hard to measure, hard even to find—the biology of life slowed and almost frozen, maturation arrested and even reversed, the disease-patient dyad rejecting the impositions and effeminations of the teen years—age, adulthood, weight—those shared enemies, fusing into one and denied as one, rejected as a force from without. Children in mid-teen years with preteen appearance and demeanor—and yet socially smart, even in the depths of the disease still verbally swift, adept, expert navigators of cliques and culture, deft at argument, while failing at that most simple math: the basic topology of survival, the taking in of food.

Many come near death, and some die. Why, ask the families, please tell us.

Why not start by asking the patient, the host of the disease? Anything verbalized would help our understanding, even if (or perhaps especially if) in the uncomplicated language and perspective of a child. But symptoms are hard for patients to explain in anorexia, as in any psychiatric disease. We can no more expect an explanation from the anorexia patient than from a person with schizophrenia when we ask how a hand can feel under alien control, or from someone with borderline when we ask for insight into the exhilaration and release of cutting. Some people simply cannot exist as others wish.

As family and doctors try to step in, to intervene, the patient-disease pair develops deceptions and dodges, whipped hard and harder from within. Together they have reframed desire, reshaped the meaning of need—as can happen with meditation, or with faith—but unsustainably. Anorexia is strong but causes fragility, and defends itself lethally. Anorexia preaches loudly in front of the mirror, and then later, off the pulpit, still whispers relentlessly with sibilant words learned in secret—a mimic, a hustler, a charlatan within—until in the end the lie is accepted. The pretense first gains leverage for its utility, but then grows rapidly to meet the monumental scope of its task. Once commissioned, the neural mercenaries cannot be recalled, but spin out of control into a rogue army ravaging the countryside.

These are not simple delusions. In the end, the patient somehow knows but does not understand, is aware but has no control. The idea lives as a layering, a battle mask adhered, fused by fire to the face of life. It is a lie compelling to the patient's life in every way that matters, measured in the clinic as thoughts, mass, and actions. The doctor elicits and records anorexia's way of thinking, one of distorted self-image:

the patient states and believes one thing, while body mass index reports the opposite. The patient's actions too can be measured—reports on the restriction of food intake, which we can track as the patient does, rigorously counting all the tiny caloric ticktocks.

Immersive cognitive and behavioral therapies can help in anorexia nervosa—especially if prolonged, for months at a stretch—using words, and building insights, to slowly shift the distortions within the patient. The goal is to identify, and address, intertwined behavioral and cognitive and social factors, and to monitor nutrition with a touch of coercion. Medications are used not as cures, not to strike at the heart of the disease but to blunt symptoms; for example, serotonin-modulating drugs are typically brought in to treat depression that is often present. In some cases antipsychotic medications are provided that additionally target dopamine signals, and can favor reorganization of thinking, to help break the rigid loops and chains of the distortion; these agents can also cause weight gain, and so an otherwise-harmful side effect becomes a side benefit, to some extent.

There is much at risk. If including mortality from medical complications—the starvation-related organ failures—alongside the suicides, then eating disorders together show the highest death rates of any psychiatric disease. Decline and death come by failure of starving cells, all across the afflicted human body. Depression and suicide, if the first to fail is the brain. Infection, if the immune system falters. Cardiac arrest, if the electrical cells of the heart, already weakened from malnourishment, can no longer cope with the distorted salts of the blood—imbalances in levels of ions that had been set billions of years ago by the rocks dissolved in the ocean of our evolution, and now fishtailing free, diluted and fluctuating in the daily vagaries of starvation.

But for the survivors, the grip of the inner tyrant fades over time. The patient can writhe free, and impose by force new thinking and new action patterns—another layer of masking, perhaps, but still reaching at last a point, over years, when the story can be told like a nightmare.

•

Medications are just as off target for bulimia nervosa—which I suspected was Emily's secret—as for anorexia: able to blunt some comorbid symptoms, but still missing the heart of it all. Bulimia is also a killer with ion imbalance—wild swings in potassium and heart rhythm that come with the purge. Bulimia sometimes becomes mixed up with anorexia, as in Micah, together creating even more extreme shifts in fluids and charged particles—calcium and magnesium derangements too, in traces of rocks and metals needed to keep excitable tissues like heart and brain and muscle stable. These cells that twitch and spike need calcium and magnesium to function properly; otherwise spasms of spontaneous activity result: fibrillations in muscle, arrhythmias in the heart, and seizures in the brain—some ending in death.

The purge can come in many forms: self-induced vomiting, or laxatives, or even excessive exercise—anything that drives down mass balance. The mass balance credit is then used for intake—often with binges of food, piling the plate again and again, caloric reward multiplied by the illicit thrill of loopholing, from knowing the purge is coming, that nothing can stop its rush.

I knew that bulimia rush, that excited torture, from my time working with pediatric inpatients, and seeing it here in Emily I wanted to let her know I knew. If I were right, and if we could get it out into the open, together we could form a kind of partnership—a therapeutic alliance. From there, it would be a matter of logistics: starting some foundational therapy, building some insight, and discharging when ready to the right outpatient or residential program for her.

"Will you be able to tell us about it?" I asked, finally pressing. "I can tell you need to."

She was fully avoiding my gaze now, back to the bedspread. "I can't, really."

"Is it somehow related to why you can't stay in class?" I looked briefly over at Sonia the strong. She seemed enthralled.

"Yes, it is kind of the same."

Time to push a little harder; on the inpatient unit, we did not have the weeks or months of time that outpatient therapy would allow, and there were other patients too. "Emily, you mentioned earlier that a long time ago you sometimes would throw up after big meals." She had described this as remote, and minor, and not connected to her current symptoms; but now it made sense as a reason to leave class. "Is it possible that's happening again?" Her finger, which had been tracing infinities and parabolas on the bedspread, paused; her eyes remained on the bed, now fixed at a point, frozen.

"What would happen if you were alone, Emily?" I asked. She looked up at Sonia.

"I don't know," Emily said, to Sonia. "Maybe it would be okay. But probably not."

I let a few more beats go by, and shifted in my seat. Sonia picked up this call and responded. "Emily," she said, "do you want me to sit with you and talk? I think the doctor has to go see some other patients pretty soon."

"Sure, that sounds okay," she said. "It's no big deal." She sounded a bit diffident, but it was the biggest of deals; it seemed that Emily probably wanted to get better. Another page had come from ortho, I really did have to go, but I could leave Sonia behind to find out more, to work her new craft, its course now well defined. I buttoned up, fared them well, and shuffled out of the room. There was no rush now; time and space were needed for alliances to grow.

As I made my way to the orthopedic surgery unit, I pondered the contrasting appearances of Micah and Emily. Micah suffered both anorexia and bulimia, but his bulimia purge strategy involved not regurgitation but walking whenever he could: pacing, circling, and even surreptitiously clenching his leg muscles while seated—all forms of burning calories. A cryptic purge, subtle, not classic bulimia—and overall he seemed mostly dominated by anorexia. He was inward-directed, a tight little bundle of sticks.

Emily could hardly have been more different. She was strong, extroverted, energetic, at a perfectly healthy weight—though who knew, perhaps she swung from one disease to the other too. During our interview, she had mentioned some caloric restriction patterns from years earlier.

Was there shared biology, despite how different these two diseases, these two patients, seemed? Anorexia was a rigid accountant, tracking every calorie and every gram, suppressing the reward of food; bulimia was natural reward embraced, amplified, repeated furiously through a cloud of calories. Yet there was a paradoxical commonality—these two could still coexist, and even work together. Both were content to kill, but the compatibility seemed to me to be deeper yet; both achieved a toxic liberation, an expression of self as dominant over the self's needs.

What brain but of a human being could make such a thing happen? At what moment in evolution did the balance of power finally tip toward cognition becoming stronger than hunger? There was no way of knowing, but I guessed it could not have been long before we emerged, not long before we became modern humans. Wanting such a thing is not enough. Wanting to live beyond want—that is unremarkable, and universal. The hard part is making it happen, for anything as funda-mental as feeding. But the modern human mind has vast and versatile reserves standing by, waiting to engage, to solve anything—calculus, poetry, space travel.

Motive force might be drawn from many different regions across the rich landscape of the human brain. Defiance of hunger is no small task, but for a nation of ninety billion cells it is perhaps not too hard to arouse powerful million-strong ensembles. Many different brain cir-cuits could even individually suffice for the uprising, each in its own right a massive and well-connected neural structure, each adapting its own mechanisms, its own culture, its own strengths.

And so diverse paths might be taken to anorexia nervosa in different patients, depending on each individual's unique genetic and social environment—a complexity already hinted at by the diversity of genes that can be involved, as with many psychiatric disorders. One patient might raise an army against hunger by drafting circuits in the frontal cortex devoted to self-restraint; another might instead work through a self-taught cross-linking of deep pleasure circuits with survival-need circuits, learning to affix the attribute of pleasure onto hunger itself; still others, like Micah, with both bulimia and anorexia, working with both motion and thought, might find their way by recruiting rhythm-generating circuits, ancient oscillators in the striatum and midbrain built for repetitive behavioral cycles. Controlling the walking rhythms of the brainstem and spinal cord, via compulsive exercise, could suborn the pleasing rhythms of counting—for both steps and calories. With bulimia and anorexia, Micah would be counting both—the calories coming in and the steps going out, the tick and the tock. Micah had woven a soft repeating rhythm of the two, their rough-knit interlocked texture absorbing all his blood and salt.

Repetition is immensely compelling. Circuitry for repetitive grooming in birds—maintaining feathers in form for flight—does not need to provide awareness of any underlying rationale. Evolution just confers motivation, to loop the action without logic or understanding, front to back, again and again and again, pleasing and inexplicable. Or the digging behaviors of the ground squirrel, badger, and burrowing spider— each of these species locks the rhythm of the dig to its own specialized frequency, its tuned neural cycle from central pattern generators. Or scratching in mammals like us—every animal has a different dig— getting to the parasite and rooting it out, driven by the flush of reward that comes with the scratch as the itch is hit, once started barely stoppable, the rhythm only heightened in intensity by the necessary damage done to the skin. A full valence flip—raw pain now raw reward.

Our brains play out more complex rhythms too, spanning time and space, using the metaphor of these basic motor actions. The same frontal cortex that plans and guides our scratch with a hand, in lockstep with its deeper partner the striatum, is also an executive for planning the daily routines, the seasonal rituals, the yearly cycles. The reward of rhythm shows up across every timescale, and in nearly every human endeavor: in knitting and suturing, in music and math, in the conceptual rituals of planning and organization. Not only actions but repetitive thoughts too can become as compelling as any tic; the extension of ancient rhythms to new kinds of conceptual digging may help us build civilizations—but when the rhythms grow too strong, some of us become collateral damage: the obsessive-compulsive cleaners, the hyperaware counters, the groomers, the scrutineers, all the suffering relentless.

My pager went off again as I entered the ortho unit—it was the psychiatry housestaff office. I picked up a phone at the nearest nurses' station and called back. It was Sonia. "She's gone."

"Uh . . . what? Gone?"

"As soon as you left, she said she wanted to sketch her problem for me." Sonia's voice was tremulous, fear gasping out through every inter-syllable. "She asked me to get some markers, so I ran to the housestaff office, and came right back." She had imagined the thrill of diagnosis, maybe a publishable case report, an epic win for her residency inter-views. "I was only away thirty seconds, and when I came back she was just gone. She wasn't on a hold, so nobody was watching, and none of the nurses saw her leave."

"I'm coming back now," I said. "Sit tight, it's okay." But it was not okay. I had read her all wrong. Emily had been the cagiest of the psy-chotic depressed, suicidal but just wary enough to snooker me. In her own hidden craft, she had set out alone. The excitement of her final liberation was what I had been picking up, not knowing, misdiagnos-ing. My house of cards had come down, and I was responsible. I double-timed it back to the unit, just short of a run. Weak.

•

It was a complicated situation, but Sonia was right that we had no con-trol. Emily was eighteen and not on a legal hold. She had never ex-pressed suicidality, and had the freedom to come and go. There was no recourse.

We buzzed around the unit, looking for clues. She had taken noth-ing, and she had even left her laptop and phone exactly where I had seen them by the bed a few minutes earlier. Not what someone leaving against medical advice would typically do, if she were just headed back home or to a friend's house. There was no time, and no need, to speak our deepest fear.

We paged the attending to update him, though there would be noth-ing he could do either. It was on us, on me.

Only ten minutes had passed. The hospital was buttoned-down pretty tightly; even where there was no locked unit, the windows were generally sealed. If suicide were the goal, it wasn't clear what route she could take. We were on the second-floor open unit—I knew how to get to the roof of the fifth floor, through the hidden rathole of our resident gym, but there was no way she would find her way there.

Sharp edges . . . the hospital cafeteria, first floor, almost exactly under our feet? Or worse, just past the cafeteria, there was a balcony, an overlook into a vast atrium—it was a long way down from that balcony to the basement floor below. She could have gotten there in thirty seconds, and anything—everything—could have happened since then.

Sonia knew the stakes and was feeling it; her face was hard and I could see, just under the surface, cracking fault lines of failure and self-doubt. "Okay," I said, as reassuringly as I could. "She is probably just going to get a cigarette. In fact, that's probably what this whole thing is—the school stuff too." It was almost plausible—a flash recall brought me back to second-year residency, when I had been called in a panic by the labor and delivery unit; a new mother was demanding to leave right after her C-section and the whole floor was in a tumult. I had been called as the consult-liaison psychiatrist to—as the obstetrics resident put it—"*I don't know, place her on a hold or something.*" After speaking with the patient in her mother tongue for just ten minutes I got to the real reason—she only needed to go have a cigarette, and had been too embarrassed to ask. I savored that small victory for years, in part as crystallization of a curious and recurring lifelong theme— I had noticed that truth can always be discovered just by letting people speak.

But not this time, and that wasn't Emily. When you're just desperate to sneak off and smoke, you don't tell authority figures to sit with you. I kept that thought in, for now. "Hang on," I said to Sonia. "Let's split up. You go check the ER and the parking lot. I'll head toward the other side of the ground floor. Don't run." On task, Sonia, high ponytail describing frenetic horizontal figure eights in the air, was gone.

When she turned the corner, I speedwalked to the escalator, trying to project professional calm as I headed down to the ground floor. Ten seconds to the cafeteria, twenty to the atrium. I turned right, one more hallway to go. Counting steps. Listening for screams. The only sound a ticktock, each step a small victory, each step burns calories. Each step is a win. Nobody can stop you from taking more steps—and every step is closer to death.

I had been so close, but I had betrayed my undeserved gift, the inescapable theme of my life, that people seem to unburden themselves with me—and this time, someone needing help had started to connect, and I had walked away. Why? Only because orthopedic surgery had paged me once too often about a transfer that could wait.

Here. Sharp edges around this corner, at the sunlit cafeteria entrance. I allowed myself to think: it was a beautiful day, as was every day here. Sunlight was coming, but I was ready for that darkness, for that crow shadowbird.

The sun streamed in from the cafeteria patio as I turned right again, and there she was, just an arm's length in front of me: Emily. We nearly collided.

She had been intercepted, hustling out of the cafeteria entrance. Standing there, we locked eyes and then both looked down. She let herself giggle in relief. In her hand was a plate of food, piled high, nearly architecturally impossible. Fried chicken drumsticks, cake, pizza—an edifice of pure caloric reward.

She told me later it had been her third round-trip in ten minutes. Duck into the cafeteria, stack food, come back out through the entrance without paying—then to the patio to gorge, purge, and return. A cycle of reward and release, without consequence—yet hoping, needing, to be caught. Loopholing: victory over the body and the equations of mass balance. That was everything, and there was no stopping. But she felt it to be crazy, knew it to be dangerous, and did not want to be alone.

•

I was on call that night, and at the first quiet moment I went out alone onto the roof, through the door near the call rooms where residents could get a few minutes of sleep between admissions and consults, and onto the moonlit expanse of concrete and railings and vents. On rare quiet nights we would go out there together sometimes, two or three of us, residents or interns or students, and sit under the stars, leaning back against hard metal scaffolds in our thin scrubs.

The roof was uncomfortable but had the feeling of a sanctuary—a space apart before the next burst of calls and pages. That night it felt important to be still and alone, to consider what had happened with Emily. Something about the biology of this disordered eating felt hard and unallowable—and when that feeling comes, I have found, it is best to seek a moment to sit with the mystery.

This disorder seemed to me unique, and important, and a clue to something scientifically deep, but first I had to ask myself: how much of this strong reaction I was feeling—that neuroscience needed to learn much from this disease—was driven by my own parental sympathies, a drive to care for Emily, displaced? I relived another scene: of a father at his fourteen-year-old's bedside on the pediatric anorexia unit, in his oil-change-shop shirt—Nick, it says above the left pocket—after her heart attack and pneumothorax. The possibility of death has been spoken, and is known to him. He's no longer able to look at her; he is only just holding her, touch his only sense, seeing nothing, focusing only on the frail sparrowlike form of her scapula, her intermittent heartbeat felt faintly through to his chest, every two seconds, and her weak cool breath on his shoulder. No—he is remembering the sound of before she was born, the thumping whoosh-whoosh of her heart coming from the ultrasound like a war drum, filling the room, fierce and strong and fast, she couldn't be held back, she was his and coming, and the tears crashed out through his eyes, then and now. She was, she had to be always, unstoppable.

With the heels of my hands I squeezed my eyes and blinked at the moon. Here was the essential conflict I saw: the self was at war with its own needs.

To understand the biology of disordered eating, it seemed, we would have to understand something even more fundamental, and no more accessible—the biological basis of the self. And if the self could be separable from its needs, what was the self then? What lay within and without its boundaries? An ancient question, unsolved. We feel at home here—we are natives; we are the self, we think—and yet we cannot precisely draw our borders, nor name our capital. Not as human beings, not as neuroscientists, not even today.

Some bounds can be guessed. The self does not extend outside the skin, for example. But even that distinction is not as obvious as it seems. Parenting may seem to blur that line. Nor does the self fill the whole volume under the skin, nor even the whole brain. The self feels the body's needs—but these needs are broadcast by some agent that is other, yet still within the body. And pain or pleasure, doled out by some deep and dour neural banker—our suffering when drives are unfulfilled, our joy when drives are met—these seem only currencies that motivate the self to act, but are no more self than any monetary instrument: assets and debts, incentives.

Philosophy, psychiatry, psychology, law, religion: all have their own perspectives on the self. Just imagination, without exception, though each fantasy nevertheless describes truth of a sort. But neuroscience, with its power to know a new kind of truth, and to make that truth known, has not quite weighed in with an answer. Caution is needed—the right scientific words might not even exist yet. Perhaps there is no such thing as a self, after all.

We do feel at times an especially strong sense of self—for example, when we struggle with, and resist, and overcome a drive—but that sense of self could be illusory, and the victorious entity just a shifting alliance of other competing drives. Still, studying the process of resisting primary drives (with eating disorders as extreme examples) might be useful, since in late-stage anorexia, the entity that resists food is not obviously a rival drive. There seemed to me no clear natural process competing against the hunger—no reason to resist that the patients knew or understood or could express—and yet hunger could still be resisted. True, the resistance to food had started for a reason, as a primal drive—social pressure, leading to a weight-loss goal—but that was only the trigger, starting the conscription of cells and circuits into that vast new army, at the end with no more reason for its final ravaging of the body than the fact of its own existence. And yet in the magnitude of its blind destructive power perhaps deep biology was revealed—just as an earthquake exposes shattered strata that show how the earth was made, in the very act of breaking the earth itself.

Biologists speak of genetic mutations that are "gain of function" or "loss of function"—this means that a change has happened, a mutation, that turns the function of the gene up or down. These mutations help reveal what the gene is for. Knowing what happens with too much or too little of something reveals a great deal about that thing's role. For Micah's severe intake restriction, despite all he had lost, I could start with thinking of this behavior as a gain of function in the self, in whatever can resist the natural drive to eat when hungry or to drink when thirsty (of course with no implication that this self's distorted form is good for the human being, any more than a gain-of-function mutation of a gene is good, rather than destructive). But if one could eavesdrop on the activity of neurons throughout the brain, one could listen for, and localize, a circuit that stands out for resisting the impositions of the drive, at least under some conditions—and that could recruit allies, other circuits, to help suppress drive-satisfying actions.

Interesting enough for a starting point, I thought—and with a tractability lending itself well to exploration. But this starting point would be understood, from the beginning, to be only a simplification, since the self includes more abstract and complex representations of drive control than eating or drinking—extending to all principles and priorities, roles and values. And there was, I realized, a different dimension as well—also within the self, and helping to define the self, but wholly separate from priorities and primary drive adjudication. This separate dimension of the self was its memories.

Starting to feel the chill of night but unwilling to leave the moonlit roof just yet—the night having a perfection of its own, in a moment and a memory that might last—it seemed to me that memories of what we have felt, and have done, might be as important a part of the self, and just as fundamental, as priorities. If an external force were to change my memories, I might feel even more a loss of self than if my priorities were instead changed.

When answering which is the most important part of a self, it might matter who is asking.

On that rooftop, among the metal gantries and humming vents, when I thought about almost everyone else in their world—co-workers, leaders of society, strangers on the street—their priorities seemed a more important aspect of their selves than their memories. *More* important, actually, in that any change to those principles would matter more to me. The selves of others were in a different category, since for my own self, the opposite was true: memories mattered more than priorities. Loved ones were perhaps in between; my son's memories seemed as important as his priorities. A little blurring of self-boundaries, perhaps. Relationships extend the self into the world, through love.

Why do our memories, of personal past experiences, matter so much to our sense of self, with significance that is at least comparable to our principles? Since we don't control our memories, it is odd that we see them as essential to our selves—even the experiences that are clearly external and brought upon us, like a surprise kiss or a rogue wave.

In considering this puzzle, out alone under the just perceptible stars, a unifying answer began to emerge: perhaps our sense of self comes not from priorities alone, nor from memories alone, but from the two together defining our path through the world. The self could even be seen as identical to this path—not a path just through space, but through some higher-dimensional realm, through three dimensions of space, one of time, and perhaps a final dimension of value— that of worth or cost in the world, with valleys of reward and ridges of pain.

We are not defined by obstacles and passageways that were laid down by others, by nature, and by the body's inner drives. These details are not us. Other people, and storms, and needs come and go, and as they do, they alter the hills and valleys of the landscape—but the self chooses the route taken. Priorities pick the path. Our selves are not the contour of that landscape available to us, in this complex topography we travel—rather, they are the chosen path. And memories serve to mark the path along the way, so we can find ourselves, embodied as where we have passed.

In this way I could see self as the fusion of memories and principles, collapsed into the unitary element of path.

It wasn't clear how to make progress right away with any of this, and I didn't get far that night before the pager, once again, summoned me to the hospital below. Though I asked myself these questions all the way through training, it took fifteen years from the day I met Emily for neuroscience to respond to me, to say anything in return at all. And when the words of science were spoken on this at last, they were consummatory, spoken in the tongue of intake: of food and water, of hunger and thirst.

•

Milton's fallen angel in *Paradise Lost* considered worldly losses as trivial compared with the stability and surety of self, of *a mind not to be changed by place or time*—even when freshly fallen into hell, a setting known to eating disorder patients and their families. Most of us are familiar with, and have used from time to time, this psychological defense. *Here at least we shall be free*: suffering is tolerable if it is the price of freedom.

This perspective helps define the self in a useful way, as that which will accept suffering rather than serve the tyranny of needs and comforts. The self makes, and is, its own place in space and time: defined not by need or circumstance, but by choosing a path that resists need. What then are the brain cells and regions that might have the capability, and agency, to pick such a path: to define a trajectory through the world that resists intense need (without just satisfying another drive)? Such circuitry would bring about a special kind of freedom, and in some patients enable a special kind of hell. Neuroscience has recently brought just a crack of light to this problem, illuminating the line between need and self, edging open this door to mystery.

Hunger and thirst, two of the most powerful drivers of animal action, begin in the brain as neural signals from small but potent populations of neurons deep in the brain, cells mixed together in a dense jumble with diverse roles that seem unrelated to one another, in and around a structure called the hypothalamus. The hypothalamus lies deep; the prefix *hypo* reflects its steadily progressing evolutionary burial *under* eons of neural sediments—under the larger thalamus, which itself is under the much larger striatum, which in turn lies under the most recently laid-down cortex forming the densely woven neural fabric on the surface of our brains.

Some of the first optogenetic experiments were carried out in these depths—in fact, the first optogenetic control of free mammalian behavior was in the hypothalamus. In 2007 only one kind of neuron here—the hypocretin cell population—was made responsive to light delivered through a fiberoptic. Control of waking and sleeping, and the REM of dreams, resulted; providing millisecond-scale pulses of blue light, twenty times per second, to these specific cells in this part of the hypothalamus caused sleeping mice, even in REM sleep, to awaken earlier than they would have otherwise.

This new precision had been needed, here as much as anywhere in the brain—since the hypothalamus holds, within its seemingly chaotic mix, not just neurons involved in sleep but also cells for sex, aggression, and body temperature, as well as hunger and thirst, and virtually every primal survival drive. All of these cells serve as broadcasters of individual needs—imposing (or trying to impose) their message on the broader brain, on the self wherever it may lie, to drive action addressing that need, working the levers of suffering and joy as needed to reinforce that action. But all of these cells are intertwined with one another in the hypothalamus, not separately accessible in real time by scientists seeking to test for roles in behavior.

Yet with optogenetics, gain- or loss-of-function experiments were enabled, to reveal how primal survival drives arise from specific activity patterns in single kinds of cells—or even single cells. Neuroscientists could control—provide or take away—the electrical activity of any one of these diverse types of intermingled cells selectively, using the same optogenetic principle that had illuminated anxiety, and motivation, and social behavior, and sleep: in which genes from microorganisms cause production of light-activated electrical currents only in the cells of interest.

Optogenetics allowed testing which of these deeply buried hypothalamic cells—known to be naturally active during the state of need—in fact cause the hunger or thirst behaviors, actually driving the consumption of food or water. Spots of laser light were delivered into the brain by fiberoptics to turn on or off targeted cell types in the hypothalamic region as animal actions were chosen in the world. With the flick of a switch to drive optogenetic excitation, a food-sated mouse immediately began to eat voraciously, and the opposite experiment—an inhibitory optogenetic intervention—suppressed food consumption even in a hungry mouse, underscoring the natural importance of these cells.

Similar experiments were carried out on different hypothalamic cells: those for thirst. These experiments showed, in the starkest of ways, how the choices of action made by an animal can be determined by electrical activity in certain very specific, and very few, neurons deep in the middle of the brain. The conundrum of agency (does free will meaningfully exist or not?), while not answered, is particularly well framed here. That a few spikes of electrical activity in a few cells control choices and actions of the individual—this now cannot be denied.

Watching these effects in real time in mice, a psychiatrist can become awash in personal memories—heartrending clinical images of bulimia and anorexia, seeing an individual gorging on food not needed, or suppressing food intake desperately needed. The hunger and thirst optogenetics experiments provided proof of principle that a local cluster of cells deep in the brain could cause and suppress such symptoms—and so, perhaps, that we might be able to design medicines or other treatments to target these cells.

But there was a key difference between experiments with optogenetics and realities of the disease—a distinction important for treatment, and for understanding the basic science of the self. In the optogenetics experiments, we directly accessed—turning up or down—the deep need cells that broadcast the drives of thirst or hunger. But bulimia and anorexia patients, despite their extreme thoughts and actions, still know the hunger—or at least the emptiness—is there. What the patients may do is counteract the effects of that feeling—associating positivity with the emptiness. If patients can't get to the need cells in the hypothalamus directly—outside the self's conscious control—this is how it must be done. Bring opposing resources to bear, fighting the effects of those need cells, forming a large enough and strong enough crowd in the town hall to win, to outshout hunger.

Is this how anorexia and bulimia become endowed with personhood? Riding atop the self circuitry, while clearly separate—a parasite, a virus recruiting the machinery of the host cell, a shell running atop an operating system, an emulation of a self. Only in this way can the disease access the problem-solving capability of the human mind. The disease recruits all the brain that the self normally can access, and must access—by turning hunger into a problem to be solved.

This simple subversion, initially endorsed by the patient—turning hunger into a challenge—allows recruitment of what our brains seem so well evolved for: solving problems, in a general and abstract way, to address needs that could never have been anticipated by evolution. And perhaps if we were not such versatile problem solvers, we would never have developed the ability to suffer this class of disease. As I had considered the day we lost—and found—Emily, different patients may solve the problem with different tricks—some by using circuits that are expert in discrete repeated actions like the striatum (to bring in the OCD-like pleasure of the rhythms of the count, and strike, and dig, and scratch, and weave), perhaps others by using restraint drives located in the frontal cortex (to bring in powerful executive-function circuits that suppress feeding in the context of social cues).

These are intriguing possibilities, but not far-fetched; in 2019, optogenetics experiments directly revealed groups of individual cells in the frontal cortex that were naturally active during social interaction but not feeding—and when directly activated by optogenetics, these specific social cells could suppress feeding, driving a resistance, even in naturally hungry mice. But regardless of specific provenance for one patient or another, the militia called up are strong circuits, and expansive, even though some have only emerged recently in evolutionary time, like those of the neocortex—that thin and vast sheet of cells including frontal cortex, a problem solver partnering with the deeper and older striatum, its enforcer and link to action.

Rodents have much smaller brains than we do, and relatively less neocortex, so mice may be less suited to resist drives. But neocortex they do have, and in a separate stream of optogenetics experiments from 2019, it was discovered that certain parts of the neocortex can stand apart from even strongly driven primal drives. When a mouse is fully water-sated but the deep thirst neurons are optogenetically driven, intense water-seeking behavior results—and yet a few parts of the brain are not fooled, and seem to know the animal is not truly thirsty. These circuits listen to the drive, without buying in; their local neural activity patterns are only mildly affected. This result was one of several discoveries resulting from the kind of brainwide listening experiment I had hoped for years earlier: using long electrodes to listen in on tens of thousands of individual neurons across the brain, while optogenetically stimulating the deep thirst neurons.

The first important finding from this brainwide eavesdropping, and a big surprise, was that most of the brain—including those sectors thought to be primarily sensory, or just movement related, or neither— was actively engaged in the simple state of seeking water when thirsty. Perhaps this finding revealed an important natural process by which the brain keeps all parts of itself informed on all planned movements and goals, so that even simple actions would be experienced by every part of the brain as generated from the self, and there would be no confusion as to the source of the drive for action. This unitary quality can go awry in disorders like schizophrenia, where simple actions can feel alien—as if generated from outside the self.

More than half of all the neurons recorded across the brain showed engagement with the task of acquiring water—both when the animal was truly needing water and also when, with optogenetics, we created a thirst-like state. So now not only are those old tales (usually thought to be false) claiming that only half, or even 10 percent, of our brains are used for this or that, demonstrably wrong—but it also seems likely that almost the entire brain is activated in specific patterns during every specific experience or action (since we now know a task as simple as drinking water when thirsty involves most of the neurons throughout much of the brain).

The second key finding was localization of the resistance: that identification of brain regions refusing to be intimidated by the imposed deep drive. Although clearly affected and so undeniably hearing the thirst signal sent from below, those few cortical structures, recently evolved and at the surface of the brain, stood out. These were not fully responding, not matching the state they would have entered into for an animal naturally seeking water when thirsty. The resistance was revealed like a shadow thrown, across both the *prefrontal cortex* (a region already known to be responsible for the generation of plans or paths through the world, and locating oneself on those paths) and the *retrosplenial cortex* (a region already known to be tightly linked to the entorhinal cortex and hippocampus, two structures involved in navigation and memory of paths in space and time). Both prefrontal and retrosplenial cortex thus fit the idea of self as path, and were already well known to be active during stimulus-independent thought—when a human subject is asked to sit quietly and think of nothing in particular, to simply be with one's self. This pattern contrasted with that in neighboring cortical areas (insular cortex, anterior cingulate cortex, and others), which showed neural activity patterns nearly indistinguishable from when the mouse truly needed water, when thirst was real.

So it seems many brain areas are able to feel and encode the state of natural thirst, as they should in order to help guide appropriate action to keep the animal alive. But at least two—prefrontal and retrosplenial cortex, perhaps in their role of self- (or path-) creation and navigation— in some sense know more about what the priorities of the animal should be, in terms of where it has been and is going, separate from the deep thirst drive. These two regions reside in recently evolved brain regions—quintessentially mammalian, and massively expanded in our lineage.

It is on the backs of such resistance that the eating disorders may find their strength—a standing army, quartered in neural barracks but always restless and poised to be called up by disease. Like the self-circuitry I imagined years earlier on the frigid metal gantries of the moonlit rooftop—thinking of, and recovering from, Emily—these parts can come to war with the whole, and win.

I walked Emily from the cafeteria to her room—she was relieved to come back. We lined up staff members to sit with her, which required some negotiation; there was no compelling legal authority against bingeing and purging, though we had some leverage since she had been stealing food. Sonia stayed with her first, Sonia who had been transformed back to her old self, with all her strength and even her serenity restored. And Emily at last could rest, cut off from access to the actions of bulimia for the time being; she could begin to recover and participate in developing a long-term plan for full healing. Even as we worked to make sure Emily was not left alone, our social worker began charting the path to an outpatient program. Bulimia had not dwelt long in Emily, and we were hopeful when she was discharged two days later.

For Micah, who was in his forties with behavior that seemed so entrenched, I was much less sanguine. We had already tried everything at our disposal. We could continue to occasionally place the nasogastric tube for feeding, when his blood pressure and heart rate skewed dangerously low—but the legal basis for doing this was always shaky and depended upon his inconsistent consent. He was not suicidal or homicidal, which is all the law addresses in allowing compulsion of psychiatry-based treatment—either these or grave disability, the inability to provide for his own basic needs. But Micah could provide perfectly well for his own needs; he only chose not to. Doctors can also compel emergency care if the patient is unable to understand the nature and consequences of treatment and cannot make an informed decision—but here again, Micah understood perfectly all the choices and consequences. He was not in delirium or psychotic. He simply wished his body to take a certain unusual form—with all the attendant risks. Here at least, he could be free.

As Micah continued to occasionally accept the NG tube—apparently only to toy with me, removing it himself later at night—I wondered how I seemed to him during all this. Hapless and childlike, arrogant and threatening—or more likely, I was not even worth that much thought. Micah's double disease set a course for him that was so strongly overdetermined he could chart his own path up the steepest hills of pain in that realm of space and time and value, and anything I said or did was beneath notice, just a slight shift of gravel under his feet. He refused a last-ditch medication that we hoped could help organize his thoughts, a low dose of olanzapine—which we also thought would put some weight on him as a side effect. I rotated off the service a week later, leaving Sonia to work with Micah. He was discharged to an outpatient facility a few days later, no better for all our ministrations.

•

Sonia collapsed during a psychiatry team dinner at another resident's apartment later that month. I hadn't seen her for three weeks. David, a neurosurgery resident, partner to another psychiatrist there, was standing next to her and leapt into action. Sonia had not quite lost consciousness, but David did a quick check there on the carpet, and then a fuller exam after we brought her to the couch and gave her orange juice. We hung back and let him work her up, until he finally stepped back, satisfied she had only fainted and was stable—and then, in a surreal moment, apparently because I knew Sonia best, David came over to present the case to me as if I were the attending rather than just another resident like him.

As worried as I was, and wanting to talk quietly with her myself, I remember thinking in that dimly lit room what an elegant thing his presentation was. David ticked through the history he had acquired, summarizing the medical and neurological exam he had tapped out in the miraculously intimate sonar of the physician without instruments, the pianist-like rhythmic fingertip percussing of internal air and water and organs, of reflexes, of heart rate and blood pressure—and concluded Sonia was severely dehydrated. She had been working out hard, admitting to eight- or nine-mile runs every morning and eating little— just not enough time, she had said. That day, there had been just carrots and some coffee.

Trying to peer around David, I did my best to see Sonia through the gloom as she lay on the couch across the room. She looked the same as when we had been on the team together, not thin or weak. What had I missed, then, about Sonia the strong? Or perhaps instead, she had only recently come to this way of being, in the past few weeks having been joined by another, now sharing her journey.

If anybody could solve the equations of mass balance and create a path, a state in defiance of a primary drive, it would be Sonia. She was her movement, she was her path, and there can be no self without movement along the path. Resist? One may as well. She had that part that moves, and fights back, and for it goes to hell.

CHAPTER 7

MORO

The broken dike, the levee washed away,
The good fields flooded and the cattle drowned,
Estranged and treacherous all the faithful ground,
And nothing left but floating disarray
Of tree and home uprooted,—was this the day
Man dropped upon his shadow without a sound
And died, having labored well and having found
His burden heavier than a quilt of clay?
No, no. I saw him when the sun had set
In water, leaning on his single oar
Above his garden faintly glimmering yet . . .
There bulked the plough, here washed the updrifted weeds . . .
And scull across his roof and make for shore,
With twisted face and pocket full of seeds.

—EDNA ST. VINCENT MILLAY, "Epitaph for the Race of Man"

"Mr. Norman, he's on 4A. Eighty-year-old veteran, long history of multi-infarct dementia. Brought to emergency yesterday, by family." The medicine resident's voice over the phone was pressured—getting his work done, trying to check off this consult request as quickly as possible. "They report that he slowly stopped talking, progressing to total silence over the course of a couple months. That's the only new symptom."

In my mind, that history was already concerning for neurological disease, raising the specter of a new stroke—especially with the apparent history of brain infarcts in the past—but it would be odd for a stroke-related process to evolve over months this way. I noticed in myself a mildly rewarding feeling of intrigue—a sensation I recalled from chess, when encountering an unconventional opening move. It was such a pleasant sensation, I even felt a bit guilty for feeling it. I leaned back in my chair and looked up at the grimy, flaking ceiling of the hospital sandwich shop. "Interesting," I began to reply, only to be cut off as the resident brusquely continued.

"The patient just moved here from Seattle after his wife died," he said. "Been living with his son's family in Modesto for a few months now. The family was worried about another stroke but we saw nothing new on the scan last night—just old white-matter lesions. He did have a UTI, so we're treating it, and we admitted him last night for that and to work up whatever happened with his talking. And now, guess what?"

A pause for effect—despite the pace of his pressured speech, the resident could not hide that he had found this one interesting too. Moments of intellectual reward can be frustratingly short-lived on inpatient call shifts, with little time to satisfy human curiosity; here, for what it was worth, one such moment seemed to have come.

"I got him to talk," the resident continued. "Turns out he can when he wants to. Just a real unpleasant character—he doesn't care about anyone, didn't care that his family was worried. Extremely cold, actually. I think antisocial personality. Guess even you guys can't unfuck that." Riffling sounds. "Still in the process of getting his records from Seattle, but their little clinic is closed till Monday. His son's here but doesn't know much of the medical history; they weren't a close family. Not a big surprise. My attending wanted me to call you, to see if you could evaluate for psychiatric explanations, since we can't find anything else. I don't really think it's delirium, since he seems oriented, though you could still suggest a trial of haloperidol—his QTc is 520, so let's be careful. Anyway, I think he just doesn't like people. This should be quick."

The resident had thought about side effects on heart rhythms, and rightly so—if the interval between two peaks on the electrocardiogram was already as long as 520 milliseconds, the treatment team risked causing a serious heart arrythmia with certain medications such as haloperidol—but his antisocial personality disorder idea didn't sound right to me, and diagnoses I favored more began volunteering themselves, populating my mental workspace. It was more likely, I thought, to be a form of delirium that did not fit the resident's expectations—

a quiet subtype of the waxing-and-waning disorientation often seen in the elderly, sometimes arising as a medication side effect, or caused by a moderate illness like his urinary tract infection. The medicine team might have assessed him by chance during a lucid phase of the delirium cycle, and so found him to be oriented.

The quiet ones are often missed; many doctors expect a highly active, vocal, demonstrative state of delirium, but the presentation we call hypoactive delirium is one of withdrawal, silence, and stillness on the outside—while deep inside, a storm of confusion churns.

On the other hand, if the resident had been partly right—in the sense that there was not delirium but rather a personality issue—then the personality change that comes with dementia was more likely to be relevant here than antisocial personality disorder. That empathy-deficient trait of antisocial personality would have been part of a life-long pattern—and though unpleasant, would not have struck the family as unusual now. Also favoring the dementia explanation, our brain imaging had apparently confirmed the underlying process: blood flow blockages (lasting long enough to kill cells) in vessels that supply the depths of the brain with sugar and oxygen.

These infarcts, spots of dead tissue that are the outcome of strokes, can be detected by computed tomography even years after the blockages, as scattered holes in the dense silkwork of interconnecting fibers that link brain cells across long distances—showing up on CT scans as lakelike black gaps called lacunae. Even in patients without a known stroke, more sensitive technologies like magnetic resonance imaging (MRI) can show the small vessel blockade of vascular dementia in a different way, as a profusion of intense white spots—scattered across the brain, marking the end of day with light, like stars in the early evening.

Personality change in dementia—well, common things are common. These changes appear in all the dementia syndromes, along the way and especially toward the end, when individual parts of the brain that manage predilections and values begin to break down. I had seen Alzheimer's disease patients with newly aggressive—even explosive—anger syndromes; Parkinson's disease patients with sudden risk-seeking tendencies; and fronto-temporal dementia patients with almost-infantile self-centeredness, verging on antisocial behavior, that the resident might have sensed.

In dementia, memory loss is the most widely recognized symptom, but dementia does not mean just amnesia. Rather more fundamentally, the word means loss of the mind itself. Memories—the stored senses and feelings and knowledge from along the journey of life that infuse the path with color and meaning—are effaced along with the values that set the path's boundaries and direction. And the latter—changing personalities and upended value systems—can be as shocking as the memory loss: a fundamental transformation in the identity, the essence of the self, of the person known and depended upon for so long.

This was, I thought, the more plausible syndrome. But without seeing the patient I could not be sure; there was also a chance the resident had actually nailed the full diagnosis—perhaps a well-disguised antisocial personality disorder had been unmasked by another process, like his urinary tract infection. I began imagining the distinct chill of the antisocial, and reflexively steeled myself to prepare for that slick indifference, that simulation of social grace, that viperish gaze unwittingly revealing to me how little I mattered, showing that one cannot conceal what one does not understand.

It was a quiet late-spring Saturday afternoon, the regular weekday psychiatry consult team was off, and I was the on-call resident for all things psychiatry. It was on me, so I stood up from my small table in the cramped hospital café, donned my armor—starched white coat, stethoscope, reflex hammer, pen—cleared away my coffee cup, and headed to the fourth-floor medicine inpatient unit.

•

Each major medical specialty in the hospital provides an on-call consult service to help fellow physicians with complex cases. In psychiatry this service is called the consult-liaison team, and training in psychiatry involves a heavy dose of C-L, fielding calls across the hospital—from intensive care and medicine units for managing delirium, from the obstetrics floor for evaluating postpartum psychosis, from surgery for sorting out competency and consent issues, and sometimes just for patient transfer when a unit with a truly closed and lockable door is needed.

Highly interdisciplinary or mysterious cases, pan-consulted, can bring the hospital together—in a kind of block party of clinical care, with many services buzzing around. This had not been obviously one of those cases—with its seeming simplicity—though when I pulled the chart from the rack at the nurses' station, I discovered that several consult teams had already been called before me—the neurology service most recently. I was the last resort for Mr. N. (as the notes referred to him, in the veterans hospital culture of anonymous respect).

Among the possibilities not mentioned by the resident, but discussed in chart notes left by the various teams, were forms of parkinsonism; the speech therapy team had correctly noted that Parkinson's disease can involve slow movements and reduced vocalization. The neurology consult team, ultimate arbiters of Parkinson's, had then come and gone, confirming poor short-term memory and multi-infarct dementia—but they found no signs of Parkinson's, noting as they signed off that although Mr. N. never smiled spontaneously, he could move his facial muscles when requested; this was not the frozen, masklike state of parkinsonism.

Neurology had commented also on the brain imaging confirmation of his multi-infarct dementia; recent and distant strokes look very different with these scans, and since no new stroke was apparent with CT, Mr. N.'s new reluctance to speak needed some other explanation. So psychiatry was called last—completing the usual progression through medical specialties, ending in the realm of the unknown.

I found Mr. N. in bed, looking straight ahead, and oddly still. His bristly bald head was propped up on three pillows, and his corrugated cheeks seemed to glisten slightly under the fluorescent lights. I also thought this was not Parkinson's after my own physical exam—there was no parkinsonian rigidity of the limbs and no tremor. Nor did I see signs of catatonia, a rare syndrome of immobility I needed to rule out, which can arise from psychosis or depression; he could move all his muscles readily when asked, nerve by nerve.

Delirium could also be mostly excluded—with the unlikely caveat that this might be, by chance, just another lucid moment. As the medicine resident had said, Mr. N. could speak, and he spoke a few words to me, choosing to answer only when asked repeatedly and the question was simply factual—but this was enough to establish that he was mostly oriented to time and place. Mr. N. knew he was in a hospital, he knew who the president was, he even knew the state we were in. He knew his son's name—Adam, from Modesto—the one who had taken him to the hospital this time, the one who had brought two grandchildren into Mr. N.'s life.

Though he refused to answer questions on his internal state—by remaining impassive, or with a brief head shake—one of his refusals came with a subtle feature that I could have easily missed had I not been watching carefully. As part of the full mental status examination in psychiatry, we probe participation in everyday interests and hobbies—asking if these are being pursued and enjoyed. The question sounds conversational, but reveals a great deal about motivation, and the ability to feel pleasure. His response to this, my query if he was enjoying his normal interests and activities in life, was nonverbal—just a downward twitch of one corner of his mouth in a hint of grimace—a half beat of self-disgust that seemed to me incompatible with delirium or antisocial personality.

I then had an urgent responsibility, one neither the medicine resident nor I had anticipated. Having caught a glimpse of his inner state, I now had to rule out depression, perhaps with an accompanying paranoia (this can be caused by severe depression and could explain his reticence to speak)—and I had somehow to address this life-threatening possibility in a mostly nonverbal patient, despite the fact that every diagnostic criterion in psychiatry is ultimately verbal in nature.

If Mr. N. were traveling deeper into a storm of psychotic depression, more and more stoic on the outside as he became increasingly paralyzed internally by hallucinations and paranoia, this syndrome would be a disaster to miss—especially since the condition would be elegantly treatable, with straightforward medication strategies. Alternatively, even if there were no psychosis, but only a severely depressed state suppressing effort allocation—making it too much of a motivational challenge to articulate words, to move lips and tongue and diaphragm enough to maintain a simple conversation—this state would have to be ruled out as well. Such a severe nonpsychotic depression could be fatal, but would also certainly be treatable.

I needed an approach that did not require the patient to form words. Seeing a framed photograph at his bedside—a Modesto High School basketball player, she seemed to be maybe fifteen—probably left by his son, I asked Mr. N. to show me a picture of his granddaughter. Displaying no grandfatherly excitement or pride, just shouldering the burden of my request, he complied—but he had no interest in looking himself. He just directed me with his eyes toward the evidence—and was done. No hint of the disorganization of psychosis.

I picked up the photo and showed it to him, pointing to her, asking for her name, watching closely. There was not a twitch of a smile, nor a softening of the eyes; but his gaze was not as dry as it had seemed. Up close I could track the almost imperceptible glistening of his cheeks; I had thought it the faintest sheen of perspiration, but the hospital room was chilly and now I could divine the source, track its scattered and discontinuous path up through crevasses and forks to headwaters in the corners of his eyes. He remained quiet, and could not say her name. Silence crashed around us—deafening, negative, noise.

•

In major depressive disorder, loss of pleasure is a classical symptom, and a classical-sounding name is given: anhedonia, the absence of beauty and joy from life. As cleanly and completely as senses of taste and smell are lost during the common cold, pleasure can be somehow detached from experience.

Though I had seen the anhedonia of depression—this inability to find reward or motivation in natural joys—many times before, it was unsettling every time. I could see how the resident had been guided down the wrong diagnostic path. Such a symptom could have appeared to manifest as a sort of inhumanity to physicians, friends and family—with a seemingly reptilian lack of warmth, even for his own grandchild.

How many millions of people with depression, over the course of human history, have had their isolation and suffering compounded this way, by helplessly eliciting anger and frustration in others—exacerbating all the other challenges and agonies of their disease? Even with this perspective, I still had to work on my own cognitions, to not react negatively to him as a person. Knowing is one thing, but understanding is another. I knew but still didn't understand, not deeply, neither as a human animal nor as a scientist.

To understand how pleasure can be detached from human experiences so universal and fundamental, we might begin by asking how value is linked to experience in the first place—where and why, in the human brain? And where and why, in the story of humanity? The answers, if we could find them, might explain the fragility of joy.

Sometimes the allocation of joy is automatic. We can feel powerful innate rewards, which serve as natural reinforcers of behavior important for survival and reproduction. One of these preset rewards may be pleasure at interacting with a grandchild—an experience that seems naturally positive in valence for us, though heightened further by experience. This response (not universal among mammals) might have acquired survival value in our lineage only as primates became more long-lived and social, for its utility in encouraging protection and education of the young. Those with increased ability to link reward circuitry to representations of the extended family could have benefited enormously from such an inborn wiring innovation. But all such connections, as physical structures, are vulnerable like any other part of the brain to a stroke—and depending on the exact location of the infarct, the effect could appear to be either specific to one kind of reward and motivation (causing an upheaval in priorities, and so an apparent personality change) or a more general and pervasive loss of pleasure in life (like the nonspecific anhedonia of depression).

Other innate pleasures seem to make little evolutionary sense—their existence only underscoring our ignorance. The reward of seeing the wild rough seashore—without the promise of food, water, or company—does not explain itself well. It is not the joy of returning home, not as we know it, not even in an evolutionary sense. Our fish-like forebears learned to breathe at the brink of land and water, but not at the pounding interface of cliff and wave. That part of our story is more in the shallow swamps of 350 million years ago, when the first air-breathing fishes emerged onto land.

Why, then, do nearly all of us see beauty in the seashore? Is there innate intrigue in the stark contrast of cliff and crashing wave, the power and peril of momentum versus bulwark? Or perhaps the waves in some way evoke the windsway of an arboreal canopy, or the reliable repetition of a lullaby, soothing with its rhythm and inevitability. Whatever its meaning, this joy is real. It is widely shared, and runs deep, and yet no logic seems fully explanatory. There are many such examples.

Natural selection provides one potential answer for the meaning of joy, which is that there is none. Meaning is an elusive, even absurd quantity in evolution; there was no meaning underlying the emergence of mammals to dominate the world after the dinosaurs—it was just chance, a giant meteor strike compounded by other natural disasters sixty-five million years ago that killed off most life as ejected dust blocked out the sun. It was meaningless, but consequential, how suddenly valuable it was to be small, fast-breeding, warm-blooded, fur-covered—and to have a strong innate drive to live in holes.

Some feelings, and the resulting behavioral drives, might arise from such chance associations, just vagaries of the environment. If a small group of human ancestors had a spontaneous affinity for—and crafted their lives around—the seashore, then the unrelated bottleneck contraction of human populations many tens of thousands of years ago could have created a founder effect: a small set of survivors exerting a large effect on the subsequent population. If most of those human beings who survived hung on via mussels and tide pool debris, scraping along like limpets on wet rocks as the rich plant life and large game animals on land died off, surviving humanity might carry within a joy and an affinity for the seashore, an intense appreciation for its imagined singular beauty—a joy not caused by the population crash but simply allowed to persist and propagate for the time being, due to humanity's close call with extinction. Not to say we know anything like that happened—though from paleogenetics we can see that there were indeed bottlenecks for us, including that global collapse in human populations bottoming out only fifty thousand years ago. Our most mysterious instinctual impressions of loveliness, then, may be just accidental fingerprints—left by artists of survival, on the cave wall of our genome.

When we all do feel joy or reward without learning, this is a trace of the past, cast forward over millennia of experience in our lineage; our forebears, at some point, most likely felt that joy, and those who were able to feel this way were able to create us. But learned rewards are another matter, arising within a lifetime, even within a minute. The brain seems designed to ingest new information, and to swiftly alter itself in response—this is how memories are made, and behaviors learned or changed in the life of an individual—and these fast physical changes can be studied in the laboratory, providing a short-timescale model for what evolution might work with on longer timescales. Learned behaviors can be rapidly tuned by modulating the strength of connections in the brain, and the groundwork for innate reward-seeking behaviors might be set over millennia in a similar way—as evolved and genetically prescribed connection strengths inside the brain. Whether learned or innate, feelings may be attached (or detached) from experience via the physical expedient of changing the strength of certain connections across the brain. And so two distinct concepts—feeling and memory—powerfully converge, both in health and in their disordered states: anhedonia and dementia.

•

We needed Mr. N.'s medical records to see if depression had been detected before, if any hints of psychosis or catatonia had been observed, and if any psychiatric treatments had been tried—with success or failure or side effects. These data points could be essential in finding a safe medication and avoiding harmful attempts at treatment (an especially important consideration in geriatric psychiatry).

The Seattle clinic was closed until Monday, the resident had said, and it was still only Saturday night. I needed that information before suggesting a medication. The next step was for me to connect with the primary treatment team and put together a plan—but it was getting late; time for Mr. N. to sleep. For the moment he was stable and safe, and so I took my leave, letting him know I'd come back to him tomorrow with a plan. He did not respond.

As I reached and opened the door, already looking out into the hallway, I heard a voice behind me:

"It's going to be a long night."

I froze at the door. Unprompted, a full sentence had come forth—from this patient who had not spoken on his own at all before, and with only one or two syllables at a time when pressed.

I turned and looked back across the room. He was now eerily upright and looking straight at me. The glisten on his cheeks was more intense, only on his upper cheeks, near the inner corners of his eyes. The room dropped away. I saw him fully—his veiny, bald head rocking gently with each breath, the symmetric sag of his eyes and mouth, his steady gaze on me. He did not speak again. He had said something important that he needed me to know.

After a long pause, I gave him my warmest smile and a reassuring nod. "Don't worry, Mr. Norman, we'll be with you all the way through."

It's going to be a long night. The last sentence he would ever speak.

•

The long course of dementia—whether spanning years or decades—is almost certainly a new phenomenon of life on earth, willed into existence by modern medicine and effective extended-family care. Via supportive social structures built with our brains, we have made the persistence of dementia possible, and have not yet found a solution. There are no cures, and the few medications available only slightly slow the steady progression of the disease.

In psychiatry, dementia is today (and this will change again) called major neurocognitive disorder, which for diagnosis requires the conjunction of both a loss of independent functioning and a loss of cognition (which can include nearly anything related to memory, language, social/perceptual/motor function, attention, planning, or decision-making). This long list, and the diversity of the symptoms that are permitted for making the diagnosis, in turn allow dementia—or major neurocognitive disorder as a medical construct—to encompass all the small and large disruptions in brain communication that can occur over a lifetime: by lacunae from strokes, by plaques and tangles in Alzheimer's disease, by spots of focal damage from accumulated injuries.

Disconnection, miscommunication, lost pathways. But what is actually missing?

Although brain cells certainly die in the dementias, it is not known if memory loss is always due to something like the loss of cells or synapses responsible for holding the memories—akin to wiping a computer drive. It is possible that instead, for at least some stages of white-matter damage like multi-infarct dementia, memories remain intact—but lie isolated from input or output projections, with only their connectivity lost.

With only interrupted input—access to the memory lost, just the pointer or lookup information—the memory would be present but not reactivatable. Or perhaps only interrupted output could occur: memories might be reactivated perfectly well, but find themselves unable to reach back into the conscious mind. Slumbering in the snow, or screaming into the void—either way, a memory could still live intact but in isolation, with connectivity lost due to the dark lakelets, the lacunae, the focal infarcts severing long-range fibers spanning the brain.

Clinically, a substantial fraction of multi-infarct dementia patients also exhibit anhedonia—a surprising correlation for two seemingly unrelated syndromes. Studies have found considerably increased anhedonia in senior populations with cognitive impairment, versus cognitively intact comparison groups—even manyfold increased in patients with frank dementia. This connection between feeling and memory runs yet deeper; in these populations, the greater the accumulated volume of those lacunae in white matter—showing greater loss of long-range connections, the carriers and controllers of information—the more anhedonia was seen. When memory fails, feeling can follow.

Optogenetics experiments have shown that value, or valence as we say, can be attached to brain states by long-range connections across the brain—for example, that valence of release from anxiety is set in part by projections from the BNST to reward circuitry deep in the midbrain. And these intriguing human epidemiological linkages—the association between anhedonia and dementia, and the association in dementia between lacunar volume and anhedonia—could be explained if the same process that causes the decline in memory (damage to long-range white-matter tracts, inputs and outputs) also causes the decline in feeling. Cells that could provide feelings may still be present but cut off, in the same ways that memories may be lost: by becoming voiceless.

Memory also needs feeling, in some sense. There may be little justification to store and recall a memory of an experience, unless the experience matters enough to elicit a feeling. Information storage takes space, uses energy, and creates curational challenges; no such cost can be borne for long on evolutionary timescales without manifesting some benefit. So the very act of storing and recalling information, of making and using a memory, is often entangled with the fact that the experience *matters*—which in conscious beings like us often means association with a feeling. Thus anhedonia could not only arise from the same process underlying dementia, but also impair memory itself, further increasing the correlation of these two states.

Many neuroscientists today believe that remembering involves a reactivation of some of the very same neurons that were active during the initial experience. Several investigators have used optogenetics to explore this idea, not in sensory regions of the brain but instead in memory-related structures called the hippocampus and the amygdala, by tagging cells that were strongly active during a learning experience (such as a fearful episode in a particular context), and then reactivating a subset of those tagged cells with light, much later, far from the fearful context across both space and time.

Mice can be seen exhibiting fear in these cases, even in the absence of anything related to the initial fear-inducing experience—that is, absent everything but the optogenetic reactivation of a few of the fear-memory neurons. So remembering, it seems, can happen when the right combination of brain cells—called an ensemble—speaks together.

If this is remembering, then what is the memory itself when it is not being actively remembered? Within which molecules, cells, or projections do the bits reside? Where is the actual information of a memory—of the stored experience, or knowledge, or feeling—as it lies dormant, awaiting recall?

Many in the field today think an answer to this question lies in a quantity called *synaptic strength*—a measure of how strongly a neuron can influence another neuron, defined as the *gain* from broadcaster to receiver. The stronger a synapse, or functional connection, between two cells, the greater the response in the receiving cell will be to a fixed pulse of activity in the broadcasting cell. As abstract as it seems, this change in influence at the synapses could *be* the memory, in a real and physical sense.

There are many interesting features to synaptic strength that make this idea plausible. First, theoretical neuroscientists have proven that synaptic strength changes indeed can store memories in an automatic way during experiences (without requiring intelligent supervision) and in a form that allows easy recall. Second, synaptic strength changes of the right kind can happen in the real world—in fact, very readily and swiftly in living neurons and brains—in response to bursts of activity or neurotransmitters. Certain patterns of synchronous or high-frequency activity pulses can drive increases—potentiation—in synaptic strength, while asynchronous or low-frequency pulses can drive decreases— depression—in synaptic strength. Both effects are plausibly useful for memory storage, based on the theoretical work.

It had only been a tantalizing hypothesis, that synaptic strength along a path from one part of the mammalian brain to another could be specifically and directly adjusted to change behavior. This idea had not been formally testable without a way to selectively provide activity pulses to change synaptic strength in projections defined by origin and target in the mammalian brain. But optogenetics enabled this intervention: a connection from one part of the brain to another can be made light-sensitive, and then high- or low-frequency light pulses can be provided along these pathways. By 2014 several groups working with mammals were optogenetically applying these principles from memory, and had confirmed that powerful and selective effects on behavior can be exerted by projection-specific synaptic strength changes themselves.

Projections fundamentally embody how effectively different parts of the brain can engage with each other, whether in health or disease; for example, it is known that interregional connectivity strength predicts interregional activity correlations. It is also known that interregional activity correlations can be linked to specific states of enjoyment—for example, reduced coordination between the auditory cortex and a deep reward-related structure (the nucleus accumbens) predicts anhedonia for music in human beings. Likewise, the specific basic reward of caring for a grandchild could be enabled by a capability for strong synaptic connectivity (and thus effective engagement) between one brain region responsible for addressing drives or rewards (like the hypothalamus or VTA/nucleus accumbens circuitry) and another brain region representing hierarchies of kinship relationships (like the lateral septum). Projection-specific synaptic strengths may allow such specific behaviors to become favored and rewarding, especially with learned positive experience.

In this way, synaptic strength at the level of brain region interconnection is an interesting quantity relevant to development and evolution of our internal feelings, since evolution is well suited to working with such interregional connection strengths. Though evolution knows nothing of music or grandchildren per se, it could set up the conditions allowing either or both to be enjoyed—to a certain level, with the right life experience. And there is no shortage of genetic complexity available to lay these specific foundations, in the richness of gene expression patterns that determine how cellular diversity and axon guidance implement brain wiring.

Value—whether negative for aversion, or positive for reward—in the end is only a neural label of sorts, one that can be attached to, or detached from, elements like experiences or memories. This flexibility is crucial for learning, for development, and for evolution. But what can be readily attached may be just as easily detached—for good or ill, in health or disease—and we now have a path for understanding how this flexibility can be enabled. Memories and values alike may both reside in synaptic strengths, learned or evolved as physical structures. And the path to the synapse—along the axon, the long-range fiber emerging from one cell to touch other cells—is set up and directed and grown according to instructions from genes (which follow all of evolution's rules) at which point the synapse itself can be powerfully tuned by the specificity of experience. Our paths, our joys, our values all lie along thin threads that can be cut—connections bearing our memories, projections that are our selves.

•

I signed out to the night psychiatry resident, whose Saturday swing shift was sandwiched between my two daytime Saturday and Sunday shifts. I had not met him before; he looked excessively sporty and energetic. Tired but thinking myself tolerant, I walked him through a summary of the patients on our unit with active issues before driving home to get a few hours of rest.

Driving back to the hospital again the following morning, along the deserted streets of early Sunday in Palo Alto, my thoughts drifted back to Mr. N. There remained challenging logistical issues if we were to initiate administration of a medication. We had to determine who was legally able to provide consent, and if Mr. N. was not able, the primary team needed to have a discussion with his son—someone I had not yet met. There was little I could do in the moment; I was technically only a consultant on this case, not a decision-maker.

After getting sign-out from the now-haggard night resident for the patients on our psychiatry unit and managing to listen with benign interest as he troweled on thickly the stories of his overnight valor, I went to a workstation to see if anything new had appeared regarding Mr. N. His location had changed, surprisingly—his name no longer appeared on the 4A medicine unit roster. A moment later I saw he was in the ICU—the intensive care unit.

Mr. N. had suffered a massive stroke the night before, an hour after I had left him. His body was alive, but it was unlikely he would ever recover independent living. His son had power of attorney. Code status had been set: do not resuscitate; do not intubate.

I stood dumb, staring, impotent. He had been right and needed to tell me. His night would be very long.

•

Only at the very end of life—only when we have put away the chessboard, with all moves made, with no more surprises to come, with most consequences played out—can we fairly judge ourselves and assign credit to actions that ultimately brought success or failure. But it is also here at the end where the memories of our moves fall away, forgotten—a cruel twist, for without memory, how then can we make sense of the lives we have lived, and find meaning in the paths we took, amid the pathos?

We cannot, and so we end where we begin, helpless and uncertain.

Mr. N. surprised us by living on for several weeks before passing. I saw a man whom I presumed to be his son two or three times around the hospice unit, walking in and out—and once as he was pushing Mr. N., supine on his gurney, down the corridor. I remember that day pausing to watch them, as they eased toward a patch of sunlight by a window, and I remember hearing his son's gentle whisper: *Here's some sun for you, Daddy.*

Mr. N. looked older than I remembered—lying flat, utterly limp, his skin a paler gray, eyes closed and mouth open, atonal, utterly still. Cashed out and gone home. His bristly head, the only part of him not covered with the blanket and sheet, seemed proud and dignified to me, though. It evoked the memory of his final move, sitting up in his hospital bed, telling me something that mattered through the fog of dementia and depth of depression, with nearly everything already taken away from him.

As they neared the window and its broad sunbeam, I could hear a medicine team hustling our way, chattering about atrial flutter. Mr.

N.'s son could hear them too—he pushed a little faster to make space, clumsily guiding the gurney toward the window at the corridor's edge.

As the team swept past me, humming along in a crescendo of discussion, the gurney jolted gently to a halt as its bumpered corner tapped the wall. At that moment of impact, both of Mr. N.'s arms suddenly swept up toward the ceiling, askew but together—the sheet dropping away as one arm ended firmly skyward, the other weaker, halfway up, both hands open and fingers splayed. Stable and strong. A frantic reach, a shocking strength.

A stunned moment of silence seized the hallway, and its motley collection of spectators, as Mr. N.'s son and the interns and I looked on at the reaching, grasping arms, all of us locked together in the surreal scene for a beat or two—and then the arms eased back to the gurney, together. Mr. N. was once again at rest.

The medicine team had slowed but never stopped. It took a few seconds for their chatter to build and re-form, as they turned a corner at the end of the hall, but now humming in a minor key, the neurology of reflexes surfacing in their minds from a whirlpool of memories and desires.

•

In dementia, the infantile reflexes come back, movements choreographed by evolution for the survival of primate babies: the *Moro* reflex (arms sweep up when the body is suddenly dropped or accelerated, a relic from our tree-climbing forebears, saving infant lives of those who became our ancestors) and the *root* (light touch on the cheek triggering a turn of the head and an opening of the mouth, to find milk). Falling from height, and losing contact with mother—the basic unlearned fears of human newborns.

Both action patterns disappear after a few months of life but come back with dementia or brain damage—not re-created at the end of life, but rather never really gone, always present but latent for decades, layered over with higher function, coated with inhibition and cognitive control, with all the threads of lived life. As the fabric frays and texture is lost, the original self finds voice again in a heart-wrenching grasp for safety, reaching for a long-dead mother.

All the details of life that mattered so much over the years, that brought moments of happiness or pain, had only covered her over, weaving across with so many weft threads that she could no longer be seen. But always there, and now at the end, the framework for everything surfaces again. As the fine threads fall away, she becomes, once more, the whole world. She might be reachable again, the mammal who kindled her baby to life, who shakingly held, and nursed, and shielded her child—from the rain and sun.

As the threads of the mind disintegrate, as massive insulated fibers fragment and fray, when memory and agency have dissolved away, what was there since birth is all that is left . . . a human infant in a thin cloth of gray, now exposed again to the cold.

Now all there is, in the confused darkness, is a gentle sway. . . . And when balance suddenly shifts, as the dry weak branch snaps, the baby is released into the night, unpinned from the world, and falls—hands sweeping, in a desperate grasp.

A branch breaks, and this is all at the end. A tree-dwelling baby, a grasping for mother, a falling through space.

EPILOGUE

My great blue bedroom, the air so quiet, scarce a cloud. In peace and silence. I could have stayed up there for always only. It's something fails us. First we feel. Then we fall. And let her rain now if she likes. Gently or strongly as she likes. Anyway let her rain for my time is come. . . .

So. Avelaval. My leaves have drifted from me. All. But one clings still. I'll bear it on me.

—JAMES JOYCE, *Finnegans Wake*

The shuttle swings on, ticking back and forth at the leading edge of the tapestry, marking time in space like a pendulum, embedding moments and feelings. Warp threads point the way into unformed space, framing—but not determining—what happens next.

This steady progression of experience clarifies patterns and buries structural threads. Either outcome serves as a resolution of sorts.

My oldest son, with whom I lived as a single father for many of these experiences—and whose broken home frightened me in the context of what I was seeing clinically—has now grown into a hardworking computer scientist and medical student, with caring relationships and a talent for guitar. Intersecting threads can either interrupt, or create, a pattern—and life gives no explanation. I now have four lovely younger children with an eminent physician-scientist—also at my university—whose mission is studying, and treating, the very same brainstem tumor that had grown in the little girl with eyes misaligned, who had almost brought to an end my path in medicine. At the heart of every story here, there is a lost child—but one who might still be found.

Every sensation described here, each individual feeling and thought that guided me to this point, now seems more richly textured than when first experienced, and more deeply interwoven. But is the original feeling better defined by, or instead obscured by, these connections formed with time? In some ways it doesn't matter—any more than buried warp threads can be meaningfully revealed without destroying a tapestry, any more than we can expose and experience our original feelings again without cutting connections and memories, and losing ourselves.

Ongoing scientific developments will continue to provide more textured interpretations for the stories told here. With each new discovery, our own construction by evolution becomes ever less simply described, and even the extinction of Neanderthals acquires more dimensionality as paleogenetics progresses. Of course they live on in us, and so are not extinct in any definitive sense, but an even more profound truth has now become apparent. We now know that when the last Neanderthals died, they were already part modern human—because the intermingling went both ways, and the last Neanderthal may have been also the last survivor of a wave of modern humans that had left Africa first. Their extinction is truly human, our own.

Most of the medical discoveries described here will, over time, be identified as just elements of a much larger picture—and those will be the success stories. A few will be forgotten, or found flawed enough to require patching and replacement. But this process of discovery and repair of flaws in our understanding is identical with the progress of science. Gaps and flaws by their very nature—like the disease processes themselves—illuminate and reveal.

Light in the natural world passes only through gaps already present—like cracks in the cloud cover or passages through the forest canopy blown open. But with this biology, and in these stories, visible light inverts that paradigm by physically opening a gate—information creating a path for itself, illuminating the whole human family as it streams through. Sometimes it seems the channel is only clumsily stuck open, a rural cow gate in damp sod; we have not fully prepared the pathway, or ourselves, to deal with the information coming through. But the gate is open.

Recent years have even brought insight into the gate itself. Hearkening back to feelings experienced near the very beginning of my scientific journey—crossing scales, exploring mysteries of the whole brain while grounded all the way down at the cellular level in our scientific methods—we have also now delved even deeper, to the molecular and atomic levels of resolution, in exploring how the light-gated protein called channelrhodopsin actually works. We have been able to elucidate the mystery of how light can be detected by a molecule and then turned into electrical current flowing through a pore in that same individual molecule. These experiments use intense beams of X-rays—the same kind of scientific method, crystallography, that enabled the discovery of the double-helical structure of DNA.

There had been intense controversy: some prominent investigators had claimed that there was not a light-gated pore within the channelrhodopsin molecule. But X-ray crystallography allowed us not only to see the pore directly and prove its existence, but also to use that knowledge to redesign the pore and show the depth of our understanding in many ways: changing atoms around—reupholstering the pore's inner lining—to create channelrhodopsins that conduct negatively charged instead of positively charged ions, or to make these molecules responsive to red rather than just blue light, or to change the timescale of the electricity elicited, speeding or slowing the currents manyfold. These new channelrhodopsins have already proven useful for neuroscience across a broad range of applications, and so cracking the structural code of this mysterious light-gated channel—thereby solving a fundamental mystery rooted in the basic biology of a most amazing plant—also opened up a scientific pathway to new explorations of the natural world, and of ourselves.

Today, even as science in my own lab at Stanford progresses, I still treat patients in an outpatient clinic focusing on depression and autism (and serve as attending physician for a block of inpatient call time every year)—all the while working with a new generation of psychiatry residents, teaching and learning as we journey together through a field that still feels as enthralling and mysterious as it did in my first moment with the schizoaffective disorder patient. We achieve cures in many patients, and in others we can only manage symptoms—a path followed in many fields of medicine, where we manage intractable diseases because we can, and because if we don't, the patient dies. We are honest peddlers of herbs that help—of feverweed and foxglove.

As our understanding of psychiatry and our insight into the neural circuit control of behavior progress together, we might be wise to begin awkward conversations for which we feel unready. We will need to stay philosophically, and morally, ahead—rather than trying to catch up once it is too late. An uncertain world is already demanding from psychiatry answers to difficult questions about ourselves in health, not only in disease. The reasons for this pressure are important—to discover, and then grapple with, and then embrace, humanity's uplifting and disturbing contradictions.

And so here, in the form of epilogue, we can look briefly to the future, along three dark and deeply forested paths only dimly illuminated by the stories in this volume that each need more profound exploration soon: our process of science, our struggle with violence, and the understanding of our own awareness.

•

Scientific breakthroughs are difficult to predict or to control—forming an odd contrast with much of the process of science, which is an exercise in controlled, and ordered, thought. Indeed, ordered thought seems natural to the human mind in general, and control over the flow of complex thoughts is taken for granted, just as we assume the steady forward passage of time. And yet we cannot use our appetite for order and control to plan the process of science completely. This is a major lesson from most scientific breakthroughs, including that of optogenetics—revealing the need to support basic research that at some level is unplanned. It would have been impossible to predict the impact—on neuroscience—of research into microbial light responses over the past 150 years. Similarly unexpected developments have launched many scientific fields; indeed, because this volume is partly memoir the stories focus on optogenetics, but other pioneering fields have also converged from unexpected directions to define the landscape of biology today.

Thus optogenetics has revealed not only a great deal about the brain but also, in an accessible way, the nature of the basic scientific process. This idea is important to keep at the forefront of our minds as we move together into the future: scientific truth—a force that can rescue us from weaknesses of our own construction—arises from free expression and pure discovery. That, and perhaps also from a little bit of disordered thinking.

I recall an alcoholic cirrhosis patient, in my care but without prospect of a new liver, who is reaching his endgame. He is drowning on dry land in liquid of his own creation. His belly is turgid and tense with ascites—the brownish-yellow fluid of hepatic failure, perhaps ten liters or more, distending his abdomen, compressing his lungs and diaphragm from below. He is only forty-eight but struggling to breathe, gasping in the bed before me.

I hold a crude tool, a trocar. Medieval, heavy in my hands, it is all we have. Illuminated by the harsh, bright procedure light at the bedside, the trocar is still dull as pewter—sterile but stained, tarnished, a blunt cylinder for placing a drain in the abdominal wall. I can take off five or six liters of fluid from his abdomen at a time, but this buys him space to breathe for only two or three days before the steady accumulation of ascites fills him up again. I cannot cure the illness, but I can do something, steadily and carefully, until we know more.

Truth is our trocar, for now. Truth that we can get to, as soon as we can get to it, through the open conversations that we know, of free argument and creative discovery.

Science, like songs and stories, serves as such a free form of human communication. Science also differs in that the conversation seems at first limited to the fraction of human beings trained to appreciate its full meaning. But like the performance artist Joan Jonas said about her art in 2018, science is "a conversation with the past and the future, and with a public." Scientists are not recluses shouting data into the void, nor automatons filling drives with bits. We seek truth, but truth to communicate in ways that we think and hope may matter. The meaning in our work comes from human partners we imagine and direct our voice toward, with awareness that these conversations will not be one-way.

Even completing a major breakthrough requires understanding of how it will be communicated, which in turn requires consideration of the listeners as well as the speaker, and the volatile context—the dynamic frame of the world beyond, its time and place in the human story. In unformed open spaces that bring no judgment or posturing, our path forward is that of a patient in talk therapy, where insight is achieved only through engaging freely and frankly, and without possibility of penalty. Otherwise immature defenses are the resort; walls are erected, evincing no understanding, isolating our own feelings—walls built because honest and free conversation, engaging all human family members, has not been prioritized. We need to be what we might be, so we can discover who we are.

·

Not far beneath the surface, part of what we can be is violent toward one another. There are many—too many—paths that lead to violence, with societal complexity that is important to understand, and this is perhaps the subject of another, different text. But when violence is visited upon human beings by human beings, without an obvious reason, seemingly for its own sake, then psychiatry (and thus neuroscience) would seem as close to the front lines as any school of human thought. This situation is usually framed in psychiatry as antisocial personality disorder, which is largely overlapping in meaning with *sociopathy*, a term widely used in the general public. We have no answers to the natural human questions—why does this disorder exist, and what can be done?—while it seems the need to understand this condition grows more urgent every day.

What proportion of humanity is capable of causing pain, or death, with utter disregard for human feeling? Estimates vary enormously depending on the study or population, from 1 to 7 percent, likely due to matters of degree—and variance in opportunity, which may be all that separates the active cases from those in a latent state.

In psychiatry, the definition of antisocial personality disorder includes "a long-term pattern of disregard for, or violation of, the rights of others," and so the criteria can be met in a person with both cruelty to animals as a child and disregard for physical or psychological integrity of other human beings as an adult. Both bits of history can be concealed, but both often are uncovered with surprising ease in the psychiatric interview, and the trained psychiatrist can come to a tentative diagnosis quite quickly.

What do we do with 1 to 7 percent: this high number, and this broad range? Are we good at heart, or original sinners? Either way, a strong argument makes itself for setting up societies so that no one person is ever fully trusted or empowered—with checks at all levels: personal, institutional, and governmental. But at even a few percent, this means the condition is deeply baked into the population. This seems a heavy burden for our species, explaining a great deal about human history and the present day—but one hopes, less so about the future, for how else can one imagine a future for humanity?—as the consequences of our actions become more global and more permanent.

Astrophysicists ask a related question in thinking about the cosmos: with its innumerable planets and its billions of years, if total technological transformation of a species and of a world takes only a few hundred years as we know, just a moment, an eyeblink, why does the universe seem so quiet? An easy explanation is that extinction follows very quickly from technology. No amount of institutional restraint is ever enough—the drives that support survival, in the end also drive extinction. Evolution creates intelligence that is unsuited for the world that intelligence, in turn, creates.

Can deeper scientific understanding of the biology save us? Little is known about the biology of antisocial personality. There is a heritable component (accounting for as much as 50 percent) revealed by studies of twins, and some evidence for reduced volume of cells in the prefrontal cortex, where aspects of restraint and sociability operate. Specific genes have been linked to sociopathy or aggression, including those encoding proteins that process neurotransmitters like serotonin in the synapse—and altered brain activity patterns have been observed, including changes in coordination between the prefrontal cortex and reward-related structures like the nucleus accumbens. But we lack deep understanding or clearly identified paths of action. Contradictions in the field still abound—for example, disagreement as to whether impulsive violence or its polar opposite (calculating, manipulative violence) is the more relevant core symptom. Each concept points to opposing ideas for diagnosis and treatment.

Modern neuroscience, however, has begun to illuminate the circuits underlying violence directed to another member of the same species—in studies that (while revealing) verge on the deeply disturbing. In a striking example of such a discovery that could not have been accomplished with prior methods, one group of researchers tried in rodents to test electrical stimulation of a tiny sliver of mammalian brain thought to modulate aggression—the ventrolateral subdivision of the ventromedial hypothalamus, or VMHvl. The research team was unable to observe aggressive responses despite numerous attempts at stimulating with an electrode, likely because the VMHvl is a small structure that is closely surrounded by other structures that elicit defensive measures instead, such as freezing or fleeing; these surrounding structures or their fibers would also be activated by electrical stimulation of the VMHvl, confounding and confusing the behavioral results. But when the team next made use of the precision of optogenetics to target only VMHvl cells with an excitatory microbial opsin, stimulation of these cells with light elicited a frenzy of violent aggression toward another mouse in the cage (a smaller nonthreatening member of the same species, the same strain, that the optogenetically controlled mouse had been perfectly content to leave alone, until the moment of flipping on the laser light).

The fact that individuals can be so instantaneously and powerfully altered in their expression of violence points to deep questions of moral philosophy. In teaching optogenetics to undergraduates, I have found it striking to see the responses they exhibit upon seeing videos—peer-reviewed and published in major journals—of instantaneous optogenetic control of violent aggression in mice. Afterward, the students often need a period of discussion, almost a dose of therapy, simply to process and incorporate into their worldviews what has been observed.

What does it mean about us, that violent aggression can be so specifically and powerfully induced by turning on a few cells deep in the brain? As the professor I can transmit the perspective that this is not entirely a new effect—aggression has previously been modulated to varying degrees, over decades, with genetic, pharmacological, surgical, and electrical means. But such knowledge seems to be of little value to the students in the moment. With these prior interventions, there has always been a veneer of nonspecificity and side effects. In contrast, the more precise an optogenetic intervention becomes, in the context of a seeming lack of self-limitation, the more problematic are its implications, and the better posed certain conundrums seem to be.

And what exactly are those conundrums? Optogenetics is too complex to be a weapon; rather, the issue is what the animals seem to be telling us about ourselves: the change in violent behavior, in its power and speed and specificity, seems disconnected from, or unconnectable to, ways we seek to combat violence in our civilization—that is, these powerful neural circuit processes seem destined to ultimately overpower fragile societal structures set up to prevent moral detachment. What can be done? What hope is there? What are we, really, when murderous violence can be instantly induced by only a few electrical blips in a few cells?

But violence can be suppressed by a few spikes too, and so at least there is now a path forward: using optogenetics and related methods to elucidate the cells and circuits that *suppress* aggression. And even if not immediately practical or therapeutic, this neuroscience-based dimension of insight enables us to move beyond intense societal debates of the past (while building on what has come before). We can now begin to unify the intersecting influences of genes and culture in a concrete and causal framework. We now understand enough about behavioral causation to see how elements of neurophysiology underlying behaviors as complex as violent aggression can be manifested in well-defined physical components of the brain: projections endowed with form (direction and strength) by individual brain development on the one hand, and learned life experience on the other.

Because we do not fully control either our brain development or our life experience, the precise nature of personal responsibility for action is still an interesting and contentious matter. A modern neuroscience perspective informed by the kind of work described in this volume might hold that there is no personal responsibility for some actions that involve the brain (like startle responses) because circuitry involving the self was never consulted, in contrast to other kinds of action where priorities and memories weigh in—that is, where circuits are engaged that define one's path through the world, such as the retrosplenial cortex and prefrontal cortex. Since such a sentence, describing causal and measurable concepts, can be reasonably written without using words like *consciousness* or *free will*, which are difficult to quantify, modern neuroscience may indeed be able to make headway on these hard questions, that until now have inhabited only the fascinating domain of the philosophical treatise.

There is unlikely to be a single location in the brain that explains freely chosen actions; indeed, we are increasingly able to grapple with more widely distributed circuitry for decision-making and path-selection, as we attain ever-broader perspectives on the activity of cells and projections throughout the brain during behavior. In 2020, recording the activity of cells broadly across mouse and human brains brought insight into the circuit-level construction of the self, by probing the fascinating process of dissociation—in which the inner sense of one's self is separated from physical experience, and so individuals feel dissociated from their own bodies. The self is aware of but detached from sensations—no longer feeling ownership of, or responsibility for, the body. With optogenetics and other methods, activity patterns in the retrosplenial cortex (consistent with ideas described in the story on eating disorders) and certain of its far-flung projection partners were found to be important for regulating the unified nature of the self and its experience. And so one can accept that there may be a distributed origin of any action, and of the self as well, without abandoning the idea of the self as a real and biological agent subject to precise scientific investigation.

Meeting this complexity head-on may eventually allow us to understand and treat (and feel empathy for) the antisocial, who may have as much free will and personal responsibility as any other person but who can often be cruel to themselves, to their own selves, as well—perhaps through a biologically definable form of detachment, or dissociation, from the feelings of both self and others. As a physician, understanding this last trait—more than any other aspect—helps me care as I should, and do, for these fellow human beings, despite everything.

•

The future of this scientific journey—given our accelerating progress toward accessing all the cells, connections, and activity patterns of brain cells in animals during behavior—is leading us not only to understanding and treatment of our own difficult and dangerous design, but also to insight into one of the most profound mysteries of the universe. Rivaling the question of *Why are we here?* is *Why are we aware?*

In 2019 optogenetic technology began to enable control of mammalian behavior in a wholly new way, no longer just allowing control of cells by type—the workhorse of optogenetics for its first fifteen years—but also allowing control of activity in many single cells, or individually specified neurons. Now we can pick, at will, tens or hundreds of single cells for optogenetic control—cells selected from among millions of neighbors by virtue of their location, their type, and even their natural activity during experiences.

This effect was achieved by developing new microscopes, including holographic devices based on liquid crystals. These machines take a massive leap beyond fiberoptics to use holograms as the interface between light and the brain, allowing a sort of sculpting of complex distributions of light even in three dimensions—to control individual opsin-producing neurons during behavior in a mammal such as a mouse.

In one application of this method, we can cause animals in complete darkness to behave as if they were seeing specific visual objects of our own design. For example, we can pick the cells that normally respond to vertical (but not horizontal) stripes in the visual environment and then, without any such visual stimulus, optogenetically turn on just those cells with our holographic spots of light, testing to see if the mouse acts as if there were vertical stripes present. Both the mouse and the mouse's brain in fact behave as if the vertical stripes were there; peering into the activity of many thousands of individual neurons in the primary visual cortex (that part of the cortex that first receives information from the retina), we can see that the rest of this circuitry—with all the complexity of its immense number of cells—acts as it does during natural perception of real vertical (but not horizontal) stripes.

We now find ourselves in an astonishing position: we can pick out groups of cells that are naturally active during an experience and then (using light and single-cell optogenetics) insert their activity patterns back in *without* the experience; when we do so, the animal (and its brain) both behave naturalistically as they would when perceiving a real stimulus. The animal behavior showing correct discrimination is similar whether the sensory stimulus is natural or provided entirely by optogenetics—and the detailed, real-time, cellular-level internal representation of the sensory discrimination across volumes of the brain is also similar, whether the sensory stimulus is natural or provided entirely by optogenetics. As far as we can tell, then (with the caveat that I will never know what another animal, human or not, is truly experiencing subjectively), we are directly inserting something resembling a specific sensation as defined by natural behavior and natural internal representation.

We were intrigued to see how few cells we could stimulate to mimic the percept, and we found that a handful was enough—as little as two to twenty cells, depending on how well trained the animal had been. So few cells sufficed, in fact, that a new question had to be asked: why are mammals not frequently distracted by chance synchrony events among a few cells that happen to have similar natural responsivity— thus fooling the brain into concluding (wrongly) that the object these cells are designed to detect must be present? In some people that may happen, as in Charles Bonnet syndrome, where people who suffer adult-onset blindness can experience complex visual hallucinations; the visual system seems to act as if all is too quiet, reaching to create something, anything, out of the noise. I treated a patient at the VA hospital with this syndrome: an amiable and elderly veteran, entirely blind, who would see fully formed visions, often of sheep and goats grazing harmlessly in the middle distance. We found his visions could be reduced with an antiepileptic medication called valproic acid, but in the end we discharged him with no prescription; he had grown attached to what his deprived visual cortex had decided to provide for him.

More broadly, such spontaneous unwanted output—of any part of the brain due to spurious correlations of a few of its cells—could be a principle underlying many psychiatric disorders, ranging from the actual auditory hallucinations of schizophrenia, to unwanted motor outputs and thoughts of tic disorders and Tourette's syndrome, to out-of-control cognitions like those of eating and anxiety disorders. The mammalian brain is poised perilously close to the level where noise might escape to be treated like a signal—an insight important both for the basic neuroscience of natural mammalian behavioral variability and for clinical psychiatry.

Beyond science and medicine, philosophical puzzles surrounding subjective awareness suddenly become better posed with this multiple-single-cell control. Indeed, new life has even been breathed into philosophical thought experiments (*Gedankenexperimente*, as the physicists Ernst Mach and Albert Einstein might have said, following a tradition extending back at least to Galileo), ancient in formulation and discussion. The modernized version of an old story might run as follows:

Suppose one could control (as with this new form of single-cell optogenetics) the exact pattern of activity, over some period of time, of every cell in the brain of an animal capable of subjective sensation— say, of a pleasurable, intensely rewarding, internal feeling. And suppose such control could even be precisely guided by first observing and recording those activity patterns in the same animal during natural exposure to a real, rewarding stimulus—just as we already know we can do for simple visual percepts in the visual cortex.

The seemingly trivial question, then, is: would the animal feel the same subjective sensation? We already know that a mouse and its visual cortex will both behave as if it had received and processed the real stimulus—but would the animal also feel the same internal awareness,

experiencing its quality beyond the information itself, like natural subjective consciousness except now when the activity pattern is presented
artificially?

It is important that this be a thought experiment—of course we cannot fully know the subjective experience of another individual, even of
another human being, nor have we yet achieved the total control con-
templated here—but like Einstein's original *Gedankenexperimente*
that illuminated relativity so powerfully, this thought experiment rapidly brings us to a conceptual crisis—one that, in its eventual resolution, could be highly informative.

The problem is that answering either yes or no to this question seems
essentially impossible. Saying no implies there is more to subjective
sensations than the cellular patterns of activity in the brain—since in
the thought experiment, we are allowed to match the precise patterns
of all physical phenomena that cellular activity elicits, including neu-
romodulators, biochemical events, and so on that are the natural consequences of neural activity. As a result, we have no framework to
understand how that answer could be no. How can there be more to
what the cells of the brain do than what they do?

Saying yes raises equally unsettling questions. If all the cells are actively controlled and a subjective sensation is being felt, then there is
no reason the cells all need to be in the head of the animal. They could
be spread all around the world, and controlled in the same way with
the same relative timing, over as long a time period as was interesting,
and the subjective sensation should still somehow be felt, somewhere,
somehow, by the animal—an animal no longer existing in any discrete
physical form. In a natural brain, neurons are near one another, or connected to one another, only to influence one another. But in this
thought experiment, neurons no longer need to influence one
another—the exact effect of what that influence would have been, over
any period of time, is already being provided by the artificial stimulus.

This answer intuitively seems wrong, as well, though we are not sure
how—it just seems to fail an absurdity test. How, and why, could individual neurons spread around the world still give rise to the inner feelings of a mouse or a human? The question is only interesting because

we are considering an inner feeling. If instead we were to divide a basketball into a hundred billion cell-like parts to be distributed around the world and controlled individually to move as they would during a bounce, there would be no philosophical debate as to whether this new system feels as though it were bouncing. The answer would be, presumably: no more or less than the original ball.

We are left with a philosophical problem, one that optogenetics has framed sharply and clearly. There are certain to be many such mysteries about the brain, like the nature of our inner subjective states, that don't fall into current scientific frameworks: questions that are deep and unanswered, but some that—it seems now—can be well posed.

And those subjective states, called qualia or feelings, are not just abstract or academic concepts. These are the same inner states that were the central focus of this volume, that first brought me to psychiatry years ago, each one inseparable from its own projection across time—over seconds, and over generations. These subjective experiences underlie our common identity and define the path we have traveled, together, as humanity—even if shared only as stories, in a book or around a fire.

ACKNOWLEDGMENTS

I am deeply indebted to so many people who helped nurture this work, and who provided motivation and energy through difficult times.

Heartfelt gratitude to Aaron Andalman, Sarah Caddick, Patricia Churchland, Louise Deisseroth, Scott Delp, Lief Fenno, Lindsay Halladay, Alizeh Iqbal, Karina Keus, Tina Kim, Anatol Kreitzer, Chris Kroeger, Rob Malenka, Michelle Monje, Laura Roberts, Neil Shubin, Vikaas Sohal, Kay Tye, Xiao Wang, and Moriel Zelikowsky for their notes and comments—along with my perceptive and tireless literary agent Jeff Silberman, and my deeply thoughtful editor and publisher Andy Ward, whose belief in these stories was always greater than my own.

I am most grateful to all the people who shared this path with me— merging their stories with my own, for a time.

NOTES

Brief references, for background on the science within each story, are included here. All of the articles are freely accessible; you can either copy and paste the link into a browser search bar (if you're reading on a connected device) or for the notes labeled PMC (for PubMedCentral) go to https://www.ncbi.nlm.nih.gov/pmc/articles/ and at the search bar enter the digital identifier shown (for PMC4790845, enter 4790845), whereupon articles can be read online or free pdfs downloaded.

PROLOGUE

8 **actual memory storage needing no guidance or supervision:** https://en.wikipedia.org/wiki/Hopfield_network; https://en.wikipedia.org/wiki/Back propagation.

12 **In optogenetics we borrow genes from diverse microbes:** https://www.ncbi.nlm.nih.gov/pmc/articles/PMC4790845/.

13 **tricks from chemistry are used to build transparent hydrogels:** https://www.ncbi.nlm.nih.gov/pmc/articles/PMC5846712/.

13 **All the interesting parts remain locked in place, still within 3-D tissue:** https://www.ncbi.nlm.nih.gov/pmc/articles/PMC6359929/.

13 **national and global initiatives to understand brain circuitry:** https://braininitiative.nih.gov/sites/default/files/pdfs/brain2025_508c.pdf; https://braininitiative.nih.gov/strategic-planning/acd-working-group/brain-research-through-advancing-innovative-neurotechnologies.

14 **many thousands of insights into how cells give rise to brain function and behavior:** https://www.ncbi.nlm.nih.gov/pmc/articles/PMC4069282/; https://www.ncbi.nlm.nih.gov/pmc/articles/PMC4790845/.

14 **connections defined by their origin and trajectory through the brain could now be precisely controlled:** https://www.ncbi.nlm.nih.gov/pmc/articles/PMC4780260/; https://www.ncbi.nlm.nih.gov/pmc/articles/PMC5729206/.

CHAPTER 1: STOREHOUSE OF TEARS

25 **they traveled into, and dwelt within, our cellular forebears more than two billion years ago:** https://www.ncbi.nlm.nih.gov/pmc/articles/PMC5426843/.

26 **with optogenetics, microbial DNA has yet again returned to animal cells:** https://www.ncbi.nlm.nih.gov/pmc/articles/PMC5723383/.

29 how much of modern Eurasian human genomes arose from this interaction—about 2 percent: https://www.ncbi.nlm.nih.gov/pmc/articles/PMC5100745/.

30 a hidden cave, alone in a final redoubt near the coast of Iberia: https://en.wikipedia.org/wiki/Gorham%27s_Cave; https://www.ncbi.nlm.nih.gov/pmc/articles/PMC6485383/; https://www.ncbi.nlm.nih.gov/pmc/articles/PMC5935692/.

31 from an extension of the amygdala called the bed nucleus of the stria terminalis: https://www.ncbi.nlm.nih.gov/pmc/articles/PMC6690364/.

32 A fiberoptic can be placed not in the BNST but in an outlying region: https://www.ncbi.nlm.nih.gov/pmc/articles/PMC4069282/; https://www.ncbi.nlm.nih.gov/pmc/articles/PMC3154022/; https://www.ncbi.nlm.nih.gov/pmc/articles/PMC3775282/.

34 In the mouse version of place preference: https://www.ncbi.nlm.nih.gov/pmc/articles/PMC5262197/; https://www.ncbi.nlm.nih.gov/pmc/articles/PMC4743797/.

35 Thus a complex inner state can be deconstructed into independent features: https://www.ncbi.nlm.nih.gov/pmc/articles/PMC6690364/.

35 parenting, in the form of intimate care of mammals for their young, was soon deconstructed into component parts, mapped onto projections across the brain: https://www.ncbi.nlm.nih.gov/pmc/articles/PMC5908752/.

37 Tears are powerful for driving emotional connection: https://www.ncbi.nlm.nih.gov/pmc/articles/PMC4882350/; https://www.ncbi.nlm.nih.gov/pmc/articles/PMC5363367/.

38 missing even this one part of the conversation may come at a cost: https://www.ncbi.nlm.nih.gov/pmc/articles/PMC4934120/; https://www.ncbi.nlm.nih.gov/pmc/articles/PMC6402489/.

39 collections of cells, sixth and seventh and parabrachial, jostle together in a small spot in the pons: https://en.wikipedia.org/wiki/Cranial_nerves.

43 In 2019 cells were studied across the entire brain of the tiny zebrafish: https://www.ncbi.nlm.nih.gov/pmc/articles/PMC6726130/.

43 optogenetics and other methods had implicated these same two structures in mammals: https://www.ncbi.nlm.nih.gov/pmc/articles/PMC5929119/.

43 Even the tiny nematode worm *Caenorhabditis elegans* appears to calculate: https://www.ncbi.nlm.nih.gov/pmc/articles/PMC3942133/.

46 Each mammalian species, on average, gets a run of about a million years: https://en.wikipedia.org/wiki/Background_extinction_rate.

46 population sizes around the world may have plummeted to a few thousand individuals: https://www.ncbi.nlm.nih.gov/pmc/articles/PMC5161557/; https://www.ncbi.nlm.nih.gov/pmc/articles/PMC4381518/.

CHAPTER 2: FIRST BREAK

49 the 767, slowly banking harborward, nearing the burning steel tower: https://en.wikipedia.org/wiki/United_Airlines_Flight_175.

55 Mood elevation has the capability to bring forth energy: https://www.ncbi .nlm.nih.gov/pmc/articles/PMC3137243/; https://www.ncbi.nlm.nih.gov/pmc/ articles/PMC2847485/.

57 mania is often not threat-triggered at all, and does not even approach utility: https://www.ncbi.nlm.nih.gov/pmc/articles/PMC2796427/.

57 *bouffée délirante* in West Africa and Haiti, a state of sudden agitated behavior: https://www.ncbi.nlm.nih.gov/pmc/articles/PMC4421900/.

59 broken fragments of the yolk genes persist, even within our own genomes: https://www.ncbi.nlm.nih.gov/pmc/articles/PMC2267819/; https://www.ncbi .nlm.nih.gov/pmc/articles/PMC5474779/.

59 Cave fish and cave salamanders—in sunless colonies, blocked off from the surface world: https://www.ncbi.nlm.nih.gov/pmc/articles/PMC5182419/.

60 dopamine neurons have attracted attention for their known roles in guiding motivation and reward seeking: https://www.ncbi.nlm.nih.gov/pmc/ articles/PMC4160519/; https://www.ncbi.nlm.nih.gov/pmc/articles/ PMC4188722/.

61 In 2015 the dopamine and circadian aspects were brought together with optogenetics: https://www.ncbi.nlm.nih.gov/pmc/articles/PMC4492925/.

61 the dopamine neuron population is not monolithic but composed of many distinct types that can be separably identified early in mammalian brain development: https://www.ncbi.nlm.nih.gov/pmc/articles/ PMC6362095/.

61 ankyrin 3 (also known as ankyrin G), which organizes the electrical infrastructure: https://www.ncbi.nlm.nih.gov/pmc/articles/PMC3856665/; https:// www.ncbi.nlm.nih.gov/pmc/articles/PMC2703780/.

62 In 2017 a mouse line was created with "knocked out"—insufficient— ankyrin 3: https://www.ncbi.nlm.nih.gov/pmc/articles/PMC5625892/.

CHAPTER 3: CARRYING CAPACITY

67 Two or three hundred milliseconds elapse before the response to a ping: https://www.ncbi.nlm.nih.gov/pmc/articles/PMC166261/; https://www.ncbi .nlm.nih.gov/pmc/articles/PMC4467230/.

74 Despite anxiety and cognitive impairment, Williams patients can seem extremely socially adept: https://www.ncbi.nlm.nih.gov/pmc/articles/ PMC4896837/; https://www.ncbi.nlm.nih.gov/pmc/articles/PMC3378107/.

80 "That incredibly thin, hairlike wasp waist": https://www.ncbi.nlm.nih.gov/ pmc/articles/PMC3016887/.

80 "ants and hornets and bees, all the social groups—later reverted away from

this life cycle": https://www.sciencedirect.com/science/article/pii/
S0960982217300593?via%3Dihub; https://www.sciencedirect.com/science/
article/pii/S0960982213010567?via%3Dihub.

81 researchers studying parenting in mice had used optogenetics: https://www
.ncbi.nlm.nih.gov/pmc/articles/PMC5908752/.

84 many of the genes linked to autism are related to these processes of electrical and chemical excitability: https://www.ncbi.nlm.nih.gov/pmc/articles/
PMC4402723/; https://www.ncbi.nlm.nih.gov/pmc/articles/PMC4624267/;
https://www.biorxiv.org/content/10.1101/484113v3.

84 people on the autism spectrum exhibit signs of increased excitability:
https://www.ncbi.nlm.nih.gov/pmc/articles/PMC4105225/.

85 speculated that a unifying theme in autism could be an increased power of
neuronal excitation—relative to countervailing influences like inhibition:
https://www.ncbi.nlm.nih.gov/pmc/articles/PMC6748642/; https://www.ncbi
.nlm.nih.gov/pmc/articles/PMC6742424/.

86 elevating the activity of *excitatory* cells in the prefrontal cortex caused an
enormous deficit in social behavior: https://www.ncbi.nlm.nih.gov/pmc/
articles/PMC4155501/.

86 mice (altered in a single gene called *Cntnap2*): https://www.ncbi.nlm.nih
.gov/pmc/articles/PMC3390029/.

87 this autism-related social deficit could be *corrected* by optogenetic interventions: https://www.ncbi.nlm.nih.gov/pmc/articles/PMC5723386/.

89 causing high excitability of prefrontal excitatory cells (an intervention that
elicited social deficits) actually did reduce the information-carrying capacity of the cells themselves: https://www.ncbi.nlm.nih.gov/pmc/articles/
PMC4155501/.

91 "The tree thrives in salt, and makes the soil salty too": https://www.ncbi
.nlm.nih.gov/pmc/articles/PMC5570027/; https://www.ncbi.nlm.nih.gov/pmc/
articles/PMC4836421/.

94 PTSD (a common and deadly disease that is often resistant to treatment
by medication): https://www.ncbi.nlm.nih.gov/pmc/articles/PMC5126802/.

CHAPTER 4: BROKEN SKIN

107 Skin arises from ectoderm, in embryos: https://en.wikipedia.org/wiki/Germ
_layer.

107 a meteor strike upended everything: https://www.youtube.com/watch?v=
tRPu5u_Pizk.

108 sensory skin organs then spread across the body: https://www.ncbi.nlm.nih
.gov/pmc/articles/PMC4245816/.

109 the patient or the psychiatrist might fit into a role from the past: https://
www.ncbi.nlm.nih.gov/pmc/articles/PMC6481907/.

110 Suicide is more common in borderline than in any other psychiatric disorder: https://www.ncbi.nlm.nih.gov/pmc/articles/PMC4102288/.

110 an unjust burden: psychological or physical trauma at a young age: https://www.ncbi.nlm.nih.gov/pmc/articles/PMC3402130/.

111 trauma during dependency—early in life when warmth and care are needed at all costs—predicts nonsuicidal self-injury later: https://www.ncbi.nlm.nih.gov/pmc/articles/PMC5201161/.

111 Our brains are building even basic structure—the electrical insulation, the myelin: https://www.sciencedirect.com/science/article/pii/S0092867414012987?via%3Dihub.

112 an individual can instead be guided chiefly by suppression of internal discomfort as the motivation for action: https://www.ncbi.nlm.nih.gov/pmc/articles/PMC5723384/.

113 cause animals to become more or less aggressive, defensive, social, sexual, hungry, thirsty, sleepy, or energetic: https://www.ncbi.nlm.nih.gov/pmc/articles/PMC5708544/; https://www.ncbi.nlm.nih.gov/pmc/articles/PMC4790845/.

113 swift to react strongly with value assignments: https://www.ncbi.nlm.nih.gov/pmc/articles/PMC5472065/.

114 causes the animal to begin to avoid the harmless room, as if it were a source of intense suffering: https://www.ncbi.nlm.nih.gov/pmc/articles/PMC4743797/.

114 turning down the dopamine neurons in the midbrain naturally, just as optogenetics does experimentally: https://www.ncbi.nlm.nih.gov/pmc/articles/PMC3493743/.

115 early-life stress and helplessness can increase habenula activity: https://www.ncbi.nlm.nih.gov/pmc/articles/PMC6726130/.

120 outpatient referral for a specialized group behavioral therapy: https://www.ncbi.nlm.nih.gov/pmc/articles/PMC6584278/.

CHAPTER 5: THE FARADAY CAGE

123 installing a true modern Faraday cage as a shield: https://en.wikipedia.org/wiki/Faraday_cage.

135 the Kalman filter, an algorithm for modeling complex unknown systems: https://en.wikipedia.org/wiki/Kalman_filter.

137 "Optimal filters will still block a few things that you actually wanted to go through": https://en.wikipedia.org/wiki/Chebyshev_filter; https://en.wikipedia.org/wiki/Butterworth_filter.

141 Matthews had imagined something he called an "Air Loom": https://en.wikipedia.org/wiki/James_Tilly_Matthews.

147 schizophrenia genetics: the collection of DNA sequence information from

human genomes: https://www.ncbi.nlm.nih.gov/pmc/articles/PMC4112379/; https://www.ncbi.nlm.nih.gov/pmc/articles/PMC4912829/.

150 evidence that disease symptoms are more common and strong in city dwellers: https://www.ncbi.nlm.nih.gov/pmc/articles/PMC3494055/.

CHAPTER 6: CONSUMMATION

165 cognitive and behavioral therapies can help in anorexia nervosa: https://www.ncbi.nlm.nih.gov/pmc/articles/PMC6181276/.

165 Medications are used not as cures, not to strike at the heart of the disease: https://www.ncbi.nlm.nih.gov/pmc/articles/PMC4418625/.

165 then eating disorders together show the highest death rates of any psychiatric disease: https://www.ncbi.nlm.nih.gov/pmc/articles/PMC2907776/.

168 the diversity of genes that can be involved, as with many psychiatric disorders: https://www.ncbi.nlm.nih.gov/pmc/articles/PMC5581217/; https://www.ncbi.nlm.nih.gov/pmc/articles/PMC6097237/.

168 Controlling the walking rhythms of the brainstem and spinal cord: https://www.ncbi.nlm.nih.gov/pmc/articles/PMC5937258/; https://www.ncbi.nlm.nih.gov/pmc/articles/PMC4844028/.

177 the first optogenetic control of free mammalian behavior was in the hypothalamus: https://www.ncbi.nlm.nih.gov/pmc/articles/PMC6744371/.

178 cause the hunger or thirst behaviors, actually driving the consumption of food or water: https://www.ncbi.nlm.nih.gov/pmc/articles/PMC5723384/.

180 specific social cells could suppress feeding, driving a resistance, even in naturally hungry mice: https://www.ncbi.nlm.nih.gov/pmc/articles/PMC6447429/.

180 When a mouse is fully water-sated but the deep thirst neurons are optogenetically driven: https://www.ncbi.nlm.nih.gov/pmc/articles/PMC6711472.

182 entorhinal cortex and hippocampus, two structures involved in navigation and memory: https://escholarship.org/uc/item/4w36z6rj.

182 a human subject is asked to sit quietly and think of nothing in particular, to simply be with one's self: https://www.ncbi.nlm.nih.gov/pmc/articles/PMC1157105/.

CHAPTER 7: MORO

188 infarcts, spots of dead tissue that are the outcome of strokes, can be detected by computed tomography: https://en.wikipedia.org/wiki/Vascular_dementia.

188 magnetic resonance imaging (MRI) can show the small vessel blockade of vascular dementia: https://www.ncbi.nlm.nih.gov/pmc/articles/PMC3405254/.

194 **350 million years ago, when the first air-breathing fishes emerged onto land:** https://www.ncbi.nlm.nih.gov/pmc/articles/PMC3903263/.

195 **global collapse in human populations bottoming out only fifty thousand years ago:** https://www.ncbi.nlm.nih.gov/pmc/articles/PMC5161557/; https://www.ncbi.nlm.nih.gov/pmc/articles/PMC4381518/.

196 **the few medications available only slightly slow the steady progression of the disease:** https://www.ncbi.nlm.nih.gov/pmc/articles/PMC6309083/.

197 **anhedonia in senior populations with cognitive impairment:** https://www.ncbi.nlm.nih.gov/pmc/articles/PMC2575050; https://www.ncbi.nlm.nih.gov/pmc/articles/PMC4326597/.

197 **the greater the accumulated volume of those lacunae in white matter:** https://www.ncbi.nlm.nih.gov/pmc/articles/PMC2575050/.

198 **valence of release from anxiety is set in part by projections from the BNST to reward circuitry:** https://www.ncbi.nlm.nih.gov/pmc/articles/PMC6690364/.

198 **absent everything but the optogenetic reactivation of a few of the fear-memory neurons:** https://www.ncbi.nlm.nih.gov/pmc/articles/PMC3331914/; https://www.ncbi.nlm.nih.gov/pmc/articles/PMC6737336/; https://www.ncbi.nlm.nih.gov/pmc/articles/PMC4825678/.

199 **synaptic strength changes indeed can store memories in an automatic way:** https://en.wikipedia.org/wiki/Hopfield_network; https://en.wikipedia.org/wiki/Backpropagation.

199 **synaptic strength changes of the right kind can happen in the real world:** https://www.ncbi.nlm.nih.gov/pmc/articles/PMC1693150/; https://www.sciencedirect.com/science/article/pii/S0092867400804845?via%3Dihub; https://www.ncbi.nlm.nih.gov/pmc/articles/PMC1693149/.

199 **Both effects are plausibly useful for memory storage, based on the theoretical work:** https://www.ncbi.nlm.nih.gov/pmc/articles/PMC5318375/.

199 **a connection from one part of the brain to another can be made light-sensitive, and then high- or low-frequency light pulses can be provided:** https://www.ncbi.nlm.nih.gov/pmc/articles/PMC3154022/; https://www.ncbi.nlm.nih.gov/pmc/articles/PMC3775282/; https://www.ncbi.nlm.nih.gov/pmc/articles/PMC6744370/.

200 **selective effects on behavior can be exerted by projection-specific synaptic strength changes:** https://archive-ouverte.unige.ch/unige:38251; https://archive-ouverte.unige.ch/unige:26937; https://www.ncbi.nlm.nih.gov/pmc/articles/PMC4210354/.

200 **Projections fundamentally embody how effectively different parts of the brain can engage with each other, whether in health or disease:** https://www.ncbi.nlm.nih.gov/pmc/articles/PMC4069282/.

200 **interregional connectivity strength predicts interregional activity correlations:** https://www.biorxiv.org/content/10.1101/422477v2.

200 **anhedonia for music in human beings:** https://www.ncbi.nlm.nih.gov/pmc/articles/PMC5135354/.

200 **brain region representing hierarchies of kinship relationships:** https://www.nature.com/articles/s41467-020-16489-x/.

200 **gene expression patterns that determine how cellular diversity and axon guidance implement brain wiring:** https://www.ncbi.nlm.nih.gov/pmc/articles/PMC6086934/; https://www.ncbi.nlm.nih.gov/pmc/articles/PMC6447408/; https://www.biorxiv.org/content/10.1101/2020.03.31.016972v2; https://www.biorxiv.org/content/10.1101/2020.07.02.184051v1; https://www.ncbi.nlm.nih.gov/pmc/articles/PMC5292032/.

203 **the *Moro* reflex:** https://en.wikipedia.org/wiki/Moro_reflex.

EPILOGUE

205 **the very same brainstem tumor that had grown in the little girl with eyes misaligned:** https://www.ncbi.nlm.nih.gov/pmc/articles/PMC5891832; https://www.ncbi.nlm.nih.gov/pmc/articles/PMC5462626; https://www.ncbi.nlm.nih.gov/pmc/articles/PMC6214371.

206 **the last Neanderthal may have been also the last survivor of a wave of modern humans:** https://www.ncbi.nlm.nih.gov/pmc/articles/PMC4933530/; https://www.biorxiv.org/content/10.1101/687368v1.

207 **exploring how the light-gated protein called channelrhodopsin actually works:** https://www.ncbi.nlm.nih.gov/pmc/articles/PMC5723383/; https://www.ncbi.nlm.nih.gov/pmc/articles/PMC6340299/; https://www.ncbi.nlm.nih.gov/pmc/articles/PMC6317992/; https://www.ncbi.nlm.nih.gov/pmc/articles/PMC4160518/.

208 **research into microbial light responses over the past 150 years:** https://www.ncbi.nlm.nih.gov/pmc/articles/PMC5723383/.

209 **like the performance artist Joan Jonas said about her art in 2018:** https://twitter.com/KyotoPrize/status/1064378354168606721.

210 **depending on the study or population, from 1 to 7 percent:** https://www.ncbi.nlm.nih.gov/books/NBK55333/.

211 **An easy explanation is that extinction follows very quickly from technology:** https://en.wikipedia.org/wiki/Fermi_paradox.

211 **There is a heritable component:** https://www.ncbi.nlm.nih.gov/pmc/articles/PMC6309228/; https://www.ncbi.nlm.nih.gov/pmc/articles/PMC5048197/.

211 **linked to sociopathy or aggression:** https://www.ncbi.nlm.nih.gov/pmc/articles/PMC2430409/; https://www.ncbi.nlm.nih.gov/pmc/articles/PMC6274606/; https://www.ncbi.nlm.nih.gov/pmc/articles/PMC6433972/; https://www.ncbi.nlm.nih.gov/pmc/articles/PMC5796650/.

212 **a frenzy of violent aggression toward another mouse:** https://www.ncbi.nlm.nih.gov/pmc/articles/PMC3075820/.

214 the fascinating domain of the philosophical treatise: https://www.science
direct.com/science/article/pii/S0896627313011355?via%3Dihub.

214 In 2020, recording the activity of cells broadly across mouse and human
brains: https://www.ncbi.nlm.nih.gov/pmc/articles/PMC7553818/.

215 control of cells by type—the workhorse of optogenetics for its first fifteen
years: https://www.ncbi.nlm.nih.gov/pmc/articles/PMC5296409/.

215 but also allowing control of activity in many single cells, or individually
specified neurons: https://www.ncbi.nlm.nih.gov/pmc/articles/PMC5734860/;
https://www.ncbi.nlm.nih.gov/pmc/articles/PMC3518588/.

215 Now we can pick, at will, tens or hundreds of single cells for optogenetic
control: https://www.ncbi.nlm.nih.gov/pmc/articles/PMC6447429/; https://
www.ncbi.nlm.nih.gov/pmc/articles/PMC6711485; https://www.biorxiv.org/
content/10.1101/394999v1.

215 we can pick the cells that normally respond to vertical (but not horizontal)
stripes: https://www.ncbi.nlm.nih.gov/pmc/articles/PMC6711485.

217 new life has even been breathed into philosophical thought experiments:
https://en.wikipedia.org/wiki/Einstein%27s_thought_experiments.

ABOUT THE AUTHOR

KARL DEISSEROTH is professor of bioengineering and psychiatry at Stanford University. He received his undergraduate degree summa cum laude at Harvard, and his MD/PhD at Stanford, where he completed psychiatry training and is board-certified by the American Board of Psychiatry and Neurology. Deisseroth is known for creating and applying new technologies for studying the brain, including optogenetics—for which he was the winner of the 2018 Kyoto Prize and the 2020 Heineken Prize, among many other major international awards. Deisseroth has five children and lives near Stanford University, where he teaches and directs Stanford's undergraduate degree in bioengineering, and treats patients with mood disorders and autism. Deisseroth helped craft the multibillion-dollar ongoing U.S. national BRAIN Initiative, and is a member of the National Academy of Medicine, the National Academy of Sciences, and the National Academy of Engineering.

ABOUT THE TYPE

This book was set in Electra, a typeface designed for Linotype by W. A. Dwiggins, the renowned type designer (1880–1956). Electra is a fluid typeface, avoiding the contrasts of thick and thin strokes that are prevalent in most modern typefaces.